400 Sensational Cookies

Linda J. Amendt

Dedication

I dedicate this book and delicious collection of special recipes
to home bakers and cookie lovers everywhere.

For complete cataloguing information, see page 563.

Design and Production: Joseph Gisini/PageWave Graphics Inc.
Editor: Susan Girvan
Proofreader: Sheila Wawanash
Indexer: Elaine Melnick
Photography: Colin Erricson
Food Styling: Kathryn Robertson
Prop Styling: Charlene Erricson

Cover image: (front to back) Cranberry Orange Spirals (page 532), Raspberry Heart Cookies (page 464) and Chocolate Cookies (page 78).

We acknowledge the financial support of the Government of Canada through the Book Publishing Industry Development Program (BPIDP) for our publishing activities.

Published by Robert Rose Inc.
120 Eglinton Avenue East, Suite 800, Toronto, Ontario, Canada M4P 1E2
Tel: (416) 322-6552   Fax: (416) 322-6936

Printed and bound in Canada

1 2 3 4 5 6 7 8 9   CPL   17 16 15 14 13 12 11 10 09

Contents

• • •

Acknowledgements 4

Introduction 5

Baking Great Cookies
    Cookie Baking Equipment and Tools 6
    Ingredients for Flavor-Packed Cookies 12
    Baking Perfect Cookies 27

Recipes for Cookie-Lovers of All Ages
    Drop Cookies 41
    Hand-Shaped Cookies 71
    Chocolate Chip Heaven 117
    Oatmeal Cookie Delights 145
    Dream Cookies. 169
    Rolled Cutout Cookies 203
    Refrigerator Slice-and-Bake Cookies 249
    Bars and Squares. 275
    Brownies, Brownies and More Brownies. 335
    Biscotti. 393
    Shortbreads 427
    Extra-Special Cookies 461

Appendicies
    Blue Ribbon Cookies 555
    Packaging Cookies for Mailing 558
    Cookie Problem Solver 560
    Cookie Supply Sources 562

Index 564

Acknowledgements

This book was a longtime dream and a labor of love. I would like to express my thanks to some of the many people who helped to make it possible.

To my dad and official cookie taster, Lee Amendt, for your endless hours of reading and proofreading my manuscript and recipes for this book. You encouraged me every step of the way, and I'm very grateful for your help and support.

To my brothers Bruce and Brion and to family and friends who have always been there to offer encouragement and eagerly try new cookie recipes.

To my friend Michael Marks ("Your Produce Man") for sharing your mother Thelma's wonderful recipe for persimmon cookies.

Special thanks to all of my recipe tasters! To my neighbors, who never turned me away when I showed up at your doors with plates full of cookies after a session of recipe testing.

To Willie Garrett, Nancy, Pam, Joyce, and everyone at the California State Fair for making judging baked foods and preserved foods such a pleasure. To Michael Marks and Laura McIntire for your excellent job of making these open judgings interactive and entertaining for the audience. To Iris Dimond, Sarah Morelli, Drew, Theresa, Kathy and all the other judges who graciously share your time and expertise to make these judgings so special and educational for all.

To Lisa Ekus-Saffer, my literary agent, and everyone at The Lisa Ekus Group for your friendship, representation, assistance and confidence in my abilities.

To Bob Dees, for publishing this book and sharing my love of cookies, Marian Jarkovich and everyone at Robert Rose Inc. To my editor Susan Girvan, who was a delight to work with on this project. To Joseph Gisini and PageWave Graphics for your wonderful book design. And to Colin Erricson, Kathryn Robertson and Charlene Erricson for your beautiful photographs and food and prop styling.

Introduction

Imagine the tantalizing aroma of fresh-baked, homemade cookies wafting through the house. Envision the wonderful sensation of biting into a delicious, chewy, flavor-packed morsel, still warm from the oven. Cookie heaven!

Cookies are North America's favorite and easiest dessert, and these delectable, tender, tasty delights have legions of fans. Hundreds of millions of cookies are baked every year in kitchens across the continent. That's a lot of cookies!

Ever wonder why some people seem to bake cookies with little effort, with every batch turning out perfect, while others struggle as their cookies turn out bland, flat and burned? It's because baking cookies is both a creative art and a science. It takes skill and practice to master the art, but it also requires an understanding of the key elements of baking to comprehend the science. With the right recipes, clear instructions and essential baking information, anyone can perfect the art and science of cookies and become a great cookie baker.

I've written this book specifically for home bakers of all skill levels, from novice to experienced. As a highly successful and knowledgeable home baker, I've filled these pages with lots of helpful information, an extensive collection of tantalizing recipes and expert tips on all aspects of cookie baking.

Detailed chapters on equipment, ingredients and baking great cookies will provide you with a solid foundation for success. The recipe chapters include special preparation techniques and advice on attaining the best results with each type of cookie. The flavorful recipes also contain step-by-step instructions to ensure great results.

I'll reveal to you the secrets of great cookie baking and tell you how to use the right ingredients and preparation methods to bake cookies with outstanding flavor. From the butter to the sugar to the extracts to the chocolate and nuts and fruit, each flavor builds on and enhances the others to create tantalizing cookies. Layers of flavor give these cookies that extra-special taste to please cookie enthusiasts of any age.

Altering the ingredients used in a recipe or adjusting the proportions of just one ingredient can significantly affect the cookie's flavor and texture. I'll not only share with you which ingredients are best to use in making cookies, but I will also explain how these ingredients interact with each other. Using the right ingredients, in the right amounts, can determine the success or failure of your cookies.

My cookie recipes range from special versions of traditional favorites and modern classics to numerous new and tempting original creations. All have a strong emphasis on flavor. No bland, boring or overly complicated cookies here. These are recipes designed for cookie lovers and contain all the information home bakers need to create great-tasting cookies.

Filled with delicious, family-oriented, kid-friendly cookies, you'll find recipes sure to please every member of the family. Many of the recipes can be prepared quickly and without a lot of fuss, making it easy to whip up a batch of fresh homemade cookies for an after-school treat, a family dessert or a special occasion.

I have earned over 900 awards, including over 600 blue ribbons and special awards for excellence, in food competitions at state and county fairs across the United States. I retired from competition after the publication of my first cookbook, *Blue Ribbon Preserves*, and I now enjoy sharing my food knowledge and expertise by serving as a state and county fair judge of both baked foods and preserved foods.

I hope this book, and the recipes and information it contains, will excite your cookie imagination and inspire you to become a great cookie baker. Your family, friends and neighbors will be delighted and thrilled to help sample your delightful cookie creations.

Happy cookie baking!

— Linda Amendt

Cookie Baking Equipment and Tools

Baking cookies is a pleasurable experience. Turning out fabulous cookies is easily accomplished if you have the right baking equipment in your kitchen. You don't have to spend a lot of money on equipment and tools. Just make sure the items are sturdy enough to stand up to years of baking.

Electric Mixers and Food Processors

The key to a great cookie is properly mixing the dough. While most cookie doughs can be mixed by hand, an electric mixer makes the job a lot faster and easier. You can use either a stand mixer or a hand-held mixer to make cookies; however, there are certain advantages to using a stand mixer.

Stand Mixers

An electric stand mixer does a great job of mixing cookie doughs and brownie batters and can also handle heavy-duty tasks such as kneading bread doughs. It frees up your hands during the creaming process, allowing you to do other things, and also does an excellent job of blending and beating ingredients.

While stand mixers are expensive, they are an indispensable piece of equipment and well worth the investment, especially if you plan to do a lot of baking. They last for years, and you'll wonder how you ever got by without one. My first mixer has been going strong for nearly 20 years, and I recently purchased a second one with an even more powerful motor.

Hand-held Mixers

Hand-held mixers are good for light jobs, such as whipping cream, creaming butter and sugar and mixing soft cookie doughs. When adding flour, mix in as much as you can with the hand-held mixer, then stir in any remaining flour by hand to avoid burning out the motor.

Food Processors Are Not for Cookies

Food processors are great for grinding nuts but should not be used to mix cookie doughs. They're not effective for creaming butter and sugar mixtures, which is essential for good cookie texture, and it's too easy to overmix the dough, resulting in tough cookies.

Cookie Sheets and Baking Pans

Cookie sheets and baking pans also play a big role in the success or failure of your cookies. The right size and type of pan can prevent a number of baking problems and help produce outstanding cookies.

Cookie Sheets

Flat, heavy gauge, shiny metal cookie sheets are the best choice for baking cookies as they allow cookies to brown and bake evenly. Dark cookie sheets and those with a darker nonstick finish can cause the bottoms of cookies to turn too brown or even burn before the cookies finish baking. Dark cookie sheets absorb more heat from the oven, while shiny sheets reflect some of the heat and help cookies bake more evenly. Shiny sheets also

---

You Can Never Have Too Many Mixer Bowls

If you like to bake more than one kind of cookie at a time, make recipes that require beating egg whites separately from the batter or do a lot of holiday baking, invest in an extra bowl or two for your electric stand mixer and extra beaters to go with them. It saves a lot of time in washing up before getting the next recipe in the oven. I own three mixer bowls and beaters and frequently have them all in use.

yield cookies with a softer texture, while cookies baked on dark sheets tend to be drier and crunchier.

Baking sheets that have a low rim around the edge are intended for baking jelly-roll cakes and some types of bar cookies but are not designed for baking drop, shaped, rolled, sliced or other types of cookies. The rim can inhibit air circulation around the cookies and cause the cookies to bake unevenly. If you must use a rimmed pan, turn it upside down and bake the cookies on the bottom of the pan.

Insulated cookie sheets are great for baking rolled cutout cookies, drop or shaped cookies and other cookies that brown easily. If you have trouble with the bottoms of your cookies browning before the rest of the cookie is done, try using insulated cookie sheets. Insulated sheets are actually two thin cookie sheets molded together with a pocket of air in between that keeps the top sheet from getting too hot. This prevents burning on the underside of the cookies. You can also create the same insulating effect by stacking two flat sheets together. I personally don't like cookies with dark bottoms and frequently use insulated cookies sheets to bake chewy drop cookies and delicate cutouts.

Choose cookie sheets that will fit in your oven and still leave at least 2 inches (5 cm) of space between the pan and the oven walls. This space will allow air to circulate around the pan so the cookies will bake and brown evenly. If you bake a lot, then you know how important it is to have several cookie sheets on hand when baking big batches of cookies.

Baking Pans

Brownies, bars and squares turn out best when baked in sturdy, shiny, single-wall metal pans, preferably made of aluminum. Shiny metal pans reflect heat. This action slows down the browning process and allows baked goods to bake all the way through to the middle without overbrowning the outside. Dark or dull-finish metal pans absorb more heat than shiny pans, and glass pans are even better heat conductors. The outside edges and bottoms of bars and brownies will cook faster and brown quicker in a dark or dull metal or glass pan. If you use a dark metal or glass pan, some adjustments should be made: lower the

oven temperature by 25°F (14°C) and line the pan with foil to reflect some of the heat and help the bars bake and brown more evenly.

The bar and brownie recipes in this book use standard-sized pans, either 13- by 9-inch (3 L) rectangular or 9-inch (2.5 L) square metal baking pans. For best results, use the size and shape of pan indicated in the recipe. Changing the pan size will produce a different result.

Mini-Muffin Pans

In cookie baking, mini-muffin pans or tins are used for baking specialty cookies like tassies, which are small, sweet pastry cups filled with tasty fillings. As with other baking pans, the best mini-muffin pans are made of shiny aluminum and have 12 or 24 mini-cups per pan. Each cup has a capacity of $1\frac{1}{2}$ tablespoons (22 mL). Dark metal pans may cause the cookie crusts to brown too much.

Fluted Tart Pan with Removable Bottom

Originally designed for making tarts, these versatile pans have many uses, including being great for shaping and baking shortbread. The removable bottom makes it easy to unmold shortbread after baking, while the fluted edge adds a nice decorative touch to the cookies. A 9-inch (23 cm) round tart pan is perfect for baking shortbread. As with other baking pans, choose one that is sturdy and made of shiny metal to keep the cookies from burning.

Other Baking Equipment

Cookie baking requires a few pieces of basic kitchen and baking equipment. These items make the job a lot easier and help keep your ingredients and kitchen organized.

Mixing Bowls

A set of nested mixing bowls is invaluable for cookie baking. The bowls are used for everything from combining dry ingredients to mixing brownie batters. They come in sets of three or four bowls. Three-bowl sets have small, medium and large bowls, with an extra-large bowl included in the larger set. Bowls should be made of glass, ceramic or stainless steel. Do not use plastic bowls — they can absorb flavors from ingredients. My personal preference is for glass bowls that allow you to see if all the ingredients are blended evenly, or ceramic bowls. I do a lot of baking and have four sets of mixing bowls. During holiday baking, they're all in use.

Small Ingredient Bowls

These look like a miniature set of nested glass mixing bowls and are used for holding small amounts of measured ingredients that are to be added to the cookie dough or batter. They help keep ingredients organized, free up measuring cups for measuring other ingredients and can be lined up in the order ingredients should be added to the mixing bowl. Small and large custard or dessert cups also work well for holding measured ingredients.

Cutting Boards

Cutting boards protect your countertops from damage and prolong the sharpness of your knives. Boards can be made of wood, durable plastic or acrylic. The newer, flexible plastic cutting mats are great for chopping nuts, dried fruit and chocolate. After chopping, you can pick up the mat, bend it and slide the ingredients right into the measuring cup. They're inexpensive, too, making it easy to set aside one or two just for baking.

Cookie ingredients are quick to absorb strong flavors like onions and garlic, so it's very important to keep one cutting board or mat just for preparing baking ingredients. Never cut chocolate, nuts, dried fruit or other baking ingredients, or roll out cookies or any other pastry, on a board that has been used to prepare meat, fish or poultry.

Rolling Pins

Rolling pins come in a variety of types and sizes. Many cooks like to work with marble rolling pins when making pastry; however, hardwood rolling pins are best for making cookies. A light touch is needed for rolling tender cookies, and the heavy weight of a marble pin makes it too easy to roll the edges of the dough too thin. My favorite rolling pin is a traditional two-handled wooden pin with handles that roll on ball bearings. I've had it for years, and it feels like an extension of my own hands. Some bakers prefer the French-style rolling pin, which is a simple pin without separate handles, that you control with the palm of your hands. One type is about 18 inches (45 cm) long and 2 inches (5 cm) in diameter. Another is about 1½ inches (4 cm) thick, very long and tapered at both ends.

The rolling pin you feel most comfortable with and is the easiest to use is the right choice. When caring for your wooden rolling pin, never wash it with soap because the wood can absorb some of the soap and transfer it to the next batch of cookies. Instead, scrape off any dough and rub the rolling pin with a paper towel to remove any remaining flour or residue.

Pastry Boards

In addition to a designated cutting board, a special board reserved only for rolling out cookie doughs, pie crusts and other pastries is a nice addition to a baker's kitchen. Hardwood, marble and smooth plastic or acrylic are all good surfaces for rolling doughs. I have a large round wooden board with rubber feet that is perfect for rolling cutout cookies and pie crusts. A pastry board will also protect your counter, preventing knife cuts, cookie cutter scars and damage from metal spatulas and utensils.

A smooth-surface countertop or kitchen table can be used as a rolling surface if you don't have a board, but care needs to be taken to be sure these surfaces are free from any

Pastry Cloths and Rolling Pin Covers

If you consistently have trouble with rolled cookies and pie crusts sticking to your pastry board, try covering it with a pastry cloth. When lightly dusted with flour, the tightly woven cloth makes an excellent surface for rolling dough. Rolling pin covers, also called stockings, are made from a stretchy cloth that slides over the end of the pin. As with a pastry cloth, when coated with flour, the cover makes dough less likely to stick to the rolling pin.

To store pastry cloths and rolling pin covers, shake out any excess flour, place the covers in a zippered storage bag and seal and keep in the freezer until the next use to prevent any fat particles from turning rancid. Hand wash cloths and covers as needed, rinsing well under running water to remove all soap residue, as any remaining soap in the fabric can be absorbed by the cookie dough during rolling. Dry thoroughly before storing.

cleaning chemicals or other food particles and residue, particularly meat juices, that could contaminate cookie doughs.

Wire Cooling Racks
Wire cooling racks are an essential piece of equipment in cookie baking. The sturdiest racks have two sets of wires attached in a grid pattern. Racks with one set of wires placed close together are also good. Wide-set wires will allow warm cookies to bend into the gaps in the rack. Large rectangular cooling racks will hold a whole cookie sheet's worth of cookies and are much better than small square or round racks. As with cookie sheets, if you do a lot of cookie baking, you can never have too many large wire cooling racks.

Measuring Equipment
Using the correct types of measuring cups to measure the different ingredients in cookie recipes is crucial to successfully baking these wonderful treats. The measurements of ingredients must be accurate in order for the cookies to have the best texture and flavor.

Liquid Measuring Cups
Use standard glass or plastic liquid measuring cups with pour spouts to measure milk, buttermilk, corn syrup, molasses, oil and other liquid ingredients.

Dry Measuring Cups
Use plastic or metal dry measuring cups with flat rims to measure flour, sugar, cocoa powder and other dry ingredients. These come in sets of graduated sizes. It is very important to use measuring cups that are designed specifically for dry ingredients. The top of these measuring cups is flat so you can use a straight utensil or scraper with a straight edge to level ingredients with the top edge for an exact measure. Dry measuring cups should also be used to measure solid ingredients, such as shortening, chopped chocolate, chocolate chips, nuts, dried fruits and coconut.

Measuring Spoons and Glasses
Use a set of measuring spoons in graduated sizes to measure small quantities of ingredients. Small measuring glasses are now readily available in many stores and are quite handy for measuring small quantities of liquid ingredients such as fruit juice and cream.

Kitchen Scale
A small kitchen scale is a handy tool for measuring chocolate sold in large bars or blocks.

Standard Baking Utensils and Tools
Some of the common utensils and tools already found in most kitchens are very helpful for baking cookies. If you don't have these items, they would be a good addition to your kitchen.

Oven Thermometer
An oven thermometer is essential to test the accuracy of your oven temperature control and allow you to make adjustments in temperature and/or baking time to achieve the best results.

Instant-Read Thermometer
An instant-read thermometer is helpful in determining the temperature of butter and other ingredients.

Kitchen Timer
An accurate kitchen timer is an absolute must for cookie baking. The texture of cookies can go from chewy to crisp in as little as a minute or two.

Mixing Spoons
A sturdy long-handled mixing spoon makes it easier to mix flour or oats into cookie dough and to fold in chocolate or chocolate chips, nuts and dried fruit. Spoons can be made of wood or metal.

Wire Whisk
A wire whisk is the perfect tool for quickly combining flour and other dry ingredients, such as baking powder, baking soda, salt, spices and sugars. It's also excellent for lightly beating eggs and blending in other ingredients by hand.

Pastry Blender
A pastry blender is used to cut butter or shortening into dry ingredients to create a crumbly mixture. It is basically a set of U-shaped wires attached to a handle that fits

snugly into the palm of your hand. Helpful in making bars and squares, a pastry blender is essential for making great pie crusts. If you don't have a pastry blender, two knives drawn together in scissor motion or a three-tined pastry fork can be used to cut in butter.

Silicone Spatula

A good spatula is essential for scraping down the bowl while mixing ingredients. It is also helpful to get all of the melted chocolate into cookie dough, to scrape brownie batter into the baking pan and smooth the top, or to gather that last bit of dough in the bottom of the bowl to make one more cookie. Silicone spatulas are sturdy, flexible and can withstand temperatures of up to 500°F (260°C). There are even silicone spatulas contoured to fit the sides of mixing bowls.

Rubber or plastic spatulas also work for scraping bowls, but they are not as sturdy and should not be used for making curds or other heated preparations because they can melt.

Metal Spatula

A wide-bladed metal spatula with a thin blade is ideal for moving warm, soft or delicate cookies to a cooling rack. It also helps maintain the shape of cutout cookies while you're transferring them from the pastry board to the cookie sheet.

Parchment Paper

Parchment paper, also known as silicone paper, is a cooking paper with a nonstick silicone coating. It comes in rolls and is found in grocery stores alongside foil and plastic wrap. Parchment paper is great to use for lining cookie sheets because it allows cookies to both spread properly and release easily from the paper without sticking. It helps cookies hold their shape and keep them from spreading too wide and thin. The paper also insulates the bottoms of cookies from the heat of the cookie sheet and helps keep them from becoming too dark during baking. It eliminates the need to grease cookie sheets and keeps the pans clean, saving on cleanup.

Parchment paper is moisture-proof, grease- and heat-resistant and can tolerate oven temperatures of up to 420°F (215°C). Cut parchment paper so it fits the cookie sheet but does not extend over the edges of the sheet or touch the oven rack or side walls of the oven. Parchment paper should never be used under the broiler because it may burn. Never use wax paper in place of parchment paper. Wax paper is not designed to handle oven temperatures. It will melt and burn and could cause an oven fire.

Heavy-Duty Foil

Heavy-duty foil is a very handy and useful tool in the kitchen and can be used to line baking pans when making bars and brownies. Lining the baking pan with foil makes it easy to remove the cookies, and cleanup is a breeze. However, foil should not be used as a substitute for parchment paper to line cookie sheets. The cookies will spread more on foil, and the foil will reflect heat onto the cookies, which can cause them to brown too much on the bottom.

Nonstick Foil

The newer nonstick foil is perfect for lining baking pans, and I highly recommend it. This foil has a nonstick coating on one side and does not need to be greased to keep bars and brownies from sticking to the foil. It is a real time-saver.

Special Utensils for Cookie Baking

While most of the essentials needed to prepare and bake cookies are standard kitchen tools, there are a few specialty items that will make the job a lot easier and faster and will yield more uniform results. Some are invaluable if you do a lot of cookie baking.

Cookie Scoop

A cookie scoop is the perfect tool for making drop cookies. It looks like a mini ice cream scoop but is designed for cookie baking. Because the cookies are all the same size and shape, they bake evenly and have a uniform appearance.

Cookie Cutters

Cookie cutters are a great way to personalize your cutout cookies. They come in every shape imaginable and a variety of sizes. There's a cookie cutter out there for every event, holiday and occasion, and they're great fun to collect. Metal cookie cutters with sharp edges make the cleanest cuts. Hand wash cookie cutters and dry them thoroughly before storing to prevent rusting.

Cookie Press
A cookie press consists of a hollow plastic or metal cylinder with a plunger at one end and a shaped disk template at the other end. It is used to make Swedish spritz and other piped or pressed cookies. Presses come with a selection of pretty templates that help you create cookies in various shapes and designs. A soft dough is spooned into the press, and then the plunger is pressed to push the dough through the template to form the cookies.

Dough Tamper
A dough tamper is designed to evenly press balls of dough into miniature muffin cups to shape the crust for tassie-type cookies. It's usually made of wood and is about 6 inches (15 cm) in length with a tapered head that is the perfect size to fit into the little cups of a miniature muffin pan.

Microplane Grater
A Microplane grater is a very sharp, fine grater that is perfect for grating the citrus zest used in cookies and pastry.

Icing Spatula
A small offset icing spatula makes easy work of spreading icing on cutout cookies. These can be found where cake decorating supplies are sold.

Silicone Baking Mats
Flexible, nonstick rubberized silicone mats can be used in place of parchment paper to line cookie sheets. They can withstand oven temperatures of up to 600°F (300°C). While silicone mats can be used over and over, quality ones don't come cheap and having several on hand for cookie baking can be quite expensive.

Kitchen Equipment for Baking Cookies

- Cookie sheets without raised sides
- Baking pans for bars, squares and brownies
- Chef's knife for chopping chocolate, nuts and dried fruit
- Cutting boards for preparing ingredients
- Dry and liquid measuring cups and measuring spoons
- Small kitchen scale
- Adjustable-speed stand mixer or hand-held mixer
- Large mixing bowls for combining cookie dough ingredients
- Large, medium and small bowls for holding measured ingredients
- Microwave-safe glass or ceramic bowl for melting chocolate
- Double-boiler for making fillings or melting chocolate
- Wire whisk for mixing dry and liquid ingredients
- Pastry blender for cutting butter into mixtures for crusts
- Flexible silicone spatula for scraping down mixing bowls
- Long-handled, large spoon for folding nuts and chocolate into cookie dough
- Rolling pin
- Pastry board or solid surface for rolling cookie dough
- Round, scalloped and shaped cookie cutters
- Cookie scoop or small spoons for portioning cookie dough
- Wire cooling racks for cooling cookies
- Oven thermometer
- Kitchen timer
- Pot holders or oven mitts to protect your hands when moving hot pans
- Hot pads or trivets for hot pans
- Small, wire-mesh sieve for sifting cocoa powder or dusting confectioner's sugar over cookies
- Small icing spatula or knife for spreading icings and glazes
- Long serrated knife for cutting bars, squares, brownies and biscotti

Ingredients for Flavor-Packed Cookies

● ● ●

Each ingredient in a cookie recipe has a specific purpose and influences the success or failure of the recipe. To make cookies with outstanding flavor and perfect texture, you need to use the appropriate ingredients. The selection of these ingredients, how they are combined and in what proportion determines the flavor and texture of the finished cookie.

In the following sections, we'll take a look at each ingredient, its particular role in baking and how ingredients interact and contribute to making great cookies.

Flours

Flour separates and evenly distributes ingredients throughout the dough or batter and binds all the ingredients. Flour also contains starches that absorb liquids and act as a thickener. Natural sugars in flour caramelize during baking and aid in browning.

The proteins in flour help produce the texture of baked goods. These proteins contribute to the structure and crumb of cookies and help determine whether cookies will be soft and tender or tough and chewy. Each type of flour has its own protein composition and lends its own characteristic to cookies.

Unopened packages of flour can be stored in a cool, dry cupboard or pantry for up to 2 years. Once opened, transfer flour to an airtight container or seal it in a plastic bag for use within 8 months or by the date marked on the original package, whichever is sooner.

All-purpose Flour

All-purpose flour is the flour of choice for baking cookies. It is made with a blend of "soft" low-protein wheat and "hard" high-protein wheat.

There are two types of all-purpose flour: bleached and unbleached. Bleaching makes the flour slightly acidic. This acidity interacts with the leavener, adding to the texture of the cookies. If you use unbleached flour in a recipe leavened with baking soda and your cookies or baked goods do not rise properly, you may need to add a touch of acid, such as a pinch of cream of tartar, to get the proper results.

Because of the acidity, cookies made with bleached flour spread less than cookies made with unbleached flour. In addition to spreading more, cookies made with unbleached flour tend to be darker and crisper. Unbleached flours are preferred by most bakers for making breads, so some flour manufacturers formulate their unbleached all-purpose flour with a higher protein content than their bleached all-purpose flour. These high-protein, all-purpose flours will yield slightly tougher cookies with a significantly darker color.

The choice of bleached or unbleached flour is a personal preference and may be determined by the finished cookie texture and appearance you prefer. I prefer to use bleached all-purpose flour when I make cookies. You can use bleached or unbleached all-purpose flour in the cookie recipes in this book.

Cake Flour

Cake flour is bleached flour that contains more "soft," or low-protein, wheat than all-purpose flour has and is used in baked goods where a light, non-chewy structure is preferred. Cookies made with cake flour tend to be soft, tender and pale.

Cake flour is frequently used in shortbread recipes to create a very tender cookie. Part cake flour is also used in some cookies to reduce their spread, particularly in recipes with a high ratio of sugar and fat compared to the amount of flour.

Bread Flour

Bread flour is made with high-protein wheat that absorbs more liquid than all-purpose flour absorbs. This characteristic gives breads their chewy texture because the protein develops into gluten, the strands that give loaves of bread their structure. The higher protein in bread flour yields cookies with a tougher texture and significantly darker color. Bread flour is not recommended for cookie baking.

Other Grains

Oats and cornstarch are two other grain ingredients that bind ingredients and add to the texture and flavor of cookies.

Oats

Oatmeal cookies have many fans. Old-fashioned (large flake) and quick-cooking rolled oats may be used interchangeably in cookie recipes. They are the same product except that quick-cooking oats have been cut into smaller pieces so they cook faster.

I call for quick-cooking oats in these recipes because I like the texture they produce in the cookies. Cookies have a short baking time, and quick-cooking oats absorb moisture and cook faster than old-fashioned oats. Cookies made with old-fashioned oats can be tougher, drier and more crumbly.

In any recipe calling for oats, you can use the type you prefer and have on hand, with two exceptions. Never use instant oats for baking. They are preprocessed and turn gummy in cookies. Steel-cut oats, also called Irish or Scottish oats, should not be used in baked goods either. They will remain hard after baking and ruin the texture of your cookies.

Cornstarch

Cornstarch is a very fine, powdery flour made from corn kernels. It is most commonly used in sauces and fillings as a thickener. In cookies, cornstarch is used as a tenderizing agent. Adding cornstarch lowers the protein content of the all-purpose flour to produce a more tender cookie. Cornstarch will also make a cookie spread a bit more. Cookies with large amounts of cornstarch will be very tender and more fragile than those made without cornstarch.

Store cornstarch in its original container in a cool, dry cupboard or pantry. Cornstarch can lose some of its thickening power after a year but will still work fine for tenderizing cookies. To preserve freshness, look for cornstarch in the new resealable plastic containers.

Sugars and Sweeteners

Sugars and sweeteners play a far greater role in cookie baking than just adding sweetness. Sugar provides both flavor and structure to baked goods. It also helps make cookies and other baked goods tender and enhances their texture and crumb. Sugar attracts and retains moisture, prolonging freshness and helping cookies maintain their flavor.

During baking, sugar chemically reacts with the proteins in flour and other ingredients. When heated above the melting point, sugar caramelizes, taking on an amber color that browns the surface of the cookies and produces a delicious, rich flavor and aroma.

The type and amount of sugar used in a recipe affects the crispness of the cookies. Cookies with a high sugar content, no acid ingredients and a low moisture level will turn crisp and crunchy as they cool. Sugar also liquefies during baking, causing cookies with a high sugar content to spread more. Liquid sweeteners such as molasses, maple syrup, corn syrup and honey add moisture, resulting in soft cookies.

Refined sugar is produced from two main sources — sugar cane and sugar beets. Sugar cane is a tropical plant that grows in tall, thick, woody stalks similar to bamboo. Sugar beets are a root crop grown underground. Growing sugar beets is less expensive than growing sugar cane, so the price of beet sugar is a little less than cane sugar. However, beet sugar can have a slightly earthy flavor. Cane sugar absorbs fewer odors and has a purer flavor. It also blends easily with other ingredients and has a low melting point so cookies brown better.

I prefer the smooth, pleasant flavor of cane sugar over the flavor of beet sugar, and I use only 100% pure cane sugar for all of my baking. Labeling laws do not require sugar refiners to identify whether their product is made from sugar beets or sugar cane. If the package does not indicate the source of the sugar, odds are it is made from beets. Pure cane sugar is usually clearly labeled.

Sugars should never be stored in the refrigerator. The humidity in the refrigerator can cause mold and other organisms to grow in sugar.

Granulated Sugar

Granulated sugar is the all-purpose sugar most frequently used in baking. The particles in granulated sugar provide friction with the butter in creamed cookie doughs and batters, incorporating air into the mixture and creating light and tender cookies. It makes cookies that are more delicate, crisper and slightly drier than cookies made with brown sugar.

Granulated sugar is made by extracting the juice from sugar cane or sugar beets and clarifying it to reduce impurities. The juice is cooked down until sugar crystals form. The remaining juice is removed, to be made into molasses later, and the crystals are further refined and purified to make granulated white sugar.

Moisture can make granulated sugar turn hard and lumpy. Store it tightly sealed in a cool, dry location. Properly stored, granulated sugar will keep indefinitely.

Baker's Sugar

Baker's sugar is the type of granulated sugar used most often by professional bakers. It is an ultrafine gourmet sugar designed specifically for baking. The grains are slightly coarser than superfine sugar.

Baker's sugar mixes, blends and melts more evenly than regular granulated sugar. It is an excellent choice for baking many types of cookies, brownies and other baked goods and may be used in place of regular granulated sugar in most recipes. Cookies made with baker's sugar tend to spread less than those made with granulated sugar. I have had excellent results using this sugar in all manner of baked goods.

Made from pure cane sugar, baker's sugar is refined for the highest grade of purity. It requires more curing time than regular granulated sugar, making it slightly more expensive. Originally created for and marketed only to professional bakers, baker's sugar is now commonly found in most large supermarkets.

Superfine Sugar

An extremely fine-grained sugar, superfine sugar is also known as bar sugar because it is used by bartenders to make mixed drinks and coffee drinks. It is sometimes called preserving sugar because its fine grains dissolve rapidly in fruit and juice mixtures when making jams and jellies.

Superfine sugar is the finest granulated sugar sold commercially. It can be substituted in recipes in equal amounts for regular granulated sugar. Available in many supermarkets, superfine sugar is usually sold in 1-pound (500 g) boxes and has a higher price per pound than granulated sugar.

It dissolves quickly in hot or cold liquids, butter, eggs and melted chocolate. Because it dissolves so quickly, superfine sugar is an excellent choice for making curd fillings. Use it whenever an extra-light, super-smooth texture is important.

Brown Sugar

Brown sugar is basically refined granulated sugar with molasses added. It is made by one of two processes: molasses is boiled until sugar crystals form, or more commonly, the molasses syrup is combined with granulated sugar crystals. Brown sugar has the same sweetening power as granulated sugar.

Whenever possible, I advise using brown sugar made from sugar cane. Brown sugar from sugar cane is a natural combination of sugar and molasses, formed using the traditional method of crystallization. Brown sugar from sugar beets is frequently made with added colorings, flavors and coatings. Molasses made from sugar beets has a harsher flavor than molasses made from sugar cane, affecting the overall quality and flavor of the brown sugar.

Dark brown sugar contains more molasses than light brown sugar, which is also called golden brown sugar. In addition to being lighter in color, light brown sugar has a more delicate caramel flavor than the richer dark brown sugar. Light and dark brown sugars can be used interchangeably. Use light brown sugar when you want a subtler, milder flavor. Use dark brown sugar for a stronger, more intense flavor.

With four times the moisture content of granulated white sugar, brown sugar is an excellent choice for baking rich, moist and chewy cookies. Brownies and other cookies made with brown sugar stay soft and moist longer than those made with granulated sugar. In some cookie recipes, brown sugar may be substituted for all or part of the granulated sugar to add flavor and moistness.

Brown sugar, as well as molasses, is higher in acid than granulated sugar. Depending on the quantity of brown sugar in the recipe, it can act alone or in partnership with other ingredients to provide the acidity level necessary to activate baking soda.

When brown sugar loses its moisture and dries out, it can become as hard as a rock. To prevent this from happening, store bags and boxes of brown sugar tightly sealed in a heavy-duty zippered plastic storage bag or in an airtight container. Store the sugar in a dark location and use within six months of purchase for maximum flavor and moisture.

While hardened brown sugar can be rescued, I don't believe it is really worth the effort. With the loss of moisture, brown sugar also loses much of its fresh flavor. Remoistened brown sugar is never as good as fresh brown sugar. Cookies made with it will not be as flavorful as they could have been,

nor will they be as moist and tender. It is much better to replace dried out brown sugar with fresh.

Confectioner's Sugar

Confectioner's sugar, also known as powdered sugar, 10X sugar or icing sugar, is primarily used for making icings, frostings and glazes. It can also be dusted on the tops of bars and cookies for decoration and flavor. Using all or part confectioner's sugar in a shortbread dough creates cookies with a fine, delicate, tender texture. To create confectioner's sugar, granulated sugar is processed until it is ground 10 times finer than regular granulated sugar. Cornstarch is added, usually about 3% of the sugar's volume, to absorb moisture from the air and prevent the sugar from becoming lumpy.

Confectioner's sugar cannot be directly substituted for granulated sugar. It does not have the same sweetening power as granulated sugar, so it must be used in larger quantities in baking. The cornstarch in confectioner's sugar also affects the texture and flavor of cookies and other baked goods.

Confectioner's sugar can absorb odors from foods and other products. Store it in a dry location away from any items with strong odors. Even with the addition of the cornstarch, confectioner's sugar can become lumpy when stored in a moist location.

Raw Sugar

Raw sugar, also known as washed raw sugar or turbinado sugar, is commonly sold in grocery stores. It is made from the first pressing of crystallized sugar obtained in the refining process. Raw sugar retains some of the natural color and flavor of the sugar juice but no more nutrients than granulated sugar. Today's raw sugars have been refined to the point where they retain little or no nutritional value.

The coarse crystals and higher melting temperature of raw sugar make it a good decorating sugar for the tops of cookies. However, raw sugar's crunchy texture is not recommended for use when making cookie doughs. It should not be substituted for granulated sugar in baking recipes. The large crystals do not cream well with butter and eggs, and it does not dissolve easily during baking, which can significantly affect

---

Softening Hardened Brown Sugar

If you want to try to remoisten dried and hardened brown sugar, there are two basic methods. The first is to add a slice of apple, a slice of bread, or a few drops of water, or a damp white paper towel to the box or container, then reseal the package and let it sit for a day or two. To soften brown sugar quickly for immediate use, spread the sugar in a covered ovenproof container and heat in the oven at 250°F (120°C) until the sugar is soft. Watch it carefully to keep it from melting. Or, to soften sugar in a microwave, place the sugar in a microwave-safe container and cover it with a wet (but not dripping) white paper towel. Microwave on High power, checking the sugar every 20 to 30 seconds, until soft.

As soon as the heated sugar is soft, measure and use it. The sugar will harden again when it starts to cool. Please use caution — sugar heated in the oven or microwave will be very hot! Do not use heated brown sugar in creamed cookie doughs as it will melt the butter or shortening and may cook the eggs, seriously affecting the texture and spread of the cookies.

the taste and texture of the cookies. Light molasses flavors in the sugar can alter the flavor balance in cookies normally made with granulated sugar.

Molasses

Molasses is the residue, or by-product, created during the sugar-refining process. The juice that remains after the sugar crystals are removed is boiled down to create molasses. It is most often made from sugar cane juice. The high moisture content in molasses makes tender cookies. In addition to moistness, molasses also adds a rich flavor and color.

Molasses is sold in two forms, sulfured and unsulfured. Sulfured molasses has a stronger, more robust flavor. It contains sulfur dioxide that is used in the sugar-refining process. The flavor of unsulfured molasses is milder and lighter. It is the most commonly used molasses, and the smooth flavor makes it the best choice for baking.

There are three strengths of molasses — light, dark and blackstrap. Light molasses, also called fancy molasses, is made in the first refining stage. The color is dark amber and the flavor is similar to burnt sugar. Dark molasses is made during the second refining stage and is darker in color, less sweet, with a heartier, somewhat bitter flavor. Light molasses is the best choice for use in most recipes, while the stronger flavor of dark molasses works well in gingerbread. Thick and rather bitter, blackstrap molasses has an intense flavor that overpowers the flavors of other cookie ingredients.

Molasses should be stored at room temperature.

Honey

Honey has nearly the same sweetening power as granulated sugar. It absorbs moisture from the air, so cookies made with honey will be soft and moist. Crisp cookies containing honey lose their crispness and soften rapidly.

Because honey is a liquid sweetener, it does not contain the particles needed to create friction with the butter during creaming. Baked goods made with honey tend to be more dense and heavier than those made with granulated sugar or brown sugar. It is difficult to create light, fluffy cookies using honey as the sweetener. Honey caramelizes

quickly and at lower temperatures than sugar, causing cookies to brown faster and sometimes burn. In addition, the flavor of honey can change when it is exposed to high oven temperatures.

I find the strong taste of honey overpowers the flavor balance of most cookies. The flavor of honey is determined by the type of flowers harvested by the bees. Some honeys, such as buckwheat, have a flavor that is too intense for cookies. If you chose to use honey when baking cookies, select a mild-flavored honey, such as clover.

While I do not recommend substituting honey for sugar in any cookie recipe, in some cases it can be done if you are willing to sacrifice the flavor, texture and appearance of your cookies. Replace no more than half of the sugar in a recipe with a mild honey. For each $1/2$ cup (125 mL) of honey used, reduce the liquid called for in the recipe by 2 tablespoons (25 mL).

Honey should be stored at room temperature. If honey crystallizes, it may be warmed in the microwave on medium power just until the crystals dissolve. Cool the honey to room temperature before using.

Corn Syrup

Corn syrup is made from cornstarch that is converted into corn sugar and then turned into a liquid. It is available in both light and dark varieties that can be used interchangeably. Clarified and flavored with vanilla, light corn syrup is used most frequently in baking. Dark corn syrup has a more pronounced caramel flavor and a deeper color.

Frequently used in icings and candies, corn syrup helps prevent the recrystallization of granulated sugars. A small quantity of corn syrup is sometimes added to cookies to make them moist. It browns at a lower temperature than sugar, making cookies that are crispy on the outside and soft on the inside.

Corn syrup should be stored at room temperature.

Artificial Sweeteners Do Not Make Good Cookies

Artificial sweeteners and low-calorie sweeteners are not recommended for baking and should not be substituted for the sugar in any of the recipes in this book. While sugar provides many important characteristics, such as texture, color, volume, moisture and, most importantly, flavor, artificial sweeteners lack these characteristics, do not interact well with other cookie ingredients and produce only mediocre results.

Artificial sweeteners only provide sweetness, which means that cookies made with artificial sweeteners lack the richness of flavor that develops as sugar caramelizes during the baking process. Because artificial sweeteners do not provide the rich flavor of sugar, substituting artificial sweeteners for sugar in baked goods means that extracts and other flavor ingredients need to be increased to compensate for the lack of flavor. The composition of artificial sweeteners changes when exposed to the heat of baking, which can cause them to turn bitter or develop an unpleasant flavor.

Artificial sweeteners do not have the same volume as sugar. As a result, they do not aerate and lighten cookie doughs and batters during the creaming process the way sugar does. This volume difference significantly alters the proportions of the recipe, and baking results can be very disappointing, producing cookies that are heavy and dense. Cookies made with artificial sweeteners are also not as tender and have a tougher texture than cookies made with sugar. Additional leavening is needed to improve the texture of the cookies.

Sugar caramelizes and browns as it bakes, adding color. Cookies made with artificial sweeteners are very pale in color and do not brown like cookies made with sugar. The doneness of the cookies cannot easily be determined by color or appearance. Because cookies made with artificial sweeteners bake faster than cookies made with sugar, it can be difficult to determine when the cookies are done.

Sugar also acts as a preservative in cookies and other baked goods, helping them retain their moisture, flavor and freshness, and prolonging shelf life. Artificial sweeteners cannot provide these natural preservative properties, and these baked goods can quickly turn stale. Cookies made with artificial sweeteners need to be eaten or frozen within 24 hours of baking to prevent them from becoming dry and hard.

Fats

There are two basic types of fats used in cookie baking — solid fats and liquid fats. Butter is a solid fat that is soft at room temperature. Shortening is a solid fat that holds its shape and maintains its texture at room temperature. Vegetable oil is a liquid fat.

Fats play several key roles in baking cookies. They influence a cookie's flavor and color, add moisture to cookies and help keep them fresh. Fats are also an important element in determining the texture and spread of a cookie. They make cookies tender by keeping the proteins in the flour from developing into gluten. When creamed with sugar, solid fats trap the air that lightens the cookies, adds structure and gives them their tender crumb. During baking, solid and liquid fats release moisture in the form of steam that helps cookies cook, set and crisp.

Different fats react differently when exposed to heat. Cookies made with butter, which melts at a low temperature, will tend to spread more, while cookies made with shortening, which melts at a higher temperature, will hold their shape better. To take advantage of their different characteristics, some recipes will call for a combination of butter and shortening to get the best cookie texture.

Cookie recipes are formulated to balance all of the ingredients, including their specific characteristics and reactions, to achieve the best results. Reducing the amount of fat in a recipe will make the cookies tougher and less flavorful, and they'll dry out sooner. The different types of fats are not interchangeable in recipes. Substituting one fat for another will yield significantly different results.

Butter

Butter is the perfect fat to use in so many cookie recipes. It contributes significantly to a cookie's tender texture and provides moisture that is essential during baking. But butter has an even more important part to play in cookie baking. It adds an amazingly rich, delicious and wonderful flavor to cookies that no other fat can provide, making it the fat of choice for many cookie bakers. Butter also browns as it bakes, helping give cookies their lovely golden color. Cookies made with butter are crisper than cookies made with shortening.

Only use butter in stick or brick form for baking. Not only is it easy to measure, but stick butter contains a high fat content that allows the butter to hold its shape. Butter sold in tubs has a higher ratio of water or air than stick butter and will significantly alter the texture of cookies.

Salt is added to butter to increase the shelf life of the product. The amount of salt in salted butters can vary quite a bit and significantly alter the flavor balance in cookies and other baked goods. Salted butter can also sometimes develop an unpleasant taste during long storage.

Unsalted butter is the best choice for cookies and all manner of baked goods. It has a fresh, sweet, cream flavor that adds immeasurably to the overall taste of the cookie. Using unsalted butter gives you control over the amount of salt in the recipe. Also, unsalted butter has a lower water content and higher fat content than salted butter, so cookies tend to spread less during baking. Because butter adds so much flavor and texture, always choose a high-quality unsalted butter for cookie baking.

Be sure your butter is fresh before using it to bake cookies. Fresh butter has a uniform color and texture all the way through the stick. If the outside of the butter is darker in color than the inside, the butter has started to oxidize from air exposure. Oxidized butter can taste stale and alter the flavor of cookies. Always taste butter, especially if it has been frozen, before using it in baking. If the butter is old or has absorbed flavors from other items in the refrigerator or freezer, it can develop an unpleasant "off" taste.

Don't use "light" butter as it contains a high percentage of water that will alter the structure of cookies. Whipped butter shouldn't be used for baking cookies because it's mostly air and has little fat content. Cookies made with whipped butter won't hold their shape during baking and will lack in flavor.

Store butter in the refrigerator at a temperature below 40°F (4°C) to maintain its freshness. Always use butter by the date stamped on the package. For longer storage, butter may be frozen for up to 4 months. Freezing longer may affect the quality of the butter's flavor and texture.

Margarine Is Not Recommended

I do not use margarine in my cookies, and I strongly advise against substituting margarine in any cookie recipe that calls for butter. In cookie baking, butter adds so much to the flavor and texture. You just won't get the same results with margarine.

Margarine is made from vegetable oil and contains a significant amount of water that will alter both the flavor and the texture of cookies. Margarines with a high water content yield tougher cookies that will dry out faster. Cookie doughs made with margarine may require additional chilling before shaping and baking. In an attempt to improve their flavor, nearly all margarines also contain a significant amount of salt, which can upset the flavor balance of cookies and other baked goods.

If you chose to use margarine in your cookies for dietary reasons, buy margarine in stick form only and be sure it contains at least 80% vegetable oil. Never use any product labeled as a "spread." These contain higher proportions of air and water and will not make good cookies.

Shortening

Hydrogenated vegetable shortening, referred to as vegetable shortening in this book, is a solid fat made from vegetable oil. It produces cookies with a softer, more cake-like texture than cookies made with butter. Because shortening melts at a higher temperature than butter, the structure of the cookies partially sets before the shortening fully melts, so the

Freezing Butter for Longer Storage

To freeze butter, tightly wrap the carton of butter or individual sticks in heavy-duty foil. Place in a plastic freezer bag, remove the air and seal tightly. Date the bag and store in the back of freezer, where the temperature is more constant. Store butter for up to 4 months. Freezing longer may affect the butter's flavor and texture.

To thaw frozen butter, remove foil and place unopened cartons or sticks in the refrigerator and allow them to thaw overnight. Thaw only enough butter for immediate use or for use within 1 week. Always taste butter before use in baking to determine freshness.

cookies don't spread as much. Cookies made with shortening get their flavor from other ingredients, such as chocolate, extracts and spices.

While both plain and butter-flavored shortenings are commonly available, I prefer to use plain shortening and add other ingredients to flavor the cookies. Butter-flavored shortenings are artificially flavored and can sometimes develop an "off," or rancid, taste, especially if stored at warm room temperatures.

Shortening is sold in packages of sticks that measure 1 cup (250 mL) each and in cans of various sizes. Store shortening in a cool, dry cupboard or pantry for up to a year.

Oil

Some cookie recipes call for vegetable oil. Like butter and shortening, oil provides moisture and makes cookies tender. Oil does not aid in leavening because it cannot be creamed to incorporate air.

Always use an oil with a neutral flavor, such as canola, corn or safflower oil. Oils labeled simply as vegetable oil are usually a blend of neutral-flavored oils and are a good choice for cookie baking. Do not bake with oils that have a strong or distinct flavor, such as olive oil or peanut oil. These oils will significantly alter the flavor of cookies and other baked goods in an unpleasant way.

Store oil in a cool, dark cupboard or pantry. Don't store it in the refrigerator as the oil will turn cloudy. Always smell oil before you use it to make sure it has not turned rancid.

Leaveners

Baking soda and baking powder are chemical leaveners that lighten the texture of cookies. These two leaveners have different chemical compositions and react with ingredients in different ways. The leavening strength of baking soda is four times as powerful as baking powder, and these leaveners are not interchangeable. If the recipe calls for baking powder and all you have in the cupboard is baking soda, it's time for a trip to the store.

When combined with liquid, both baking soda and baking powder release carbon dioxide, which causes cookies and other baked goods to rise. Baking powder is a universal leavening agent, while baking soda works best when an acid is present to trigger the action of the leavener. In recipes containing both baking powder and baking soda, the baking powder does most of the leavening. The baking soda is added to neutralize acids in the recipe, add tenderness to the cookies and provide some leavening.

Baking powder and baking soda should be stored in a cool, dry cupboard or pantry, away from moisture, and replaced every 6 months to ensure freshness and full leavening power in your baked goods.

Baking Soda

Baking soda is a natural alkaline that, when combined with liquid and an acid ingredient, immediately releases carbon dioxide. In recipes calling for baking soda as the only leavener, in order to work properly the recipe must include an acid ingredient, such as brown sugar, molasses, chocolate, natural cocoa powder, citrus juice, buttermilk or sour cream.

If there is too little acid in the recipe to neutralize the alkalinity of the baking soda, the cookies may not rise properly and can develop a soapy taste. In turn, baking soda balances the acid, which helps the cookies to develop a golden brown color as they bake. Cookies containing too much baking soda will spread out quite a bit, be very thin and may contain air pockets. Excessive amounts of baking soda can also make cookies taste too salty. It is important to measure ingredients accurately.

Because the leavening process begins immediately after contact with liquid, baking soda should not be used as the primary leavener in recipes that require chilling prior to baking. Any delay in baking will make the baking soda less effective.

Baking Powder

Baking powder is a compound leavener. The primary ingredient is baking soda, but baking powder also contains cornstarch and an acid, usually cream of tartar, to activate the baking soda. The cornstarch acts as a buffer to delay the reaction of the baking soda and acid after combination with the liquid.

Because the baking soda and acid ratio is already sufficient in baking powder, the amount of acid in the recipe doesn't need to be balanced to the proportion of baking powder as it does with baking soda. Baking powder does not neutralize the acid ingredients in the cookie dough. A higher acid level makes cookies spread less, bake faster and be lighter in color.

Double-acting baking powder, the most common variety found in stores, packs a double punch of leavening power. It starts to react when it comes in contact with liquid during mixing and again when the cookies are placed in the oven and the baking powder is heated. This makes it the ideal leavening choice for cookie doughs that are chilled before baking.

Adding an excessive amount of baking powder to a recipe can result in cookies with a metallic aftertaste.

Are baking powder and baking soda still fresh?

Have you had those containers of baking soda and baking powder in the cabinet for a while? Are you wondering if they're still good for baking? Here's a quick test to check their effectiveness.

Baking Soda

In a small bowl or glass, mix 2 teaspoons (10 mL) white vinegar and ¼ teaspoon (1 mL) baking soda. If the mixture immediately bubbles up, your baking soda is good.

Baking Powder

In a small bowl or glass, mix ¼ cup (50 mL) hot water and ½ teaspoon (2 mL) baking powder. If the mixture immediately bubbles up, your baking powder is good.

Cream of Tartar

Cream of tartar (tartaric acid) is an acid. Tartaric acid is a by-product of winemaking. During fermentation, a white sediment develops and lines the inside of the wine casks. After the wine is removed from the casks, this sediment is collected and purified and then ground to produce the very fine white powder that we know as cream of tartar.

Cream of tartar reacts with baking soda to make it work when combined with a liquid. It is the acid ingredient commonly found in most baking powders. In cookie recipes leavened with baking soda alone and containing no other acid ingredients, cream of

tartar is added to activate the baking soda.

Cream of tartar can be found in the spice section of most grocery stores. Stored in a cool, dry location away from moisture, cream of tartar will keep indefinitely.

Eggs

Eggs provide proteins, fat and moisture and contribute to the structure and texture of cookies. Like flour, eggs bind other ingredients. They help hold cookies together and keep them from spreading too much in the oven. As eggs are beaten, their proteins create a structure that traps the air and liquids that help define a cookie's texture. During baking, the trapped air bubbles expand and make the cookies rise. Eggs also add richness, tenderness and color to baked goods.

Egg yolks add moisture to cookies and encourage browning. They also act as an emulsifier, helping to blend the fat with the liquid ingredients. Egg whites dry out cookies and make them crisper. Never substitute all egg whites for the whole eggs in a recipe; those cookies will be very dry and crumbly. Using egg substitute in place of fresh eggs in cookies and baked goods is not recommended. Egg substitutes are made primarily from egg whites and will significantly affect the quality of your cookies.

All of the recipes in this book use large eggs, the standard size used for baking. If you do not have large eggs, then lightly beat your eggs and substitute ¼ cup (50 mL) beaten egg for each large egg called for in the recipe.

Store eggs, in their original carton, on a shelf in the refrigerator and use them within 3 to 5 weeks of purchase. Eggs should not be stored in the refrigerator door, where they're subjected to temperature changes every time the door is opened.

Dairy

Liquid dairy products play a minor flavor and texture role in most cookie recipes. However, adding too much liquid can cause cookies to spread too thin. In recipes calling for larger quantities, dairy products add moisture, flavor and texture. Moisture in dairy products works to activate the leavening agents in the dough. Solid dairy items, such as sour cream and cream cheese, contribute to the structure, texture and flavor of the cookies.

Milk

Recipes in this book calling for milk were tested using whole milk, which contains $3\frac{1}{2}$% milk fat. The fat contributes to the structure of the cookies. Lower-fat milks may be substituted, but there will be a difference in flavor and texture.

Half-and-Half (10%) Cream

Half-and-half (10%) cream is a blend of whole milk and cream and contains $10\frac{1}{2}$% to 18% milk fat. It lends richness and flavor to cookies. Whole milk may be substituted, but its lower milk fats will alter the flavor and texture of the cookies.

Whipping (35%) Cream

Whipping (35%) cream contributes flavor and texture in cookie recipes. Milk or half-and-half (10%) cream should not be substituted for whipping (35%) cream as the reduction in fat will alter the cookie's structure. Some grocery stores carry products labeled "light" and "heavy" whipping cream. Light whipping cream contains 30% milk fat and heavy whipping cream contains between 36% and 49% milk fat. When a recipe calls for whipping (35%) cream, light whipping cream may be used. If the recipe specifies heavy whipping cream, then that is what should be used to achieve the right texture.

Buttermilk

Buttermilk, a thick and creamy cultured milk, adds a special flavor and tenderness to cookies, bars and brownies. It is usually made from lower-fat milk and has an acidic tang. Choose a high-quality buttermilk with a good, fresh flavor.

Sweetened Condensed Milk

Sweetened condensed milk is a thick, sweet canned milk product. It is made by removing about 50% of the water from whole milk, then combining up to 40% sugar with the thick milk. Regular, reduced-fat or nonfat sweetened condensed milk may be used in the recipes calling for sweetened condensed milk without any noticeable difference in results.

Evaporated Milk

Evaporated milk is a canned milk product in which 60% of the water has been removed. Do not substitute evaporated milk for any other milk product in a cookie as the results will be significantly different.

Sour Cream

Sour cream has a milk fat content of 14% and is made by souring cream with an acidifier. It contributes to the flavor, texture and moisture of baked goods. Reduced-fat and nonfat sour creams contain thickeners and have a stronger sour flavor. Substituting these for regular sour cream may alter the flavor and texture of cookies.

Cream Cheese

Cream cheese is a fresh cheese made from cream and has a milk fat content of 33%. It adds wonderful flavor and gives cookies a very tender texture. Cream cheese is used in cookie doughs, bar and brownie fillings, and frostings. Reduced-fat and nonfat cream cheese products contain thickeners that can alter the product's texture and flavor when baked. Because the fat in cream cheese is an integral part of the recipe, substituting reduced-fat and nonfat varieties can significantly affect the quality of the finished cookie.

Chocolates and Cocoa Powders

For many chocolate-lovers, there is no other flavor for cookies and cakes. There are two ingredients responsible for bringing that luxurious flavor to cookies, brownies and bars — chocolate and cocoa powder. Let's take a closer look at both of these wonderful ingredients.

Chocolate

Chocolate has been enchanting people for over 3000 years. Chocolate, from the Aztec word *xocolatl*, is made from the seeds, called beans, of the *Theobroma cacao* tree, which is native to the tropical regions of Central and South America. The Olmec Indians are believed to be the first culture to have grown cocoa beans as a domestic crop.

Chocolate is made by drying or roasting, then husking and grinding the cacao beans.

Heat is applied during the grinding process, causing the beans to release cocoa butter. This mixture of ground beans and cocoa butter, called chocolate liquor, is the base from which all chocolate is made. The higher the chocolate liquor content in a chocolate, the more intense the flavor. Emulsifiers are added to the cocoa particles to make the chocolate smooth.

There are many flavors of chocolate, each with its own unique taste characteristics. Traditionally, unsweetened chocolate was considered the standard for baking. However, many unsweetened chocolates are not high-quality and require a significant amount of additional sugar and fat in the baked goods to make the flavor palatable.

Many professional bakers now choose bittersweet chocolate instead of unsweetened chocolate for all their baking. I fall into this category. I don't like to bake with a chocolate that doesn't have a good flavor when eaten out-of-hand. Too much effort and other ingredients have to be put in to make the final product taste good. The recipes in this book are designed to use bittersweet chocolate or semisweet chocolate, both of which are readily available, as the primary baking chocolate. In most recipes, bittersweet chocolate and semisweet chocolate can be used interchangeably, depending on your preference.

A chocolate's flavor depends on the quality of the beans and how they were grown, roasted and processed. The flavor of chocolate can vary significantly from one brand to another. Some contain more chocolate liquor and cocoa butter, while others contain more sugar. The very best chocolates contain pure vanilla extract rather than artificial vanilla flavoring. Which brand of chocolate to use in baking is very much a personal choice. Taste several different chocolates and bake with what you like best.

Chocolate chips contain less cocoa butter than chocolate shaped in bar form, which helps them retain their chip shape when heated during baking. This makes chocolate chips great for making chocolate chip cookies but not a good choice for melting. Bar chocolate melts more uniformly with a smoother texture and combines better with the other ingredients in cookie dough.

Chocolate can sometimes develop a harmless powdery coating called bloom. When stored in a warm or humid location, a small amount of cocoa butter can separate from the chocolate. This cocoa butter bloom is harmless and will reincorporate back into the chocolate when it is melted. To prevent bloom, store chocolate in a cool, dry place. Never store chocolate in the refrigerator or freezer. When melted, moisture on the chocolate will cause it to seize up and harden into lumps. It will not melt smoothly and will become unusable for baking.

Unsweetened Baking Chocolate
Unsweetened chocolate, also called baking chocolate, is made entirely of chocolate liquor and contains no sugar, cream or flavorings. It is very bitter and meant for baking only, not for eating.

Bittersweet Chocolate
Bittersweet chocolate contains a minimum of 35% chocolate liquor, with many brands around 50% and some even higher. The more chocolate liquor, the more intense the flavor. Bittersweet chocolate also differs from unsweetened chocolate in that it contains some sugar and additional cocoa butter to make it richer and smoother.

Semisweet Chocolate
Semisweet chocolate contains a minimum of 15% to 35% chocolate liquor, added cocoa butter and more sugar than bittersweet chocolate.

Sweet Dark Chocolate
Sweet dark chocolate contains as much as 70% chocolate liquor and added cocoa butter. It has more sugar than bittersweet chocolate but less sugar than semisweet chocolate. This is my favorite chocolate for baking and eating.

Milk Chocolate
Milk chocolate contains a minimum of 10% chocolate liquor, added cocoa butter and a fair amount of sugar. It also contains between 12% and 20% cream or milk solids.

Chocolate Chips
Chocolate chips are available in all chocolate flavors, and semisweet chocolate chips even come in a fun miniature size. There are also chocolate chips containing artificial flavorings, but I don't recommend using these for baking

cookies as they can develop an "off" flavor during baking. Some lesser known or generic brands of chocolate chips use a lower-quality chocolate and no cocoa butter in their chips. Always check the ingredient label to make sure the chocolate chips contain cocoa butter. Do not bake with any chocolate chips that don't have a really good chocolate flavor.

White Chocolate

White chocolate is technically not a chocolate because it does not contain any chocolate liquor. It is made from cocoa butter, sugar, cream or milk solids and flavorings. If it doesn't contain cocoa butter, then it isn't white chocolate. Read the ingredients label to be sure you are buying real white chocolate with cocoa butter.

Imitation products, frequently made with palm kernel oil, are usually labeled as white confectionery bars. Imitation chips are called vanilla baking chips or simply white chips. These bland coatings are not worth the money. They have little flavor, poor texture, do not melt well and should not be used in baking cookies.

Cocoa Powder

Cocoa powder is made from the solid particles that are left after cocoa butter has been removed from crushed and roasted cacao beans. These particles are finely ground and sieved to produce a powder. The quantity of cocoa butter remaining in the cocoa powder varies by brand and can range from virtually nothing to nearly 35%.

There are two standard types of unsweetened cocoa powder available in stores — natural and Dutch-process. For best results, use the type of cocoa powder called for in the recipe. Always use unsweetened cocoa powder for baking. Don't use a cocoa drink mix or powdered ground chocolate. Both contain high amounts of sugar, and some contain powdered milk as well. Store cocoa powder in a cool, dry place. Exposure to moisture can cause cocoa powder to clump.

Natural Cocoa Powder

Natural cocoa powder is slightly acidic and has a somewhat bitter flavor. Recipes using natural cocoa powder contain more sugar to balance the sharper flavor of the cocoa. While natural cocoa powder may be substituted for Dutch-process cocoa powder in most recipes, the flavor of the finished cookies or baked goods will be slightly bitter.

Dutch-Process Cocoa Powder

Dutch-process cocoa powder is a refined cocoa treated with a small amount of an alkali solution to neutralize the natural acids. This process improves the flavor and color of the cocoa. The darker color and mellower flavor make Dutch-process cocoa powder the perfect choice for baking rich, intense brownies and cookies. All of the recipes in this book using cocoa are made with Dutch-process cocoa powder.

Black Cocoa Powder

Black cocoa is the very darkest cocoa powder. A standard in the baking industry, black cocoa is a Dutch-process cocoa powder treated with additional alkali to deepen the color and mellow the flavor even more. If you've wondered how professional bakers make those really dark, chocolaty cakes and cookies, the answer is black cocoa. It is now available by mail-order to home bakers. (See Cookie Supply Sources, page 562) Black cocoa powder may be substituted in a recipe for part or all of the regular Dutch-process cocoa powder.

The newer special dark cocoa blends available in many grocery stores are a combination of natural cocoa and black cocoa powders. I love to use it in my recipes to make decadent, fudgy brownies.

Nuts

Nuts add a tantalizing crunchy texture and a special flavor to many varieties of cookies. Each type of nut has its own characteristics and unique taste. Toasting or roasting dries the natural oils in nuts, enhances their flavor and helps maintain their crunch. Salt is great on nuts that will be eaten out-of-hand, but only unsalted nuts should be used in baking. Salted nuts can give cookies an unpleasant, overly salty taste.

Cookie bakers have a great advantage over years past in that many nuts can now be purchased already toasted or roasted and ready for baking. If you live in the United States and are fortunate to have a Trader Joe's store in your area, they are a great place for buying nuts and have a very wide selection. (See Cookie Supply Sources, page 562.)

Some people have serious allergies to nuts, while others just don't like the flavor of nuts. Except in cases where nuts are an integral part of the recipe, nuts can usually be added to or omitted from cookies and brownies without altering the texture too much.

Nut oils can turn rancid quickly. Always taste nuts to make sure they are fresh before adding them to your cookies. If you are not planning to use your nuts within 2 to 3 weeks of purchase, wrap the nuts well and seal in freezer bags and freeze until ready to use. Frozen nuts thaw quickly. Bring them to room temperature before adding to cookie doughs and batters.

Walnuts
Walnuts are a universal nut and a great choice for all kinds of baked goods. English walnuts, the kind typically found in grocery stores, have a mild flavor and are the best ones to use in cookies. The intense and slightly bitter taste of black walnuts can overpower the flavor of other cookie ingredients.

Pecans
Pecans have a sweet, buttery flavor. These higher-fat nuts add a wonderful richness to cookies. Pecans can be used interchangeably with walnuts in most recipes.

Almonds
Almonds have a pale color and a delicate flavor. Toasting almonds helps them stay crunchy.

Pistachio Nuts
Like almonds, pistachios have a mild, sweet flavor. The nut meat has a distinctive light green color that makes them a fun choice for baking.

Cashews
Cashews have a distinct, buttery flavor and curved shape. Always buy roasted unsalted cashews for use in baking cookies.

Macadamia Nuts
Macadamia nuts have a rich, buttery, sweet flavor. Thought of as Hawaiian, where most of the crop is grown, macadamia nuts are actually native to Australia. For baking

cookies, purchase macadamia nuts already roasted and unsalted.

Peanuts
Peanuts are not actually a nut but a shelled legume grown underground. For cookie baking, buy roasted, unsalted peanuts that have already had the skins removed.

Hazelnuts
Hazelnuts, or filberts, are a mild nut with a somewhat sweet flavor. Buy hazelnuts that have already had the bitter skins removed.

Almond Paste
Almond paste is a sweet, granular mixture of ground almonds and sugar. It is used in some cookie recipes and frequently as a filling for pastries.

Fruit Ingredients
There are many fruit ingredients that can be added to cookies to enhance their flavor and provide a nice texture. Choose high-quality fruit and fruit products to get the best results.

Dried Fruit
Dried fruits, such as apricots, cherries, cranberries, blueberries, dates and raisins, add incredible bursts of flavor to cookies. Choose dried fruit that is plump, tender and soft. Fruit that is dried out will be tough and draw moisture from the cookies, making them dry. If the dried fruit in your cupboard is past its prime, it's time to buy new fruit.

Coconut
Coconut is a terrific ingredient to add to cookies to give them a tropical flair. A number of recipes in this book are built around coconut and its sweet flavor. When coconut is used as an ingredient, the recipe specifies sweetened flaked coconut. This is the standard coconut found in the baking aisle at grocery stores. The recipe is designed to take into account the sweetness of the coconut. Desiccated or unsweetened coconut should not be substituted for sweetened flaked coconut in these recipes.

Citrus Fruit
Citrus juice and zest give cookies a bright, fresh, tangy flavor. Use only the outer, colored portion of citrus peel, called the zest. This

colored zest contains all the flavorful citrus oils. The white pith underneath the zest is very bitter and will cause the cookies to taste quite bitter and unpleasant. Citrus fruit purchased at the store is coated with a light vegetable wax to protect and prolong the freshness of the fruit. Before zesting the fruit, remove this wax by gently scrubbing the fruit with a soft brush and drying it thoroughly.

Freshly squeezed citrus juices have the best taste. Never use the lemon or lime juice that comes in those little plastic, fruit-shaped containers or bottles. It is very sour and will ruin the flavor of your cookies. When juicing citrus fruits, be careful not to squeeze or ream the fruit so much that you press into the outer white pith, as this can turn the juice bitter. Freshly squeezed citrus juices should be strained to remove any seeds.

Jams

Jams play a major role as fillings in cookies, particularly in bars and squares. Because the jam is so essential to the overall taste of the cookie, it is important to use a quality jam with a great flavor. If you make your own jams, cookies are a great way to showcase your homemade creations. While there are a number of fruit spreads on the market, those with very low sugar contents may be too tart to balance with the sweetness of the cookies. I recommend using a regular jam in these recipes.

Extracts and Flavorings

There are a number of extracts and flavorings used in baking that give incredible flavor to cookies. Whenever available, use only pure extracts. These are made from the essence of the fruit, herb or other ingredient; have the best, cleanest, purest flavor; and will taste wonderful in your cookies and other baked goods. Imitation flavorings can't compare to the real thing.

Flavorings like maple, rum and brandy give cookies a stronger flavor than their liquid counterparts. A teaspoon (5 mL) of maple flavoring will give as much maple flavor as ¼ cup (125 mL) maple syrup without adding so much liquid. This allows you to make intensely flavored cookies without them spreading all over the cookie sheet.

Vanilla Extract

Vanilla comes from a tropical orchid plant, *Vanilla planifolla*, that grows within the 20° band on either side of the equator and is native to the Americas. The Totonaca people of the Gulf Coast of Mexico are believed to be the first people to cultivate vanilla. The Spaniards introduced vanilla to the rest of the world when they brought it from Mexico to Spain in the early 1500s. It is now grown in many countries, with the largest of the world's vanilla crops being produced in Madagascar and Indonesia. Though there are about 150 varieties of vanilla, only two — Bourbon and Tahitian — are used commercially.

Vanilla is the most labor-intensive agricultural crop in the world, which is why it is so expensive. A vanilla plant blooms for the first time three years after planting, and the fruit, long slender pods that resemble green beans, must mature for 9 months before it can be harvested. The harvested beans are treated with hot water or heat and sun-dried for several weeks or months. The dried beans are then allowed to rest for a couple of months to fully develop their flavor.

Pure vanilla extract is made by circulating diluted alcohol through finely chopped, dried vanilla beans, then straining the extract. It has a strong, rich flavor and tantalizing aroma that is unmistakable. Vanilla extract can stand on its own as the primary flavor in a cookie and also enhances and enriches the flavor of other ingredients, such as chocolate.

Imitation vanilla is an artificial flavoring made from synthetic flavors and colors. The taste of imitation vanilla cannot even come close to the flavor of pure vanilla extract. It may be cheap, but it's still not worth the money. I strongly advise using only pure vanilla extract in baking. If you're going to take the time and spend the money to bake cookies for yourself, your family and friends, why use an artificial ingredient that leaves your cookies lacking in flavor?

Almond Extract

After vanilla, almond extract is the most frequently used extract in cookie baking. Almond extract is made from bitter almonds, not the sweet kind of almond that we eat and add to baked goods. The oil from the almonds is processed, destroying a toxic substance (prussic acid) that is found in bitter almonds, and then combined with alcohol to create almond extract.

As with imitation vanilla, imitation almond extract is not an extract. It is an artificial flavoring made from synthetic flavors and colors and should not be used as a substitute for pure almond extract in cookies.

Instant Espresso Powder

While not really a flavoring, instant espresso powder adds immense flavor to cookies. Love coffee and want to give your cookies a rich coffee flavor? Instant espresso powder packs an intense coffee taste without adding liquid that can cause cookies to spread. The powder is made by spray-drying brewed espresso, a concentrated coffee made from darkly roasted coffee beans, and then processing it into very fine granules.

Salt

In cookies, salt acts as a flavor enhancer. In a small quantity, it balances and intensifies the flavor of other ingredients in the dough or batter. In larger amounts, salt has a distinct flavor all its own that can easily upset a cookie's delicate flavor balance and overpower the other ingredients. Salt shouldn't be eliminated from cookie recipes. Without salt, some cookies will taste bland and unexciting.

A small amount of salt is also frequently added to frostings to cut the intensity of the sugar's sweetness.

Table salt is the preferred choice for use in cookies because its fine grains distribute well through the dry ingredients. Kosher salt has coarser grains that don't dissolve evenly during baking and can create salty pockets in cookies. Sea salt usually has a stronger flavor than table salt and can make cookies taste too salty.

Spices

Spices like cinnamon, ginger and nutmeg contribute amazing flavor to cookies. Because they are so strong and can easily overpower the flavors of other ingredients, spices need to be used in small quantities and with great restraint. Cloves are a prime example. Nothing ruins the taste of a cookie quite like the overwhelming flavor of cloves. As a state and county fair judge, I can't count the number of unpalatable cookies that have failed to win awards because the intense flavor of cloves smothered the taste of all other ingredients.

The flavor of spices deteriorates over time, and exposure to heat and moisture causes them to fade rapidly. Buy spices in small quantities, store them in tightly sealed containers in a cool, dry place and use them within 1 year of purchase for the best flavor.

Baking Perfect Cookies

• • •

It's easy to become a great cookie baker. Learn and follow a few basic rules and techniques, and you'll soon be the envy of your family and friends for your wonderful cookies. They'll be lining up for more!

The temperature and measurement of the ingredients, the order they are added, the method of combining them, the correct size and type of pan, the oven temperature and the rack position are all crucial elements of great cookie baking. We will take a close look at these fundamentals and more, and the important role they each play in baking perfect cookies.

Understanding Baking Terms

In order to create great cookies and baked goods, an understanding and working knowledge of the baking terms used in recipes is essential. Some terms have multiple meanings that depend on the type of cooking. The terms below are defined as they are used in baking.

Bake: To cook food using the dry heat of an oven.

Beat: To rapidly stir or whip a single ingredient or mixture of ingredients in a circular motion with a spoon, fork, wire whisk or electric mixer.

Cookie Baking 101

Being organized, following steps in order and paying attention to details are essential to great cookie baking. Below is a quick overview of the cookie-baking process.

- Review the recipe to be sure you have all ingredients.
- Gather all equipment and ingredients needed for the recipe.
- Use the type and size of pan specified in the recipe.
- Prepare cookie sheets or pans according to recipe directions.
- Prepare all ingredients needed for recipe.
- Soften butter and bring eggs and dairy ingredients to room temperature.
- Chop chocolate, nuts and dried fruit.
- Accurately measure all ingredients before starting to mix the cookies.
- Preheat oven for 15 minutes before baking cookies.
- Check oven temperature with a reliable oven thermometer.
- Prepare recipe according to recipe instructions.
- Use proper mixing techniques, baking equipment and utensils.
- Avoid overmixing dough to prevent tough cookies.
- Chill dough, if directed to do so in recipe.
- Make cookies the same size and uniform thickness.
- Place cookie dough on cool cookie sheets, spacing according to recipe instructions.
- Spread brownie batters and bar crust evenly in pan.
- Bake as instructed in recipe.
- Bake only one cookie sheet or baking pan in the oven at a time.
- Use a kitchen timer to accurately time baking.
- Check doneness at shortest baking time.
- Transfer baked cookies to a wire rack to cool.
- Let cookie sheets cool completely between batches.
- Cool cookies completely before icing and/or storing.

Blend: To combine two or more ingredients with a spoon, wire whisk or electric mixer until smooth and evenly mixed.

Chop: To cut chocolate, nuts, dried fruit or other ingredients into $\frac{1}{4}$- to $\frac{1}{2}$-inch (0.5 to 1 cm) pieces.

Combine: To place two or more ingredients in a bowl or container and thoroughly mix together.

Cream: To beat together softened butter or shortening with sugar to incorporate air into the mixture.

Cut in: To combine butter or shortening into a flour mixture until it is evenly distributed in small pieces and the mixture resembles coarse crumbs and starts to come together. This can be done using your fingers, a pastry blender or two knives.

Dash: A small measure of a liquid ingredient, equal to about $\frac{1}{16}$ teaspoon (0.25 mL).

Drizzle: To slowly pour a thin stream of icing over top of finished baked goods or a liquid ingredient into a mixture of other ingredients.

Dust: To lightly sift an ingredient, such as confectioner's sugar, over baked goods to give them a decorative appearance and a sweet finish.

Fold: To gently and slowly blend light or delicate ingredients, such as beaten egg whites or whipped cream, into a mixture with a spoon or spatula by cutting down through the mixture and across the bottom, bringing part of the mixture back up to the top in a circular motion. Or to lightly and evenly incorporate chopped ingredients, such as chocolate or nuts, into a mixed dough or batter without overworking the mixture.

Glaze: To apply a light, even coating of an ingredient or a thin icing to baked goods.

Grate: To rub an ingredient, such as citrus zest, over a grater to make very fine pieces.

Grease: To lightly coat the inside of a baking pan with butter, shortening or nonstick cooking spray to prevent baked goods from sticking.

Mix: To stir or beat together two or more ingredients with a spoon or electric mixer until thoroughly combined.

Pinch: A small measure of a dry ingredient, such as salt, that can be picked up and held between the thumb and forefinger. A pinch is less than $\frac{1}{8}$ teaspoon (0.5 mL).

Preheat: To bring the oven up to the full temperature stated in the recipe before baking.

Room temperature: In terms of baking, 72°F (22°C) is considered room temperature.

Scant: An amount of an ingredient slightly less than the indicated measurement.

Separate: Refers to eggs, meaning to separate the egg white from the egg yolk.

Sift: To pass dry ingredients, such as confectioner's sugar and cocoa powder, through a fine-meshed sieve or a sifter to remove any lumps. Ingredients are also sifted to combine and aerate them.

Soften: To bring chilled butter to a beatable temperature by letting it stand at room temperature until it reaches about 65°F (18°C).

Stir: To gently blend a combination of ingredients by hand, using a spoon or wire whisk in a circular motion.

Whip: To rapidly beat a single ingredient or mixture of ingredients using a wire whisk or an electric mixer fitted with the whip attachment, to incorporate air and increase the volume.

Whisk: To mix two or more ingredients together using a wire whisk until well combined and smooth.

Preparing Cookie Sheets and Baking Pans

Proper preparation of cookie sheets and baking pans will ensure even baking and keep cookies, bars and brownies from sticking to the sheets and pans.

Cookie Sheets

To prevent cookies from sticking, line cookie sheets with parchment paper. This will not only help the cookies release effortlessly but will help keep the bottoms of the cookies from overbrowning and make it quick and easy to transfer them to the cooling rack by simply sliding the parchment paper off the pan and onto the rack. You can grease cookie sheets with shortening or nonstick cooking spray if you prefer, but greased sheets will cause the cookies to spread out and lose their shape. Because exposed butter can burn easily, it should not be used for greasing cookie sheets. Never use salted butter to grease cookie sheets as it will cause the cookies to stick.

Baking Pans

For the bar-type recipes in this book, I like to line the baking pans with heavy-duty foil. Not only does it make it really easy to remove bars, squares, brownies and shortbreads from the pan in one piece, it also protects pans from knife cuts and makes cleanup a breeze. For bars and brownies made in a 13- by 9-inch (3 L) baking pan, and squares with heavy ingredients, line the pan with two layers of foil. The double foil provides extra support to keep the bars from bending in the middle when removed from the pan.

To easily shape the foil to fit the pan, fold the foil over the outside of the pan, leaving 1 to 2 inches (2.5 to 5 cm) of foil extending over edges on at least two opposite sides. Carefully fit the shaped foil into the pan, pressing tightly against the pan bottom and sides, and fold the foil extensions down over the outside of the pan.

After lining, the bottom and sides of the pan should be greased to prevent the bars from sticking. If you choose not to line your pan, it should still be greased to prevent sticking. Nonstick cooking spray and unsalted butter are both good choices for greasing pans; however, do not use salted butter — the salt will make the bars stick to the foil or pan.

I have fallen in love with the nonstick foil now readily available in grocery stores. If you use nonstick foil to line the pan, there is

no need to grease it. Bars and brownies won't stick!

Preheating the Oven

Properly preheating the oven is a crucial step to successful cookie baking. Never put cookies into an oven that isn't fully preheated. If the oven isn't hot enough, the fat in the cookies will melt too much before the cookies can set, resulting in flat, thin, wide-spread cookies. The cookies won't brown as well and take longer to bake, which can dry them out and make them tough and crumbly.

Checking Your Oven's Temperature

If you have trouble with your cookies taking a longer time to bake than indicated in the recipe or browning too quickly before the center is done, check the accuracy of your oven's temperature control.

Place the oven rack in the center position and set a freestanding oven thermometer on the rack. Set the oven temperature to 350°F (180°C) and let it heat up for 15 minutes before checking the temperature. If the thermometer reads lower than 350°F (180°C), make note of the temperature difference and increase the oven setting by that number of degrees. If the thermometer reads higher than 350°F (180°C), then reduce the oven setting by that number of degrees. Each time you bake, adjust your oven setting so that it heats to the correct temperature. If your oven is off by more than 25°F (14°C), you may want to have the thermostat recalibrated.

Before turning on the oven, set the top oven rack in the center position to ensure the cookies bake evenly. Always turn the oven on before starting to mix or roll the cookie dough, following the recipe instructions. Some new ovens preheat very quickly, but most ovens need about 15 minutes to heat up to 350°F (180°C) and longer for higher temperatures. It's always better to have a hot oven waiting for the cookies rather than cookies warming up on the counter waiting for the oven to reach temperature.

After the oven comes to temperature, open the door only when needed and only for as long as necessary. Bring the cookie sheet to the oven, and then open the door. If you open the oven door, then cross the kitchen

---

Baking Pan Size Matters

Choosing the appropriate size of baking pan can make the difference between success and failure. All of the recipes in this book call for standard-sized baking pans. Always use the size and shape of pan specified in the recipe. Changing the pan will yield different results. A smaller pan will cause bars or squares to underbake and they may overflow the pan, while using a larger pan will produce thin bars or squares that overbake or burn. Some bars or squares may overcook on the outside, yet remain undercooked in the center.

to pick up the cookie sheet to put it in the oven, by the time you shut the door the oven temperature can drop as much as 25°F (14°C). During baking, if you open the door to check on the cookies, take a quick peek, then shut the door again to keep in the heat.

Preparing Ingredients

The ingredients you chose to bake with and how you prepare them has a direct impact on the way your cookies will turn out. Paying attention to these details will give you the best possible results.

Quality Counts

Always use quality ingredients for baking. You truly can taste the difference. Cookies are all about flavor, and you can't get great flavor from discount and imitation ingredients. Yes, a good butter and pure vanilla extract cost more money than their lesser counterparts, but they also pack a flavor wallop that you can't get from the cheap stuff.

Just as important as the quality of the ingredients is how you handle and prepare them for mixing. Some ingredients require special care in their preparation. We'll take a closer look at these ingredients and techniques.

Temperature Matters

Heat is the enemy in cookie mixing, and the temperature of ingredients can make or break the success of a batch of cookies. For baking purposes, room temperature is considered to be 72°F (22°C). If you're baking in a warm kitchen, you'll need to pay extra-close attention to the temperature of your ingredients. Certain key ingredients and their temperature determine how the cookies will bake.

Softening Butter

Butter needs to be the right temperature for the type of cookies being made. If the butter is too warm, the cookie dough will be soft and sticky and the cookies will not hold their shape when baking. Warm butter will not hold air bubbles well and will not develop a light texture during creaming. The cookies will turn out flat and heavy. If the butter is too cold, it will be difficult to cream the butter with other ingredients, and it will be too cold to hold air pockets.

Most cookie recipes using the creaming method of combining ingredients call for butter to be softened. Butter is considered softened when it reaches 65°F (18°C). Butter warms as it is beaten, so starting with the butter at this temperature prevents it from getting too warm and soft during mixing.

To soften butter, let it sit in its wrapper on the counter for 15 to 30 minutes. The warmer your kitchen, the faster the butter will soften. If you forget to set butter out to soften, cut it into small pieces, separate them to allow air circulation and let the butter stand at room temperature for 10 minutes. Butter stored in the freezer will take longer to soften. Set the butter in the refrigerator the night before baking to let it defrost, then soften as described above. Or frozen butter may be cut into pieces and thawed on the counter for 15 to 30 minutes. Never try to soften butter in the microwave. It won't warm evenly, will start to melt and be too soft for cookie baking.

In recipes calling for room temperature butter, the butter should be no warmer than 72°F (22°C). Butter starts to melt at about 85°F (29°C), which is why it melts from the

---

When is butter the right temperature?

The following methods will help determine when your butter is warmed to the right temperature for cookie baking.

Softened Butter

Gently press your thumb or fingertip into the wrapped stick of butter. If it is firm but leaves a slight indentation, the butter is softened.

Insert an instant-read thermometer into the center of the stick of butter. If it reads 65°F (18°C), the butter is softened.

Room Temperature Butter

If the stick of butter feels firm but will bend slightly, it is at room temperature.

Insert an instant-read thermometer into the center of the stick of butter. If it reads 72°F (22°C), the butter is at room temperature.

If butter appears greasy on the surface, it has warmed past room temperature and started to melt. The butter is too warm for cookie baking. If butter melts, use it for other purposes. Butter that has melted and been rechilled should not be used in any recipe calling for softened or room temperature butter because the structure of the butter has been altered and won't beat the same way.

heat of your hand when you touch it. If it's a very hot day, you don't have air conditioning and your kitchen is really warm, it's not the day for baking cookies containing butter.

Chilled Butter
Butter is usually classified as "chilled" at a temperature of 40°F (4°C). Chilled butter is taken straight from the refrigerator, then usually cut into small pieces and used right away in the recipe. The cold temperature of the butter will help regulate the temperature of the mixture.

Shortening
For cookie recipes, shortening should be used at room temperature of 72°F (22°C). Shortening does not start to melt until about 100°F (38°C), making it solid until it reaches the oven.

Eggs
Large eggs are the standard size used for baking, and these recipes were developed using large eggs. The eggs should be brought to room temperature before beating or adding to other ingredients. Room temperature eggs beat to a higher volume and incorporate into doughs and batters better and faster than cold eggs. If eggs are cold when added to creamed butter and sugar, they will cause the mixture to curdle, or "break." For meringues and other recipes using beaten egg whites, you'll get a higher volume and lighter texture if the whites are at room temperature before you whip them. Eggs, however, separate more easily when they're cold. If you're making a recipe that calls for separated eggs, or egg yolks or egg whites only, separate the eggs when they're cold and let them come up to room temperature before using. For food safety reasons, eggs should not stand at room temperature for more than 2 hours.

Dairy Products
All dairy products should be brought to room temperature, 72°F (22°C), before adding them to cookie doughs. Adding cold milk, buttermilk, cream or sour cream to a creamed mixture of butter, sugar and eggs may cause the mixture to curdle, or "break."

Chocolate
Chocolate is the heart and soul of many of the cookie recipes in this book. Touch and handle chocolate as little as possible as your body heat will melt the chocolate.

Chopping Chocolate
When chopping chocolate, make sure your knife and work surface are completely dry. Contact with even a tiny amount of water will cause chocolate to seize up and harden rather than melt smoothly when exposed to heat. When preparing chocolate for melting, chop it into pieces about $\frac{1}{2}$ inch (1 cm) in size. When preparing chopped chocolate that will be added to cookie dough, cut it into pieces about $\frac{1}{4}$ inch (0.5 cm) in size.

Melting Chocolate
There are a few ways to melt chocolate. I have found the best way is to melt chocolate in the microwave on reduced power. The recipes requiring melted chocolate provide detailed melting directions. The chocolate may not appear melted when you take it out of the microwave, but it will soften when stirred. Chocolate will have a shiny appearance as it melts.

Melting chocolate in the top of a double boiler will keep the chocolate from burning; however, the water in the steam will frequently cause it to seize up. Keep the water at a low simmer to avoid this problem. It's not a good idea to melt chocolate in a pan over direct heat as the chocolate can quickly and easily scorch. If chocolate overheats or scorches, it cannot be used because it will have an unpleasant flavor that will ruin the cookies.

Butter or cream is frequently melted with the chocolate. Melting chocolate with butter or cream helps protect the chocolate from burning. It also keeps the chocolate from seizing if it comes in contact with water or any other liquids.

Cooling the melted chocolate for a few minutes before adding it to a creamed mixture will prevent the chocolate from melting the butter and curdling or partially cooking the eggs before the batter makes it into the oven. If the chocolate cools off too much, reheat it quickly in the microwave for 5 to 10 seconds and stir until smooth.

Nuts and Dried Fruit
Nuts and dried fruit should always be chopped before measuring. Some fruits, such

as raisins and dried cranberries, are frequently used whole. The size of the chopped pieces is important to give the cookies a good texture.

Chopping Nuts
Chop nuts into uniform pieces about $\frac{1}{4}$ to $\frac{1}{2}$ inch (0.5 to 1 cm) in size. Finely chopped nuts should be cut into $\frac{1}{8}$-inch (3 mm) pieces. Chopped nuts may be toasted to bring out their flavor. Finely chopped nuts should not be toasted after chopping as they can easily burn and spoil the flavor of the cookies.

Toasting Nuts
Preheat oven to 350°F (180°C). Line a baking sheet with foil and spread chopped nuts evenly over the foil in a single layer. Bake for 5 minutes, stirring halfway through so the nuts will toast evenly. Remove nuts from the pan and let cool on paper towels. Cool completely before using in cookies.

Chopping Dried Fruit
If a recipe calls for dried fruit to be chopped, cut it into uniform pieces about $\frac{1}{4}$ to $\frac{1}{2}$ inch (0.5 to 1 cm) in size.

Dried fruit tends to stick to the knife and make quite a gummy mess when it's being chopped. This is caused by the fruit's high sugar content. To reduce sticking, make it easier to chop dried fruit and make cleanup a lot faster, lightly coat the knife blade with nonstick cooking spray.

The strands of sweetened flaked coconut can sometimes be very long. Before measuring the coconut, spread it out on a cutting board and give it a quick chop with a large knife. This will make it easier to stir the coconut into the cookie dough and create cookies with a more uniform texture.

Measuring Ingredients
When it comes to measuring ingredients for cookies and other baked goods, accuracy counts. It is critical to successful cookie baking, and incorrect or inconsistent measuring can lead to cookie failure. Always use the correct type of measuring cup to measure ingredients. Make sure your measuring utensils are clean and completely dry before starting to measure ingredients.

A graduated set of dry measuring cups should be used to measure flour, sugar and other dry ingredients. Use a dry measuring cup or spoon that matches the exact capacity of the amount of ingredient you need. Gently spoon the ingredients into the measuring cup. Do not measure flour or other dry ingredients by dipping measuring cups into canisters or bags and scraping off the top. This method of measuring, called the dip-and-scoop method, is not as reliable and will yield measured amounts that are significantly different from those produced by spooning the ingredients into the cup.

Use a glass liquid measuring cup to measure all liquid ingredients. Set the measuring cup on a level surface, such as a countertop or table. Pour liquid ingredients into the cup and bend down to read the markings at eye level. Don't raise the cup up to eye level to read it; you won't get an accurate measurement. You can also use the newer liquid measuring cups that let you read the markings from above.

Never measure ingredients over top of a mixing bowl containing any other ingredients. If the ingredient you're measuring spills over into the bowl, it will alter the recipe balance and may ruin your cookies.

Flour
Due to the advances in flour production, it's no longer necessary to sift flour to aerate it before measuring. However, flour does settle and compact a little during shipping and storage. Before measuring flour, give it a quick stir with a fork or spoon to loosen the flour pack. Spoon flour into a dry measuring cup until overflowing, then level it off by sweeping a straight knife blade or thin spatula across the top rim of the cup. Don't tap the cup on the counter as this will settle and compact the flour and give you an inaccurate measurement.

Oats
Spoon or pour oats into a dry measuring cup. Sweep a straight knife blade or thin spatula across the rim of the cup to level off the top.

Granulated Sugar
Spoon or pour granulated sugar into a dry measuring cup and sweep a straight knife blade or thin spatula across the rim of the cup to level off the top.

Brown Sugar

Spoon brown sugar into a dry measuring cup. Using your fingers or the back of a spoon, firmly press the brown sugar into the cup until it is tightly packed and even with the rim. The sugar should hold its shape when unmolded from the cup. If you won't be using the brown sugar shortly after measuring, cover it with plastic wrap to keep it from drying out.

Confectioner's Sugar

Confectioner's (powdered/icing) sugar can settle during shipping and storage. Give it a quick stir with a fork or whisk to fluff it and break up any large lumps. Spoon the confectioner's sugar into a dry measuring cup and sweep a straight knife blade or thin spatula across the rim of the cup to level off the top.

Confectioner's Sugar: To Sift or Not to Sift

Confectioner's (powdered/icing) sugar should not be sifted before measuring for the recipes in this book. Sifting incorporates air into the sugar, changing its volume. Sifted confectioner's sugar doesn't yield the same measurement as unsifted sugar and will affect the way the cookies bake. If even after stirring, your confectioner's sugar is particularly lumpy, sift it after measuring and before combining with other ingredients.

Cocoa Powder

Spoon cocoa powder into a dry measuring cup and sweep a straight knife blade or thin spatula across the rim of the cup to level off the top. To remove lumps, sift cocoa powder by pressing it through a fine-meshed sieve after measuring.

Butter or Shortening Sticks

Use a sharp knife to cut off the desired amount along the marking lines on the wrapper.

Bulk Shortening or Peanut Butter

Press shortening or peanut butter firmly into a dry measuring cup until it is solidly packed and any air bubbles have been removed. Sweep a straight knife blade or thin spatula across the rim of the cup to level off the top. To make it easier to remove these ingredients from the cup, spray the cup with nonstick cooking spray before measuring. If refrigerated, bring shortening or peanut butter to room temperature before using it in baking.

Sour Cream

Spoon sour cream into a dry measuring cup. Press it down with the back of the spoon to remove any large air bubbles. Sweep a straight knife blade or thin spatula across the rim of the cup to level off the top.

Chopped Ingredients

Measure chopped or coarse ingredients, such as chopped chocolate, chocolate chips, nuts, dried fruits and coconut, by spooning or pouring the ingredients into a dry measuring cup until they are level with the rim of the cup.

Corn Syrup, Molasses or Honey

Use a liquid measuring cup placed on a level surface to measure corn syrup, molasses or honey. Pour the ingredient into the cup and bend over to read the measurement line at eye level. To easily measure these thick, sticky ingredients and get the right amount into your cookies, lightly spray the measuring cup with nonstick cooking spray before measuring. The ingredient will slide right out of the cup.

Liquid Ingredients

Use a liquid measuring cup placed on a level surface to measure all liquid ingredients, including milk and vegetable oil. Pour the ingredient into the cup and bend down to read the measurement line at eye level.

Measuring Spoons and Glasses

Dip the measuring spoon into dry ingredients, such as flour, sugar, baking powder, baking soda or spices, and sweep a straight knife blade or thin spatula across the rim of the spoon to level off the top. Pour liquid ingredients, such as extracts, into the measuring spoon just until full and even with the rim of the spoon. Measuring glasses may also be used to measure small quantities of liquid ingredients. Bend down to read the measurement line on the glass at eye level.

Standard Measure Equivalents

½ tbsp	=	1½ tsp	=	7 mL
1 tbsp	=	3 tsp	=	15 mL
1½ tbsp	=	4½ tsp	=	22 mL
⅛ cup	=	2 tbsp	=	25 mL
¼ cup	=	4 tbsp	=	50 mL
⅓ cup	=	5⅓ tbsp	=	75 mL
½ cup	=	8 tbsp	=	125 mL
⅔ cup	=	10⅔ tbsp	=	150 mL
¾ cup	=	12 tbsp	=	175 mL
⅞ cup	=	14 tbsp	=	210 mL
1 cup	=	16 tbsp	=	250 mL

Measurement and Weight Equivalents

For those of you who prefer to weigh your baking ingredients rather than using measuring cups, the following equivalents are provided to help you convert the volume measurements in these recipes to weight measurements. As volume-to-weight measurements can vary, you may need to make minor adjustments in ingredient quantities to achieve the desired results.

Volume	Ingredient	Ounces	Grams
Dry Ingredients			
1 cup	all-purpose flour	4.25	120
1 cup	cake flour	4	113
1 cup	rolled oats	3.5	100
1 cup	cornstarch	4.5	128
1 tbsp	cornstarch	0.3	8.5
1 tsp	baking powder	0.15	4
1 tsp	baking soda	0.18	5
1 tsp	salt	0.25	7
1 tsp	ground spices	0.07	2

Volume	Ingredient	Ounces	Grams
Sugars			
1 cup	granulated sugar	7	200
1 cup	packed brown sugar	7.5	213
1 cup	confectioner's sugar	4	113
1 cup	corn syrup	11	312
1 cup	molasses	12	340
Fats			
1 cup	butter	8	227
1 tbsp	butter	0.5	14
1 cup	shortening	6.7	190
1 tbsp	shortening	0.4	11.3
1 cup	vegetable oil	7.5	213
Dairy			
1 cup	milk	8	227
1 cup	buttermilk	8	227
1 cup	sour cream	8	227
Chocolate, Nuts and Dried Fruits			
1 cup	chopped chocolate	6	170
1 cup	chocolate chips	6	170
1 cup	cocoa powder	3	85
1 cup	chopped almonds	5	142
1 cup	chopped cashews	4	113
1 cup	chopped macadamia nuts	4.5	128
1 cup	chopped pecans	4	113
1 cup	chopped walnuts	4	113
1 cup	peanut butter	9.5	270
1 cup	chopped apricots	3	85
1 cup	dried cranberries	2	56
1 cup	sweetened flaked coconut	3	85
1 cup	raisins	6	170

Combining Ingredients

Using the correct techniques to combine your ingredients will ensure that your cookies are tender and bake well in the oven.

Mixing Cookie Doughs

There are three primary mixing methods used for combining fat into a dough or batter: creaming, one-bowl and cut-in. Each method is used for making a different type of cookie dough and creates specific cookie characteristics.

Creaming Method

Creaming is the most common method used to mix cookies. The process of creaming combines the fat and sugar in a way that creates a wonderful texture in cookies. The fat may be butter, shortening, cream cheese or a combination of these fats. As butter is the most common fat used in cookies, I'm going to use butter as the example in explaining the method of creaming. The process is the same for shortening or cream cheese, with the exception that shortening can be used at room temperature.

To achieve the best results, the butter needs to be softened before you start the creaming process. Softened butter, at a temperature of 65°F (18°C), creams better and holds more air than butter at room temperature of 72°F (22°C), while butter that is very soft or warm won't hold much air at all. Melting changes the structure of butter. Never use melted butter for creaming as it won't hold any air. If your butter has warmed up too much and started to melt, don't use it for creaming. Even if you chill the butter to firm it up, it won't have the same texture after resolidifying nor will it have the same ability to hold air. It's time to get out a fresh stick of butter.

Softened butter and sugar are combined in a mixing bowl and beaten continuously with an electric mixer on medium speed for 2 to 4 minutes, depending on the cookie recipe. Butter and sugar can be creamed by hand, but it is a laborious process and the results are not as good as those using either a stand or hand-held mixer. As the mixture beats, sugar crystals cut into the butter, creating air pockets. This trapped air expands as the cookies bake. Baking powder and baking soda will enlarge these air bubbles and help the dough rise. It's this process that gives creamed cookies their tender texture.

When butter and sugar are properly creamed, the mixture is referred to as being light and fluffy. Light means that the butter has turned pale in color and is lighter in texture. Fluffy means that the mixture now contains lots of trapped air pockets and has increased in volume.

> **Butter and sugar are creamed together for three reasons:**
> - To thoroughly combine the butter and sugar before adding other ingredients
> - To help the sugar start to dissolve into the butter
> - To incorporate air into the mixture to make a light, tender cookie with a good crumb

After the butter and sugar have been beaten until light and fluffy, the eggs are added one at a time. Each egg should be thoroughly beaten in before adding the next egg. This allows the mixture of creamed butter and sugar to retain its light texture, improves the texture of the cookies and ensures that the eggs are fully incorporated. After adding the last egg, continue beating until the mixture is smooth and creamy before adding the dry ingredients.

When you add eggs to creamed butter and sugar, there is a chance that the mixture will appear curdled. This is referred to as the mixture "breaking," and it happens when the eggs are too cold. Don't worry, your cookies will be fine. Just keep beating until the mixture is smooth before adding any more eggs. Adding the eggs one at a time and beating well in between additions will help prevent breaking. If the mixture doesn't smooth out after beating in the eggs, gradually start to add the dry ingredients. The flour will help bind the mixture, bring it together and turn it smooth.

Gradually stir in the dry ingredients to blend them evenly into the mixture without forming lumps. Use the low-speed setting on the mixer to keep the flour from flying out of the bowl and to prevent overworking the dough. After adding the last of the dry ingredients, stir just until well combined and no streaks of flour remain in the bowl. Overmixing the flour will develop gluten and make the cookies tough.

While it is most common that butter and sugar are creamed together, there are times when the sugar is creamed with eggs instead of butter. This occurs most often in chocolate recipes, brownies in particular, when the butter is melted with the chocolate and later added to the creamed mixture. In this case, whole eggs and sugar are creamed until the mixture is light and smooth, using the same process as for creaming butter and sugar until the mixture is light and smooth. Because eggs don't trap as much air as butter does, the egg mixture doesn't reach the same stage of fluffiness as a mixture of creamed butter and sugar.

> **A Note About Food Processors**
> I know some people love to use their food processor for everything, but I advise against using a food processor to make cookie dough. Cookies mixed in a food processor may not cook properly, as processors are not designed to cream butter and sugar mixtures to lighten and aerate them. Overprocessing will toughen cookie doughs, while underprocessing won't effectively combine the ingredients.

One-Bowl Method

In the one-bowl method, used to mix many brownie recipes, the chocolate and butter are melted in a large bowl. The other ingredients are then added to the bowl with the melted chocolate mixture. A wire whisk or wooden spoon is used to mix the batter as each ingredient is added in the order given in the recipe, blending well before adding the next one to the bowl.

Sugar is sometimes mixed with the other dry ingredients to prevent the flour mixture from clumping when combined with the wet ingredients. This allows the flour mixture to be blended into the other ingredients with a minimum amount of mixing, thereby reducing the development of gluten and yielding tender, fudgy brownies.

Cut-In Method

In the cut-in method, also called rubbing, the dry ingredients are thoroughly whisked together in a bowl and the fat, usually butter, is worked into the dry mixture. It is the technique used for making flaky pie crusts. When baking cookies, this method is primarily used for making crusts and crumb toppings for bars and squares. There is, however, a difference between a cookie crust and a pie crust. A cookie crust gets all its moisture from the butter, which holds the crust together. A pie crust has a smaller ratio of butter to flour, and water or another liquid is added to pull the crust together.

The cut-in method yields very tender cookie crusts and crumbly toppings. Butter, the best fat to use for making bar crusts and toppings, should be well chilled and cut into pieces. If the butter is too soft, it will start to melt as you work it into the flour mixture, yielding a tougher crust or a soft topping.

For cookie crusts, the best tool for working the fat into the dry ingredients is your hands. By using your hands, you can quickly rub all the butter evenly into the flour and bring the whole mixture together into a crumbly dough. You can also use a pastry blender or two table knives in a slicing motion to cut the butter in until the mixture resembles a coarse meal and then use your hands to bring it together into a dough. The process is the same for making a crumb topping.

Other Mixing Techniques

There are a few other techniques that are standard to the process of mixing cookie doughs. Each one contributes to the texture of the cookies.

Whisking Dry Ingredients

Sifting flour aerates it, trapping air between the particles. Older recipes always called for sifting flour because flour was ground more coarsely and settled quite a lot during shipping and storage. Modern flour has a much finer grain and does not require sifting before use. Sifting flour will yield cookies with a very light, spongy texture.

To easily combine flour and other dry ingredients, place the ingredients in a bowl and use vigorous strokes to mix them together with a wire whisk. Whisking leaveners, baking powder and baking soda into the flour will ensure that they are evenly distributed throughout the cookie dough. Even distribution of the leaveners is important to prevent large air bubbles and tunnels from forming in the cookies. This process of whisking the dry ingredients together also means that less mixing is required when they are added to the cookie dough, yielding tender cookies with better texture.

Lightly Beating Eggs

With an electric mixer or wire whisk, beat eggs until the yolk and white are thoroughly combined and frothy with no streaks of white remaining.

Adding Dry Ingredients

Dry ingredients should be gradually added to a mixture just until no streaks of flour remain visible. This should be done with an electric mixer on low speed or by hand. If you're using a hand-held mixer, you may want to begin the process with your mixer and switch to the hand method as the dough becomes stiffer. Overmixing a dough or batter after adding the flour will develop gluten and make the cookies tough. For oatmeal cookies, the oats should be stirred in just until blended and evenly distributed throughout the mixture.

Folding

Folding is the process of gently combining ingredients into a mixture without deflating the air incorporated during creaming. In non-creamed batters, adding ingredients through gentle folding prevents overmixing the batter, keeping brownies and cookies from becoming tough. Folding is always done by hand so you can control the blending process. A silicone or rubber spatula, wooden spoon or large metal spoon all work well for folding.

Chocolate chips, chopped chocolate, nuts, coconut, raisins and other dried fruits are the most common ingredients folded into cookie doughs and batters.

Scraping Down the Bowl

It is important to periodically scrape down the bowl during mixing to be sure all the ingredients are fully incorporated into the dough. The bowl should always be scraped down after mixing the wet ingredients — butter, eggs, dairy, extracts, melted chocolate — before adding the dry ingredients. This ensures that there are no clumps of the creamed mixture or other ingredients clinging to the side or bottom of the bowl and not mixed into the dough. It also reduces the amount of stirring needed when adding in the dry ingredients.

To Chill or Not to Chill

Many recipes call for chilling the dough before shaping or baking the cookies. This is common for drop cookies, hand-shaped cookies, rolled cutout cookies and slice-and-bake cookies containing butter and some recipes made with shortening. This step should not be skipped. Chilling firms the fat in the dough and makes it easier to handle and shape. When the fat is cold, the cookies also don't spread as much in the oven as they bake. If the fat is too warm, then the cookies will spread very thin before they have a chance to set.

If your kitchen is warm, above 72°F (22°C), you may have trouble with some other cookie doughs being too soft and your cookies spreading too much. In this case, you may find it helpful to chill the dough for other cookie recipes before shaping or baking. However, cookie doughs that use baking soda as the only leavener should not be chilled. Baking soda starts working as soon as it comes into contact with liquid, and its leavening ability dissipates quickly.

Baking Cookies

Always work with cool cookie sheets. If the sheets are warm, the butter or other fat in the cookie dough will begin to melt and the cookies will start to bake before the pan goes in the oven. This will result in unevenly baked, flat cookies with thin edges. Always let cookie sheets cool completely between batches. The sheet should be cool to the touch before putting the next batch of cookies on it.

Cooling Cookie Sheets

Hot cookie sheets can take up to 30 minutes to cool to room temperature. Place hot cookie sheets on wire cooling racks so that air can circulate around and under the sheets to help them cool faster. Cookie sheets should feel cool to the touch before you use them again.

For best baking results, position the oven rack in the center of the oven and bake only one cookie sheet in the oven at a time. With only one sheet in the oven, the heated air will circulate freely around the pan and the cookies will bake uniformly and brown more evenly. Baking two sheets at a time will inhibit air circulation. It will cause the cookies on the upper sheet to brown too much on the top and the ones on the lower sheet to burn on the bottom.

If you choose to bake two sheets at a time, place the oven racks in the top third and bottom third of the oven. Halfway through the baking time, swap the position of the cookie sheets so that the cookies don't brown too much on the top or bottom. Because opening

Refrigerating Cookie Dough

If you're not ready to bake the cookies right away, many cookie doughs can be stored in the refrigerator for up to a week. Choose a recipe that is leavened with baking powder as baking soda quickly loses its leavening power after the dough is mixed. Shape the dough for rolled cutout cookies into a flat disk, slice-and-bake cookies into a log, or drop cookies and shaped cookies into a ball and wrap tightly in plastic wrap. You can also spoon drop and shaped cookie doughs into a zippered plastic storage bag, remove the air and tightly seal. If a drop cookie recipe does not include instructions to chill the dough before portioning it, then bring the refrigerated dough back to room temperature before baking the cookies.

the door to swap the pans will lower the oven temperature, you'll need to increase the baking time and watch the cookies carefully. Swapping the pans during baking can also cause the partially baked cookies to fall when exposed to the cooler room air temperature, resulting in flat, dense cookies.

Bars and brownies should also be baked on the center rack in the oven and not be baked more than one pan at a time. Like cookies baked on a cookie sheet, bar-type cookies need good air circulation in order to bake properly. If the bottom of the pan is blocked from the heating element, the bottom crust won't cook completely and will be soggy.

Timing Is Everything

It is important to use an accurate kitchen timer to time cookies while they bake. Timing is key in baking. Just a few minutes in baking time can make the difference between underdone cookies, perfect cookies and overdone cookies. Underbaked cookies will be limp and doughy, while overbaked cookies quickly turn dry, hard and tough. If you get distracted, your cookies may end up ruined. A timer will remind you to take the cookies out of the oven and save you a lot of frustration and grief.

Soft or Crispy?

Do you like your cookies soft or crispy? Both types have many fans, and both can be equally yummy. If you like your cookies soft, check them at the shortest baking time given in the recipe. If you like them crispy, bake a minute or two longer than the time indicated in the recipe. Remember that cookies will continue baking for a minute or two after you have removed them from the oven.

Cooling Cookies

Remove the cookies from the hot cookie sheet and place them on a wire cooling rack in a single layer. Never stack or overlap cookies as they cool. Cookies need air circulation to allow steam and heat to escape and to keep the cookies from becoming soggy. Piling warm cookies on top of each other can also cause them to bend in shape, squash the cookies underneath or stick together.

Bar cookies and brownies should be cooled completely in their baking pans on a wire rack. Elevating the pan off the countertop on a rack allows air to circulate under the pan and cool the bars from both the top and bottom. Bars and brownies will be much easier to remove from the pan after they are cool.

Finishing Touches

Cookies are the perfect medium for letting your creativity loose and having fun. You can dress up cookies in a variety of ways. Sprinkle the tops with sugar before baking to give them a glistening appearance and sweet crunch. Top baked cookies with a glaze, drizzle with icing or melted chocolate, dip edges in melted chocolate, sandwich two cookies together with a frosting or jam filling, or dust with confectioner's sugar to give them a new dimension and a different twist. Icings add an extra layer of flavor and make some cookies even prettier than they already are. Have fun decorating rolled cutout cookies and slice-and-bake cookies with colored icings for a special occasion or as a rainy day project.

In most cases, you want to let cookies cool completely before you start frosting or icing so the frosting holds its shape and the icing doesn't melt. There are a few bar and square recipes where the glaze is spread over the warm cookies. This helps the glaze spread out in a thin, even layer and be partially absorbed into the top of the bars.

The consistency of a frosting, icing or glaze can depend on the accuracy of measuring ingredients, the amount of liquid added and even the weather. Too much or too little confectioner's sugar will make an icing too stiff or too thin. Always start with the smallest amount of liquid listed in the recipe and add more only as needed. Too much liquid will make the icing runny. If the weather is hot and humid, icings can be soft and sticky, hard to work with and take a long time to set. To avoid this problem, it's better to let the temperature cool off a bit and ice the cookies later in the day.

Storing Cookies

By properly storing your cookies, you can keep them from quickly turning stale. Store cookies in airtight containers to maintain their freshness and flavor. Exposure to air will soften crisp cookies and cause soft cookies to dry out. Plastic storage containers with tight-fitting lids, zippered storage bags that seal tightly, cookie tins with snug lids and small cookie jars with a gasket-type seal are all good choices. Cookies can also be wrapped tightly in plastic wrap or foil. Soft cookies stored on plates loosely covered with plastic wrap will dry out quickly.

Allow frostings and icings to set completely before storing cookies. Separate cookie layers with parchment paper or waxed paper to prevent iced cookies from sticking to each other.

Uncut bar cookies and brownies may be stored in their baking pan, tightly covered with foil or plastic wrap. After cutting, store bars and brownies in tightly sealed storage containers. Separate the layers with parchment paper or waxed paper to keep them from sticking together.

Store crisp cookies and soft cookies in separate containers to maintain their texture. Otherwise, the crisp cookies will absorb some of the moisture from the soft cookies. The crisp cookies will soften, and the soft cookies will partially dry out. Flavors can blend during storage, so it is best to store each flavor of cookie in a different container. Be sure to store cookies with strong flavors, such as mint or ginger, in separate containers so their flavor won't be absorbed by other cookies.

Most cookies can be stored at room temperature for up to 3 days and still maintain freshness. All cookies, bars and brownies with perishable ingredients, such as a cream cheese or curd filling, a cream cheese frosting or a sour cream topping, must be stored in the refrigerator to prevent spoilage. Perishable cookies will keep well in the refrigerator for up to 3 days.

Freezing Cookies and Cookie Doughs

While nothing beats the flavor of cookies fresh from the oven, most baked cookies and a lot of cookie doughs can be frozen for later use.

Packaging Cookies for the Freezer
Before packaging cookies for the freezer, make sure they are completely cooled. This will keep excess trapped moisture from turning the cookies soggy when they're defrosted. Don't ice or glaze cookies before freezing. Many icings don't freeze well and can become sticky when defrosted. Wait until after the cookies are thawed to frost or ice them.

Like other foods, frozen cookies are susceptible to freezer burn. Freezer burn occurs when foods dry out in the freezer. It can significantly affect both the flavor and texture of cookies. Wrapping the cookies well and sealing in an airtight container or tightly wrapping in foil will lessen the effects of freezer burn. It will also keep them from absorbing odors during storage.

For best results, use sturdy containers specifically designed for freezer storage. You can also use freezer storage bags and heavy foil for packaging cookies for the freezer. Wrap cookies in plastic wrap to prevent moisture loss before sealing them in containers or storage bags or wrapping in foil. Be sure to label the packages with the date and contents. Cookies can usually be frozen for up to 3 months without significant flavor or moisture loss.

Freeze bar cookies and brownies uncut or in large pieces. Cut bar cookies should be wrapped in plastic wrap, with parchment paper or waxed paper separating the layers so they don't stick together, and packed in freezer storage containers. Bar cookies can also be packed into zippered freezer bags and wrapped in heavy foil.

A great way to keep soft cookies from sticking together during freezing is to place the cookies in a single layer on a cookie sheet or tray lined with parchment paper or foil and freeze for 1 to 2 hours. When frozen, wrap the cookies well, label and immediately return them to the freezer. This also works well for cut bar cookies.

To defrost cookies, remove them from the container or unwrap the foil and let plastic-wrapped cookies thaw at room temperature on the counter for 15 to 30 minutes. Defrost cookies containing perishable ingredients in the refrigerator overnight. After defrosting, cookies should be eaten within 1 to 2 days for the best flavor and texture.

Mix Now, Bake Later
For baking at a later date, many cookie doughs can be mixed and then tightly wrapped and

frozen, either shaped or unshaped, for up to 3 months. Cookie doughs containing double-acting baking powder are the best choice for freezing as baking soda will lose its leavening ability quickly during freezer storage.

Shape cookie doughs for rolled cutout cookies into a flat disk. Wrap the dough tightly in plastic wrap, then seal in heavy foil to prevent freezer burn and label with the date and contents. To use, remove the foil and thaw the plastic-wrapped dough in the refrigerator overnight.

Rolls of slice-and-bake cookie dough are great for freezing. Wrap the rolls tightly in plastic wrap, then seal in heavy foil and label. To bake the cookies, remove the foil and thaw the plastic-wrapped rolls in the refrigerator overnight, or slice the frozen dough and bake, adding 1 to 3 minutes to the baking time, depending on the thickness of the slices.

For drop cookies, use a cookie scoop or spoons to drop individual portions of dough onto a parchment paper– or foil-lined cookie sheet or tray and freeze for at least 2 hours. For hand-shaped cookies, roll dough into balls or other shapes and freeze. Transfer frozen dough portions to a zippered freezer bag, remove the air and seal tightly. Wrap the bag in heavy foil and label. There's no need to defrost before baking. Just remove enough frozen dough portions for the number of cookies you want and bake, adding 2 to 3 minutes to the baking time. You can also freeze drop and hand-shaped cookie doughs by packing the dough into a zippered freezer bag, squeezing out all the air, tightly sealing the bag and wrapping it in heavy foil. Defrost the bag of dough in the refrigerator before portioning or shaping it for baking.

High Altitude Adjustments for Baking

Cookies are pretty forgiving at lower altitudes and don't need much, if any, adjustment for altitudes below 3000 feet (915 m). If you have trouble with your cookies at higher altitudes, try these suggestions.

If your cookies are too pale, try increasing the oven temperature by 25°F (14°C) and reducing the baking time by a minute or two to compensate for the higher temperature. If your cookies puff up too much, reduce the amount of baking powder or baking soda by $\frac{1}{8}$ teaspoon (0.5 mL) for each 3000 feet (915 m) in elevation.

Because liquids evaporate faster at higher elevations, if your cookies are dry or the dough doesn't come together well, increase the amount of liquid or add another egg. For each additional 1000 feet (305 m), add an additional $1\frac{1}{2}$ tsp (7 mL) of liquid. If the dough seems to be the right consistency, but your cookies are still dry, add an extra egg to the recipe. Reducing the amount of sugar in the recipe by 1 to 2 tablespoons (15 to 30 mL) may also improve the texture.

Local Altitude Adjustments

For specific information on high altitude adjustments for your area, contact your local county extension office. You can also send questions regarding baking at high altitude to: Colorado State University, Food Science Extension Office, Fort Collins, CO 80523-1571.

Drop Cookies

●●●

White Chocolate Coconut
  Cookies. 43
Pumpkin Spice Cookies 44
Mocha Fudge Truffle Cookies 46
Cranberry Nut Cookies. 47
Lemon Drops 48
Peanut Butter Cookies 49
Coconut Cookies 50
Maple Walnut Cookies 51
Orange Marmalade Cookies. 52
Fudgy Brownie Cookies 53
Pineapple Cookies 54
Coconut Macaroons. 55
Cranberry Orange Cookies. 56

Tangy Lime Cookies 57
Michael's Mom's Persimmon
  Cookies. 58
Toffee Cookies 59
Amaretti 60
Orange Cookies 61
Hawaiian Cookies. 62
Butterscotch Pecan Cookies 63
Cashew Cookies 64
Mini M&M Candy Cookies 65
Blueberry Lemon Cookies 66
Mincemeat Cookies 67
Apple Walnut Cookies 68
Malted Milk Cookies 70

About Drop Cookies

The simplest kind of cookie to make, drop cookies are named for the way the dough is transferred from the mixing bowl to the cookie sheet by dropping it from a spoon. You can also use a cookie scoop to make drop cookies. Drop cookies are made using the creaming method of mixing to combine the butter and sugar, giving these delightful cookies their wonderful texture and structure.

Drop cookies lend themselves to a wide variety of flavors and added ingredients. Many of our favorite cookies — chocolate chip, oatmeal and peanut butter — are easy-to-make drop cookies. Making drop cookies is a great activity to share with kids, and baking these cookies often rekindles our own fond childhood memories.

Two-Spoon Method

This traditional, simple process of making drop cookies requires only two tableware spoons, either teaspoons or tablespoons. Fill one spoon with about a tablespoon (15 mL) of cookie dough and use the other spoon to push the dough off onto the cookie sheet in a neat mound. Space the dough 2 inches (5 cm) apart to keep the cookies from spreading into each other during baking. If the dough sticks to the spoons and won't drop off easily, chill the dough for a few minutes to firm the fat before portioning it onto the cookie sheet.

Cookie Scoop Method

A cookie scoop makes the job of transferring the dough to the cookie sheet quick and easy. It also produces nice round cookies with a consistent size and shape that bake evenly. A 1-tablespoon (15 mL) cookie scoop will yield a standard-sized 2- to $2\frac{1}{2}$-inch (5 to 6 cm) cookie, depending on the spread of the dough.

Dip the cookie scoop into the cookie dough and level off any excess dough, making the dough even with the rim of the scoop. Squeeze the scoop handle to release the formed dough onto a prepared cookie sheet and space the cookies 2 inches (5 cm) apart.

The cookies should release easily from the scoop. If you have trouble with the dough sticking, chill it as directed in the recipe before scooping it onto the pan. If the dough is properly chilled and you're still having a problem with the dough not releasing from the scoop, lightly coat the inside of the scoop with nonstick cooking spray.

Giant Cookies

If you want to bake giant cookies, use a standard ice cream scoop or a $\frac{1}{4}$-cup (50 mL) measuring cup to portion the dough and space the cookies 4 inches (10 cm) apart on the cookie sheet. You'll need to increase the baking time, which will vary depending on the size and type of cookie you're making. Bake a test batch of two cookies to determine the baking time needed, and use this as a guide for baking the remaining cookies. Watch the cookies through the oven window, and try not to open the door too many times as this will lower the oven temperature and make it difficult to establish an accurate baking time.

White Chocolate Coconut Cookies

White chocolate is a perfect companion for coconut, and the two flavors blend beautifully to give these cookies their luxurious flavor.

Tip

For the best flavor, use chopped white chocolate or white chocolate chips rather than baking chips labeled as "white" or "vanilla." These imitation chips do not contain the high ratio of cocoa butter that gives white chocolate its special flavor.

- Preheat oven to 350°F (180°C)
- Cookie sheets, lined with parchment paper

2⅓ cups	all-purpose flour	575 mL
1½ tsp	baking powder	7 mL
½ tsp	baking soda	2 mL
¼ tsp	salt	1 mL
1⅓ cups	sweetened flaked coconut	325 mL
1 cup	unsalted butter, softened	250 mL
½ cup	granulated sugar	125 mL
½ cup	packed light brown sugar	125 mL
2	eggs	2
1 tsp	vanilla extract	5 mL
½ tsp	almond extract	2 mL
1½ cups	chopped white chocolate or white chocolate chips	375 mL

1. In a bowl, whisk together flour, baking powder, baking soda and salt until well combined. Stir in coconut. Set aside.

2. In a large bowl, using an electric mixer on medium speed, cream butter, granulated sugar and brown sugar until light and fluffy, about 3 minutes. Add eggs one at a time, beating well after each addition. Beat in vanilla and almond extract. Scrape down sides of bowl. On low speed or using a wooden spoon, gradually add flour mixture, beating just until blended. By hand, fold in white chocolate.

3. Using a cookie scoop or spoons, drop tablespoonfuls (15 mL) of dough about 2 inches (5 cm) apart on prepared cookie sheets. Bake one sheet at a time in preheated oven for 10 to 12 minutes or until edges start to turn lightly golden.

4. Immediately slide parchment paper onto a wire cooling rack. Cool cookies for 5 minutes, then transfer from parchment paper to cooling rack and cool completely.

Pumpkin Spice Cookies

Makes about 4 dozen cookies ● ● ●

These slightly spicy, soft, chewy, cake-like cookies are a perfect fall treat.

Tips

Let icing set before storing cookies between layers of wax paper in a tightly sealed container. If cookies will be frozen, do not ice them. Completely defrost the cookies before drizzling icing over them.

Pumpkin can be sold by volume (fl. oz/mL) or weight (oz/g). A 15 oz (425 g) can is equal to 14 fl. oz (398 mL).

- ● **Preheat oven to 350°F (180°C)**
- ● **Cookie sheets, lined with parchment paper**

Cookies

2½ cups	all-purpose flour	625 mL
2 tsp	baking powder	10 mL
1 tsp	ground cinnamon	5 mL
½ tsp	ground nutmeg	2 mL
¼ tsp	ground ginger	1 mL
¼ tsp	baking soda	1 mL
¼ tsp	salt	1 mL
½ cup	unsalted butter, softened	125 mL
¾ cup	packed dark brown sugar	175 mL
½ cup	granulated sugar	125 mL
2	eggs	2
1 tsp	vanilla extract	5 mL
1	can (15 oz or 398 mL) solid pack (purée) pumpkin	1
1 cup	chopped pecans	250 mL

Icing

1 cup	confectioner's (powdered/icing) sugar	250 mL
1 to 2 tbsp	half-and-half (10%) cream or milk	15 to 25 mL
½ tsp	maple flavoring	2 mL

1. **Cookies:** In a bowl, whisk together flour, baking powder, cinnamon, nutmeg, ginger, baking soda and salt until well combined. Set aside.

2. In a large bowl, using an electric mixer on medium speed, cream butter, brown sugar and granulated sugar until light and fluffy, about 3 minutes. Add eggs one at a time, beating well after each addition. Beat in vanilla. Add pumpkin and stir until well combined. Scrape down sides of bowl. On low speed or using a wooden spoon, gradually add flour mixture, beating just until blended. By hand, fold in pecans.

3. Using a cookie scoop or spoons, drop tablespoonfuls (15 mL) of dough about 2 inches (5 cm) apart on prepared cookie sheets. Bake one sheet at a time in preheated oven for 12 to 15 minutes or until edges start to turn lightly golden.

4. Immediately slide parchment paper onto a wire cooling rack. Cool cookies for 5 minutes, then transfer from parchment paper to cooling rack and cool completely.

5. *Icing:* In a small bowl, combine confectioner's sugar, 1 tablespoon (15 mL) of the cream and maple flavoring. Using a small whisk or a fork, blend until icing is smooth and thin enough to drizzle from a fork. Add more cream as needed to achieve the right consistency. Drizzle icing over cooled cookies.

Mocha Fudge Truffle Cookies

Makes about 3½ dozen cookies ● ● ●

Rich, soft and chocolaty, these luscious cookies are sure to satisfy chocolate lovers.

Tips

Homemade cookies make a great gift for family and friends and are perfect for every occasion.

Sweet dark chocolate contains up to 70% chocolate liquor and added cocoa butter. It also has more sugar than bittersweet chocolate but less than semisweet.

Variation

Substitute chopped walnuts for chopped pecans.

- ● **Preheat oven to 325°F (160°C)**
- ● **Cookie sheets, lined with parchment paper**

12 oz	sweet dark chocolate, chopped	375 g
2 tbsp	unsalted butter, melted	25 mL
1½ tsp	instant espresso powder or instant coffee granules	7 mL
¾ cup	all-purpose flour	175 mL
1 tsp	baking powder	5 mL
½ tsp	salt	2 mL
3	eggs	3
1¼ cups	granulated sugar	300 mL
1½ tsp	vanilla extract	7 mL
1 cup	chopped pecans	250 mL

1. In the top of a double boiler, combine chocolate and butter. Place pan over simmering water and heat, stirring frequently, until chocolate softens and begins to melt. Remove pan from heat and stir in espresso powder. Stir until chocolate is completely melted and mixture is smooth. Set aside to cool.

2. In a bowl, whisk together flour, baking powder and salt until well combined. Set aside.

3. In a large bowl, using an electric mixer on medium speed, lightly beat eggs. Add granulated sugar and beat until light and lemon-colored, about 4 minutes. Add cooled chocolate mixture and beat until smooth. Beat in vanilla. Scrape down sides of bowl. On low speed or using a wooden spoon, gradually add flour mixture, beating just until blended. By hand, fold in pecans.

4. Using a cookie scoop or spoons, drop tablespoonfuls (15 mL) of dough about 2 inches (5 cm) apart on prepared cookie sheets. Bake one sheet at a time in preheated oven for 15 to 18 minutes or until set around the edges but slightly soft in the center.

5. Immediately slide parchment paper onto a wire cooling rack. Cool cookies for 5 minutes, then transfer from parchment paper to cooling rack and cool completely.

Cranberry Nut Cookies

Makes about 4 dozen cookies ● ● ●

There is something very special about combining the flavors of dried cranberries and white chocolate. Add in crunchy pecans and the flavor goes to a whole new level.

Tip

Prepare and measure all of the ingredients before you start mixing the cookies.

- ● **Preheat oven to 350°F (180°C)**
- ● **Cookie sheets, lined with parchment paper**

2 ¾ cups	all-purpose flour	675 mL
2 tsp	baking powder	10 mL
½ tsp	baking soda	2 mL
½ tsp	salt	2 mL
½ cup	unsalted butter, softened	125 mL
½ cup	vegetable shortening	125 mL
⅔ cup	granulated sugar	150 mL
⅔ cup	packed light brown sugar	150 mL
2	eggs	2
1 tsp	vanilla extract	5 mL
1 cup	dried cranberries	250 mL
1 cup	chopped white chocolate or white chocolate chips	250 mL
1 cup	chopped pecans	250 mL

1. In a bowl, whisk together flour, baking powder, baking soda and salt until well combined. Set aside.

2. In a large bowl, using an electric mixer on medium speed, cream butter, shortening, granulated sugar and brown sugar until light and fluffy, about 3 minutes. Add eggs one at a time, beating well after each addition. Beat in vanilla. Scrape down sides of bowl. On low speed or using a wooden spoon, gradually add flour mixture, beating just until blended. By hand, fold in cranberries, white chocolate and pecans.

3. Using a cookie scoop or spoons, drop tablespoonfuls (15 mL) of dough about 2 inches (5 cm) apart on prepared cookie sheets. Bake one sheet at a time in preheated oven for 10 to 12 minutes or until edges start to turn lightly golden.

4. Immediately slide parchment paper onto a wire cooling rack. Cool cookies for 5 minutes, then transfer from parchment paper to cooling rack and cool completely.

Lemon Drops

Makes about 2½ dozen cookies ● ● ●

These delightful cookies are brimming with tangy lemon flavor.

Tips

This recipe requires the zest and juice of 2 lemons. Prepare the zest and juice and set aside.

A ripe medium lemon will yield about 2 teaspoons (10 mL) finely grated zest and 2 to 3 tablespoons (25 to 45 mL) juice. A lemon at room temperature will yield more juice than a lemon straight from the refrigerator.

Let icing set before storing cookies between layers of wax paper in a tightly sealed container.

● **Cookie sheets, lined with parchment paper**

Cookies

1 cup	granulated sugar	250 mL
2 tbsp	grated lemon zest	25 mL
2 cups	all-purpose flour	500 mL
1½ tsp	baking powder	7 mL
¼ tsp	baking soda	1 mL
¼ tsp	salt	1 mL
½ cup	unsalted butter, softened	125 mL
2	eggs	2
3 tbsp	freshly squeezed lemon juice	45 mL

Icing

1½ cups	confectioner's (powdered/icing) sugar	375 mL
2 tbsp	unsalted butter, at room temperature	25 mL
2 tsp	grated lemon zest	10 mL
1½ tbsp	freshly squeezed lemon juice	22 mL

1. **Cookies:** In a small bowl, combine granulated sugar and lemon zest until well blended. Set aside.
2. In a bowl, whisk together flour, baking powder, baking soda and salt until well combined. Set aside.
3. In a large bowl, using an electric mixer on medium speed, cream butter and sugar mixture until light and fluffy, about 3 minutes. Add eggs one at a time, beating well after each addition. Beat in lemon juice. Scrape down sides of bowl. On low speed or using a wooden spoon, gradually add flour mixture, beating just until blended. Cover dough with plastic wrap and chill for at least 1 hour.
4. Preheat oven to 350°F (180°C). Using a cookie scoop or spoons, drop tablespoonfuls (15 mL) of dough about 2 inches (5 cm) apart on prepared cookie sheets. Bake one sheet at a time in preheated oven for 10 to 12 minutes or until edges start to turn lightly golden.
5. Immediately slide parchment paper onto a wire cooling rack. Cool cookies for 5 minutes, then transfer from parchment paper to cooling rack and cool completely.
6. **Icing:** In a small bowl, combine confectioner's sugar, butter, lemon zest and lemon juice. Using a small whisk or a fork, beat until icing is smooth. Spread icing over cooled cookies.

Peanut Butter Cookies

What peanut butter lover can resist a handful of chewy peanut butter cookies fresh from the oven?

Tip

You can use chunky peanut butter in this recipe.

Variation

By hand, fold 1 cup (250 mL) chopped unsalted peanuts into cookie dough.

- Preheat oven to 350°F (180°C)
- Cookie sheets, lined with parchment paper

2 cups	all-purpose flour	500 mL
1 tsp	baking powder	5 mL
½ tsp	baking soda	2 mL
¼ tsp	salt	1 mL
¾ cup	peanut butter	175 mL
½ cup	vegetable shortening	125 mL
¾ cup	packed light brown sugar	175 mL
½ cup	granulated sugar	125 mL
2	eggs	2
2 tsp	vanilla extract	10 mL

1. In a bowl, whisk together flour, baking powder, baking soda and salt until well combined. Set aside.

2. In a large bowl, using an electric mixer on medium speed, cream peanut butter, shortening, brown sugar and granulated sugar until light and fluffy, about 3 minutes. Add eggs one at a time, beating well after each addition. Beat in vanilla. Scrape down sides of bowl. On low speed or using a wooden spoon, gradually add flour mixture, beating just until blended.

3. Using a cookie scoop or spoons, drop tablespoonfuls (15 mL) of dough about 2 inches (5 cm) apart on prepared cookie sheets. Flatten slightly in crisscross pattern with tines of a fork. Bake one sheet at a time in preheated oven for 8 to 10 minutes or until edges start to turn lightly golden.

4. Immediately slide parchment paper onto a wire cooling rack. Cool cookies for 5 minutes, then transfer from parchment paper to cooling rack and cool completely.

Coconut Cookies

Makes about 3 dozen cookies

● ● ●

If you like coconut, you'll love these coconut-packed gems!

Tip
Chopping the coconut will give the cookies a more uniform texture.

Variation
By hand, fold 1 cup (250 mL) chopped unsalted almonds into cookie dough.

● **Cookie sheets, lined with parchment paper**

2¼ cups	all-purpose flour	550 mL
½ tsp	baking soda	2 mL
¼ tsp	salt	1 mL
2 cups	sweetened flaked coconut, coarsely chopped	500 mL
1 cup	unsalted butter, softened	250 mL
1 cup	granulated sugar	250 mL
2	eggs	2
½ tsp	vanilla extract	2 mL
½ tsp	almond extract	2 mL

1. In a bowl, whisk together flour, baking soda and salt until well combined. Stir in coconut. Set aside.

2. In a large bowl, using an electric mixer on medium speed, cream butter and granulated sugar until light and fluffy, about 3 minutes. Add eggs one at a time, beating well after each addition. Beat in vanilla and almond extract. Scrape down sides of bowl. On low speed or using a wooden spoon, gradually add flour mixture, beating just until blended. Cover dough with plastic wrap and chill for at least 1 hour.

3. Preheat oven to 350°F (180°C). Using a cookie scoop or spoons, drop tablespoonfuls (15 mL) of dough about 2 inches (5 cm) apart on prepared cookie sheets. Bake one sheet at a time in preheated oven for 13 to 15 minutes or until edges turn lightly golden.

4. Immediately slide parchment paper onto a wire cooling rack. Cool cookies for 5 minutes, then transfer from parchment paper to cooling rack and cool completely.

Maple Walnut Cookies

Makes about 3½ dozen cookies ● ● ●

Maple and walnuts are two flavors that just seem to be meant to go together.

Tips

Flavorings such as maple, rum and brandy give cookies a stronger flavor than their liquid counterparts. A teaspoon (5 mL) of maple flavoring will give as much maple flavor as ¼ cup (125 mL) maple syrup without adding that much liquid.

Fold in the nuts by hand to keep from overworking the dough after the flour is mixed in. Overworking the dough will make the cookies tough.

Let icing set before storing cookies between layers of wax paper. Do not ice if cookies are to be frozen.

- Preheat oven to 350°F (180°C)
- Cookie sheets, lined with parchment paper

Cookies

2¾ cups	all-purpose flour	675 mL
2 tsp	baking powder	10 mL
½ tsp	baking soda	2 mL
½ tsp	salt	2 mL
½ cup	unsalted butter, softened	125 mL
½ cup	vegetable shortening	125 mL
1¼ cups	packed light brown sugar	300 mL
2	eggs	2
3 tbsp	light (golden) corn syrup	45 mL
4 tsp	maple flavoring	20 mL
½ tsp	vanilla extract	2 mL
1½ cups	chopped walnuts	375 mL

Icing

1 cup	confectioner's (powdered/icing) sugar	250 mL
1 to 2 tbsp	half-and-half (10%) cream or milk	15 to 25 mL
1 tsp	maple flavoring	5 mL

1. *Cookies:* In a bowl, whisk together flour, baking powder, baking soda and salt until well combined. Set aside.

2. In a large bowl, using an electric mixer on medium speed, cream butter, shortening and brown sugar until light and fluffy, about 3 minutes. Add eggs one at a time, beating well after each addition. Beat in corn syrup, maple flavoring and vanilla. Scrape down sides of bowl. On low speed or using a wooden spoon, gradually add flour mixture, beating just until blended. By hand, fold in walnuts.

3. Using a cookie scoop or spoons, drop tablespoonfuls (15 mL) of dough about 2 inches (5 cm) apart on prepared cookie sheets. Bake one sheet at a time in preheated oven for 10 to 12 minutes or until edges start to turn lightly golden.

4. Immediately slide parchment paper onto a wire cooling rack. Cool cookies for 5 minutes, then transfer from parchment paper to cooling rack and cool completely.

5. *Icing:* In a small bowl, combine confectioner's sugar, 1 tablespoon (15 mL) of the cream and maple flavoring. Using a small whisk or a fork, blend until icing is smooth and thin enough to drizzle from a fork. Add more cream as needed to achieve the right consistency. Drizzle icing over cooled cookies.

Orange Marmalade Cookies

Makes about 3 dozen cookies

These are one of my all-time favorite cookies. The marmalade adds an extra dimension of flavor and texture with the pieces of rind and fruit intensifying the orange flavor in both the cookie and the glaze. I like to use homemade marmalade in this recipe when I have an extra jar on the shelf.

Tips

Use a high-quality orange marmalade with thin strips or small pieces of peel for the best texture and prettiest presentation.

Always let cookie sheets cool completely before placing the next batch of cookie dough on the sheet.

Let glaze set before storing cookies between layers of wax paper in a tightly sealed container.

● Cookie sheets, lined with parchment paper

Cookies

2 cups	all-purpose flour	500 mL
2 tsp	baking powder	10 mL
1/2 tsp	salt	2 mL
1/2 cup	unsalted butter, softened	125 mL
2/3 cup	granulated sugar	150 mL
1	egg	1
1 tsp	vanilla extract	5 mL
1 tsp	orange extract	5 mL
2/3 cup	orange marmalade	150 mL

Glaze

1 1/2 cups	confectioner's (powdered/icing) sugar	375 mL
1 tbsp	half-and-half (10%) cream or milk	15 mL
3/4 tsp	orange extract	3 mL
1/3 cup	orange marmalade	75 mL

1. **Cookies:** In a bowl, whisk together flour, baking powder and salt until well combined. Set aside.

2. In a large bowl, using an electric mixer on medium speed, cream butter and granulated sugar until light and fluffy, about 3 minutes. Add egg and beat well. Beat in vanilla and orange extract. On low speed or using a wooden spoon, beat in orange marmalade until well combined. Scrape down sides of bowl. Gradually add flour mixture, beating just until blended. Cover dough with plastic wrap and chill for at least 1 hour.

3. Preheat oven to 375°F (190°C). Using a cookie scoop or spoons, drop tablespoonfuls (15 mL) of dough about 2 inches (5 cm) apart on prepared cookie sheets. Bake one sheet at a time in preheated oven for 8 to 10 minutes or until edges start to turn lightly golden.

4. Immediately slide parchment paper onto a wire cooling rack. Cool cookies for 5 minutes, then transfer from parchment paper to cooling rack and cool completely.

5. **Glaze:** In a small bowl, combine confectioner's sugar, cream and orange extract. Using a small whisk or a fork, blend until smooth. Stir in orange marmalade. Spread glaze over cooled cookies.

Fudgy Brownie Cookies

Makes about 3 dozen cookies

These cookies have a brownie-like texture. For gooey cookies, slightly underbake the cookies. For more of a cake-like texture, bake the cookies for an extra minute or two.

Tips

Dutch-process cocoa powder is a refined cocoa treated with a small amount of an alkali solution to neutralize the natural acids. This process improves the flavor and color of the cocoa.

Use a cookie scoop to uniformly portion cookie dough and ensure even baking.

Variation

By hand, fold 1 cup (250 mL) chopped semisweet chocolate or semisweet chocolate chips into cookie dough along with walnuts.

- Preheat oven to 350°F (180°C)
- Cookie sheets, lined with parchment paper

1¾ cups	all-purpose flour	425 mL
½ cup	unsweetened Dutch-process cocoa powder, sifted	125 mL
1 tsp	baking powder	5 mL
½ tsp	baking soda	2 mL
½ tsp	salt	2 mL
⅓ cup	unsalted butter, softened	75 mL
⅓ cup	vegetable shortening	75 mL
1¼ cups	packed dark brown sugar	300 mL
3	eggs	3
2 tsp	vanilla extract	10 mL
1 cup	chopped walnuts	250 mL

1. In a bowl, whisk together flour, cocoa powder, baking powder, baking soda and salt until well combined. Set aside.

2. In a large bowl, using an electric mixer on medium speed, cream butter, shortening and brown sugar until light and fluffy, about 3 minutes. Add eggs one at a time, beating well after each addition. Beat in vanilla. Scrape down sides of bowl. On low speed or using a wooden spoon, gradually add flour mixture, beating just until blended. By hand, fold in walnuts.

3. Using a cookie scoop or spoons, drop tablespoonfuls (15 mL) of dough about 2 inches (5 cm) apart on prepared cookie sheets. Bake one sheet at a time in preheated oven for 10 to 12 minutes or just until set.

4. Immediately slide parchment paper onto a wire cooling rack. Cool cookies for 5 minutes, then transfer from parchment paper to cooling rack and cool completely.

Pineapple Cookies

● ● ●

These treats are infused with pineapple flavor in both the cookies and the frosting.

Tips

A small offset spatula is the perfect tool to quickly and easily spread frosting on the cookies.

Let frosting set before storing cookies between layers of wax paper in a tightly sealed container.

- ● **Preheat oven to 350°F (180°C)**
- ● **Cookie sheets, lined with parchment paper**

Cookies

2½ cups	all-purpose flour	625 mL
1 tsp	baking powder	5 mL
½ tsp	baking soda	2 mL
¼ tsp	salt	1 mL
⅔ cup	unsalted butter, softened	150 mL
⅔ cup	granulated sugar	150 mL
⅔ cup	packed light brown sugar	150 mL
2	eggs	2
½ tsp	vanilla extract	2 mL
1	can (20 oz or 540 mL) juice-packed crushed pineapple, drained (reserve pineapple juice for frosting)	1

Frosting

2 cups	confectioner's (powdered/icing) sugar	500 mL
2 tbsp	unsalted butter, at room temperature	25 mL
2 to 3 tbsp	pineapple juice	25 to 45 mL
¼ tsp	vanilla extract	1 mL

1. ***Cookies:*** In a bowl, whisk together flour, baking powder, baking soda and salt until well combined. Set aside.

2. In a large bowl, using an electric mixer on medium speed, cream butter, granulated sugar and brown sugar until light and fluffy, about 3 minutes. Add eggs one at a time, beating well after each addition. Beat in vanilla. Scrape down sides of bowl. On low speed or using a wooden spoon, gradually add flour mixture, beating just until blended. By hand, fold in pineapple.

3. Using a cookie scoop or spoons, drop tablespoonfuls (15 mL) of dough about 2 inches (5 cm) apart on prepared cookie sheets. Bake one sheet at a time in preheated oven for 10 to 12 minutes or until edges start to turn lightly golden.

4. Immediately slide parchment paper onto a wire cooling rack. Cool cookies for 5 minutes, then transfer from parchment paper to cooling rack and cool completely.

5. ***Frosting:*** In a small bowl, combine confectioner's sugar, butter, 2 tablespoons (25 mL) of the pineapple juice and vanilla. Using a small whisk or a fork, blend until frosting is smooth and spreadable. Add more pineapple juice as needed to achieve the right consistency. Spread frosting over cooled cookies.

Coconut Macaroons

Drizzled with chocolate, these moist and chewy coconut cookies are a big hit.

Tips

Chocolate can be melted in the top of a double boiler placed over simmering water. Stir frequently, until chocolate is completely melted and mixture is smooth. Set aside to cool.

Once glaze has set, cookies should be stored between layers of wax paper.

- Preheat oven to 325°F (160°C)
- Cookie sheets, lined with parchment paper

Cookies

²⁄₃ cup	all-purpose flour	150 mL
½ cup	granulated sugar	125 mL
¼ tsp	salt	1 mL
2²⁄₃ cups	sweetened flaked coconut	650 mL
1	egg	1
2	egg whites	2
1 tsp	vanilla extract	5 mL

Chocolate Glaze

1 cup	chopped semisweet chocolate or semisweet chocolate chips	250 mL
1 tsp	vegetable shortening	5 mL

1. **Cookies:** In a large bowl, whisk together flour, granulated sugar and salt until well combined. Stir in coconut. Set aside.

2. In a small bowl, using a small whisk or a fork, lightly beat egg and egg whites. Stir in vanilla. Add to flour mixture and stir until well blended.

3. Using spoons, drop rounded teaspoonfuls (5 mL) of dough about 2 inches (5 cm) apart on prepared cookie sheets. Bake one sheet at a time in preheated oven for 18 to 20 minutes or until lightly golden.

4. Immediately slide parchment paper onto a wire cooling rack. Cool cookies for 5 minutes, then transfer from parchment paper to cooling rack and cool completely.

5. **Glaze:** In a 1-quart (1 L) microwave-safe zippered storage bag, combine semisweet chocolate and vegetable shortening. Microwave on High power for 1 minute. Knead bag until completely combined and smooth, microwaving an additional 10 seconds at a time as needed to fully melt chocolate. Cut off a small corner of bag and drizzle chocolate over tops of cooled cookies. Place on parchment or wax paper to set. Allow chocolate to set completely before serving or storing.

Cranberry Orange Cookies

The orange juice and orange zest in these scrumptious cookies blend beautifully with the cranberries.

Tip

Eggs help hold cookies together and keep them from spreading too much in the oven by binding the other ingredients. As eggs are beaten, their proteins create a structure that traps air and liquids and help define a cookie's texture. During baking, the trapped air bubbles expand and cause cookies to rise.

- Preheat oven to 350°F (180°C)
- Cookie sheets, lined with parchment paper

3 cups	all-purpose flour	750 mL
2 tsp	baking powder	10 mL
½ tsp	baking soda	2 mL
½ tsp	salt	2 mL
1 cup	unsalted butter, softened	250 mL
1½ cups	granulated sugar	375 mL
1 tbsp	grated orange zest	15 mL
2	eggs	2
¼ cup	freshly squeezed orange juice	50 mL
1½ cups	dried cranberries	375 mL
1 cup	chopped walnuts	250 mL

1. In a bowl, whisk together flour, baking powder, baking soda and salt until well combined. Set aside.

2. In a large bowl, using an electric mixer on medium speed, cream butter, granulated sugar and orange zest until light and fluffy, about 3 minutes. Add eggs one at a time, beating well after each addition. Scrape down sides of bowl. On low speed or using a wooden spoon, alternately add flour mixture and orange juice, beating after each addition, just until blended. By hand, fold in cranberries and walnuts.

3. Using a cookie scoop or spoons, drop tablespoonfuls (15 mL) of dough about 2 inches (5 cm) apart on prepared cookie sheets. Bake one sheet at a time in preheated oven for 10 to 12 minutes or until edges start to turn lightly golden.

4. Immediately slide parchment paper onto a wire cooling rack. Cool cookies for 5 minutes, then transfer from parchment paper to cooling rack and cool completely.

Tangy Lime Cookies

These refreshing cookies have a bright and zesty lime flavor.

Tips

A Microplane grater will finely zest the lime peel for a wonderful texture in cookies.

Let glaze set before storing cookies between layers of wax paper in a tightly sealed container.

- Cookie sheets, lined with parchment paper

Cookies

2¾ cups	all-purpose flour	675 mL
1 tsp	baking powder	5 mL
½ tsp	baking soda	2 mL
¼ tsp	salt	1 mL
¾ cup	unsalted butter, softened	175 mL
1¼ cups	granulated sugar	300 mL
2	eggs	2
2½ tbsp	grated lime zest	37 mL
2 tbsp	freshly squeezed lime juice	25 mL

Glaze

¾ cup	confectioner's (powdered/icing) sugar	175 mL
½ tsp	grated lime zest	2 mL
1½ tbsp	freshly squeezed lime juice	22 mL

1. **Cookies:** In a bowl, whisk together flour, baking powder, baking soda and salt until well combined. Set aside.

2. In a large bowl, using an electric mixer on medium speed, cream butter and granulated sugar until light and fluffy, about 3 minutes. Add eggs one at a time, beating well after each addition. Beat in lime zest and juice. Scrape down sides of bowl. On low speed or using a wooden spoon, gradually add flour mixture, beating just until blended. Cover dough with plastic wrap and chill for at least 1 hour.

3. Preheat oven to 350°F (180°C). Using a cookie scoop or spoons, drop tablespoonfuls (15 mL) of dough about 2 inches (5 cm) apart on prepared cookie sheets. Bake one sheet at a time in preheated oven for 10 to 12 minutes or until edges start to turn lightly golden.

4. Immediately slide parchment paper onto a wire cooling rack. Cool cookies for 5 minutes, then transfer from parchment paper to cooling rack and cool completely.

5. **Glaze:** In a small bowl, combine confectioner's sugar, lime zest and juice. Using a small whisk or a fork, blend until glaze is smooth and thin enough to drizzle from a fork. Drizzle glaze over cooled cookies.

Michael's Mom's Persimmon Cookies

Makes about 4 dozen cookies ● ● ●

My friend Michael Marks, known as Your Produce Man in the United States, absolutely loves persimmon cookies. His mom, Mrs. Thelma L. Marks, made a batch of her special soft and spicy persimmon cookies for Michael every Christmas season. Michael graciously shared his mom's wonderful cookie recipe and his helpful persimmon tips.

Tips

Be sure to use the Hachiya variety of persimmon in these cookies. Set them out at room temperature to ripen. When they feel like a water balloon, they are ready to use.

To purée persimmons, remove the stems and place persimmons, peel and all, in a blender. Blend until a smooth pulp forms. The pulp may be sealed in zippered freezer storage bags and frozen for up to a year.

- **Preheat oven to 375°F (190°C)**
- **Cookie sheets, lined with parchment paper**

2 cups	all-purpose flour	500 mL
1 tsp	baking soda	5 mL
1 tsp	ground cinnamon	5 mL
1 tsp	ground nutmeg	5 mL
1 tsp	ground cloves	5 mL
1 tsp	salt	5 mL
1/2 cup	unsalted butter, softened	125 mL
1 cup	granulated sugar	250 mL
1	egg	1
1 cup	persimmon pulp (see Tips, at left)	250 mL
1 cup	raisins	250 mL
1 cup	chopped walnuts	250 mL

1. In a bowl, whisk together flour, baking soda, cinnamon, nutmeg, cloves and salt until well combined. Set aside.

2. In a large bowl, using an electric mixer on medium speed, cream butter, granulated sugar, egg and persimmon pulp until smooth and creamy, about 2 minutes. Scrape down sides of bowl. On low speed or using a wooden spoon, gradually add flour mixture, beating just until blended. By hand, fold in raisins and walnuts.

3. Using spoons, drop rounded teaspoonfuls (5 mL) of dough about 2 inches (5 cm) apart on prepared cookie sheets. Bake one sheet at a time in preheated oven for 15 to 20 minutes or until edges turn lightly golden.

4. Immediately slide parchment paper onto a wire cooling rack. Cool cookies for 5 minutes, then transfer from parchment paper to cooling rack and cool completely.

Toffee Cookies

Sweet and crunchy toffee bits highlight these brown sugar cookies.

Tip

Toffee bits can be found in the baking aisle of most grocery stores.

- Preheat oven to 350°F (180°C)
- Cookie sheets, lined with parchment paper

2¾ cups	all-purpose flour	675 mL
1½ tsp	baking powder	7 mL
½ tsp	baking soda	2 mL
½ tsp	salt	2 mL
1 cup	unsalted butter, softened	250 mL
1¼ cups	packed light brown sugar	300 mL
2	eggs	2
1½ tsp	vanilla extract	7 mL
2 cups	toffee bits	500 mL

1. In a bowl, whisk together flour, baking powder, baking soda and salt until well combined. Set aside.

2. In a large bowl, using an electric mixer on medium speed, cream butter and brown sugar until light and fluffy, about 3 minutes. Add eggs one at a time, beating well after each addition. Beat in vanilla. Scrape down sides of bowl. On low speed or using a wooden spoon, gradually add flour mixture, beating just until blended. By hand, fold in toffee bits.

3. Using a cookie scoop or spoons, drop tablespoonfuls (15 mL) of dough about 2 inches (5 cm) apart on prepared cookie sheets. Bake one sheet at a time in preheated oven for 10 to 12 minutes or until edges start to turn lightly golden.

4. Immediately slide parchment paper onto a wire cooling rack. Cool cookies for 5 minutes, then transfer from parchment paper to cooling rack and cool completely.

Amaretti

These are delightfully crispy cookies with a full almond flavor.

Tips

If you prefer, substitute $\frac{1}{2}$ teaspoon (2 mL) almond extract and 1 teaspoon (5 mL) water for the amaretto.

Almond paste is a sweet, granular mixture of ground almonds and sugar. It can be found in the baking aisle of most grocery stores.

● **Cookie sheets, lined with parchment paper**

1 cup	granulated sugar	250 mL
1	package (7 oz or 210 g) almond paste	1
2	egg whites	2
1½ tsp	amaretto liqueur	7 mL
¼ cup	all-purpose flour	50 mL
	Additional granulated sugar	

1. In a large bowl, using an electric mixer on medium speed, cream granulated sugar and almond paste until almond paste is broken into small pieces. Add egg whites and amaretto and beat on high speed until smooth, about 4 minutes. Scrape down sides of bowl. On low speed or using a wooden spoon, gradually add flour, beating just until blended. Cover dough with plastic wrap and chill for at least 1 hour.

2. Preheat oven to 350°F (180°C). Using spoons, drop rounded teaspoonfuls (5 mL) of dough about 2 inches (5 cm) apart on prepared cookie sheets. Sprinkle tops of cookies with granulated sugar. Bake one sheet at a time in preheated oven for 12 to 14 minutes or until edges turn lightly golden.

3. Immediately slide parchment paper onto a wire cooling rack. Cool cookies for 5 minutes, then transfer from parchment paper to cooling rack and cool completely.

Orange Cookies

Layers of orange flavors give these cookies their delightful citrus aroma and taste.

Tips

When zesting oranges, remove only the colored (outer) part of the peel. The white part underneath, called the pith, is very bitter and will give cookies an unpleasant flavor.

Let icing set before storing cookies between layers of wax paper in a tightly sealed container.

● **Cookie sheets, lined with parchment paper**

Cookies

1 cup	granulated sugar	250 mL
2 tbsp	grated orange zest	25 mL
3 cups	all-purpose flour	750 mL
1½ tsp	baking powder	7 mL
½ tsp	baking soda	2 mL
¼ tsp	salt	1 mL
⅓ cup	unsalted butter, softened	75 mL
⅓ cup	vegetable shortening	75 mL
2	eggs	2
¼ tsp	orange extract	1 mL
½ cup	freshly squeezed orange juice	125 mL

Icing

1½ cups	confectioner's (powdered/icing) sugar	375 mL
2 tbsp	unsalted butter, at room temperature	25 mL
2 tsp	grated orange zest	10 mL
1½ tbsp	freshly squeezed orange juice	22 mL

1. *Cookies:* In a small bowl, combine granulated sugar and orange zest until well blended. Set aside.
2. In a bowl, whisk together flour, baking powder, baking soda and salt until well combined. Set aside.
3. In a large bowl, using an electric mixer on medium speed, cream butter, shortening and sugar mixture until light and fluffy, about 3 minutes. Add eggs one at a time, beating well after each addition. Beat in orange extract. Scrape down sides of bowl. On low speed or using a wooden spoon, alternately stir in flour mixture and orange juice, beating after each addition, just until blended. Cover dough with plastic wrap and chill for at least 1 hour.
4. Preheat oven to 350°F (180°C). Using a cookie scoop or spoons, drop tablespoonfuls (15 mL) of dough about 2 inches (5 cm) apart on prepared cookie sheets. Bake one sheet at a time in preheated oven for 10 to 12 minutes or until edges start to turn lightly golden.
5. Immediately slide parchment paper onto a wire cooling rack. Cool cookies for 5 minutes, then transfer from parchment paper to cooling rack and cool completely.
6. *Icing:* In a small bowl, combine confectioner's sugar, butter, orange zest and orange juice. Using a small whisk or a fork, beat until icing is smooth. Spread icing over cooled cookies.

Hawaiian Cookies

Makes about 3½ dozen cookies

Pineapple, coconut and macadamia nuts give these cookies a tropical flair and make them a perfect finish for an outdoor meal on a summer evening.

Tip

If you only have crushed pineapple packed in syrup, it may be substituted for the juice-packed pineapple, although the cookies will be a bit sweeter.

Variation

Piña Colada Cookies: Substitute 1½ tsp (7 mL) rum flavoring for almond extract. Increase the coconut to 1½ cups (375 mL) and omit macadamia nuts.

- **Preheat oven to 375°F (190°C)**
- **Cookie sheets, lined with parchment paper**

2 cups	all-purpose flour	500 mL
1 tsp	baking powder	5 mL
½ tsp	baking soda	2 mL
¼ tsp	salt	1 mL
½ cup	unsalted butter, softened	125 mL
½ cup	granulated sugar	125 mL
½ cup	packed light brown sugar	125 mL
1	egg	1
½ tsp	vanilla extract	2 mL
¼ tsp	almond extract	1 mL
1	can (20 oz or 540 mL) juice-packed crushed pineapple, drained	1
1 cup	sweetened flaked coconut	250 mL
1 cup	chopped roasted unsalted macadamia nuts	250 mL

1. In a bowl, whisk together flour, baking powder, baking soda and salt until well combined. Set aside.

2. In a large bowl, using an electric mixer on medium speed, cream butter, granulated sugar and brown sugar until light and fluffy, about 3 minutes. Add egg and beat well. Beat in vanilla and almond extract. Scrape down sides of bowl. On low speed or using a wooden spoon, gradually add flour mixture, beating just until blended. By hand, fold in pineapple, coconut and macadamia nuts.

3. Using a cookie scoop or spoons, drop tablespoonfuls (15 mL) of dough about 2 inches (5 cm) apart on prepared cookie sheets. Bake one sheet at a time in preheated oven for 8 to 10 minutes or until edges start to turn lightly golden.

4. Immediately slide parchment paper onto a wire cooling rack. Cool cookies for 5 minutes, then transfer from parchment paper to cooling rack and cool completely.

Butterscotch Pecan Cookies

Dark brown sugar, butterscotch chips and pecans make these cookies sweet and flavorful.

Tips

Butterscotch chips can be found in the baking aisle of most grocery stores.

Brown sugar adds moisture and rich flavor to cookies.

● **Cookie sheets, lined with parchment paper**

2½ cups	all-purpose flour	625 mL
1 tsp	baking powder	5 mL
½ tsp	baking soda	2 mL
¼ tsp	salt	1 mL
¾ cup	unsalted butter, softened	175 mL
1 cup	packed dark brown sugar	250 mL
2	eggs	2
1 tsp	vanilla extract	5 mL
1½ cups	butterscotch chips	375 mL
1 cup	chopped pecans	250 mL

1. In a bowl, whisk together flour, baking powder, baking soda and salt until well combined. Set aside.

2. In a large bowl, using an electric mixer on medium speed, cream butter and brown sugar until light and fluffy, about 3 minutes. Add eggs one at a time, beating well after each addition. Beat in vanilla. Scrape down sides of bowl. On low speed or using a wooden spoon, gradually add flour mixture, beating just until blended. By hand, fold in butterscotch chips and pecans. Cover dough with plastic wrap and chill for at least 1 hour.

3. Preheat oven to 350°F (180°C). Using a cookie scoop or spoons, drop tablespoonfuls (15 mL) of dough about 2 inches (5 cm) apart on prepared cookie sheets. Bake one sheet at a time in preheated oven for 10 to 12 minutes or until edges start to turn lightly golden.

4. Immediately slide parchment paper onto a wire cooling rack. Cool cookies for 5 minutes, then transfer from parchment paper to cooling rack and cool completely.

Cashew Cookies

● ● ●

Cashews are one of my favorite nuts, and I love to use them in cookies. The Browned Butter Frosting is the perfect finish for these treats.

Tips

Always taste nuts before adding them to cookies to make sure they are fresh.

Let frosting set before storing cookies between layers of wax paper in a tightly sealed container.

- ● **Preheat oven to 350°F (180°C)**
- ● **Cookie sheets, lined with parchment paper**

Cookies

2½ cups	all-purpose flour	625 mL
1 tsp	baking powder	5 mL
½ tsp	baking soda	2 mL
¼ tsp	salt	1 mL
⅔ cup	unsalted butter, softened	150 mL
1 cup	packed dark brown sugar	250 mL
2	eggs	2
1 tsp	vanilla extract	5 mL
1½ cups	chopped unsalted cashews	375 mL

Browned Butter Frosting

⅓ cup	unsalted butter	75 mL
3 tbsp	half-and-half (10%) cream or milk	45 mL
¼ tsp	vanilla extract	1 mL
2 cups	confectioner's (powdered/icing) sugar	500 mL
¼ cup	finely chopped unsalted cashews	50 mL

1. ***Cookies:*** In a bowl, whisk together flour, baking powder, baking soda and salt until well combined. Set aside.

2. In a large bowl, using an electric mixer on medium speed, cream butter and brown sugar until light and fluffy, about 3 minutes. Add eggs one at a time, beating well after each addition. Beat in vanilla. Scrape down sides of bowl. On low speed or using a wooden spoon, gradually add flour mixture, beating just until blended. By hand, fold in cashews.

3. Using a cookie scoop or spoons, drop tablespoonfuls (15 mL) of dough about 2 inches (5 cm) apart on prepared cookie sheets. Bake one sheet at a time in preheated oven for 10 to 12 minutes or until edges start to turn lightly golden.

4. Immediately slide parchment paper onto a wire cooling rack. Cool cookies for 5 minutes, then transfer from parchment paper to cooling rack and cool completely.

5. ***Frosting:*** In a small saucepan, over medium heat, lightly brown butter. Remove pan from heat and stir in cream and vanilla. Add confectioner's sugar and beat until frosting is smooth and creamy. Spread frosting over cooled cookies. Sprinkle with chopped cashews.

Mini M&M Candy Cookies

I love using mini M&Ms to make these cookies. The tiny chocolate candies distribute well through the dough so there are candies in every bit of colorful cookie.

Tip

Line cookie sheets with parchment paper to keep cookies from sticking.

● **Preheat oven to 350°F (180°C)**
● **Cookie sheets, lined with parchment paper**

2½ cups	all-purpose flour	625 mL
2 tsp	baking powder	10 mL
½ tsp	baking soda	2 mL
½ tsp	salt	2 mL
¾ cup	unsalted butter, softened	175 mL
1 cup	packed dark brown sugar	250 mL
½ cup	granulated sugar	125 mL
2	eggs	2
2 tsp	vanilla extract	10 mL
1	package (12 oz or 275 g) mini M&M candies	1

1. In a bowl, whisk together flour, baking powder, baking soda and salt until well combined. Set aside.

2. In a large bowl, using an electric mixer on medium speed, cream butter, brown sugar and granulated sugar until light and fluffy, about 3 minutes. Add eggs one at a time, beating well after each addition. Beat in vanilla. Scrape down sides of bowl. On low speed or using a wooden spoon, gradually add flour mixture, beating just until blended. By hand, fold in M&M candies.

3. Using a cookie scoop or spoons, drop tablespoonfuls (15 mL) of dough about 2 inches (5 cm) apart on prepared cookie sheets. Bake one sheet at a time in preheated oven for 8 to 10 minutes or until edges start to turn lightly golden.

4. Immediately slide parchment paper onto a wire cooling rack. Cool cookies for 5 minutes, then transfer from parchment paper to cooling rack and cool completely.

Blueberry Lemon Cookies

● ● ●

The flavor of lemon is an excellent complement to blueberries.

Tips

Be sure your oven is fully preheated before baking your first batch of cookies. Most ovens take up to 15 minutes to heat up to 350°F (180°C).

Let icing set before storing cookies between layers of wax paper in a tightly sealed container.

● **Preheat oven to 350°F (180°C)**
● **Cookie sheets, lined with parchment paper**

Cookies

2⅔ cups	all-purpose flour	650 mL
1 tsp	baking powder	5 mL
½ tsp	baking soda	2 mL
½ tsp	salt	2 mL
½ cup	unsalted butter, softened	125 mL
½ cup	vegetable shortening	125 mL
¾ cup	granulated sugar	175 mL
¾ cup	packed light brown sugar	175 mL
2	eggs	2
2 tsp	grated lemon zest	10 mL
½ tsp	vanilla extract	2 mL
1½ cups	dried blueberries	375 mL

Icing

1½ cups	confectioner's (powdered/icing) sugar	375 mL
2 tbsp	unsalted butter, at room temperature	25 mL
2 tbsp	freshly squeezed lemon juice	25 mL

1. *Cookies:* In a bowl, whisk together flour, baking powder, baking soda and salt until well combined. Set aside.

2. In a large bowl, using an electric mixer on medium speed, cream butter, shortening, granulated sugar and brown sugar until light and fluffy, about 3 minutes. Add eggs one at a time, beating well after each addition. Beat in lemon zest and vanilla. Scrape down sides of bowl. On low speed or using a wooden spoon, gradually add flour mixture, beating just until blended. By hand, fold in blueberries.

3. Using a cookie scoop or spoons, drop tablespoonfuls (15 mL) of dough about 2 inches (5 cm) apart on prepared cookie sheets. Bake one sheet at a time in preheated oven for 10 to 12 minutes or until edges start to turn lightly golden.

4. Immediately slide parchment paper onto a wire cooling rack. Cool cookies for 5 minutes, then transfer from parchment paper to cooling rack and cool completely.

5. *Icing:* In a small bowl, combine confectioner's sugar, butter and lemon juice. Using a small whisk or a fork, beat until icing is smooth. Spread icing over cooled cookies.

Mincemeat Cookies

These are a wonderful treat to add to a holiday cookie tray.

Tips

Jars of canned mincemeat can be found in grocery stores throughout the year. Look for it in the baking aisle or canned fruit aisle.

Let glaze set before storing cookies between layers of wax paper in a tightly sealed container.

- Preheat oven to 350°F (180°C)
- Cookie sheets, lined with parchment paper

Cookies

2 cups	all-purpose flour	500 mL
1 tsp	baking powder	5 mL
½ tsp	baking soda	2 mL
½ tsp	ground cinnamon	2 mL
¼ tsp	ground nutmeg	1 mL
¼ tsp	salt	1 mL
½ cup	unsalted butter, softened	125 mL
¾ cup	packed light brown sugar	175 mL
2	eggs	2
1 tsp	rum flavoring	5 mL
½ tsp	vanilla extract	2 mL
1 cup	mincemeat	250 mL
¾ cup	chopped walnuts	175 mL

Glaze

1½ cups	confectioner's (powdered/icing) sugar	375 mL
1 to 2 tbsp	half-and-half (10%) cream or milk	15 to 25 mL
1 tsp	rum flavoring	5 mL

1. **Cookies:** In a bowl, whisk together flour, baking powder, baking soda, cinnamon, nutmeg and salt until well combined. Set aside.

2. In a large bowl, using an electric mixer on medium speed, cream butter and brown sugar until light and fluffy, about 3 minutes. Add eggs one at a time, beating well after each addition. Beat in rum flavoring and vanilla extract. Scrape down sides of bowl. On low speed or using a wooden spoon, gradually add flour mixture, beating just until blended. By hand, fold in mincemeat and walnuts.

3. Using a cookie scoop or spoons, drop tablespoonfuls (15 mL) of dough about 2 inches (5 cm) apart on prepared cookie sheets. Bake one sheet at a time in preheated oven for 10 to 12 minutes or until edges start to turn lightly golden.

4. Immediately slide parchment paper onto a wire cooling rack. Cool cookies for 5 minutes, then transfer from parchment paper to cooling rack and cool completely.

5. **Glaze:** In a small bowl, combine confectioner's sugar, 1 tablespoon (15 mL) of the cream and rum flavoring. Using a small whisk or a fork, blend until glaze is smooth and thin enough to drizzle from a fork. Add more cream as needed to achieve the right consistency. Drizzle glaze over cooled cookies.

Apple Walnut Cookies

Makes about 3½ dozen cookies   ● ● ●

This is a great autumn cookie to make when the fresh apple harvest comes in, as well as anytime throughout the year.

Tip

A tart baking apple such as Granny Smith is a good choice for this recipe. Prepare the apple after measuring all the other ingredients and just before mixing the cookie dough to help keep the apple from turning brown.

- **Preheat oven to 350°F (180°C)**
- **Cookie sheets, lined with parchment paper**

Cookies

2¾ cups	all-purpose flour	675 mL
1½ tsp	baking powder	7 mL
½ tsp	baking soda	2 mL
½ tsp	ground cinnamon	2 mL
¼ tsp	ground nutmeg	1 mL
¼ tsp	salt	1 mL
⅔ cup	unsalted butter, softened	150 mL
⅔ cup	granulated sugar	150 mL
⅔ cup	packed light brown sugar	150 mL
2	eggs	2
3 tbsp	unsweetened apple cider or apple juice	45 mL
½ tsp	vanilla extract	2 mL
1¼ cups	finely chopped peeled and cored apple	300 mL
¾ cup	chopped walnuts	175 mL

Frosting

2 cups	confectioner's (powdered/icing) sugar	500 mL
2 tbsp	unsalted butter, at room temperature	25 mL
2 to 3 tbsp	unsweetened apple cider or apple juice	25 to 45 mL
¼ tsp	vanilla extract	1 mL
Pinch	ground nutmeg	Pinch
¼ cup	finely chopped walnuts	50 mL

1. **Cookies:** In a bowl, whisk together flour, baking powder, baking soda, cinnamon, nutmeg and salt until well combined. Set aside.

2. In a large bowl, using an electric mixer on medium speed, cream butter, granulated sugar and brown sugar until light and fluffy, about 3 minutes. Add eggs one at a time, beating well after each addition. Beat in apple cider and vanilla. Scrape down sides of bowl. On low speed or using a wooden spoon, gradually add flour mixture, beating just until blended. By hand, fold in apple and walnuts.

Tip
Let frosting set before storing cookies between layers of wax paper in a tightly sealed container.

3. Using a cookie scoop or spoons, drop tablespoonfuls (15 mL) of dough about 2 inches (5 cm) apart on prepared cookie sheets. Bake one sheet at a time in preheated oven for 12 to 14 minutes or until edges start to turn lightly golden.

4. Immediately slide parchment paper onto a wire cooling rack. Cool cookies for 5 minutes, then transfer from parchment paper to cooling rack and cool completely.

5. *Frosting:* In a small bowl, combine confectioner's sugar, butter, 2 tablespoons (25 mL) of the apple cider, vanilla and nutmeg. Using a small whisk or a fork, blend until frosting is smooth and spreadable. Add more apple cider as needed to achieve the right consistency. Spread frosting over cooled cookies. Sprinkle with chopped walnuts.

"Welcome to the Neighborhood" Gift

Are there new neighbors moving in next door or down the street? Nothing says "Welcome to the neighborhood! We're glad you're here!" quite like a pretty plate piled high with fresh homemade brownies. You're sure make a great impression and make some new friends.

Malted Milk Cookies

These cookies are popular with kids of all ages.

Tips

Easily crush malted milk balls by placing them in a zippered storage bag, sealing the bag and tapping the balls lightly with a rolling pin, large spoon or other kitchen utensil to break them into small pieces.

Before making cookies, taste malted milk balls to make sure they are fresh and have good flavor.

- Preheat oven to 350°F (180°C)
- Cookie sheets, lined with parchment paper

2½ cups	all-purpose flour	625 mL
½ cup	malted milk powder	125 mL
2 tsp	baking powder	10 mL
½ tsp	baking soda	2 mL
½ tsp	salt	2 mL
½ cup	unsalted butter, softened	125 mL
½ cup	vegetable shortening	125 mL
1 cup	packed light brown sugar	250 mL
2	eggs	2
2 tsp	vanilla extract	10 mL
2 cups	chocolate-coated malted milk balls, broken into small pieces	500 mL

1. In a bowl, whisk together flour, malted milk powder, baking powder, baking soda and salt until well combined. Set aside.

2. In a large bowl, using an electric mixer on medium speed, cream butter, shortening and brown sugar until light and fluffy, about 3 minutes. Add eggs one at a time, beating well after each addition. Beat in vanilla. Scrape down sides of bowl. On low speed or using a wooden spoon, gradually add flour mixture, beating just until blended. By hand, fold in malted milk ball pieces.

3. Using a cookie scoop or spoons, drop tablespoonfuls (15 mL) of dough about 2 inches (5 cm) apart on prepared cookie sheets. Bake one sheet at a time in preheated oven for 10 to 12 minutes or until edges start to turn lightly golden.

4. Immediately slide parchment paper onto a wire cooling rack. Cool cookies for 5 minutes, then transfer from parchment paper to cooling rack and cool completely.

Hand-Shaped Cookies

Ultimate Dark Chocolate Espresso
  Cookies. 73
Chewy Peanut Butter Cookies 74
Pecan Sandies 75
Lemon Crinkles 76
Snickerdoodles. 77
Chocolate Cookies 78
Molasses Cookies 79
Cranberry Coconut Cookies 80
Favorite Sugar Cookies. 81
Brown Sugar Cookies. 82
Chocolate-Dipped Cappuccino
  Sticks 83
Viennese Vanilla Crescents 84
Spice Cookies 85
Coconut Lime Cookies 86
Gary's Chocolate Cookies 87
Lemon Sugar Cookies 88
Thumbprint Cookies 89
Chocolate Thumbprint Cookies 90
Peanut Butter Jam Thumbprints 91
White Chocolate Raspberry
  Thumbprints 92

Mexican Wedding Cake
  Cookies. 94
Orange Wedding Cake Cookies 95
Classic Peanut Butter Cookies 96
Rum Cookies 97
Double Almond Cookies. 98
Glazed Lime Cookies 99
Coconut Pecan Cookies. 100
Lemon Balls 101
Cream Cheese Walnut Cookies 102
Ginger Cookies. 103
Peanut Butter Chews 104
Coffee Almond Rounds 105
English Toffee Cookies 106
Swedish Tea Cookies 108
White Chocolate Cookies 109
Butter Pecan Cookies. 110
Chinese Almond Cookies 111
Festive Sugar Cookies 112
Eggnog Sugar Cookies. 113
Almond Logs 114
Spritz Cookies 115
Chocolate Spritz Cookies 116

About Hand-Shaped Cookies

Shaped cookies are formed by hand into a variety of shapes, including balls, logs and crescents. The cookie dough is usually chilled first to make it easier to shape. These "hands on" cookies are fun to make and are a great project for the whole family. Hand-shaped cookies can be baked unadorned or rolled in a variety of sugars, nuts or other toppings before baking.

The dough needs to be cold when you start to shape it. If the dough is too warm, the heat from your hands will soften the butter in the dough and cause the cookies to lose their shape when they bake. If the cookie dough starts to soften and becomes too sticky to work with, return it to the refrigerator for a few minutes to firm the butter.

Chilled dough can be formed into many shapes, but round balls are the most common shape for this type of cookie. Shaping the dough into balls before baking produces attractive cookies that are uniform in size and appearance.

To shape the cookies, roll a portion of dough between your palms to form it into a ball. About 2 teaspoons (10 mL) of dough will make a 1-inch (2.5 cm) ball. To keep the dough from sticking to your hands, coat them with nonstick vegetable spray before starting to shape the dough. You can dust your hands with flour if you prefer, but the cookies will absorb more flour and may become dry or tough when baked.

This category also includes cookies, such as spritz, where the dough is pressed through a cookie press. Any soft-dough cookie can be shaped using a cookie press as long as the dough doesn't contain chocolate chips, nuts, dried fruit or other pieces that would clog the press.

Ultimate Dark Chocolate Espresso Cookies

Makes about 5 dozen cookies

Intensely chocolate and flavored with espresso powder for an extra kick, these fudgy cookies are even better the next day!

Tip

These cookies are very sticky, so it is important to lightly spray hands with nonstick cooking spray to prevent dough from sticking while shaping cookies.

● **Cookie sheets, lined with parchment paper**

10 oz	bittersweet chocolate, chopped	300 g
2¼ cups	all-purpose flour	550 mL
½ cup	unsweetened Dutch-process cocoa powder, sifted	125 mL
2½ tsp	baking powder	12 mL
½ tsp	salt	2 mL
⅔ cup	unsalted butter, softened	150 mL
1½ cups	packed dark brown sugar	375 mL
½ cup	granulated sugar	125 mL
2½ tsp	instant espresso powder	12 mL
4	eggs	4
2½ tsp	vanilla extract	12 mL

1. In a microwave-safe bowl, heat chopped chocolate in microwave at Medium-High (75%) power for 1 minute. Stir chocolate until smooth. If necessary, heat at Medium (50%) power for 10 seconds at a time, stirring between each heating, just until chocolate is melted. Set aside to cool.

2. In a bowl, whisk together flour, cocoa powder, baking powder and salt until well combined. Set aside.

3. In a large bowl, using an electric mixer on medium speed, cream butter, brown sugar, granulated sugar and espresso powder until light and fluffy, about 3 minutes. Add eggs one at a time, beating well after each addition. Beat in vanilla. Scrape down sides of bowl. Add melted chocolate and stir until thoroughly combined. On low speed or using a wooden spoon, gradually add flour mixture, beating just until blended. Cover dough with plastic wrap and chill for at least 1 hour.

4. Preheat oven to 350°F (180°C). Lightly grease hands with nonstick cooking spray. Roll pieces of dough into 1-inch (2.5 cm) balls. Place about 2 inches (5 cm) apart on prepared cookie sheets. Bake one sheet at a time in preheated oven for 10 to 12 minutes or until set around the edges but slightly soft in the center.

5. Immediately slide parchment paper onto a wire cooling rack. Cool cookies for 5 minutes, then transfer from parchment paper to cooling rack and cool completely.

Chewy Peanut Butter Cookies

● ● ●

This is one of my favorite peanut butter cookies.

Tip
Creamy peanut butter gives these cookies a smooth texture. You can use chunky peanut butter if you prefer more texture in your cookies.

● **Cookie sheets, lined with parchment paper**

2½ cups	all-purpose flour	625 mL
2 tsp	baking powder	10 mL
½ tsp	baking soda	2 mL
¼ tsp	salt	1 mL
1 cup	creamy peanut butter	250 mL
½ cup	vegetable shortening	125 mL
1½ cups	packed light brown sugar	375 mL
2	eggs	2
1 tbsp	vanilla extract	15 mL

1. In a bowl, whisk together flour, baking powder, baking soda and salt until well combined. Set aside.

2. In a large bowl, using an electric mixer on medium speed, cream peanut butter, shortening and brown sugar until light and fluffy, about 3 minutes. Add eggs one at a time, beating well after each addition. Beat in vanilla. Scrape down sides of bowl. On low speed or using a wooden spoon, gradually add flour mixture, beating just until blended. Cover dough with plastic wrap and chill for at least 30 minutes.

3. Preheat oven to 350°F (180°C). Lightly grease hands with nonstick cooking spray. Roll pieces of dough into 1¼-inch (3 cm) balls. Place about 2 inches (5 cm) apart on prepared cookie sheets. Using a fork, make crisscross marks on top of cookie, pressing dough to ½ inch (1 cm) thick. Bake one sheet at a time in preheated oven for 10 to 12 minutes or until edges start to turn lightly golden.

4. Immediately slide parchment paper onto a wire cooling rack. Cool cookies for 5 minutes, then transfer from parchment paper to cooling rack and cool completely.

Pecan Sandies

Baking these cookies at a low oven temperature allows them to crisp without burning.

Tip

Always taste nuts before adding them to cookies to make sure they are fresh.

• **Cookie sheets, lined with parchment paper**

2 cups	all-purpose flour	500 mL
1 tsp	baking powder	5 mL
½ tsp	salt	2 mL
¾ cup	unsalted butter, softened	175 mL
⅔ cup	confectioner's (powdered/icing) sugar	150 mL
2 tsp	vanilla extract	10 mL
1 cup	chopped pecans	250 mL
	Additional confectioner's (powdered/icing) sugar	

1. In a bowl, whisk together flour, baking powder and salt until well combined. Set aside.

2. In a large bowl, using an electric mixer on medium speed, cream butter and confectioner's sugar until light and fluffy, about 2 minutes. Beat in vanilla. Scrape down sides of bowl. On low speed or using a wooden spoon, gradually add flour mixture, beating just until blended. By hand, fold in pecans. Cover dough with plastic wrap and chill for at least 30 minutes.

3. Preheat oven to 300°F (150°C). Lightly grease hands with nonstick cooking spray. Roll pieces of dough into 1-inch (2.5 cm) balls. Place about 2 inches (5 cm) apart on prepared cookie sheets. Flatten balls slightly with bottom of a glass dipped in confectioner's sugar. Bake one sheet at a time in preheated oven for 18 to 20 minutes or until edges start to turn lightly golden.

4. Immediately slide parchment paper onto a wire cooling rack. Cool cookies for 5 minutes, then transfer from parchment paper to cooling rack and cool completely. Dust lightly with confectioner's sugar.

Lemon Crinkles

I love the little flecks of lemon zest in these attractive cookies.

Tip

A microplane grater will finely zest the lemon peel for a wonderful texture in cookies. Be sure to include only the colored part of the outer peel.

• Cookie sheets, lined with parchment paper

1⅔ cups	all-purpose flour	400 mL
1 tsp	baking powder	5 mL
½ tsp	cream of tartar	2 mL
¼ tsp	baking soda	1 mL
¼ tsp	salt	1 mL
¼ cup	unsalted butter, softened	50 mL
¼ cup	vegetable shortening	50 mL
1 cup	granulated sugar	250 mL
1	egg	1
1 tbsp	lemon zest	15 mL
1 tbsp	freshly squeezed lemon juice	15 mL
	Additional granulated sugar	

1. In a bowl, whisk together flour, baking powder, cream of tartar, baking soda and salt until well combined. Set aside.

2. In a large bowl, using an electric mixer on medium speed, cream butter, shortening and granulated sugar until light and fluffy, about 3 minutes. Add egg and beat well. Beat in lemon zest and lemon juice. Scrape down sides of bowl. On low speed or using a wooden spoon, gradually add flour mixture, beating just until blended. Cover dough with plastic wrap and chill for at least 1 hour.

3. Preheat oven to 350°F (180°C). Lightly grease hands with nonstick cooking spray. Roll pieces of dough into 1-inch (2.5 cm) balls. Roll balls in granulated sugar. Place about 2 inches (5 cm) apart on prepared cookie sheets. Bake one sheet at a time in preheated oven for 10 to 12 minutes or until edges start to turn lightly golden.

4. Immediately slide parchment paper onto a wire cooling rack. Cool cookies for 5 minutes, then transfer from parchment paper to cooling rack and cool completely.

Snickerdoodles

A childhood classic, snickerdoodles are tender sugar cookies rolled in cinnamon sugar to create a delicious coating.

Tip

Lightly coat the dough balls with the sugar mixture for a mild cinnamon flavor. For a stronger cinnamon topping, roll the dough balls in the sugar mixture until they are very well coated.

● Cookie sheets, lined with parchment paper

Cookies

2½ cups	all-purpose flour	625 mL
1 tsp	baking soda	5 mL
½ tsp	cream of tartar	2 mL
1 cup	unsalted butter, softened	250 mL
1¼ cups	granulated sugar	300 mL
1	egg	1
1 tsp	vanilla extract	5 mL

Cinnamon Sugar

¼ cup	granulated sugar	50 mL
2 tsp	ground cinnamon	10 mL

1. **Cookies:** In a bowl, whisk together flour, baking soda and cream of tartar until well combined. Set aside.

2. In a large bowl, using an electric mixer on medium speed, cream butter and granulated sugar until light and fluffy, about 3 minutes. Add egg and beat well. Beat in vanilla. Scrape down sides of bowl. On low speed or using a wooden spoon, gradually add flour mixture, beating just until blended. Cover dough with plastic wrap and chill for at least 1 hour.

3. Preheat oven to 350°F (180°C).

4. **Cinnamon Sugar:** In a shallow dish, using a fork or wire whisk, combine granulated sugar and cinnamon until well blended.

5. Lightly grease hands with nonstick cooking spray. Roll pieces of dough into 1-inch (2.5 cm) balls. Roll balls in cinnamon sugar. Place about 2 inches (5 cm) apart on prepared cookie sheets. Bake one sheet at a time in preheated oven for 10 to 12 minutes or until edges start to turn lightly golden.

6. Immediately slide parchment paper onto a wire cooling rack. Cool cookies for 5 minutes, then transfer from parchment paper to cooling rack and cool completely.

Chocolate Cookies

Makes about 3½ dozen cookies ● ● ●

The tops of these lovely, intensely chocolate cookies have a pretty, crackled appearance.

Tip

Bittersweet chocolate contains a minimum of 35% chocolate liquor, with many brands around 50% and some even higher. The more chocolate liquor is included, the more intense the flavor. Bittersweet chocolate differs from unsweetened chocolate in that it contains some sugar and additional cocoa butter to make it richer and smoother. For a milder chocolate flavor, lighter color and slightly sweeter cookie, semisweet chocolate may be substituted for the bittersweet chocolate.

● **Cookie sheets, lined with parchment paper**

6 oz	bittersweet chocolate, chopped	175 g
1¼ cups	all-purpose flour	300 mL
1 cup	cake flour	250 mL
½ tsp	baking powder	2 mL
½ tsp	baking soda	2 mL
½ tsp	salt	2 mL
½ cup	unsalted butter, softened	125 mL
1⅓ cups	granulated sugar	325 mL
2	eggs	2
1½ tsp	vanilla extract	7 mL
	Additional granulated sugar	

1. In a microwave-safe bowl, heat chopped chocolate in microwave at Medium-High (75%) power for 1 minute. Stir chocolate until smooth. If necessary, heat at Medium (50%) power for 10 seconds at a time, stirring between each heating, just until chocolate is melted. Set aside to cool.

2. In a bowl, whisk together all-purpose flour, cake flour, baking powder, baking soda and salt until well combined. Set aside.

3. In a large bowl, using an electric mixer on medium speed, cream butter and granulated sugar until light and fluffy, about 3 minutes. Add eggs one at a time, beating well after each addition. Beat in melted chocolate and vanilla. Scrape down sides of bowl. On low speed or using a wooden spoon, gradually add flour mixture, beating just until blended. Cover dough with plastic wrap and chill for at least 1 hour.

4. Preheat oven to 350°F (180°C). Lightly grease hands with nonstick cooking spray. Roll pieces of dough into 1-inch (2.5 cm) balls. Roll balls in granulated sugar. Place about 2 inches (5 cm) apart on prepared cookie sheets. Bake one sheet at a time in preheated oven for 10 to 12 minutes or until set and tops are cracked

5. Immediately slide parchment paper onto a wire cooling rack. Cool cookies for 5 minutes, then transfer from parchment paper to cooling rack and cool completely.

Molasses Cookies

Warm spices and the rustic flavor of molasses blend nicely in these gems. They are a perfect treat with a piping hot cup of tea or coffee on a cold winter day.

Tip

Store eggs in their original carton on a shelf in the refrigerator. Do not store eggs in the door because the temperature fluctuates every time the door is opened.

● **Cookie sheets, lined with parchment paper**

2¾ cups	all-purpose flour	675 mL
1 tsp	baking powder	5 mL
1 tsp	baking soda	5 mL
½ tsp	ground cinnamon	2 mL
¼ tsp	ground ginger	1 mL
¼ tsp	ground nutmeg	1 mL
¼ tsp	salt	1 mL
½ cup	vegetable shortening	125 mL
1 cup	packed dark brown sugar	250 mL
½ cup	fancy molasses	125 mL
2	eggs	2
1 tsp	vanilla extract	5 mL
	Additional granulated sugar	

1. In a bowl, whisk together flour, baking powder, baking soda, cinnamon, ginger, nutmeg and salt until well combined. Set aside.

2. In a large bowl, using an electric mixer on medium speed, cream shortening and brown sugar until light and fluffy, about 3 minutes. Beat in molasses. Add eggs one at a time, beating well after each addition. Beat in vanilla. Scrape down sides of bowl. On low speed or using a wooden spoon, gradually add flour mixture, beating just until blended. Cover dough with plastic wrap and chill for at least 1 hour.

3. Preheat oven to 350°F (180°C). Lightly grease hands with nonstick cooking spray. Roll pieces of dough into 1-inch (2.5 cm) balls. Roll balls in granulated sugar. Place about 2 inches (5 cm) apart on prepared cookie sheets. Bake one sheet at a time in preheated oven for 10 to 12 minutes or until edges start to turn lightly golden.

4. Immediately slide parchment paper onto a wire cooling rack. Cool cookies for 5 minutes, then transfer from parchment paper to cooling rack and cool completely.

Cranberry Coconut Cookies

Makes about 3½ dozen cookies

The sweetness of the coconut balances the tanginess of the dried cranberries in these delights that are crispy on the outside and chewy on the inside.

Tip

Unsalted butter is the best choice for baked goods. It has a fresh, sweet cream flavor that adds immeasurably to the overall taste of the cookie. Because butter adds so much flavor, always choose a high-quality unsalted butter for cookie baking. Unsalted butter has a lower water content and higher fat content than salted butter, so cookies tend to spread less on the cookie sheet.

Variation

Cranberry Apricot Coconut Cookies: Use 1 cup (250 mL) dried cranberries and add 1 cup (250 mL) chopped dried apricots.

- **Cookie sheets, lined with parchment paper**

2 cups	all-purpose flour	500 mL
1 tsp	baking powder	5 mL
¼ tsp	salt	1 mL
¾ cup	unsalted butter, softened	175 mL
1 cup	granulated sugar	250 mL
1	egg	1
1 tsp	vanilla extract	5 mL
½ tsp	almond extract	2 mL
1½ cups	dried cranberries	375 mL
1½ cups	sweetened flaked coconut	375 mL
	Additional granulated sugar	

1. In a bowl, whisk together flour, baking powder and salt until well combined. Set aside.

2. In a large bowl, using an electric mixer on medium speed, cream butter and granulated sugar until light and fluffy, about 3 minutes. Add egg and beat well. Beat in vanilla and almond extract. Scrape down sides of bowl. On low speed or using a wooden spoon, gradually add flour mixture, beating just until blended. By hand, fold in cranberries and coconut. Cover dough with plastic wrap and chill for at least 1 hour.

3. Preheat oven to 350°F (180°C). Lightly grease hands with nonstick cooking spray. Roll pieces of dough into 1-inch (2.5 cm) balls. Roll balls in granulated sugar. Place about 2 inches (5 cm) apart on prepared cookie sheets. Bake one sheet at a time in preheated oven for 10 to 12 minutes or until edges start to turn lightly golden.

4. Immediately slide parchment paper onto a wire cooling rack. Cool cookies for 5 minutes, then transfer from parchment paper to cooling rack and cool completely.

Favorite Sugar Cookies

This is my favorite sugar cookie recipe — a tender butter cookie with just enough sugar and lots of vanilla.

Tip

Use only pure extracts. These are made from the essence of the fruit, herb or other ingredient and have the best, cleanest, purest flavor and will taste wonderful in your cookies and other baked goods. Imitation flavorings can't compare to an extract.

● **Cookie sheets, lined with parchment paper**

2½ cups	all-purpose flour	625 mL
1 tsp	baking soda	5 mL
½ tsp	cream of tartar	2 mL
1 cup	unsalted butter, softened	250 mL
1¼ cups	granulated sugar	300 mL
1	egg	1
2 tsp	vanilla extract	10 mL
	Additional granulated sugar	

1. In a bowl, whisk together flour, baking soda and cream of tartar until well combined. Set aside.

2. In a large bowl, using an electric mixer on medium speed, cream butter and granulated sugar until light and fluffy, about 3 minutes. Add egg and beat well. Beat in vanilla. Scrape down sides of bowl. On low speed or using a wooden spoon, gradually add flour mixture, beating just until blended. Cover dough with plastic wrap and chill for at least 1 hour.

3. Preheat oven to 350°F (180°C). Lightly grease hands with nonstick cooking spray. Roll pieces of dough into 1-inch (2.5 cm) balls. Roll balls in granulated sugar. Place about 2 inches (5 cm) apart on prepared cookie sheets. Bake one sheet at a time in preheated oven for 10 to 12 minutes or until edges start to turn lightly golden.

4. Immediately slide parchment paper onto a wire cooling rack. Cool cookies for 5 minutes, then transfer from parchment paper to cooling rack and cool completely.

Brown Sugar Cookies

A sweet, chewy, slightly gooey cookie with lots of brown sugar. I love these!

Tips

For crisp cookies, bake for 10 to 14 minutes.

Brown sugar adds moisture and rich flavor to cookies.

• **Cookie sheets, lined with parchment paper**

2¾ cups	all-purpose flour	675 mL
1 tsp	baking soda	5 mL
⅔ cup	unsalted butter, softened	150 mL
⅓ cup	vegetable shortening	75 mL
2 cups	packed dark brown sugar	500 mL
2	eggs	2
1½ tsp	vanilla extract	7 mL

1. In a bowl, whisk together flour and baking soda until well combined. Set aside.

2. In a large bowl, using an electric mixer on medium speed, cream butter, shortening and brown sugar until light and fluffy, about 3 minutes. Add eggs one at a time, beating well after each addition. Beat in vanilla. Scrape down sides of bowl. On low speed or using a wooden spoon, gradually add flour mixture, beating just until blended. Cover dough with plastic wrap and chill for at least 1 hour.

3. Preheat oven to 350°F (180°C). Lightly grease hands with nonstick cooking spray. Roll pieces of dough into 1-inch (2.5 cm) balls. Place about 2 inches (5 cm) apart on prepared cookie sheets. Bake one sheet at a time in preheated oven for 8 to 10 minutes or until edges start to turn lightly golden.

4. Immediately slide parchment paper onto a wire cooling rack. Cool cookies for 5 minutes, then transfer from parchment paper to cooling rack and cool completely.

Chocolate-Dipped Cappuccino Sticks

Makes about 4½ dozen cookies ● ● ●

Espresso, cream and chocolate — a great combination of flavors.

Tip

Cookie recipes are formulated to balance all of the ingredients and take advantage of their specific characteristics and reactions. Reducing the amount of fat in a recipe will make the cookies tougher and less flavorful, and they'll dry out sooner. The different types of fats are not interchangeable in recipes. Substituting one fat for another will yield significantly different results.

Variation

After dipping in chocolate, roll cookies in 1½ cups (375 mL) finely chopped walnuts, pecans or almonds.

● **Cookie sheets, lined with parchment paper**

Cookies

2½ cups	all-purpose flour	625 mL
½ tsp	baking powder	2 mL
½ tsp	salt	2 mL
½ cup	unsalted butter, softened	125 mL
¾ cup	packed light brown sugar	175 mL
½ cup	granulated sugar	125 mL
1 tbsp	instant espresso powder	15 mL
½ tsp	vanilla extract	2 mL
¼ cup	half-and-half (10%) cream	50 mL

Glaze

1½ cups	chopped semisweet chocolate or semisweet chocolate chips	375 mL
2 tsp	vegetable shortening	10 mL

1. **Cookies:** In a bowl, whisk together flour, baking powder and salt until well combined. Set aside.

2. In a large bowl, using an electric mixer on medium speed, cream butter, brown sugar and granulated sugar until light and fluffy, about 3 minutes. Beat in espresso powder and vanilla. Scrape down sides of bowl. On low speed or using a wooden spoon, gradually add flour mixture, alternating with half-and-half, beating in each addition completely. Cover dough with plastic wrap and chill for at least 1 hour.

3. Preheat oven to 350°F (180°C). Lightly grease hands with nonstick cooking spray. Roll tablespoonfuls (15 mL) of dough into 2½-inch (6 cm) long logs. Place about 2 inches (5 cm) apart on prepared cookie sheets. Bake one sheet at a time in preheated oven for 10 to 12 minutes or until lightly golden.

4. Immediately slide parchment paper onto a wire cooling rack. Cool cookies for 5 minutes, then transfer from parchment paper to cooling rack and cool completely.

5. **Glaze:** In a small microwave-safe bowl, combine chocolate and vegetable shortening. Microwave on Medium-High (75%) power for 1 minute. Stir until completely combined and smooth, microwaving an additional 10 seconds at a time as needed to fully melt chocolate. Dip one end of each cooled cookie in chocolate. Place on parchment or wax paper to set. Allow chocolate to set before serving or storing.

Viennese Vanilla Crescents

These traditional holiday cookies are flavored with vanilla and almonds and coated in vanilla sugar.

Tip

The leftover vanilla pods contain lots of flavor. Add them to a small canister of granulated or confectioner's sugar and let sit for a week or two to create vanilla sugar that can be used in baking and beverages.

• **Cookie sheets, lined with parchment paper**

Vanilla Sugar

2 cups	confectioner's (powdered/icing) sugar	500 mL
1	whole vanilla bean	1

Cookies

2 cups	all-purpose flour	500 mL
1 cup	unsalted blanched almonds, finely ground	250 mL
¾ cup	confectioner's (powdered/icing) sugar	175 mL
¼ tsp	salt	1 mL
1 cup	unsalted butter, cut into small pieces	250 mL
1 tsp	vanilla extract	5 mL

1. *Vanilla Sugar:* Place confectioner's sugar in a bowl. Using a sharp, pointed knife, split vanilla bean in half lengthwise. Scrape seeds into sugar. Whisk until sugar and seeds are well combined. Cover with plastic wrap and set aside. Save vanilla pods for other use (see Tip, at left).

2. *Cookies:* In a large bowl, whisk together flour, ground almonds, confectioner's sugar and salt until well combined. Add butter and vanilla. Using your fingers, work butter into flour mixture until evenly blended and dough comes together in a ball. Cover dough with plastic wrap and chill for at least 1 hour.

3. Preheat oven to 350°F (180°C). Lightly grease hands with nonstick cooking spray. Roll tablespoonfuls (15 mL) of dough into 2½-inch (6 cm) long logs. Shape each log into a small crescent. Place about 2 inches (5 cm) apart on prepared cookie sheets. Bake one sheet at a time in preheated oven for 12 to 14 minutes or until edges turn lightly golden.

4. Immediately slide parchment paper onto a wire cooling rack. Cool for 1 minute; then dredge hot cookies, a few at a time, in vanilla sugar until well coated. Place on cooling rack and cool completely. Dredge again in vanilla sugar.

Spice Cookies

● ● ●

Warm spice notes make these cookies a perfect accompaniment to a hot cup of tea.

Tip

The flavor of spices deteriorates over time, and exposure to heat and moisture causes them to fade rapidly. For the best flavor, buy spices in small quantities, store in tightly sealed containers in a cool, dry place and use within 1 year of purchase.

● **Cookie sheets, lined with parchment paper**

2½ cups	all-purpose flour	625 mL
1½ tsp	baking powder	7 mL
1 tsp	ground cinnamon	5 mL
½ tsp	ground nutmeg	2 mL
½ tsp	baking soda	2 mL
¼ tsp	ground ginger	1 mL
¼ tsp	salt	1 mL
½ cup	unsalted butter, softened	125 mL
½ cup	vegetable shortening	125 mL
¾ cup	granulated sugar	175 mL
¾ cup	packed dark brown sugar	175 mL
2	eggs	2
1 tsp	vanilla extract	5 mL
	Additional granulated sugar	

1. In a bowl, whisk together flour, baking powder, cinnamon, nutmeg, baking soda, ginger and salt until well combined. Set aside.

2. In a large bowl, using an electric mixer on medium speed, cream butter, shortening, granulated sugar and brown sugar until light and fluffy, about 3 minutes. Add eggs one at a time, beating well after each addition. Beat in vanilla. Scrape down sides of bowl. On low speed or using a wooden spoon, gradually add flour mixture, beating just until blended. Cover dough with plastic wrap and chill for at least 1 hour.

3. Preheat oven to 350°F (180°C). Lightly grease hands with nonstick cooking spray. Roll pieces of dough into 1-inch (2.5 cm) balls. Roll balls in granulated sugar. Place about 2 inches (5 cm) apart on prepared cookie sheets. Bake one sheet at a time in preheated oven for 10 to 12 minutes or until edges start to turn lightly golden.

4. Immediately slide parchment paper onto a wire cooling rack. Cool cookies for 5 minutes, then transfer from parchment paper to cooling rack and cool completely.

Coconut Lime Cookies

Makes about 3 dozen cookies ● ● ●

The refreshing blend of coconut and lime gives these cookies a tantalizing flavor.

Tip

Chopping the coconut will give the cookies a more uniform texture.

Variation

Coconut Lemon Cookies: Substitute grated lemon zest for the grated lime zest.

● **Cookie sheets, lined with parchment paper**

1¾ cups	all-purpose flour	425 mL
1 tsp	baking powder	5 mL
¼ tsp	baking soda	1 mL
¼ tsp	cream of tartar	1 mL
¼ tsp	salt	1 mL
¾ cup	sweetened flaked coconut, chopped	175 mL
⅔ cup	unsalted butter, softened	150 mL
¾ cup	granulated sugar	175 mL
1	egg	1
1 tbsp	grated lime zest	15 mL
1½ cups	sweetened flaked coconut, finely chopped	375 mL

1. In a bowl, whisk together flour, baking powder, baking soda, cream of tartar and salt until well combined. Stir in the ¾ cup (175 mL) of chopped coconut. Set aside.

2. In a large bowl, using an electric mixer on medium speed, cream butter and granulated sugar until light and fluffy, about 3 minutes. Add egg and beat well. Beat in lime zest. Scrape down sides of bowl. On low speed or using a wooden spoon, gradually add flour mixture, beating just until blended. Cover dough with plastic wrap and chill for at least 1 hour.

3. Preheat oven to 350°F (180°C). Spread the 1½ cups (375 mL) finely chopped coconut in a thin layer on a large plate or in a pie pan. Lightly grease hands with nonstick cooking spray. Roll pieces of dough into 1-inch (2.5 cm) balls. Roll balls in coconut. Place about 2 inches (5 cm) apart on prepared cookie sheets. Bake one sheet at a time in preheated oven for 10 to 12 minutes or until edges start to turn lightly golden.

4. Immediately slide parchment paper onto a wire cooling rack. Cool cookies for 5 minutes, then transfer from parchment paper to cooling rack and cool completely.

Gary's Chocolate Cookies

● ● ●

I created this special recipe for my good friend and civic leader Gary Thomasian. We both really love chocolate, and these terrific cookies satisfy even the strongest of chocolate cravings.

Tip

Sugar adds flavor and texture to cookies and helps keep them fresh longer. Brown sugar adds moisture and even more flavor to cookies.

● **Cookie sheets, lined with parchment paper**

2 cups	all-purpose flour	500 mL
2/3 cup	unsweetened Dutch-process cocoa powder, sifted	150 mL
1/2 tsp	baking powder	2 mL
1/2 tsp	baking soda	2 mL
1/4 tsp	salt	1 mL
1 cup	vegetable shortening	250 mL
1 cup	granulated sugar	250 mL
1 cup	packed dark brown sugar	250 mL
3	eggs	3
2 tsp	vanilla extract	10 mL
	Additional granulated sugar	

1. In a bowl, whisk together flour, cocoa powder, baking powder, baking soda and salt until well combined. Set aside.

2. In a large bowl, using an electric mixer on medium speed, cream shortening, granulated sugar and brown sugar until light and fluffy, about 2 minutes. Add eggs one at a time, beating well after each addition. Beat in vanilla. Scrape down sides of bowl. On low speed or using a wooden spoon, gradually add flour mixture, beating just until blended. Cover dough with plastic wrap and chill for at least 2 hours.

3. Preheat oven to 350°F (180°C). Lightly grease hands with nonstick cooking spray. Roll pieces of dough into 1-inch (2.5 cm) balls. Roll balls in granulated sugar. Place about 2 inches (5 cm) apart on prepared cookie sheets. Bake one sheet at a time in preheated oven for 8 to 10 minutes or until set and tops are cracked.

4. Immediately slide parchment paper onto a wire cooling rack. Cool cookies for 5 minutes, then transfer from parchment paper to cooling rack and cool completely.

Lemon Sugar Cookies

Makes about 4½ dozen cookies

Lemon is one of my favorite flavors. These sugar cookies have a fresh lemon aroma and pleasing lemon flavor.

Tip

After removing the zest from the lemon, gently press down on the lemon with the palm of your hand and roll it back and forth on a cutting board. This will break the inner cells of the fruit and release more juice.

Variation

Orange Sugar Cookies: Substitute orange zest for lemon zest and orange juice for lemon juice.

• **Cookie sheets, lined with parchment paper**

3 cups	all-purpose flour	750 mL
1 tsp	baking soda	5 mL
½ tsp	cream of tartar	2 mL
1 cup	unsalted butter, softened	250 mL
1¼ cups	granulated sugar	300 mL
1	egg	1
2 tbsp	grated lemon zest	25 mL
2 tbsp	freshly squeezed lemon juice	25 mL
½ tsp	vanilla extract	2 mL
	Additional granulated sugar	

1. In a bowl, whisk together flour, baking soda and cream of tartar until well combined. Set aside.

2. In a large bowl, using an electric mixer on medium speed, cream butter and granulated sugar until light and fluffy, about 3 minutes. Add egg and beat well. Beat in lemon zest, lemon juice and vanilla. Scrape down sides of bowl. On low speed or using a wooden spoon, gradually add flour mixture, beating just until blended. Cover dough with plastic wrap and chill for at least 1 hour.

3. Preheat oven to 350°F (180°C). Lightly grease hands with nonstick cooking spray. Roll pieces of dough into 1-inch (2.5 cm) balls. Roll balls in granulated sugar. Place about 2 inches (5 cm) apart on prepared cookie sheets. Bake one sheet at a time in preheated oven for 10 to 12 minutes or until edges start to turn lightly golden.

4. Immediately slide parchment paper onto a wire cooling rack. Cool cookies for 5 minutes, then transfer from parchment paper to cooling rack and cool completely.

Thumbprint Cookies

These filled cookies are also known as "thimble cookies" because a thimble was often used to make the indentation in the center.

Tips

Any flavor of jam works well in these cookies. Try blueberry, strawberry, seedless blackberry, peach or pineapple.

Store cookies between layers of wax paper in a tightly sealed container.

If cookies will be frozen, do not fill them. The filling should be added after the frozen cookies are completely defrosted.

Variation

Roll dough balls in 1 cup (250 mL) finely chopped pecans before baking.

● **Cookie sheets, lined with parchment paper**

2 cups	all-purpose flour	500 mL
2 tsp	baking powder	10 mL
½ tsp	salt	2 mL
1 cup	vegetable shortening	250 mL
¾ cup	granulated sugar	175 mL
3	egg yolks	3
2 tsp	vanilla extract	10 mL
¼ cup	seedless raspberry jam	50 mL
¼ cup	apricot jam	50 mL

1. In a bowl, whisk together flour, baking powder and salt until well combined. Set aside.

2. In a large bowl, using an electric mixer on medium speed, cream shortening and granulated sugar until light and fluffy, about 3 minutes. Add egg yolks one at a time, beating well after each addition. Beat in vanilla. Scrape down sides of bowl. On low speed or using a wooden spoon, gradually add flour mixture, beating just until blended. Cover dough with plastic wrap and chill for at least 1 hour.

3. Preheat oven to 350°F (180°C). Lightly grease hands with nonstick cooking spray. Roll pieces of dough into 1¼-inch (3 cm) balls. Place about 2 inches (5 cm) apart on prepared cookie sheets. Using the handle of a wooden spoon, a thimble or your finger, make a deep indentation in center of each ball, being careful not to press all the way through the dough. Bake one sheet at a time in preheated oven for 8 to 10 minutes or until edges start to turn lightly golden.

4. If needed, quickly remake indentations using the end of a wooden spoon. Immediately slide parchment paper onto a wire cooling rack. Cool cookies for 5 minutes, then transfer from parchment paper to cooling rack and cool completely. Fill the center of each cooled cookie with a small spoonful of jam.

Chocolate Thumbprint Cookies

This chocolaty version of the classic thumbprint cookie is very good made with strawberry jam, but seedless raspberry jam is also an excellent choice for the filling.

Tips

Keep brown sugar soft by storing it in an airtight container or putting a piece of bread in with it.

Store cookies between layers of wax paper in a tightly sealed container.

If cookies will be frozen, do not fill them. The filling should be added after the frozen cookies are completely defrosted.

● **Cookie sheets, lined with parchment paper**

1 cup	chopped semisweet chocolate or semisweet chocolate chips	250 mL
2 cups	all-purpose flour	500 mL
1 tsp	baking powder	5 mL
¼ tsp	baking soda	1 mL
¼ tsp	salt	1 mL
½ cup	unsalted butter, softened	125 mL
1 cup	packed dark brown sugar	250 mL
1	egg	1
1 tsp	vanilla extract	5 mL
1 cup	finely chopped pecans	250 mL
½ cup	strawberry jam	125 mL

1. In a microwave-safe bowl, heat chopped chocolate in microwave at Medium-High (75%) power for 1 minute. Stir chocolate until smooth. If necessary, heat at Medium (50%) power for 10 seconds at a time, stirring between each heating, just until chocolate is melted. Set aside to cool.

2. In a bowl, whisk together flour, baking powder, baking soda and salt until well combined. Set aside.

3. In a large bowl, using an electric mixer on medium speed, cream butter and brown sugar until light and fluffy, about 3 minutes. Add egg and beat well. Beat in melted chocolate and vanilla. Scrape down sides of bowl. On low speed or using a wooden spoon, gradually add flour mixture, beating just until blended. Cover dough with plastic wrap and chill for at least 1 hour.

4. Preheat oven to 350°F (180°C). Lightly grease hands with nonstick cooking spray. Roll pieces of dough into 1¼-inch (3 cm) balls. Roll balls in chopped pecans. Place about 2 inches (5 cm) apart on prepared cookie sheets. Using the handle of a wooden spoon, a thimble or your finger, make a deep indentation in center of each ball, being careful not to press all the way through the dough. Bake one sheet at a time in preheated oven for 8 to 10 minutes or until set.

5. If needed, quickly remake indentations using the end of a wooden spoon. Immediately slide parchment paper onto a wire cooling rack. Cool cookies for 5 minutes, then transfer from parchment paper to cooling rack and cool completely. Fill the center of each cooled cookie with a small spoonful of jam.

Peanut Butter Jam Thumbprints

A winning flavor combination for an outstanding cookie. This one is a hit with kids of all ages.

Tips

Use different types of jam for variety and a colorful presentation on cookie trays.

These are also wonderful made with grape jelly.

Store cookies between layers of wax paper in a tightly sealed container.

If cookies will be frozen, do not fill them. The filling should be added after the frozen cookies are completely defrosted.

● **Cookie sheets, lined with parchment paper**

2 cups	all-purpose flour	500 mL
1 tsp	baking powder	5 mL
¼ tsp	baking soda	1 mL
¼ tsp	salt	1 mL
½ cup	unsalted butter, softened	125 mL
½ cup	creamy peanut butter	125 mL
½ cup	packed light brown sugar	125 mL
¼ cup	granulated sugar	50 mL
1	egg	1
1 tsp	vanilla extract	5 mL
	Additional granulated sugar	
½ cup	seedless raspberry jam, apricot jam or favorite flavor of jam	125 mL

1. In a bowl, whisk together flour, baking powder, baking soda and salt until well combined. Set aside.

2. In a large bowl, using an electric mixer on medium speed, cream butter, peanut butter, brown sugar and granulated sugar until light and fluffy, about 3 minutes. Add egg and beat well. Beat in vanilla. Scrape down sides of bowl. On low speed or using a wooden spoon, gradually add flour mixture, beating just until blended. Cover dough with plastic wrap and chill for at least 1 hour.

3. Preheat oven to 350°F (180°C). Lightly grease hands with nonstick cooking spray. Roll pieces of dough into 1½-inch (4 cm) balls. Roll balls in granulated sugar. Place about 2 inches (5 cm) apart on prepared cookie sheets. Using the handle of a wooden spoon, a thimble or your finger, make a deep indentation in center of each ball, being careful not to press all the way through the dough. Bake one sheet at a time in preheated oven for 8 to 10 minutes or until edges start to turn lightly golden.

4. If needed, quickly remake indentations using the end of a wooden spoon. Immediately slide parchment paper onto a wire cooling rack. Cool cookies for 5 minutes, then transfer from parchment paper to cooling rack and cool completely. Fill the center of each cooled cookie with a small spoonful of jam.

White Chocolate Raspberry Thumbprints

●●●

White chocolate and raspberry make a wonderful pairing. The white chocolate drizzled over the top gives these cookies a pretty appearance and an extra layer of chocolate.

Tips

Chocolate can be melted in the top of a double boiler placed over simmering water. Stir frequently, until chocolate is completely melted and mixture is smooth. Set aside to cool.

Store cookies between layers of wax paper. Do not freeze glazed cookies.

- **Cookie sheets, lined with parchment paper**

Cookies

1 cup	chopped white chocolate or white chocolate chips	250 mL
2 cups	all-purpose flour	500 mL
1 tsp	baking powder	5 mL
¼ tsp	baking soda	1 mL
¼ tsp	salt	1 mL
½ cup	unsalted butter, softened	125 mL
¾ cup	granulated sugar	175 mL
2	egg yolks	2
½ tsp	vanilla extract	2 mL
½ tsp	almond extract	2 mL
½ cup	seedless raspberry jam	125 mL

Glaze

1 cup	chopped white chocolate or white chocolate chips	250 mL
1 tsp	vegetable shortening	5 mL

1. **Cookies:** In the top of a double boiler, over simmering water, heat white chocolate, stirring frequently, until chocolate softens and begins to melt. Remove pan from heat and stir until chocolate is fully melted and smooth. Set aside to cool.

2. In a bowl, whisk together flour, baking powder, baking soda and salt until well combined. Set aside.

3. In a large bowl, using an electric mixer on medium speed, cream butter and granulated sugar until light and fluffy, about 3 minutes. Add egg yolks one at a time, beating well after each addition. Beat in melted chocolate, vanilla and almond extract. Scrape down sides of bowl. On low speed or using a wooden spoon, gradually add flour mixture, beating just until blended. Cover dough with plastic wrap and chill for at least 1 hour.

Tip

If cookies will be frozen, do not fill them. The filling and glaze should be added after the frozen cookies are completely defrosted.

4. Preheat oven to 350°F (180°C). Lightly grease hands with nonstick cooking spray. Roll pieces of dough into $1\frac{1}{4}$-inch (3 cm) balls. Place about 2 inches (5 cm) apart on prepared cookie sheets. Using the handle of a wooden spoon, a thimble or your finger, make a deep indentation in center of each ball, being careful not to press all the way through the dough. Bake one sheet at a time in preheated oven for 8 to 10 minutes or until edges start to turn lightly golden.

5. If needed, quickly remake indentations using the end of a wooden spoon. Immediately slide parchment paper onto a wire cooling rack. Cool cookies for 5 minutes, then transfer from parchment paper to cooling rack and cool completely. Fill the center of each cooled cookie with a small spoonful of jam.

6. *Glaze:* In the top of a double boiler, combine white chocolate and vegetable shortening. Place pan over simmering water and heat, stirring frequently, until chocolate softens and begins to melt. Remove pan from heat and stir until completely combined and smooth. Spoon melted chocolate into a zippered storage bag. Cut off a small corner of bag and drizzle chocolate over tops of cooled cookies. Place on parchment or wax paper to set. Allow chocolate to set before serving or storing.

Mexican Wedding Cake Cookies

● ● ●

Also called Snowballs, these cookies have many variations and a number of countries claim their origin. This version, made with pecans, is believed to have originated in Mexico.

Tip

Store unopened packages of flour in a cool, dry place for up to 2 years. Always use flour before the expiry date stamped on the package.

Variation

Chocolate Chip Wedding Cookies: By hand, fold 1 cup (250 mL) mini semisweet chocolate chips into cookie dough.

● **Cookie sheets, lined with parchment paper**

1 cup	all-purpose flour	250 mL
1 cup	finely chopped pecans	250 mL
1/2 cup	unsalted butter, softened	125 mL
1/4 cup	confectioner's (powdered/icing) sugar	50 mL
1/2 tsp	vanilla extract	2 mL
	Additional confectioner's (powdered/icing) sugar	

1. In a bowl, whisk together flour and pecans until well combined. Set aside.

2. In a large bowl, using an electric mixer on medium speed, cream butter and confectioner's sugar until light and fluffy, about 2 minutes. Beat in vanilla. Scrape down sides of bowl. On low speed or using a wooden spoon, gradually add flour mixture, beating just until blended. Cover dough with plastic wrap and chill for at least 1 hour.

3. Preheat oven to 325°F (160°C). Lightly grease hands with nonstick cooking spray. Roll pieces of dough into 1-inch (2.5 cm) balls. Place about 2 inches (5 cm) apart on prepared cookie sheets. Bake one sheet at a time in preheated oven for 14 to 18 minutes or until edges turn lightly golden.

4. Immediately slide parchment paper onto a wire cooling rack. Cool for 2 minutes, then dredge hot cookies, a few at a time, in confectioner's sugar until well coated. Place on cooling rack and cool completely. Dredge again in confectioner's sugar.

Orange Wedding Cake Cookies

Makes about 3 dozen cookies ● ● ●

This citrus version of wedding cake cookies is flavored with fragrant orange zest.

Tips

A Microplane grater will finely zest the orange peel for a wonderful texture in cookies. Be sure to include only the colored part of the outer peel.

Using extract in these cookies gives them great flavor without adding too much liquid.

Variation

Lemon Wedding Cake Cookies: Substitute lemon zest for orange zest and lemon extract for orange extract.

● **Cookie sheets, lined with parchment paper**

1⅓ cups	all-purpose flour	325 mL
⅔ cup	finely chopped unsalted blanched almonds	150 mL
½ cup	unsalted butter, softened	125 mL
⅓ cup	confectioner's (powdered/icing) sugar	75 mL
1 tbsp	grated orange zest	15 mL
¼ tsp	orange extract	1 mL

1. In a bowl, whisk together flour and almonds until well combined. Set aside.

2. In a large bowl, using an electric mixer on medium speed, cream butter and confectioner's sugar until light and fluffy, about 2 minutes. Beat in orange zest and orange extract. Scrape down sides of bowl. On low speed or using a wooden spoon, gradually add flour mixture, beating just until blended. Cover dough with plastic wrap and chill for at least 1 hour.

3. Preheat oven to 325°F (160°C). Lightly grease hands with nonstick cooking spray. Roll pieces of dough into 1-inch (2.5 cm) balls. Place about 2 inches (5 cm) apart on prepared cookie sheets. Bake one sheet at a time in preheated oven for 14 to 18 minutes or until edges turn lightly golden.

4. Immediately slide parchment paper onto a wire cooling rack. Cool for 2 minutes, then dredge hot cookies, a few at a time, in confectioner's sugar until well coated. Place on cooling rack and cool completely. Dredge again in confectioner's sugar.

Classic Peanut Butter Cookies

● ● ●

These yummy cookies are a favorite with big kids as well as the little ones.

Tips

Both creamy and crunchy peanut butters work well in this recipe.

Lightly coat the measuring cup with nonstick cooking spray to make it easier to remove the peanut butter.

● **Cookie sheets, lined with parchment paper**

2 cups	all-purpose flour	500 mL
1 tsp	baking powder	5 mL
½ tsp	baking soda	2 mL
¼ tsp	salt	1 mL
½ cup	unsalted butter, softened	125 mL
½ cup	peanut butter	125 mL
½ cup	granulated sugar	125 mL
½ cup	packed dark brown sugar	125 mL
1	egg	1

1. In a bowl, whisk together flour, baking powder, baking soda and salt until well combined. Set aside.

2. In a large bowl, using an electric mixer on medium speed, cream butter, peanut butter, granulated sugar and brown sugar until light and fluffy, about 3 minutes. Add egg and beat well. Scrape down sides of bowl. On low speed or using a wooden spoon, gradually add flour mixture, beating just until blended. Cover dough with plastic wrap and chill for at least 1 hour.

3. Preheat oven to 375°F (190°C). Lightly grease hands with nonstick cooking spray. Roll pieces of dough into 1-inch (2.5 cm) balls. Place about 2 inches (5 cm) apart on prepared cookie sheets. Using a fork, make crisscross marks on top of cookie, pressing dough to ½ inch (1 cm) thick. Bake one sheet at a time in preheated oven for 10 to 12 minutes or until edges turn lightly golden.

4. Immediately slide parchment paper onto a wire cooling rack. Cool cookies for 5 minutes, then transfer from parchment paper to cooling rack and cool completely.

Rum Cookies

The flavor of these cookies is even better the second day.

Tip

Baking powder and baking soda are not interchangeable. Always use the specified type and amount of leavener called for in the recipe.

● **Cookie sheets, lined with parchment paper**

2½ cups	all-purpose flour	625 mL
2 tsp	baking powder	10 mL
1 tsp	ground cinnamon	5 mL
½ tsp	ground nutmeg	2 mL
¼ tsp	baking soda	1 mL
¼ tsp	salt	1 mL
⅓ cup	unsalted butter, softened	75 mL
⅓ cup	vegetable shortening	75 mL
1 cup	packed dark brown sugar	250 mL
2	eggs	2
1½ tbsp	dark rum	22 mL
	Additional granulated sugar	

1. In a bowl, whisk together flour, baking powder, cinnamon, nutmeg, baking soda and salt until well combined. Set aside.

2. In a large bowl, using an electric mixer on medium speed, cream butter, shortening and brown sugar until light and fluffy, about 3 minutes. Add eggs one at a time, beating well after each addition. Beat in rum. Scrape down sides of bowl. On low speed or using a wooden spoon, gradually add flour mixture, beating just until blended. Cover dough with plastic wrap and chill for at least 1 hour.

3. Preheat oven to 350°F (180°C). Lightly grease hands with nonstick cooking spray. Roll pieces of dough into 1-inch (2.5 cm) balls. Roll balls in granulated sugar. Place about 2 inches (5 cm) apart on prepared cookie sheets. Bake one sheet at a time in preheated oven for 10 to 12 minutes or until edges start to turn lightly golden.

4. Immediately slide parchment paper onto a wire cooling rack. Cool cookies for 5 minutes, then transfer from parchment paper to cooling rack and cool completely.

Double Almond Cookies

These iced cookies have a big nutty taste.

Tips

Make cookies the same size and shape so they will bake evenly.

Let icing set before storing cookies between layers of wax paper in a tightly sealed container.

• Cookie sheets, lined with parchment paper

Cookies

2½ cups	all-purpose flour	625 mL
1 tsp	baking powder	5 mL
½ tsp	baking soda	2 mL
½ tsp	salt	2 mL
½ cup	unsalted butter, softened	125 mL
½ cup	vegetable shortening	125 mL
1⅓ cups	granulated sugar	325 mL
2	eggs	2
1½ tsp	almond extract	7 mL
1½ cups	chopped unsalted almonds	375 mL

Icing

1 cup	confectioner's (powdered/icing) sugar	250 mL
1 to 2 tbsp	half-and-half (10%) cream or milk	15 to 25 mL
½ tsp	almond extract	2 mL

1. **Cookies:** In a bowl, whisk together flour, baking powder, baking soda and salt until well combined. Set aside.

2. In a large bowl, using an electric mixer on medium speed, cream butter, shortening and granulated sugar until light and fluffy, about 3 minutes. Add eggs one at a time, beating well after each addition. Beat in almond extract. Scrape down sides of bowl. On low speed or using a wooden spoon, gradually add flour mixture, beating just until blended. By hand, fold in almonds. Cover dough with plastic wrap and chill for at least 1 hour.

3. Preheat oven to 350°F (180°C). Lightly grease hands with nonstick cooking spray. Roll pieces of dough into 1-inch (2.5 cm) balls. Place about 2 inches (5 cm) apart on prepared cookie sheets. Bake one sheet at a time in preheated oven for 10 to 12 minutes or until edges start to turn lightly golden.

4. Immediately slide parchment paper onto a wire cooling rack. Cool cookies for 5 minutes, then transfer from parchment paper to cooling rack and cool completely.

5. **Icing:** In a small bowl, combine confectioner's sugar, 1 tablespoon (15 mL) of the cream and almond extract. Using a small whisk or a fork, blend until icing is smooth and thin enough to drizzle from a fork. Add more cream as needed to achieve the right consistency. Drizzle icing over cooled cookies.

Glazed Lime Cookies

● ● ●

The hint of almond extract really enhances the lime flavor.

Tips

A ripe medium lime will yield about 1 teaspoon (5 mL) finely grated zest and 1½ to 2 tablespoons (22 to 25 mL) juice.

Let glaze set before storing cookies between layers of wax paper in a tightly sealed container.

● **Cookie sheets, lined with parchment paper**

Cookies

3 cups	all-purpose flour	750 mL
1½ tsp	baking powder	7 mL
½ tsp	baking soda	2 mL
¼ tsp	salt	1 mL
1 cup	unsalted butter, softened	250 mL
1⅓ cups	granulated sugar	325 mL
2	eggs	2
1 tbsp	grated lime zest	15 mL
1 tbsp	freshly squeezed lime juice	15 mL
¼ tsp	almond extract	1 mL

Glaze

1½ cups	confectioner's (powdered/icing) sugar	375 mL
1 tbsp	grated lime zest	15 mL
3 tbsp	freshly squeezed lime juice	45 mL

1. **Cookies:** In a bowl, whisk together flour, baking powder, baking soda and salt until well combined. Set aside.

2. In a large bowl, using an electric mixer on medium speed, cream butter and granulated sugar until light and fluffy, about 3 minutes. Add eggs one at a time, beating well after each addition. Beat in lime zest, lime juice and almond extract. Scrape down sides of bowl. On low speed or using a wooden spoon, gradually add flour mixture, beating just until blended. Cover dough with plastic wrap and chill for at least 1 hour.

3. Preheat oven to 350°F (180°C). Lightly grease hands with nonstick cooking spray. Roll pieces of dough into 1-inch (2.5 cm) balls. Place about 2 inches (5 cm) apart on prepared cookie sheets. Bake one sheet at a time in preheated oven for 10 to 12 minutes or until edges start to turn lightly golden.

4. Immediately slide parchment paper onto a wire cooling rack. Cool cookies for 5 minutes, then transfer from parchment paper to cooling rack and cool completely.

5. **Glaze:** In a small bowl, combine confectioner's sugar, lime zest and lime juice. Using a small whisk or a fork, blend until glaze is smooth. Spread glaze over cooled cookies.

Coconut Pecan Cookies

Chewy coconut and crunchy pecans are combined in this recipe to make a lovely cookie.

Tip

Use table salt for baking. It has a balanced flavor and very fine grains that blend well into the other ingredients.

Variations

Coconut Walnut Cookies: Substitute chopped walnuts for chopped pecans.

Coconut Almond Cookies: Substitute 1 tsp (5 mL) almond extract for 2 tsp (10 mL) vanilla extract and substitute chopped unsalted almonds for chopped pecans.

● **Cookie sheets, lined with parchment paper**

2½ cups	all-purpose flour	625 mL
1 tsp	baking powder	5 mL
½ tsp	baking soda	2 mL
½ tsp	salt	2 mL
¾ cup	unsalted butter, softened	175 mL
¾ cup	packed light brown sugar	175 mL
½ cup	granulated sugar	125 mL
2	eggs	2
2 tsp	vanilla extract	10 mL
1⅓ cups	sweetened flaked coconut	325 mL
1⅓ cups	chopped pecans	325 mL

1. In a bowl, whisk together flour, baking powder, baking soda and salt until well combined. Set aside.

2. In a large bowl, using an electric mixer on medium speed, cream butter, brown sugar and granulated sugar until light and fluffy, about 3 minutes. Add eggs one at a time, beating well after each addition. Beat in vanilla. Scrape down sides of bowl. On low speed or using a wooden spoon, gradually add flour mixture, beating just until blended. By hand, fold in coconut and pecans. Cover dough with plastic wrap and chill for at least 1 hour.

3. Preheat oven to 375°F (190°C). Lightly grease hands with nonstick cooking spray. Roll pieces of dough into 1-inch (2.5 cm) balls. Place about 2 inches (5 cm) apart on prepared cookie sheets. Bake one sheet at a time in preheated oven for 8 to 10 minutes or until edges start to turn lightly golden.

4. Immediately slide parchment paper onto a wire cooling rack. Cool cookies for 5 minutes, then transfer from parchment paper to cooling rack and cool completely.

Lemon Balls

● ● ●

Rolling these cookies in a lemon sugar topping gives them an extra burst of flavor.

Tip

Grate lemon zest for topping very fine or give it a quick chop with a chef's knife. Zest will then blend evenly with granulated sugar.

Variation

Orange Balls: Substitute orange zest for lemon zest and orange juice for lemon juice in cookies. Use orange zest instead of lemon zest in topping.

● Cookie sheets, lined with parchment paper

Cookies

¾ cup	unsalted butter, softened	175 mL
¾ cup	confectioner's (powdered/icing) sugar	175 mL
1 tbsp	grated lemon zest	15 mL
1 tbsp	freshly squeezed lemon juice	15 mL
2½ cups	all-purpose flour	625 mL

Topping

⅔ cup	granulated sugar	150 mL
1 tbsp	finely grated lemon zest	15 mL
3 tbsp	milk	45 mL

1. **Cookies:** In a large bowl, using an electric mixer on medium speed, cream butter and confectioner's sugar until light and fluffy, about 3 minutes. Beat in lemon zest and lemon juice. Scrape down sides of bowl. On low speed or using a wooden spoon, gradually add flour, beating just until blended. Cover dough with plastic wrap and chill for at least 1 hour.

2. Preheat oven to 325°F (160°C). Lightly grease hands with nonstick cooking spray. Roll pieces of dough into 1-inch (2.5 cm) balls. Place about 2 inches (5 cm) apart on prepared cookie sheets. Bake one sheet at a time in preheated oven for 14 to 16 minutes or until edges turn lightly golden.

3. Immediately slide parchment paper onto a wire cooling rack. Cool cookies for 1 minute.

4. **Topping:** In a small bowl, whisk together granulated sugar and lemon zest until well combined. Brush tops of warm cookies with milk and dip cookies in sugar mixture. Transfer cookies to cooling rack and cool completely.

Cream Cheese Walnut Cookies

Makes about 4 dozen cookies ● ● ●

Walnuts add a nutty crunch and flavor to these tender cookies.

Tip

To prevent tops or bottoms of cookies from becoming too brown, bake one sheet at a time with the oven rack positioned in the center of the oven.

● **Cookie sheets, lined with parchment paper**

2⅔ cups	all-purpose flour	650 mL
2 tsp	baking powder	10 mL
½ tsp	salt	2 mL
⅔ cup	unsalted butter, softened	150 mL
3 oz	cream cheese, softened	90 g
1⅓ cups	granulated sugar	325 mL
2	eggs	2
1 tsp	vanilla extract	5 mL
½ tsp	almond extract	2 mL
2 cups	chopped walnuts	500 mL
	Confectioner's (powdered/icing) sugar	

1. In a bowl, whisk together flour, baking powder and salt until well combined. Set aside.

2. In a large bowl, using an electric mixer on medium speed, cream butter, cream cheese and granulated sugar until light and fluffy, about 3 minutes. Add eggs one at a time, beating well after each addition. Beat in vanilla and almond extract. Scrape down sides of bowl. On low speed or using a wooden spoon, gradually add flour mixture, beating just until blended. By hand, fold in walnuts. Cover dough with plastic wrap and chill for at least 1 hour.

3. Preheat oven to 350°F (180°C). Lightly grease hands with nonstick cooking spray. Roll pieces of dough into 1-inch (2.5 cm) balls. Place about 2 inches (5 cm) apart on prepared cookie sheets. Bake one sheet at a time in preheated oven for 12 to 14 minutes or until edges turn lightly golden.

4. Immediately slide parchment paper onto a wire cooling rack. Cool cookies for 2 minutes, then dust tops with confectioner's sugar. Transfer cookies from parchment paper to cooling rack and cool completely.

Ginger Cookies

Makes about 2½ dozen cookies ● ● ●

These cookies are soft and chewy and have an intense ginger flavor.

Tips

For crisper cookies, bake 10 to 12 minutes.

For easier handling and measuring, molasses should be at room temperature.

Flavors can blend during storage, so store cookies with strong flavors in separate containers.

● **Cookie sheets, lined with parchment paper**

2 cups	all-purpose flour	500 mL
2 tsp	ground ginger	10 mL
1 tsp	baking soda	5 mL
½ tsp	ground cinnamon	2 mL
½ cup	vegetable shortening	125 mL
¼ cup	unsalted butter, softened	50 mL
1 cup	granulated sugar	250 mL
1	egg	1
¼ cup	fancy molasses	50 mL
	Additional granulated sugar	

1. In a bowl, whisk together flour, ginger, baking soda and cinnamon until well combined. Set aside.

2. In a large bowl, using an electric mixer on medium speed, cream shortening, butter and granulated sugar until light and fluffy, about 3 minutes. Add egg and beat well. Beat in molasses. Scrape down sides of bowl. On low speed or using a wooden spoon, gradually add flour mixture, beating just until blended. Cover dough with plastic wrap and chill for at least 1 hour.

3. Preheat oven to 350°F (180°C). Lightly grease hands with nonstick cooking spray. Roll pieces of dough into 1-inch (2.5 cm) balls. Roll balls in granulated sugar. Place about 2 inches (5 cm) apart on prepared cookie sheets. Bake one sheet at a time in preheated oven for 8 to 10 minutes or until edges start to turn lightly golden.

4. Immediately slide parchment paper onto a wire cooling rack. Cool cookies for 5 minutes, then transfer from parchment paper to cooling rack and cool completely.

Peanut Butter Chews

These cookies have a nice peanut butter flavor, a chewy texture and a pretty look.

Tip

Always taste peanut butter to make sure it's fresh before using it for baking. The nut oil in peanut butter can turn stale or rancid after the jar has been open awhile.

● **Cookie sheets, lined with parchment paper**

1¾ cups	all-purpose flour	425 mL
1 tsp	baking soda	5 mL
¼ tsp	salt	1 mL
½ cup	vegetable shortening	125 mL
½ cup	chunky peanut butter	125 mL
½ cup	granulated sugar	125 mL
½ cup	packed light brown sugar	125 mL
2	eggs	2
1 tsp	vanilla extract	5 mL
	Additional granulated sugar	

1. In a bowl, whisk together flour, baking soda and salt until well combined. Set aside.

2. In a large bowl, using an electric mixer on medium speed, cream shortening, peanut butter, granulated sugar and brown sugar until light and fluffy, about 3 minutes. Add eggs one at a time, beating well after each addition. Beat in vanilla. Scrape down sides of bowl. On low speed or using a wooden spoon, gradually add flour mixture, beating just until blended. Cover dough with plastic wrap and chill for at least 1 hour.

3. Preheat oven to 350°F (180°C). Lightly grease hands with nonstick cooking spray. Roll pieces of dough into 1-inch (2.5 cm) balls. Roll balls in granulated sugar. Place about 2 inches (5 cm) apart on prepared cookie sheets. Bake one sheet at a time in preheated oven for 10 to 12 minutes or until edges start to turn lightly golden.

4. Immediately slide parchment paper onto a wire cooling rack. Cool cookies for 5 minutes, then transfer from parchment paper to cooling rack and cool completely.

Coffee Almond Rounds

● ● ●

I like the balance of coffee and almond flavors in these small bites.

Tip

For even baking, cookie sheets should fit inside your oven with at least 2 inches (5 cm) of space between the sheet and the sides of the oven.

● **Cookie sheets, lined with parchment paper**

2 cups	all-purpose flour	500 mL
1 tsp	baking powder	5 mL
1/4 tsp	baking soda	1 mL
1/4 tsp	salt	1 mL
1/2 cup	vegetable shortening	125 mL
1/2 cup	granulated sugar	125 mL
1/2 cup	packed light brown sugar	125 mL
1	egg	1
1/2 tsp	vanilla extract	2 mL
1/3 cup	strong brewed coffee	75 mL
3/4 cup	chopped unsalted almonds	175 mL
	Additional granulated sugar	

1. In a bowl, whisk together flour, baking powder, baking soda and salt until well combined. Set aside.

2. In a large bowl, using an electric mixer on medium speed, cream shortening, granulated sugar and brown sugar until light and fluffy, about 3 minutes. Add egg and beat well. Beat in vanilla. Scrape down sides of bowl. On low speed or using a wooden spoon, gradually add flour mixture, alternating with coffee, beating well after each addition. By hand, fold in almonds. Cover dough with plastic wrap and chill for at least 1 hour.

3. Preheat oven to 350°F (180°C). Lightly grease hands with nonstick cooking spray. Roll pieces of dough into 1-inch (2.5 cm) balls. Roll balls in granulated sugar. Place about 2 inches (5 cm) apart on prepared cookie sheets. Bake one sheet at a time in preheated oven for 10 to 12 minutes or until edges start to turn lightly golden.

4. Immediately slide parchment paper onto a wire cooling rack. Cool cookies for 5 minutes, then transfer from parchment paper to cooling rack and cool completely.

English Toffee Cookies

These cookies are reminiscent of English toffee candies.

Tips

Chocolate can be melted in the top of a double boiler placed over simmering water. Stir frequently, until chocolate is completely melted and mixture is smooth. Set aside to cool.

To measure flour properly, stir the flour in the package or container to add some air, then gently spoon the flour into a dry measuring cup. Use a knife or spatula to level off the flour even with the rim of the cup.

● **Cookie sheets, lined with parchment paper**

Cookies

2¾ cups	all-purpose flour	675 mL
2 tsp	baking powder	10 mL
¼ tsp	baking soda	1 mL
¼ tsp	salt	1 mL
1 cup	unsalted butter, softened	250 mL
⅔ cup	granulated sugar	150 mL
⅔ cup	packed light brown sugar	150 mL
2	eggs	2
2 tsp	vanilla extract	10 mL
1 cup	toffee bits	250 mL
½ cup	chopped unsalted almonds	125 mL
	Additional granulated sugar	

Glaze

1 cup	chopped semisweet chocolate or semisweet chocolate chips	250 mL
1 tsp	vegetable shortening	5 mL
¼ cup	finely chopped unsalted almonds	50 mL

1. *Cookies:* In a bowl, whisk together flour, baking powder, baking soda and salt until well combined. Set aside.

2. In a large bowl, using an electric mixer on medium speed, cream butter, granulated sugar and brown sugar until light and fluffy, about 3 minutes. Add eggs one at a time, beating well after each addition. Beat in vanilla. Scrape down sides of bowl. On low speed or using a wooden spoon, gradually add flour mixture, beating just until blended. By hand, fold in toffee bits and almonds. Cover dough with plastic wrap and chill for at least 1 hour.

3. Preheat oven to 350°F (180°C). Lightly grease hands with nonstick cooking spray. Roll pieces of dough into 1-inch (2.5 cm) balls. Roll balls in granulated sugar. Place about 2 inches (5 cm) apart on prepared cookie sheets. Bake one sheet at a time in preheated oven for 10 to 12 minutes or until edges start to turn lightly golden.

Tip
Store cookies between layers of wax paper in a tightly sealed container.

4. Immediately slide parchment paper onto a wire cooling rack. Cool cookies for 5 minutes, then transfer from parchment paper to cooling rack and cool completely.

5. *Glaze:* In a 1-quart (1 L) microwave-safe zippered storage bag, combine semisweet chocolate and vegetable shortening. Microwave on Medium-High (75%) power for 1 minute. Knead bag until completely combined and smooth, microwaving an additional 10 seconds at a time as needed to fully melt chocolate. Cut off a small corner of bag and drizzle chocolate over tops of cooled cookies. Sprinkle with finely chopped almonds. Place on parchment or wax paper to set. Allow chocolate to set before serving or storing.

Creative Gift Idea

There are so many pretty cookie jars to choose from that it is easy to find one that is appropriate for the person who will receive your thoughtful gift. Cookie jars are fun and fanciful gifts sure to be appreciated by cookie bakers everywhere.

To make your gift extra-special, fill the jar with a batch of fresh, homemade cookies! This may sound like an obvious idea, but giving cookies in a cookie jar is not done very often. Most people either give cookies or a cookie jar but rarely combine the two. This combination will make a unique gift that will stand out from the rest.

Swedish Tea Cookies

These traditional holiday cookies are usually served at Christmas.

Tip

Eggs should be at room temperature when added to the creamed butter and sugar mixture. Cold eggs can cause the mixture to break and appear curdled.

● **Cookie sheets, lined with parchment paper**

2 cups	all-purpose flour	500 mL
2 tsp	baking powder	10 mL
¼ tsp	salt	1 mL
¾ cup	unsalted butter, softened	175 mL
¾ cup	packed light brown sugar	175 mL
2	egg yolks	2
1 tsp	vanilla extract	5 mL
2	egg whites, lightly beaten	2
1 cup	finely chopped unsalted almonds	250 mL
½ cup	currant or raspberry jelly	125 mL

1. In a bowl, whisk together flour, baking powder and salt until well combined. Set aside.

2. In a large bowl, using an electric mixer on medium speed, cream butter and brown sugar until light and fluffy, about 3 minutes. Add eggs yolks one at a time, beating well after each addition. Beat in vanilla. Scrape down sides of bowl. On low speed or using a wooden spoon, gradually add flour mixture, beating just until blended. Cover dough with plastic wrap and chill for at least 1 hour.

3. Preheat oven to 350°F (180°C). Lightly grease hands with nonstick cooking spray. Roll pieces of dough into 1¼-inch (3 cm) balls. Dip balls in egg white and roll in chopped almonds. Place about 2 inches (5 cm) apart on prepared cookie sheets. Using the handle of a wooden spoon, a thimble or your finger, make a deep indentation in center of each ball, being careful not to press all the way through the dough. Bake one sheet at a time in preheated oven for 8 to 10 minutes or until edges start to turn lightly golden.

4. If needed, quickly remake indentations using the end of a wooden spoon. Immediately slide parchment paper onto a wire cooling rack. Cool cookies for 5 minutes, then transfer from parchment paper to cooling rack and cool completely. Fill the center of each cooled cookie with a small spoonful of jelly.

White Chocolate Cookies

A tender white chocolate cookie filled with chunks of white chocolate and crunchy macadamia nuts.

Tip

Real white chocolate contains cocoa butter. Always check the ingredients for cocoa butter to be sure you are using white chocolate. Avoid any product labeled as "white" or "vanilla" baking chips.

● Cookie sheets, lined with parchment paper

6 oz	white chocolate, chopped	175 g
1¼ cups	cake flour	300 mL
1 cup	all-purpose flour	250 mL
2 tsp	baking powder	10 mL
½ tsp	salt	2 mL
½ cup	unsalted butter, softened	125 mL
½ cup	granulated sugar	125 mL
2	eggs	2
½ tsp	vanilla extract	2 mL
1 cup	chopped white chocolate or white chocolate chips	250 mL
⅔ cup	chopped roasted unsalted macadamia nuts	150 mL

1. In the top of a double boiler, over simmering water, heat the 6 oz (175 g) white chocolate, stirring frequently, until chocolate softens and begins to melt. Remove pan from heat and stir until chocolate is completely melted and smooth. Set aside to cool.

2. In a bowl, whisk together cake flour, all-purpose flour, baking powder and salt until well combined. Set aside.

3. In a large bowl, using an electric mixer on medium speed, cream butter and granulated sugar until light and fluffy, about 3 minutes. Add eggs one at a time, beating well after each addition. Beat in vanilla. Scrape down sides of bowl. On low speed or using a wooden spoon, gradually add flour mixture, beating just until blended. Add melted white chocolate and beat until thoroughly combined. By hand, fold in the 1 cup (250 mL) white chocolate and macadamia nuts. Cover dough with plastic wrap and chill for at least 1 hour.

4. Preheat oven to 350°F (180°C). Lightly grease hands with nonstick cooking spray. Roll pieces of dough into 1-inch (2.5 cm) balls. Place about 2 inches (5 cm) apart on prepared cookie sheets. Bake one sheet at a time in preheated oven for 10 to 12 minutes or until edges start to turn lightly golden.

5. Immediately slide parchment paper onto a wire cooling rack. Cool cookies for 5 minutes, then transfer from parchment paper to cooling rack and cool completely.

Butter Pecan Cookies

These tasty cookies are loaded with pecans.

Tips

Unsalted butter is the best choice for baking. It gives cookies a rich, fresh flavor and helps them develop a light golden brown color.

Let frosting set before storing cookies between layers of wax paper in a tightly sealed container.

• Cookie sheets, lined with parchment paper

Cookies

2½ cups	all-purpose flour	625 mL
1½ tsp	baking powder	7 mL
½ tsp	baking soda	2 mL
¼ tsp	salt	1 mL
¾ cup	unsalted butter, softened	175 mL
1¼ cups	packed light brown sugar	300 mL
2	eggs	2
1 tsp	vanilla extract	5 mL
1½ cups	chopped pecans	375 mL

Browned Butter Frosting

⅓ cup	unsalted butter	75 mL
3 tbsp	half-and-half (10%) cream or milk	45 mL
¼ tsp	vanilla extract	1 mL
2 cups	confectioner's (powdered/icing) sugar	500 mL
1 cup	pecan halves	250 mL

1. **Cookies:** In a bowl, whisk together flour, baking powder, baking soda and salt until well combined. Set aside.

2. In a large bowl, using an electric mixer on medium speed, cream butter and brown sugar until light and fluffy, about 3 minutes. Add eggs one at a time, beating well after each addition. Beat in vanilla. Scrape down sides of bowl. On low speed or using a wooden spoon, gradually add flour mixture, beating just until blended. By hand, fold in chopped pecans. Cover dough with plastic wrap and chill for at least 1 hour.

3. Preheat oven to 350°F (180°C). Lightly grease hands with nonstick cooking spray. Roll pieces of dough into 1-inch (2.5 cm) balls. Place about 2 inches (5 cm) apart on prepared cookie sheets . Bake one sheet at a time in preheated oven for 10 to 12 minutes or until edges start to turn lightly golden.

4. Immediately slide parchment paper onto a wire cooling rack. Cool cookies for 5 minutes, then transfer from parchment paper to cooling rack and cool completely.

5. **Frosting:** In a small saucepan, over medium heat, lightly brown butter. Remove pan from heat and stir in cream and vanilla. Add confectioner's sugar and beat until frosting is smooth and creamy. Spread frosting over cooled cookies. Place a pecan half in center of each frosted cookie and press gently to set pecan into frosting.

Chinese Almond Cookies

Makes 4 dozen cookies

These classic cookies have a wonderful almond flavor.

Tip

Nuts can turn rancid quickly. If you're not going to use them within a couple of weeks of purchase, tightly wrap the nuts and store them in the freezer to preserve their flavor.

● **Cookie sheets, lined with parchment paper**

2½ cups	all-purpose flour	625 mL
1 tsp	baking powder	5 mL
½ tsp	salt	2 mL
1 cup	vegetable shortening	250 mL
1 cup	granulated sugar	250 mL
1	egg	1
2 tsp	almond extract	10 mL
48	whole unsalted blanched almonds	48
1	egg white	1
2 tsp	water	10 mL

1. In a bowl, whisk together flour, baking powder and salt until well combined. Set aside.

2. In a large bowl, using an electric mixer on medium speed, cream shortening and granulated sugar until light and fluffy, about 3 minutes. Add egg and beat well. Beat in almond extract. Scrape down sides of bowl. On low speed or using a wooden spoon, gradually add flour mixture, beating just until blended. Cover dough with plastic wrap and chill for at least 30 minutes.

3. Preheat oven to 350°F (180°C). Lightly grease hands with nonstick cooking spray. Roll tablespoonfuls (15 mL) of dough into 48 balls. Place about 2 inches (5 cm) apart on prepared cookie sheets . Place a whole almond in center of each ball. Using a glass, press the flat bottom on balls to flatten to ½ inch (1 cm) thick.

4. In a small bowl, whisk together egg white and water until well blended. Lightly brush egg white mixture over top of each cookie. Bake one sheet at a time in preheated oven for 12 to 14 minutes or until edges turn lightly golden.

5. Immediately slide parchment paper onto a wire cooling rack. Cool cookies for 5 minutes, then transfer from parchment paper to cooling rack and cool completely.

estive Sugar Cookies

These cookies make a colorful treat for any holiday.

Tip

Prepare cookies for any holiday and use sugar colors appropriate for the celebration.

● **Cookie sheets, lined with parchment paper**

2¾ cups	all-purpose flour	675 mL
1 tsp	baking soda	5 mL
1 tsp	cream of tartar	5 mL
¼ tsp	salt	1 mL
1 cup	unsalted butter, softened	250 mL
½ cup	granulated sugar	125 mL
½ cup	packed light brown sugar	125 mL
2	eggs	2
1 tsp	vanilla extract	5 mL
	Colored granulated sugar	

1. In a bowl, whisk together flour, baking soda, cream of tartar and salt until well combined. Set aside.

2. In a large bowl, using an electric mixer on medium speed, cream butter, granulated sugar and brown sugar until light and fluffy, about 3 minutes. Add eggs one at a time, beating well after each addition. Beat in vanilla. Scrape down sides of bowl. On low speed or using a wooden spoon, gradually add flour mixture, beating just until blended. Cover dough with plastic wrap and chill for at least 1 hour.

3. Preheat oven to 350°F (180°C). Lightly grease hands with nonstick cooking spray. Roll pieces of dough into 1-inch (2.5 cm) balls. Roll balls in colored sugar. Place about 2 inches (5 cm) apart on prepared cookie sheets . Bake one sheet at a time in preheated oven for 10 to 12 minutes or until edges start to turn lightly golden.

4. Immediately slide parchment paper onto a wire cooling rack. Cool cookies for 5 minutes, then transfer from parchment paper to cooling rack and cool completely.

Eggnog Sugar Cookies

Make these cookies during the holiday season when cartons of eggnog are available in the grocery store dairy case.

Tip

Using 2 egg yolks instead of a whole egg gives these lovely cookies enhanced flavor and great texture.

● Cookie sheets, lined with parchment paper

Cookies

2¾ cups	all-purpose flour	675 mL
1½ tsp	baking powder	7 mL
½ tsp	baking soda	2 mL
½ tsp	ground nutmeg	2 mL
¼ tsp	salt	1 mL
⅔ cup	unsalted butter, softened	150 mL
1 cup	granulated sugar	250 mL
2	egg yolks	2
1 tsp	vanilla extract	5 mL
½ cup	dairy eggnog	125 mL

Nutmeg Sugar

¼ cup	granulated sugar	50 mL
1 tsp	ground nutmeg	5 mL

1. *Cookies:* In a bowl, whisk together flour, baking powder, baking soda, nutmeg and salt until well combined. Set aside.

2. In a large bowl, using an electric mixer on medium speed, cream butter and granulated sugar until light and fluffy, about 3 minutes. Add egg yolks one at a time, beating well after each addition. Beat in vanilla. Scrape down sides of bowl. On low speed or using a wooden spoon, gradually add flour mixture, alternating with eggnog, stirring well after each addition. Cover dough with plastic wrap and chill for at least 1 hour.

3. Preheat oven to 350°F (180°C).

4. *Nutmeg Sugar:* In a shallow dish, using a fork or wire whisk, combine granulated sugar and nutmeg until well blended.

5. Lightly grease hands with nonstick cooking spray. Roll pieces of dough into 1-inch (2.5 cm) balls. Roll balls in nutmeg sugar. Place about 2 inches (5 cm) apart on prepared cookie sheets . Bake one sheet at a time in preheated oven for 10 to 12 minutes or until edges start to turn lightly golden.

6. Immediately slide parchment paper onto a wire cooling rack. Cool cookies for 5 minutes, then transfer from parchment paper to cooling rack and cool completely.

Almond Logs

These attractive nutty cookie sticks are a traditional holiday treat and add variety to party cookie trays and packages of cookies for gift-giving.

Tips

For best flavor, use a quality pure almond extract. Imitation extracts can give cookies an unpleasant taste.

Dark-colored cookie sheets can cause cookies to burn. Use a heavy-gauge aluminum cookie sheet to prevent cookies from overbrowning.

- Preheat oven to 325°F (160°C)
- Cookie sheets, lined with parchment paper

3 cups	all-purpose flour	750 mL
1 cup	granulated sugar	250 mL
1 cup	finely chopped unsalted almonds	250 mL
1 cup	unsalted butter, cut into small pieces	250 mL
1 tsp	almond extract	5 mL
	Confectioner's (powdered/icing) sugar	

1. In a large bowl, whisk together flour, sugar and almonds until well combined. Add butter and almond extract. Using your fingers, work butter into flour mixture until evenly blended and dough comes together in a ball.

2. Lightly grease hands with nonstick cooking spray. Roll tablespoonfuls (15 mL) of dough into 2½-inch (6 cm) long logs. Place about 2 inches (5 cm) apart on prepared cookie sheets. Bake one sheet at a time in preheated oven for 15 to 18 minutes or until lightly golden.

3. Immediately slide parchment paper onto a wire cooling rack. Cool for 2 minutes, then dredge hot cookies, a few at a time, in confectioner's sugar until well coated. Place on cooling rack and cool completely. Dredge again in confectioner's sugar.

Spritz Cookies

A traditional Scandinavian cookie, spritz cookies are shaped by pushing the soft dough through a cookie press. Different templates can be used to create a variety of fun and pretty cookie shapes.

Tip

The dough should be soft enough to easily push through the press, yet firm enough to hold its shape and design on the cookie sheet.

- Preheat oven to 375°F (190°C)
- Cookie sheets, lined with parchment paper
- Cookie press

2 cups	all-purpose flour	500 mL
½ tsp	baking powder	2 mL
¼ tsp	salt	1 mL
1 cup	unsalted butter, softened	250 mL
¾ cup	granulated sugar	175 mL
1	egg	1
1 tsp	vanilla extract	5 mL
	Colored sugar	

1. In a bowl, whisk together flour, baking powder and salt until well combined. Set aside.

2. In a large bowl, using an electric mixer on medium speed, cream butter and granulated sugar until light and fluffy, about 3 minutes. Add egg and beat well. Beat in vanilla. Scrape down sides of bowl. On low speed or using a wooden spoon, gradually add flour mixture, beating just until blended.

3. Fit cookie press with desired template and spoon cookie dough into press. Pipe cookies onto prepared cookie sheets about 1 inch (2.5 cm) apart. Sprinkle with colored sugar. Bake one sheet at a time in preheated oven for 8 to 12 minutes or until edges start to turn lightly golden.

4. Immediately slide parchment paper onto a wire cooling rack. Cool cookies for 5 minutes, then transfer from parchment paper to cooling rack and cool completely.

Variations

Lemon Spritz: Reduce vanilla to ½ tsp (2 mL) and add 4 tsp (20 mL) finely grated lemon zest or ½ tsp (2 mL) lemon extract to dough. Substitute coarse sugar for colored sugar.

Orange Spritz: Reduce vanilla to ½ tsp (2 mL) and add 4 tsp (20 mL) finely grated orange zest or ½ tsp (2 mL) orange extract to dough. Substitute coarse sugar for colored sugar.

Chocolate Spritz Cookies

● ● ●

These delicious chocolate cookies are a charming adaptation of the classic Spritz cookie.

Tip

The dough should be soft enough to easily push through the press, yet firm enough to hold its shape and design on the cookie sheet.

- Preheat oven to 375°F (190°C)
- Cookie sheets, lined with parchment paper
- Cookie press

1¾ cups	all-purpose flour	425 mL
¼ cup	unsweetened Dutch-process cocoa powder, sifted	50 mL
½ tsp	baking powder	2 mL
¼ tsp	salt	1 mL
1 cup	unsalted butter, softened	250 mL
¾ cup	granulated sugar	175 mL
1	egg	1
1 tsp	vanilla extract	5 mL
	Coarse sugar	

1. In a bowl, whisk together flour, cocoa powder, baking powder and salt until well combined. Set aside.

2. In a large bowl, using an electric mixer on medium speed, cream butter and granulated sugar until light and fluffy, about 3 minutes. Add egg and beat well. Beat in vanilla. Scrape down sides of bowl. On low speed or using a wooden spoon, gradually add flour mixture, beating just until blended.

3. Fit cookie press with desired template and spoon cookie dough into press. Pipe cookies onto prepared cookie sheets about 1 inch (2.5 cm) apart. Sprinkle with coarse sugar. Bake, one sheet at a time in preheated oven for 8 to 12 minutes or until edges start to turn lightly golden.

4. Immediately slide parchment paper onto a wire cooling rack. Cool cookies for 5 minutes, then transfer from parchment paper to cooling rack and cool completely.

Chocolate Chip Heaven

●●●

Chocolate Chip Heaven Cookies . . . 119
Blue Ribbon Chocolate Chip
   Cookies. 120
Double Chocolate Chip Cookies. . . . 121
Buttermilk Chocolate Chip
   Cookies. 122
Chewy Chocolate Chip Cookies 123
Chocolate Chip Walnut Cookies 124
White Chocolate Chip Cookies 125
Chocolate Chunk Cookies 126
Sweet Dark Chocolate Chip
   Cookies. 127
Chocolate Chip Orange Cookies . . . 128
Triple Chocolate Chip Cookies 129
Glazed Chocolate Chip Cookies 130
Classic Chocolate Chip Cookies. . . . 131
Bittersweet Chocolate Chunk
   Cookies. 132

Chocolate Chip Almond
   Cookies. 133
Milk Chocolate Chip Cookies 134
Jumbo Chocolate Chip Cookies 135
Tender Chocolate Chip Cookies 136
Deluxe Chocolate Chip Cookies 137
Chocolate Chocolate Chip
   Cookies. 138
Cream Cheese Chocolate Chip
   Cookies. 139
Peanut Butter Chocolate Chippers . . 140
Crispy Chocolate Chip Cookies 141
Sour Cream Chocolate Chip
   Cookies. 142
Chocolate Chip Espresso
   Cookies. 143
Special Chocolate Chip
   Cookies. 144

About Chocolate Chip Cookies

For some people there is only one kind of cookie — chocolate chip! These heavenly cookies have legions of devoted fans. Of all the types of cookies baked every year, chocolate chip are by far the most popular. Over 90 million bags of chocolate chips are sold in North America each year. That's a lot of chocolate chip cookies!

I have so many excellent versions of these delightful cookies that they deserve their own chapter. This special chocolate chip cookie collection uses both drop cookie and hand-shaped cookie techniques to create these deliciously tempting treats. Lightly crispy on the outside and soft and chewy on the inside, these buttery cookies are studded with a variety of heavenly morsels of luscious chocolate.

I like to use chopped chocolate in my chocolate chip cookies because of the way the chocolate enhances the flavor and texture of the cookies. You may happily substitute chocolate chips for the chopped chocolate in any of these recipes. Just be sure to use real chocolate chips made from a high-quality chocolate.

Nuts or No Nuts

Some people absolutely love nuts in their chocolate chip cookies. Others consider it an offense against the chocolate to include nuts, and they won't touch a chocolate chip cookie that contains them. Some of these recipes contain nuts, and others do not. In most cases, the nuts are optional and can easily be left out. In some recipes, the nuts are needed for texture and the cookies will spread too much if they're omitted. You can solve this problem by replacing all or part of the nuts with more chocolate.

The First Chocolate Chip Cookie

The chocolate chip cookie is considered to be an American creation. In 1930 in Whitman, Massachusetts, Kenneth and Ruth Wakefield opened a lodge and restaurant in a historic colonial house. Built in 1709, the Toll House originally served as a rest stop where weary travelers could get a good meal and pay their tolls for travel on the road between Boston and New Bedford.

Ruth Wakefield quickly became known throughout New England for her wonderful desserts. One day, while baking a batch of colonial-era Butter Drop Do cookies, Ruth ran out of nuts. The resourceful innkeeper broke up a Nestlé semisweet chocolate bar and added the pieces to her cookie dough. Expecting the chocolate to melt into the cookies as they baked, she was surprised that the bits of gooey melted chocolate held their shape. The Toll House Cookie was born. Lodge guests were thrilled with Ruth's new creation, and word about her cookies quickly spread. Several New England newspapers happily published Ruth's recipe for cookies with broken bits of chocolate in them.

In 1939, Nestlé introduced Toll House Semi-Sweet Chocolate Morsels, tiny pieces of chocolate in convenient, ready-to-use packages. There are now many different brands of quality chocolate chips available in an assortment of kinds of chocolate.

Chocolate Chip Heaven Cookies

Makes about 4 dozen cookies ● ● ●

This is one of my favorite chocolate chip recipes. (It's so hard to pick just one!) I love the richness of the brown sugar and vanilla and the soft, chewy texture of the cookie.

Tip

Use a high-quality vanilla extract for the best flavor, never an imitation vanilla flavoring!

Variations

Substitute chopped pecans for chopped walnuts.

Ultimate Chocolate Chip Heaven Cookies: Omit walnuts and use 3 cups (750 mL) chopped semisweet chocolate or semisweet chocolate chips.

- Cookie sheets, lined with parchment paper

2¾ cups	all-purpose flour	675 mL
2 tsp	baking powder	10 mL
½ tsp	baking soda	2 mL
¼ tsp	salt	1 mL
¾ cup	unsalted butter, softened	175 mL
1½ cups	packed dark brown sugar	375 mL
3	eggs	3
1 tbsp	vanilla extract	15 mL
2 cups	chopped semisweet chocolate or semisweet chocolate chips	500 mL
1 cup	chopped walnuts	250 mL

1. In a bowl, whisk together flour, baking powder, baking soda and salt until well combined. Set aside.

2. In a large bowl, using an electric mixer on medium speed, cream butter and brown sugar until light and fluffy, about 3 minutes. Add eggs one at a time, beating well after each addition. Beat in vanilla. Scrape down sides of bowl. On low speed or using a wooden spoon, gradually add flour mixture, beating just until blended. By hand, fold in chocolate and walnuts. Cover dough with plastic wrap and chill for at least 1 hour.

3. Preheat oven to 350°F (180°C). Using a cookie scoop or spoons, drop tablespoonfuls (15 mL) of dough about 2 inches (5 cm) apart on prepared cookie sheets. Bake one sheet at a time in preheated oven for 10 to 12 minutes or until edges start to turn lightly golden.

4. Immediately slide parchment paper onto a wire cooling rack. Cool cookies for 5 minutes, then transfer from parchment paper to cooling rack and cool completely.

Blue Ribbon Chocolate Chip Cookies

An award-winning cookie with great flavor and texture, these are perfect any day of the week.

Tip

Any flavor of chocolate works really well in these delicious cookies.

- Preheat oven to 350°F (180°C)
- Cookie sheets, lined with parchment paper

3 cups	all-purpose flour	750 mL
1 tbsp	baking powder	15 mL
½ tsp	baking soda	2 mL
½ tsp	salt	2 mL
⅔ cup	vegetable shortening	150 mL
½ cup	unsalted butter, softened	125 mL
¾ cup	granulated sugar	175 mL
¾ cup	packed dark brown sugar	175 mL
3	eggs	3
1 tbsp	vanilla extract	15 mL
2 cups	chopped semisweet chocolate or semisweet chocolate chips	500 mL

1. In a bowl, whisk together flour, baking powder, baking soda and salt until well combined. Set aside.

2. In a large bowl, using an electric mixer on medium speed, cream shortening, butter, granulated sugar and brown sugar until light and fluffy, about 3 minutes. Add eggs one at a time, beating well after each addition. Beat in vanilla. Scrape down sides of bowl. On low speed or using a wooden spoon, gradually add flour mixture, beating just until blended. By hand, fold in chocolate.

3. Using a cookie scoop or spoons, drop tablespoonfuls (15 mL) of dough about 2 inches (5 cm) apart on prepared cookie sheets. Bake one sheet at a time in preheated oven for 10 to 12 minutes or until edges start to turn lightly golden.

4. Immediately slide parchment paper onto a wire cooling rack. Cool cookies for 5 minutes, then transfer from parchment paper to cooling rack and cool completely.

Double Chocolate Chip Cookies

Two flavors of chocolate give these cookies a double chocolate punch.

Tip

Use a cookie scoop to uniformly portion cookie dough to and ensure even baking.

Variation

Substitute chopped milk chocolate or milk chocolate chips for the bittersweet chocolate.

- Preheat oven to 350°F (180°C)
- Cookie sheets, lined with parchment paper

2¾ cups	all-purpose flour	675 mL
1 tsp	baking powder	5 mL
½ tsp	baking soda	2 mL
¼ tsp	salt	1 mL
½ cup	unsalted butter, softened	125 mL
½ cup	vegetable shortening	125 mL
¾ cup	granulated sugar	175 mL
¾ cup	packed light brown sugar	175 mL
2	eggs	2
1½ tsp	vanilla extract	7 mL
1 cup	chopped semisweet chocolate or semisweet chocolate chips	250 mL
1 cup	chopped bittersweet chocolate or bittersweet chocolate chips	250 mL

1. In a bowl, whisk together flour, baking powder, baking soda and salt until well combined. Set aside.

2. In a large bowl, using an electric mixer on medium speed, cream butter, shortening, granulated sugar and brown sugar until light and fluffy, about 3 minutes. Add eggs one at a time, beating well after each addition. Beat in vanilla. Scrape down sides of bowl. On low speed or using a wooden spoon, gradually add flour mixture, beating just until blended. By hand, fold in semisweet and bittersweet chocolate.

3. Using a cookie scoop or spoons, drop tablespoonfuls (15 mL) of dough about 2 inches (5 cm) apart on prepared cookie sheets. Bake one sheet at a time in preheated oven for 10 to 12 minutes or until edges start to turn lightly golden.

4. Immediately slide parchment paper onto a wire cooling rack. Cool cookies for 5 minutes, then transfer from parchment paper to cooling rack and cool completely.

Buttermilk Chocolate Chip Cookies

● ● ●

Creamy buttermilk adds a nice flavor that blends beautifully with the chocolate in these lovely cookies.

Tip

To measure flour properly, stir the flour in the package or container to give it some air, then gently spoon the flour into a dry measuring cup. Use a knife or spatula to level off the flour even with the rim.

Variation

Substitute chopped walnuts or chopped almonds for chopped pecans.

- Preheat oven to 350°F (180°C)
- Cookie sheets, lined with parchment paper

3½ cups	all-purpose flour	875 mL
1 tsp	baking powder	5 mL
1 tsp	baking soda	5 mL
¼ tsp	salt	1 mL
1 cup	vegetable shortening	250 mL
1 cup	granulated sugar	250 mL
1 cup	packed light brown sugar	250 mL
2	eggs	2
2 tsp	vanilla extract	10 mL
½ cup	buttermilk	125 mL
2 cups	chopped semisweet chocolate or semisweet chocolate chips	500 mL
1 cup	chopped pecans	250 mL

1. In a bowl, whisk together flour, baking powder, baking soda and salt until well combined. Set aside.

2. In a large bowl, using an electric mixer on medium speed, cream shortening, granulated sugar and brown sugar until light and fluffy, about 3 minutes. Add eggs one at a time, beating well after each addition. Beat in vanilla. Scrape down sides of bowl. On low speed or using a wooden spoon, gradually add flour mixture, alternating with buttermilk, beating just until blended. By hand, fold in chocolate and pecans.

3. Using a cookie scoop or spoons, drop tablespoonfuls (15 mL) of dough about 2 inches (5 cm) apart on prepared cookie sheets. Bake one sheet at a time in preheated oven for 10 to 12 minutes or until edges start to turn lightly golden.

4. Immediately slide parchment paper onto a wire cooling rack. Cool cookies for 5 minutes, then transfer from parchment paper to cooling rack and cool completely.

Chewy Chocolate Chip Cookies

Makes about 4 dozen cookies

● ● ●

A combination of all-purpose and cake flour plus butter and shortening adds lots of texture to these flavorful cookies.

Tips

For crispier cookies, bake for 13 to 15 minutes.

Eggs add to the structure and texture of cookies and help bind the ingredients.

- Preheat oven to 350°F (180°C)
- Cookie sheets, lined with parchment paper

1½ cups	all-purpose flour	375 mL
1½ cups	cake flour	375 mL
1½ tsp	baking powder	7 mL
½ tsp	baking soda	2 mL
½ tsp	salt	2 mL
½ cup	unsalted butter, softened	125 mL
½ cup	vegetable shortening	125 mL
¾ cup	granulated sugar	175 mL
¾ cup	packed light brown sugar	175 mL
2	eggs	2
2 tsp	vanilla extract	10 mL
2 cups	chopped semisweet chocolate or semisweet chocolate chips	500 mL

1. In a bowl, whisk together all-purpose flour, cake flour, baking powder, baking soda and salt until well combined. Set aside.

2. In a large bowl, using an electric mixer on medium speed, cream butter, shortening, granulated sugar and brown sugar until light and fluffy, about 3 minutes. Add eggs one at a time, beating well after each addition. Beat in vanilla. Scrape down sides of bowl. On low speed or using a wooden spoon, gradually add flour mixture, beating just until blended. By hand, fold in chocolate.

3. Using a cookie scoop or spoons, drop tablespoonfuls (15 mL) of dough about 2 inches (5 cm) apart on prepared cookie sheets. Bake one sheet at a time in preheated oven for 10 to 12 minutes or until edges start to turn lightly golden.

4. Immediately slide parchment paper onto a wire cooling rack. Cool cookies for 5 minutes, then transfer from parchment paper to cooling rack and cool completely.

Chocolate Chip Walnut Cookies

These crunchy chocolate chip cookies are perfect for nut lovers.

Tip

Always taste nuts to make sure they are fresh. For added flavor, walnuts may be toasted before making cookies (see page 32).

• Cookie sheets, lined with parchment paper

2½ cups	all-purpose flour	625 mL
1 tsp	baking soda	5 mL
1 tsp	cream of tartar	5 mL
1 cup	unsalted butter, softened	250 mL
¾ cup	granulated sugar	175 mL
¾ cup	packed light brown sugar	175 mL
2	eggs	2
2 tsp	vanilla extract	10 mL
2 cups	chopped walnuts	500 mL
1 cup	chopped semisweet chocolate or semisweet chocolate chips	250 mL

1. In a bowl, whisk together flour, baking soda and cream of tartar until well combined. Set aside.

2. In a large bowl, using an electric mixer on medium speed, cream butter, granulated sugar and brown sugar until light and fluffy, about 3 minutes. Add eggs one at a time, beating well after each addition. Beat in vanilla. Scrape down sides of bowl. On low speed or using a wooden spoon, gradually add flour mixture, beating just until blended. By hand, fold in walnuts and chocolate. Cover dough with plastic wrap and chill for at least 1 hour.

3. Preheat oven to 350°F (180°C). Using a cookie scoop or spoons, drop tablespoonfuls (15 mL) of dough about 2 inches (5 cm) apart on prepared cookie sheets. Bake one sheet at a time in preheated oven for 10 to 12 minutes or until edges start to turn lightly golden.

4. Immediately slide parchment paper onto a wire cooling rack. Cool cookies for 5 minutes, then transfer from parchment paper to cooling rack and cool completely.

White Chocolate Chip Cookies

Makes about 3½ dozen cookies

I love the flavor combination of white chocolate and macadamia nuts with a touch of almond extract.

Tip

Real white chocolate contains cocoa butter. Always check the ingredients for cocoa butter to be sure you are using white chocolate. Avoid any product labeled as "white" or "vanilla" baking chips.

Variations

Substitute chopped unsalted almonds for chopped macadamia nuts.

White Chocolate Chip Coconut Cookies: By hand, fold ¾ cup (175 mL) sweetened flaked coconut into dough along with white chocolate and macadamia nuts.

- Preheat oven to 350°F (180°C)
- Cookie sheets, lined with parchment paper

2⅔ cups	all-purpose flour	650 mL
2 tsp	baking powder	10 mL
¼ tsp	baking soda	1 mL
¼ tsp	salt	1 mL
½ cup	unsalted butter, softened	125 mL
½ cup	vegetable shortening	125 mL
1 cup	packed light brown sugar	250 mL
½ cup	granulated sugar	125 mL
2	eggs	2
1 tsp	vanilla extract	5 mL
½ tsp	almond extract	2 mL
2 cups	chopped white chocolate or white chocolate chips	500 mL
1 cup	chopped roasted unsalted macadamia nuts	250 mL

1. In a bowl, whisk together flour, baking powder, baking soda and salt until well combined. Set aside.

2. In a large bowl, using an electric mixer on medium speed, cream butter, shortening, brown sugar and granulated sugar until light and fluffy, about 3 minutes. Add eggs one at a time, beating well after each addition. Beat in vanilla and almond extract. Scrape down sides of bowl. On low speed or using a wooden spoon, gradually add flour mixture, beating just until blended. By hand, fold in chocolate and macadamia nuts.

3. Using a cookie scoop or spoons, drop tablespoonfuls (15 mL) of dough about 2 inches (5 cm) apart on prepared cookie sheets. Bake one sheet at a time in preheated oven for 10 to 12 minutes or until edges start to turn lightly golden.

4. Immediately slide parchment paper onto a wire cooling rack. Cool cookies for 5 minutes, then transfer from parchment paper to cooling rack and cool completely.

Chocolate Chunk Cookies

Chocolate-lovers will enjoy the big chunks in these wonderful cookies

Tip

Always let a cookie sheet cool completely before placing the next batch of cookie dough on it.

- Preheat oven to 350°F (180°C)
- Cookie sheets, lined with parchment paper

1¾ cups	all-purpose flour	425 mL
1 cup	cake flour	250 mL
1 tbsp	baking powder	15 mL
½ tsp	salt	2 mL
½ cup	unsalted butter, softened	125 mL
6 tbsp	vegetable shortening	90 mL
1 cup	packed light brown sugar	250 mL
½ cup	granulated sugar	125 mL
2	eggs	2
1½ tsp	vanilla extract	7 mL
2 cups	coarsely chopped semisweet chocolate	500 mL

1. In a bowl, whisk together all-purpose flour, cake flour, baking powder and salt until well combined. Set aside.

2. In a large bowl, using an electric mixer on medium speed, cream butter, shortening, brown sugar and granulated sugar until light and fluffy, about 3 minutes. Add eggs one at a time, beating well after each addition. Beat in vanilla. Scrape down sides of bowl. On low speed or using a wooden spoon, gradually add flour mixture, beating just until blended. By hand, fold in chocolate.

3. Using a cookie scoop or spoons, drop tablespoonfuls (15 mL) of dough about 2 inches (5 cm) apart on prepared cookie sheets. Bake one sheet at a time in preheated oven for 10 to 12 minutes or until edges start to turn lightly golden.

4. Immediately slide parchment paper onto a wire cooling rack. Cool cookies for 5 minutes, then transfer from parchment paper to cooling rack and cool completely.

Sweet Dark Chocolate Chip Cookies

Makes about 2½ dozen cookies ● ● ●

I love sweet dark chocolate, so I created this special cookie recipe to satisfy my craving. The cookies are not as sweet as some other chocolate chip cookies.

Tip

Brown sugar adds moisture and rich flavor to cookies.

- Preheat oven to 350°F (180°C)
- Cookie sheets, lined with parchment paper

2½ cups	all-purpose flour	625 mL
1 tsp	baking powder	5 mL
½ tsp	baking soda	2 mL
¼ tsp	salt	1 mL
6 tbsp	unsalted butter, softened	90 mL
6 tbsp	vegetable shortening	90 mL
1 cup	packed dark brown sugar	250 mL
2	eggs	2
1 tbsp	vanilla extract	15 mL
2 cups	chopped sweet dark chocolate or sweet dark chocolate chips	500 mL

1. In a bowl, whisk together flour, baking powder, baking soda and salt until well combined. Set aside.

2. In a large bowl, using an electric mixer on medium speed, cream butter, shortening and brown sugar until light and fluffy, about 3 minutes. Add eggs one at a time, beating well after each addition. Beat in vanilla. Scrape down sides of bowl. On low speed or using a wooden spoon, gradually add flour mixture, beating just until blended. By hand, fold in chocolate.

3. Using a cookie scoop or spoons, drop tablespoonfuls (15 mL) of dough about 2 inches (5 cm) apart on prepared cookie sheets. Bake one sheet at a time in preheated oven for 10 to 12 minutes or until edges start to turn lightly golden.

4. Immediately slide parchment paper onto a wire cooling rack. Cool cookies for 5 minutes, then transfer from parchment paper to cooling rack and cool completely.

Chocolate Chip Orange Cookies

Makes about 3½ dozen cookies ● ● ●

Chocolate and orange are a heavenly combination in these moist, chewy cookies.

Tip

When zesting oranges, remove only the outer colored part of the peel. The white part underneath, called the pith, is very bitter and will give cookies an unpleasant flavor.

Variation

Substitute finely chopped bittersweet chocolate for sweet dark chocolate.

- Preheat oven to 350°F (180°C)
- Cookie sheets, lined with parchment paper

2¾ cups	all-purpose flour	675 mL
2 tsp	baking powder	10 mL
½ tsp	baking soda	2 mL
¼ tsp	salt	1 mL
½ cup	unsalted butter, softened	125 mL
½ cup	vegetable shortening	125 mL
1 cup	packed dark brown sugar	250 mL
½ cup	granulated sugar	125 mL
2	eggs	2
2 tbsp	grated orange zest	25 mL
½ tsp	vanilla extract	2 mL
2 cups	finely chopped sweet dark chocolate	500 mL

1. In a bowl, whisk together flour, baking powder, baking soda and salt until well combined. Set aside.

2. In a large bowl, using an electric mixer on medium speed, cream butter, shortening, brown sugar and granulated sugar until light and fluffy, about 3 minutes. Add eggs one at a time, beating well after each addition. Beat in orange zest and vanilla. Scrape down sides of bowl. On low speed or using a wooden spoon, gradually add flour mixture, beating just until blended. By hand, fold in chocolate.

3. Using a cookie scoop or spoons, drop tablespoonfuls (15 mL) of dough about 2 inches (5 cm) apart on prepared cookie sheets. Bake one sheet at a time in preheated oven for 10 to 12 minutes or until edges start to turn lightly golden.

4. Immediately slide parchment paper onto a wire cooling rack. Cool cookies for 5 minutes, then transfer from parchment paper to cooling rack and cool completely.

Triple Chocolate Chip Cookies

Makes about 3½ dozen cookies ● ● ●

Three flavors of chocolate give these cookies a pretty appearance and great flavor.

Tip

Homemade cookies make a great gift for family and friends and are perfect for every occasion.

Variations

Substitute chopped bittersweet or sweet dark chocolate or bittersweet or dark chocolate chips for milk chocolate.

Triple Chocolate Chip Nut Cookies: By hand, fold 1 cup (250 mL) chopped walnuts or pecans or chopped unsalted almonds into dough along with chocolate.

- ● **Preheat oven to 350°F (180°C)**
- ● **Cookie sheets, lined with parchment paper**

2¾ cups	all-purpose flour	675 mL
1 tsp	baking powder	5 mL
½ tsp	baking soda	2 mL
½ tsp	salt	2 mL
½ cup	unsalted butter, softened	125 mL
½ cup	vegetable shortening	125 mL
1 cup	packed dark brown sugar	250 mL
⅓ cup	granulated sugar	75 mL
2	eggs	2
2 tbsp	light (golden) corn syrup	25 mL
2 tsp	vanilla extract	10 mL
½ cup	chopped semisweet chocolate or semisweet chocolate chips	125 mL
½ cup	chopped white chocolate or white chocolate chips	125 mL
½ cup	chopped milk chocolate or milk chocolate chips	125 mL

1. In a bowl, whisk together flour, baking powder, baking soda and salt until well combined. Set aside.

2. In a large bowl, using an electric mixer on medium speed, cream butter, shortening, brown sugar and granulated sugar until light and fluffy, about 3 minutes. Add eggs one at a time, beating well after each addition. Beat in corn syrup and vanilla. Scrape down sides of bowl. On low speed or using a wooden spoon, gradually add flour mixture, beating just until blended. By hand, fold in semisweet, white and milk chocolate.

3. Using a cookie scoop or spoons, drop tablespoonfuls (15 mL) of dough about 2 inches (5 cm) apart on prepared cookie sheets. Bake one sheet at a time in preheated oven for 10 to 12 minutes or until edges start to turn lightly golden.

4. Immediately slide parchment paper onto a wire cooling rack. Cool cookies for 5 minutes, then transfer from parchment paper to cooling rack and cool completely.

Glazed Chocolate Chip Cookies

● ● ●

The chocolate glaze on top of the cookies adds an extra dimension and makes a pretty presentation.

Tips

Line cookie sheets with parchment paper to keep cookies from sticking.

Chocolate can be melted in the top of a double boiler placed over simmering water. Stir frequently, until chocolate is completely melted and mixture is smooth. Set aside to cool.

Variation

Substitute chopped pecans for chopped walnuts.

- Preheat oven to 350°F (180°C)
- Cookie sheets, lined with parchment paper

Cookies

2¾ cups	all-purpose flour	675 mL
1 tsp	baking soda	5 mL
¼ tsp	salt	1 mL
1 cup	unsalted butter, softened	250 mL
¾ cup	granulated sugar	175 mL
¾ cup	packed light brown sugar	175 mL
2	eggs	2
1 tsp	vanilla extract	5 mL
1 cup	chopped semisweet chocolate or semisweet chocolate chips	250 mL
1 cup	chopped walnuts	250 mL

Glaze

1 cup	chopped semisweet chocolate or semisweet chocolate chips	250 mL
1 tsp	vegetable shortening	5 mL

1. *Cookies:* In a bowl, whisk together flour, baking soda and salt until well combined. Set aside.

2. In a large bowl, using an electric mixer on medium speed, cream butter, granulated sugar and brown sugar until light and fluffy, about 3 minutes. Add eggs one at a time, beating well after each addition. Beat in vanilla. Scrape down sides of bowl. On low speed or using a wooden spoon, gradually add flour mixture, beating just until blended. By hand, fold in chocolate and walnuts.

3. Using a cookie scoop or spoons, drop tablespoonfuls (15 mL) of dough about 2 inches (5 cm) apart on prepared cookie sheets. Bake one sheet at a time in preheated oven for 10 to 12 minutes or until edges start to turn lightly golden.

4. Immediately slide parchment paper onto a wire cooling rack. Cool cookies for 5 minutes, then transfer from parchment paper to cooling rack and cool completely.

5. *Glaze:* In a 1-quart (1 L) microwave-safe zippered storage bag, combine semisweet chocolate and vegetable shortening. Microwave on Medium-High (75%) power for 1 minute. Knead bag until completely combined and smooth, microwaving an additional 10 seconds at a time as needed to fully melt chocolate. Cut off a small corner of bag and drizzle chocolate over tops of cooled cookies. Place on parchment or wax paper to set. Allow chocolate to set before serving or storing.

Classic Chocolate Chip Cookies

● ● ●

Evoking fond memories of childhood, these chocolate chip cookies are soft, thin and chewy.

Tip

Always use pure vanilla extract in cookies. Imitation vanilla is made from synthetic flavors and colors, and the taste cannot compare to pure vanilla extract.

Variation

Classic Chocolate Chip Nut Cookies: By hand, fold in 1 cup (250 mL) chopped walnuts or pecans along with chocolate.

- **Preheat oven to 350°F (180°C)**
- **Cookie sheets, lined with parchment paper**

2¼ cups	all-purpose flour	550 mL
1 tsp	baking soda	5 mL
½ tsp	salt	2 mL
1 cup	unsalted butter, softened	250 mL
¾ cup	granulated sugar	175 mL
¾ cup	packed light brown sugar	175 mL
2	eggs	2
1 tsp	vanilla extract	5 mL
2 cups	chopped semisweet chocolate or semisweet chocolate chips	500 mL

1. In a bowl, whisk together flour, baking soda and salt until well combined. Set aside.

2. In a large bowl, using an electric mixer on medium speed, cream butter, granulated sugar and brown sugar until light and fluffy, about 3 minutes. Add eggs one at a time, beating well after each addition. Beat in vanilla. Scrape down sides of bowl. On low speed or using a wooden spoon, gradually add flour mixture, beating just until blended. By hand, fold in chocolate.

3. Using a cookie scoop or spoons, drop tablespoonfuls (15 mL) of dough about 2 inches (5 cm) apart on prepared cookie sheets. Bake one sheet at a time in preheated oven for 10 to 12 minutes or until edges start to turn lightly golden.

4. Immediately slide parchment paper onto a wire cooling rack. Cool cookies for 5 minutes, then transfer from parchment paper to cooling rack and cool completely.

Bittersweet Chocolate Chunk Cookies

Chunks of chocolate give these cookies a rustic appearance, and they pack a hefty chocolate wallop.

Tip

Use a cookie scoop to uniformly portion cookie dough and ensure even baking.

- Preheat oven to 350°F (180°C)
- Cookie sheets, lined with parchment paper

2¾ cups	all-purpose flour	675 mL
1 tbsp	baking powder	15 mL
½ tsp	salt	2 mL
½ cup	unsalted butter, softened	125 mL
½ cup	vegetable shortening	125 mL
1 cup	packed dark brown sugar	250 mL
½ cup	granulated sugar	125 mL
2	eggs	2
2 tsp	vanilla extract	10 mL
2 cups	coarsely chopped bittersweet chocolate	500 mL

1. In a bowl, whisk together flour, baking powder and salt until well combined. Set aside.

2. In a large bowl, using an electric mixer on medium speed, cream butter, shortening, brown sugar and granulated sugar until light and fluffy, about 3 minutes. Add eggs one at a time, beating well after each addition. Beat in vanilla. Scrape down sides of bowl. On low speed or using a wooden spoon, gradually add flour mixture, beating just until blended. By hand, fold in chocolate.

3. Using a cookie scoop or spoons, drop tablespoonfuls (15 mL) of dough about 2 inches (5 cm) apart on prepared cookie sheets. Bake one sheet at a time in preheated oven for 10 to 12 minutes or until edges start to turn lightly golden.

4. Immediately slide parchment paper onto a wire cooling rack. Cool cookies for 5 minutes, then transfer from parchment paper to cooling rack and cool completely.

Chocolate Chip Almond Cookies

The almonds and almond extract give these cookies a special nutty flavor.

Tip

Fold in the chocolate and nuts by hand to keep from overworking the dough after the flour is mixed in. Overworking the dough will make the cookies tough.

● **Preheat oven to 350°F (180°C)**
● **Cookie sheets, lined with parchment paper**

2½ cups	all-purpose flour	625 mL
1 tsp	baking powder	5 mL
½ tsp	baking soda	2 mL
¼ tsp	salt	1 mL
¾ cup	unsalted butter, softened	175 mL
¾ cup	granulated sugar	175 mL
¾ cup	packed light brown sugar	175 mL
2	eggs	2
1 tsp	vanilla extract	5 mL
¼ tsp	almond extract	1 mL
1½ cups	chopped semisweet chocolate or semisweet chocolate chips	375 mL
1½ cups	chopped unsalted almonds	375 mL

1. In a bowl, whisk together flour, baking powder, baking soda and salt until well combined. Set aside.

2. In a large bowl, using an electric mixer on medium speed, cream butter, granulated sugar and brown sugar until light and fluffy, about 3 minutes. Add eggs one at a time, beating well after each addition. Beat in vanilla and almond extract. Scrape down sides of bowl. On low speed or using a wooden spoon, gradually add flour mixture, beating just until blended. By hand, fold in chocolate and almonds.

3. Using a cookie scoop or spoons, drop tablespoonfuls (15 mL) of dough about 2 inches (5 cm) apart on prepared cookie sheets. Bake one sheet at a time in preheated oven for 10 to 12 minutes or until edges start to turn lightly golden.

4. Immediately slide parchment paper onto a wire cooling rack. Cool cookies for 5 minutes, then transfer from parchment paper to cooling rack and cool completely.

Milk Chocolate Chip Cookies

Makes about 3½ dozen cookies

Milk chocolate has a mild chocolate flavor, making these cookies a hit with young kids.

Tip

Use table salt for baking. It has a balanced flavor and very fine grains that blend well into the other ingredients.

● **Cookie sheets, lined with parchment paper**

2½ cups	all-purpose flour	625 mL
1 tsp	baking powder	5 mL
½ tsp	baking soda	2 mL
¼ tsp	salt	1 mL
1 cup	unsalted butter, softened	250 mL
1 cup	granulated sugar	250 mL
½ cup	packed light brown sugar	125 mL
2	eggs	2
1 tsp	vanilla extract	5 mL
2 cups	chopped milk chocolate or milk chocolate chips	500 mL

1. In a bowl, whisk together flour, baking powder, baking soda and salt until well combined. Set aside.

2. In a large bowl, using an electric mixer on medium speed, cream butter, granulated sugar and brown sugar until light and fluffy, about 3 minutes. Add eggs one at a time, beating well after each addition. Beat in vanilla. Scrape down sides of bowl. On low speed or using a wooden spoon, gradually add flour mixture, beating just until blended. By hand, fold in chocolate. Cover dough with plastic wrap and chill for at least 1 hour.

3. Preheat oven to 350°F (180°C). Using a cookie scoop or spoons, drop tablespoonfuls (15 mL) of dough about 2 inches (5 cm) apart on prepared cookie sheets. Bake one sheet at a time in preheated oven for 10 to 12 minutes or until edges start to turn lightly golden.

4. Immediately slide parchment paper onto a wire cooling rack. Cool cookies for 5 minutes, then transfer from parchment paper to cooling rack and cool completely.

Jumbo Chocolate Chip Cookies

Makes about 1½ dozen cookies ● ● ●

This is a great recipe for big cookies.

Tips

For crispier cookies, bake an additional 2 to 3 minutes.

Baking powder and baking soda are not interchangeable. Always use the specified type and amount of leavener called for in the recipe.

● **Cookie sheets, lined with parchment paper**

2¾ cups	all-purpose flour	675 mL
1 tsp	baking soda	5 mL
¼ tsp	salt	1 mL
1 cup	unsalted butter, softened	250 mL
1 cup	granulated sugar	250 mL
½ cup	packed light brown sugar	125 mL
2	eggs	2
1 tbsp	vanilla extract	15 mL
1½ cups	chopped semisweet chocolate or semisweet chocolate chips	375 mL
¾ cup	chopped walnuts	175 mL

1. In a bowl, whisk together flour, baking soda and salt until well combined. Set aside.

2. In a large bowl, using an electric mixer on medium speed, cream butter, granulated sugar and brown sugar until light and fluffy, about 3 minutes. Add eggs one at a time, beating well after each addition. Beat in vanilla. Scrape down sides of bowl. On low speed or using a wooden spoon, gradually add flour mixture, beating just until blended. By hand, fold in chocolate and walnuts. Cover dough with plastic wrap and chill for at least 1 hour.

3. Preheat oven to 350°F (180°C). Using a ¼-cup (50 mL) ice cream scoop, drop scoopfuls of dough about 4 inches (10 cm) apart on prepared cookie sheets. Bake one sheet at a time in preheated oven for 15 to 18 minutes or until edges start to turn lightly golden.

4. Immediately slide parchment paper onto a wire cooling rack. Cool cookies for 5 minutes, then transfer from parchment paper to cooling rack and cool completely.

Tender Chocolate Chip Cookies

● ● ●

Cake flour gives these cookies a tender crumb and more of a cake-like texture than traditional chocolate chip cookies.

Tip

Space cookies 2 inches (5 cm) apart on cookie sheets to allow enough room for spreading and air circulation for even baking.

● **Cookie sheets, lined with parchment paper**

2¾ cups	cake flour	675 mL
2¼ tsp	baking powder	11 mL
1 tsp	salt	5 mL
½ cup	vegetable shortening	125 mL
6 tbsp	unsalted butter, softened	90 mL
¾ cup	packed light brown sugar	175 mL
⅓ cup	granulated sugar	75 mL
2	eggs	2
3 tbsp	light (golden) corn syrup	45 mL
2 tsp	vanilla extract	10 mL
2 cups	chopped semisweet chocolate or semisweet chocolate chips	500 mL
1 cup	chopped walnuts	250 mL

1. In a bowl, whisk together cake flour, baking powder and salt until well combined. Set aside.

2. In a large bowl, using an electric mixer on medium speed, cream shortening, butter, brown sugar and granulated sugar until light and fluffy, about 3 minutes. Add eggs one at a time, beating well after each addition. Beat in corn syrup and vanilla. Scrape down sides of bowl. On low speed or using a wooden spoon, gradually add flour mixture, beating just until blended. By hand, fold in chocolate and walnuts. Cover dough with plastic wrap and chill for at least 1 hour.

3. Preheat oven to 350°F (180°C). Using a cookie scoop or spoons, drop tablespoonfuls (15 mL) of dough about 2 inches (5 cm) apart on prepared cookie sheets. Bake one sheet at a time in preheated oven for 10 to 12 minutes or until edges start to turn lightly golden.

4. Immediately slide parchment paper onto a wire cooling rack. Cool cookies for 5 minutes, then transfer from parchment paper to cooling rack and cool completely.

Deluxe Chocolate Chip Cookies

These cookies are loaded with three flavors of chocolate chips and two kinds of nuts and are sure to please cookie-lovers of all ages!

Tip

Parchment paper is a heat- and grease-resistant baking paper used to line cookie sheets to prevent cookies from sticking and burning on the bottom. It can be found in most grocery stores.

- Preheat oven to 350°F (180°C)
- Cookie sheets, lined with parchment paper

2⅔ cups	all-purpose flour	650 mL
1 tsp	baking powder	5 mL
½ tsp	baking soda	2 mL
½ tsp	salt	2 mL
½ cup	unsalted butter, softened	125 mL
½ cup	vegetable shortening	125 mL
1 cup	packed light brown sugar	250 mL
½ cup	granulated sugar	125 mL
2	eggs	2
1½ tsp	vanilla extract	7 mL
½ cup	chopped semisweet chocolate or semisweet chocolate chips	125 mL
½ cup	chopped bittersweet chocolate or bittersweet chocolate chips	125 mL
½ cup	chopped milk chocolate or milk chocolate chips	125 mL
½ cup	chopped pecans	125 mL
½ cup	chopped walnuts	125 mL

1. In a bowl, whisk together flour, baking powder, baking soda and salt until well combined. Set aside.

2. In a large bowl, using an electric mixer on medium speed, cream butter, shortening, brown sugar and granulated sugar until light and fluffy, about 3 minutes. Add eggs one at a time, beating well after each addition. Beat in vanilla. Scrape down sides of bowl. On low speed or using a wooden spoon, gradually add flour mixture, beating just until blended. By hand, fold in semisweet, bittersweet and milk chocolate, pecans and walnuts.

3. Using a cookie scoop or spoons, drop tablespoonfuls (15 mL) of dough about 2 inches (5 cm) apart on prepared cookie sheets. Bake one sheet at a time in preheated oven for 10 to 12 minutes or until edges start to turn lightly golden.

4. Immediately slide parchment paper onto a wire cooling rack. Cool cookies for 5 minutes, then transfer from parchment paper to cooling rack and cool completely.

Chocolate Chocolate Chip Cookies

● ● ●

These luscious cookies are sure to satisfy a big chocolate craving.

Tip

Creaming the butter and sugar beats air into the mixture. These air pockets give cookies a tender texture.

Variation

By hand, fold 1 cup (250 mL) chopped walnuts or chopped pecans into dough with chocolate.

● **Cookie sheets, lined with parchment paper**

2½ cups	all-purpose flour	625 mL
6 tbsp	unsweetened Dutch-process cocoa powder, sifted	90 mL
1 tsp	baking powder	5 mL
½ tsp	salt	2 mL
¾ cup	unsalted butter, softened	175 mL
1½ cups	packed dark brown sugar	375 mL
3	eggs	3
1 tbsp	vanilla extract	15 mL
2 cups	chopped semisweet chocolate or semisweet chocolate chips	500 mL

1. In a bowl, whisk together flour, cocoa powder, baking powder and salt until well combined. Set aside.

2. In a large bowl, using an electric mixer on medium speed, cream butter and brown sugar until light and fluffy, about 3 minutes. Add eggs one at a time, beating well after each addition. Beat in vanilla. Scrape down sides of bowl. On low speed or using a wooden spoon, gradually add flour mixture, beating just until blended. By hand, fold in chocolate. Cover dough with plastic wrap and chill for at least 1 hour.

3. Preheat oven to 350°F (180°C). Using a cookie scoop or spoons, drop tablespoonfuls (15 mL) of dough about 2 inches (5 cm) apart on prepared cookie sheets. Bake one sheet at a time in preheated oven for 10 to 12 minutes or just until set.

4. Immediately slide parchment paper onto a wire cooling rack. Cool cookies for 5 minutes, then transfer from parchment paper to cooling rack and cool completely.

Cream Cheese Chocolate Chip Cookies

The cream cheese makes these cookies very tender and rich.

Tip

Store unopened packages of flour in a cool, dry place for up to 2 years. Always use flour before the date stamped on the package.

● **Cookie sheets, lined with parchment paper**

2⅔ cups	all-purpose flour	650 mL
2 tsp	baking powder	10 mL
½ tsp	salt	2 mL
⅔ cup	unsalted butter, softened	150 mL
3 oz	cream cheese, softened	90 g
1⅓ cups	granulated sugar	325 mL
2	eggs	2
2 tsp	vanilla extract	10 mL
2 cups	chopped semisweet chocolate or semisweet chocolate chips	500 mL

1. In a bowl, whisk together flour, baking powder and salt until well combined. Set aside.

2. In a large bowl, using an electric mixer on medium speed, cream butter, cream cheese and granulated sugar until light and fluffy, about 3 minutes. Add eggs one at a time, beating well after each addition. Beat in vanilla. Scrape down sides of bowl. On low speed or using a wooden spoon, gradually add flour mixture, beating just until blended. By hand, fold in chocolate. Cover dough with plastic wrap and chill for at least 1 hour.

3. Preheat oven to 350°F (180°C). Using a cookie scoop or spoons, drop tablespoonfuls (15 mL) of dough about 2 inches (5 cm) apart on prepared cookie sheets. Bake one sheet at a time in preheated oven for 12 to 14 minutes or until edges start to turn lightly golden.

4. Immediately slide parchment paper onto a wire cooling rack. Cool cookies for 5 minutes, then transfer from parchment paper to cooling rack and cool completely.

Peanut Butter Chocolate Chippers

● ● ●

Peanut butter and chocolate, oh yeah! This classic pairing of flavors is popular with kids of all ages.

Tip

Lightly coat the measuring cup with nonstick cooking spray to make it easier to remove the peanut butter.

- Preheat oven to 350°F (180°C)
- Cookie sheets, lined with parchment paper

2²⁄₃ cups	all-purpose flour	650 mL
1 tsp	baking powder	5 mL
½ tsp	baking soda	2 mL
¼ tsp	salt	1 mL
½ cup	vegetable shortening	125 mL
½ cup	creamy peanut butter	125 mL
¾ cup	granulated sugar	175 mL
½ cup	packed light brown sugar	125 mL
2	eggs	2
1 tsp	vanilla extract	5 mL
2 cups	chopped semisweet chocolate or semisweet chocolate chips	500 mL
1 cup	chopped unsalted peanuts	250 mL

1. In a bowl, whisk together flour, baking powder, baking soda and salt until well combined. Set aside.

2. In a large bowl, using an electric mixer on medium speed, cream shortening, peanut butter, granulated sugar and brown sugar until light and fluffy, about 3 minutes. Add eggs one at a time, beating well after each addition. Beat in vanilla. Scrape down sides of bowl. On low speed or using a wooden spoon, gradually add flour mixture, beating just until blended. By hand, fold in chocolate and peanuts.

3. Using a cookie scoop or spoons, drop tablespoonfuls (15 mL) of dough about 2 inches (5 cm) apart on prepared cookie sheets. Bake one sheet at a time in preheated oven for 10 to 12 minutes or until edges start to turn lightly golden.

4. Immediately slide parchment paper onto a wire cooling rack. Cool cookies for 5 minutes, then transfer from parchment paper to cooling rack and cool completely.

Crispy Chocolate Chip Cookies

If you prefer crispy chocolate chip cookies rather than soft and chewy cookies, this recipe is for you.

Tip

For even baking, cookie sheets should fit inside oven with at least 2 inches (5 cm) of space between the sheet and the sides of the oven.

Variation

Crispy Chocolate Chip Nut Cookies: By hand, fold 1 cup (250 mL) chopped walnuts or pecans into dough with chocolate.

- **Preheat oven to 350°F (180°C)**
- **Cookie sheets, lined with parchment paper**

2½ cups	all-purpose flour	625 mL
1 tsp	baking soda	5 mL
¼ tsp	salt	1 mL
1 cup	unsalted butter, softened	250 mL
1 cup	granulated sugar	250 mL
½ cup	packed light brown sugar	125 mL
2	eggs	2
1 tsp	vanilla extract	5 mL
1½ cups	chopped semisweet chocolate or semisweet chocolate chips	375 mL

1. In a bowl, whisk together flour, baking soda and salt until well combined. Set aside.

2. In a large bowl, using an electric mixer on medium speed, cream butter, granulated sugar and brown sugar until light and fluffy, about 3 minutes. Add eggs one at a time, beating well after each addition. Beat in vanilla. Scrape down sides of bowl. On low speed or using a wooden spoon, gradually add flour mixture, beating just until blended. By hand, fold in chocolate.

3. Using a cookie scoop or spoons, drop tablespoonfuls (15 mL) of dough about 2 inches (5 cm) apart on prepared cookie sheets. Bake one sheet at a time in preheated oven for 15 to 18 minutes or until edges and tops turn golden brown.

4. Cool cookies on pan for 2 minutes, then slide parchment paper onto a wire cooling rack. Cool cookies for 5 minutes, then transfer from parchment paper to cooling rack and cool completely.

Sour Cream Chocolate Chip Cookies

Sour cream gives these lovely cookies a moist texture and slight tang.

Tip

Use a cookie scoop to uniformly portion cookie dough and ensure even baking.

● **Cookie sheets, lined with parchment paper**

2¾ cups	all-purpose flour	675 mL
1 tsp	baking powder	5 mL
½ tsp	baking soda	2 mL
¼ tsp	salt	1 mL
⅔ cup	unsalted butter, softened	150 mL
⅔ cup	granulated sugar	150 mL
⅔ cup	packed light brown sugar	150 mL
2	eggs	2
½ cup	sour cream	125 mL
1½ tsp	vanilla extract	7 mL
1½ cups	chopped semisweet chocolate or semisweet chocolate chips	375 mL

1. In a bowl, whisk together flour, baking powder, baking soda and salt until well combined. Set aside.

2. In a large bowl, using an electric mixer on medium speed, cream butter, granulated sugar and brown sugar until light and fluffy, about 3 minutes. Add eggs one at a time, beating well after each addition. Beat in sour cream and vanilla. Scrape down sides of bowl. On low speed or using a wooden spoon, gradually add flour mixture, beating just until blended. By hand, fold in chocolate. Cover dough with plastic wrap and chill for at least 1 hour.

3. Preheat oven to 350°F (180°C). Using a cookie scoop or spoons, drop tablespoonfuls (15 mL) of dough about 2 inches (5 cm) apart on prepared cookie sheets. Bake one sheet at a time in preheated oven for 10 to 12 minutes or until edges start to turn lightly golden.

4. Immediately slide parchment paper onto a wire cooling rack. Cool cookies for 5 minutes, then transfer from parchment paper to cooling rack and cool completely.

Chocolate Chip Espresso Cookies

● ● ●

Chocolate and coffee in a cookie — what a heavenly combination!

Tip
Use the appropriate measuring tools and techniques to accurately measure ingredients.

Variation
By hand, fold 1 cup (250 mL) chopped walnuts or pecans into dough with chocolate.

● **Preheat oven to 350°F (180°C)**
● **Cookie sheets, lined with parchment paper**

2½ cups	all-purpose flour	625 mL
2 tbsp	instant espresso powder	25 mL
1 tsp	baking powder	5 mL
½ tsp	baking soda	2 mL
½ tsp	salt	2 mL
½ cup	unsalted butter, softened	125 mL
½ cup	vegetable shortening	125 mL
1 cup	packed dark brown sugar	250 mL
¾ cup	granulated sugar	175 mL
2	eggs	2
2 tsp	vanilla extract	10 mL
1½ cups	chopped semisweet chocolate or semisweet chocolate chips	375 mL

1. In a bowl, whisk together flour, espresso powder, baking powder, baking soda and salt until well combined. Set aside.
2. In a large bowl, using an electric mixer on medium speed, cream butter, shortening, brown sugar and granulated sugar until light and fluffy, about 3 minutes. Add eggs one at a time, beating well after each addition. Beat in vanilla. Scrape down sides of bowl. On low speed or using a wooden spoon, gradually add flour mixture, beating just until blended. By hand, fold in chocolate.
3. Using a cookie scoop or spoons, drop tablespoonfuls (15 mL) of dough about 2 inches (5 cm) apart on prepared cookie sheets. Bake one sheet at a time in preheated oven for 10 to 12 minutes or until edges start to turn lightly golden.
4. Immediately slide parchment paper onto a wire cooling rack. Cool cookies for 5 minutes, then transfer from parchment paper to cooling rack and cool completely.

Special Chocolate Chip Cookies

● ● ●

A small amount of corn syrup helps give these lovely chocolate chip cookies a slightly crispy outside and a soft, chewy inside.

Tip

Fold in the chocolate chips by hand to keep from overworking the dough after the flour is mixed in. Overworking the dough will make the cookies tough.

- Preheat oven to 350°F (180°C)
- Cookie sheets, lined with parchment paper

2½ cups	all-purpose flour	625 mL
1 tsp	baking powder	5 mL
½ tsp	baking soda	2 mL
¼ tsp	salt	1 mL
¾ cup	vegetable shortening	175 mL
1¼ cups	packed dark brown sugar	300 mL
2	eggs	2
3 tbsp	light corn syrup	45 mL
2 tsp	vanilla extract	10 mL
2 cups	chopped semisweet chocolate or semisweet chocolate chips	500 mL
1 cup	chopped walnuts	250 mL

1. In a bowl, whisk together flour, baking powder, baking soda and salt until well combined. Set aside.

2. In a large bowl, using an electric mixer on medium speed, cream shortening and brown sugar until light and fluffy, about 3 minutes. Add eggs one at a time, beating well after each addition. Beat in corn syrup and vanilla. Scrape down sides of bowl. On low speed or using a wooden spoon, gradually add flour mixture, beating just until blended. By hand, fold in chocolate and walnuts.

3. Using a cookie scoop or spoons, drop tablespoonfuls (15 mL) of dough about 2 inches (5 cm) apart on prepared cookie sheets. Bake, one sheet at a time in preheated oven for 10 to 12 minutes or until edges start to turn lightly golden.

4. Immediately slide parchment paper onto a wire cooling rack. Cool cookies for 5 minutes, then transfer from parchment paper to cooling rack and cool completely.

Oatmeal Cookie Delights

●●●

Oatmeal Raisin Cookies 147

Chewy Oatmeal Cookies 148

Oatmeal Walnut Cookies 149

Oatmeal Chippers. 150

Cranberry Oat Cookies. 151

Pineapple Apricot Oatmeal Drops. . . 152

Old-Fashioned Oatmeal Cookies . . . 153

White Chocolate Oatmeal Cookies . . 154

Coconut Oat Chews. 155

Peanut Butter Oat Chippers 156

Oatmeal Pumpkin Cookies 157

Tropical Oat Cookies 158

Chocolate-Glazed Oatmeal Cookies. 159

Banana Rum Oatmeal Cookies. 160

Lots of Oats Cookies 161

Molasses Oat Cookies 162

Orange Oat Drops 163

Oatmeal Almond Cookies. 164

Banana Walnut Oatmeal Cookies . . . 165

Apricot Coconut Oatmeal Drops. . . . 166

Applesauce Oatmeal Cookies. 167

Frosted Marmalade Oat Cookies . . . 168

About Oatmeal Cookies

Oatmeal cookies are a special treat and the ultimate in cookie comfort food. For many, they evoke fond memories of childhood and happy thoughts of brisk fall days and warm, cozy kitchens. Many oatmeal cookies are scented with cinnamon and make the whole house smell wonderful as they bake.

Made with drop cookie and shaped cookie baking techniques, these treasures are moist and chewy. Many get their richness of flavor from brown sugar, molasses and vanilla. Adding to their appeal, the gems in this collection are filled with wonderful ingredients like nuts, raisins, dried apricots and cranberries, coconut and even chocolate, along with lots of chewy oats. These recipes are sure to appeal to oatmeal cookie fans, and they may even convert a few people who claim not to like oatmeal cookies.

Quick-cooking oats have a finer texture and faster cooking time than old-fashioned oats, making them an excellent choice for tender oatmeal cookies. If you only have old-fashioned, or large flake, oats on hand, they may be used in place of quick-cooking oats in these cookie recipes. Instant oats are preprocessed and turn gummy when used in baked goods. Steel-cut oats, also called Irish or Scottish oats, remain hard when baked and should not be used for making cookies.

The Origins of the Oatmeal Cookie

The ancient Romans planted the first domesticated crop of oats, and when they traveled to the British Isles, the Romans brought oats with them. The oats survived and prospered as one of the few food crops that could thrive in the cool, damp climate of Scotland. The origins of today's oatmeal cookies can be traced back to the ancient oatcakes and bannocks eaten by the Scottish people.

In 1620, the Pilgrims brought oats with them on the *Mayflower* when they came to America to establish the first European colony. In Europe and England, until about 1900, oats continued to be considered a crop fit only to be eaten by horses and peasants, while the rich ate breads made of wheat.

It wasn't until the late 1800s that oats were used in confectionery baking and the first oatmeal cookies appeared. Since then, the popularity of oatmeal cookies has grown by leaps and bounds, and they are now enjoyed by people all over the world. Their popularity is so strong in the United States that April 30th has been designated as National Oatmeal Cookie Day.

Oatmeal Raisin Cookies

These wonderful, cinnamon-scented cookies are sweet reminders of childhood.

Tips

Pecans may be omitted.

Use plump, moist raisins to make cookies with the best flavor and texture. If the raisins you have in the cupboard are dried out, then it's time to buy fresh.

- Preheat oven to 350°F (180°C)
- Cookie sheets, lined with parchment paper

2 cups	all-purpose flour	500 mL
1½ tsp	baking powder	7 mL
½ tsp	ground cinnamon	2 mL
½ tsp	baking soda	2 mL
¼ tsp	salt	1 mL
1 cup	unsalted butter, softened	250 mL
1⅓ cups	granulated sugar	325 mL
⅔ cup	packed light brown sugar	150 mL
2	eggs	2
2 tsp	vanilla extract	10 mL
2½ cups	quick-cooking rolled oats	625 mL
1⅓ cups	raisins	325 mL
1 cup	chopped pecans	250 mL

1. In a bowl, whisk together flour, baking powder, cinnamon, baking soda and salt until well combined. Set aside.

2. In a large bowl, using an electric mixer on medium speed, cream butter, granulated sugar and brown sugar until light and fluffy, about 3 minutes. Add eggs one at a time, beating well after each addition. Beat in vanilla. Scrape down sides of bowl. On low speed or using a wooden spoon, gradually add flour mixture, beating just until blended. Gradually stir in oats. By hand, fold in raisins and pecans.

3. Using a cookie scoop or spoons, drop tablespoonfuls (15 mL) of dough about 2 inches (5 cm) apart on prepared cookie sheets. Bake one sheet at a time in preheated oven for 10 to 12 minutes or until edges start to turn lightly golden.

4. Immediately slide parchment paper onto a wire cooling rack. Cool cookies for 5 minutes, then transfer from parchment paper to cooling rack and cool completely.

Chewy Oatmeal Cookies

I love using golden raisins in oatmeal cookies because of their sweet, fruity flavor.

Tip

Use a cookie scoop to uniformly portion cookie dough and ensure even baking.

Variation

Substitute chopped walnuts for chopped pecans.

- **Preheat oven to 350°F (180°C)**
- **Cookie sheets, lined with parchment paper**

1¼ cups	all-purpose flour	300 mL
1 tbsp	baking powder	15 mL
½ tsp	salt	2 mL
1 cup	vegetable shortening	250 mL
1½ cups	packed light brown sugar	375 mL
2	eggs	2
2 tsp	vanilla extract	10 mL
3 cups	quick-cooking rolled oats	750 mL
1 cup	golden raisins	250 mL
1 cup	chopped pecans	250 mL

1. In a bowl, whisk together flour, baking powder and salt until well combined. Set aside.

2. In a large bowl, using an electric mixer on medium speed, cream shortening and brown sugar until light and fluffy, about 3 minutes. Add eggs one at a time, beating well after each addition. Beat in vanilla. Scrape down sides of bowl. On low speed or using a wooden spoon, gradually add flour mixture, beating just until blended. Gradually stir in oats. By hand, fold in raisins and pecans.

3. Using a cookie scoop or spoons, drop tablespoonfuls (15 mL) of dough about 2 inches (5 cm) apart on prepared cookie sheets. Bake one sheet at a time in preheated oven for 10 to 12 minutes or until edges start to turn lightly golden.

4. Immediately slide parchment paper onto a wire cooling rack. Cool cookies for 5 minutes, then transfer from parchment paper to cooling rack and cool completely.

Oatmeal Walnut Cookies

●●●

There is something very special about blending the flavors of oats, brown sugar, maple and walnuts.

Tip

Toasting nuts brings out their flavor and makes them crunchy.

Variation

Substitute chopped pecans for chopped walnuts

- Preheat oven to 350°F (180°C)
- Cookie sheets, lined with parchment paper

1½ cups	all-purpose flour	375 mL
2 tsp	baking powder	10 mL
½ tsp	baking soda	2 mL
¼ tsp	salt	1 mL
¾ cup	unsalted butter, softened	175 mL
1⅓ cups	packed dark brown sugar	325 mL
2	eggs	2
1½ tsp	vanilla extract	7 mL
1 tsp	maple flavoring	5 mL
2½ cups	quick-cooking rolled oats	625 mL
2 cups	chopped walnuts	500 mL

1. In a bowl, whisk together flour, baking powder, baking soda and salt until well combined. Set aside.

2. In a large bowl, using an electric mixer on medium speed, cream butter and brown sugar until light and fluffy, about 3 minutes. Add eggs one at a time, beating well after each addition. Beat in vanilla and maple flavoring. Scrape down sides of bowl. On low speed or using a wooden spoon, gradually add flour mixture, beating just until blended. Gradually stir in oats. By hand, fold in walnuts.

3. Using a cookie scoop or spoons, drop tablespoonfuls (15 mL) of dough about 2 inches (5 cm) apart on prepared cookie sheets. Bake one sheet at a time in preheated oven for 10 to 12 minutes or until edges start to turn lightly golden.

4. Immediately slide parchment paper onto a wire cooling rack. Cool cookies for 5 minutes, then transfer from parchment paper to cooling rack and cool completely.

Oatmeal Chippers

Chocolate chips are a wonderful addition to an oatmeal cookie rich in brown sugar.

Tip

Fold in the chocolate by hand to keep from overworking the dough after the flour and oats are mixed in. Overworking the dough will make the cookies tough.

Variation

Oatmeal Nut Chippers: By hand, fold 1 cup (250 mL) of chopped walnuts or pecans into dough along with the chocolate.

- Preheat oven to 350°F (180°C)
- Cookie sheets, lined with parchment paper

1¾ cups	all-purpose flour	425 mL
1 tsp	baking powder	5 mL
1 tsp	baking soda	5 mL
¼ tsp	salt	1 mL
1 cup	unsalted butter, softened	250 mL
1½ cups	packed dark brown sugar	375 mL
2	eggs	2
2 tsp	vanilla extract	10 mL
2¾ cups	quick-cooking rolled oats	675 mL
2 cups	chopped semisweet chocolate or semisweet chocolate chips	500 mL

1. In a bowl, whisk together flour, baking powder, baking soda and salt until well combined. Set aside.

2. In a large bowl, using an electric mixer on medium speed, cream butter and brown sugar until light and fluffy, about 3 minutes. Add eggs one at a time, beating well after each addition. Beat in vanilla. Scrape down sides of bowl. On low speed or using a wooden spoon, gradually add flour mixture, beating just until blended. Gradually stir in oats. By hand, fold in chocolate.

3. Using a cookie scoop or spoons, drop tablespoonfuls (15 mL) of dough about 2 inches (5 cm) apart on prepared cookie sheets. Bake one sheet at a time in preheated oven for 10 to 12 minutes or until edges start to turn lightly golden.

4. Immediately slide parchment paper onto a wire cooling rack. Cool cookies for 5 minutes, then transfer from parchment paper to cooling rack and cool completely.

Cranberry Oat Cookies

Makes about 4 dozen cookies

● ● ●

I love the taste of cranberries and pecans in this chewy oatmeal cookie. These make a perfect fall treat.

Tip

Always taste nuts before adding them to cookies to make sure they are fresh.

- ● **Preheat oven to 350°F (180°C)**
- ● **Cookie sheets, lined with parchment paper**

1½ cups	all-purpose flour	375 mL
1½ tsp	baking powder	7 mL
½ tsp	baking soda	2 mL
¼ tsp	salt	1 mL
¾ cup	unsalted butter, softened	175 mL
1⅓ cups	granulated sugar	325 mL
2	eggs	2
2 tsp	grated orange zest	10 mL
1½ tsp	vanilla extract	7 mL
2½ cups	quick-cooking rolled oats	625 mL
1½ cups	dried cranberries	375 mL
1 cup	chopped pecans	250 mL

1. In a bowl, whisk together flour, baking powder, baking soda and salt until well combined. Set aside.

2. In a large bowl, using an electric mixer on medium speed, cream butter and granulated sugar until light and fluffy, about 3 minutes. Add eggs one at a time, beating well after each addition. Beat in orange zest and vanilla. Scrape down sides of bowl. On low speed or using a wooden spoon, gradually add flour mixture, beating just until blended. Gradually stir in oats. By hand, fold in cranberries and pecans.

3. Using a cookie scoop or spoons, drop tablespoonfuls (15 mL) of dough about 2 inches (5 cm) apart on prepared cookie sheets. Bake one sheet at a time in preheated oven for 10 to 12 minutes or until edges start to turn lightly golden.

4. Immediately slide parchment paper onto a wire cooling rack. Cool cookies for 5 minutes, then transfer from parchment paper to cooling rack and cool completely.

Pineapple Apricot Oatmeal Drops

Pineapple and apricots are a great flavor combination. Add them to oatmeal cookies, and the cookies become an award-winning treat.

Tip

To keep dried apricots from sticking to the chopping knife, lightly spray the blade with nonstick cooking spray.

- Preheat oven to 350°F (180°C)
- Cookie sheets, lined with parchment paper

1½ cups	canned juice-packed crushed pineapple	375 mL
1 cup	chopped dried apricots	250 mL
1¾ cups	all-purpose flour	425 mL
1½ tsp	baking powder	7 mL
¾ tsp	baking soda	3 mL
¼ tsp	salt	1 mL
⅔ cup	unsalted butter, softened	150 mL
⅔ cup	vegetable shortening	150 mL
¾ cup	granulated sugar	175 mL
¾ cup	packed light brown sugar	175 mL
2	eggs	2
3 cups	quick-cooking rolled oats	750 mL
⅔ cup	chopped roasted unsalted macadamia nuts	150 mL
½ cup	sweetened flaked coconut	125 mL

1. In a bowl, combine pineapple and apricots. Set aside and let soak for 30 minutes.
2. In a bowl, whisk together flour, baking powder, baking soda and salt until well combined. Set aside.
3. In a large bowl, using an electric mixer on medium speed, cream butter, shortening, granulated sugar and brown sugar until light and fluffy, about 3 minutes. Add eggs one at a time, beating well after each addition. Scrape down sides of bowl. On low speed or using a wooden spoon, gradually add flour mixture, beating just until blended. Gradually stir in oats. By hand, fold in macadamia nuts and coconut. Drain apricots and pineapple well and fold into dough.
4. Using a cookie scoop or spoons, drop tablespoonfuls (15 mL) of dough about 2 inches (5 cm) apart on prepared cookie sheets. Bake one sheet at a time in preheated oven for 10 to 12 minutes or until edges start to turn lightly golden.
5. Immediately slide parchment paper onto a wire cooling rack. Cool cookies for 5 minutes, then transfer from parchment paper to cooling rack and cool completely.

Old-Fashioned Oatmeal Cookies

Makes about 3 dozen cookies

These are like the cookies grandmother used to make.

Tip

Sugar caramelizes as it bakes and helps give cookies their lovely golden color.

- **Preheat oven to 350°F (180°C)**
- **Cookie sheets, lined with parchment paper**

1½ cups	all-purpose flour	375 mL
1 tsp	baking powder	5 mL
1 tsp	ground cinnamon	5 mL
½ tsp	baking soda	2 mL
¼ tsp	salt	1 mL
¾ cup	unsalted butter, softened	175 mL
⅔ cup	granulated sugar	150 mL
⅔ cup	packed dark brown sugar	150 mL
2	eggs	2
1 tsp	vanilla extract	5 mL
2½ cups	quick-cooking rolled oats	625 mL

1. In a bowl, whisk together flour, baking powder, cinnamon, baking soda and salt until well combined. Set aside.

2. In a large bowl, using an electric mixer on medium speed, cream butter, granulated sugar and brown sugar until light and fluffy, about 3 minutes. Add eggs one at a time, beating well after each addition. Beat in vanilla. Scrape down sides of bowl. On low speed or using a wooden spoon, gradually add flour mixture, beating just until blended. Gradually stir in oats.

3. Using a cookie scoop or spoons, drop tablespoonfuls (15 mL) of dough about 2 inches (5 cm) apart on prepared cookie sheets. Bake one sheet at a time in preheated oven for 10 to 12 minutes or until edges start to turn lightly golden.

4. Immediately slide parchment paper onto a wire cooling rack. Cool cookies for 5 minutes, then transfer from parchment paper to cooling rack and cool completely.

White Chocolate Oatmeal Cookies

Makes about 3½ dozen cookies ● ● ●

Adding white chocolate and almond extract to the mix elevates these cookies to a whole new level.

Tip

To prevent tops or bottoms of cookies from becoming too brown, bake one sheet at a time on an oven rack positioned in the center of the oven.

Variation

By hand, fold 1 cup (250 mL) chopped unsalted almonds or roasted unsalted macadamia nuts into dough with white chocolate.

- Preheat oven to 350°F (180°C)
- Cookie sheets, lined with parchment paper

1¾ cups	all-purpose flour	425 mL
1 tsp	baking powder	5 mL
1 tsp	baking soda	5 mL
1 cup	unsalted butter, softened	250 mL
¾ cup	granulated sugar	175 mL
¾ cup	packed light brown sugar	175 mL
2	eggs	2
1 tsp	vanilla extract	5 mL
½ tsp	almond extract	2 mL
2¾ cups	quick-cooking rolled oats	675 mL
2 cups	chopped white chocolate or white chocolate chips	500 mL

1. In a bowl, whisk together flour, baking powder and baking soda until well combined. Set aside.

2. In a large bowl, using an electric mixer on medium speed, cream butter, granulated sugar and brown sugar until light and fluffy, about 3 minutes. Add eggs one at a time, beating well after each addition. Beat in vanilla and almond extract. Scrape down sides of bowl. On low speed or using a wooden spoon, gradually add flour mixture, beating just until blended. Gradually stir in oats. By hand, fold in white chocolate.

3. Using a cookie scoop or spoons, drop tablespoonfuls (15 mL) of dough about 2 inches (5 cm) apart on prepared cookie sheets. Bake one sheet at a time in preheated oven for 10 to 12 minutes or until edges start to turn lightly golden.

4. Immediately slide parchment paper onto a wire cooling rack. Cool cookies for 5 minutes, then transfer from parchment paper to cooling rack and cool completely.

Coconut Oat Chews

Add chewy coconut to a yummy oatmeal dough, and you have a delightful cookie.

Tips

Dark-colored cookie sheets can cause cookies to burn. Use a heavy-gauge aluminum cookie sheet to prevent cookies from overbrowning.

Use a mild-flavored oil, such as canola oil, for baking. Olive oil and other strong-flavored oils like peanut oil will give cookies an unpleasant taste.

- Preheat oven to 350°F (180°C)
- Cookie sheets, lined with parchment paper

1 1/3 cups	all-purpose flour	325 mL
1 1/2 tsp	baking powder	7 mL
1/2 tsp	baking soda	2 mL
1/4 tsp	salt	1 mL
2	eggs	2
2/3 cup	vegetable oil	150 mL
1 cup	packed light brown sugar	250 mL
1/3 cup	granulated sugar	75 mL
1 tsp	vanilla extract	5 mL
1/2 tsp	coconut flavoring	2 mL
2 2/3 cups	quick-cooking rolled oats	650 mL
1 1/2 cups	sweetened flaked coconut	375 mL

1. In a bowl, whisk together flour, baking powder, baking soda and salt until well combined. Set aside.

2. In a large bowl, using an electric mixer on medium speed, lightly beat eggs. Gradually beat in oil. Add brown sugar and granulated sugar and cream until light and fluffy, about 3 minutes. Beat in vanilla extract and coconut flavoring. Scrape down sides of bowl. On low speed or using a wooden spoon, gradually add flour mixture, beating just until blended. Gradually stir in oats. By hand, fold in coconut.

3. Using a cookie scoop or spoons, drop tablespoonfuls (15 mL) of dough about 2 inches (5 cm) apart on prepared cookie sheets. Bake one sheet at a time in preheated oven for 10 to 12 minutes or until edges start to turn lightly golden.

4. Immediately slide parchment paper onto a wire cooling rack. Cool cookies for 5 minutes, then transfer from parchment paper to cooling rack and cool completely.

Peanut Butter Oat Chippers

Makes about 5 dozen cookies

Packed with peanut butter and chocolate, these wonderful cookies are a hit with both kids and adults.

Tip

You may use creamy peanut butter instead of chunky peanut butter, if you prefer.

- Preheat oven to 350°F (180°C)
- Cookie sheets, lined with parchment paper

1½ cups	all-purpose flour	375 mL
1 tbsp	baking powder	15 mL
½ tsp	salt	2 mL
¾ cup	unsalted butter, softened	175 mL
¾ cup	chunky peanut butter	175 mL
⅔ cup	granulated sugar	150 mL
⅔ cup	packed light brown sugar	150 mL
3	eggs	3
2 tsp	vanilla extract	10 mL
3½ cups	quick-cooking rolled oats	875 mL
1½ cups	chopped semisweet chocolate or semisweet chocolate chips	375 mL
1½ cups	peanut butter chips	375 mL

1. In a bowl, whisk together flour, baking powder and salt until well combined. Set aside.

2. In a large bowl, using an electric mixer on medium speed, cream butter, peanut butter, granulated sugar and brown sugar until light and fluffy, about 3 minutes. Add eggs one at a time, beating well after each addition. Beat in vanilla. Scrape down sides of bowl. On low speed or using a wooden spoon, gradually add flour mixture, beating just until blended. Gradually stir in oats. By hand, fold in chocolate and peanut butter chips.

3. Using a cookie scoop or spoons, drop tablespoonfuls (15 mL) of dough about 2 inches (5 cm) apart on prepared cookie sheets. Bake one sheet at a time in preheated oven for 12 minutes or until edges start to turn lightly golden.

4. Immediately slide parchment paper onto a wire cooling rack. Cool cookies for 5 minutes, then transfer from parchment paper to cooling rack and cool completely.

Oatmeal Pumpkin Cookies

Makes about 3½ dozen cookies ● ● ●

A festive, lightly spiced cookie that makes a perfect treat any time of year.

Tip

Use the appropriate measuring tools and techniques to accurately measure ingredients.

Variation

Substitute chopped pecans for chopped walnuts.

- Preheat oven to 350°F (180°C)
- Cookie sheets, lined with parchment paper

2 cups	all-purpose flour	500 mL
1 tsp	baking powder	5 mL
½ tsp	ground cinnamon	2 mL
½ tsp	baking soda	2 mL
¼ tsp	ground ginger	1 mL
¼ tsp	ground nutmeg	1 mL
¼ tsp	salt	1 mL
⅔ cup	unsalted butter, softened	150 mL
⅔ cup	granulated sugar	150 mL
⅔ cup	packed light brown sugar	150 mL
1	egg	1
1 cup	solid pack (purée) canned pumpkin (not pie filling)	250 mL
2 tsp	grated orange zest	10 mL
1 tsp	vanilla extract	5 mL
2½ cups	quick-cooking rolled oats	625 mL
1 cup	chopped walnuts	250 mL

1. In a bowl, whisk together flour, baking powder, cinnamon, baking soda, ginger, nutmeg and salt until well combined. Set aside.

2. In a large bowl, using an electric mixer on medium speed, cream butter, granulated sugar and brown sugar until light and fluffy, about 3 minutes. Beat in egg. Beat in pumpkin, orange zest and vanilla. Scrape down sides of bowl. On low speed or using a wooden spoon, gradually add flour mixture, beating just until blended. Gradually stir in oats. By hand, fold in walnuts.

3. Using a cookie scoop or spoons, drop tablespoonfuls (15 mL) of dough about 2 inches (5 cm) apart on prepared cookie sheets. Flatten dough slightly with a fork or the bottom of a glass. Bake one sheet at a time in preheated oven for 12 minutes or until edges start to turn lightly golden.

4. Immediately slide parchment paper onto a wire cooling rack. Cool cookies for 5 minutes, then transfer from parchment paper to cooling rack and cool completely.

Tropical Oat Cookies

● ● ●

Pineapple, coconut and macadamia nuts make these oatmeal cookies extra-special.

Tip

Use a cookie scoop to uniformly portion cookie dough and ensure even baking.

- Preheat oven to 350°F (180°C)
- Cookie sheets, lined with parchment paper

1⅔ cups	all-purpose flour	400 mL
1 tbsp	baking powder	15 mL
½ tsp	salt	2 mL
1 cup	unsalted butter, softened	250 mL
¾ cup	granulated sugar	175 mL
¾ cup	packed light brown sugar	175 mL
2	eggs	2
1 tsp	almond extract	5 mL
3 cups	quick-cooking rolled oats	750 mL
1 cup	drained canned juice-packed crushed pineapple	250 mL
¾ cup	sweetened flaked coconut	175 mL
¾ cup	chopped roasted unsalted macadamia nuts	175 mL

1. In a bowl, whisk together flour, baking powder and salt until well combined. Set aside.

2. In a large bowl, using an electric mixer on medium speed, cream butter, granulated sugar and brown sugar until light and fluffy, about 3 minutes. Add eggs one at a time, beating well after each addition. Beat in almond extract. Scrape down sides of bowl. On low speed or using a wooden spoon, gradually add flour mixture, beating just until blended. Gradually stir in oats. By hand, fold in pineapple, coconut and macadamia nuts.

3. Lightly grease hands with nonstick cooking spray. Roll pieces of dough into 1-inch (2.5 cm) balls. Place on prepared cookie sheets. Bake one sheet at a time in preheated oven for 10 to 12 minutes or until edges start to turn lightly golden.

4. Immediately slide parchment paper onto a wire cooling rack. Cool cookies for 5 minutes, then transfer from parchment paper to cooling rack and cool completely.

Chocolate-Glazed Oatmeal Cookies

Drizzled with chocolate and sweetened with coconut, these cookies are a big hit around my house.

Tips

Brown sugar adds moisture and rich flavor to cookies.

Let glaze set before storing cookies between layers of wax paper in a tightly sealed container.

- Preheat oven to 350°F (180°C)
- Cookie sheets, lined with parchment paper

Cookies

1⅔ cups	all-purpose flour	400 mL
1½ tsp	baking powder	7 mL
½ tsp	baking soda	2 mL
¼ tsp	salt	1 mL
⅔ cup	unsalted butter, softened	150 mL
1¼ cups	packed dark brown sugar	300 mL
2	eggs	2
1 tsp	vanilla extract	5 mL
¾ cup	sweetened flaked coconut	175 mL
2 cups	quick-cooking rolled oats	500 mL

Glaze

1 cup	confectioner's (powdered/icing) sugar	250 mL
¼ cup	unsweetened Dutch-process cocoa powder, sifted	50 mL
1 to 2 tbsp	half-and-half (10%) cream or milk	15 to 25 mL
2 tsp	unsalted butter, at room temperature	10 mL
½ tsp	vanilla extract	2 mL

1. **Cookies:** In a bowl, whisk together flour, baking powder, baking soda and salt until well combined. Set aside.

2. In a large bowl, using an electric mixer on medium speed, cream butter and brown sugar until light and fluffy, about 3 minutes. Add eggs one at a time, beating well after each addition. Beat in vanilla. Scrape down sides of bowl. On low speed or using a wooden spoon, gradually add flour mixture, beating just until blended. Beat in coconut. Gradually stir in oats.

3. Lightly grease hands with nonstick cooking spray. Roll pieces of dough into 1-inch (2.5 cm) balls. Place on prepared cookie sheets. Bake one sheet at a time in preheated oven for 10 to 12 minutes or until edges start to turn lightly golden.

4. Immediately slide parchment paper onto a wire cooling rack. Cool cookies for 5 minutes, then transfer from parchment paper to cooling rack and cool completely.

5. **Glaze:** In a small bowl, combine confectioner's sugar, cocoa powder, 1 tablespoon (15 mL) of the cream, butter and vanilla. Using a small whisk or a fork, blend until glaze is smooth and thin enough to drizzle from a fork. Add more cream as needed to achieve the right consistency. Drizzle glaze over cooled cookies.

Banana Rum Oatmeal Cookies

With a South Seas island flavor, these cookies are a great way to use ripe bananas.

Tip

Store unopened packages of flour in a cool, dry place for up to 2 years. Always use flour before the date stamped on the package.

- **Preheat oven to 350°F (180°C)**
- **Cookie sheets, lined with parchment paper**

1¹/₄ cups	all-purpose flour	300 mL
2¹/₂ tsp	baking powder	12 mL
¹/₂ tsp	salt	2 mL
¹/₄ cup	unsalted butter, softened	50 mL
¹/₄ cup	vegetable shortening	50 mL
²/₃ cup	granulated sugar	150 mL
²/₃ cup	packed light brown sugar	150 mL
2	eggs	2
2 tsp	rum flavoring	10 mL
1 tsp	vanilla extract	5 mL
1¹/₂ cups	mashed ripe bananas	375 mL
³/₄ cup	sweetened flaked coconut	175 mL
3 cups	quick-cooking rolled oats	750 mL

1. In a bowl, whisk together flour, baking powder and salt until well combined. Set aside.

2. In a large bowl, using an electric mixer on medium speed, cream butter, shortening, granulated sugar and brown sugar until light and fluffy, about 3 minutes. Add eggs one at a time, beating well after each addition. Beat in rum flavoring and vanilla. Beat in bananas and coconut until thoroughly combined. Scrape down sides of bowl. On low speed or using a wooden spoon, gradually add flour mixture, beating just until blended. Gradually stir in oats.

3. Using a cookie scoop or spoons, drop tablespoonfuls (15 mL) of dough about 2 inches (5 cm) apart on prepared cookie sheets. Bake one sheet at a time in preheated oven for 12 minutes or until edges start to turn lightly golden.

4. Immediately slide parchment paper onto a wire cooling rack. Cool cookies for 5 minutes, then transfer from parchment paper to cooling rack and cool completely.

Lots of Oats Cookies

These yummy cookies are packed with oats and raisins.

Tip

Dark or golden raisins are both good choices for use in this recipe.

- Preheat oven to 350°F (180°C)
- Cookie sheets, lined with parchment paper

1¼ cups	all-purpose flour	300 mL
2 tsp	baking powder	10 mL
1 tsp	ground cinnamon	5 mL
1 tsp	baking soda	5 mL
¼ tsp	salt	1 mL
¼ tsp	ground nutmeg	1 mL
1 cup	unsalted butter, softened	250 mL
1½ cups	packed dark brown sugar	375 mL
3	eggs	3
2 tsp	vanilla extract	10 mL
4 cups	quick-cooking rolled oats	1 L
1½ cups	raisins	375 mL

1. In a bowl, whisk together flour, baking powder, cinnamon, baking soda, salt and nutmeg until well combined. Set aside.

2. In a large bowl, using an electric mixer on medium speed, cream butter and brown sugar until light and fluffy, about 3 minutes. Add eggs one at a time, beating well after each addition. Beat in vanilla. Scrape down sides of bowl. On low speed or using a wooden spoon, gradually add flour mixture, beating just until blended. Gradually stir in oats. By hand, fold in raisins.

3. Using a cookie scoop or spoons, drop tablespoonfuls (15 mL) of dough about 2 inches (5 cm) apart on prepared cookie sheets. Bake one sheet at a time in preheated oven for 10 to 12 minutes or until edges start to turn lightly golden.

4. Immediately slide parchment paper onto a wire cooling rack. Cool cookies for 5 minutes, then transfer from parchment paper to cooling rack and cool completely.

Molasses Oat Cookies

● ● ●

Brown sugar and molasses give these cookies their rich flavor.

Tip

Parchment paper is a heat- and grease-resistant baking paper used to line cookie sheets to prevent cookies from sticking and burning on the bottom. It can be found in most grocery stores.

- Preheat oven to 350°F (180°C)
- Cookie sheets, lined with parchment paper

1½ cups	all-purpose flour	375 mL
1½ tsp	baking powder	7 mL
½ tsp	baking soda	2 mL
¼ tsp	salt	1 mL
⅔ cup	vegetable shortening	150 mL
1¼ cups	packed dark brown sugar	300 mL
⅓ cup	fancy molasses	75 mL
2	eggs	2
1 tsp	vanilla extract	5 mL
2½ cups	quick-cooking rolled oats	625 mL

1. In a bowl, whisk together flour, baking powder, baking soda and salt until well combined. Set aside.

2. In a large bowl, using an electric mixer on medium speed, cream shortening and brown sugar until light and fluffy, about 3 minutes. Beat in molasses. Add eggs one at a time, beating well after each addition. Beat in vanilla. Scrape down sides of bowl. On low speed or using a wooden spoon, gradually add flour mixture, beating just until blended. Gradually stir in oats.

3. Using a cookie scoop or spoons, drop tablespoonfuls (15 mL) of dough about 2 inches (5 cm) apart on prepared cookie sheets. Bake one sheet at a time in preheated oven for 10 to 12 minutes or until edges start to turn lightly golden.

4. Immediately slide parchment paper onto a wire cooling rack. Cool cookies for 5 minutes, then transfer from parchment paper to cooling rack and cool completely.

Orange Oat Drops

A touch of orange makes these cookies special.

Tip

For crisp cookies, bake for 12 to 15 minutes.

Variation

Orange Chocolate Oat Drops: By hand, fold 1 cup (250 mL) chopped semisweet chocolate or semisweet chocolate chips into cookie dough.

- **Preheat oven to 350°F (180°C)**
- **Cookie sheets, lined with parchment paper**

1½ cups	all-purpose flour	375 mL
2 tsp	baking powder	10 mL
½ tsp	baking soda	2 mL
¼ tsp	salt	1 mL
¾ cup	unsalted butter, softened	175 mL
⅔ cup	granulated sugar	150 mL
⅔ cup	packed light brown sugar	150 mL
2	eggs	2
1 tsp	vanilla extract	5 mL
3 tbsp	grated orange zest	45 mL
2⅔ cups	quick-cooking rolled oats	650 mL

1. In a bowl, whisk together flour, baking powder, baking soda and salt until well combined. Set aside.

2. In a large bowl, using an electric mixer on medium speed, cream butter, granulated sugar and brown sugar until light and fluffy, about 3 minutes. Add eggs one at a time, beating well after each addition. Beat in vanilla and orange zest. Scrape down sides of bowl. On low speed or using a wooden spoon, gradually add flour mixture, beating just until blended. Gradually stir in oats.

3. Using a cookie scoop or spoons, drop tablespoonfuls (15 mL) of dough about 2 inches (5 cm) apart on prepared cookie sheets. Bake one sheet at a time in preheated oven for 10 to 12 minutes or until edges start to turn lightly golden.

4. Immediately slide parchment paper onto a wire cooling rack. Cool cookies for 5 minutes, then transfer from parchment paper to cooling rack and cool completely.

Oatmeal Almond Cookies

Makes about 3½ dozen cookies

These cookies have lots of great almond flavor.

Tip

Eggs should be at room temperature when added to the creamed butter and sugar mixture. Cold eggs can cause the mixture to break and appear curdled.

- Preheat oven to 350°F (180°C)
- Cookie sheets, lined with parchment paper

1½ cups	all-purpose flour	375 mL
1½ tsp	baking powder	7 mL
½ tsp	baking soda	2 mL
¼ tsp	salt	1 mL
¾ cup	unsalted butter, softened	175 mL
1 cup	granulated sugar	250 mL
1	egg	1
1 tsp	almond extract	5 mL
½ tsp	vanilla extract	2 mL
2½ cups	quick-cooking rolled oats	625 mL
1 cup	chopped unsalted almonds	250 mL

1. In a bowl, whisk together flour, baking powder, baking soda and salt until well combined. Set aside.

2. In a large bowl, using an electric mixer on medium speed, cream butter and granulated sugar until light and fluffy, about 3 minutes. Beat in egg. Beat in almond extract and vanilla. Scrape down sides of bowl. On low speed or using a wooden spoon, gradually add flour mixture, beating just until blended. Gradually stir in oats. By hand, fold in almonds.

3. Lightly grease hands with nonstick cooking spray. Roll pieces of dough into 1-inch (2.5 cm) balls. Place on prepared cookie sheets. Bake one sheet at a time in preheated oven for 10 to 12 minutes or until edges start to turn lightly golden.

4. Immediately slide parchment paper onto a wire cooling rack. Cool cookies for 5 minutes, then transfer from parchment paper to cooling rack and cool completely.

Banana Walnut Oatmeal Cookies

I really like the comforting blend of bananas and walnuts in these oatmeal cookies.

Tip

For the fullest flavor, use bananas with peels that are golden in color with small flecks of brown.

● **Preheat oven to 350°F (180°C)**
● **Cookie sheets, lined with parchment paper**

1¾ cups	all-purpose flour	425 mL
1½ tsp	baking powder	7 mL
1 tsp	baking soda	5 mL
¼ tsp	salt	1 mL
½ cup	unsalted butter, softened	125 mL
½ cup	vegetable shortening	125 mL
¾ cup	granulated sugar	175 mL
¾ cup	packed light brown sugar	175 mL
2	eggs	2
1 tsp	vanilla extract	5 mL
2	medium-size ripe bananas, mashed	2
3½ cups	quick-cooking rolled oats	875 mL
1 cup	chopped walnuts	250 mL

1. In a bowl, whisk together flour, baking powder, baking soda and salt until well combined. Set aside.

2. In a large bowl, using an electric mixer on medium speed, cream butter, shortening, granulated sugar and brown sugar until light and fluffy, about 3 minutes. Add eggs one at a time, beating well after each addition. Beat in vanilla and bananas. Scrape down sides of bowl. On low speed or using a wooden spoon, gradually add flour mixture, beating just until blended. Gradually stir in oats. By hand, fold in walnuts.

3. Using a cookie scoop or spoons, drop tablespoonfuls (15 mL) of dough about 2 inches (5 cm) apart on prepared cookie sheets. Bake one sheet at a time in preheated oven for 12 minutes or until edges start to turn lightly golden.

4. Immediately slide parchment paper onto a wire cooling rack. Cool cookies for 5 minutes, then transfer from parchment paper to cooling rack and cool completely.

Apricot Coconut Oatmeal Drops

Packed with apricots, coconut and almonds, these cookies are very satisfying and make a great afternoon snack.

Tip

Use a cookie scoop to uniformly portion cookie dough and ensure even baking.

- Preheat oven to 350°F (180°C)
- Cookie sheets, lined with parchment paper

1⅔ cups	all-purpose flour	400 mL
2 tsp	baking powder	10 mL
½ tsp	salt	2 mL
1 cup	unsalted butter, softened	250 mL
¾ cup	granulated sugar	175 mL
¾ cup	packed light brown sugar	175 mL
2	eggs	2
1 tsp	vanilla extract	5 mL
1 tsp	almond extract	5 mL
3 cups	quick-cooking rolled oats	750 mL
1¼ cups	chopped dried apricots	300 mL
1¼ cups	sweetened flaked coconut	300 mL
1 cup	chopped unsalted almonds	250 mL

1. In a bowl, whisk together flour, baking powder and salt until well combined. Set aside.

2. In a large bowl, using an electric mixer on medium speed, cream butter, granulated sugar and brown sugar until light and fluffy, about 3 minutes. Add eggs one at a time, beating well after each addition. Beat in vanilla and almond extract. Scrape down sides of bowl. On low speed or using a wooden spoon, gradually add flour mixture, beating just until blended. Gradually stir in oats. By hand, fold in apricots, coconut and almonds.

3. Using a cookie scoop or spoons, drop tablespoonfuls (15 mL) of dough about 2 inches (5 cm) apart on prepared cookie sheets. Bake one sheet at a time in preheated oven for 10 to 12 minutes or until edges start to turn lightly golden.

4. Immediately slide parchment paper onto a wire cooling rack. Cool cookies for 5 minutes, then transfer from parchment paper to cooling rack and cool completely.

Applesauce Oatmeal Cookies

Makes about 4 dozen cookies ● ● ●

The addition of applesauce makes these cookies moist and flavorful.

Tip

Be sure to use unsweetened applesauce in these cookies. Sweetened applesauce will make the cookies too sweet, and reducing the sugar to compensate will alter cookie texture.

Variations

Applesauce Raisin Oatmeal Cookies: Omit cinnamon and substitute raisins for walnuts.

Applesauce Cranberry Oatmeal Cookies: Omit cinnamon and substitute dried cranberries for walnuts.

- Preheat oven to 350°F (180°C)
- Cookie sheets, lined with parchment paper

2½ cups	all-purpose flour	625 mL
2 tsp	baking powder	10 mL
1½ tsp	ground cinnamon	7 mL
½ tsp	baking soda	2 mL
¼ tsp	salt	1 mL
¾ cup	unsalted butter, softened	175 mL
¾ cup	granulated sugar	175 mL
¾ cup	packed light brown sugar	175 mL
2	eggs	2
1 cup	unsweetened applesauce	250 mL
1 tsp	vanilla extract	5 mL
2½ cups	quick-cooking rolled oats	625 mL
1½ cups	chopped walnuts	375 mL

1. In a bowl, whisk together flour, baking powder, cinnamon, baking soda and salt until well combined. Set aside.

2. In a large bowl, using an electric mixer on medium speed, cream butter, granulated sugar and brown sugar until light and fluffy, about 3 minutes. Add eggs one at a time, beating well after each addition. Beat in applesauce and vanilla. Scrape down sides of bowl. On low speed or using a wooden spoon, gradually add flour mixture, beating just until blended. Gradually stir in oats. By hand, fold in walnuts.

3. Using a cookie scoop or spoons, drop tablespoonfuls (15 mL) of dough about 2 inches (5 cm) apart on prepared cookie sheets. Bake one sheet at a time in preheated oven for 12 minutes or until edges start to turn lightly golden.

4. Immediately slide parchment paper onto a wire cooling rack. Cool cookies for 5 minutes, then transfer from parchment paper to cooling rack and cool completely.

Frosted Marmalade Oat Cookies

Makes about 4½ dozen cookies

*Orange marmalade
in the cookies and
a drizzle of orange
icing overtop give
these oatmeal gems a
delightful citrus flavor.*

Tip

These oatmeal cookies
spread out during
baking, so give them
space on the pan to
expand.

- Preheat oven to 350°F (180°C)
- Cookie sheets, lined with parchment paper

Cookies

2 cups	all-purpose flour	500 mL
1½ tsp	baking powder	7 mL
½ tsp	baking soda	2 mL
¼ tsp	salt	1 mL
½ cup	unsalted butter, softened	125 mL
½ cup	vegetable shortening	125 mL
½ cup	granulated sugar	125 mL
½ cup	packed light brown sugar	125 mL
2	eggs	2
¾ cup	orange marmalade	175 mL
1 tsp	vanilla extract	5 mL
3¼ cups	quick-cooking rolled oats	800 mL

Icing

1½ cups	confectioner's (powdered/icing) sugar	375 mL
2 tbsp	unsalted butter, melted	25 mL
3 tbsp	freshly squeezed orange juice	45 mL

1. **Cookies:** In a bowl, whisk together flour, baking powder, baking soda and salt until well combined. Set aside.

2. In a large bowl, using an electric mixer on medium speed, cream butter, shortening, granulated sugar and brown sugar until light and fluffy, about 3 minutes. Add eggs one at a time, beating well after each addition. Beat in orange marmalade and vanilla. Scrape down sides of bowl. On low speed or using a wooden spoon, gradually add flour mixture, beating just until blended. Gradually stir in oats.

3. Using a cookie scoop or spoons, drop tablespoonfuls (15 mL) of dough about 3 inches (7.5 cm) apart on prepared cookie sheets. Bake one sheet at a time in preheated oven for 11 to 13 minutes or until edges start to turn lightly golden.

4. Immediately slide parchment paper onto a wire cooling rack. Cool cookies for 5 minutes, then transfer from parchment paper to cooling rack and cool completely.

5. **Icing:** In a small bowl, combine confectioner's sugar, butter and orange juice. Using a small whisk or a fork, beat until icing is smooth. Drizzle icing over cooled cookies.

Dream Cookies

●●●

Chocolate Chip Dreams 171

Chocolate Dreams 172

Double Chocolate Dreams 173

Oatmeal Dreams. 174

Apricot Dreams 175

Maple Pecan Dreams 176

Chocolate Decadence Dreams 177

White Chocolate Chip Dreams 178

Double White Chocolate Dreams . . . 179

Oatmeal Cranberry Pecan
  Dreams 180

Chocolate Almond Dreams. 181

Chocolate Chip Oatmeal Dreams . . . 182

Coconut Dreams 183

Espresso Dreams 184

Black and White Chocolate
  Dreams 185

Butterscotch Dreams 186

Apricot Coconut Dreams 187

Golden Oatmeal Dreams 188

CocoMac Dreams 189

Orange Dreams 190

Cranberry Apricot Dreams 191

Oatmeal Ambrosia Dreams. 192

Mocha Fudge Dreams 193

Coconut Oat Dreams 194

Lemon Dreams. 195

Tropical Dreams 196

Doodle Dreams 197

Cherry Oatmeal Dreams 198

Pistachio Dreams 199

Pineapple Dreams 200

Apricot Cranberry Oat Dreams 201

Toffee Dreams 202

About Dream Cookies

Dream cookies are a unique type of drop cookie. They are rich, moist, tender and chewy and loaded with flavor. The secret to creating these wonderful cookies is the instant pudding mix added to the cookie dough. It not only adds flavor but gives the cookies their special texture and helps keep them moist. Dream cookies are easy to make, and the results are simply terrific.

Because the instant pudding in the dough adds to the structure of the cookies, the dough doesn't need to be chilled before baking. In fact, these cookies turn out better if you don't chill the dough. They need to go into the oven before the pudding sets, which is what will happen if you chill the dough.

If slightly underbaked, these cookies are delightfully chewy and gooey. If baked a little longer, they have a moist, more cake-like texture. Both textures are a result of the pudding in the dough. It gives these cookies an exceptional texture and structure that cannot be found in any other type of cookie.

These cookies bake up really well on insulated cookie sheets and also do well on heavy-gauge, shiny metal sheets. Be sure to line the cookie sheet with parchment paper or a silicone mat. The pudding mix in the cookie dough makes them a little more prone to sticking than other types of cookies.

Choose a high-quality instant pudding mix or instant pudding and pie filling mix with great flavor to make these cookies. As with other cookie ingredients, this isn't the time to use a bargain mix. Make sure you use an instant pudding mix. Do not substitute a cook-and-serve pudding mix as this will not work in these cookies. Also, do not use a sugar-free instant pudding mix as this will significantly alter both the flavor and the texture of the cookies. The sugar in the pudding mix is necessary to create the proper structure. Cookies made with sugar-free pudding mix will be tough, flat and can easily burn.

Chocolate Chip Dreams

Makes about 3½ dozen cookies ● ● ●

I love chocolate chip cookies, and this recipe is one of my absolute favorites! The cookies are soft and chewy, have a rich chocolate flavor and do not spread all over the pan. To top that off, they are super-easy to make. The key is to not overbake the cookies. Whenever I take these to a gathering or party, I always come home with an empty plate and many requests for the recipe.

Tips

This basic recipe works well with any flavor of chopped chocolate or chocolate chips.

For an intensely chocolate cookie, omit nuts and replace with more chocolate.

Variation

Substitute chopped pecans for chopped walnuts. Nuts may be omitted, if you prefer.

- ● **Preheat oven to 375°F (190°C)**
- ● **Cookie sheets, lined with parchment paper**

2⅓ cups	all-purpose flour	575 mL
1	package (3.4 oz or 102 g) instant vanilla pudding mix	1
1 tsp	baking powder	5 mL
½ tsp	baking soda	2 mL
¼ tsp	salt	1 mL
½ cup	unsalted butter, softened	125 mL
½ cup	vegetable shortening	125 mL
⅔ cup	packed light brown sugar	150 mL
⅓ cup	granulated sugar	75 mL
2	eggs	2
2 tsp	vanilla extract	10 mL
2 cups	chopped semisweet chocolate or semisweet chocolate chips	500 mL
1 cup	chopped walnuts	250 mL

1. In a bowl, whisk together flour, pudding mix, baking powder, baking soda and salt until well combined. Set aside.

2. In a large bowl, using an electric mixer on medium speed, cream butter, shortening, brown sugar and granulated sugar until light and fluffy, about 2 minutes. Add eggs one at a time, beating well after each addition. Beat in vanilla. Scrape down sides of bowl. On low speed or using a wooden spoon, gradually add flour mixture, beating just until blended. By hand, fold in chocolate and walnuts.

3. Using a cookie scoop or spoons, drop tablespoonfuls (15 mL) of dough about 2 inches (5 cm) apart on prepared cookie sheets. Bake one sheet at a time in preheated oven for 8 to 10 minutes or until edges start to turn lightly golden.

4. Immediately slide parchment paper onto a wire cooling rack. Cool cookies for 5 minutes, then transfer from parchment paper to cooling rack and cool completely.

Chocolate Dreams

● ● ●

These cookies have a light chocolate flavor and a wonderful texture.

Tips

Sugar adds flavor and texture to cookies and helps keep them fresh.

All of the recipes in this book use large eggs, the standard size used for baking. If you do not have large eggs, then lightly beat your eggs and substitute ¼ cup (50 mL) beaten egg for each large egg called for in the recipe.

- Preheat oven to 375°F (190°C)
- Cookie sheets, lined with parchment paper

2½ cups	all-purpose flour	625 mL
1	package (3.4 oz or 102 g) instant chocolate pudding mix	1
1 tsp	baking powder	5 mL
½ tsp	baking soda	2 mL
¼ tsp	salt	1 mL
½ cup	unsalted butter, softened	125 mL
½ cup	vegetable shortening	125 mL
⅔ cup	packed light brown sugar	150 mL
⅓ cup	granulated sugar	75 mL
2	eggs	2
1 tsp	vanilla extract	5 mL

1. In a bowl, whisk together flour, pudding mix, baking powder, baking soda and salt until well combined. Set aside.

2. In a large bowl, using an electric mixer on medium speed, cream butter, shortening, brown sugar and granulated sugar until light and fluffy, about 2 minutes. Add eggs one at a time, beating well after each addition. Beat in vanilla. Scrape down sides of bowl. On low speed or using a wooden spoon, gradually add flour mixture, beating just until blended.

3. Using a cookie scoop or spoons, drop tablespoonfuls (15 mL) of dough about 2 inches (5 cm) apart on prepared cookie sheets. Bake one sheet at a time in preheated oven for 8 to 10 minutes or until set around the edges but slightly soft in the center.

4. Immediately slide parchment paper onto a wire cooling rack. Cool cookies for 5 minutes, then transfer from parchment paper to cooling rack and cool completely.

Double Chocolate Dreams

Makes about 3 dozen cookies

Loaded with dark brown sugar, chocolate and nuts, these wonderful cookies have a full chocolate flavor.

Tips

English walnuts, the kind typically found in grocery stores, have a mild flavor and are the best ones to use in cookies. The intense and slightly bitter taste of black walnuts can overpower the other ingredients.

Using a cookie scoop will uniformly portion cookie dough and ensure even baking.

Variation

Substitute chopped pecans or chopped unsalted almonds for chopped walnuts.

- **Preheat oven to 375°F (190°C)**
- **Cookie sheets, lined with parchment paper**

2¹⁄₃ cups	all-purpose flour	575 mL
1	package (3.4 oz or 102 g) instant chocolate pudding mix	1
1 tsp	baking powder	5 mL
½ tsp	baking soda	2 mL
¼ tsp	salt	1 mL
½ cup	unsalted butter, softened	125 mL
½ cup	vegetable shortening	125 mL
1 cup	packed dark brown sugar	250 mL
2	eggs	2
1½ tsp	vanilla extract	7 mL
1½ cups	chopped semisweet chocolate or semisweet chocolate chips	375 mL
1 cup	chopped walnuts	250 mL

1. In a bowl, whisk together flour, pudding mix, baking powder, baking soda and salt until well combined. Set aside.

2. In a large bowl, using an electric mixer on medium speed, cream butter, shortening and brown sugar until light and fluffy, about 2 minutes. Add eggs one at a time, beating well after each addition. Beat in vanilla. Scrape down sides of bowl. On low speed or using a wooden spoon, gradually add flour mixture, beating just until blended. By hand, fold in chocolate and walnuts.

3. Using a cookie scoop or spoons, drop tablespoonfuls (15 mL) of dough about 2 inches (5 cm) apart on prepared cookie sheets. Bake one sheet at a time in preheated oven for 8 to 10 minutes or until set around the edges but slightly soft in the center.

4. Immediately slide parchment paper onto a wire cooling rack. Cool cookies for 5 minutes, then transfer from parchment paper to cooling rack and cool completely.

Oatmeal Dreams

These delicious treats are one of my favorites.

Tip

Using egg substitute in place of fresh eggs in cookies and baked goods is not advisable. Egg substitutes are made primarily from egg whites and will significantly affect the quality of your cookies.

Variation

Oatmeal Raisin Dreams: By hand, stir 1½ cups (375 mL) dark or golden raisins into cookie dough after mixing.

- Preheat oven to 375°F (190°C)
- Cookie sheets, lined with parchment paper

1²⁄₃ cups	all-purpose flour	400 mL
1	package (3.4 oz or 102 g) instant vanilla pudding mix	1
1½ tsp	ground cinnamon	7 mL
1½ tsp	baking powder	7 mL
½ tsp	baking soda	2 mL
¼ tsp	salt	1 mL
½ cup	unsalted butter, softened	125 mL
½ cup	vegetable shortening	125 mL
1 cup	packed dark brown sugar	250 mL
2	eggs	2
1½ tsp	vanilla extract	7 mL
3¼ cups	quick-cooking rolled oats	800 mL

1. In a bowl, whisk together flour, pudding mix, cinnamon, baking powder, baking soda and salt until well combined. Set aside.

2. In a large bowl, using an electric mixer on medium speed, cream butter, shortening and brown sugar until light and fluffy, about 2 minutes. Add eggs one at a time, beating well after each addition. Beat in vanilla. Scrape down sides of bowl. On low speed or using a wooden spoon, gradually add flour mixture, beating just until blended. Gradually stir in oats.

3. Using a cookie scoop or spoons, drop tablespoonfuls (15 mL) of dough about 2 inches (5 cm) apart on prepared cookie sheets. Bake one sheet at a time in preheated oven for 8 to 10 minutes or until edges start to turn lightly golden.

4. Immediately slide parchment paper onto a wire cooling rack. Cool cookies for 5 minutes, then transfer from parchment paper to cooling rack and cool completely.

Apricot Dreams

● ● ●

I love the combination of apricots and macadamia nuts in these yummy cookies.

Tip

French vanilla pudding gives these cookies a rich flavor, but vanilla pudding may be substituted.

Variation

Substitute chopped unsalted almonds for chopped macadamia nuts.

- Preheat oven to 375°F (190°C)
- Cookie sheets, lined with parchment paper

2 cups	chopped dried apricots	500 mL
½ cup	freshly squeezed orange juice	125 mL
3 cups	all-purpose flour	750 mL
1	package (3.4 oz or 102 g) instant French vanilla pudding mix	1
2 tsp	baking powder	10 mL
½ tsp	baking soda	2 mL
¼ tsp	salt	1 mL
½ cup	unsalted butter, softened	125 mL
½ cup	vegetable shortening	125 mL
½ cup	granulated sugar	125 mL
½ cup	packed light brown sugar	125 mL
2	eggs	2
1 tsp	vanilla extract	5 mL
½ tsp	almond extract	2 mL
1 tsp	grated orange zest	5 mL
1 cup	chopped roasted unsalted macadamia nuts	250 mL

1. In a small bowl, combine apricots and orange juice. Set aside and let stand 15 minutes, stirring occasionally.
2. In a bowl, whisk together flour, pudding mix, baking powder, baking soda and salt until well combined. Set aside.
3. In a large bowl, using an electric mixer on medium speed, cream butter, shortening, granulated sugar and brown sugar until light and fluffy, about 2 minutes. Add eggs one at a time, beating well after each addition. Beat in vanilla, almond extract and orange zest. Scrape down sides of bowl. On low speed or using a wooden spoon, gradually add flour mixture, beating just until blended. By hand, fold in apricot mixture and macadamia nuts.
4. Using a cookie scoop or spoons, drop tablespoonfuls (15 mL) of dough about 2 inches (5 cm) apart on prepared cookie sheets. Bake one sheet at a time in preheated oven for 8 to 10 minutes or until edges start to turn lightly golden.
5. Immediately slide parchment paper onto a wire cooling rack. Cool cookies for 5 minutes, then transfer from parchment paper to cooling rack and cool completely.

Maple Pecan Dreams

Makes about 3 dozen cookies

The classic pairing of maple and pecans makes these chewy cookies a big hit.

Tip

Flavorings such as maple, rum and brandy give cookies a stronger flavor than their liquid counterparts. A teaspoon (5 mL) of maple flavoring will give as much maple flavor as $\frac{1}{4}$ cup (125 mL) maple syrup without adding that much liquid.

Variation

Maple Walnut Dreams: Substitute chopped walnuts for chopped pecans.

- Preheat oven to 375°F (190°C)
- Cookie sheets, lined with parchment paper

2$\frac{1}{3}$ cups	all-purpose flour	575 mL
1	package (3.4 oz or 102 g) instant vanilla pudding mix	1
1 tsp	baking powder	5 mL
$\frac{1}{2}$ tsp	baking soda	2 mL
$\frac{1}{4}$ tsp	salt	1 mL
$\frac{1}{2}$ cup	unsalted butter, softened	125 mL
$\frac{1}{2}$ cup	vegetable shortening	125 mL
1 cup	packed dark brown sugar	250 mL
2	eggs	2
2 tsp	maple flavoring	10 mL
$\frac{1}{2}$ tsp	vanilla extract	2 mL
2$\frac{1}{2}$ cups	chopped pecans	625 mL

1. In a bowl, whisk together flour, pudding mix, baking powder, baking soda and salt until well combined. Set aside.

2. In a large bowl, using an electric mixer on medium speed, cream butter, shortening and brown sugar until light and fluffy, about 2 minutes. Add eggs one at a time, beating well after each addition. Beat in maple flavoring and vanilla. Scrape down sides of bowl. On low speed or using a wooden spoon, gradually add flour mixture, beating just until blended. By hand, fold in pecans.

3. Using a cookie scoop or spoons, drop tablespoonfuls (15 mL) of dough about 2 inches (5 cm) apart on prepared cookie sheets. Bake one sheet at a time in preheated oven for 8 to 10 minutes or until edges start to turn lightly golden.

4. Immediately slide parchment paper onto a wire cooling rack. Cool cookies for 5 minutes, then transfer from parchment paper to cooling rack and cool completely.

Chocolate Decadence Dreams

Makes about 2½ dozen cookies ● ● ●

Rich, full of chocolate and decadent, these intense cookies are a chocolate-lover's dream!

Tip

These cookies are also great made with chopped white chocolate or white chocolate chips or with a combination of white chocolate and sweet dark chocolate.

Variations

Chocolate Walnut Decadence Dreams: By hand, fold in 1 cup (250 mL) chopped walnuts along with the chocolate.

- Preheat oven to 375°F (190°C)
- Cookie sheets, lined with parchment paper

2⅓ cups	all-purpose flour	575 mL
1	package (3.4 oz or 102 g) instant chocolate fudge pudding mix	1
1 tsp	baking powder	5 mL
½ tsp	baking soda	2 mL
¼ tsp	salt	1 mL
½ cup	unsalted butter, softened	125 mL
½ cup	vegetable shortening	125 mL
1 cup	packed dark brown sugar	250 mL
2	eggs	2
2 tsp	vanilla extract	10 mL
1½ cups	chopped sweet dark chocolate or sweet dark chocolate chips	375 mL

1. In a bowl, whisk together flour, pudding mix, baking powder, baking soda and salt until well combined. Set aside.

2. In a large bowl, using an electric mixer on medium speed, cream butter, shortening and brown sugar until light and fluffy, about 2 minutes. Add eggs one at a time, beating well after each addition. Beat in vanilla. Scrape down sides of bowl. On low speed or using a wooden spoon, gradually add flour mixture, beating just until blended. By hand, fold in chocolate.

3. Using a cookie scoop or spoons, drop tablespoonfuls (15 mL) of dough about 2 inches (5 cm) apart on prepared cookie sheets. Bake one sheet at a time in preheated oven for 8 to 10 minutes or until set around the edges but slightly soft in the center.

4. Immediately slide parchment paper onto a wire cooling rack. Cool cookies for 5 minutes, then transfer from parchment paper to cooling rack and cool completely.

White Chocolate Chip Dreams

● ● ●

These elegant white chocolate chip cookies are a great addition to any cookie collection.

Tips

If you have trouble with the bottom of your cookies browning too much or burning, try using insulated cookie sheets.

For the best flavor, use chopped white chocolate or white chocolate chips rather than baking chips labeled as "white" or "vanilla." These imitation chips do not contain the high ratio of cocoa butter that gives white chocolate its special flavor.

- **Preheat oven to 375°F (190°C)**
- **Cookie sheets, lined with parchment paper**

2⅓ cups	all-purpose flour	575 mL
1	package (3.4 oz or 102 g) instant vanilla pudding mix	1
1 tsp	baking powder	5 mL
½ tsp	baking soda	2 mL
¼ tsp	salt	1 mL
½ cup	unsalted butter, softened	125 mL
½ cup	vegetable shortening	125 mL
½ cup	granulated sugar	125 mL
½ cup	packed light brown sugar	125 mL
2	eggs	2
1 tsp	vanilla extract	5 mL
2 cups	chopped white chocolate or white chocolate chips	500 mL

1. In a bowl, whisk together flour, pudding mix, baking powder, baking soda and salt until well combined. Set aside.

2. In a large bowl, using an electric mixer on medium speed, cream butter, shortening, granulated sugar and brown sugar until light and fluffy, about 2 minutes. Add eggs one at a time, beating well after each addition. Beat in vanilla. Scrape down sides of bowl. On low speed or using a wooden spoon, gradually add flour mixture, beating just until blended. By hand, fold in white chocolate.

3. Using a cookie scoop or spoons, drop tablespoonfuls (15 mL) of dough about 2 inches (5 cm) apart on prepared cookie sheets. Bake one sheet at a time in preheated oven for 8 to 10 minutes or until edges start to turn lightly golden.

4. Immediately slide parchment paper onto a wire cooling rack. Cool cookies for 5 minutes, then transfer from parchment paper to cooling rack and cool completely.

Double White Chocolate Dreams

White chocolate pudding adds an extra level of flavor and richness to these special cookies.

Tip

Use regular unsalted butter in stick or brick form for making cookies. Whipped butters contain air while "light" butters contain a lot of water, both of which will produce flat, tough cookies.

- Preheat oven to 375°F (190°C)
- Cookie sheets, lined with parchment paper

2⅓ cups	all-purpose flour	575 mL
1	package (3.4 oz or 102 g) instant white chocolate pudding mix	1
1 tsp	baking powder	5 mL
½ tsp	baking soda	2 mL
¼ tsp	salt	1 mL
½ cup	unsalted butter, softened	125 mL
½ cup	vegetable shortening	125 mL
⅔ cup	granulated sugar	150 mL
⅓ cup	packed light brown sugar	75 mL
2	eggs	2
1 tsp	vanilla extract	5 mL
1½ cups	chopped white chocolate or white chocolate chips	375 mL
1 cup	chopped roasted unsalted macadamia nuts	250 mL

1. In a bowl, whisk together flour, pudding mix, baking powder, baking soda and salt until well combined. Set aside.

2. In a large bowl, using an electric mixer on medium speed, cream butter, shortening, granulated sugar and brown sugar until light and fluffy, about 2 minutes. Add eggs one at a time, beating well after each addition. Beat in vanilla. Scrape down sides of bowl. On low speed or using a wooden spoon, gradually add flour mixture, beating just until blended. By hand, fold in white chocolate and macadamia nuts.

3. Using a cookie scoop or spoons, drop tablespoonfuls (15 mL) of dough about 2 inches (5 cm) apart on prepared cookie sheets. Bake one sheet at a time in preheated oven for 8 to 10 minutes or until edges start to turn lightly golden.

4. Immediately slide parchment paper onto a wire cooling rack. Cool cookies for 5 minutes, then transfer from parchment paper to cooling rack and cool completely.

Oatmeal Cranberry Pecan Dreams

Makes about 4 dozen cookies ● ● ●

The combination of dried cranberries and crunchy pecans make these flavorful oatmeal cookies very popular. They disappear in a hurry!

Tip

Nuts can turn rancid quickly. If you're not going to use them within a couple of weeks, tightly wrap the nuts and store them in the freezer to preserve their flavor.

- Preheat oven to 375°F (190°C)
- Cookie sheets, lined with parchment paper

1⅓ cups	all-purpose flour	325 mL
1	package (3.4 oz or 102 g) instant vanilla pudding mix	1
1½ tsp	baking powder	7 mL
½ tsp	baking soda	2 mL
¼ tsp	salt	1 mL
½ cup	unsalted butter, softened	125 mL
½ cup	vegetable shortening	125 mL
1 cup	packed light brown sugar	250 mL
2	eggs	2
1½ tsp	vanilla extract	7 mL
3 cups	quick-cooking rolled oats	750 mL
1½ cups	dried cranberries	375 mL
1 cup	chopped pecans	250 mL

1. In a bowl, whisk together flour, pudding mix, baking powder, baking soda and salt until well combined. Set aside.

2. In a large bowl, using an electric mixer on medium speed, cream butter, shortening and brown sugar until light and fluffy, about 2 minutes. Add eggs one at a time, beating well after each addition. Beat in vanilla. Scrape down sides of bowl. On low speed or using a wooden spoon, gradually add flour mixture, beating just until blended. Gradually stir in oats. By hand, fold in cranberries and pecans.

3. Using a cookie scoop or spoons, drop tablespoonfuls (15 mL) of dough about 2 inches (5 cm) apart on prepared cookie sheets. Bake one sheet at a time in preheated oven for 8 to 10 minutes or until edges start to turn lightly golden.

4. Immediately slide parchment paper onto a wire cooling rack. Cool cookies for 5 minutes, then transfer from parchment paper to cooling rack and cool completely.

Chocolate Almond Dreams

These cookies have a light chocolate flavor and a wonderful texture.

Tip

Baking powder is a compound leavener. The primary ingredient is baking soda, but baking powder also contains cornstarch and an acid, usually cream of tartar, to activate the baking soda. The cornstarch acts as a buffer to delay the reaction of the baking soda and acid after combination with the liquid.

Variations

Chocolate Walnut Dreams: Substitute vanilla extract for almond extract and chopped walnuts for chopped almonds.

Chocolate Pecan Dreams: Substitute vanilla extract for almond extract and chopped pecans for chopped almonds.

Chocolate Hazelnut Dreams: Substitute chopped unsalted hazelnuts for chopped almonds.

- Preheat oven to 375°F (190°C)
- Cookie sheets, lined with parchment paper

2½ cups	all-purpose flour	625 mL
1	package (3.4 oz or 102 g) instant chocolate pudding mix	1
1 tsp	baking powder	5 mL
½ tsp	baking soda	2 mL
¼ tsp	salt	1 mL
½ cup	unsalted butter, softened	125 mL
½ cup	vegetable shortening	125 mL
1 cup	packed light brown sugar	250 mL
2	eggs	2
1 tsp	almond extract	5 mL
1½ cups	chopped unsalted almonds	375 mL

1. In a bowl, whisk together flour, pudding mix, baking powder, baking soda and salt until well combined. Set aside.

2. In a large bowl, using an electric mixer on medium speed, cream butter, shortening and brown sugar until light and fluffy, about 2 minutes. Add eggs one at a time, beating well after each addition. Beat in almond extract. Scrape down sides of bowl. On low speed or using a wooden spoon, gradually add flour mixture, beating just until blended. By hand, fold in almonds.

3. Using a cookie scoop or spoons, drop tablespoonfuls (15 mL) of dough about 2 inches (5 cm) apart on prepared cookie sheets. Bake one sheet at a time in preheated oven for 8 to 10 minutes or until set around the edges but slightly soft in the center.

4. Immediately slide parchment paper onto a wire cooling rack. Cool cookies for 5 minutes, then transfer from parchment paper to cooling rack and cool completely.

Chocolate Chip Oatmeal Dreams

Makes about 4 dozen cookies ● ● ●

For many cookie-lovers, chocolate and oatmeal are the perfect combination.

Tip

Prepare and measure all of the ingredients before you start mixing the cookies.

- Preheat oven to 375°F (190°C)
- Cookie sheets, lined with parchment paper

1½ cups	all-purpose flour	375 mL
1	package (3.4 oz or 102 g) instant vanilla pudding mix	1
1 tsp	baking powder	5 mL
½ tsp	baking soda	2 mL
¼ tsp	salt	1 mL
½ cup	unsalted butter, softened	125 mL
½ cup	vegetable shortening	125 mL
⅔ cup	packed light brown sugar	150 mL
⅓ cup	granulated sugar	75 mL
2	eggs	2
2 tsp	vanilla extract	10 mL
3¼ cups	quick-cooking rolled oats	800 mL
2 cups	chopped semisweet chocolate or semisweet chocolate chips	500 mL
1 cup	chopped walnuts	250 mL

1. In a bowl, whisk together flour, pudding mix, baking powder, baking soda and salt until well combined. Set aside.
2. In a large bowl, using an electric mixer on medium speed, cream butter, shortening, brown sugar and granulated sugar until light and fluffy, about 2 minutes. Add eggs one at a time, beating well after each addition. Beat in vanilla. Scrape down sides of bowl. On low speed or using a wooden spoon, gradually add flour mixture, beating just until blended. Gradually stir in oats. By hand, fold in chocolate and walnuts.
3. Using a cookie scoop or spoons, drop tablespoonfuls (15 mL) of dough about 2 inches (5 cm) apart on prepared cookie sheets. Bake one sheet at a time in preheated oven for 8 to 10 minutes or until edges start to turn lightly golden.
4. Immediately slide parchment paper onto a wire cooling rack. Cool cookies for 5 minutes, then transfer from parchment paper to cooling rack and cool completely.

Coconut Dreams

Coconut-lovers will flip over these flavorful, tender cookies.

Tip

Eggs add to the structure and texture of cookies and help bind the ingredients. All of the recipes in this book use large eggs, the standard size used for baking. If you do not have large eggs, then lightly beat your eggs and substitute ¼ cup (50 mL) beaten egg for each large egg called for in the recipe.

- Preheat oven to 375°F (190°C)
- Cookie sheets, lined with parchment paper

2⅓ cups	all-purpose flour	575 mL
1	package (3.4 oz or 102 g) instant vanilla pudding mix	1
1 tsp	baking powder	5 mL
½ tsp	baking soda	2 mL
¼ tsp	salt	1 mL
2 cups	sweetened flaked coconut	500 mL
½ cup	unsalted butter, softened	125 mL
½ cup	vegetable shortening	125 mL
½ cup	granulated sugar	125 mL
½ cup	packed light brown sugar	125 mL
2	eggs	2
1 tsp	vanilla extract	5 mL
1 tsp	almond extract	5 mL

1. In a bowl, whisk together flour, pudding mix, baking powder, baking soda and salt until well combined. Stir in coconut. Set aside.

2. In a large bowl, using an electric mixer on medium speed, cream butter, shortening, granulated sugar and brown sugar until light and fluffy, about 2 minutes. Add eggs one at a time, beating well after each addition. Beat in vanilla and almond extract. Scrape down sides of bowl. On low speed or using a wooden spoon, gradually add flour mixture, beating just until blended.

3. Using a cookie scoop or spoons, drop tablespoonfuls (15 mL) of dough about 2 inches (5 cm) apart on prepared cookie sheets. Bake one sheet at a time in preheated oven for 8 to 10 minutes or until edges start to turn lightly golden.

4. Immediately slide parchment paper onto a wire cooling rack. Cool cookies for 5 minutes, then transfer from parchment paper to cooling rack and cool completely.

Espresso Dreams

These delightful cookies are a coffee-lover's dream.

Tips

Instant espresso powder can be found in the coffee aisle of most major grocery stores.

Flour separates and evenly distributes ingredients throughout the dough or batter, binds all the ingredients and contains starches that absorb liquids and act as a thickener. Natural sugars in flour caramelize during baking and aid in browning.

- ● Preheat oven to 375°F (190°C)
- ● Cookie sheets, lined with parchment paper

2½ cups	all-purpose flour	625 mL
1	package (3.4 oz or 102 g) instant vanilla pudding mix	1
3 tbsp	instant espresso powder	45 mL
1 tsp	baking powder	5 mL
½ tsp	baking soda	2 mL
¼ tsp	salt	1 mL
½ cup	unsalted butter, softened	125 mL
½ cup	vegetable shortening	125 mL
½ cup	granulated sugar	125 mL
½ cup	packed light brown sugar	125 mL
2	eggs	2
1½ tsp	vanilla extract	7 mL

1. In a bowl, whisk together flour, pudding mix, espresso powder, baking powder, baking soda and salt until well combined. Set aside.

2. In a large bowl, using an electric mixer on medium speed, cream butter, shortening, granulated sugar and brown sugar until light and fluffy, about 2 minutes. Add eggs one at a time, beating well after each addition. Beat in vanilla. Scrape down sides of bowl. On low speed or using a wooden spoon, gradually add flour mixture, beating just until blended.

3. Using a cookie scoop or spoons, drop tablespoonfuls (15 mL) of dough about 2 inches (5 cm) apart on prepared cookie sheets. Bake one sheet at a time in preheated oven for 8 to 10 minutes or until edges start to turn lightly golden.

4. Immediately slide parchment paper onto a wire cooling rack. Cool cookies for 5 minutes, then transfer from parchment paper to cooling rack and cool completely.

Black and White Chocolate Dreams

Makes about 3 dozen cookies ● ● ●

Packed with lots of chocolate flavor and crunchy macadamia nuts, these cookies have a great chewy texture.

Tip

If you have problems with your cookies over- or underbaking, use an oven thermometer to check the accuracy of your oven's temperature control.

- Preheat oven to 375°F (190°C)
- Cookie sheets, lined with parchment paper

2¹⁄₃ cups	all-purpose flour	575 mL
1	package (3.4 oz or 102 g) instant chocolate pudding mix	1
1 tsp	baking powder	5 mL
½ tsp	baking soda	2 mL
¼ tsp	salt	1 mL
½ cup	unsalted butter, softened	125 mL
½ cup	vegetable shortening	125 mL
1 cup	packed dark brown sugar	250 mL
2	eggs	2
1½ tsp	vanilla extract	7 mL
1½ cups	chopped white chocolate or white chocolate chips	375 mL
1 cup	chopped roasted unsalted macadamia nuts	250 mL

1. In a bowl, whisk together flour, pudding mix, baking powder, baking soda and salt until well combined. Set aside.

2. In a large bowl, using an electric mixer on medium speed, cream butter, shortening and brown sugar until light and fluffy, about 2 minutes. Add eggs one at a time, beating well after each addition. Beat in vanilla. Scrape down sides of bowl. On low speed or using a wooden spoon, gradually add flour mixture, beating just until blended. By hand, fold in white chocolate and macadamia nuts.

3. Using a cookie scoop or spoons, drop tablespoonfuls (15 mL) of dough about 2 inches (5 cm) apart on prepared cookie sheets. Bake one sheet at a time in preheated oven for 8 to 10 minutes or until set around the edges but slightly soft in the center.

4. Immediately slide parchment paper onto a wire cooling rack. Cool cookies for 5 minutes, then transfer from parchment paper to cooling rack and cool completely.

Butterscotch Dreams

I love the combination of flavors in these special cookies.

Tip

Unsalted butter is the best choice for baked goods. It has a fresh, sweet cream flavor that adds immeasurably to the overall taste of the cookie. Because butter adds so much flavor, always choose a high-quality unsalted butter for cookie baking. Unsalted butter has a lower water content and higher fat content than salted butter, so cookies tend to spread less on the baking sheet.

Variations

Use chopped semisweet chocolate or semisweet chocolate chips in place of white chocolate and substitute chopped pecans for chopped cashews.

Double Butterscotch Dreams: Replace part or all of the white chocolate with butterscotch chips.

● **Preheat oven to 375°F (190°C)**
● **Cookie sheets, lined with parchment paper**

2⅔ cups	all-purpose flour	650 mL
1	package (3.4 oz or 102 g) instant butterscotch pudding mix	1
1 tsp	baking powder	5 mL
½ tsp	baking soda	2 mL
¼ tsp	salt	1 mL
½ cup	unsalted butter, softened	125 mL
½ cup	vegetable shortening	125 mL
1 cup	packed dark brown sugar	250 mL
2	eggs	2
1 tsp	vanilla extract	5 mL
1½ cups	chopped white chocolate or white chocolate chips	375 mL
1 cup	chopped unsalted cashews	250 mL

1. In a bowl, whisk together flour, pudding mix, baking powder, baking soda and salt until well combined. Set aside.

2. In a large bowl, using an electric mixer on medium speed, cream butter, shortening and brown sugar until light and fluffy, about 2 minutes. Add eggs one at a time, beating well after each addition. Beat in vanilla. Scrape down sides of bowl. On low speed or using a wooden spoon, gradually add flour mixture, beating just until blended. By hand, fold in chocolate and cashews.

3. Using a cookie scoop or spoons, drop tablespoonfuls (15 mL) of dough about 2 inches (5 cm) apart on prepared cookie sheets. Bake one sheet at a time in preheated oven for 8 to 10 minutes or until edges start to turn lightly golden.

4. Immediately slide parchment paper onto a wire cooling rack. Cool cookies for 5 minutes, then transfer from parchment paper to cooling rack and cool completely.

Apricot Coconut Dreams

Makes about 3½ dozen cookies ● ● ●

With a nice touch of orange, these cookies pack lots of flavor.

Tips

French vanilla pudding gives these cookies a rich flavor, but vanilla pudding may be substituted.

When grating the zest, be sure to include only the colored part of the outer peel on the orange.

- Preheat oven to 375°F (190°C)
- Cookie sheets, lined with parchment paper

1½ cups	chopped dried apricots	375 mL
6 tbsp	freshly squeezed orange juice	90 mL
3 cups	all-purpose flour	750 mL
1	package (3.4 oz or 102 g) instant French vanilla pudding mix	1
2 tsp	baking powder	10 mL
½ tsp	baking soda	2 mL
¼ tsp	salt	1 mL
½ cup	unsalted butter, softened	125 mL
½ cup	vegetable shortening	125 mL
½ cup	granulated sugar	125 mL
½ cup	packed light brown sugar	125 mL
2	eggs	2
1 tsp	vanilla extract	5 mL
½ tsp	almond extract	2 mL
1 tsp	grated orange zest	5 mL
1 cup	sweetened flaked coconut	250 mL
1 cup	chopped unsalted almonds	250 mL

1. In a small bowl, combine apricots and orange juice. Set aside and let stand 15 minutes, stirring occasionally.

2. In a bowl, whisk together flour, pudding mix, baking powder, baking soda and salt until well combined. Set aside.

3. In a large bowl, using an electric mixer on medium speed, cream butter, shortening, granulated sugar and brown sugar until light and fluffy, about 2 minutes. Add eggs one at a time, beating well after each addition. Beat in vanilla, almond extract and orange zest. Scrape down sides of bowl. On low speed or using a wooden spoon, gradually add flour mixture, beating just until blended. By hand, fold in apricot mixture, coconut and almonds.

4. Using a cookie scoop or spoons, drop tablespoonfuls (15 mL) of dough about 2 inches (5 cm) apart on prepared cookie sheets. Bake one sheet at a time in preheated oven for 8 to 10 minutes or until edges start to turn lightly golden.

5. Immediately slide parchment paper onto a wire cooling rack. Cool cookies for 5 minutes, then transfer from parchment paper to cooling rack and cool completely.

Golden Oatmeal Dreams

Makes about 4 dozen cookies ● ● ●

I like using golden raisins in these tender oatmeal cookies.

Tips

Cookies made with butter will tend to spread more than cookies made with shortening because shortening melts at a higher temperature. Cookies with only shortening will hold their shape better. Recipes calling for a combination of butter and shortening take advantage of the best qualities of both types of fat.

Dark raisins may be substituted for golden raisins.

- Preheat oven to 375°F (190°C)
- Cookie sheets, lined with parchment paper

1½ cups	all-purpose flour	375 mL
1	package (3.4 oz or 102 g) instant vanilla pudding mix	1
1 tsp	ground cinnamon	5 mL
1½ tsp	baking powder	7 mL
½ tsp	baking soda	2 mL
¼ tsp	salt	1 mL
½ cup	unsalted butter, softened	125 mL
½ cup	vegetable shortening	125 mL
⅔ cup	packed light brown sugar	150 mL
⅓ cup	granulated sugar	75 mL
2	eggs	2
1 tsp	vanilla extract	5 mL
3 cups	quick-cooking rolled oats	750 mL
1½ cups	golden raisins	375 mL
1 cup	chopped walnuts	250 mL

1. In a bowl, whisk together flour, pudding mix, cinnamon, baking powder, baking soda and salt until well combined. Set aside.

2. In a large bowl, using an electric mixer on medium speed, cream butter, shortening, brown sugar and granulated sugar until light and fluffy, about 2 minutes. Add eggs one at a time, beating well after each addition. Beat in vanilla. Scrape down sides of bowl. On low speed or using a wooden spoon, gradually add flour mixture, beating just until blended. Gradually stir in oats. By hand, fold in raisins and walnuts.

3. Using a cookie scoop or spoons, drop tablespoonfuls (15 mL) of dough about 2 inches (5 cm) apart on prepared cookie sheets. Bake one sheet at a time in preheated oven for 8 to 10 minutes or until edges start to turn lightly golden.

4. Immediately slide parchment paper onto a wire cooling rack. Cool cookies for 5 minutes, then transfer from parchment paper to cooling rack and cool completely.

CocoMac Dreams

Coconut, macadamia nuts and white chocolate make a rich, crunchy combination in these heavenly cookies.

Tip

Buy and use roasted macadamia nuts for the best flavor. Roasting brings out the nutty flavor of the macadamias.

Variation

Substitute chopped unsalted almonds for chopped macadamia nuts.

● Preheat oven to 375°F (190°C)
● Cookie sheets, lined with parchment paper

2⅓ cups	all-purpose flour	575 mL
1	package (3.4 oz or 102 g) instant vanilla pudding mix	1
1 tsp	baking powder	5 mL
½ tsp	baking soda	2 mL
¼ tsp	salt	1 mL
2 cups	sweetened flaked coconut	500 mL
½ cup	unsalted butter, softened	125 mL
½ cup	vegetable shortening	125 mL
⅔ cup	granulated sugar	150 mL
⅓ cup	packed light brown sugar	75 mL
2	eggs	2
1½ tsp	vanilla extract	7 mL
¼ tsp	almond extract	1 mL
1½ cups	chopped white chocolate or white chocolate chips	375 mL
1 cup	chopped roasted unsalted macadamia nuts	250 mL

1. In a bowl, whisk together flour, pudding mix, baking powder, baking soda and salt until well combined. Stir in coconut. Set aside.

2. In a large bowl, using an electric mixer on medium speed, cream butter, shortening, granulated sugar and brown sugar until light and fluffy, about 2 minutes. Add eggs one at a time, beating well after each addition. Beat in vanilla. Scrape down sides of bowl. On low speed or using a wooden spoon, gradually add flour mixture, beating just until blended. By hand, fold in white chocolate and macadamia nuts.

3. Using a cookie scoop or spoons, drop tablespoonfuls (15 mL) of dough about 2 inches (5 cm) apart on prepared cookie sheets. Bake one sheet at a time in preheated oven for 8 to 10 minutes or until edges start to turn lightly golden.

4. Immediately slide parchment paper onto a wire cooling rack. Cool cookies for 5 minutes, then transfer from parchment paper to cooling rack and cool completely.

Orange Dreams

Moist and tender, these citrus cookies are a big hit with both adults and children.

Tip

When creamed with sugar, solid fats trap air that lightens the cookies, adds structure and gives them their tender crumb. During baking, solid and liquid fats release moisture in the form of steam that helps cookies cook, set and crisp.

Variations

Orange Walnut Dreams: By hand, fold 1 1/2 cups (375 mL) chopped walnuts into dough after mixing.

Orange Pecan Dreams: By hand, fold 1 1/2 cups (375 mL) chopped pecans into dough after mixing.

- Preheat oven to 375°F (190°C)
- Cookie sheets, lined with parchment paper

3 1/2 cups	all-purpose flour	875 mL
1	package (3.4 oz or 102 g) instant vanilla pudding mix	1
2 tsp	baking powder	10 mL
1/2 tsp	baking soda	2 mL
1/4 tsp	salt	1 mL
1/2 cup	unsalted butter, softened	125 mL
1/2 cup	vegetable shortening	125 mL
2/3 cup	granulated sugar	150 mL
1/3 cup	packed light brown sugar	75 mL
2	eggs	2
1/2 cup	frozen orange juice concentrate, thawed	125 mL
2 tbsp	grated orange zest	25 mL
1 tsp	vanilla extract	5 mL

1. In a bowl, whisk together flour, pudding mix, baking powder, baking soda and salt until well combined. Set aside.

2. In a large bowl, using an electric mixer on medium speed, cream butter, shortening, granulated sugar and brown sugar until light and fluffy, about 2 minutes. Add eggs one at a time, beating well after each addition. Beat in orange juice concentrate, orange zest and vanilla. Scrape down sides of bowl. On low speed or using a wooden spoon, gradually add flour mixture, beating just until blended.

3. Using a cookie scoop or spoons, drop tablespoonfuls (15 mL) of dough about 2 inches (5 cm) apart on prepared cookie sheets. Bake one sheet at a time in preheated oven for 8 to 10 minutes or until edges start to turn lightly golden.

4. Immediately slide parchment paper onto a wire cooling rack. Cool cookies for 5 minutes, then transfer from parchment paper to cooling rack and cool completely.

Cranberry Apricot Dreams

Makes about 3½ dozen cookies ● ● ●

I love baking with dried cranberries and apricots. They add a lot of flavor and texture to these enticing cookies.

Tip

French vanilla pudding gives these cookies a rich flavor, but vanilla pudding may be substituted.

- Preheat oven to 375°F (190°C)
- Cookie sheets, lined with parchment paper

1 cup	dried cranberries	250 mL
1 cup	chopped dried apricots	250 mL
½ cup	freshly squeezed orange juice	125 mL
3 cups	all-purpose flour	750 mL
1	package (3.4 oz or 102 g) instant French vanilla pudding mix	1
1½ tsp	baking powder	7 mL
½ tsp	baking soda	2 mL
¼ tsp	salt	1 mL
½ cup	unsalted butter, softened	125 mL
½ cup	vegetable shortening	125 mL
½ cup	granulated sugar	125 mL
½ cup	packed light brown sugar	125 mL
2	eggs	2
1 tsp	vanilla extract	5 mL
½ tsp	almond extract	2 mL
1 tsp	grated orange zest	5 mL
1 cup	chopped roasted unsalted macadamia nuts	250 mL

1. In a small bowl, combine cranberries, apricots and orange juice. Set aside and let stand 15 minutes, stirring occasionally.

2. In a bowl, whisk together flour, pudding mix, baking powder, baking soda and salt until well combined. Set aside.

3. In a large bowl, using an electric mixer on medium speed, cream butter, shortening, granulated sugar and brown sugar until light and fluffy, about 2 minutes. Add eggs one at a time, beating well after each addition. Beat in vanilla, almond extract and orange zest. Scrape down sides of bowl. On low speed or using a wooden spoon, gradually add flour mixture, beating just until blended. By hand, fold in macadamia nuts.

4. Using a cookie scoop or spoons, drop tablespoonfuls (15 mL) of dough about 2 inches (5 cm) apart on prepared cookie sheets. Bake one sheet at a time in preheated oven for 8 to 10 minutes or until edges start to turn lightly golden.

5. Immediately slide parchment paper onto a wire cooling rack. Cool cookies for 5 minutes, then transfer from parchment paper to cooling rack and cool completely.

Oatmeal Ambrosia Dreams

When I take these fruit-packed cookies to parties and potlucks, they disappear in a hurry.

Tip

Butter is considered to be softened when it is at a temperature of 65°F (18°C).

- Preheat oven to 375°F (190°C)
- Cookie sheets, lined with parchment paper

1½ cups	all-purpose flour	375 mL
1	package (3.4 oz or 102 g) instant vanilla pudding mix	1
1½ tsp	baking powder	7 mL
½ tsp	baking soda	2 mL
¼ tsp	salt	1 mL
½ cup	unsalted butter, softened	125 mL
½ cup	vegetable shortening	125 mL
½ cup	granulated sugar	125 mL
½ cup	packed light brown sugar	125 mL
2	eggs	2
1½ tsp	vanilla extract	7 mL
3 cups	quick-cooking rolled oats	750 mL
1 cup	chopped dried apricots	250 mL
1 cup	drained canned juice-packed crushed pineapple	250 mL
1 cup	sweetened flaked coconut	250 mL
1 cup	chopped roasted unsalted macadamia nuts	250 mL

1. In a bowl, whisk together flour, pudding mix, baking powder, baking soda and salt until well combined. Set aside.

2. In a large bowl, using an electric mixer on medium speed, cream butter, shortening, granulated sugar and brown sugar until light and fluffy, about 2 minutes. Add eggs one at a time, beating well after each addition. Beat in vanilla. Scrape down sides of bowl. On low speed or using a wooden spoon, gradually add flour mixture, beating just until blended. Gradually stir in oats. By hand, fold in apricots, pineapple, coconut and macadamia nuts.

3. Using a cookie scoop or spoons, drop tablespoonfuls (15 mL) of dough about 2 inches (5 cm) apart on prepared cookie sheets. Bake one sheet at a time in preheated oven for 8 to 10 minutes or until edges start to turn lightly golden.

4. Immediately slide parchment paper onto a wire cooling rack. Cool cookies for 5 minutes, then transfer from parchment paper to cooling rack and cool completely.

Mocha Fudge Dreams

Makes about 2½ dozen cookies ● ● ●

Chocolate and coffee make a heavenly combination in these moist, chewy cookies.

Tips

Instant espresso powder can be found in the coffee aisle of most major grocery stores.

Salt should not be eliminated from cookie recipes. Without salt, some cookies will taste bland and unexciting.

- ● **Preheat oven to 375°F (190°C)**
- ● **Cookie sheets, lined with parchment paper**

2½ cups	all-purpose flour	625 mL
1	package (3.4 oz or 102 g) instant chocolate fudge pudding mix	1
1 tbsp	instant espresso powder	15 mL
1 tsp	baking powder	5 mL
½ tsp	baking soda	2 mL
¼ tsp	salt	1 mL
½ cup	unsalted butter, softened	125 mL
½ cup	vegetable shortening	125 mL
⅔ cup	packed dark brown sugar	150 mL
⅓ cup	granulated sugar	75 mL
2	eggs	2
2 tsp	vanilla extract	10 mL

1. In a bowl, whisk together flour, pudding mix, espresso powder, baking powder, baking soda and salt until well combined. Set aside.

2. In a large bowl, using an electric mixer on medium speed, cream butter, shortening, brown sugar and granulated sugar until light and fluffy, about 2 minutes. Add eggs one at a time, beating well after each addition. Beat in vanilla. Scrape down sides of bowl. On low speed or using a wooden spoon, gradually add flour mixture, beating just until blended.

3. Using a cookie scoop or spoons, drop tablespoonfuls (15 mL) of dough about 2 inches (5 cm) apart on prepared cookie sheets. Bake one sheet at a time in preheated oven for 8 to 10 minutes or until set around the edges but slightly soft in the center.

4. Immediately slide parchment paper onto a wire cooling rack. Cool cookies for 5 minutes, then transfer from parchment paper to cooling rack and cool completely.

Coconut Oat Dreams

● ● ●

I like to whip up a batch of these satisfying coconut cookies on rainy days.

Tips

Always let baking sheets cool completely before placing the next batch of cookie dough on the sheet.

I strongly advise against substituting margarine in any cookie recipe that calls for butter. In cookie baking, butter adds to the flavor and texture. You just won't get the same results with margarine.

- Preheat oven to 375°F (190°C)
- Cookie sheets, lined with parchment paper

1⅓ cups	all-purpose flour	325 mL
1	package (3.4 oz or 102 g) instant vanilla pudding mix	1
1½ tsp	baking powder	7 mL
½ tsp	baking soda	2 mL
¼ tsp	salt	1 mL
2 cups	sweetened flaked coconut	500 mL
½ cup	unsalted butter, softened	125 mL
½ cup	vegetable shortening	125 mL
⅔ cup	packed light brown sugar	150 mL
⅓ cup	granulated sugar	75 mL
2	eggs	2
1½ tsp	vanilla extract	7 mL
3 cups	quick-cooking rolled oats	750 mL

1. In a bowl, whisk together flour, pudding mix, baking powder, baking soda and salt until well combined. Stir in coconut. Set aside.

2. In a large bowl, using an electric mixer on medium speed, cream butter, shortening, brown sugar and granulated sugar until light and fluffy, about 2 minutes. Add eggs one at a time, beating well after each addition. Beat in vanilla. Scrape down sides of bowl. On low speed or using a wooden spoon, gradually add flour mixture, beating just until blended. Gradually stir in oats.

3. Using a cookie scoop or spoons, drop tablespoonfuls (15 mL) of dough about 2 inches (5 cm) apart on prepared cookie sheets. Bake one sheet at a time in preheated oven for 8 to 10 minutes or until edges start to turn lightly golden.

4. Immediately slide parchment paper onto a wire cooling rack. Cool cookies for 5 minutes, then transfer from parchment paper to cooling rack and cool completely.

Lemon Dreams

This book would not be complete without a recipe for lemon dream cookies!

Tips

Use ripe lemons for cookies with the best flavor. Ripe lemons have a deep yellow peel and strong lemon aroma.

If you have access to locally grown Meyer lemons, they are a great choice for use in this recipe. Meyer lemons have a sweeter, more intense lemon flavor than Eureka lemons, the common variety of commercially grown lemon found in most markets.

- Preheat oven to 375°F (190°C)
- Cookie sheets, lined with parchment paper

2⅔ cups	all-purpose flour	650 mL
1	package (3.4 oz or 102 g) instant vanilla pudding mix	1
1 tsp	baking powder	5 mL
½ tsp	baking soda	2 mL
¼ tsp	salt	1 mL
½ cup	unsalted butter, softened	125 mL
½ cup	vegetable shortening	125 mL
⅔ cup	granulated sugar	150 mL
⅓ cup	packed light brown sugar	75 mL
2	eggs	2
3 tbsp	grated lemon zest	45 mL
1 tbsp	freshly squeezed lemon juice	15 mL

1. In a bowl, whisk together flour, pudding mix, baking powder, baking soda and salt until well combined. Set aside.

2. In a large bowl, using an electric mixer on medium speed, cream butter, shortening, granulated sugar and brown sugar until light and fluffy, about 2 minutes. Add eggs one at a time, beating well after each addition. Beat in lemon zest and lemon juice. Scrape down sides of bowl. On low speed or using a wooden spoon, gradually add flour mixture, beating just until blended.

3. Using a cookie scoop or spoons, drop tablespoonfuls (15 mL) of dough about 2 inches (5 cm) apart on prepared cookie sheets. Bake one sheet at a time in preheated oven for 8 to 10 minutes or until edges start to turn lightly golden.

4. Immediately slide parchment paper onto a wire cooling rack. Cool cookies for 5 minutes, then transfer from parchment paper to cooling rack and cool completely.

Tropical Dreams

My dad loves the combination of coconut, pineapple and macadamia nuts in these scrumptious cookies, and I agree!

Tips

Using a cookie scoop will uniformly portion cookie dough and ensure even baking.

Fats influence a cookie's flavor and color, add moisture to cookies and help keep them fresh. Fats are also an important element in determining the texture and spread of a cookie.

● **Preheat oven to 375°F (190°C)**
● **Cookie sheets, lined with parchment paper**

2½ cups	all-purpose flour	625 mL
1	package (3.4 oz or 102 g) instant vanilla pudding mix	1
1 tsp	baking powder	5 mL
½ tsp	baking soda	2 mL
¼ tsp	salt	1 mL
½ cup	unsalted butter, softened	125 mL
½ cup	vegetable shortening	125 mL
½ cup	granulated sugar	125 mL
½ cup	packed light brown sugar	125 mL
2	eggs	2
1 tsp	vanilla extract	5 mL
1 cup	sweetened flaked coconut	250 mL
1 cup	drained canned juice-packed crushed pineapple	250 mL
1 cup	chopped roasted unsalted macadamia nuts	250 mL

1. In a bowl, whisk together flour, pudding mix, baking powder, baking soda and salt until well combined. Set aside.
2. In a large bowl, using an electric mixer on medium speed, cream butter, shortening, granulated sugar and brown sugar until light and fluffy, about 2 minutes. Add eggs one at a time, beating well after each addition. Beat in vanilla. Scrape down sides of bowl. On low speed or using a wooden spoon, gradually add flour mixture, beating just until blended. By hand, fold in coconut, pineapple and macadamia nuts.
3. Using a cookie scoop or spoons, drop tablespoonfuls (15 mL) of dough about 2 inches (5 cm) apart on prepared cookie sheets. Bake one sheet at a time in preheated oven for 8 to 10 minutes or until edges start to turn lightly golden.
4. Immediately slide parchment paper onto a wire cooling rack. Cool cookies for 5 minutes, then transfer from parchment paper to cooling rack and cool completely.

Doodle Dreams

● ● ●

These delicious cookies are a variation on traditional snickerdoodles. The pudding gives them a rich flavor.

Tip

If you prefer a stronger cinnamon flavor, increase cinnamon in the topping to 2 tablespoons (25 mL).

- Preheat oven to 375°F (190°C)
- Cookie sheets, lined with parchment paper

Cookies

2¾ cups	all-purpose flour	675 mL
1	package (3.4 oz or 102 g) instant vanilla pudding mix	1
1 tsp	baking powder	5 mL
½ tsp	baking soda	2 mL
¼ tsp	salt	1 mL
½ cup	unsalted butter, softened	125 mL
½ cup	vegetable shortening	125 mL
⅔ cup	granulated sugar	150 mL
⅓ cup	packed light brown sugar	75 mL
2	eggs	2
1½ tsp	vanilla extract	7 mL

Topping

½ cup	granulated sugar	125 mL
1 tbsp	ground cinnamon	15 mL

1. **Cookies:** In a bowl, whisk together flour, pudding mix, baking powder, baking soda and salt until well combined. Set aside.

2. In a large bowl, using an electric mixer on medium speed, cream butter, shortening, granulated sugar and brown sugar until light and fluffy, about 2 minutes. Add eggs one at a time, beating well after each addition. Beat in vanilla. Scrape down sides of bowl. On low speed or using a wooden spoon, gradually add flour mixture, beating just until blended.

3. **Topping:** In a small bowl, combine sugar and cinnamon until well blended. Spread cinnamon sugar on a large plate or sheet of wax paper.

4. Lightly grease hands with nonstick cooking spray. Roll pieces of dough into 1-inch (2.5 cm) balls. Roll dough balls in cinnamon sugar and place on prepared cookie sheets. Bake one sheet at a time in preheated oven for 8 to 10 minutes or until edges start to turn lightly golden.

5. Immediately slide parchment paper onto a wire cooling rack. Cool cookies for 5 minutes, then transfer from parchment paper to cooling rack and cool completely.

Cherry Oatmeal Dreams

Makes about 4 dozen cookies

The hint of almond flavor from the extract nicely complements the flavor of the cherries in these wonderful cookies.

Tip

Dried cherries can be found alongside raisins and dried cranberries in most major grocery stores, specialty food stores and many produce markets.

Variation

Cherry Nut Oatmeal Cookies: By hand, fold 1 cup (250 mL) chopped walnuts or pecans into cookie dough along with dried cherries.

- Preheat oven to 375°F (190°C)
- Cookie sheets, lined with parchment paper

1⅓ cups	all-purpose flour	325 mL
1	package (3.4 oz or 102 g) instant vanilla pudding mix	1
1½ tsp	baking powder	7 mL
½ tsp	baking soda	2 mL
¼ tsp	salt	1 mL
½ cup	unsalted butter, softened	125 mL
½ cup	vegetable shortening	125 mL
⅔ cup	packed light brown sugar	150 mL
⅓ cup	granulated sugar	75 mL
2	eggs	2
1 tsp	vanilla extract	5 mL
½ tsp	almond extract	2 mL
3 cups	quick-cooking rolled oats	750 mL
2 cups	chopped dried cherries	500 mL

1. In a bowl, whisk together flour, pudding mix, baking powder, baking soda and salt until well combined. Set aside.

2. In a large bowl, using an electric mixer on medium speed, cream butter, shortening, brown sugar and granulated sugar until light and fluffy, about 2 minutes. Add eggs one at a time, beating well after each addition. Beat in vanilla and almond extract. Scrape down sides of bowl. On low speed or using a wooden spoon, gradually add flour mixture, beating just until blended. Gradually stir in oats. By hand, fold in cherries.

3. Using a cookie scoop or spoons, drop tablespoonfuls (15 mL) of dough about 2 inches (5 cm) apart on prepared cookie sheets. Bake one sheet at a time in preheated oven for 8 to 10 minutes or until edges start to turn lightly golden.

4. Immediately slide parchment paper onto a wire cooling rack. Cool cookies for 5 minutes, then transfer from parchment paper to cooling rack and cool completely.

Pistachio Dreams

Loaded with nuts, these fun green-colored cookies pack a strong pistachio punch.

Tip

Store cookies in a tightly sealed container at room temperature for up to 3 days.

Variation

Pistachio Chip Dreams: Use 1 cup (250 mL) pistachio nuts and fold 1½ cups (375 mL) semisweet chocolate chips into cookie dough along with nuts.

- Preheat oven to 375°F (190°C)
- Cookie sheets, lined with parchment paper

2⅓ cups	all-purpose flour	575 mL
1	package (3.4 oz or 102 g) instant pistachio pudding mix	1
1 tsp	baking powder	5 mL
½ tsp	baking soda	2 mL
¼ tsp	salt	1 mL
½ cup	unsalted butter, softened	125 mL
½ cup	vegetable shortening	125 mL
½ cup	granulated sugar	125 mL
½ cup	packed light brown sugar	125 mL
2	eggs	2
1 tsp	vanilla extract	5 mL
2 cups	chopped unsalted pistachio nuts	500 mL

1. In a bowl, whisk together flour, pudding mix, baking powder, baking soda and salt until well combined. Set aside.

2. In a large bowl, using an electric mixer on medium speed, cream butter, shortening, granulated sugar and brown sugar until light and fluffy, about 2 minutes. Add eggs one at a time, beating well after each addition. Beat in vanilla. Scrape down sides of bowl. On low speed or using a wooden spoon, gradually add flour mixture, beating just until blended. By hand, fold in pistachio nuts.

3. Using a cookie scoop or spoons, drop tablespoonfuls (15 mL) of dough about 2 inches (5 cm) apart on prepared cookie sheets. Bake one sheet at a time in preheated oven for 8 to 10 minutes or until edges start to turn lightly golden.

4. Immediately slide parchment paper onto a wire cooling rack. Cool cookies for 5 minutes, then transfer from parchment paper to cooling rack and cool completely.

Pineapple Dreams

● ● ●

If you like pineapple, you'll love these tender treats.

Tip

Space cookies 2 inches (5 cm) apart on cookie sheets to allow enough room for spreading and for air circulation for even baking.

- Preheat oven to 375°F (190°C)
- Cookie sheets, lined with parchment paper

2⅔ cups	all-purpose flour	650 mL
1	package (3.4 oz or 102 g) instant vanilla pudding mix	1
1 tsp	baking powder	5 mL
½ tsp	baking soda	2 mL
¼ tsp	salt	1 mL
½ cup	unsalted butter, softened	125 mL
½ cup	vegetable shortening	125 mL
1 cup	packed light brown sugar	250 mL
2	eggs	2
1½ tsp	vanilla extract	7 mL
2 cups	drained canned juice-packed crushed pineapple	500 mL

1. In a bowl, whisk together flour, pudding mix, baking powder, baking soda and salt until well combined. Set aside.

2. In a large bowl, using an electric mixer on medium speed, cream butter, shortening and brown sugar until light and fluffy, about 2 minutes. Add eggs one at a time, beating well after each addition. Beat in vanilla. Scrape down sides of bowl. On low speed or using a wooden spoon, gradually add flour mixture, beating just until blended. By hand, fold in pineapple.

3. Using a cookie scoop or spoons, drop tablespoonfuls (15 mL) of dough about 2 inches (5 cm) apart on prepared cookie sheets. Bake one sheet at a time in preheated oven for 8 to 10 minutes or until edges start to turn lightly golden.

4. Immediately slide parchment paper onto a wire cooling rack. Cool cookies for 5 minutes, then transfer from parchment paper to cooling rack and cool completely.

Apricot Cranberry Oat Dreams

Oatmeal cookies are very versatile and are perfect for adding lots of colorful dried apricots and cranberries.

Tips

Bread flour has a high protein content and should not be used for baking cookies.

Store cookies in a tightly sealed container at room temperature for up to 3 days.

- Preheat oven to 375°F (190°C)
- Cookie sheets, lined with parchment paper

1⅓ cups	all-purpose flour	325 mL
1	package (3.4 oz or 102 g) instant vanilla pudding mix	1
1½ tsp	baking powder	7 mL
½ tsp	baking soda	2 mL
¼ tsp	salt	1 mL
½ cup	unsalted butter, softened	125 mL
½ cup	vegetable shortening	125 mL
1 cup	packed light brown sugar	250 mL
2	eggs	2
2 tsp	grated orange zest	10 mL
1½ tsp	vanilla extract	7 mL
3 cups	quick-cooking rolled oats	750 mL
1½ cups	chopped dried apricots	375 mL
1½ cups	dried cranberries	375 mL

1. In a bowl, whisk together flour, pudding mix, baking powder, baking soda and salt until well combined. Set aside.

2. In a large bowl, using an electric mixer on medium speed, cream butter, shortening and brown sugar until light and fluffy, about 2 minutes. Add eggs one at a time, beating well after each addition. Beat in orange zest and vanilla. Scrape down sides of bowl. On low speed or using a wooden spoon, gradually add flour mixture, beating just until blended. Gradually stir in oats. By hand, fold in apricots and cranberries.

3. Using a cookie scoop or spoons, drop tablespoonfuls (15 mL) of dough about 2 inches (5 cm) apart on prepared cookie sheets. Bake one sheet at a time in preheated oven for 8 to 10 minutes or until edges start to turn lightly golden.

4. Immediately slide parchment paper onto a wire cooling rack. Cool cookies for 5 minutes, then transfer from parchment paper to cooling rack and cool completely.

Toffee Dreams

Filled with crunchy toffee bits and pecans, these cookies are bursting with flavor.

Tips

Bags of toffee bits can be found in the baking aisle of most grocery stores.

Use unsalted butter for cookies. Salted butter can give cookies an "off" flavor or make them too salty.

- **Preheat oven to 375°F (190°C)**
- **Cookie sheets, lined with parchment paper**

2⅓ cups	all-purpose flour	575 mL
1	package (3.4 oz or 102 g) instant vanilla pudding mix	1
1 tsp	baking powder	5 mL
½ tsp	baking soda	2 mL
¼ tsp	salt	1 mL
½ cup	unsalted butter, softened	125 mL
½ cup	vegetable shortening	125 mL
1 cup	packed dark brown sugar	250 mL
2	eggs	2
2 tsp	vanilla extract	10 mL
2 cups	toffee bits	500 mL
1 cup	chopped pecans	250 mL

1. In a bowl, whisk together flour, pudding mix, baking powder, baking soda and salt until well combined. Set aside.

2. In a large bowl, using an electric mixer on medium speed, cream butter, shortening and brown sugar until light and fluffy, about 2 minutes. Add eggs one at a time, beating well after each addition. Beat in vanilla. Scrape down sides of bowl. On low speed or using a wooden spoon, gradually add flour mixture, beating just until blended. By hand, fold in toffee bits and pecans.

3. Using a cookie scoop or spoons, drop tablespoonfuls (15 mL) of dough about 2 inches (5 cm) apart on prepared cookie sheets. Bake one sheet at a time in preheated oven for 8 to 10 minutes or until edges start to turn lightly golden.

4. Immediately slide parchment paper onto a wire cooling rack. Cool cookies for 5 minutes, then transfer from parchment paper to cooling rack and cool completely.

Rolled Cutout Cookies

Blue Ribbon Sugar Cookies 206

Tender Cutouts. 207

Vanilla Cookie Cutter Cookies. 208

Cream Cheese Sugar Cookies 210

Old-time Gingerbread Cookies 212

Holiday Sugar Cookies 214

Brown Sugar Cutouts. 216

Eier Kringle. 218

Lemon Sugar Cookies 220

Almond Cutouts 222

Snowflake Cookies. 224

Sour Cream Cookies 226

Glazed Orange Cutouts 228

Maple Leaf Cookies 230

Chocolate Sandwich Cookies. 232

Spice Cookies 234

Raspberry Cream Sandwich
Cookies. 236

Lime Cutouts 238

Cinnamon Sugar Cookies. 240

Espresso Sandwich Cookies 242

Chocolate Cutouts 244

Nutmeg Cookies. 246

Peanut Butter Cutouts 248

About Rolled Cutout Cookies

Rolled cutout cookies are exactly what their name implies: the tender dough is rolled out thin and cut into shapes with cookie cutters or a pastry wheel. These fun and decorative cookies are a favorite with kids of all ages. They can be cut into an endless variety of shapes, eaten plain, sandwiched together with fillings or decorated with frostings, colored sugars and sprinkles.

Dutch and German settlers brought the first cookie cutters to America. The cutout cookie recipes in this chapter call for a 2½-inch (6 cm) cookie cutter. You may use any shape cookie cutter that is approximately this size. For cutouts made with larger or smaller cookie cutters, you will need to adjust the baking time accordingly.

Cookie doughs can absorb flavors and odors from cutting boards that have been used to prepare other foods. These flavors can remain in boards even after they have been washed. I keep a separate board specifically for rolling out cookies, pie crusts and other pastries. Never use a board that has been used for preparing meats or poultry as a surface for rolling cookies or any other dough.

Chilling the Dough

Cutout cookie doughs should be chilled for 1 to 2 hours before rolling. Chilling the dough allows the protein in the flour to relax, making the dough much easier to handle and roll out. Chilling also firms up the butter so the cookies hold their shape when baked. In addition, the moisture from the ingredients will have time to distribute through the dough and be absorbed by the flour. Chilling makes the dough less likely to stick to the pastry board and rolling pin, reducing the amount of flour needed to dust the board.

Divide the dough into two equal portions. Shape each portion of dough into a flat disk about ½ inch (1 cm) thick. This will allow the dough to chill quickly and evenly and make it easier to roll out. Wrap the dough tightly in plastic wrap to keep it from drying out or absorbing flavors and odors from the refrigerator.

Rolling the Dough

Work with only one portion of dough at a time. Keep the remaining dough in the refrigerator until you're ready to roll it. If the dough has been chilled overnight, let it sit on the counter wrapped in plastic for 10 minutes to make it easier to roll.

Lightly dust a pastry board or other flat surface and the rolling pin with flour to keep the dough, from sticking. Avoid using a lot of flour — working too much extra flour into the dough will toughen the cookies. You can dust the board and rolling pin with sifted confectioner's (powdered/icing) sugar instead of flour. This sugar will give the cookies a little extra sweetness without making them tough. This is a good alternative to use for very soft doughs or on warm days when cookie dough tends to stick to the board more. Instead of using a pastry board, you can also roll the dough out between two sheets of parchment paper on a flat surface.

Roll the dough from the center out toward the edges. Never roll back and forth across the dough as this will strengthen the gluten and make the cookies tough. As the rolling pin approaches the edge of the dough circle, relax the pressure on the pin to keep the edges from being rolled too thin. This helps keep the dough the same thickness from the center to the edge, which means the cookies will be a uniform thickness and bake evenly.

Think of the dough as the face of a clock. With the first stroke, roll out from the center to the position for 12 o'clock. Roll the next stroke from the center out to the 2 o'clock position and the next stroke to the 4 o'clock position. Keep rolling until you've gone all the way around the clock, using about six strokes. Give the dough a quarter turn and add flour to the rolling surface only as needed to prevent the dough from sticking. Continue the rolling process until the dough is the specified thickness.

If the dough becomes too soft or sticky during rolling, place the board in the refrigerator for 10 minutes or until the dough is firm enough to roll.

Cutting Cookies

If, after rolling, the dough is too soft to cut and transfer cookies to the cookie sheet, chill the board in the refrigerator for a few minutes to firm up the dough.

To prevent the dough from sticking to the cookie cutter, dip the cutter in flour or confectioner's (powdered/icing) sugar and tap off any excess before cutting the cookies. If the dough starts sticking, dip the cutter again before cutting more cookies. For chocolate cookies, dip the cutter in sifted cocoa powder to prevent white edges on the cookies.

Cut out the cookies as close to each other as possible in order to get as many cookies as you can out of the first rolling of the dough. Each time you reroll the scraps, the dough will absorb more flour, which can make the cookies tough. Make clean cuts without twisting the cookie cutter to keep from distorting the shape of the cookies and prevent them from shrinking.

Once you've cut out all the cookies you can from the dough, peel away the scraps of dough to make it easier to transfer the cookies to the cookie sheet. A large, thin-bladed spatula is useful for transferring cutouts from the pastry board to the cookie sheet. It also helps the cutouts hold their shape without stretching and becoming distorted. Place similar size cutouts on the same sheet so they bake evenly in the same amount of time.

Gather the dough scraps and gently knead them together. If the dough is soft, chill it for a few minutes before rerolling. Use as little flour as possible on the board and rolling pin to prevent the cookies from becoming tough.

Finishing Cookies

This is the time to have fun and let your creativity take over. Cutout cookies can be finished or decorated in many ways. Sprinkle the cutouts with colored sugar before baking or spread cooled cookies with colored frostings and top with candies. Fill a decorating bag with thinned frosting and pipe decorations on top of the cookies. You can improvise a decorating bag by filling a zippered storage bag with frosting and cutting a small tip off the corner. Set the frosted cookies onto a rack, tray or wax paper to dry.

Frosting can easily be thinned to the desired consistency for decorating by adding a little more cream or milk. Keep any icing not in the decorating bag covered with a damp cloth and plastic wrap to prevent it from drying out while you decorate.

Blue Ribbon Sugar Cookies

Makes about 3½ dozen cookies

These delicious, award-winning vanilla cutout cookies can be topped with colored sugars.

Tip

Chilled cookie dough is easier to roll and handle than dough at room temperature.

- Cookie sheets, lined with parchment paper
- Cookie cutters

3 cups	all-purpose flour	750 mL
½ tsp	baking powder	2 mL
½ tsp	baking soda	2 mL
¼ tsp	salt	1 mL
½ cup	unsalted butter, softened	125 mL
½ cup	vegetable shortening	125 mL
1⅓ cups	granulated sugar	325 mL
2	eggs	2
1 tbsp	vanilla extract	15 mL
	Coarse sugar or additional granulated sugar	

1. In a bowl, whisk together flour, baking powder, baking soda and salt until well combined. Set aside.

2. In a large bowl, using an electric mixer on medium speed, cream butter, shortening and granulated sugar until light and fluffy, about 3 minutes. Add eggs one at a time, beating well after each addition. Beat in vanilla. Scrape down sides of bowl. On low speed or using a wooden spoon, gradually add flour mixture, beating just until blended.

3. Divide dough in half. Shape each portion into a flat disk. Tightly wrap each disk in plastic wrap and chill for at least 1 hour.

4. Preheat oven to 350°F (180°C). Lightly dust a pastry board, clean countertop or other flat surface and a rolling pin with confectioner's (icing) sugar or flour. Working with one dough disk at a time, unwrap dough and roll out to uniform thickness of ¼ inch (0.5 cm). Halfway through rolling, rotate the dough a quarter turn and dust the board again to prevent dough from sticking.

5. Dip 2½-inch (6 cm) cookie cutters in confectioner's sugar or flour and cut dough into desired shapes. Cut out as many cookies as possible from first rolling. Carefully transfer cutouts to prepared cookie sheets, placing 1 inch (2.5 cm) apart. Gather dough remnants into a ball, reroll, cut out more cookies and transfer to cookie sheets. Sprinkle cookies with coarse sugar.

6. Bake one sheet at a time in preheated oven for 8 to 10 minutes or until edges start to turn lightly golden.

7. Immediately slide parchment paper onto a wire cooling rack. Cool cookies for 5 minutes, then transfer from parchment paper to cooling rack and cool completely.

Tender Cutouts

● ● ●

A touch of corn syrup added to the dough gives these cookies a tender texture.

Tip

Cookies may be frosted after cooling instead of dusting with confectioner's sugar.

Variation

Sprinkle cookies with colored sugar before baking.

- ● **Cookie cutters**
- ● **Cookie sheets, lined with parchment paper**

3 cups	all-purpose flour	750 mL
1/2 tsp	baking powder	2 mL
1/4 tsp	baking soda	1 mL
1/4 tsp	salt	1 mL
1 cup	unsalted butter, softened	250 mL
1 2/3 cups	confectioner's (powdered/icing) sugar	400 mL
2 tbsp	light corn syrup	25 mL
1	egg	1
1/2 tsp	vanilla extract	2 mL
1/2 tsp	almond extract	2 mL
	Additional confectioner's (powdered/icing) sugar	

1. In a bowl, whisk together flour, baking powder, baking soda and salt until well combined. Set aside.

2. In a large bowl, using an electric mixer on medium speed, cream butter, confectioner's sugar and corn syrup until light and fluffy, about 3 minutes. Add egg and beat well. Beat in vanilla and almond extract. Scrape down sides of bowl. On low speed or using a wooden spoon, gradually add flour mixture, beating just until blended.

3. Divide dough in half. Shape each portion into a flat disk. Tightly wrap each disk in plastic wrap and chill for at least 1 hour.

4. Preheat oven to 350°F (180°C). Lightly dust a pastry board, clean countertop or other flat surface and a rolling pin with confectioner's sugar or flour. Working with one dough disk at a time, unwrap dough and roll out to uniform thickness of 1/8 inch (3 mm). Halfway through rolling, rotate the dough a quarter turn and dust the board again to prevent dough from sticking.

5. Dip 2 1/2-inch (6 cm) cookie cutters in confectioner's sugar or flour and cut dough into desired shapes. Cut out as many cookies as possible from first rolling. Carefully transfer cutouts to prepared cookie sheets, placing 1 inch (2.5 cm) apart. Gather dough remnants into a ball, reroll, cut out more cookies and transfer to cookie sheets.

6. Bake one sheet at a time in preheated oven for 8 to 10 minutes or until edges start to turn lightly golden.

7. Immediately slide parchment paper onto a wire cooling rack. Cool cookies for 2 minutes, then transfer from parchment paper to cooling rack. Dust cookies with confectioner's sugar. Cool completely.

Vanilla Cookie Cutter Cookies

*I first started baking
these as a young girl,
and I bake dozens
of these wonderful
cookies for Christmas
every year.*

Tips

Always use pure vanilla
extract in cookies.
Imitation vanilla is made
from synthetic flavors
and colors, and the taste
cannot compare to pure
vanilla extract.

Let frosting set before
storing cookies between
layers of wax paper in a
tightly sealed container.

- Cookie sheets, lined with parchment paper
- Cookie cutters

Cookies

3 cups	all-purpose flour	750 mL
¾ tsp	baking powder	3 mL
½ tsp	salt	2 mL
⅔ cup	unsalted butter, softened	150 mL
⅔ cup	granulated sugar	150 mL
2	eggs	2
2 tsp	vanilla extract	10 mL
2 tbsp	half-and-half (10%) cream or milk	25 mL

Frosting

3 cups	confectioner's (powdered/icing) sugar	750 mL
3 tbsp	unsalted butter, softened	45 mL
3 to 4 tbsp	half-and-half (10%) cream or milk	45 to 50 mL
1 tsp	vanilla extract	5 mL

1. *Cookies:* In a bowl, whisk together flour, baking powder and salt until well combined. Set aside.

2. In a large bowl, using an electric mixer on medium speed, cream butter and granulated sugar until light and fluffy, about 3 minutes. Add eggs one at a time, beating well after each addition. Beat in vanilla. Scrape down sides of bowl. On low speed or using a wooden spoon, gradually add flour mixture, alternating with the cream, beating just until blended.

3. Divide dough in half. Shape each portion into a flat disk. Tightly wrap each disk in plastic wrap and chill for at least 1 hour.

4. Preheat oven to 375°F (190°C). Lightly dust a pastry board, clean countertop or other flat surface and a rolling pin with confectioner's sugar or flour. Working with one dough disk at a time, unwrap dough and roll out to uniform thickness of ⅛ inch (3 mm). Halfway through rolling, rotate the dough a quarter turn and dust the board again to prevent dough from sticking.

5. Dip 2½-inch (6 cm) cookie cutters in confectioner's sugar or flour and cut dough into desired shapes. Cut out as many cookies as possible from first rolling. Carefully transfer cutouts to prepared cookie sheets, placing 1 inch (2.5 cm) apart. Gather dough remnants into a ball, reroll, cut out more cookies and transfer to cookie sheets.

Tip

All of the recipes in this book use large eggs, the standard size used for baking. If you do not have large eggs, then lightly beat your eggs and substitute $\frac{1}{4}$ cup (50 mL) beaten egg for each large egg called for in the recipe.

6. Bake one sheet at a time in preheated oven for 5 to 7 minutes or until edges start to turn lightly golden.

7. Immediately slide parchment paper onto a wire cooling rack. Cool cookies for 5 minutes, then transfer from parchment paper to cooling rack and cool completely.

8. *Frosting:* In a bowl, combine confectioner's sugar, butter, 3 tablespoons (45 mL) of the cream and vanilla. Using an electric mixer on medium speed, beat until frosting is light and fluffy, about 2 minutes. Add more cream as needed to achieve the desired consistency. Spread frosting over tops of cooled cookies.

A Rainbow of Colors

To give your cookies a festive touch, you can tint cookie dough with either liquid or paste food colorings. Liquid food coloring can commonly be found in red, yellow, blue and green colors, is easy to use and will yield a dough with a pastel color. Paste food coloring, which is found anywhere cake decorating supplies are sold, comes in a wide variety of colors and can be used to tint dough to darker, more vibrant shades.

To tint cookie dough, add the food coloring as soon as the flour is incorporated into the dough. Start with a small amount of food coloring and add more until the desired shade is achieved, being careful not to overmix the dough. If you're using paste food coloring, use a clean toothpick each time you add color to the dough to prevent transferring raw dough into the food coloring container.

Cream Cheese Sugar Cookies

Makes about 5 dozen cookies

Tender and rich, these cookies disappear in a hurry.

Tips

Use only just as much flour as you need on your rolling surface and rolling pin to keep the cookies from sticking. If the dough absorbs too much extra flour, the cookies will be tough.

Let frosting set before storing cookies between layers of wax paper in a tightly sealed container in the refrigerator.

- Cookie sheets, lined with parchment paper
- Cookie cutters

Cookies

3 cups	all-purpose flour	750 mL
1 tsp	baking powder	5 mL
1/4 tsp	baking soda	1 mL
1/4 tsp	salt	1 mL
3/4 cup	unsalted butter, softened	175 mL
3 oz	cream cheese, softened	90 g
1 cup	granulated sugar	250 mL
1	egg yolk	1
1 tsp	vanilla extract	5 mL

Frosting

2 cups	confectioner's (powdered/icing) sugar	500 mL
3 tbsp	cream cheese, at room temperature	45 mL
2 to 3 tbsp	half-and-half (10%) cream or milk	25 to 45 mL
1 tsp	vanilla extract	5 mL

1. **Cookies:** In a bowl, whisk together flour, baking powder, baking soda and salt until well combined. Set aside.

2. In a large bowl, using an electric mixer on medium speed, cream butter, cream cheese and granulated sugar until light and fluffy, about 3 minutes. Add egg yolk and beat well. Beat in vanilla. Scrape down sides of bowl. On low speed or using a wooden spoon, gradually add flour mixture, beating just until blended.

3. Divide dough in half. Shape each portion into a flat disk. Tightly wrap each disk in plastic wrap and chill for at least 1 hour.

4. Preheat oven to 350°F (180°C). Lightly dust a pastry board, clean countertop or other flat surface and a rolling pin with confectioner's sugar or flour. Working with one dough disk at a time, unwrap dough and roll out to uniform thickness of 1/8 inch (3 mm). Halfway through rolling, rotate the dough a quarter turn and dust the board again to prevent dough from sticking.

5. Dip 2 1/2-inch (6 cm) cookie cutters in confectioner's sugar or flour and cut dough into desired shapes. Cut out as many cookies as possible from first rolling. Carefully transfer cutouts to prepared cookie sheets, placing 1 inch (2.5 cm) apart. Gather dough remnants into a ball, reroll, cut out more cookies and transfer to cookie sheets.

Tip

The combination of butter and cream cheese in the dough creates a flavorful and tender cookie.

6. Bake one sheet at a time in preheated oven for 8 to 10 minutes or until edges start to turn lightly golden.

7. Immediately slide parchment paper onto a wire cooling rack. Cool cookies for 5 minutes, then transfer from parchment paper to cooling rack and cool completely.

8. *Frosting:* In a bowl, combine confectioner's sugar, cream cheese, 2 tablespoons (25 mL) of the cream and vanilla. Using an electric mixer on medium speed, beat until frosting is light and fluffy, about 2 minutes. Add more cream as needed to achieve the desired consistency. Spread frosting over tops of cooled cookies.

Egg Paint

Decorating with egg paint is a great way to add vibrant color and decorative designs to pale cutout cookies that will not be frosted. The cutouts are painted before they go into the oven, and the design bakes onto the cookies.

To make egg paint: In a small bowl, stir together 2 egg yolks and $\frac{1}{2}$ teaspoon (2 mL) water until well blended. Divide the egg mixture among several small bowls. Add a little bit of food coloring to each bowl and stir until evenly combined.

Use a small, clean brush to paint decorative designs on unbaked cutouts before baking. Clean the brush between colors or use a different brush for each color. If the egg paint starts to thicken while you're working with it, thin it with a drop or two of water.

Old-time Gingerbread Cookies

Makes about 2½ dozen cookies

Memories of childhood are rekindled with these thick, chewy gingerbread people. Lightly spiced, these are a favorite of kids and adults alike.

Tips

Use a variety of cookie cutter sizes to create gingerbread "families."

Increase the ginger if you prefer a strong ginger flavor.

Meringue powder is sold in stores that carry cake decorating supplies and in some large supermarkets.

- Cookie sheets, lined with parchment paper
- Cookie cutters

Cookies

3 cups	all-purpose flour	750 mL
1 tsp	ground ginger	5 mL
½ tsp	ground cinnamon	2 mL
½ tsp	baking powder	2 mL
½ tsp	baking soda	2 mL
¼ tsp	salt	1 mL
½ cup	unsalted butter, softened	125 mL
⅓ cup	granulated sugar	75 mL
⅓ cup	packed light brown sugar	75 mL
1	egg	1
½ cup	fancy molasses	125 mL
½ tsp	vanilla extract	2 mL

Royal Icing

2 cups	confectioner's (powdered/icing) sugar	500 mL
1 tbsp	meringue powder	15 mL
¼ cup	water	50 mL
	Decorative candies	

1. **Cookies:** In a bowl, whisk together flour, ginger, cinnamon, baking powder, baking soda and salt until well combined. Set aside.
2. In a large bowl, using an electric mixer on medium speed, cream butter, granulated sugar and brown sugar until light and fluffy, about 3 minutes. Add egg and beat well. Beat in molasses and vanilla. Scrape down sides of bowl. On low speed or using a wooden spoon, gradually add flour mixture, beating just until blended.
3. Divide dough in half. Shape each portion into a flat disk. Tightly wrap each disk in plastic wrap and chill for at least 1 hour.
4. Preheat oven to 350°F (180°C). Lightly dust a pastry board, clean countertop or other flat surface and a rolling pin with confectioner's sugar or flour. Working with one dough disk at a time, unwrap dough and roll out to uniform thickness of ¼ inch (0.5 cm). Halfway through rolling, rotate the dough a quarter turn and dust the board again to prevent dough from sticking.

Tips

Royal icing dries out quickly. Cover bowl of icing with a damp cloth to keep it moist.

Let icing set before storing cookies between layers of wax paper in a tightly sealed container.

5. Dip 3-inch (7.5 cm) people-shaped cookie cutters in confectioner's sugar or flour and cut dough into desired shapes. Cut out as many cookies as possible from first rolling. Carefully transfer cutouts to prepared cookie sheets, placing 1 inch (2.5 cm) apart. Gather dough remnants into a ball, reroll, cut out more cookies and transfer to cookie sheets.

6. Bake one sheet at a time in preheated oven for 9 to 11 minutes or until set.

7. Immediately slide parchment paper onto a wire cooling rack. Cool cookies for 5 minutes, then transfer from parchment paper to cooling rack and cool completely.

8. *Icing:* In a bowl, combine confectioner's sugar and meringue powder until well blended. Add water. Using an electric mixer on low speed, beat until well blended. Increase speed to medium and beat until soft peaks form, about 5 to 6 minutes. Spoon icing into a pastry bag fitted with a round tip or a zippered storage bag. Cut off a small corner of storage bag. Pipe icing onto cookies and decorate with candies as desired.

Coating Cutout Cookies with Royal Icing

Fit two pastry bags with a coupler and a small decorator tip in each bag. (If using disposable pastry bags, cut the point off the bags before adding the tip.)

Fill one bag with Royal Icing (page 212). Pipe a fine bead of icing around the edge of each cookie. This outline will act as a dam and keep the icing from flowing over the edge of the cookie.

Thin the remaining icing with a few drops of water until it will flow smoothly when spread. Fill the second pastry bag with the thinned icing. With the thinned icing, fill in the centers of the cookies, letting the icing flow out to the outline. If necessary, use a small clean paintbrush to spread the icing evenly over the cookies.

Let the icing dry completely before adding any additional decorations.

Holiday Sugar Cookies

Makes about 4 dozen cookies ● ● ●

Topped with brightly colored sugar, these delicious cookies make a perfect holiday treat.

Tips

Change the color of the sugar to fit the holiday.

Cream of tartar (tartaric acid) is an acid. In cookies leavened with baking soda alone, which contain no other acid ingredients, cream of tartar is added to activate the baking soda.

- Cookie sheets, lined with parchment paper
- Cookie cutters

Cookies

2 cups	all-purpose flour	500 mL
1/2 tsp	cream of tartar	2 mL
1/4 tsp	baking soda	1 mL
1/4 tsp	salt	1 mL
1/2 cup	unsalted butter, softened	125 mL
1 cup	granulated sugar	250 mL
1	egg	1
1 tsp	vanilla extract	5 mL

Topping

1	egg white	1
1 tsp	water	5 mL
	Red– and green–colored sugar	

1. **Cookies:** In a bowl, whisk together flour, cream of tartar, baking soda and salt until well combined. Set aside.

2. In a large bowl, using an electric mixer on medium speed, cream butter and granulated sugar until light and fluffy, about 3 minutes. Add egg and beat well. Beat in vanilla. Scrape down sides of bowl. On low speed or using a wooden spoon, gradually add flour mixture, beating just until blended.

3. Divide dough in half. Shape each portion into a flat disk. Tightly wrap each disk in plastic wrap and chill for at least 1 hour.

4. Preheat oven to 350°F (180°C). Lightly dust a pastry board, clean countertop or other flat surface and a rolling pin with confectioner's (powdered/icing) sugar or flour. Working with one dough disk at a time, unwrap dough and roll out to uniform thickness of 1/4 inch (0.5 cm). Halfway through rolling, rotate the dough a quarter turn and dust the board again to prevent dough from sticking.

5. Dip 2 1/2-inch (6 cm) cookie cutters in confectioner's sugar or flour and cut dough into desired shapes. Cut out as many cookies as possible from first rolling. Carefully transfer cutouts to prepared cookie sheets, placing 1 inch (2.5 cm) apart. Gather dough remnants into a ball, reroll, cut out more cookies and transfer to cookie sheets.

6. **Topping:** In a small bowl, using a wire whisk, lightly beat egg white and water. Lightly brush tops of cookies with egg white mixture and sprinkle with colored sugar.

Tip
Sugar provides both flavor and structure to cookies.

7. Bake one sheet at a time in preheated oven for 10 to 12 minutes or until edges start to turn lightly golden.

8. Immediately slide parchment paper onto a wire cooling rack. Cool cookies for 5 minutes, then transfer from parchment paper to cooling rack and cool completely.

Hosting a Cookie Decorating Party

A cookie decorating party is an entertaining holiday event and a great way to spend time with friends and neighbors during the busy holiday season. It is also a fun activity for kids' birthday parties, if you can handle a little mess. Here are a few tips to get you started.

- Purchase a variety of colored sugars, sprinkles, decorator candies, chocolate chips and any other candy items that you think will be fun to use for decorating cookies.
- Bake the cutout cookies the day before the party and consider making two or three different kinds of cutout cookies. To make the job easier, you can prepare the doughs a few days in advance and then roll, cut out and bake the cookies the day before your event. Use a variety of shaped cookie cutters that fit the season or theme of the party.
- Make two or three large mixing bowls of frosting and consider making a large batch of Royal Icing (page 212). Divide the frosting into four or five smaller bowls and color each with a different shade of food coloring.
- Assemble several disposable pastry bags and fit them with couplers and decorating tips. Keep additional decorating tips handy so different shapes can be fitted to the icing bags. Fill each bag with a different frosting color. Reserve some frosting for icing the cookies themselves.
- Cover the table with a plastic tablecloth and set out lots of damp and dry paper towels for cleaning sticky hands.
- Set out an assortment of knives, spatulas, spoons, tweezers, toothpicks and any other tools you think would be helpful for decorating the cookies.

Brown Sugar Cutouts

● ● ●

With a rich flavor from lots of brown sugar, these are a delightful change from traditional sugar cookies.

Tips

If you have problems with your cookies overbaking or underbaking, use an oven thermometer to check the accuracy of your oven's temperature control.

Let frosting set before storing cookies between layers of wax paper in a tightly sealed container.

- Cookie sheets, lined with parchment paper
- Cookie cutters

Cookies

2½ cups	all-purpose flour	625 mL
½ tsp	baking powder	2 mL
½ tsp	baking soda	2 mL
¼ tsp	salt	1 mL
¾ cup	unsalted butter, softened	175 mL
1½ cups	packed light brown sugar	375 mL
2	eggs	2
2 tsp	vanilla extract	10 mL

Frosting

2 cups	confectioner's (powdered/icing) sugar	500 mL
2 to 3 tbsp	half-and-half (10%) cream or milk	25 to 45 mL
½ tsp	vanilla extract	2 mL

1. **Cookies:** In a bowl, whisk together flour, baking powder, baking soda and salt until well combined. Set aside.

2. In a large bowl, using an electric mixer on medium speed, cream butter and brown sugar until light and fluffy, about 3 minutes. Add eggs one at a time, beating well after each addition. Beat in vanilla. Scrape down sides of bowl. On low speed or using a wooden spoon, gradually add flour mixture, beating just until blended.

3. Divide dough in half. Shape each portion into a flat disk. Tightly wrap each disk in plastic wrap and chill for at least 1 hour.

4. Preheat oven to 350°F (180°C). Lightly dust a pastry board, clean countertop or other flat surface and a rolling pin with confectioner's sugar or flour. Working with one dough disk at a time, unwrap dough and roll out to uniform thickness of ⅛ inch (3 mm). Halfway through rolling, rotate the dough a quarter turn and dust the board again to prevent dough from sticking.

5. Dip 2½-inch (6 cm) cookie cutters in confectioner's sugar or flour and cut dough into desired shapes. Cut out as many cookies as possible from first rolling. Carefully transfer cutouts to prepared cookie sheets, placing 1 inch (2.5 cm) apart. Gather dough remnants into a ball, reroll, cut out more cookies and transfer to cookie sheets.

Tip

Bread flour has a high protein content and should not be used for baking cookies.

6. Bake one sheet at a time in preheated oven for 6 to 8 minutes or until edges start to turn lightly golden.

7. Immediately slide parchment paper onto a wire cooling rack. Cool cookies for 5 minutes, then transfer from parchment paper to cooling rack and cool completely.

8. *Frosting:* In a bowl, combine confectioner's sugar, 2 tablespoons (25 mL) of the cream and vanilla. Using an electric mixer on medium speed, beat until frosting is smooth and spreadable. Add more cream as needed to achieve the desired consistency. Spread frosting over tops of cooled cookies.

Cookie Place Cards

Add a unique touch to your dinner table and make every guest feel special with personalized cookie place cards. These are great for dinner parties and brunches, holiday dinners, birthdays, rehearsal dinners, wedding receptions, or any sit-down event.

Roll one portion of the cookie dough into a rectangle and use a scalloped pastry wheel cutter to slice the dough into rectangles of desired size. Bake and cool as directed in the recipe and ice with Royal Icing (page 212), if desired. Thin the icing to piping consistency and spoon into a pastry bag fitted with a small round decorator tip. You may also use a squeeze bottle or a zippered storage bag with a tiny corner cut off. Pipe names and any decorations onto cookies. Let icing set completely.

Eier Kringle

Flavored with aromatic spices and molasses, these German holiday cookies are traditionally cut into Santa Claus shapes and glazed with vanilla icing.

Tips

Flavors can blend during storage, so store cookies with strong flavors in separate containers.

Let icing set before storing cookies between layers of wax paper in a tightly sealed container.

- Cookie sheets, lined with parchment paper
- Cookie cutters

Cookies

2¾ cups	all-purpose flour	675 mL
1 tsp	baking powder	5 mL
1 tsp	ground cinnamon	5 mL
½ tsp	ground ginger	2 mL
½ tsp	ground nutmeg	2 mL
¼ tsp	baking soda	1 mL
¼ tsp	salt	1 mL
¼ cup	unsalted butter, softened	50 mL
½ cup	granulated sugar	125 mL
½ cup	packed light brown sugar	125 mL
⅓ cup	fancy molasses	75 mL
2	egg yolks	2
¼ cup	sour cream	50 mL
1 tsp	vanilla extract	5 mL

Icing

1½ cups	confectioner's (powdered/icing) sugar	375 mL
2 tbsp	half-and-half (10%) cream or milk	25 mL
1 tbsp	unsalted butter, softened	15 mL
½ tsp	vanilla extract	2 mL

1. **Cookies:** In a bowl, whisk together flour, baking powder, cinnamon, ginger, nutmeg, baking soda and salt until well combined. Set aside.

2. In a large bowl, using an electric mixer on medium speed, cream butter, granulated sugar, brown sugar and molasses until light and fluffy, about 3 minutes. Add egg yolks one at a time, beating well after each addition. Beat in sour cream and vanilla. Scrape down sides of bowl. On low speed or using a wooden spoon, gradually add flour mixture, beating just until blended.

3. Divide dough in half. Shape each portion into a flat disk. Tightly wrap each disk in plastic wrap and chill for at least 1 hour.

4. Preheat oven to 350°F (180°C). Lightly dust a pastry board, clean countertop or other flat surface and a rolling pin with confectioner's sugar or flour. Working with one dough disk at a time, unwrap dough and roll out to uniform thickness of ¼ inch (0.5 cm). Halfway through rolling, rotate the dough a quarter turn and dust the board again to prevent dough from sticking.

Tip

Molasses is sold in two forms, sulfured and unsulfured. The smooth flavor of light, unsulfured molasses, also called fancy molasses, makes it the best choice for baking.

5. Dip 2½-inch (6 cm) cookie cutters in confectioner's sugar or flour and cut dough into desired shapes. Cut out as many cookies as possible from first rolling. Carefully transfer cutouts to prepared cookie sheets, placing 1 inch (2.5 cm) apart. Gather dough remnants into a ball, reroll, cut out more cookies and transfer to cookie sheets.

6. Bake one sheet at a time in preheated oven for 10 to 12 minutes or until set.

7. Immediately slide parchment paper onto a wire cooling rack. Cool cookies for 5 minutes, then transfer from parchment paper to cooling rack and cool completely.

8. *Icing:* In a bowl, combine confectioner's sugar, cream, butter and vanilla. Using an electric mixer on medium speed, beat until icing is smooth and spreadable. Spread icing over tops of cooled cookies.

Painting Iced Cookies

You can express your artistic talents by adding your own painted designs to iced cutout cookies. Ice the cooled cookies with Royal Icing (page 212) and let dry completely. Using a clean fine paint brush, carefully paint designs on the icing with liquid food coloring. Rinse the brush thoroughly between colors or use a different brush for each color.

Lemon Sugar Cookies

Makes about 6 dozen cookies ● ● ●

Lusciously lemon, these cookies have a refreshing, bright citrus flavor.

Tips

For the freshest flavor, grate lemons and squeeze juice just before making the cookies. Never use bottled lemon juice as it will give the cookies a bitter, unpleasant aftertaste.

Let frosting set before storing cookies between layers of wax paper in a tightly sealed container.

● Cookie sheets, lined with parchment paper
● Cookie cutters

Cookies

3 cups	all-purpose flour	750 mL
½ tsp	baking powder	2 mL
½ tsp	baking soda	2 mL
¼ tsp	salt	1 mL
¾ cup	unsalted butter, softened	175 mL
⅔ cup	granulated sugar	150 mL
½ cup	confectioner's (powdered/icing) sugar	125 mL
2	eggs	2
1 tbsp	grated lemon zest	15 mL
3 tbsp	freshly squeezed lemon juice	45 mL
½ tsp	vanilla extract	2 mL

Frosting

2½ cups	confectioner's (powdered/icing) sugar	625 mL
2 tbsp	unsalted butter, softened	25 mL
2 to 3 tbsp	freshly squeezed lemon juice	25 to 45 mL
¼ tsp	vanilla extract	1 mL

1. ***Cookies:*** In a bowl, whisk together flour, baking powder, baking soda and salt until well combined. Set aside.

2. In a large bowl, using an electric mixer on medium speed, cream butter, granulated sugar and confectioner's sugar until light and fluffy, about 3 minutes. Add eggs one at a time, beating well after each addition. Beat in lemon zest, lemon juice and vanilla. Scrape down sides of bowl. On low speed or using a wooden spoon, gradually add flour mixture, beating just until blended.

3. Divide dough in half. Shape each portion into a flat disk. Tightly wrap each disk in plastic wrap and chill for at least 1 hour.

4. Preheat oven to 350°F (180°C). Lightly dust a pastry board, clean countertop or other flat surface and a rolling pin with confectioner's sugar or flour. Working with one dough disk at a time, unwrap dough and roll out to uniform thickness of ⅛ inch (3 mm). Halfway through rolling, rotate the dough a quarter turn and dust the board again to prevent dough from sticking.

Tip
When juicing citrus fruits, be careful not to squeeze or ream the fruit so much that you press into the white pith. This can make the juice bitter. Freshly squeezed citrus juices should be strained to remove seeds.

5. Dip $2\frac{1}{2}$-inch (6 cm) cookie cutters in confectioner's sugar or flour and cut dough into desired shapes. Cut out as many cookies as possible from first rolling. Carefully transfer cutouts to prepared cookie sheets, placing 1 inch (2.5 cm) apart. Gather dough remnants into a ball, reroll, cut out more cookies and transfer to cookie sheets.

6. Bake one sheet at a time in preheated oven for 8 to 10 minutes or until edges start to turn lightly golden.

7. Immediately slide parchment paper onto a wire cooling rack. Cool cookies for 5 minutes, then transfer from parchment paper to cooling rack and cool completely.

8. *Frosting:* In a bowl, combine confectioner's sugar, butter, 2 tablespoons (25 mL) of the lemon juice and vanilla. Using an electric mixer on medium speed, beat until frosting is light and fluffy, about 2 minutes. Add more lemon juice as needed to achieve the desired consistency. Spread frosting over tops of cooled cookies.

Sugar Sparkles

To give cookies a sparkling accent, pipe frosting outlines and patterns onto cookies. While the frosting is still soft, sprinkle colored sugar over the frosting design. Let the icing dry for several minutes, then shake off the excess sugar.

Almond Cutouts

Layers of almond flavors give these cookies their tantalizing nuttiness.

Tips

For a pretty finishing touch, use sliced unsalted almonds in place of chopped almonds and arrange almond slices in the shape of a flower on top of the iced cookies.

Let frosting set before storing cookies between layers of wax paper in a tightly sealed container.

- Cookie sheets, lined with parchment paper
- Cookie cutters

Cookies

3 cups	all-purpose flour	750 mL
1 tsp	baking powder	5 mL
½ tsp	salt	2 mL
¾ cup	unsalted butter, softened	175 mL
1¼ cups	granulated sugar	300 mL
2	eggs	2
2 tsp	almond extract	10 mL

Frosting

3 cups	confectioner's (powdered/icing) sugar	750 mL
3 tbsp	unsalted butter, softened	45 mL
3 to 4 tbsp	half-and-half (10%) cream or milk	45 to 50 mL
1 tsp	almond extract	5 mL
⅓ cup	finely chopped unsalted almonds	75 mL

1. *Cookies:* In a bowl, whisk together flour, baking powder and salt until well combined. Set aside.

2. In a large bowl, using an electric mixer on medium speed, cream butter and granulated sugar until light and fluffy, about 3 minutes. Add eggs one at a time, beating well after each addition. Beat in almond extract. Scrape down sides of bowl. On low speed or using a wooden spoon, gradually add flour mixture, beating just until blended.

3. Divide dough in half. Shape each portion into a flat disk. Tightly wrap each disk in plastic wrap and chill for at least 1 hour.

4. Preheat oven to 375°F (190°C). Lightly dust a pastry board, clean countertop or other flat surface and a rolling pin with confectioner's sugar or flour. Working with one dough disk at a time, unwrap dough and roll out to uniform thickness of ⅛ inch (3 mm). Halfway through rolling, rotate the dough a quarter turn and dust the board again to prevent dough from sticking.

5. Dip 2½-inch (6 cm) cookie cutters in confectioner's sugar or flour and cut dough into desired shapes. Cut out as many cookies as possible from first rolling. Carefully transfer cutouts to prepared cookie sheets, placing 1 inch (2.5 cm) apart. Gather dough remnants into a ball, reroll, cut out more cookies and transfer to cookie sheets.

Tip

Almond extract is made
from bitter almonds,
not the sweet kind of
almonds that we eat and
add to baked goods.

6. Bake one sheet at a time in preheated oven for 7 to 9 minutes
or until edges start to turn lightly golden.

7. Immediately slide parchment paper onto a wire cooling rack.
Cool cookies for 5 minutes, then transfer from parchment paper
to cooling rack and cool completely.

8. *Frosting:* In a bowl, combine confectioner's sugar, butter,
3 tablespoons (45 mL) of the cream and almond extract. Using
an electric mixer on medium speed, beat until frosting is light
and fluffy, about 2 minutes. Add more cream as needed to
achieve the desired consistency. Spread frosting over tops of
cooled cookies. Sprinkle chopped almonds over frosting.

Milk Paint

Milk paint can be used to paint designs on cutout cookies
before they go into the oven. Milk paint will give you designs
with softer colors than egg paint.

Pour a small amount of evaporated milk into several small
bowls. Add a little bit of food coloring to each bowl and stir
until well blended. Use a small, clean brush to paint decorative
designs on unbaked cutouts. Clean the brush between colors
or use a different brush for each color.

Snowflake Cookies

These pretty snowflake-shaped cookies are perfect to bake on a cold, blustery or snowy winter day.

Tips

These cookies are also wonderful simply dusted with confectioner's sugar in place of the icing.

Let icing set before storing cookies between layers of wax paper in a tightly sealed container.

- Cookie sheets, lined with parchment paper
- Snowflake cookie cutters

Cookies

2¾ cups	all-purpose flour	675 mL
½ tsp	cream of tartar	2 mL
½ tsp	baking soda	2 mL
¼ tsp	salt	1 mL
½ cup	unsalted butter, softened	125 mL
½ cup	vegetable shortening	125 mL
½ cup	granulated sugar	125 mL
½ cup	confectioner's (powdered/icing) sugar	125 mL
1	egg	1
1 tsp	vanilla extract	5 mL
½ tsp	almond extract	2 mL

Icing

2 cups	confectioner's (powdered/icing) sugar	500 mL
2 tbsp	unsalted butter, softened	25 mL
2 to 3 tbsp	half-and-half (10%) cream or milk	25 to 45 mL
¼ tsp	vanilla extract	1 mL
⅛ tsp	almond extract	0.5 mL
	Silver dragée candies	

1. **Cookies:** In a bowl, whisk together flour, cream of tartar, baking soda and salt until well combined. Set aside.
2. In a large bowl, using an electric mixer on medium speed, cream butter, shortening, granulated sugar and confectioner's sugar until light and fluffy, about 3 minutes. Add egg and beat well. Beat in vanilla and almond extract. Scrape down sides of bowl. On low speed or using a wooden spoon, gradually add flour mixture, beating just until blended.
3. Divide dough in half. Shape each portion into a flat disk. Tightly wrap each disk in plastic wrap and chill for at least 1 hour.
4. Preheat oven to 375°F (190°C). Lightly dust a pastry board, clean countertop or other flat surface and a rolling pin with confectioner's sugar or flour. Working with one dough disk at a time, unwrap dough and roll out to uniform thickness of ¼ inch (0.5 cm). Halfway through rolling, rotate the dough a quarter turn and dust the board again to prevent dough from sticking.

Pumpkin Spice Cookies (page 44)

Coconut Macaroons (page 55)

Chocolate Cookies (page 78), Peanut Butter Jam Thumbprints (page 91),
Cranberry Orange Spirals (page 532) and Apricot Rugelach (page 536)

Chocolate-Dipped Cappuccino Sticks (page 83)

Ginger Cookies (page 103)

Chocolate Chunk Cookies (page 126)

White Chocolate Chip Cookies (page 125),
Triple Chocolate Chip Cookies (page 129)
and Chocolate Chocolate Chip Cookies (page 138)

Oatmeal Raisin Cookies (page 147)

Tip
Vanilla extract is made
from the long slender
pods of a tropical orchid
plant.

5. Dip a 2½-inch (6 cm) snowflake-shaped cookie cutter in confectioner's sugar or flour and cut dough into desired shapes. Cut out as many cookies as possible from first rolling. Carefully transfer cutouts to prepared cookie sheets, placing 1 inch (2.5 cm) apart. Gather dough remnants into a ball, reroll, cut out more cookies and transfer to cookie sheets.

6. Bake one sheet at a time in preheated oven for 8 to 10 minutes or until edges start to turn lightly golden.

7. Immediately slide parchment paper onto a wire cooling rack. Cool cookies for 5 minutes, then transfer from parchment paper to cooling rack and cool completely.

8. *Icing:* In a bowl, combine confectioner's sugar, butter, 2 tablespoons (25 mL) of the cream, vanilla and almond extract. Using an electric mixer on medium speed, beat until icing is smooth and spreadable. Add more cream as needed to achieve the desired consistency. Spread icing over tops of cooled cookies. Decorate with silver dragées.

Cookie Cutter Ornaments

Tie a colorful ribbon around individual shaped metal cookie cutters to create ornaments that are both pretty and practical. Choose a variety of shapes or select shaped cookie cutters that fit a specific theme.

Sour Cream Cookies

Sour cream gives these delicious sugar cookies their soft and tender texture. Topped with a thick layer of creamy frosting and colorful candy sprinkles, these cookies are a big hit.

Tips

Dipping the cookie cutters in flour or confectioner's (powdered/icing) sugar before cutting out the cookies will let the dough release from the cutters and ensure nicely shaped cookies.

Let frosting set before storing cookies between layers of wax paper in a tightly sealed container.

- Cookie sheets, lined with parchment paper
- Round cookie cutters

Cookies

3½ cups	all-purpose flour	875 mL
½ tsp	baking powder	2 mL
½ tsp	baking soda	2 mL
¼ tsp	salt	1 mL
½ cup	unsalted butter, softened	125 mL
1 cup	granulated sugar	250 mL
2	eggs	2
¾ cup	sour cream	175 mL
1 tsp	vanilla extract	5 mL
¼ tsp	almond extract	1 mL

Frosting

5 cups	confectioner's (powdered/icing) sugar	1.25 L
⅓ cup	unsalted butter, softened	75 mL
5 to 6 tbsp	half-and-half (10%) cream or milk	75 to 90 mL
1½ tsp	vanilla extract	7 mL
½ tsp	almond extract	2 mL
	Candy sprinkles	

1. **Cookies:** In a bowl, whisk together flour, baking powder, baking soda and salt until well combined. Set aside.

2. In a large bowl, using an electric mixer on medium speed, cream butter and granulated sugar until light and fluffy, about 3 minutes. Add eggs one at a time, beating well after each addition. Beat in sour cream, vanilla and almond extract. Scrape down sides of bowl. On low speed or using a wooden spoon, gradually add flour mixture, beating just until blended.

3. Divide dough in half. Shape each portion into a flat disk. Tightly wrap each disk in plastic wrap and chill for at least 4 hours or overnight.

4. Preheat oven to 375°F (190°C). Lightly dust a pastry board, clean countertop or other flat surface and a rolling pin with confectioner's sugar or flour. Working with one dough disk at a time, unwrap dough and roll out to uniform thickness of ¼ inch (0.5 cm). Halfway through rolling, rotate the dough a quarter turn and dust the board again to prevent dough from sticking.

Tip

Accurately measure all ingredients for the dough before starting to mix the cookies.

5. Dip a $2\frac{1}{2}$-inch (6 cm) round cookie cutter in confectioner's sugar or flour and cut dough into desired shapes. Cut out as many cookies as possible from first rolling. Carefully transfer cutouts to prepared cookie sheets, placing 1 inch (2.5 cm) apart. Gather dough remnants into a ball, reroll, cut out more cookies and transfer to cookie sheets.

6. Bake one sheet at a time in preheated oven for 10 to 12 minutes or until edges start to turn lightly golden.

7. Immediately slide parchment paper onto a wire cooling rack. Cool cookies for 5 minutes, then transfer from parchment paper to cooling rack and cool completely.

8. *Frosting:* In a bowl, combine confectioner's sugar, butter, 5 tablespoons (75 mL) of the cream, vanilla and almond extract. Using an electric mixer on medium speed, beat until frosting is light and fluffy, about 2 minutes. Add more cream as needed to achieve the desired consistency. Spread frosting over tops of cooled cookies. Sprinkle candy sprinkles over top of frosted cookies.

Cocoa Powder Stencil Designs

A simple dusting of sifted cocoa powder can dress up light-colored, unfrosted cutout cookies or add an extra dimension to frosted cutouts.

Center a small pretty stencil (available at craft stores in a wide variety of patterns) or a paper doily on top of the cookie. Lightly sift the cocoa powder over top of the cookie. Carefully remove the stencil without disturbing the cocoa design. Decorate the cookies the same day they will be served and store the cookies in a single layer to prevent smudging the designs.

Glazed Orange Cutouts

Using orange juice concentrate in both the cookie dough and the glaze intensifies the citrus flavor of these delightful cookies.

Tips

A Microplane grater will finely zest the orange peel for a wonderful texture in cookies.

Let glaze set before storing cookies between layers of wax paper in a tightly sealed container.

● **Cookie sheets, lined with parchment paper**
● **Cookie cutters**

Cookies

3⅓ cups	all-purpose flour	825 mL
½ tsp	baking powder	2 mL
½ tsp	baking soda	2 mL
¼ tsp	salt	1 mL
¾ cup	unsalted butter, softened	175 mL
¼ cup	vegetable shortening	50 mL
⅔ cup	granulated sugar	150 mL
⅓ cup	packed light brown sugar	75 mL
1	egg	1
⅓ cup	frozen orange juice concentrate, thawed	75 mL
1 tbsp	grated orange zest	15 mL
½ tsp	vanilla extract	2 mL

Glaze

1½ cups	confectioner's (powdered/icing) sugar	375 mL
2 tbsp	unsalted butter, softened	25 mL
1 tbsp	frozen orange juice concentrate, thawed	15 mL
1 tsp	grated orange zest	5 mL
2 to 3 tsp	half-and-half (10%) cream or milk	10 to 15 mL
¼ tsp	vanilla extract	1 mL

1. **Cookies:** In a bowl, whisk together flour, baking powder, baking soda and salt until well combined. Set aside.

2. In a large bowl, using an electric mixer on medium speed, cream butter, shortening, granulated sugar and brown sugar until light and fluffy, about 3 minutes. Add egg and beat well. Beat in orange juice concentrate, orange zest and vanilla. Scrape down sides of bowl. On low speed or using a wooden spoon, gradually add flour mixture, beating just until blended.

3. Divide dough in half. Shape each portion into a flat disk. Tightly wrap each disk in plastic wrap and chill for at least 1 hour.

4. Preheat oven to 350°F (180°C). Lightly dust a pastry board, clean countertop or other flat surface and a rolling pin with confectioner's sugar or flour. Working with one dough disk at a time, unwrap dough and roll out to uniform thickness of ⅛ inch (3 mm). Halfway through rolling, rotate the dough a quarter turn and dust the board again to prevent dough from sticking.

Tip
To prevent tops or bottoms of cookies from becoming too brown, bake one sheet at a time with the oven rack positioned in the center of the oven.

5. Dip $2\frac{1}{2}$-inch (6 cm) cookie cutters in confectioner's sugar or flour and cut dough into desired shapes. Cut out as many cookies as possible from first rolling. Carefully transfer cutouts to prepared cookie sheets, placing 1 inch (2.5 cm) apart. Gather dough remnants into a ball, reroll, cut out more cookies and transfer to cookie sheets.

6. Bake one sheet at a time in preheated oven for 7 to 9 minutes or until edges start to turn lightly golden.

7. Immediately slide parchment paper onto a wire cooling rack. Cool cookies for 5 minutes, then transfer from parchment paper to cooling rack and cool completely.

8. *Glaze:* In a bowl, combine confectioner's sugar, butter, orange juice concentrate, orange zest, 2 teaspoons (10 mL) of the cream and vanilla. Using an electric mixer on medium speed, beat until glaze is smooth and spreadable. Add more cream as needed to achieve the desired consistency. Spread glaze over tops of cooled cookies.

Maple Leaf Cookies

● ● ●

A plate full of these delicious treats make an excellent gift for a friend or neighbor.

Tips

A small offset spatula is the perfect tool to quickly and easily spread icing on the cookies.

Let icing set before storing cookies between layers of wax paper in a tightly sealed container.

- Cookie sheets, lined with parchment paper
- Maple-leaf-shaped cookie cutters

Cookies

2¾ cups	all-purpose flour	675 mL
1 tsp	baking powder	5 mL
½ tsp	salt	2 mL
¾ cup	unsalted butter, softened	175 mL
½ cup	granulated sugar	125 mL
½ cup	packed dark brown sugar	125 mL
2	eggs	2
2 tsp	maple flavoring	10 mL
½ tsp	vanilla extract	2 mL

Icing

2 cups	confectioner's (powdered/icing) sugar	500 mL
3 tbsp	unsalted butter, softened	45 mL
2 to 3 tbsp	half-and-half (10%) cream or milk	25 to 45 mL
¾ tsp	maple flavoring	3 mL
½ tsp	vanilla extract	2 mL

1. **Cookies:** In a bowl, whisk together flour, baking powder and salt until well combined. Set aside.

2. In a large bowl, using an electric mixer on medium speed, cream butter, granulated sugar and brown sugar until light and fluffy, about 3 minutes. Add eggs one at a time, beating well after each addition. Beat in maple flavoring and vanilla. Scrape down sides of bowl. On low speed or using a wooden spoon, gradually add flour mixture, beating just until blended.

3. Divide dough in half. Shape each portion into a flat disk. Tightly wrap each disk in plastic wrap and chill for at least 1 hour.

4. Preheat oven to 350°F (180°C). Lightly dust a pastry board, clean countertop or other flat surface and a rolling pin with confectioner's sugar or flour. Working with one dough disk at a time, unwrap dough and roll out to uniform thickness of ¼ inch (0.5 cm). Halfway through rolling, rotate the dough a quarter turn and dust the board again to prevent dough from sticking.

5. Dip 2½-inch (6 cm) cookie cutters in confectioner's sugar or flour and cut dough into desired shapes. Cut out as many cookies as possible from first rolling. Carefully transfer cutouts to prepared cookie sheets, placing 1 inch (2.5 cm) apart. Gather dough remnants into a ball, reroll, cut out more cookies and transfer to cookie sheets.

Tip

Flavorings such as maple, rum and brandy give cookies a stronger flavor than their liquid counterparts. A teaspoon (5 mL) of maple flavoring will give as much maple flavor as $\frac{1}{4}$ cup (125 mL) of maple syrup without adding that much liquid.

6. Bake one sheet at a time in preheated oven for 10 to 12 minutes or until edges start to turn lightly golden.

7. Immediately slide parchment paper onto a wire cooling rack. Cool cookies for 5 minutes, then transfer from parchment paper to cooling rack and cool completely.

8. *Icing:* In a bowl, combine confectioner's sugar, butter, 2 tablespoons (25 mL) of the cream, maple flavoring and vanilla. Using an electric mixer on medium speed, beat until icing is smooth and spreadable. Add more cream as needed to achieve the desired consistency. Spread icing over tops of cooled cookies.

Lollipop Cookies

Like your cookies on a stick? Make lollipop cookies! Roll out cutout cookie dough to a uniform thickness of $\frac{3}{8}$-inch (0.75 cm). Using a $2\frac{1}{2}$-inch (6 cm) round cookie cutter, cut out as many cookies as possible from the first rolling. Carefully transfer the cutouts to parchment-lined cookie sheets, placing 2 inches (5 cm) apart. Carefully insert a round lollipop stick into the side of each cutout, gently pushing the stick halfway into the cutout.

Bake one cookie sheet at a time in an oven preheated to 350°F (180°C) for 10 to 12 minutes, or until the edges turn lightly golden brown. Let cookies cool on the sheet for a couple of minutes, then use a wide spatula to carefully transfer them to a wire cooling rack. Allow the cookies to cool completely before decorating as desired.

Chocolate Sandwich Cookies

Filled with a fluffy buttercream frosting, these cookies appeal to all ages.

Tip

Make cutouts close together on rolled dough to get as many cookies as possible from the first rolling. Rolling the dough scraps multiple times can toughen the cookies.

Variation

Chocolate Coffee Cream Cookies: Add 1 tsp (5 mL) instant espresso powder to filling.

● Cookie sheets, lined with parchment paper
● Cookie cutters

Cookies

2½ cups	all-purpose flour	625 mL
⅓ cup	unsweetened Dutch-process cocoa powder	75 mL
¼ tsp	baking soda	1 mL
¼ tsp	salt	1 mL
½ cup	unsalted butter, softened	125 mL
½ cup	vegetable shortening	125 mL
1⅓ cups	packed light brown sugar	325 mL
1	egg	1
1 tsp	vanilla extract	5 mL

Filling

2 cups	confectioner's (powdered/icing) sugar	500 mL
2 tbsp	unsalted butter, softened	25 mL
2 tbsp	half-and-half (10%) cream or milk	25 mL
1 tsp	vanilla extract	5 mL

1. **Cookies:** In a bowl, whisk together flour, cocoa powder, baking soda and salt until well combined. Set aside.

2. In a large bowl, using an electric mixer on medium speed, cream butter, shortening and brown sugar until light and fluffy, about 3 minutes. Add egg and beat well. Beat in vanilla. Scrape down sides of bowl. On low speed or using a wooden spoon, gradually add flour mixture, beating just until blended.

3. Divide dough in half. Shape each portion into a flat disk. Tightly wrap each disk in plastic wrap and chill for at least 1 hour.

4. Preheat oven to 350°F (180°C). Lightly dust a pastry board, clean countertop or other flat surface and a rolling pin with confectioner's sugar or flour. Working with one dough disk at a time, unwrap dough and roll out to uniform thickness of ⅛ inch (3 mm). Halfway through rolling, rotate the dough a quarter turn and dust the board again to prevent dough from sticking.

5. Dip 2½-inch (6 cm) cookie cutters in confectioner's sugar or flour and cut dough into desired shapes. Cut out as many cookies as possible from first rolling. Carefully transfer cutouts to prepared cookie sheets, placing 1 inch (2.5 cm) apart. Gather dough remnants into a ball, reroll, cut out more cookies and transfer to cookie sheets.

6. Bake one sheet at a time in preheated oven for 8 to 10 minutes or until set.

7. Immediately slide parchment paper onto a wire cooling rack. Cool cookies for 5 minutes, then transfer from parchment paper to cooling rack and cool completely.

8. *Filling:* In a bowl, combine confectioner's sugar, butter, cream and vanilla. Using an electric mixer on medium speed, beat until frosting is light and fluffy, about 3 minutes. Spread a layer of filling over the bottom side of half of the cooled cookies. Top with remaining cookies.

Changing the Shape

The great thing about rolled cutout cookies is that you can cut them into a wide variety of shapes. Most of the recommended baking times are based on cookies made with a cookie cutter that is about $2\frac{1}{2}$ inches (6 cm) in diameter. If you use cookie cutters that are larger than those indicated in the recipe, you will need to increase the baking time slightly. If the cookie cutters are smaller than $2\frac{1}{2}$ inches (6 cm), then reduce the baking time.

Spice Cookies

Scented with orange and warm spices, these cookies fill the house with their tantalizing aroma as they bake.

Tips

For crisper cookies, bake an additional 1 to 2 minutes.

Flavors can blend during storage, so store cookies with strong flavors in separate containers.

● **Cookie sheets, lined with parchment paper**
● **Cookie cutters**

2¾ cups	all-purpose flour	675 mL
2 tsp	ground cinnamon	10 mL
1 tsp	ground ginger	5 mL
½ tsp	ground nutmeg	2 mL
½ tsp	baking powder	2 mL
¼ tsp	baking soda	1 mL
¼ tsp	salt	1 mL
¾ cup	unsalted butter, softened	175 mL
⅔ cup	granulated sugar	150 mL
⅔ cup	packed dark brown sugar	150 mL
1	egg	1
1 tbsp	fancy molasses	15 mL
2 tbsp	grated orange zest	25 mL
3 tbsp	freshly squeezed orange juice	45 mL
½ tsp	vanilla extract	2 mL

1. In a bowl, whisk together flour, cinnamon, ginger, nutmeg, baking powder, baking soda and salt until well combined. Set aside.
2. In a large bowl, using an electric mixer on medium speed, cream butter, granulated sugar and brown sugar until light and fluffy, about 3 minutes. Add egg and beat well. Beat in molasses, orange zest, orange juice and vanilla. Scrape down sides of bowl. On low speed or using a wooden spoon, gradually add flour mixture, beating just until blended.
3. Divide dough in half. Shape each portion into a flat disk. Tightly wrap each disk in plastic wrap and chill for at least 1 hour.
4. Preheat oven to 350°F (180°C). Lightly dust a pastry board, clean countertop or other flat surface and a rolling pin with confectioner's (powdered/icing) sugar or flour. Working with one dough disk at a time, unwrap dough and roll out to uniform thickness of ⅛ inch (3 mm). Halfway through rolling, rotate the dough a quarter turn and dust the board again to prevent dough from sticking.

Tip

Buy spices in small quantities and use them within 1 year of purchase for the best flavor.

5. Dip 2½-inch (6 cm) cookie cutters in confectioner's sugar or flour and cut dough into desired shapes. Cut out as many cookies as possible from first rolling. Carefully transfer cutouts to prepared cookie sheets, placing 1 inch (2.5 cm) apart. Gather dough remnants into a ball, reroll, cut out more cookies and transfer to cookie sheets.

6. Bake one sheet at a time in preheated oven for 8 to 10 minutes or until edges start to turn lightly golden.

7. Immediately slide parchment paper onto a wire cooling rack. Cool cookies for 5 minutes, then transfer from parchment paper to cooling rack and cool completely.

Cookie Ornaments

Cookie ornaments are a fun decoration for Christmas or for other holidays and special events. They can also be given as party favors for birthdays, wedding receptions and baby showers.

After cutting cookies into desired shapes, transfer them to the cookie sheet. Use a plastic drinking straw to punch a hole in each cutout about ¼ inch (0.5 cm) from the top. Bake as directed in the recipe. After baking check the hole to be sure it didn't partly close during baking. If necessary, quickly re-cut the hole before transferring the cookies to the cooling rack.

Decorate the cookies to suit the holiday or event. After the decorations are completely dry, thread a thin ribbon or cord through the hole and tie to form an ornament hanger.

Raspberry Cream Sandwich Cookies

The blend of almond-scented cookies with a raspberry filling make these pretty cookies a special treat.

Tip

To keep cutout shapes from becoming distorted, use a metal spatula to support cookies as you transfer them to the cookie sheet.

Variation

Apricot Cream Sandwich Cookies: Substitute apricot jam for seedless raspberry jam in the filling.

- Cookie sheets, lined with parchment paper
- Cookie cutters

Cookies

3 cups	all-purpose flour	750 mL
½ tsp	baking powder	2 mL
½ tsp	baking soda	2 mL
¼ tsp	salt	1 mL
½ cup	unsalted butter, softened	125 mL
½ cup	granulated sugar	125 mL
½ cup	confectioner's (powdered/icing) sugar	125 mL
2	egg yolks	2
⅔ cup	sour cream	150 mL
1 tsp	vanilla extract	5 mL
½ tsp	almond extract	2 mL

Filling

2¼ cups	confectioner's (powdered/icing) sugar	550 mL
2 tbsp	unsalted butter, softened	25 mL
2 tbsp	half-and-half (10%) cream or milk	25 mL
¼ tsp	vanilla extract	1 mL
¼ tsp	almond extract	1 mL
½ cup	seedless raspberry jam	125 mL
	Additional confectioner's (powdered/icing) sugar	

1. **Cookies:** In a bowl, whisk together flour, baking powder, baking soda and salt until well combined. Set aside.

2. In a large bowl, using an electric mixer on medium speed, cream butter, granulated sugar and confectioner's sugar until light and fluffy, about 2 minutes. Add egg yolks one at a time, beating well after each addition. Beat in sour cream, vanilla and almond extract. Scrape down sides of bowl. On low speed or using a wooden spoon, gradually add flour mixture, beating just until blended.

3. Divide dough in half. Shape each portion into a flat disk. Tightly wrap each disk in plastic wrap and chill for at least 2 hours.

4. Preheat oven to 350°F (180°C). Lightly dust a pastry board, clean countertop or other flat surface and a rolling pin with confectioner's sugar or flour. Working with one dough disk at a time, unwrap dough and roll out to uniform thickness of ⅛ inch (3 mm). Halfway through rolling, rotate the dough a quarter turn and dust the board again to prevent dough from sticking.

Tip

Let filling set before storing cookies between layers of wax paper in a tightly sealed container.

5. Dip $2\frac{1}{2}$-inch (6 cm) cookie cutters in confectioner's sugar or flour and cut dough into desired shapes. Cut out as many cookies as possible from first rolling. Carefully transfer cutouts to prepared cookie sheets, placing 1 inch (2.5 cm) apart. Gather dough remnants into a ball, reroll, cut out more cookies and transfer to cookie sheets.

6. Bake one sheet at a time in preheated oven for 7 to 9 minutes or until edges start to turn lightly golden.

7. Immediately slide parchment paper onto a wire cooling rack. Cool cookies for 5 minutes, then transfer from parchment paper to cooling rack and cool completely.

8. *Filling:* In a bowl, combine confectioner's sugar, butter, cream, vanilla and almond extract. Using an electric mixer on medium speed, beat until frosting is light and fluffy, about 2 minutes. Stir in raspberry jam. Spread a layer of filling over the bottom side of half of the cooled cookies. Top with remaining cookies. Dust with confectioner's sugar.

Keep Frosting Soft While Decorating

To keep bowls of frostings and icings from drying out while decorating cookies, cover the frosting with a damp, but not wet, paper towel pressed down on the surface. If the paper towel starts to dry out, lightly remoisten it.

Lime Cutouts

Flavored with fresh lime juice and flecked with lime zest, these tangy frosted cookies are a refreshing treat any time of day.

Tips

A ripe medium lime will yield about 1 teaspoon (5 mL) finely grated zest and 1 1/2 to 2 tablespoons (22 to 25 mL) juice.

Let frosting set before storing cookies between layers of wax paper in a tightly sealed container in the refrigerator.

- Cookie sheets, lined with parchment paper
- Cookie cutters

Cookies

3 cups	all-purpose flour	750 mL
1/2 tsp	baking powder	2 mL
1/4 tsp	baking soda	1 mL
1/4 tsp	salt	1 mL
3/4 cup	unsalted butter, softened	175 mL
1 cup	granulated sugar	250 mL
1	egg	1
1 tbsp	grated lime zest	15 mL
1/4 cup	freshly squeezed lime juice	50 mL

Frosting

1 1/2 cups	confectioner's (powdered/icing) sugar	375 mL
3 oz	cream cheese, softened	90 g
2 tsp	freshly squeezed lime juice	10 mL

1. *Cookies:* In a bowl, whisk together flour, baking powder, baking soda and salt until well combined. Set aside.

2. In a large bowl, using an electric mixer on medium speed, cream butter and granulated sugar until light and fluffy, about 3 minutes. Add egg and beat well. Beat in lime zest and lime juice. Scrape down sides of bowl. On low speed or using a wooden spoon, gradually add flour mixture, beating just until blended.

3. Divide dough in half. Shape each portion into a flat disk. Tightly wrap each disk in plastic wrap and chill for at least 2 hours.

4. Preheat oven to 350°F (180°C). Lightly dust a pastry board, clean countertop or other flat surface and a rolling pin with confectioner's sugar or flour. Working with one dough disk at a time, unwrap dough and roll out to uniform thickness of 1/4 inch (0.5 cm). Halfway through rolling, rotate the dough a quarter turn and dust the board again to prevent dough from sticking.

5. Dip 2 1/2-inch (6 cm) cookie cutters in confectioner's sugar or flour and cut dough into desired shapes. Cut out as many cookies as possible from first rolling. Carefully transfer cutouts to prepared cookie sheets, placing 1 inch (2.5 cm) apart. Gather dough remnants into a ball, reroll, cut out more cookies and transfer to cookie sheets.

Tip

Store eggs in their original carton on a shelf in the refrigerator. Do not store eggs in the door because the temperature fluctuates every time the door is opened.

6. Bake one sheet at a time in preheated oven for 8 to 10 minutes or until edges start to turn lightly golden.

7. Immediately slide parchment paper onto a wire cooling rack. Cool cookies for 5 minutes, then transfer from parchment paper to cooling rack and cool completely.

8. *Frosting:* In a bowl, combine confectioner's sugar, cream cheese and lime juice. Using an electric mixer on medium speed, beat until frosting is light and fluffy, about 3 minutes. Spread frosting over tops of cooled cookies.

A Calendar of Reasons to Decorate Cookies

Decorated cookies are not just for Christmas or birthdays. They are a perfect treat for so many special events throughout the year. Here are some excuses to get out your shaped cookie cutters, decorating tools and food coloring and let your creativity flow.

Hanukkah	Graduation
Kwanza	Engagement parties
New Year's Eve	Weddings
New Year's Day	Baby showers
Valentine's Day	Teacher appreciation
St. Patrick's Day	Luau
Easter	Tea Party
Independence Day	Mardi Gras
Thanksgiving	Super Bowl
Halloween	Bon voyage party
International holidays	Retirement party

Cinnamon Sugar Cookies

● ● ●

With cinnamon in the cookies and sprinkled on top, these cutouts have just the right touch of spice.

Tip

If you have trouble with the bottom of your cookies browning too much or burning, try using insulated cookie sheets.

- Cookie sheets, lined with parchment paper
- Cookie cutters

Cookies

2 cups	all-purpose flour	500 mL
½ tsp	baking powder	2 mL
½ tsp	ground cinnamon	2 mL
¼ tsp	baking soda	1 mL
¼ tsp	salt	1 mL
⅔ cup	unsalted butter, softened	150 mL
¾ cup	granulated sugar	175 mL
1	egg	1
1 tsp	vanilla extract	5 mL

Topping

3 tbsp	granulated sugar	45 mL
1½ tsp	ground cinnamon	7 mL

1. *Cookies:* In a bowl, whisk together flour, baking powder, cinnamon, baking soda and salt until well combined. Set aside.

2. In a large bowl, using an electric mixer on medium speed, cream butter and granulated sugar until light and fluffy, about 3 minutes. Add egg and beat well. Beat in vanilla. Scrape down sides of bowl. On low speed or using a wooden spoon, gradually add flour mixture, beating just until blended.

3. Divide dough in half. Shape each portion into a flat disk. Tightly wrap each disk in plastic wrap and chill for at least 1 hour.

4. Preheat oven to 350°F (180°C). Lightly dust a pastry board, clean countertop or other flat surface and a rolling pin with confectioner's (powdered/icing) sugar or flour. Working with one dough disk at a time, unwrap dough and roll out to uniform thickness of ⅛ inch (3 mm). Halfway through rolling, rotate the dough a quarter turn and dust the board again to prevent dough from sticking.

5. Dip 2½-inch (6 cm) cookie cutters in confectioner's sugar or flour and cut dough into desired shapes. Cut out as many cookies as possible from first rolling. Carefully transfer cutouts to prepared cookie sheets, placing 1 inch (2.5 cm) apart. Gather dough remnants into a ball, reroll, cut out more cookies and transfer to cookie sheets.

Tip

The flavor of spices deteriorates over time as exposure to heat and moisture causes it to fade rapidly.

6. *Topping:* In a small bowl, whisk together granulated sugar and cinnamon. Sprinkle topping evenly over cookies.

7. Bake one sheet at a time in preheated oven for 8 to 10 minutes or until edges start to turn lightly golden.

8. Immediately slide parchment paper onto a wire cooling rack. Cool cookies for 5 minutes, then transfer from parchment paper to cooling rack and cool completely.

Decorating with a Pastry Bag

Using a pastry bag is a great way to add colorful decorations to rolled cutout cookies.

For each frosting color you will be working with, fit a pastry bag with a coupler and a small decorator tip. If using disposable pastry bags, cut the point off the bags before adding the tip and filling the bag. The advantage of using a coupler is that you can change the shape of tip on the bag. Place a bag in a measuring cup or a sturdy mug and roll down the top edge of the bag to form a cuff. Spoon the frosting into the bag, pushing it down to the tip to remove any air bubbles. Fill the bag no more than two-thirds full. Roll up the cuff and twist the top of the bag closed.

To achieve the best designs, hold the bag at a 45-degree angle to the cookie and apply steady, even pressure from the top of the bag. Release the pressure on the bag before lifting it from the cookie surface. If the frosting becomes too warm and soft, place the bag in the refrigerator for several minutes. Note: If the frosting is too thick to press out through the tip, thin the frosting with a small amount of milk or corn syrup before filling the bag. (If using Royal Icing, thin it with a few drops of water.)

Espresso Sandwich Cookies

Coffee cookies filled with a creamy coffee frosting are a coffee-lover's dream!

Tips

Instant espresso powder can be found in the coffee aisle of most grocery stores.

Let filling set before storing cookies between layers of wax paper in a tightly sealed container.

- Cookie sheets, lined with parchment paper
- Cookie cutters

Cookies

2²⁄₃ cups	all-purpose flour	650 mL
1 tbsp	instant espresso powder	15 mL
1 tsp	baking powder	5 mL
¹⁄₂ tsp	salt	2 mL
¹⁄₂ cup	unsalted butter, softened	125 mL
¹⁄₂ cup	vegetable shortening	125 mL
1¹⁄₃ cups	granulated sugar	325 mL
1	egg	1
1 tsp	vanilla extract	5 mL

Filling

3 cups	confectioner's (powdered/icing) sugar	750 mL
2 tsp	instant espresso powder	10 mL
3 tbsp	unsalted butter, softened	45 mL
3 tbsp	half-and-half (10%) cream or milk	45 mL
1 tsp	vanilla extract	5 mL

1. **Cookies:** In a bowl, whisk together flour, espresso powder, baking powder and salt until well combined. Set aside.

2. In a large bowl, using an electric mixer on medium speed, cream butter, shortening and granulated sugar until light and fluffy, about 3 minutes. Add egg and beat well. Beat in vanilla. Scrape down sides of bowl. On low speed or using a wooden spoon, gradually add flour mixture, beating just until blended.

3. Divide dough in half. Shape each portion into a flat disk. Tightly wrap each disk in plastic wrap and chill for at least 1 hour.

4. Preheat oven to 350°F (180°C). Lightly dust a pastry board, clean countertop or other flat surface and a rolling pin with confectioner's sugar or flour. Working with one dough disk at a time, unwrap dough and roll out to uniform thickness of ¹⁄₈ inch (3 mm). Halfway through rolling, rotate the dough a quarter turn and dust the board again to prevent dough from sticking.

5. Dip 2¹⁄₂-inch (6 cm) cookie cutters in confectioner's sugar or flour and cut dough into desired shapes. Cut out as many cookies as possible from first rolling. Carefully transfer cutouts to prepared cookie sheets, placing 1 inch (2.5 cm) apart. Gather dough remnants into a ball, reroll, cut out more cookies and transfer to cookie sheets.

Tip

Tightly wrapped in plastic wrap, this cookie dough can be stored in the refrigerator for up to 1 week.

6. Bake one sheet at a time in preheated oven for 8 to 10 minutes or until edges start to turn lightly golden.

7. Immediately slide parchment paper onto a wire cooling rack. Cool cookies for 5 minutes, then transfer from parchment paper to cooling rack and cool completely.

8. *Filling:* In a bowl, combine confectioner's sugar and espresso powder until well blended. Add butter, cream and vanilla. Using an electric mixer on medium speed, beat until filling is light and fluffy, about 3 minutes. Spread a layer of filling over the bottom side of half of the cooled cookies. Top with remaining cookies.

Creative Gift Idea

To create a hostess gift for a bridge club or card party, cut cookies into heart, diamond, spade and club shapes. Or you can cut the dough into rectangles and decorate the baked cookies like playing cards. Pack the cookies into a decorative tin or pretty basket and add a deck of cards.

Chocolate Cutouts

Makes about 3 dozen cookies

● ● ●

These delightful chocolate cookies are topped with a wonderful chocolate frosting.

Tips

Unsweetened Dutch-process cocoa powder gives these cookies a rich, chocolaty flavor without any bitterness. Regular unsweetened cocoa powder may be substituted if you do not have unsweetened Dutch-process cocoa powder.

Let frosting set before storing cookies between layers of wax paper in a tightly sealed container.

● **Cookie sheets, lined with parchment paper**
● **Cookie cutters**

Cookies

1¾ cups	all-purpose flour	425 mL
½ cup	unsweetened Dutch-process cocoa powder	125 mL
1 tsp	baking powder	5 mL
¼ tsp	baking soda	1 mL
¼ tsp	salt	1 mL
½ cup	unsalted butter, softened	125 mL
⅓ cup	vegetable shortening	75 mL
½ cup	granulated sugar	125 mL
½ cup	packed light brown sugar	125 mL
1	egg	1
1½ tsp	vanilla extract	7 mL

Frosting

2½ cups	confectioner's (powdered/icing) sugar	625 mL
2 tbsp	unsweetened Dutch-process cocoa powder	25 mL
3 tbsp	unsalted butter, softened	45 mL
3 tbsp	half-and-half (10%) cream or milk	45 mL
1 tsp	vanilla extract	5 mL

1. *Cookies:* In a bowl, whisk together flour, cocoa powder, baking powder, baking soda and salt until well combined. Set aside.

2. In a large bowl, using an electric mixer on medium speed, cream butter, shortening, granulated sugar and brown sugar until light and fluffy, about 3 minutes. Add egg and beat well. Beat in vanilla. Scrape down sides of bowl. On low speed or using a wooden spoon, gradually add flour mixture, beating just until blended.

3. Divide dough in half. Shape each portion into a flat disk. Tightly wrap each disk in plastic wrap and chill for at least 1 hour.

4. Preheat oven to 375°F (190°C). Lightly dust a pastry board, clean countertop or other flat surface and a rolling pin with confectioner's sugar or flour. Working with one dough disk at a time, unwrap dough and roll out to uniform thickness of ¼ inch (0.5 cm). Halfway through rolling, rotate the dough a quarter turn and dust the board again to prevent dough from sticking.

Tip

Dutch-process cocoa powder is a refined cocoa treated with a small amount of an alkali solution to neutralize the natural acids. This process improves the flavor and color of the cocoa.

5. Dip $2\frac{1}{2}$-inch (6 cm) cookie cutters in confectioner's sugar or flour and cut dough into desired shapes. Cut out as many cookies as possible from first rolling. Carefully transfer cutouts to prepared cookie sheets, placing 1 inch (2.5 cm) apart. Gather dough remnants into a ball, reroll, cut out more cookies and transfer to cookie sheets.

6. Bake one sheet at a time in preheated oven for 7 to 9 minutes or until set.

7. Immediately slide parchment paper onto a wire cooling rack. Cool cookies for 5 minutes, then transfer from parchment paper to cooling rack and cool completely.

8. *Frosting:* In a bowl, combine confectioner's sugar and cocoa powder until well blended. Add butter, cream and vanilla. Using an electric mixer on medium speed, beat until frosting is light and fluffy, about 3 minutes. Spread frosting over tops of cooled cookies.

Sugar Stencil Designs

A simple dusting of sifted confectioner's (powdered/icing) sugar can dress up dark-colored unfrosted cutout cookies or add an extra dimension to cookies iced with chocolate or colored frosting.

Center a small, pretty stencil (available at craft stores in a wide variety of patterns) or a paper doily on top of the cookie. Lightly sift the confectioner's sugar over top of the cookie. Carefully remove the stencil without disturbing the sugar design. Decorate the cookies the same day they will be served and store the cookies in a single layer to prevent smudging the designs.

Nutmeg Cookies

Makes about 3 dozen cookies

● ● ●

Lightly scented with fragrant nutmeg, these cookies are a nice treat on cool fall afternoons.

Tips

Butter is considered to be softened when it is at a temperature of 65°F (18°C).

Let frosting set before storing cookies between layers of wax paper in a tightly sealed container.

● Cookie sheets, lined with parchment paper
● Cookie cutters

Cookies

2⅓ cups	all-purpose flour	575 mL
1 tsp	ground nutmeg	5 mL
½ tsp	baking powder	2 mL
½ tsp	baking soda	2 mL
¼ tsp	salt	1 mL
¾ cup	unsalted butter, softened	175 mL
1 cup	granulated sugar	250 mL
2	eggs	2
1 tsp	vanilla extract	5 mL
1 tsp	rum flavoring	5 mL

Frosting

2 cups	confectioner's (powdered/icing) sugar	500 mL
3 tbsp	unsalted butter, softened	45 mL
2 tbsp	half-and-half (10%) cream or milk	25 mL
1 tsp	vanilla extract	5 mL
½ tsp	rum flavoring	2 mL
	Ground nutmeg	

1. **Cookies:** In a bowl, whisk together flour, nutmeg, baking powder, baking soda and salt until well combined. Set aside.

2. In a large bowl, using an electric mixer on medium speed, cream butter and granulated sugar until light and fluffy, about 3 minutes. Add eggs one at a time, beating well after each addition. Beat in vanilla and rum flavoring. Scrape down sides of bowl. On low speed or using a wooden spoon, gradually add flour mixture, beating just until blended.

3. Divide dough in half. Shape each portion into a flat disk. Tightly wrap each disk in plastic wrap and chill for at least 1 hour.

4. Preheat oven to 350°F (180°C). Lightly dust a pastry board, clean countertop or other flat surface and a rolling pin with confectioner's sugar or flour. Working with one dough disk at a time, unwrap dough and roll out to uniform thickness of ¼ inch (0.5 cm). Halfway through rolling, rotate the dough a quarter turn and dust the board again to prevent dough from sticking.

Tip

All of the recipes in this book use large eggs, the standard size used for baking. If you do not have large eggs, then lightly beat your eggs and substitute $\frac{1}{4}$ cup (50 mL) beaten egg for each large egg called for in the recipe.

5. Dip $2\frac{1}{2}$-inch (6 cm) cookie cutters in confectioner's sugar or flour and cut dough into desired shapes. Cut out as many cookies as possible from first rolling. Carefully transfer cutouts to prepared cookie sheets, placing 1 inch (2.5 cm) apart. Gather dough remnants into a ball, reroll, cut out more cookies and transfer to cookie sheets.

6. Bake one sheet at a time in preheated oven for 10 to 12 minutes or until edges start to turn lightly golden.

7. Immediately slide parchment paper onto a wire cooling rack. Cool cookies for 5 minutes, then transfer from parchment paper to cooling rack and cool completely.

8. *Frosting:* In a bowl, combine confectioner's sugar, butter, cream, vanilla and rum extract. Using an electric mixer on medium speed, beat until frosting is light and fluffy, about 2 minutes. Spread frosting over tops of cooled cookies. Lightly sprinkle nutmeg over top of frosted cookies.

Creative Gift Idea

Fill a colorful beach pail with pretty cookies shaped and decorated like sailboats, seashells and sea creatures. Wrap the pail in clear cellophane and tie the top with a raffia bow.

Peanut Butter Cutouts

Makes about 4 dozen cookies ● ● ●

Yummy peanut butter cookies are perfect for cutting into fun shapes.

Tip

Delicious without any adornment, Peanut Butter Cutouts may also be sprinkled with sugar before baking or spread with icing and topped with decorative sprinkles after baking and cooling.

● Cookie sheets, lined with parchment paper
● Cookie cutters

2 cups	all-purpose flour	500 mL
$\frac{1}{2}$ tsp	baking powder	2 mL
$\frac{1}{2}$ tsp	baking soda	2 mL
$\frac{2}{3}$ cup	creamy peanut butter	150 mL
$\frac{1}{3}$ cup	unsalted butter, softened	75 mL
$\frac{1}{2}$ cup	granulated sugar	125 mL
$\frac{1}{2}$ cup	packed light brown sugar	125 mL
2	eggs	2
1 tsp	vanilla extract	5 mL

1. In a bowl, whisk together flour, baking powder and baking soda until well combined. Set aside.

2. In a large bowl, using an electric mixer on medium speed, cream peanut butter, butter, granulated sugar and brown sugar until light and fluffy, about 3 minutes. Add eggs one at a time, beating well after each addition. Beat in vanilla. Scrape down sides of bowl. On low speed or using a wooden spoon, gradually add flour mixture, beating just until blended.

3. Divide dough in half. Shape each portion into a flat disk. Tightly wrap each disk in plastic wrap and chill for at least 1 hour.

4. Preheat oven to 375°F (190°C). Lightly dust a pastry board, clean countertop or other flat surface and a rolling pin with confectioner's (icing) sugar or flour. Working with one dough disk at a time, unwrap dough and roll out to uniform thickness of $\frac{1}{8}$ inch (3 mm). Halfway through rolling, rotate the dough a quarter turn and dust the board again to prevent dough from sticking.

5. Dip $2\frac{1}{2}$-inch (6 cm) cookie cutters in confectioner's sugar or flour and cut dough into desired shapes. Cut out as many cookies as possible from first rolling. Carefully transfer cutouts to prepared cookie sheets, placing 1 inch (2.5 cm) apart. Gather dough remnants into a ball, reroll, cut out more cookies and transfer to cookie sheets.

6. Bake one sheet at a time in preheated oven for 7 to 9 minutes or until edges start to turn lightly golden.

7. Immediately slide parchment paper onto a wire cooling rack. Cool cookies for 5 minutes, then transfer from parchment paper to cooling rack and cool completely.

Refrigerator Slice-and-Bake Cookies

●●●

Lemon Slices 251

Butterscotch Slices. 252

Cinnamon Crisps 253

Eggnog Cookies. 254

Chocolate Mint Thins 256

Maple Nut Wafers. 257

Vanilla Slices. 258

Orange Clouds 259

Chocolate Chip Slices 260

Glazed Almond Slices. 261

Lemon Sandwich Cookies 262

Coconut Crisps 263

Date Walnut Slices 264

Pecan Rounds 265

Mocha Chip Thins 266

Cream Cheese Citrus Rounds 267

Cranberry Almond Slices 268

Chocolate-Glazed Coffee
   Cookies. 269

Molasses Slices 270

White Chocolate Rounds 271

Sugar Cookie Slices 272

Apricot Slices 273

Margarita Cookies 274

About Refrigerator Slice-and-Bake Cookies

Shaped into logs and chilled, refrigerator slice-and-bake cookies can be quickly baked in large or small quantities. Slice-and-bake cookie dough freezes well. With a batch or two or three of slice-and-bake cookie doughs in the fridge or freezer, it's easy to have hot, fresh homemade cookies anytime you want them. They're great to have on hand for drop-in guests during the busy holiday season and throughout the year.

Also called icebox cookies, refrigerator slice-and-bake cookies lend themselves to many combinations of ingredients and flavors. Chocolate, nuts and dried fruits should be finely chopped to make it easier to cut the dough into slices. If the pieces are too large, the dough may break apart when sliced.

These versatile cookie slices can be served plain, dusted with confectioner's (powdered/icing) sugar, iced, or filled with frosting or jam to make sandwich cookies. They're sure to satisfy cookie cravings both big and small.

Shaping the Dough
After mixing the dough for slice-and-bake cookies, it needs to be shaped into a log, then tightly wrapped and refrigerated until firm enough to cut into slices that will hold their shape. If the dough is too soft to roll into a log, chill the dough for 10 minutes or more to firm it up a bit and make it easier to handle.

To easily shape the dough into a log, spoon the dough onto a piece of parchment paper within 1 inch (2.5 cm) of the long edge, leaving 2 to 3 inches (5 to 7.5 cm) at each end. Slowly roll the parchment paper around the dough, shaping it into a log as you go. Wrap the parchment tightly around the log and twist the ends to seal. A twist-tie wrapped around each end will help keep the parchment tightly sealed. After wrapping, roll the log back and forth on the counter until it's smooth and is uniform in diameter.

The dough can also be wrapped in plastic wrap using the same technique; however, the plastic wrap will not support the log as well as the parchment paper.

The dough log needs to be chilled for several hours or overnight to firm it up for slicing. During chilling, the dough tends to flatten on the underside of the log. To keep the dough round, I slide the log into an empty cardboard wrapping paper tube, cut into 12-inch (30 cm) lengths. The tube maintains the round shape of the log as it chills. Heavy-duty cardboard tubes work better than lightweight tubes. If the diameter of the tube is too narrow for the dough log, split the tube lengthwise with scissors so that it will wrap around the log. These cardboard tubes are great for protecting dough logs in the freezer as well and keep them from getting bent or dented. They also add an extra layer of protection from freezer burn.

Dough logs may be refrigerated for up to a week if they're wrapped tightly to keep the dough from drying out. For longer storage, wrap parchment-covered logs in heavy-duty foil, seal tightly and store in the freezer for up to 3 months.

Slicing the Dough Log
Work with one log of dough at a time, keeping any remaining dough in the refrigerator until you're ready to cut it. To get a clean cut, use a sharp, thin-bladed knife to slice the chilled dough. To maintain the round shape of the cookies, roll the log slightly after cutting each slice. This will keep the downward pressure of the knife from flattening the bottom of the roll and making the cookies lopsided.

Cut the dough into $1/8$-inch (3 mm) slices to produce crispier cookies. Thicker $1/4$-inch (0.5 cm) slices will yield softer, chewier cookies. Space the dough rounds 1 inch (2.5 cm) apart on the cookie sheet for even baking and browning.

Lemon Slices

These lovely cookies have a pleasingly light lemon flavor and scent.

Tip

When zesting lemons, remove only the outer colored part of the peel. The white part underneath, called the pith, is very bitter and will give cookies an unpleasant flavor.

• Cookie sheets, lined with parchment paper

2¼ cups	all-purpose flour	550 mL
1½ tsp	baking powder	7 mL
¼ tsp	salt	1 mL
¾ cup	unsalted butter, softened	175 mL
¾ cup	granulated sugar	175 mL
1	egg	1
1 tbsp	grated lemon zest	15 mL
1 tbsp	freshly squeezed lemon juice	15 mL

1. In a bowl, whisk together flour, baking powder and salt until well combined. Set aside.

2. In a large bowl, using an electric mixer on medium speed, cream butter and granulated sugar until light and fluffy, about 3 minutes. Add egg and beat well. Stir in lemon zest and lemon juice. Scrape down sides of bowl. On low speed or using a wooden spoon, gradually add flour mixture, beating just until blended.

3. Divide dough in half. Shape each portion of dough into a log 2 inches (5 cm) in diameter. Tightly wrap each dough log in parchment paper or plastic wrap and chill for 2 to 3 hours or overnight.

4. Preheat oven to 350°F (180°C). Working with one dough log at a time, remove parchment paper or plastic wrap. Using a sharp knife, cut log into ¼-inch (0.5 cm) slices. Place about 1 inch (2.5 cm) apart on prepared cookie sheets. Bake one sheet at a time in preheated oven for 10 to 12 minutes or until edges start to turn lightly golden.

5. Immediately slide parchment paper onto a wire cooling rack. Cool cookies for 5 minutes, then transfer from parchment paper to cooling rack and cool completely.

Butterscotch Slices

These easy rounds get their flavor from dark brown sugar.

Tips

To keep logs round as they chill, place wrapped and shaped dough inside a cardboard wrapping paper tube. The curved shape of the tube will keep the bottom of the dough log from flattening out.

To prevent tops or bottoms of cookies from becoming too brown, bake one sheet at a time with the oven rack positioned in the center of the oven.

● **Cookie sheets, lined with parchment paper**

2¼ cups	all-purpose flour	550 mL
½ tsp	baking powder	2 mL
¼ tsp	baking soda	1 mL
¼ tsp	salt	1 mL
¾ cup	unsalted butter, softened	175 mL
1 cup	packed dark brown sugar	250 mL
1	egg	1
1 tsp	vanilla extract	5 mL

1. In a bowl, whisk together flour, baking powder, baking soda and salt until well combined. Set aside.

2. In a large bowl, using an electric mixer on medium speed, cream butter and brown sugar until light and fluffy, about 3 minutes. Add egg and beat well. Beat in vanilla. Scrape down sides of bowl. On low speed or using a wooden spoon, gradually add flour mixture, beating just until blended.

3. Divide dough in half. Shape each portion of dough into a log 2 inches (5 cm) in diameter. Tightly wrap each dough log in parchment paper or plastic wrap and chill for 2 to 3 hours or overnight.

4. Preheat oven to 350°F (180°C). Working with one dough log at a time, remove parchment paper or plastic wrap. Using a sharp knife, cut log into ¼-inch (0.5 cm) slices. Place about 1 inch (2.5 cm) apart on prepared cookie sheets. Bake one sheet at a time in preheated oven for 10 to 12 minutes or until edges start to turn lightly golden.

5. Immediately slide parchment paper onto a wire cooling rack. Cool cookies for 5 minutes, then transfer from parchment paper to cooling rack and cool completely.

Cinnamon Crisps

With cinnamon in both the cookies and the icing, these cookies pack a nice cinnamon punch.

Tips

Wrap logs of slice-and-bake dough tightly to keep them from drying out in the refrigerator.

Let icing set before storing cookies between layers of wax paper in a tightly sealed container.

● **Cookie sheets, lined with parchment paper**

Cookies

2 cups	all-purpose flour	500 mL
1¼ tsp	ground cinnamon	6 mL
½ tsp	baking powder	2 mL
¼ tsp	salt	1 mL
⅔ cup	unsalted butter, softened	150 mL
¾ cup	granulated sugar	175 mL
2	eggs	2
1 tsp	vanilla extract	5 mL

Icing

1 cup	confectioner's (powdered/icing) sugar	250 mL
½ tsp	ground cinnamon	2 mL
2 to 3 tbsp	half-and-half (10%) cream or milk	25 to 45 mL

1. **Cookies:** In a bowl, whisk together flour, cinnamon, baking powder and salt until well combined. Set aside.

2. In a large bowl, using an electric mixer on medium speed, cream butter and granulated sugar until light and fluffy, about 3 minutes. Add eggs one at a time, beating well after each addition. Beat in vanilla. Scrape down sides of bowl. On low speed or using a wooden spoon, gradually add flour mixture, beating just until blended.

3. Divide dough in half. Shape each portion of dough into a log 2 inches (5 cm) in diameter. Tightly wrap each dough log in parchment paper or plastic wrap and chill for 2 to 3 hours or overnight.

4. Preheat oven to 350°F (180°C). Working with one dough log at a time, remove parchment paper or plastic wrap. Using a sharp knife, cut log into ¼-inch (0.5 cm) slices. Place about 1 inch (2.5 cm) apart on prepared cookie sheets. Bake one sheet at a time in preheated oven for 10 to 12 minutes or until edges start to turn lightly golden.

5. Immediately slide parchment paper onto a wire cooling rack. Cool cookies for 5 minutes, then transfer from parchment paper to cooling rack and cool completely.

6. **Icing:** In a small bowl, combine confectioner's sugar and cinnamon. Add 2 tablespoons (25 mL) of the cream. Using a small whisk or a fork, blend until icing is smooth and thin enough to drizzle from a fork. Add more cream as needed to achieve the desired consistency. Drizzle icing over cooled cookies.

Eggnog Cookies

Lightly spiced, these fragrant cookies are a special treat around the holidays.

Tips

When slicing the dough, roll the log slightly after each cut to maintain the round shape of the cookies.

Let icing set before storing cookies between layers of wax paper in a tightly sealed container.

● **Cookie sheets, lined with parchment paper**

Cookies

4 cups	all-purpose flour	1 L
1 tsp	baking powder	5 mL
¼ tsp	ground nutmeg	1 mL
¼ tsp	salt	1 mL
¾ cup	unsalted butter, softened	175 mL
1⅓ cups	granulated sugar	325 mL
2	egg yolks	2
½ tsp	vanilla extract	2 mL
¾ cup	dairy eggnog	175 mL

Icing

2 cups	confectioner's (powdered/icing) sugar	500 mL
2 tbsp	unsalted butter, softened	25 mL
1 to 2 tbsp	dairy eggnog	15 to 25 mL
¼ tsp	vanilla extract	1 mL

1. ***Cookies:*** In a bowl, whisk together flour, baking powder, nutmeg and salt until well combined. Set aside.

2. In a large bowl, using an electric mixer on medium speed, cream butter and granulated sugar until light and fluffy, about 3 minutes. Add egg yolks one at a time, beating well after each addition. Beat in vanilla. Scrape down sides of bowl. On low speed or using a wooden spoon, gradually add flour mixture, alternating with eggnog, beating after each addition just until blended.

3. Divide dough in half. Shape each portion of dough into a log 2 inches (5 cm) in diameter. Tightly wrap each dough log in parchment paper or plastic wrap and chill for 4 hours or overnight.

4. Preheat oven to 375°F (190°C). Working with one dough log at a time, remove parchment paper or plastic wrap. Using a sharp knife, cut log into ¼-inch (0.5 cm) slices. Place about 1 inch (2.5 cm) apart on prepared cookie sheets. Bake one sheet at a time in preheated oven for 8 to 10 minutes or until edges start to turn lightly golden.

Tip

Cartons of fresh eggnog can be found in the grocery store dairy case during the fall and winter holidays.

5. Immediately slide parchment paper onto a wire cooling rack. Cool cookies for 5 minutes, then transfer from parchment paper to cooling rack and cool completely.

6. *Icing:* In a small bowl, combine confectioner's sugar, butter, 1 tablespoon (15 mL) of the eggnog and vanilla. Using a small whisk or a fork, blend until icing is smooth and spreadable. Add more eggnog as needed to achieve the desired consistency. Spread icing over cooled cookies.

Think Beyond the Round

For variety, shape the cookie dough into shapes other than round logs. To create square cookies, wrap the dough log in plastic wrap and twist the ends of the plastic wrap to seal. Place it on a small cutting board, tray or other solid flat surface and press gently to flatten the bottom side of the log. Turn the log over and flatten the opposite side, then turn the log and flatten the two remaining sides to form a square-shaped log. Holding the twisted ends of the plastic, continue to turn the dough and flatten until all sides are flat and of uniform size. Place the cutting board in the refrigerator and chill the dough for at least 4 hours before slicing.

You can use the same technique to form triangular-shaped cookies by turning and flattening the dough log on three sides to create a triangle.

Chocolate Mint Thins

Makes about 2 dozen cookies ● ● ●

Chocolate cookies filled with a chocolate mint frosting — a heavenly combination.

Tips

Flavors can blend during storage, so store cookies with strong flavors in separate containers.

Let filling set before storing cookies between layers of wax paper in a tightly sealed container.

● **Cookie sheets, lined with parchment paper**

Cookies

2⅓ cups	all-purpose flour	575 mL
½ cup	unsweetened Dutch-process cocoa powder	125 mL
¼ tsp	baking soda	1 mL
¼ tsp	salt	1 mL
½ cup	unsalted butter, softened	125 mL
½ cup	vegetable shortening	125 mL
1¼ cups	packed dark brown sugar	300 mL
1	egg	1
1 tsp	vanilla extract	5 mL

Filling

3 cups	confectioner's (powdered/icing) sugar	750 mL
2 tbsp	unsweetened Dutch-process cocoa powder	25 mL
¼ cup	unsalted butter, softened	50 mL
2 tbsp	half-and-half (10%) cream or milk	25 mL
½ tsp	mint extract	2 mL

1. **Cookies:** In a bowl, whisk together flour, cocoa powder, baking soda and salt until well combined. Set aside.

2. In a large bowl, using an electric mixer on medium speed, cream butter, shortening and brown sugar until light and fluffy, about 3 minutes. Add egg and beat well. Beat in vanilla. Scrape down sides of bowl. On low speed or using a wooden spoon, gradually add flour mixture, beating just until blended.

3. Divide dough in half. Shape each portion of dough into a log 2 inches (5 cm) in diameter. Tightly wrap each dough log in parchment paper or plastic wrap and chill for 2 to 3 hours or overnight.

4. Preheat oven to 350°F (180°C). Working with one dough log at a time, remove parchment paper or plastic wrap. Using a sharp knife, cut log into ¼-inch (0.5 cm) slices. Place about 1 inch (2.5 cm) apart on prepared cookie sheets. Bake one sheet at a time in preheated oven for 10 to 12 minutes or until set.

5. Immediately slide parchment paper onto a wire cooling rack. Cool cookies for 5 minutes, then transfer from parchment paper to cooling rack and cool completely.

6. **Filling:** In a medium bowl, combine confectioner's sugar, cocoa powder, butter, cream and mint extract. Using an electric mixer on medium speed, beat until the filling is light and fluffy, about 3 to 4 minutes. Spread a thick layer of filling over the bottom side of half of the cooled cookies. Top with remaining cookies.

Maple Nut Wafers

Makes about 4 dozen cookies ● ● ●

Studded with finely chopped walnuts, these cookies have a good maple flavor.

Tips

Nuts can turn rancid quickly. If you're not going to use them within a couple of weeks, tightly wrap the nuts and store them in the freezer to preserve their flavor.

Let glaze set before storing cookies between layers of wax paper in a tightly sealed container.

Variation

Substitute chopped pecans for chopped walnuts.

● **Cookie sheets, lined with parchment paper**

Cookies

2¾ cups	all-purpose flour	675 mL
½ tsp	baking powder	2 mL
¼ tsp	baking soda	1 mL
¼ tsp	salt	1 mL
1 cup	unsalted butter, softened	250 mL
½ cup	granulated sugar	125 mL
½ cup	packed light brown sugar	125 mL
1	egg	1
2 tsp	maple flavoring	10 mL
¾ cup	finely chopped walnuts	175 mL

Glaze

1½ cups	confectioner's (powdered/icing) sugar	375 mL
2 tbsp	half-and-half (10%) cream or milk	25 mL
1 tsp	maple flavoring	5 mL

1. **Cookies:** In a bowl, whisk together flour, baking powder, baking soda and salt until well combined. Set aside.

2. In a large bowl, using an electric mixer on medium speed, cream butter, granulated sugar and brown sugar until light and fluffy, about 3 minutes. Add egg and beat well. Stir in maple flavoring. Scrape down sides of bowl. On low speed or using a wooden spoon, gradually add flour mixture, beating just until blended. By hand, fold in walnuts.

3. Divide dough in half. Shape each portion of dough into a log 2 inches (5 cm) in diameter. Tightly wrap each dough log in parchment paper or plastic wrap and chill for 2 to 3 hours or overnight.

4. Preheat oven to 350°F (180°C). Working with one dough log at a time, remove parchment paper or plastic wrap. Using a sharp knife, cut log into ¼-inch (0.5 cm) slices. Place about 1 inch (2.5 cm) apart on prepared cookie sheets. Bake one sheet at a time in preheated oven for 10 to 12 minutes or until edges start to turn lightly golden.

5. Immediately slide parchment paper onto a wire cooling rack. Cool cookies for 5 minutes, then transfer from parchment paper to cooling rack and cool completely.

6. **Glaze:** In a small bowl, combine confectioner's sugar, cream and maple flavoring. Using a small whisk or a fork, blend until glaze is smooth and spreadable. Spread glaze over cooled cookies.

Vanilla Slices

These pretty little cookies are definitely comfort food.

Tips

Always use pure vanilla extract in cookies. Imitation vanilla is made from synthetic flavors and colors, and the taste cannot compare to pure vanilla extract.

Let frosting set before storing cookies between layers of wax paper in a tightly sealed container.

• Cookie sheets, lined with parchment paper

Cookies

2¼ cups	all-purpose flour	550 mL
½ tsp	baking powder	2 mL
¼ tsp	salt	1 mL
¾ cup	unsalted butter, softened	175 mL
¾ cup	granulated sugar	175 mL
1	egg	1
2 tsp	vanilla extract	10 mL

Frosting

3 cups	confectioner's (powdered/icing) sugar	750 mL
¼ cup	unsalted butter, softened	50 mL
3 tbsp	half-and-half (10%) cream or milk	45 mL
1 tsp	vanilla extract	5 mL
⅛ tsp	salt	0.5 mL
	Candy sprinkles	

1. **Cookies:** In a bowl, whisk together flour, baking powder and salt until well combined. Set aside.

2. In a large bowl, using an electric mixer on medium speed, cream butter and granulated sugar until light and fluffy, about 3 minutes. Add egg and beat well. Beat in vanilla. Scrape down sides of bowl. On low speed or using a wooden spoon, gradually add flour mixture, beating just until blended.

3. Divide dough in half. Shape each portion of dough into a log 2 inches (5 cm) in diameter. Tightly wrap each dough log in parchment paper or plastic wrap and chill for 2 to 3 hours or overnight.

4. Preheat oven to 350°F (180°C). Working with one dough log at a time, remove parchment paper or plastic wrap. Using a sharp knife, cut log into ¼-inch (0.5 cm) slices. Place about 1 inch (2.5 cm) apart on prepared cookie sheets. Bake one sheet at a time in preheated oven for 10 to 12 minutes or until edges start to turn lightly golden.

5. Immediately slide parchment paper onto a wire cooling rack. Cool cookies for 5 minutes, then transfer from parchment paper to cooling rack and cool completely.

6. **Frosting:** In a small bowl, combine confectioner's sugar, butter, cream, vanilla and salt. Using a small whisk or a fork, blend until frosting is smooth and spreadable. Spread frosting over cooled cookies. Top with candy sprinkles.

Orange Clouds

The addition of cornstarch to the dough gives these citrusy cookies a very light texture.

Tips

A ripe medium orange will yield about 1 tablespoon (15 mL) finely grated zest and 3 to 4 tablespoons (45 to 50 mL) juice.

Let glaze set before storing cookies between layers of wax paper in a tightly sealed container.

● **Cookie sheets, lined with parchment paper**

Cookies

1¾ cups	all-purpose flour	425 mL
½ cup	cornstarch	125 mL
½ tsp	baking powder	2 mL
¼ tsp	salt	1 mL
⅔ cup	unsalted butter, softened	150 mL
½ cup	granulated sugar	125 mL
⅓ cup	confectioner's (powdered/icing) sugar	75 mL
1	egg yolk	1
1 tbsp	frozen orange juice concentrate, thawed	15 mL
2 tsp	grated orange zest	10 mL

Glaze

1 cup	confectioner's (powdered/icing) sugar	250 mL
2 tbsp	unsalted butter, softened	25 mL
1 tbsp	frozen orange juice concentrate, thawed	15 mL
1 tsp	grated orange zest	5 mL

1. *Cookies:* In a bowl, whisk together flour, cornstarch, baking powder and salt until well combined. Set aside.

2. In a large bowl, using an electric mixer on medium speed, cream butter, granulated sugar and confectioner's sugar until light and fluffy, about 3 minutes. Add egg yolk and beat well. Stir in orange juice concentrate and orange zest. Scrape down sides of bowl. On low speed or using a wooden spoon, gradually add flour mixture, beating just until blended.

3. Divide dough in half. Shape each portion of dough into a log 2 inches (5 cm) in diameter. Tightly wrap each dough log in parchment paper or plastic wrap and chill for 2 to 3 hours or overnight.

4. Preheat oven to 350°F (180°C). Working with one dough log at a time, remove parchment paper or plastic wrap. Using a sharp knife, cut log into ¼-inch (0.5 cm) slices. Place about 1 inch (2.5 cm) apart on prepared cookie sheets. Bake one sheet at a time in preheated oven for 8 to 10 minutes or until edges start to turn lightly golden.

5. Immediately slide parchment paper onto a wire cooling rack. Cool cookies for 5 minutes, then transfer from parchment paper to cooling rack and cool completely.

6. *Glaze:* In a small bowl, combine confectioner's sugar, butter, orange juice concentrate and orange zest. Using a small whisk or a fork, blend until smooth. Spread glaze over cooled cookies.

Chocolate Chip Slices

Using mini chocolate chips will keep these rounds from breaking apart when you slice them.

Tip

Fold in the chocolate chips by hand to keep from overworking the dough after the flour is mixed in. Overworking the dough will make the cookies tough.

Cookie sheets, lined with parchment paper

2 cups	all-purpose flour	500 mL
½ tsp	baking powder	2 mL
½ tsp	salt	2 mL
¾ cup	unsalted butter, softened	175 mL
1 cup	packed light brown sugar	250 mL
1	egg	1
1 tsp	vanilla extract	5 mL
1½ cups	mini semisweet chocolate chips	375 mL

1. In a bowl, whisk together flour, baking powder and salt until well combined. Set aside.

2. In a large bowl, using an electric mixer on medium speed, cream butter and brown sugar until light and fluffy, about 3 minutes. Add egg and beat well. Beat in vanilla. Scrape down sides of bowl. On low speed or using a wooden spoon, gradually add flour mixture, beating just until blended. By hand, fold in chocolate chips.

3. Divide dough in half. Shape each portion of dough into a log 2 inches (5 cm) in diameter. Tightly wrap each dough log in parchment paper or plastic wrap and chill for 2 to 3 hours or overnight.

4. Preheat oven to 375°F (190°C). Working with one dough log at a time, remove parchment paper or plastic wrap. Using a sharp knife, cut log into ¼-inch (0.5 cm) slices. Place about 1 inch (2.5 cm) apart on prepared cookie sheets. Bake one sheet at a time in preheated oven for 8 to 10 minutes or until edges start to turn lightly golden.

5. Immediately slide parchment paper onto a wire cooling rack. Cool cookies for 5 minutes, then transfer from parchment paper to cooling rack and cool completely.

Glazed Almond Slices

Almond is one of my favorite flavors, and these glazed cookies are very satisfying.

Tips

Logs of slice-and-bake dough may be tightly wrapped and stored in the freezer for 3 months.

Let glaze set before storing cookies between layers of wax paper in a tightly sealed container.

- Cookie sheets, lined with parchment paper

Cookies

2½ cups	all-purpose flour	625 mL
½ tsp	baking powder	2 mL
¼ tsp	salt	1 mL
½ cup	unsalted butter, softened	125 mL
½ cup	vegetable shortening	125 mL
1 cup	granulated sugar	250 mL
1	egg	1
1 tsp	almond extract	5 mL
½ cup	finely chopped unsalted almonds	125 mL

Glaze

1½ cups	confectioner's (powdered/icing) sugar	375 mL
2 tbsp	half-and-half (10%) cream or milk	25 mL
1 tsp	almond extract	5 mL

1. **Cookies:** In a bowl, whisk together flour, baking powder and salt until well combined. Set aside.

2. In a large bowl, using an electric mixer on medium speed, cream butter, shortening and granulated sugar until light and fluffy, about 3 minutes. Add egg and beat well. Stir in almond extract. Scrape down sides of bowl. On low speed or using a wooden spoon, gradually add flour mixture, beating just until blended. By hand, fold in almonds.

3. Divide dough in half. Shape each portion of dough into a log 2 inches (5 cm) in diameter. Tightly wrap each dough log in parchment paper or plastic wrap and chill for 2 to 3 hours or overnight.

4. Preheat oven to 375°F (190°C). Working with one dough log at a time, remove parchment paper or plastic wrap. Using a sharp knife, cut log into ¼-inch (0.5 cm) slices. Place about 1 inch (2.5 cm) apart on prepared cookie sheets. Bake one sheet at a time in preheated oven for 8 to 10 minutes or until edges start to turn lightly golden.

5. Immediately slide parchment paper onto a wire cooling rack. Cool cookies for 5 minutes, then transfer from parchment paper to cooling rack and cool completely.

6. **Glaze:** In a small bowl, combine confectioner's sugar, cream and almond extract. Using a small whisk or a fork, blend until glaze is smooth and spreadable. Spread glaze over cooled cookies.

Lemon Sandwich Cookies

Tender lemon cookies are filled with a lemon butter cream to create a delightful sandwich cookie. These are a nice treat with tea, milk or coffee.

Tips

A Microplane grater will finely zest the lemon peel for a wonderful texture in cookies.

Let filling set before storing cookies between layers of wax paper in a tightly sealed container.

● Cookie sheets, lined with parchment paper

Cookies

2⅔ cups	all-purpose flour	650 mL
½ tsp	baking powder	2 mL
¼ tsp	salt	1 mL
1 cup	unsalted butter, softened	250 mL
⅔ cup	granulated sugar	150 mL
½ cup	confectioner's (powdered/icing) sugar	125 mL
2	egg yolks	2
2 tsp	grated lemon zest	10 mL
3 tbsp	freshly squeezed lemon juice	45 mL

Filling

2 cups	confectioner's (powdered/icing) sugar	500 mL
¼ cup	unsalted butter, softened	50 mL
1 tsp	grated lemon zest	5 mL
2 tsp	freshly squeezed lemon juice	10 mL

1. **Cookies:** In a bowl, whisk together flour, baking powder and salt until well combined. Set aside.

2. In a large bowl, using an electric mixer on medium speed, cream butter, granulated sugar and confectioner's sugar until light and fluffy, about 3 minutes. Add egg yolks one at a time, beating well after each addition. Stir in lemon zest and lemon juice. Scrape down sides of bowl. On low speed or using a wooden spoon, gradually add flour mixture, beating just until blended.

3. Divide dough in half. Shape each portion of dough into a log 2 inches (5 cm) in diameter. Tightly wrap each dough log in parchment paper or plastic wrap and chill for 2 to 3 hours or overnight.

4. Preheat oven to 350°F (180°C). Working with one dough log at a time, remove parchment paper or plastic wrap. Using a sharp knife, cut log into ¼-inch (0.5 cm) slices. Place about 1 inch (2.5 cm) apart on prepared cookie sheets. Bake one sheet at a time in preheated oven for 10 to 12 minutes or until edges start to turn lightly golden.

5. Immediately slide parchment paper onto a wire cooling rack. Cool cookies for 5 minutes, then transfer from parchment paper to cooling rack and cool completely.

6. **Filling:** In a bowl, combine confectioner's sugar, butter, lemon zest and juice. Using an electric mixer on medium speed, beat until light and fluffy. Spread a thick layer over the bottom side of half of the cooled cookies. Top with remaining cookies.

Coconut Crisps

● ● ●

Coconut gives these slices a tropical flair.

Tips

Tightly wrapped, slice-and-bake dough can be stored in the refrigerator for up to 1 week.

Cookies can be stored in a tightly sealed container at room temperature for up to 3 days.

● **Cookie sheets, lined with parchment paper**

2¼ cups	all-purpose flour	550 mL
½ tsp	baking powder	2 mL
¼ tsp	salt	1 mL
1 cup	sweetened flaked coconut, coarsely chopped	250 mL
1 cup	unsalted butter, softened	250 mL
⅔ cup	granulated sugar	150 mL
1	egg	1
½ tsp	vanilla extract	2 mL
¼ tsp	coconut extract	1 mL

1. In a bowl, whisk together flour, baking powder and salt until well combined. Stir in coconut. Set aside.

2. In a large bowl, using an electric mixer on medium speed, cream butter and granulated sugar until light and fluffy, about 3 minutes. Add egg and beat well. Beat in vanilla and coconut extract. Scrape down sides of bowl. On low speed or using a wooden spoon, gradually add flour mixture, beating just until blended.

3. Divide dough in half. Shape each portion of dough into a log 2 inches (5 cm) in diameter. Tightly wrap each dough log in parchment paper or plastic wrap and chill for 2 to 3 hours or overnight.

4. Preheat oven to 350°F (180°C). Working with one dough log at a time, remove parchment paper or plastic wrap. Using a sharp knife, cut log into ¼-inch (0.5 cm) slices. Place about 1 inch (2.5 cm) apart on prepared cookie sheets. Bake one sheet at a time in preheated oven for 10 to 12 minutes or until edges start to turn lightly golden.

5. Immediately slide parchment paper onto a wire cooling rack. Cool cookies for 5 minutes, then transfer from parchment paper to cooling rack and cool completely.

Date Walnut Slices

Dates and walnuts are a good flavor pairing, and they add a lot of character to these delightful cookies.

Tips

To keep dates from sticking to your knife when you chop them, give the knife blade a light coat of nonstick cooking spray.

Cookies can be stored in a tightly sealed container at room temperature for up to 3 days.

● **Cookie sheets, lined with parchment paper**

2½ cups	all-purpose flour	625 mL
½ tsp	baking powder	2 mL
¼ tsp	baking soda	1 mL
¼ tsp	salt	1 mL
½ cup	unsalted butter, softened	125 mL
½ cup	vegetable shortening	125 mL
¾ cup	granulated sugar	175 mL
½ cup	packed light brown sugar	125 mL
1	egg	1
1 tsp	vanilla extract	5 mL
⅔ cup	finely chopped dates	150 mL
½ cup	finely chopped walnuts	125 mL

1. In a bowl, whisk together flour, baking powder, baking soda and salt until well combined. Set aside.

2. In a large bowl, using an electric mixer on medium speed, cream butter, shortening, granulated sugar and brown sugar until light and fluffy, about 3 minutes. Add egg and beat well. Beat in vanilla. Scrape down sides of bowl. On low speed or using a wooden spoon, gradually add flour mixture, beating just until blended. By hand, fold in dates and walnuts

3. Divide dough in half. Shape each portion of dough into a log 2 inches (5 cm) in diameter. Tightly wrap each dough log in parchment paper or plastic wrap and chill for 2 to 3 hours or overnight.

4. Preheat oven to 350°F (180°C). Working with one dough log at a time, remove parchment paper or plastic wrap. Using a sharp knife, cut log into ¼-inch (0.5 cm) slices. Place about 1 inch (2.5 cm) apart on prepared cookie sheets. Bake one sheet at a time in preheated oven for 10 to 12 minutes or until edges start to turn lightly golden.

5. Immediately slide parchment paper onto a wire cooling rack. Cool cookies for 5 minutes, then transfer from parchment paper to cooling rack and cool completely.

Pecan Rounds

These nut cookies can be soft or crisp depending on how long you bake them. Either way, they are very good.

Tips

Toasting nuts (see page 32) brings out their flavor and makes them crunchy.

Cookies can be stored in a tightly sealed container at room temperature for up to 3 days.

● Cookie sheets, lined with parchment paper

2¼ cups	all-purpose flour	550 mL
1 tsp	baking powder	5 mL
¼ tsp	salt	1 mL
¾ cup	unsalted butter, softened	175 mL
¾ cup	granulated sugar	175 mL
1	egg	1
1 tsp	vanilla extract	5 mL
¾ cup	finely chopped toasted pecans	175 mL

1. In a bowl, whisk together flour, baking powder and salt until well combined. Set aside.

2. In a large bowl, using an electric mixer on medium speed, cream butter and granulated sugar until light and fluffy, about 3 minutes. Add egg and beat well. Beat in vanilla. Scrape down sides of bowl. On low speed or using a wooden spoon, gradually add flour mixture, beating just until blended. By hand, fold in pecans.

3. Divide dough in half. Shape each portion of dough into a log 2 inches (5 cm) in diameter. Tightly wrap each dough log in parchment paper or plastic wrap and chill for 2 to 3 hours or overnight.

4. Preheat oven to 350°F (180°C). Working with one dough log at a time, remove parchment paper or plastic wrap. Using a sharp knife, cut log into ¼-inch (0.5 cm) slices. Place about 1 inch (2.5 cm) apart on prepared cookie sheets. Bake one sheet at a time in preheated oven for 10 to 12 minutes or until edges start to turn lightly golden.

5. Immediately slide parchment paper onto a wire cooling rack. Cool cookies for 5 minutes, then transfer from parchment paper to cooling rack and cool completely.

Butterfly Cookies

After cutting the dough logs into ¼-inch (0.5 cm) slices, cut each slice in half. Place the rounded edges of two half-slices together to form a butterfly shape. Gently press the slices together and bake as directed in the recipe.

Mocha Chip Thins

The pairing of chocolate and espresso gives these simple cookies a bold flavor.

Tip

For a crispier texture, bake cookies 2 minutes longer.

● **Cookie sheets, lined with parchment paper**

2 cups	all-purpose flour	500 mL
⅓ cup	unsweetened Dutch-process cocoa powder	75 mL
1 tsp	instant espresso powder	5 mL
½ tsp	baking powder	2 mL
¼ tsp	salt	1 mL
¾ cup	unsalted butter, softened	175 mL
1 cup	packed light brown sugar	250 mL
1	egg	1
1 tsp	vanilla extract	5 mL
1½ cups	mini semisweet chocolate chips	375 mL

1. In a bowl, whisk together flour, cocoa powder, espresso powder, baking powder and salt until well combined. Set aside.

2. In a large bowl, using an electric mixer on medium speed, cream butter and brown sugar until light and fluffy, about 3 minutes. Add egg and beat well. Beat in vanilla. Scrape down sides of bowl. On low speed or using a wooden spoon, gradually add flour mixture, beating just until blended. By hand, fold in chocolate chips.

3. Divide dough in half. Shape each portion of dough into a log 2 inches (5 cm) in diameter. Tightly wrap each dough log in parchment paper or plastic wrap and chill for 2 to 3 hours or overnight.

4. Preheat oven to 375°F (190°C). Working with one dough log at a time, remove parchment paper or plastic wrap. Using a sharp knife, cut log into ¼-inch (0.5 cm) slices. Place about 1 inch (2.5 cm) apart on prepared cookie sheets. Bake one sheet at a time in preheated oven for 8 to 10 minutes or until set.

5. Immediately slide parchment paper onto a wire cooling rack. Cool cookies for 5 minutes, then transfer from parchment paper to cooling rack and cool completely.

Cream Cheese Citrus Rounds

Makes about 4 dozen cookies ● ● ●

Orange and lemon pleasingly scent these tender rounds. They are great accompaniment to a cup of hot tea or a cold glass of milk.

Tip

When slicing the dough, roll the log slightly after each cut to maintain the round shape of the cookies

● **Cookie sheets, lined with parchment paper**

2½ cups	all-purpose flour	625 mL
½ tsp	baking powder	2 mL
¼ tsp	salt	1 mL
⅔ cup	unsalted butter, softened	150 mL
3 oz	cream cheese, softened	90 g
½ cup	granulated sugar	125 mL
½ cup	confectioner's (powdered/icing) sugar	125 mL
1	egg	1
1 tbsp	grated orange zest	15 mL
2 tsp	grated lemon zest	10 mL
½ tsp	vanilla extract	2 mL

1. In a bowl, whisk together flour, baking powder and salt until well combined. Set aside.

2. In a large bowl, using an electric mixer on medium speed, cream butter, cream cheese, granulated sugar and confectioner's sugar until light and fluffy, about 3 minutes. Add egg and beat well. Stir in orange zest, lemon zest and vanilla. Scrape down sides of bowl. On low speed or using a wooden spoon, gradually add flour mixture, beating just until blended.

3. Divide dough in half. Shape each portion of dough into a log 2 inches (5 cm) in diameter. Tightly wrap each dough log in parchment paper or plastic wrap and chill for 2 to 3 hours or overnight.

4. Preheat oven to 350°F (180°C). Working with one dough log at a time, remove parchment paper or plastic wrap. Using a sharp knife, cut log into ¼-inch (0.5 cm) slices. Place about 1 inch (2.5 cm) apart on prepared cookie sheets. Bake one sheet at a time in preheated oven for 10 to 12 minutes or until edges start to turn lightly golden.

5. Immediately slide parchment paper onto a wire cooling rack. Cool cookies for 5 minutes, then transfer from parchment paper to cooling rack and cool completely.

Cranberry Almond Slices

With flecks of ruby-colored cranberries and pieces of almond, these slices are very pretty as well as tasty.

Tips

Finely chop nuts and dried fruit for slice-and-bake cookies. If the pieces are too big, the dough may crack or crumble when sliced.

Wrap logs of slice-and-bake dough tightly to keep them from drying out in the refrigerator.

● Cookie sheets, lined with parchment paper

2¼ cups	all-purpose flour	550 mL
½ tsp	baking powder	2 mL
½ tsp	salt	2 mL
¾ cup	unsalted butter, softened	175 mL
1 cup	granulated sugar	250 mL
1	egg	1
½ tsp	vanilla extract	2 mL
½ tsp	almond extract	2 mL
¾ cup	finely chopped dried cranberries	175 mL
½ cup	finely chopped unsalted almonds	125 mL

1. In a bowl, whisk together flour, baking powder and salt until well combined. Set aside.
2. In a large bowl, using an electric mixer on medium speed, cream butter and granulated sugar until light and fluffy, about 3 minutes. Add egg and beat well. Beat in vanilla and almond extract. Scrape down sides of bowl. On low speed or using a wooden spoon, gradually add flour mixture, beating just until blended. By hand, fold in cranberries and almonds.
3. Divide dough in half. Shape each portion of dough into a log 2 inches (5 cm) in diameter. Tightly wrap each dough log in parchment paper or plastic wrap and chill for 2 to 3 hours or overnight.
4. Preheat oven to 350°F (180°C). Working with one dough log at a time, remove parchment paper or plastic wrap. Using a sharp knife, cut log into ¼-inch (0.5 cm) slices. Place about 1 inch (2.5 cm) apart on prepared cookie sheets. Bake one sheet at a time in preheated oven for 10 to 12 minutes or until edges start to turn lightly golden.
5. Immediately slide parchment paper onto a wire cooling rack. Cool cookies for 5 minutes, then transfer from parchment paper to cooling rack and cool completely.

Chocolate-Glazed Coffee Cookies

Makes about 4 dozen cookies
● ● ●

The chocolate glaze is a nice finishing touch and complements the coffee flavor.

Tips

Chocolate can be melted in the top of a double boiler placed over simmering water. Stir frequently, until chocolate is completely melted and mixture is smooth. Set aside to cool slightly before drizzling over cooled cookies.

Let chocolate set before storing cookies between layers of wax paper in a tightly sealed container.

● **Cookie sheets, lined with parchment paper**

Cookies

2½ cups	all-purpose flour	625 mL
1 tbsp	instant espresso powder	15 mL
½ tsp	baking powder	2 mL
½ tsp	salt	2 mL
¾ cup	unsalted butter, softened	175 mL
¾ cup	granulated sugar	175 mL
1	egg	1
1 tsp	vanilla extract	5 mL

Glaze

1 cup	chopped semisweet chocolate or semisweet chocolate chips	250 mL
1 tsp	vegetable shortening	5 mL

1. ***Cookies:*** In a bowl, whisk together flour, espresso powder, baking powder and salt until well combined. Set aside.

2. In a large bowl, using an electric mixer on medium speed, cream butter and granulated sugar until light and fluffy, about 3 minutes. Add egg and beat well. Beat in vanilla. Scrape down sides of bowl. On low speed or using a wooden spoon, gradually add flour mixture, beating just until blended.

3. Divide dough in half. Shape each portion of dough into a log 2 inches (5 cm) in diameter. Tightly wrap each dough log in parchment paper or plastic wrap and chill for 2 to 3 hours or overnight.

4. Preheat oven to 350°F (180°C). Working with one dough log at a time, remove parchment paper or plastic wrap. Using a sharp knife, cut log into ¼-inch (0.5 cm) slices. Place about 1 inch (2.5 cm) apart on prepared cookie sheets. Bake one sheet at a time in preheated oven for 10 to 12 minutes or until edges start to turn lightly golden.

5. Immediately slide parchment paper onto a wire cooling rack. Cool cookies for 5 minutes, then transfer from parchment paper to cooling rack and cool completely.

6. ***Glaze:*** In a 1-quart (1 L) microwave-safe zippered storage bag, combine semisweet chocolate and vegetable shortening. Microwave on High power for 1 minute. Knead bag until completely combined and smooth, microwaving an additional 10 seconds at a time as needed to fully melt chocolate. Cut off a small corner of bag and drizzle chocolate over tops of cooled cookies. Place on parchment or wax paper to set.

Molasses Slices

Rich molasses and brown sugar give these cookies depth in flavor and color.

Tip

To keep logs round as they chill, place wrapped and shaped dough inside a cardboard tube. The curved shape of the tube will keep the bottom of the dough log from flattening out.

● **Cookie sheets, lined with parchment paper**

2¾ cups	all-purpose flour	675 mL
½ tsp	baking powder	2 mL
¼ tsp	baking soda	1 mL
¼ tsp	salt	1 mL
⅓ cup	unsalted butter, softened	75 mL
⅓ cup	vegetable shortening	75 mL
¾ cup	packed light brown sugar	175 mL
1	egg	1
½ cup	fancy molasses	125 mL
1 tsp	vanilla extract	5 mL

1. In a bowl, whisk together flour, baking powder, baking soda and salt until well combined. Set aside.

2. In a large bowl, using an electric mixer on medium speed, cream butter, shortening and brown sugar until light and fluffy, about 3 minutes. Add egg and beat well. Stir in molasses and vanilla. Scrape down sides of bowl. On low speed or using a wooden spoon, gradually add flour mixture, beating just until blended.

3. Divide dough in half. Shape each portion of dough into a log 2 inches (5 cm) in diameter. Tightly wrap each dough log in parchment paper or plastic wrap and chill for 2 to 3 hours or overnight.

4. Preheat oven to 350°F (180°C). Working with one dough log at a time, remove parchment paper or plastic wrap. Using a sharp knife, cut log into ¼-inch (0.5 cm) slices. Place about 1 inch (2.5 cm) apart on prepared cookie sheets. Bake one sheet at a time in preheated oven for 10 to 12 minutes or until set.

5. Immediately slide parchment paper onto a wire cooling rack. Cool cookies for 5 minutes, then transfer from parchment paper to cooling rack and cool completely.

White Chocolate Rounds

Keep rolls of dough for these wonderful cookies on hand in the refrigerator or freezer. You can quickly bake fresh cookies up as a special treat for unexpected guests.

Tips

Real white chocolate contains cocoa butter. Always check the ingredients for cocoa butter to be sure you are using white chocolate. Avoid any product labeled as "white" or "vanilla" baking chips.

Defrost frozen dough logs in the refrigerator overnight. The dough can also be sliced and baked while still frozen; just add a couple minutes to the baking time.

● **Cookie sheets, lined with parchment paper**

2 cups	all-purpose flour	500 mL
½ tsp	baking powder	2 mL
½ tsp	salt	2 mL
¾ cup	unsalted butter, softened	175 mL
1 cup	granulated sugar	250 mL
1	egg	1
1 tsp	vanilla extract	5 mL
¼ tsp	almond extract	1 mL
1 cup	finely chopped white chocolate	250 mL

1. In a bowl, whisk together flour, baking powder and salt until well combined. Set aside.

2. In a large bowl, using an electric mixer on medium speed, cream butter and granulated sugar until light and fluffy, about 3 minutes. Add egg and beat well. Beat in vanilla and almond extract. Scrape down sides of bowl. On low speed or using a wooden spoon, gradually add flour mixture, beating just until blended. By hand, fold in white chocolate.

3. Divide dough in half. Shape each portion of dough into a log 2 inches (5 cm) in diameter. Tightly wrap each dough log in parchment paper or plastic wrap and chill for 2 to 3 hours or overnight.

4. Preheat oven to 375°F (190°C). Working with one dough log at a time, remove parchment paper or plastic wrap. Using a sharp knife, cut log into ¼-inch (0.5 cm) slices. Place about 1 inch (2.5 cm) apart on prepared cookie sheets. Bake one sheet at a time in preheated oven for 8 to 10 minutes or until edges start to turn lightly golden.

5. Immediately slide parchment paper onto a wire cooling rack. Cool cookies for 5 minutes, then transfer from parchment paper to cooling rack and cool completely.

Sugar Cookie Slices

These are great cookies to make for holidays or special occasions.

Tip

Use a sugar color that fits the event, holiday or time of year.

● **Cookie sheets, lined with parchment paper**

2½ cups	all-purpose flour	625 mL
½ tsp	baking powder	2 mL
¼ tsp	baking soda	1 mL
¼ tsp	salt	1 mL
¾ cup	unsalted butter, softened	175 mL
1 cup	granulated sugar	250 mL
1	egg	1
2 tsp	vanilla extract	10 mL
½ cup	colored sugar	125 mL

1. In a bowl, whisk together flour, baking powder, baking soda and salt until well combined. Set aside.

2. In a large bowl, using an electric mixer on medium speed, cream butter and granulated sugar until light and fluffy, about 3 minutes. Add egg and beat well. Beat in vanilla. Scrape down sides of bowl. On low speed or using a wooden spoon, gradually add flour mixture, beating just until blended.

3. Divide dough in half. Shape each portion of dough into a log 2 inches (5 cm) in diameter. Roll each dough log in colored sugar. Tightly wrap each dough log in parchment paper or plastic wrap and chill for 2 to 3 hours or overnight.

4. Preheat oven to 350°F (180°C). Working with one dough log at a time, remove parchment paper or plastic wrap. Using a sharp knife, cut log into ¼-inch (0.5 cm) slices. Place about 1 inch (2.5 cm) apart on prepared cookie sheets. Bake one sheet at a time in preheated oven for 10 to 12 minutes or until edges start to turn lightly golden.

5. Immediately slide parchment paper onto a wire cooling rack. Cool cookies for 5 minutes, then transfer from parchment paper to cooling rack and cool completely.

Apricot Slices

With a hint of orange, these pretty slices have a lovely fruit flavor.

Tip

To keep dried apricots from sticking to your knife when you chop them, give the knife blade a light coat of nonstick cooking spray.

● **Cookie sheets, lined with parchment paper**

2¼ cups	all-purpose flour	550 mL
½ tsp	baking powder	2 mL
½ tsp	salt	2 mL
¾ cup	unsalted butter, softened	175 mL
1 cup	granulated sugar	250 mL
1	egg	1
1 tbsp	grated orange zest	15 mL
½ tsp	vanilla extract	2 mL
¾ cup	finely chopped dried apricots	175 mL

1. In a bowl, whisk together flour, baking powder and salt until well combined. Set aside.

2. In a large bowl, using an electric mixer on medium speed, cream butter and granulated sugar until light and fluffy, about 3 minutes. Add egg and beat well. Stir in orange zest and vanilla. Scrape down sides of bowl. On low speed or using a wooden spoon, gradually add flour mixture, beating just until blended. By hand, fold in apricots.

3. Divide dough in half. Shape each portion of dough into a log 2 inches (5 cm) in diameter. Tightly wrap each dough log in parchment paper or plastic wrap and chill for 2 to 3 hours or overnight.

4. Preheat oven to 350°F (180°C). Working with one dough log at a time, remove parchment paper or plastic wrap. Using a sharp knife, cut log into ¼-inch (0.5 cm) slices. Place about 1 inch (2.5 cm) apart on prepared cookie sheets. Bake one sheet at a time in preheated oven for 10 to 12 minutes or until edges start to turn lightly golden.

5. Immediately slide parchment paper onto a wire cooling rack. Cool cookies for 5 minutes, then transfer from parchment paper to cooling rack and cool completely.

Margarita Cookies

These adult cookies are infused with the flavors that make margaritas so popular.

Tip

Cointreau and triple sec are orange-flavored liqueurs used to make margaritas. Either liqueur will work well in this intoxicating recipe.

● **Cookie sheets, lined with parchment paper**

2½ cups	all-purpose flour	625 mL
½ tsp	baking powder	2 mL
¼ tsp	baking soda	1 mL
¼ tsp	salt	1 mL
⅔ cup	unsalted butter, softened	150 mL
¾ cup	granulated sugar	175 mL
1	egg	1
4 tsp	tequila	20 mL
1 tbsp	grated lime zest	15 mL
2 tsp	freshly squeezed lime juice	10 mL
2 tsp	Cointreau or triple sec	10 mL

1. In a bowl, whisk together flour, baking powder, baking soda and salt until well combined. Set aside.

2. In a large bowl, using an electric mixer on medium speed, cream butter and granulated sugar until light and fluffy, about 3 minutes. Add egg and beat well. Stir in tequila, lime zest, lime juice and cointreau. Scrape down sides of bowl. On low speed or using a wooden spoon, gradually add flour mixture, beating just until blended.

3. Divide dough in half. Shape each portion of dough into a log 2 inches (5 cm) in diameter. Tightly wrap each dough log in parchment paper or plastic wrap and chill for 2 to 3 hours or overnight.

4. Preheat oven to 350°F (180°C). Working with one dough log at a time, remove parchment paper or plastic wrap. Using a sharp knife, cut log into ¼-inch (0.5 cm) slices. Place about 1 inch (2.5 cm) apart on prepared cookie sheets. Bake one sheet at a time in preheated oven for 10 to 12 minutes or until edges start to turn lightly golden.

5. Immediately slide parchment paper onto a wire cooling rack. Cool cookies for 5 minutes, then transfer from parchment paper to cooling rack and cool completely.

Bars and Squares

●●●

Apple Pie Crumb Squares 277

Apricot Pineapple Bars 278

Raspberry Streusel Squares 280

Coconut Pecan Bars 282

Cherry Cheesecake Squares 283

Sunshine Lemon Squares 284

Tropical Oat Squares 285

Sour Cream Blueberry Squares 286

Cranberry Almond Bars 287

Nutty Chocolate Squares 288

Apricot Crunch Squares 289

Cream Cheese Blondies 290

Chocolate Mint Bars 291

Coconut Pineapple Bars 292

Lime Squares 293

Pecan Pie Bars 294

Chocolate Almond Toffee Bars 295

Boysenberry Squares 296

Peanut Butter Oat Bars 297

Chocolate Walnut Bars 298

Nutty Fruit Bars 299

Sour Cream Lemon Squares 300

Cherry Crumb Squares 301

Pumpkin Crunch Bars 302

Deluxe Nut Bars 304

Cashew Caramel Blondies 305

Buttermilk Spice Bars 306

Maple Date Pecan Squares 307

Chocolate Chip Coffee Bars 308

Peaches and Cream Squares 310

Oatmeal Coconut Bars 311

Strawberry Squares 312

Almond Squares 313

Pineapple Nut Cheese Squares 314

Golden Coconut Cashew Squares . . 316

White Chocolate Pumpkin
    Blondies 318

Cappuccino Cheesecake Bars 320

Marmalade Crumb Bars 321

Cranberry Coconut Squares 322

Maple Walnut Squares 323

Apricot Pineapple Crumb Bars 324

Raspberry Oat Squares 326

Creamy Lemon Oat Squares 327

Applesauce Walnut Bars 328

White Chocolate Raspberry Crumb
    Squares 329

Blueberry Pie Bars 330

Lime Coconut Squares 331

Pineapple Squares 332

Caramel Pecan Squares 333

Mincemeat Bars 334

About Bars and Squares

Many bars and squares are cookies baked in a rectangular or square baking pan. They get their names from the shapes they're cut into for serving. But don't feel limited to just bar and square shapes. These wonderful cookies can be cut into diamonds and triangles for variety and a pretty appearance on cookie trays.

A favorite of many cookie enthusiasts, these multilayered cookies usually start with a bottom crust that is topped with a luscious fruit, nut, chocolate or cream cheese filling. Some bars and squares are then finished with a crumb topping, glaze or light dusting of confectioner's (powdered/icing) sugar.

Another type of bar, known as blondies, are a batter cookie made like brownies but without the chocolate. They can be made in a variety of flavors and are frequently loaded with nuts and fruit. Their textures can range from dense and chewy to light and velvety.

Tender cake bars are strong on flavor and similar in texture to snack cakes. Frequently served unadorned, they can also be finished with a glaze, frosting, streusel or nut topping, or even dusted with confectioner's (powdered/icing) sugar.

Preparing Baking Pans

Preparing the baking pan by lining it with foil makes it much easier to remove the bars or squares from the pan after baking and protects the pan from damage from knife cuts. It also makes cleanup a breeze.

Line square baking pans with one sheet of heavy-duty foil. For 13- by 9-inch (3 L) pans, use two layers of foil for additional support. Carefully fit the sheet of foil into the pan, leaving 1 to 2 inches (2.5 to 5 cm) of foil extending over the pan edge on at least two opposite sides. Fold these extensions down over the outside of the pan. They will be used to lift the cooled bars from the pan before cutting. After lining the pan, grease it with nonstick cooking spray or unsalted butter. Another option is to use the nonstick foil now available in grocery stores. It works well for bar cookies, and no greasing is required.

If you choose not to line your pan with foil, it should be greased with nonstick cooking spray or unsalted butter to prevent sticking.

Making Crusts and Crumb Toppings

The crusts for bars and squares are made using the cut-in method of combining ingredients (see page 36), which produces a tender base for the cookies. The chilled butter is worked into the flour mixture until it creates a crumbly dough. This method is also used for making the crumb toppings. The crust dough is then pressed into the baking pan in an even layer to make a crust of uniform thickness. Push the dough all the way into the corners of the pan and make sure there are no high or low spots in the crust. It is important that the crust be uniform so that it will bake evenly.

Some recipes call for the crust to be baked before the filling is added, while others bake the crust and filling together. The oven rack should be positioned in the center of the oven so that the crust will bake all the way through without overly browning and drying out.

Cutting Bars and Squares

Allow the bar cookies to cool completely in the pan before cutting. This will make it easier to cut the cookies into bars and squares or other shapes. Using the extended edges of the foil, carefully lift the cookies from the pan and place them on a sturdy cutting board. Gently pull the edges of the foil away from the sides of the bars. If the foil sticks, run a knife blade between the bars and foil to loosen. A knife with a long, thin, sharp blade will do the cleanest job as you cut the cookies into bars. Wipe the knife with a towel between cuts to keep the blade clean and prevent the bars from sticking to the knife.

Apple Pie Crumb Squares

These tender, flavorful bars with a hint of cinnamon are reminiscent of fresh apple pie with a crumb topping.

Tips

Granny Smith apples or other firm varieties of cooking apples work well in this recipe.

Cut into small bars for cookie portions; cut them into large squares and serve topped with a scoop of ice cream for a satisfying dessert.

Store squares between layers of wax paper in a tightly sealed container at room temperature. Squares can be stored at room temperature for up to 2 days or in the refrigerator for up to 3 days.

- Preheat oven to 350°F (180°C)
- 9-inch (2.5 L) square baking pan, lined with foil, greased

Crust

2¼ cups	all-purpose flour	550 mL
½ cup	granulated sugar	125 mL
½ cup	packed light brown sugar	125 mL
1 tsp	baking powder	5 mL
⅛ tsp	ground cinnamon	0.5 mL
⅛ tsp	salt	0.5 mL
1 cup	quick-cooking rolled oats	250 mL
1 cup	unsalted butter, cut into pieces	250 mL

Filling

½ cup	packed light brown sugar	125 mL
¼ cup	granulated sugar	50 mL
2½ tbsp	cornstarch	37 mL
½ tsp	ground cinnamon	2 mL
⅛ tsp	ground nutmeg	0.5 mL
4 cups	thinly sliced peeled apples	1 L
3 tbsp	unsalted butter, melted	45 mL
2 tsp	freshly squeezed lemon juice	10 mL

1. **Crust:** In a large bowl, whisk together flour, granulated sugar, brown sugar, baking powder, cinnamon and salt until well combined. Stir in oats. Using a pastry blender, a fork or your fingers, cut in butter until evenly combined. Mixture will resemble coarse crumbs and start to come together. Using the back of a spoon or your fingers, press two-thirds of crust mixture evenly into bottom of prepared pan. Reserve remaining crust mixture for topping.

2. **Filling:** In a small bowl, whisk together brown sugar, granulated sugar, cornstarch, cinnamon and nutmeg until well combined. Set aside.

3. In a large bowl, combine apples, melted butter and lemon juice, tossing until apples are well coated. Gradually stir in the sugar mixture until well combined. Spread filling evenly over crust. Crumble reserved crust mixture over filling.

4. Bake in preheated oven for 35 to 40 minutes or until lightly golden. Let cool completely in baking pan on a wire rack.

5. Using foil, lift cooled squares from pan and place on a cutting board. Cut into 1½-inch (4 cm) squares.

Apricot Pineapple Bars

● ● ●

Luscious apricots and pineapple, blended with a hint of orange, give these fruity bars lots of flavor.

Tips

I prefer to use juice-packed pineapple in this recipe as syrup-packed pineapple can make the bars too sweet.

Let icing set completely before storing bars between layers of wax paper in a tightly sealed container. Bars can be stored in the refrigerator for up to 3 days.

- Preheat oven to 350°F (180°C)
- 13- by 9-inch (3 L) baking pan, lined with foil, greased

Crust

2 cups	all-purpose flour	500 mL
6 tbsp	confectioner's (powdered/icing) sugar	90 mL
1/8 tsp	baking powder	0.5 mL
1 cup	unsalted butter, cut into pieces	250 mL

Filling

1 cup	chopped dried apricots	250 mL
1/3 cup	freshly squeezed orange juice	75 mL
6 tbsp	all-purpose flour	90 mL
1 tsp	baking powder	5 mL
1/4 tsp	salt	1 mL
4	eggs	4
1 1/2 cups	granulated sugar	375 mL
1/2 tsp	vanilla extract	2 mL
3/4 cup	drained canned juice-packed crushed pineapple	175 mL

Icing

2 cups	confectioner's (powdered/icing) sugar	500 mL
2 tbsp	unsalted butter, melted	25 mL
2 tsp	grated orange zest	10 mL
2 tbsp	freshly squeezed orange juice	25 mL

1. *Crust:* In a bowl, whisk together flour, confectioner's sugar and baking powder until well combined. Using a pastry blender, a fork or your fingers, cut in butter until evenly combined. Mixture will resemble coarse crumbs and start to come together. Using the back of a spoon or your fingers, press crust evenly into bottom of prepared pan. Bake in preheated oven for 15 minutes or until lightly golden. Let cool completely on a wire rack.

2. *Filling:* In a small bowl, thoroughly combine apricots and orange juice. Set aside.

3. In a small bowl, whisk together flour, baking powder and salt. Set aside.

4. In a large bowl, using an electric mixer on medium speed, lightly beat eggs. Add granulated sugar and beat until smooth and creamy, about 1 minute. Beat in vanilla. Scrape down sides of bowl. On low speed or using a wooden spoon, gradually add flour mixture, beating just until blended. By hand, fold in apricot mixture and pineapple. Pour filling over cooled crust and spread evenly.

5. Bake for 28 to 32 minutes or until lightly golden brown around edges. Let cool completely in baking pan on a wire rack.

6. *Icing:* In a small bowl, combine confectioner's sugar, melted butter, orange zest and orange juice. Using a small whisk or a fork, blend until icing is smooth and thin enough to drizzle from a fork. Drizzle icing over cooled bars. Let stand 20 minutes or until icing is set.

7. Using foil, lift bars from pan and place on a cutting board. Cut into 1- by $2\frac{1}{4}$-inch (2.5 by 5.5 cm) bars.

Raspberry Streusel Squares

● ● ●

A tender crust with almonds, raspberry filling and a crumbly streusel topping combine to make great squares. This is one of my favorite cookies.

Tips

For a pretty appearance, cut cookies into diamond or triangle shapes.

Let icing set completely before storing squares between layers of wax paper in a tightly sealed container. Squares can be stored at room temperature for up to 3 days.

● Preheat oven to 350°F (180°C)
● 9-inch (2.5 L) square baking pan, lined with foil, greased

Crust

1½ cups	all-purpose flour	375 mL
6 tbsp	confectioner's (powdered/icing) sugar	90 mL
⅛ tsp	baking powder	0.5 mL
¼ cup	finely chopped roasted unsalted almonds	50 mL
⅔ cup	unsalted butter, cut into pieces	150 mL

Filling

1 cup	seedless raspberry jam	250 mL

Topping

1 cup	all-purpose flour	250 mL
⅓ cup	granulated sugar	75 mL
¼ tsp	almond extract	1 mL
⅓ cup	unsalted butter, cut into pieces	75 mL

Icing

¾ cup	confectioner's (powdered/icing) sugar	175 mL
1 to 2 tbsp	half-and-half (10%) cream or milk	15 to 25 mL
⅛ tsp	almond extract	0.5 mL

1. **Crust:** In a bowl, whisk together flour, confectioner's sugar and baking powder until well combined. Stir in almonds. Using a pastry blender, a fork or your fingers, cut in butter until evenly combined. Mixture will resemble coarse crumbs and start to come together. Using the back of a spoon or your fingers, press crust evenly into bottom of prepared pan.

2. **Filling:** Stir raspberry jam to loosen it. Spread jam evenly over crust.

3. **Topping:** In a small bowl, whisk together flour and granulated sugar until well blended. Stir in almond extract. Using a fork or your fingers, work in butter until evenly combined. Mixture will resemble coarse crumbs and start to come together. Crumble topping over jam.

4. Bake in preheated oven for 20 to 24 minutes or until lightly golden. Let cool completely in baking pan on a wire rack.

Tip

The small amount of cornstarch in confectioner's sugar helps create a very tender crust for bars and squares.

5. *Icing:* In a small bowl, combine confectioner's sugar, 1 tablespoon (15 mL) of the cream and almond extract. Using a small whisk or a fork, blend until icing is smooth and thin enough to drizzle from a fork. Add more cream as needed to achieve the desired consistency. Drizzle icing over cooled squares. Let stand 20 minutes or until the icing is set.

6. Using foil, lift squares from pan and place on a cutting board. Cut into $1\frac{1}{2}$-inch (4 cm) squares.

Squares into Triangles

When cutting squares into serving pieces, think outside the classic square shape. Cut the cookies into squares, and then cut each square in half to form two triangles.

Coconut Pecan Bars

These scrumptious, rich bars are a family favorite. Packed with coconut and pecans, they make a great addition to holiday cookie trays and are a wonderful pleasure throughout the year.

Tips

I also make these bars with maple flavoring used in place of the vanilla extract for a special flavor treat.

Let icing set completely before storing bars between layers of wax paper in a tightly sealed container. Bars can be stored in the refrigerator for up to 3 days. Bring to room temperature before serving.

- **Preheat oven to 350°F (180°C)**
- **13- by 9-inch (3 L) baking pan, lined with foil, greased**

Crust

2 cups	all-purpose flour	500 mL
1 tbsp	granulated sugar	15 mL
¼ tsp	baking powder	1 mL
1 cup	unsalted butter, cut into pieces	250 mL

Filling

1¾ cups	packed light brown sugar	425 mL
1½ cups	chopped pecans	375 mL
¾ cup	sweetened flaked coconut	175 mL
2	eggs	2
1 tbsp	unsalted butter, melted	15 mL
1 tsp	vanilla extract	5 mL
¼ tsp	baking powder	1 mL

Icing

½ cup	confectioner's (powdered/icing) sugar	125 mL
2 tsp	half-and-half (10%) cream or milk	10 mL
½ tsp	vanilla extract	2 mL

1. **Crust:** In a bowl, whisk together flour, granulated sugar and baking powder until well combined. Using a pastry blender, a fork or your fingers, cut in butter until evenly combined. Mixture will resemble coarse crumbs and start to come together. Using the back of a spoon or your fingers, press crust evenly into bottom of prepared pan. Bake in preheated oven for 15 minutes or until lightly golden. Place on a wire cooling rack.

2. **Filling:** In a large bowl, combine brown sugar, pecans and coconut until well blended. Set aside.

3. In a small bowl, using a wire whisk, lightly beat eggs. Whisk in melted butter, vanilla and baking powder until well combined and smooth. Add egg mixture to brown sugar mixture and stir just until well blended. Spoon filling over warm crust and carefully spread evenly to edges of pan.

4. Bake for 20 to 22 minutes or until lightly golden brown around edges. Let cool completely in baking pan on a wire rack.

5. **Icing:** In a small bowl, combine confectioner's sugar, cream and vanilla. Using a small whisk or a fork, blend until icing is smooth and thin enough to drizzle from a fork. Drizzle icing over cooled bars. Let stand 20 minutes or until icing is set.

6. Using foil, lift bars from pan and place on a cutting board. Cut into 1- by 2¼-inch (2.5 by 5.5 cm) bars.

Cherry Cheesecake Squares

Makes 36 squares

Simple to make, these squares pack a full cheesecake and fruit flavor in a small treat.

Tips

These squares can be made using almost any flavor of sweet jam, offering an endless variety of flavors.

Chilling the pan of squares for a couple of hours makes them easier to cut.

Store squares between layers of wax paper in a tightly sealed container. Squares can be stored in the refrigerator for up to 3 days.

- Preheat oven to 350°F (180°C)
- 9-inch (2.5 L) square baking pan, lined with foil, greased

Crust

1 cup	finely crushed vanilla wafer crumbs	250 mL
1/3 cup	ground roasted unsalted almonds	75 mL
3 tbsp	granulated sugar	45 mL
1/4 cup	unsalted butter, melted	50 mL

Filling

8 oz	cream cheese, softened	250 g
1/4 cup	granulated sugar	50 mL
1	egg	1
1/8 tsp	almond extract	0.5 mL
1/3 cup	cherry jam or cherry preserves	75 mL

1. **Crust:** In a bowl, whisk together cookie crumbs, ground almonds and granulated sugar until well combined. Add melted butter and stir until evenly combined. Mixture will resemble coarse crumbs and start to come together. Using the back of a spoon or your fingers, press crust evenly into bottom of prepared pan. Bake in preheated oven for 8 minutes or until lightly golden. Place pan on a wire cooling rack.

2. **Filling:** In a large bowl, using an electric mixer on medium speed, beat cream cheese and granulated sugar until smooth and creamy, about 2 minutes. Add egg and beat well. Beat in almond extract. Pour filling over warm crust and spread evenly.

3. Stir cherry jam to loosen it. Drop teaspoonfuls (5 mL) of jam over cream cheese filling. Insert a knife halfway down through filling. Draw knife in a swirl pattern through filling to create a marbled effect.

4. Bake for 20 to 25 minutes, or just until filling is set. Let cool completely in baking pan on a wire rack. Refrigerate for 2 hours before cutting.

5. Using foil, lift chilled squares from pan and place on a cutting board. Cut into 1 1/2-inch (4 cm) squares.

Sunshine Lemon Squares

● ● ●

These delightful lemon squares have a heavenly, tangy citrus flavor, and the lemon glaze takes them to a higher level.

Tips

If you have access to Meyer lemons, they are perfect for use in these excellent squares. Meyer lemons are a cross between a lemon and an orange. They are golden yellow in color and have a fragrant, flavorful juice that is less tart than standard lemon varieties found in grocery stores.

A ripe medium lemon will yield about 2 teaspoons (10 mL) finely grated zest and 2 to 3 tablespoons (25 to 45 mL) juice. Always prepare sufficient lemon zest before juicing the lemons.

Let glaze set completely before storing squares in a single layer in a tightly sealed container. Squares can be stored in the refrigerator for up to 3 days.

- Preheat oven to 350°F (180°C)
- 9-inch (2.5 L) square baking pan, lined with foil, greased

Crust

1½ cups	all-purpose flour	375 mL
¼ cup	granulated sugar	50 mL
¼ tsp	salt	1 mL
2 tsp	grated lemon zest	10 mL
½ cup	unsalted butter, cut into pieces	125 mL

Filling

1⅓ cups	granulated sugar	325 mL
3 tbsp	cornstarch	45 mL
4	eggs	4
2	egg yolks	2
2 tsp	grated lemon zest	10 mL
1 cup	freshly squeezed lemon juice	250 mL

Glaze

1 cup	confectioner's (powdered/icing) sugar	250 mL
4 tsp	freshly squeezed lemon juice	20 mL
2 tsp	unsalted butter, melted	10 mL

1. **Crust:** In a bowl, whisk together flour, granulated sugar and salt until well combined. Stir in lemon zest. Using a pastry blender, a fork or your fingers, cut in butter until evenly combined. Mixture will resemble coarse crumbs and start to come together. Using the back of a spoon or your fingers, press crust evenly into bottom of prepared pan. Bake in preheated oven for 12 minutes or until lightly golden. Let cool completely on a wire rack.

2. **Filling:** In a small bowl, whisk together granulated sugar and cornstarch. Set aside.

3. In a bowl, lightly beat eggs and egg yolks. Add sugar mixture and beat until well blended. Stir in lemon zest. Gradually whisk in lemon juice until well combined. Pour filling over cooled crust.

4. Bake for 22 to 26 minutes, or just until filling is set. Let cool completely in baking pan on a wire rack.

5. **Glaze:** In a small bowl, combine confectioner's sugar, lemon juice and melted butter. Using a small whisk or a fork, blend until glaze is smooth. Spread glaze evenly over cooled squares. Let stand 20 minutes or until the glaze is set.

6. Using foil, lift squares from pan and place on a cutting board. Cut into 1½-inch (4 cm) squares.

Tropical Oat Squares

● ● ●

Extra coconut added to the topping of these lovely bars gives them an extra crunch.

Tips

Apricot pineapple preserves, apricot jam or apricot preserves may be substituted for the apricot pineapple jam.

Store squares between layers of wax paper in a tightly sealed container. Squares can be stored at room temperature for up to 3 days.

- Preheat oven to 350°F (180°C)
- 9-inch (2.5 L) square baking pan, lined with foil, greased

Crust

1½ cups	all-purpose flour	375 mL
⅔ cup	granulated sugar	150 mL
1 tsp	baking powder	5 mL
¼ tsp	baking soda	1 mL
¼ tsp	salt	1 mL
1 cup	quick-cooking rolled oats	250 mL
¾ cup	sweetened flaked coconut, coarsely chopped	175 mL
¾ cup	unsalted butter, melted	175 mL
1 tsp	vanilla extract	5 mL
¼ tsp	coconut extract	1 mL

Filling

1 cup	apricot pineapple jam	250 mL

Topping

⅓ cup	sweetened flaked coconut, coarsely chopped	75 mL

1. **Crust:** In a large bowl, whisk together flour, granulated sugar, baking powder, baking soda and salt until well combined. Stir in oats and coconut.

2. In a small bowl, whisk together melted butter, vanilla and coconut extract until well blended. Drizzle butter mixture over flour mixture. Using a fork, stir until well combined and crumbly. Reserve ¾ cup (175 mL) of crust mixture for topping. Using the back of a spoon or your fingers, press the remaining crust mixture evenly into bottom of prepared pan.

3. **Filling:** Stir apricot pineapple jam to loosen it. Spread jam evenly over crust.

4. **Topping:** Add chopped coconut to reserved crust mixture and stir until well combined. Crumble topping mixture over jam.

5. Bake in preheated oven for 22 to 25 minutes or until lightly golden. Let cool completely in baking pan on a wire rack.

6. Using foil, lift cooled squares from pan and place on a cutting board. Cut into 1½-inch (4 cm) squares.

Sour Cream Blueberry Squares

A flavorful blueberry filling sandwiched between a tender crust and a creamy topping makes for a special square.

Tips

Cooling the squares for 10 minutes before adding the sour cream layer helps keep the filling from bleeding into the topping.

Unsalted butter is the best choice for baking. It gives cookie crusts a rich, fresh flavor and helps them develop a light golden color.

Store squares in a single layer in a tightly sealed container in the refrigerator for up to 3 days.

- Preheat oven to 350°F (180°C)
- 9-inch (2.5 L) square baking pan, lined with foil, greased

Crust

1½ cups	all-purpose flour	375 mL
½ cup	granulated sugar	125 mL
¼ tsp	salt	1 mL
½ cup	unsalted butter, cut into pieces	125 mL

Filling

1½ cups	blueberry pie filling	375 mL
⅛ tsp	ground cinnamon	0.5 mL

Topping

1½ cups	sour cream	375 mL
¼ cup	granulated sugar	50 mL
½ tsp	vanilla extract	2 mL

1. **Crust:** In a bowl, whisk together flour, granulated sugar and salt until well combined. Using a pastry blender, a fork or your fingers, cut in butter until evenly combined. Mixture will resemble coarse crumbs and start to come together. Using the back of a spoon or your fingers, press crust mixture evenly into bottom of prepared pan. Bake in preheated oven for 12 minutes or until lightly golden. Place pan on a wire cooling rack and allow to cool.

2. **Filling:** In a bowl, combine blueberry pie filling and cinnamon until well blended. Pour filling over cooled crust and spread evenly.

3. Bake for 12 minutes. Place pan on a wire rack and cool for 10 minutes.

4. **Topping:** In a small bowl, whisk together sour cream, granulated sugar and vanilla until well blended. Spread topping over hot squares.

5. Bake for 5 minutes. Let cool completely in baking pan on a wire rack.

6. Using foil, lift cooled squares from pan and place on a cutting board. Cut into 1½-inch (4 cm) squares.

Cranberry Almond Bars

Makes about 28 bars

● ● ●

These cake-like bars blend tangy cranberries and almonds into a yummy snack.

Tips

Thawed chopped frozen cranberries may be substituted for fresh cranberries. Chop cranberries while still partially frozen to keep them from getting mushy.

Store bars between layers of wax paper in a tightly sealed container at room temperature. Bars can be stored for up to 3 days.

- Preheat oven to 350°F (180°C)
- 13- by 9-inch (3 L) baking pan, lined with foil, greased

2 cups	all-purpose flour	500 mL
1½ tsp	baking powder	7 mL
¼ tsp	baking soda	1 mL
¼ tsp	salt	1 mL
1 cup	unsalted butter, softened	250 mL
2 cups	granulated sugar	500 mL
3	eggs	3
1 tsp	almond extract	5 mL
½ tsp	vanilla extract	2 mL
1 cup	chopped fresh cranberries	250 mL
¾ cup	chopped unsalted almonds	175 mL

1. In a bowl, whisk together flour, baking powder, baking soda and salt until well combined. Set aside.

2. In a large bowl, using an electric mixer on medium speed, cream butter and granulated sugar until light and fluffy, about 3 minutes. Add eggs one at a time, beating well after each addition. Beat in almond extract and vanilla. Scrape down sides of bowl. On low speed or using a wooden spoon, gradually add flour mixture, stirring just until blended. By hand, fold in cranberries and almonds. Spread batter evenly into prepared pan.

3. Bake in preheated oven for 30 to 35 minutes or until a wooden pick inserted into the center comes out with a few moist crumbs. Let cool completely in baking pan on a wire rack.

4. Using foil, lift cooled bars from pan and place on a cutting board. Cut into approximately 1¾- by 2¼-inch (4.5 by 5.5 cm) bars.

Nutty Chocolate Squares

Rich, fudgy and nutty, these squares are wonderful with a hot cup of coffee or an ice-cold glass of milk.

Tips

Lining the pan with foil makes it easy to remove squares from the pan after cooling and makes cleanup a breeze.

Store squares between layers of wax paper in a tightly sealed container. Squares can be stored at room temperature for up to 3 days.

- Preheat oven to 350°F (180°C)
- 9-inch (2.5 L) square baking pan, lined with foil, greased

Crust

1¾ cups	all-purpose flour	425 mL
⅓ cup	granulated sugar	75 mL
⅛ tsp	baking powder	0.5 mL
⅛ tsp	salt	0.5 mL
½ tsp	vanilla extract	2 mL
⅔ cup	unsalted butter, cut into pieces	150 mL

Filling

1 cup	sweetened condensed milk	250 mL
½ cup	dark sweet chocolate, chopped	125 mL
1 tsp	vanilla extract	5 mL
½ cup	chopped pecans	125 mL
⅓ cup	sweetened flaked coconut, coarsely chopped	75 mL

1. **Crust:** In a bowl, whisk together flour, granulated sugar, baking powder and salt until well combined. Stir in vanilla. Using a pastry blender, a fork or your fingers, cut in butter until evenly combined. Mixture will resemble coarse crumbs and start to come together. Using the back of a spoon or your fingers, press crust evenly into bottom of prepared pan.

2. **Filling:** In a microwave-safe bowl, heat sweetened condensed milk and chocolate in a microwave at Medium-High (75%) power for 30 seconds. Stir until chocolate is melted and mixture is smooth and well combined. If necessary, heat at Medium (50%) power for 10 seconds at a time, stirring between each heating, just until chocolate is melted. Do not overheat. Stir in vanilla. Fold in pecans and coconut. Spread filling evenly over crust.

3. Bake in preheated oven for 28 to 30 minutes, or just until center of filling is set. Let cool completely in baking pan on a wire rack.

4. Using foil, lift cooled squares from pan and place on a cutting board. Cut into 1½-inch (4 cm) squares.

Apricot Crunch Squares

The coconut in the topping adds a nice crunchy texture and another dimension in flavor.

Tips

Use shiny or light-colored metal baking pans for making squares. Dark pans absorb more heat and can cause squares to overbake.

Store squares between layers of wax paper in a tightly sealed container at room temperature for up to 3 days.

- Preheat oven to 350°F (180°C)
- 9-inch (2.5 L) square baking pan, lined with foil, greased

Crust

2²⁄₃ cups	all-purpose flour	650 mL
²⁄₃ cup	granulated sugar	150 mL
1¹⁄₄ tsp	baking powder	6 mL
¹⁄₈ tsp	salt	0.5 mL
¹⁄₂ tsp	almond extract	2 mL
1 cup	unsalted butter, cut into pieces	250 mL

Filling

1 cup	apricot jam or apricot preserves	250 mL

Topping

¹⁄₂ cup	sweetened flaked coconut, coarsely chopped	125 mL

1. **Crust:** In a bowl, whisk together flour, granulated sugar, baking powder and salt until well combined. Stir in almond extract. Using a pastry blender, a fork or your fingers, cut in butter until evenly combined. Mixture will resemble coarse crumbs and start to come together. Reserve 1 cup (250 mL) of crust mixture for topping. Using the back of a spoon or your fingers, press remaining crust mixture evenly into bottom of prepared pan.

2. **Filling:** Stir apricot jam to loosen it. Spread jam evenly over crust.

3. **Topping:** Add chopped coconut to reserved crust mixture and stir until well combined. Crumble topping mixture over jam.

4. Bake in preheated oven for 24 to 27 minutes or until lightly golden. Let cool completely in baking pan on a wire rack.

5. Using foil, lift cooled squares from pan and place on a cutting board. Cut into 1¹⁄₂-inch (4 cm) squares.

Cream Cheese Blondies

Marbled with a cream cheese filling, these lovely blondies are a great choice to serve for a brunch or a special occasion, or as an evening dessert for family and friends.

Tips

For best results, use the pan size and shape called for in the recipe. If you use a different pan, you will need to adjust the baking time to reduce the chance of burning or undercooking.

Store blondies between layers of wax paper in a tightly sealed container. Blondies can be stored in the refrigerator for up to 3 days.

● **Preheat oven to 350°F (180°C)**
● **9-inch (2.5 L) square baking pan, lined with foil, greased**

Cream Cheese Filling

8 oz	cream cheese, softened	250 g
1/3 cup	granulated sugar	75 mL
1	egg	1
1/4 cup	sour cream	50 mL
1 tsp	vanilla extract	5 mL

Blondie Batter

1 1/3 cups	all-purpose flour	325 mL
1 tsp	baking powder	5 mL
1/4 tsp	salt	1 mL
1/2 cup	chopped pecans	125 mL
2	eggs	2
1/2 cup	unsalted butter, melted	125 mL
2/3 cup	packed light brown sugar	150 mL
1/3 cup	granulated sugar	75 mL
2 tsp	vanilla extract	10 mL

1. *Filling:* In a large bowl, using an electric mixer on medium speed, beat cream cheese and granulated sugar until smooth and creamy, about 2 minutes. Add egg and beat well. Stir in sour cream and vanilla. Cover and set aside.

2. *Blondies:* In a bowl, whisk together flour, baking powder and salt until well combined. Stir in pecans. Set aside.

3. In a bowl, using a wire whisk, lightly beat eggs. Gradually whisk in melted butter. Add brown sugar and granulated sugar and beat until well combined. Beat in vanilla. Scrape down sides of bowl. Gradually add flour mixture, stirring just until blended.

4. Spread two-thirds of blondie batter evenly into prepared pan. Carefully spread cream cheese filling evenly over blondie batter. Spoon tablespoonfuls (15 mL) of remaining blondie batter over filling. Insert a knife halfway down through filling. Draw the knife in a swirl pattern to create a marbled effect.

5. Bake in preheated oven for 25 to 30 minutes or until a wooden pick inserted near the center comes out with a few moist crumbs. Let cool completely in baking pan on a wire rack.

6. Using foil, lift cooled blondies from pan and place on a cutting board. Cut into 1 1/2-inch (4 cm) squares.

Chocolate Mint Bars

These pretty layered bars have a dark chocolate base cookie covered with a fluffy mint filling and topped with melted chocolate.

Tips

Add a festive green tint to mint filling by adding 2 or 3 drops of green food coloring.

Chocolate can be melted in the top of a double boiler placed over simmering water. Stir frequently, until chocolate is completely melted and mixture is smooth. Use a spoon to drizzle the chocolate over chilled mint filling.

Store bars in a single layer in a tightly sealed container. Keep bars in the refrigerator for up to 3 days.

- Preheat oven to 350°F (180°C)
- 13- by 9-inch (3 L) baking pan, lined with foil, greased

Chocolate Cookie Base

1½ cups	all-purpose flour	375 mL
1 cup	granulated sugar	250 mL
½ cup	unsweetened Dutch-process cocoa powder, sifted	125 mL
1 tsp	baking powder	5 mL
¼ tsp	salt	1 mL
2	eggs	2
¾ cup	unsalted butter, melted	175 mL

Mint Filling

2½ cups	confectioner's (powdered/icing) sugar	625 mL
3 tbsp	half-and-half (10%) cream or milk	45 mL
2 tbsp	unsalted butter, softened	25 mL
½ tsp	mint extract	2 mL
⅛ tsp	salt	0.5 mL

Chocolate Topping

8 oz	sweet dark chocolate, chopped	250 g
1 tbsp	vegetable shortening	15 mL

1. **Base:** In a bowl, whisk together flour, granulated sugar, cocoa powder, baking powder and salt until well combined. In a small bowl, using a wire whisk, lightly beat eggs. Whisk in melted butter. Add egg mixture to flour mixture and stir until well blended. Spread batter evenly into prepared pan.

2. Bake in preheated oven for 15 to 18 minutes or until set. Let cool completely on a wire rack.

3. **Filling:** In a bowl, combine confectioner's sugar, cream, butter, mint extract and salt. Using an electric mixer on medium speed, beat until filling is light and fluffy, about 4 minutes. Spread filling evenly over cooled crust. Refrigerate 30 minutes or until filling is set.

4. **Topping:** In a 1-quart (1 L) micro-wave safe zippered storage bag, combine chocolate and shortening. Microwave on High power for 1 minute. Knead bag until completely combined and smooth, microwaving an additional 10 seconds at a time as needed to fully melt chocolate. Cut off a small corner of bag and drizzle chocolate over chilled mint filling. Refrigerate bars for 20 minutes or until chocolate is set.

5. Using foil, lift chilled bars from pan and place on a cutting board. Cut into 1- by 2¼-inch (2.5 by 5.5 cm) bars.

Coconut Pineapple Bars

I love the blending of flavors in these tropical bars.

Tips

Save the juice drained from the canned pineapple in the filling to use in making the icing.

Store bars between layers of wax paper in a tightly sealed container. Bars can be kept in the refrigerator for up to 3 days.

- Preheat oven to 350°F (180°C)
- 13- by 9-inch (3 L) baking pan, lined with foil, greased

Crust

2 cups	all-purpose flour	500 mL
3/4 cup	granulated sugar	175 mL
1/2 tsp	baking powder	2 mL
3/4 cup	unsalted butter, cut into pieces	175 mL

Filling

3 tbsp	all-purpose flour	45 mL
1/2 tsp	baking powder	2 mL
1/4 tsp	salt	1 mL
3	eggs	3
1/2 cup	granulated sugar	125 mL
1/2 cup	packed light brown sugar	125 mL
1 1/2 cups	sweetened flaked coconut	375 mL
1	can (20 oz or 540 mL) juice-packed crushed pineapple, drained, juice reserved	1

Icing

1 1/4 cups	confectioner's (powdered/icing) sugar	300 mL
2 tbsp	reserved pineapple juice	25 mL
1 tbsp	unsalted butter, melted	15 mL

1. **Crust:** In a bowl, whisk together flour, granulated sugar and baking powder until well combined. Using a pastry blender, a fork or your fingers, cut in butter until evenly combined. Mixture will resemble coarse crumbs and start to come together. Using the back of a spoon or your fingers, press crust evenly into bottom of prepared pan. Bake in preheated oven for 15 minutes or until lightly golden. Let cool completely on a wire rack.

2. **Filling:** In a bowl, whisk together flour, baking powder and salt until well combined. Set aside.

3. In a large bowl, using a wire whisk, lightly beat eggs. Add granulated sugar and brown sugar and stir until well combined. Whisk in flour mixture. Stir in coconut and pineapple. Pour filling over cooled crust and spread evenly.

4. Bake for 25 to 27 minutes or until lightly golden brown around edges. Let cool for 20 minutes on a wire rack.

5. **Icing:** In a small bowl, combine confectioner's sugar, pineapple juice and melted butter. Using a small whisk or a fork, blend until smooth. Spread icing over warm filling. Let cool completely.

6. Using foil, lift cooled bars from pan and place on a cutting board. Cut into 1- by 2 1/4-inch (2.5 by 5.5 cm) bars.

Lime Squares

Sweet and tangy, these squares have lots of lime flavor.

Tips

A ripe medium lime will yield about 1 teaspoon (5 mL) finely grated zest and 1½ to 2 tablespoons (22 to 25 mL) juice.

If desired, lightly dust tops of cooled squares with confectioner's sugar.

Store squares between layers of wax paper in a tightly sealed container. Squares can be stored in the refrigerator for up to 3 days.

- **Preheat oven to 350°F (180°C)**
- **9-inch (2.5 L) square baking pan, lined with foil, greased**

Crust

1½ cups	all-purpose flour	375 mL
⅓ cup	granulated sugar	75 mL
¼ tsp	salt	1 mL
1 tsp	grated lime zest	5 mL
½ cup	unsalted butter, cut into pieces	125 mL

Filling

1 cup	granulated sugar	250 mL
2 tbsp	cornstarch	25 mL
4	eggs	4
1 tsp	grated lime zest	5 mL
⅔ cup	freshly squeezed lime juice	150 mL

1. **Crust:** In a bowl, whisk together flour, granulated sugar and salt until well combined. Stir in lime zest. Using a pastry blender, a fork or your fingers, cut in butter until evenly combined. Mixture will resemble coarse crumbs and start to come together. Using the back of a spoon or your fingers, press crust evenly into bottom of prepared pan. Bake in preheated oven for 12 minutes or until lightly golden. Place pan on a wire cooling rack.

2. **Filling:** In a small bowl, whisk together granulated sugar and cornstarch. Set aside.

3. In a bowl, lightly beat eggs. Add sugar mixture and beat until well blended. Stir in lime zest. Gradually whisk in lime juice until well combined. Spread filling evenly over warm crust.

4. Bake for 14 to 17 minutes, or just until filling is set. Let cool completely in baking pan on a wire rack.

5. Using foil, lift cooled squares from pan and place on a cutting board. Cut into 1½-inch (4 cm) squares.

Pecan Pie Bars

Makes 52 bars

● ● ●

A classic bar recipe. I like mine with lots of nuts.

Tips

Nuts can turn rancid quickly. If you're not going to use them within a couple of weeks, tightly wrap the nuts and store them in the freezer to preserve their flavor.

Store bars between layers of wax paper in a tightly sealed container. Bars can be stored in the refrigerator for up to 3 days.

● Preheat oven to 350°F (180°C)
● 13- by 9-inch (3 L) baking pan, lined with foil, greased

Crust

2 cups	all-purpose flour	500 mL
1/2 cup	confectioner's (powdered/icing) sugar	125 mL
1/4 tsp	baking powder	1 mL
1/4 tsp	salt	1 mL
2/3 cup	unsalted butter, cut into pieces	150 mL

Filling

3	eggs	3
1/2 cup	packed light brown sugar	125 mL
1/3 cup	granulated sugar	75 mL
1 cup	light (golden) corn syrup	250 mL
2 tbsp	unsalted butter, melted	25 mL
1 1/2 tsp	vanilla extract	7 mL
1 3/4 cups	chopped pecans	425 mL

1. **Crust:** In a bowl, whisk together flour, confectioner's sugar, baking powder and salt until well combined. Using a pastry blender, a fork or your fingers, cut in butter until evenly combined. Mixture will resemble coarse crumbs and start to come together. Using the back of a spoon or your fingers, press crust evenly into bottom of prepared pan. Bake in preheated oven for 15 minutes or until lightly golden. Place pan on a wire cooling rack.

2. **Filling:** In a large bowl, using a wire whisk, lightly beat eggs. Add brown sugar and granulated sugar and beat until well combined. Gradually whisk in corn syrup. Beat in melted butter and vanilla. Scrape down sides of bowl. Fold in pecans. Spread filling evenly over baked crust.

3. Bake for 25 to 30 minutes or until filling is set. Let cool completely in baking pan on a wire rack.

4. Using foil, lift cooled bars from pan and place on a cutting board. Cut into 1- by 2 1/4-inch (2.5 by 5.5 cm) bars.

Chocolate Almond Toffee Bars

The chocolate and almond topping makes these bars special.

Tips

Use the appropriate measuring tools and techniques to accurately measure ingredients.

Store bars between layers of wax paper in a tightly sealed container. Bars can be stored at room temperature for up to 3 days.

- ● **Preheat oven to 350°F (180°C)**
- ● **13- by 9-inch (3 L) baking pan, lined with foil, greased**

Bars

2½ cups	all-purpose flour	625 mL
¼ tsp	baking powder	1 mL
¼ tsp	salt	1 mL
½ cup	unsalted butter, softened	125 mL
½ cup	vegetable shortening	125 mL
1 cup	packed light brown sugar	250 mL
2	eggs	2
½ tsp	vanilla extract	2 mL
½ tsp	almond extract	2 mL

Topping

1¼ cups	semisweet chocolate chips	300 mL
½ cup	finely chopped unsalted almonds	125 mL

1. ***Bars:*** In a bowl, whisk together flour, baking powder and salt until well combined. Set aside.

2. In a large bowl, using an electric mixer on medium speed, cream butter, shortening and brown sugar until smooth and creamy, about 2 minutes. Add eggs one at a time, beating well after each addition. Beat in vanilla and almond extract. Scrape down sides of bowl. On low speed or using a wooden spoon, gradually add flour mixture, stirring just until blended. Spread batter evenly into prepared pan.

3. Bake in preheated oven for 18 to 20 minutes or until lightly golden. Place pan on a wire cooling rack.

4. ***Topping:*** Sprinkle chocolate chips over hot bars. Let stand for 2 minutes or until chocolate is melted. Spread melted chocolate evenly over bars. Sprinkle almonds over chocolate. Let cool completely in baking pan on a wire rack.

5. Using foil, lift cooled bars from pan and place on a cutting board. Cut into 1- by 2¼-inch (2.5 by 5.5 cm) bars.

Boysenberry Squares

A touch of coconut enhances these excellent berry squares.

Tips

Bread flour has a high protein content and should not be used for baking bars and squares.

Let icing set completely before storing squares between layers of wax paper in a tightly sealed container. Squares can be stored at room temperature for up to 3 days.

Variation

Blackberry Squares: Substitute seedless blackberry jam for seedless boysenberry jam in filling.

- ● Preheat oven to 350°F (180°C)
- ● 9-inch (2.5 L) square baking pan, lined with foil, greased

Crust

1¾ cups	all-purpose flour	425 mL
6 tbsp	confectioner's (powdered/icing) sugar	90 mL
⅛ tsp	baking powder	0.5 mL
⅔ cup	unsalted butter, cut into pieces	150 mL

Filling

1 cup	seedless boysenberry jam	250 mL

Topping

1 cup	all-purpose flour	250 mL
⅓ cup	granulated sugar	75 mL
¼ cup	sweetened flaked coconut, finely chopped	50 mL
½ tsp	vanilla extract	2 mL
⅓ cup	unsalted butter, cut into pieces	75 mL

Icing

¾ cup	confectioner's (powdered/icing) sugar	175 mL
1 to 2 tbsp	half-and-half (10%) cream or milk	15 to 25 mL
¼ tsp	vanilla extract	1 mL

1. **Crust:** In a bowl, whisk together flour, confectioner's sugar and baking powder until well combined. Using a pastry blender, a fork or your fingers, cut in butter until evenly combined. Mixture will resemble coarse crumbs and start to come together. Using the back of a spoon or your fingers, press crust evenly into bottom of prepared pan.

2. **Filling:** Stir boysenberry jam to loosen it. Spread over crust.

3. **Topping:** In a small bowl, whisk together flour and granulated sugar until well blended. Add coconut and stir until well combined. Stir in vanilla. Using a fork or your fingers, work in butter until evenly combined. Mixture will resemble coarse crumbs and start to come together. Crumble topping over jam.

4. Bake in preheated oven for 20 to 24 minutes or until lightly golden. Let cool completely in baking pan on a wire rack.

5. **Icing:** In a small bowl, combine confectioner's sugar, 1 tablespoon (15 mL) of the cream and vanilla. Using a small whisk or a fork, blend until icing is smooth and thin enough to drizzle from a fork. Add more cream as needed to achieve the desired consistency. Drizzle icing over cooled squares. Let stand 20 minutes or until the icing is set.

6. Using foil, lift squares from pan and place on a cutting board. Using a long knife, cut into 1½-inch (4 cm) squares.

Peanut Butter Oat Bars

These yummy bars blend two flavors that were made for each other — peanut butter and chocolate.

Tips

Lightly coat the measuring cup with nonstick cooking spray to make it easier to remove the peanut butter after measuring.

Store bars between layers of wax paper in a tightly sealed container. Bars can be stored at room temperature for up to 3 days.

● **Preheat oven to 350°F (180°C)**
● **13- by 9-inch (3 L) baking pan, lined with foil, greased**

1½ cups	all-purpose flour	375 mL
2 tsp	baking powder	10 mL
½ tsp	salt	2 mL
6 oz	semisweet chocolate, chopped	175 g
1 cup	creamy peanut butter	250 mL
½ cup	unsalted butter, softened	125 mL
1¼ cups	packed light brown sugar	300 mL
2	eggs	2
1 tsp	vanilla extract	5 mL
2 cups	quick-cooking rolled oats	500 mL
1 cup	mini semisweet chocolate chips	250 mL

1. In a bowl, whisk together flour, baking powder and salt until well combined. Set aside.

2. In a small microwave-safe bowl, heat chopped chocolate in a microwave at Medium-High (75%) power for 1 minute. Stir chocolate until smooth. If necessary, heat at Medium (50%) power for 10 seconds at a time, stirring between each heating, just until chocolate is melted. Do not overheat. Set aside.

3. In a large bowl, using an electric mixer on medium speed, cream peanut butter, butter and brown sugar until light and fluffy, about 3 minutes. Add eggs one at a time, beating well after each addition. Beat in vanilla. Scrape down sides of bowl. On low speed or using a wooden spoon, gradually add flour mixture, stirring just until blended. By hand, stir in oats. Reserve 1½ cups (375 mL) of dough mixture for topping.

4. Fold mini chocolate chips into remaining dough. Spread dough evenly into prepared pan. Pour melted chocolate over dough and spread evenly. Crumble reserved dough mixture over chocolate.

5. Bake for 30 to 35 minutes or until lightly golden brown around edges. Let cool completely in baking pan on a wire rack.

6. Using foil, lift cooled bars from pan and place on a cutting board. Cut into 1- by 2¼-inch (2.5 by 5.5 cm) bars.

Chocolate Walnut Bars

● ● ●

These bars have a rich fudgy, nutty filling.

Tips

Sweetened condensed milk is sold by weight in the U.S. and by volume in Canada. A U.S. 14-oz can contains $1\frac{1}{3}$ cups (325 mL).

Lining the pan with foil makes it easy to remove bars from the pan after cooling and makes cleanup a breeze.

Store bars between layers of wax paper in a tightly sealed container. Bars can be stored in the refrigerator for up to 3 days.

- Preheat oven to 350°F (180°C)
- 13- by 9-inch (3 L) baking pan, lined with foil, greased

Crust

2 cups	all-purpose flour	500 mL
$\frac{1}{2}$ cup	packed light brown sugar	125 mL
$\frac{2}{3}$ cup	unsalted butter, cut into pieces	150 mL

Filling

3 oz	dark sweet chocolate, chopped	90 g
1	egg	1
$1\frac{1}{3}$ cups	sweetened condensed milk	325 mL
1 tsp	vanilla extract	5 mL
$1\frac{1}{3}$ cups	chopped walnuts	325 mL

1. **Crust:** In a bowl, whisk together flour and brown sugar until well combined. Using a pastry blender, a fork or your fingers, cut in butter until evenly combined. Mixture will resemble coarse crumbs and start to come together. Using the back of a spoon or your fingers, press crust evenly into bottom of prepared pan. Bake in preheated oven for 15 minutes or until lightly golden. Place pan on a wire cooling rack.

2. **Filling:** In a small microwave-safe bowl, heat chocolate in a microwave at Medium-High (75%) power for 1 minute. Stir chocolate until smooth. If necessary, heat at Medium (50%) power for 10 seconds at a time, stirring between each heating, just until chocolate is melted. Do not overheat. Set aside.

3. In a large bowl, using a wire whisk, lightly beat egg. Whisk in sweetened condensed milk until well combined. Stir in melted chocolate and vanilla. Fold in walnuts. Spread filling evenly over baked crust.

4. Bake for 20 to 25 minutes or until lightly golden brown around edges. Let cool completely in baking pan on a wire rack.

5. Using foil, lift cooled bars from pan and place on a cutting board. Cut into 1- by $2\frac{1}{4}$-inch (2.5 by 5.5 cm) bars.

Nutty Fruit Bars

Makes 52 bars

● ● ●

Packed with lots of fruit and nuts, these wonderful treats are as colorful as they are tasty.

Tips

Sweetened condensed milk is sold by weight in the U.S. and by volume in Canada. A U.S. 14-oz can contains $1\frac{1}{3}$ cups (325 mL).

Store unopened packages of flour in a cool, dry place for up to 2 years. Always use flour before the date stamped on the package.

Store bars between layers of wax paper in a tightly sealed container. Bars can be stored in the refrigerator for up to 3 days.

● **Preheat oven to 350°F (180°C)**
● **13- by 9-inch (3 L) baking pan, lined with foil, greased**

Filling

1 cup	chopped dried apricots	250 mL
1 cup	dried cranberries	250 mL
$\frac{1}{2}$ cup	freshly squeezed orange juice	125 mL
1 cup	sweetened flaked coconut	250 mL
$\frac{3}{4}$ cup	drained crushed pineapple	175 mL
$\frac{2}{3}$ cup	chopped walnuts	150 mL
$\frac{2}{3}$ cup	chopped pecans	150 mL
$1\frac{1}{3}$ cups	sweetened condensed milk	325 mL

Crust

2 cups	all-purpose flour	500 mL
$\frac{1}{4}$ tsp	salt	1 mL
$\frac{3}{4}$ cup	unsalted butter, softened	175 mL
$\frac{1}{2}$ cup	packed light brown sugar	125 mL

1. *Filling:* In a medium saucepan, combine apricots, cranberries and orange juice. Over medium heat, heat until orange juice is hot. Do not bring to a boil. Remove from heat, cover and set aside.

2. *Crust:* In a bowl, whisk together flour and salt until well combined.

3. In a large bowl, using an electric mixer on medium speed, cream butter and brown sugar until light and fluffy, about 2 minutes. On low speed or using a wooden spoon, gradually add flour mixture, stirring just until blended. Using the back of a spoon or your fingers, press crust evenly into bottom of prepared pan. Bake in preheated oven for 15 minutes or until lightly golden. Place pan on a wire cooling rack. Set aside.

4. Add coconut, pineapple, walnuts and pecans to fruit mixture and stir until well combined. Spread evenly over hot crust. Pour sweetened condensed milk over fruit filling and spread evenly.

5. Bake for 28 to 32 minutes or until lightly golden brown around edges. Let cool completely in baking pan on a wire rack.

6. Using foil, lift cooled bars from pan and place on a cutting board. Cut into 1- by $2\frac{1}{4}$-inch (2.5 by 5.5 cm) bars.

Sour Cream Lemon Squares

A layer of lemon filling is topped with a thin layer of sour cream in these sweet and tangy squares.

Tips

A Microplane grater will finely zest the lemon peel for a wonderful texture in cookies.

Store squares between layers of wax paper in a tightly sealed container. Squares can be stored in the refrigerator for up to 3 days.

- Preheat oven to 350°F (180°C)
- 9-inch (2.5 L) square baking pan, lined with foil, greased

Crust

1½ cups	all-purpose flour	375 mL
6 tbsp	confectioner's (powdered/icing) sugar	90 mL
¼ tsp	salt	1 mL
1 tsp	grated lemon zest	5 mL
½ cup	unsalted butter, cut into pieces	125 mL

Filling

¾ cup	granulated sugar	175 mL
1 tbsp	all-purpose flour	15 mL
3	eggs	3
1 tbsp	grated lemon zest	15 mL
3 tbsp	freshly squeezed lemon juice	45 mL

Topping

1 cup	sour cream	250 mL
3 tbsp	granulated sugar	45 mL
1 tbsp	freshly squeezed lemon juice	15 mL

1. **Crust:** In a bowl, whisk together flour, confectioner's sugar and salt until well combined. Stir in lemon zest. Using a pastry blender, a fork or your fingers, cut in butter until evenly combined. Mixture will resemble coarse crumbs and start to come together. Using the back of a spoon or your fingers, press crust evenly into bottom of prepared pan. Bake in preheated oven for 12 minutes or until lightly golden. Place pan on a wire cooling rack.

2. **Filling:** In a small bowl, whisk together granulated sugar and flour. Set aside.

3. In a bowl, lightly beat eggs. Add sugar mixture and beat until well blended. Stir in lemon zest. Gradually whisk in lemon juice until well combined. Spread filling evenly over warm crust.

4. Bake for 15 to 18 minutes, or just until filling is set. Place pan on a wire cooling rack.

5. **Topping:** In a small bowl, whisk together sour cream, granulated sugar and lemon juice until well blended. Spread topping over hot squares.

6. Bake for 5 minutes. Let cool completely in baking pan on a wire rack.

7. Using foil, lift cooled squares from pan and place on a cutting board. Cut into 1½-inch (4 cm) squares.

Cherry Crumb Squares

● ● ●

I love the combination of cherry and almond flavors in cookies and other baked goods.

Tips

To measure flour properly, stir the flour in the package or container to add some air, then gently spoon the flour into a dry measuring cup. Use a knife or spatula to level off the flour with the rim of the cup.

For a pretty appearance, cut cookies into diamond or triangle shapes.

Store squares between layers of wax paper in a tightly sealed container. Squares can be stored at room temperature for up to 3 days.

● **Preheat oven to 350°F (180°C)**
● **9-inch (2.5 L) square baking pan, lined with foil, greased**

Crust

2½ cups	all-purpose flour	625 mL
⅔ cup	granulated sugar	150 mL
½ tsp	almond extract	2 mL
1 cup	unsalted butter, cut into pieces	250 mL

Filling

1 cup	cherry jam or cherry preserves	250 mL

Icing

1 cup	confectioner's (powdered/icing) sugar	250 mL
4 to 5 tsp	half-and-half (10%) cream or milk	20 to 25 mL
2 tsp	unsalted butter, melted	10 mL
⅛ tsp	almond extract	0.5 mL

1. **Crust:** In a bowl, whisk together flour and granulated sugar until well combined. Stir in almond extract. Using a pastry blender, a fork or your fingers, cut in butter until evenly combined. Mixture will resemble coarse crumbs and start to come together. Using the back of a spoon or your fingers, press two-thirds of crust mixture evenly into bottom of prepared pan. Reserve remaining mixture for topping.

2. **Filling:** Stir cherry jam to loosen it. Spread evenly over crust. Crumble reserved crust mixture over jam.

3. Bake in preheated oven for 20 to 24 minutes or until lightly golden brown around edges. Let cool completely in baking pan on a wire rack.

4. **Icing:** In a small bowl, combine confectioner's sugar, 4 teaspoons (20 mL) of the cream, melted butter and almond extract. Using a small whisk or a fork, blend until icing is smooth and thin enough to drizzle from a fork. Add more cream as needed to achieve the desired consistency. Drizzle icing over cooled squares. Let stand 20 minutes or until the icing is set.

5. Using foil, lift squares from pan and place on a cutting board. Cut into 1½-inch (4 cm) squares.

Pumpkin Crunch Bars

Makes 52 bars

● ● ●

These bars are like pumpkin pie with a nut topping. The whole house smells wonderful as these treats bake in the oven.

Tips

Be sure to use canned, solid pack pumpkin rather than canned pumpkin pie mix in this recipe.

Store bars between layers of wax paper in a tightly sealed container. Bars can be stored in the refrigerator for up to 3 days.

- Preheat oven to 350°F (180°C)
- 13-by 9-inch (3 L) square baking pan, lined with foil, greased

Crust

2 cups	all-purpose flour	500 mL
2/3 cup	packed light brown sugar	150 mL
1/4 tsp	salt	1 mL
2/3 cup	unsalted butter, cut into pieces	150 mL

Filling

1/2 cup	granulated sugar	125 mL
1/4 cup	packed light brown sugar	50 mL
1/2 tsp	ground cinnamon	2 mL
1/4 tsp	ground ginger	1 mL
1/8 tsp	ground nutmeg	0.5 mL
1/8 tsp	salt	0.5 mL
3	eggs	3
1	can (15 oz or 398 mL) solid pack (purée) pumpkin	1
2/3 cup	half-and-half (10%) cream	150 mL

Topping

2 cups	finely chopped pecans	500 mL
1 cup	packed light brown sugar	250 mL
2 tbsp	all-purpose flour	25 mL
1/2 cup	unsalted butter, cut into pieces	125 mL

1. **Crust:** In a bowl, whisk together flour, brown sugar and salt until well combined. Using a pastry blender, a fork or your fingers, cut in butter until evenly combined. Mixture will resemble coarse crumbs and start to come together. Using the back of a spoon or your fingers, press crust evenly into bottom of prepared pan. Bake in preheated oven for 15 minutes or until lightly golden. Place pan on a wire cooling rack.

2. **Filling:** In a bowl, whisk together granulated sugar, brown sugar, cinnamon, ginger, nutmeg and salt. Set aside.

3. In a large bowl, using a wire whisk, lightly beat eggs. Stir in pumpkin. Gradually whisk in cream until well blended. Add sugar mixture and stir until well combined. Pour filling over crust and spread evenly.

Tip

All of the recipes in this book use large eggs, the standard size used for baking. If you do not have large eggs, then lightly beat your eggs and substitute ¼ cup (50 mL) beaten egg for each large egg called for in the recipe.

4. Bake for 20 to 24 minutes, or just until filling is set in the center. Place pan on a wire cooling rack.

5. *Topping:* In a small bowl, combine pecans, brown sugar and flour until well blended. Using a fork or your fingers, work in butter until evenly combined and crumbly. Crumble topping over hot filling. Bake for another 15 minutes. Let cool completely in baking pan on a wire rack.

6. Using foil, lift cooled bars from pan and place on a cutting board. Cut into 1- by 2¼-inch (2.5 by 5.5 cm) bars.

Host or Hostess Gift

When you are invited to a party by a special friend, it can be a challenge to find a thoughtful thank-you gift for the host or hostess. A gift of delicious, homemade cookies to enjoy the next day is always welcome.

Choose an elegant decorative plate, platter or bowl. It does not have to be large or expensive, but it should fit your host's taste and be one that he or she will appreciate and enjoy using in the future.

If you know your host's favorite flavor of cookie, tailor your gift to their personal preference, and both you and your gift will be fondly remembered. Bars and squares are an excellent choice. Be sure to let your host know if any of the bars or squares will require refrigeration. You can give a plateful of one type of bar or square or fill the dish with a variety of flavors.

Place the dish in the middle of a large piece of clear cellophane and bring the cellophane together above the dish. Tie it closed with a colorful ribbon and add a pretty gift tag.

Deluxe Nut Bars

● ● ●

If you love nuts, these are the bars for you.

Tips

Use shiny or light-colored metal baking pans for making bars. Dark pans absorb more heat and can cause bars to overbake.

Store bars between layers of wax paper in a tightly sealed container. Bars can be stored at room temperature for up to 3 days.

- Preheat oven to 350°F (180°C)
- 13- by 9-inch (3 L) baking pan, lined with foil, greased

Crust

2 cups	all-purpose flour	500 mL
1/3 cup	granulated sugar	75 mL
1/4 tsp	salt	1 mL
1 cup	unsalted butter, cut into pieces	250 mL

Filling

2/3 cup	light (golden) corn syrup	150 mL
1/2 cup	packed light brown sugar	125 mL
1/3 cup	unsalted butter, cut into pieces	75 mL
3 tbsp	whipping (35%) cream	45 mL
1 cup	walnut halves	250 mL
1 cup	pecan halves	250 mL
1 cup	roasted unsalted cashews	250 mL
1 cup	roasted unsalted almonds	250 mL

1. **Crust:** In a bowl, whisk together flour, granulated sugar and salt until well combined. Using a pastry blender, a fork or your fingers, cut in butter until evenly combined. Mixture will resemble coarse crumbs and start to come together. Using the back of a spoon or your fingers, press crust evenly into bottom of prepared pan. Bake in preheated oven for 18 to 20 minutes or until lightly golden. Let cool completely on a wire rack.

2. **Filling:** In a large saucepan, over medium heat, heat corn syrup and brown sugar, stirring constantly until brown sugar is completely dissolved. Bring to a boil. Boil for 2 minutes without stirring. Add butter and cream. Boil and stir for 1 minute. Remove pan from heat and stir in walnuts, pecans, cashews and almonds. Spread nut filling evenly over cooled crust.

3. Bake for 20 minutes. Let cool completely in baking pan on a wire rack.

4. Using foil, lift cooled bars from pan and place on a cutting board. Cut into 1- by 2¼-inch (2.5 by 5.5 cm) bars.

Cashew Caramel Blondies

● ● ●

Luscious and easy to make, these nutty squares will satisfy even the strongest caramel cravings.

Tips

If you melt the caramels in a pan on the stovetop instead of in a microwave, allow the mixture to cool for a couple of minutes before proceeding to the next step.

Homemade cookies make a great gift for family and friends and are perfect for every occasion.

Store blondies between layers of wax paper in a tightly sealed container. Blondies can be stored in the refrigerator for up to 3 days.

● **Preheat oven to 350°F (180°C)**
● **9-inch (2.5 L) square baking pan, lined with foil, greased**

1 cup	all-purpose flour	250 mL
½ tsp	baking powder	2 mL
¼ tsp	salt	1 mL
20	individually wrapped caramels, unwrapped	20
⅓ cup	unsalted butter, softened	75 mL
2 tbsp	whipping (35%) cream	25 mL
½ cup	granulated sugar	125 mL
¼ cup	packed light brown sugar	50 mL
2	eggs	2
½ tsp	vanilla extract	2 mL
1¼ cups	chopped roasted unsalted cashews	300 mL

1. In a bowl, whisk together flour, baking powder and salt until well combined. Set aside.

2. In a microwave-safe bowl, heat caramels, butter and cream in a microwave at Medium-High (75%) power for 1 minute. Stir until caramels are melted and mixture is well combined. If necessary, heat at Medium (50%) power for 10 seconds at a time, stirring between each heating, just until mixture is smooth. Do not overheat.

3. Using a wire whisk or large spoon, stir granulated sugar and brown sugar into warm caramel mixture. Add eggs one at a time, beating well after each addition. Beat in vanilla. Scrape down sides of bowl. Gradually add flour mixture, stirring just until blended. Fold in cashews. Spread batter evenly into prepared pan.

4. Bake in preheated oven for 18 to 23 minutes or until a wooden pick inserted near the center comes out with a few moist crumbs. Let cool completely in baking pan on a wire rack.

5. Using foil, lift cooled blondies from pan and place on a cutting board. Cut into 1½-inch (4 cm) squares.

Buttermilk Spice Bars

● ● ●

The buttermilk adds a great flavor to these yummy spice cake bars.

Tips

Creaming the butter and sugar beats air into the mixture. These air pockets give bars a tender texture.

Store bars between layers of wax paper in a tightly sealed container. Bars can be stored at room temperature for up to 3 days.

- **Preheat oven to 350°F (180°C)**
- **13- by 9-inch (3 L) baking pan, lined with foil, greased**

Bars

2 cups	all-purpose flour	500 mL
2 tsp	baking powder	10 mL
1½ tsp	ground cinnamon	7 mL
½ tsp	ground nutmeg	2 mL
¼ tsp	ground ginger	1 mL
¼ tsp	baking soda	1 mL
¼ tsp	salt	1 mL
⅔ cup	unsalted butter, softened	150 mL
1¼ cups	granulated sugar	300 mL
2	eggs	2
1 tsp	vanilla extract	5 mL
⅔ cup	buttermilk	150 mL

Topping

2 tbsp	granulated sugar	25 mL
½ tsp	ground cinnamon	2 mL

1. **Bars:** In a bowl, whisk together flour, baking powder, cinnamon, nutmeg, ginger, baking soda and salt until well combined. Set aside.

2. In a large bowl, using an electric mixer on medium speed, cream butter and granulated sugar until light and fluffy, about 3 minutes. Add eggs one at a time, beating well after each addition. Beat in vanilla. Scrape down sides of bowl. On low speed or using a wooden spoon, gradually add flour mixture, alternating with buttermilk, beating just until blended. Spread batter evenly into prepared pan.

3. **Topping:** In a small bowl, whisk together granulated sugar and cinnamon. Sprinkle mixture over batter.

4. Bake in preheated oven for 25 to 30 minutes or until a wooden pick inserted into the center comes out with a few moist crumbs. Let cool completely in baking pan on a wire rack.

5. Using foil, lift cooled bars from pan and place on a cutting board. Cut into approximately 1¾- by 2¼-inch (4.5 by 5.5 cm) bars.

Maple Date Pecan Squares

Makes 36 squares ● ● ●

Something magical happens when you combine the flavors of maple and dates.

Tips

To keep dates from sticking to your knife when you chop them, give the knife blade a light coat of nonstick cooking spray.

If chopped dates stick together, mix them with the pecans before adding to the filling.

Store squares between layers of wax paper in a tightly sealed container. Squares can be stored in the refrigerator for up to 3 days.

- Preheat oven to 350°F (180°C)
- 9-inch (2.5 L) square baking pan, lined with foil, greased

Crust

1½ cups	all-purpose flour	375 mL
½ cup	packed light brown sugar	125 mL
¼ tsp	salt	1 mL
½ cup	unsalted butter, cut into pieces	125 mL

Filling

⅓ cup	packed light brown sugar	75 mL
2 tbsp	all-purpose flour	25 mL
⅛ tsp	salt	0.5 mL
2	eggs	2
⅔ cup	light (golden) corn syrup	150 mL
1 tsp	maple flavoring	5 mL
½ tsp	vanilla extract	2 mL
½ cup	chopped pitted dates	125 mL
½ cup	chopped pecans	125 mL

1. **Crust:** In a bowl, whisk together flour, brown sugar and salt until well combined. Using a pastry blender, a fork or your fingers, cut in butter until evenly combined. Mixture will resemble coarse crumbs and start to come together. Using the back of a spoon or your fingers, press crust evenly into bottom of prepared pan. Bake in preheated oven for 12 minutes or until lightly golden. Let cool completely in baking pan on a wire rack.

2. **Filling:** In a small bowl, whisk together brown sugar, flour and salt. Set aside.

3. In a large bowl, using a wire whisk, lightly beat eggs. Gradually whisk in corn syrup. Add brown sugar mixture and stir until well combined. Beat in maple flavoring and vanilla. Scrape down sides of bowl. Fold in dates and pecans and stir until evenly distributed. Pour filling over cooled crust and spread evenly.

4. Bake for 30 to 32 minutes or until lightly golden brown around edges and filling is set in the center. Let cool completely in baking pan on a wire rack.

5. Using foil, lift cooled squares from pan and place on a cutting board. Cut into 1½-inch (4 cm) squares.

Chocolate Chip Coffee Bars

● ● ●

Instant espresso powder gives these bars a lovely coffee flavor.

Tips

Instant espresso powder can be found in the coffee aisle of most major grocery stores.

Let frosting set before storing bars, covered, at room temperature for up to 3 days.

Variation

Fold ½ cup (125 mL) chopped walnuts into batter along with chopped chocolate.

● **Preheat oven to 350°F (180°C)**
● **13- by 9-inch (3 L) baking pan, lined with foil, greased**

Bars

1¾ cups	all-purpose flour	425 mL
1 tsp	instant espresso powder	5 mL
½ tsp	baking powder	2 mL
½ tsp	baking soda	2 mL
¼ tsp	salt	1 mL
⅔ cup	unsalted butter, softened	150 mL
1 cup	packed light brown sugar	250 mL
2	eggs	2
3 tbsp	half-and-half (10%) cream or milk	45 mL
1 tsp	vanilla extract	5 mL
¾ cup	chopped semisweet chocolate or semisweet chocolate chips	175 mL

Frosting

2 cups	confectioner's (powdered/icing) sugar	500 mL
2 tbsp	unsweetened Dutch-process cocoa powder, sifted	25 mL
1 tsp	instant espresso powder	5 mL
3 tbsp	unsalted butter, softened	45 mL
1 to 2 tbsp	half-and-half (10%) cream or milk	15 to 25 mL
½ tsp	vanilla extract	2 mL

1. *Bars:* In a bowl, whisk together flour, espresso powder, baking powder, baking soda and salt until well combined. Set aside.

2. In a large bowl, using an electric mixer on medium speed, cream butter and brown sugar until light and fluffy, about 3 minutes. Add eggs one at a time, beating well after each addition. Beat in cream and vanilla. Scrape down sides of bowl. On low speed or using a wooden spoon, gradually add flour mixture, beating just until blended. By hand, fold in chocolate. Spread batter evenly into prepared pan.

3. Bake in preheated oven for 22 to 28 minutes or until a wooden pick inserted into the center comes out with a few moist crumbs. Let cool completely in baking pan on a wire rack.

Tip

Bread flour has a high protein content and should not be used for baking cookies.

4. *Frosting:* In a bowl, whisk together confectioner's sugar, cocoa powder and espresso powder. Set aside. In a large bowl, using an electric mixer on medium speed, beat butter until smooth. Gradually beat in confectioner's sugar mixture. Add 1 tablespoon (15 mL) of the cream and vanilla and beat until smooth and fluffy. Add more cream as needed to achieve the desired consistency. Spread frosting over cooled bars. Let stand 20 minutes or until frosting is set.

5. Using foil, lift bars from pan and place on a cutting board. Cut into approximately $1\frac{3}{4}$- by $2\frac{1}{4}$-inch (4.5 by 5.5 cm) bars.

Diamond Bars

When cutting bars into serving pieces, think outside the classic rectangle shape.

Diamonds are a great shape for bars that are baked in a rectangular pan. Make a diagonal cut from one corner of the bars to the opposite corner, slicing all the way through the bars. Make a second diagonal cut connecting the two remaining corners, creating an X pattern. Then make a series of parallel cuts, spaced 1- or $1\frac{1}{2}$-inches (2.5 or 4 cm) apart, on either side of the first cuts to create a diamond pattern. If you have trouble making straight cuts, you can use a ruler to keep the lines straight and even.

Peaches and Cream Squares

● ● ●

*Think of these
as peach-swirled
cheesecake morsels.
This is a very versatile
recipe, and each of
the variations gives
a different flavor
experience.*

Tips

Use shiny or light-
colored metal baking
pans for making squares.
Dark pans absorb more
heat and can cause
squares to overbake.

Store squares between
layers of wax paper in a
tightly sealed container.
Squares can be stored in
the refrigerator for up to
3 days.

Variations

*Blackberry Cream
Squares:* Substitute
seedless blackberry
jam for the peach
jam in filling.

*Raspberry Cream
Squares:* Substitute
seedless raspberry
jam for the peach
jam in filling.

*Orange Cream
Squares:* Substitute
orange marmalade
for the peach jam in
filling.

● Preheat oven to 350°F (180°C)
● 9-inch (2.5 L) square baking pan, lined with foil, greased

Crust

1½ cups	all-purpose flour	375 mL
½ cup	confectioner's (powdered/icing) sugar	125 mL
¼ tsp	salt	1 mL
⅔ cup	unsalted butter, cut into pieces	150 mL

Filling

8 oz	cream cheese, softened	250 g
¼ cup	granulated sugar	50 mL
1	egg	1
½ tsp	vanilla extract	2 mL
½ cup	peach jam or peach preserves	125 mL

1. **Crust:** In a bowl, whisk together flour, confectioner's sugar and salt until well combined. Using a pastry blender, a fork or your fingers, cut in butter until evenly combined. Mixture will resemble coarse crumbs and start to come together. Using the back of a spoon or your fingers, press crust evenly into bottom of prepared pan. Bake in preheated oven for 12 minutes or until lightly golden. Place pan on a wire cooling rack.

2. **Filling:** In a large bowl, using an electric mixer on medium speed, beat cream cheese and granulated sugar until smooth and creamy, about 2 minutes. Add egg and beat well. Stir in vanilla. Pour filling over warm crust and spread evenly.

3. Stir peach jam to loosen it. Drop teaspoonfuls (5 mL) of jam over cream cheese filling. Insert a knife halfway down through filling. Draw knife in a swirl pattern through filling to create a marbled effect.

4. Bake for 22 to 25 minutes, or just until filling is set. Let cool completely in baking pan on a wire rack. Refrigerate for 2 hours before cutting.

5. Using foil, lift chilled squares from pan and place on a cutting board. Cut into 1½-inch (4 cm) squares.

Oatmeal Coconut Bars

These delightful bars, loaded with coconut, rise up high and cake-like.

Tips

Quick-cooking rolled oats give these bars a nice texture, but old-fashioned rolled oats may be substituted if you do not have the quick-cooking variety.

Store bars between layers of wax paper in a tightly sealed container. Bars can be stored at room temperature for up to 3 days.

- Preheat oven to 350°F (180°C)
- 13- by 9-inch (3 L) baking pan, lined with foil, greased

1½ cups	all-purpose flour	375 mL
2 tsp	baking powder	10 mL
½ tsp	baking soda	2 mL
¼ tsp	salt	1 mL
1 cup	unsalted butter, softened	250 mL
1 cup	packed light brown sugar	250 mL
½ cup	granulated sugar	125 mL
3	eggs	3
1 tsp	vanilla extract	5 mL
1½ cups	sweetened flaked coconut, coarsely chopped	375 mL
3 cups	quick-cooking rolled oats	750 mL

1. In a bowl, whisk together flour, baking powder, baking soda and salt until well combined. Set aside.

2. In a large bowl, using an electric mixer on medium speed, cream butter, brown sugar and granulated sugar until light and fluffy, about 3 minutes. Add eggs one at a time, beating well after each addition. Beat in vanilla. Scrape down sides of bowl. On low speed or using a wooden spoon, gradually add flour mixture, beating just until blended. By hand, fold in coconut. Gradually stir in oats. Spread batter evenly into prepared pan.

3. Bake in preheated oven for 30 to 35 minutes or until a wooden pick inserted into the center comes out with a few moist crumbs. Let cool completely in baking pan on a wire rack.

4. Using foil, lift cooled bars from pan and place on a cutting board. Cut into approximately 1¾- by 2¼-inch (4.5 by 5.5 cm) bars.

Strawberry Squares

●●●

The orange zest in the crust and crumb topping adds an extra layer of flavor.

Tips

Stirring the strawberry jam to loosen the texture makes it easier to spread it over the crust.

Let glaze set completely before storing squares between layers of wax paper in a tightly sealed container. Squares can be stored at room temperature for up to 3 days.

Variation

Peach Squares: Substitute peach jam for strawberry jam in filling.

- Preheat oven to 350°F (180°C)
- 9-inch (2.5 L) square baking pan, lined with foil, greased

Crust

2¹⁄₂ cups	all-purpose flour	625 mL
1 cup	granulated sugar	250 mL
¹⁄₄ tsp	salt	1 mL
2 tsp	grated orange zest	10 mL
1 cup	unsalted butter, cut into pieces	250 mL

Filling

1 cup	strawberry jam	250 mL

Glaze

³⁄₄ cup	confectioner's (powdered/icing) sugar	175 mL
1 to 2 tbsp	half-and-half (10%) cream or milk	15 to 25 mL
¹⁄₄ tsp	vanilla extract	1 mL

1. *Crust:* In a bowl, whisk together flour, granulated sugar and salt until well combined. Stir in orange zest. Using a pastry blender, a fork or your fingers, cut in butter until evenly combined. Mixture will resemble coarse crumbs and start to come together. Using the back of a spoon or your fingers, press two-thirds of crust mixture evenly into bottom of prepared pan. Reserve remaining crust mixture for topping.

2. *Filling:* Stir strawberry jam to loosen it. Spread jam evenly over crust. Crumble reserved crust mixture over jam.

3. Bake in preheated oven for 20 to 24 minutes or until lightly golden. Let cool completely in baking pan on a wire rack.

4. *Glaze:* In a small bowl, combine confectioner's sugar, 1 tablespoon (15 mL) of the cream and vanilla. Using a small whisk or a fork, blend until icing is smooth and thin enough to spread. Add more cream as needed to achieve the desired consistency. Spread glaze evenly over cooled squares. Let stand 20 minutes or until the glaze is set.

5. Using foil, lift squares from pan and place on a cutting board. Cut into 1¹⁄₂-inch (4 cm) squares.

Almond Squares

●●●

Layers and layers of almond flavor make these wonderful squares a sure winner.

Tips

Almond paste comes in cans and tubes and can be found in the baking aisle of most grocery stores.

Store squares between layers of wax paper in a tightly sealed container. Squares can be stored at room temperature for up to 3 days.

- ● **Preheat oven to 350°F (180°C)**
- ● **9-inch (2.5 L) square baking pan, lined with foil, greased**

Crust

1½ cups	all-purpose flour	375 mL
⅓ cup	granulated sugar	75 mL
¼ tsp	salt	1 mL
⅔ cup	unsalted butter, cut into pieces	150 mL

Filling

6 oz	almond paste	175 g
⅓ cup	granulated sugar	75 mL
2	eggs	2
½ tsp	vanilla extract	2 mL
¾ cup	coarsely chopped sliced unsalted almonds	175 mL

1. **Crust:** In a bowl, whisk together flour, granulated sugar and salt until well combined. Using a pastry blender, a fork or your fingers, cut in butter until evenly combined. Mixture will resemble coarse crumbs and start to come together. Using the back of a spoon or your fingers, press crust evenly into bottom of prepared pan. Bake in preheated oven for 12 minutes or until lightly golden. Place pan on a wire cooling rack.

2. **Filling:** Crumble almond paste into a mixer bowl. Add sugar and eggs. Using an electric mixer on low speed, beat until well combined and smooth, about 3 minutes. Stir in vanilla. Spread filling evenly over warm crust. Sprinkle almonds over filling.

3. Bake for 18 to 20 minutes or until almonds start to turn lightly golden. Let cool completely in baking pan on a wire rack.

4. Using foil, lift cooled squares from pan and place on a cutting board. Cut into 1½-inch (4 cm) squares.

Pineapple Nut Cheese Squares

Makes 36 squares

● ● ●

The flavors of the Hawaiian isles are always a winner at my house.

Tips

Save the juice drained from the canned pineapple in filling to use in making the icing.

Let icing set completely before storing squares between layers of wax paper in a tightly sealed container. Squares can be stored in the refrigerator for up to 3 days.

● **Preheat oven to 350°F (180°C)**
● **9-inch (2.5 L) square baking pan, lined with foil, greased**

Crust

1¼ cups	all-purpose flour	300 mL
⅓ cup	granulated sugar	75 mL
⅛ tsp	salt	0.5 mL
½ cup	unsalted butter, cut into pieces	125 mL

Filling

8 oz	cream cheese, softened	250 g
3 tbsp	granulated sugar	45 mL
1	egg	1
1 tbsp	half-and-half (10%) cream or milk	15 mL
1 tsp	vanilla extract	5 mL
1	can (20 oz or 540 mL) juice-packed crushed pineapple, drained, juice reserved	1
⅔ cup	sweetened flaked coconut	150 mL
½ cup	chopped roasted unsalted macadamia nuts	125 mL

Icing

½ cup	confectioner's (powdered/icing) sugar	125 mL
1 tbsp	reserved pineapple juice	15 mL
1 tsp	unsalted butter, melted	5 mL

1. Crust: In a bowl, whisk together flour, granulated sugar and salt until well combined. Using a pastry blender, a fork or your fingers, cut in butter until evenly combined. Mixture will resemble coarse crumbs and start to come together. Using the back of a spoon or your fingers, press crust evenly into bottom of prepared pan. Bake in preheated oven for 12 minutes or until lightly golden. Place pan on a wire cooling rack.

2. Filling: In a bowl, using an electric mixer on medium speed, beat cream cheese and granulated sugar until smooth and creamy, about 2 minutes. Add egg and beat well. Stir in cream and vanilla. Spread cream cheese filling evenly over warm crust. Sprinkle pineapple, coconut and macadamia nuts evenly over cream cheese filling.

Tip

Bars and squares containing cream cheese should be stored in the refrigerator.

3. Bake for 18 to 20 minutes, or just until filling is set. Let cool completely in baking pan on a wire rack.

4. *Icing:* In a small bowl, combine confectioner's sugar, pineapple juice and melted butter. Using a small whisk or a fork, blend until icing is smooth and thin enough to drizzle from a fork. Drizzle icing over cooled squares. Let stand 20 minutes or until the icing is set.

5. Using foil, lift squares from pan and place on a cutting board. Cut into $1\frac{1}{2}$-inch (4 cm) squares.

Golden Coconut Cashew Squares

● ● ●

Coconut-lovers will flip for these sweet, decadent squares that have a filling similar to pecan pie, but packed with coconut and macadamia nuts.

Tips

Always taste nuts before adding them to cookies to make sure they are fresh.

Let icing set completely before storing squares between layers of wax paper in a tightly sealed container. Squares can be stored in the refrigerator for up to 3 days.

Variation

Golden Coconut Macadamia Nut Squares: Substitute chopped roasted unsalted macadamia nuts for the chopped cashews in the filling.

● **Preheat oven to 350°F (180°C)**
● **9-inch (2.5 L) square baking pan, lined with foil, greased**

Crust

1 cup	all-purpose flour	250 mL
⅓ cup	granulated sugar	75 mL
⅓ cup	sweetened flaked coconut, coarsely chopped	75 mL
½ cup	unsalted butter, cut into pieces	125 mL

Filling

2 tbsp	all-purpose flour	25 mL
¼ tsp	baking powder	1 mL
¼ tsp	salt	1 mL
2	eggs	2
¾ cup	granulated sugar	175 mL
½ cup	packed light brown sugar	125 mL
1 tsp	vanilla extract	5 mL
1½ cups	sweetened flaked coconut, coarsely chopped	375 mL
¾ cup	chopped roasted unsalted cashews	175 mL

Icing

½ cup	confectioner's (powdered/icing) sugar	125 mL
1 tbsp	half-and-half (10%) cream or milk	15 mL
¼ tsp	vanilla extract	1 mL

1. **Crust:** In a bowl, whisk together flour and granulated sugar until well combined. Stir in coconut. Using a pastry blender, a fork or your fingers, cut in butter until evenly combined. Mixture will resemble coarse crumbs and start to come together. Using the back of a spoon or your fingers, press crust evenly into bottom of prepared pan. Bake in preheated oven for 12 minutes or until lightly golden. Place pan on a wire cooling rack.

2. **Filling:** In a small bowl, whisk together flour, baking powder and salt. Set aside.

3. In a large bowl, using a wire whisk, lightly beat eggs. Add granulated sugar and brown sugar and stir until well combined. Beat in vanilla. Scrape down sides of bowl. Gradually whisk in flour mixture until well blended. Fold in coconut and cashews. Spread filling evenly over warm crust.

Tip

Lining the baking pan with foil makes it much easier to remove bars or squares from the pan after baking and protects the pan from damage from knife cuts. It also makes cleanup a breeze.

4. Bake for 20 to 22 minutes or just until filling is set. Let cool completely in baking pan on a wire rack.

5. *Icing:* In a small bowl, combine confectioner's sugar, cream and vanilla. Using a small whisk or a fork, blend until icing is smooth and thin enough to drizzle from a fork. Drizzle icing over cooled squares. Let stand 20 minutes or until the icing is set.

6. Using foil, lift squares from pan and place on a cutting board. Cut into $1\frac{1}{2}$-inch (4 cm) squares.

Creative Gift Idea

Here is a great gift for anyone who loves plants or gardening and cookies, too!

Choose a pretty plant pot large enough to hold a collection of colorful bars and squares or other types of cookies. The pot can be a simple one made of terra cotta or a more decorative one finished with a colorful glaze. Line the pot with a piece of burlap or a fabric with a garden theme.

Bake a few kinds of bars and squares with a variety of colors and textures. It is best to choose recipes that do not require refrigeration. After cutting, wrap bars and squares individually or in packages of a few each. Wrap different flavors of bars and squares separately to keep the flavors from mingling.

Arrange the packages of cookies in the pot, padding with tissue paper as needed. Wrap the pot in clear cellophane and tie with a pretty bow that coordinates with the color of the pot.

White Chocolate Pumpkin Blondies

● ● ●

Pair white chocolate with pumpkin, and you have a heavenly combination.

Tips

Be sure to use canned, solid pack pumpkin, also known as purée, not canned pumpkin pie filling, in this recipe.

Store blondies between layers of wax paper in a tightly sealed container. Blondies can be stored in the refrigerator for up to 3 days.

● **Preheat oven to 350°F (180°C)**
● **9-inch (2.5 L) square baking pan, lined with foil, greased**

Blondies

1⅓ cups	all-purpose flour	325 mL
1½ tsp	baking powder	7 mL
¾ tsp	ground cinnamon	3 mL
¼ tsp	ground ginger	1 mL
¼ tsp	ground nutmeg	1 mL
¼ tsp	salt	1 mL
2	eggs	2
1 cup	solid pack (purée) pumpkin	250 mL
¾ cup	packed light brown sugar	175 mL
½ cup	unsalted butter, melted	125 mL
½ tsp	vanilla extract	2 mL
½ cup	chopped white chocolate or white chocolate chips	125 mL
½ cup	chopped pecans	125 mL

Frosting

5 oz	white chocolate, chopped	150 g
2 tbsp	whipping (35%) cream	25 mL
8 oz	cream cheese, softened	250 g
1 cup	confectioner's (powdered/icing) sugar	250 mL
2 tbsp	finely chopped pecans	25 mL

1. ***Blondies:*** In a bowl, whisk together flour, baking powder, cinnamon, ginger, nutmeg and salt until well combined. Set aside.

2. In a large bowl, using a wire whisk, lightly beat eggs. Add pumpkin and stir until well combined. Add brown sugar and stir until well blended. Stir in melted butter and vanilla. Scrape down sides of bowl. On low speed or using a wooden spoon, gradually add flour mixture, stirring just until blended. By hand, fold in white chocolate and pecans. Spread batter evenly into prepared pan.

3. Bake in preheated oven for 30 to 35 minutes or until a wooden pick inserted near the center comes out with a few moist crumbs. Let cool completely in baking pan on a wire rack.

Tip

For the best flavor, use chopped white chocolate or white chocolate chips rather than baking chips labeled as "white" or "vanilla." These imitation chips do not contain the high ratio of cocoa butter that gives white chocolate its special flavor.

4. *Frosting:* In a large microwave-safe bowl, heat white chocolate and cream in a microwave at Medium-High (75%) power for 30 seconds. Stir until smooth. If necessary, heat at Medium (50%) power for 10 seconds at a time, stirring between each heating, just until chocolate is melted. Do not overheat. Cool for 5 minutes.

5. In a large bowl, using an electric mixer on medium speed or using a wooden spoon, gradually beat cream cheese and confectioner's sugar until light and fluffy, about 4 minutes. Scrape down sides of bowl. Add cooled melted white chocolate mixture and beat until smooth and creamy. Spread frosting over cooled blondies. Sprinkle pecans over frosting. Chill for at least 1 hour before cutting.

6. Using foil, lift chilled blondies from pan and place on a cutting board. Cut into 1½-inch (4 cm) squares.

Cappuccino Cheesecake Bars

If you enjoy the flavor of cappuccino, give these creamy bars a try.

Tips

For best results, use the pan size and shape called for in the recipe. If you use a different pan, you will need to adjust the baking time to reduce the chance of burning or undercooking.

Store bars between layers of wax paper in a tightly sealed container. Bars can be stored in the refrigerator for up to 3 days.

- Preheat oven to 350°F (180°C)
- 13- by 9-inch (3 L) baking pan, lined with foil, greased

Crust

2 cups	all-purpose flour	500 mL
¾ cup	confectioner's (powdered/icing) sugar	175 mL
3 tbsp	unsweetened Dutch-process cocoa powder, sifted	45 mL
1 tsp	instant espresso powder	5 mL
1 cup	unsalted butter, cut into pieces	250 mL

Filling

1½ tbsp	instant espresso powder	22 mL
1 tbsp	hot water	15 mL
I lb	cream cheese, softened	500 g
⅔ cup	granulated sugar	150 mL
2	eggs	2
2 tsp	vanilla extract	10 mL

1. **Crust:** In a bowl, whisk together flour, confectioner's sugar, cocoa powder and espresso powder until well combined. Using a pastry blender, a fork or your fingers, cut in butter until evenly combined. Mixture will resemble coarse crumbs and start to come together. Using the back of a spoon or your fingers, press crust evenly into bottom of prepared pan. Bake in preheated oven for 15 minutes or until lightly golden. Let cool completely on a wire rack.

2. **Filling:** In a small bowl, combine instant espresso powder and hot water. Stir until completely dissolved. Set aside to cool.

3. In a large bowl, using an electric mixer on medium speed, beat cream cheese and granulated sugar until smooth and creamy, about 2 minutes. Add eggs one at a time, beating well after each addition. Beat in vanilla.

4. Spread two-thirds of filling evenly over cooled crust. Add cooled espresso to remaining filling. Drop small spoonfuls of espresso filling over cream cheese filling. Insert a knife halfway down through filling. Draw knife in a swirl pattern to create a marbled effect.

5. Bake for 25 to 30 minutes, or just until filling is set. Let cool completely in baking pan on a wire rack. Cover and chill for at least 4 hours before cutting.

6. Using foil, lift chilled bars from pan and place on a cutting board. Cut into 1- by 2¼-inch (2.5 by 5.5 cm) bars.

Peanut Butter Oat Chippers
(page 156)

Maple Pecan Dreams (page 176)
and Cranberry Apricot Dreams (page 191)

Chocolate Decadence Dreams (page 177)

Snowflake Cookies (page 224)

Raspberry Cream
Sandwich Cookies
(page 236)

Chocolate Mint Thins (page 256),
Lemon Sandwich Cookies (page 262)
and Cranberry Almond Slices (page 268)

Raspberry Streusel Squares (page 280)
and Apricot Crunch Squares (page 289)

Deluxe Nut Bars (page 304)

Marmalade Crumb Bars

Orange marmalade keeps these scrumptious bars moist, and the addition of orange juice concentrate and orange zest packs them with flavor.

Tips

Use shiny or light-colored metal baking pans for making bars. Dark pans absorb more heat and can cause bars to overbake.

Store bars between layers of wax paper in a tightly sealed container. Bars can be stored at room temperature for up to 3 days.

- Preheat oven to 350°F (180°C)
- 13- by 9-inch (3 L) baking pan, lined with foil, greased

Topping

1 cup	all-purpose flour	250 mL
1/3 cup	granulated sugar	75 mL
2 tsp	grated orange zest	10 mL
1/3 cup	unsalted butter, cut into pieces	75 mL

Bars

1½ cups	all-purpose flour	375 mL
½ tsp	baking powder	2 mL
¼ tsp	baking soda	1 mL
¼ tsp	salt	1 mL
½ cup	unsalted butter, softened	125 mL
½ cup	granulated sugar	125 mL
½ cup	confectioner's (powdered/icing) sugar	125 mL
1	egg	1
2 tbsp	frozen orange juice concentrate, thawed	25 mL
1 tsp	grated orange zest	5 mL
⅔ cup	orange marmalade	150 mL

1. **Topping:** In a small bowl, whisk together flour and granulated sugar until well blended. Stir in orange zest. Using a fork or your fingers, work in butter until evenly combined. Mixture will resemble coarse crumbs and start to come together. Set aside.

2. **Bars:** In a bowl, whisk together flour, baking powder, baking soda and salt until well combined. Set aside.

3. In a large bowl, using an electric mixer on medium speed, cream butter, granulated sugar and confectioner's sugar until light and fluffy, about 3 minutes. Add egg and beat well. Beat in orange juice concentrate and orange zest. Scrape down sides of bowl. On low speed or using a wooden spoon, gradually add flour mixture, stirring just until blended. By hand, stir in orange marmalade. Spread batter evenly into prepared pan. Crumble topping over batter.

4. Bake in preheated oven for 30 to 35 minutes or until a wooden pick inserted into the center comes out with a few moist crumbs. Let cool completely in baking pan on a wire rack.

5. Using foil, lift cooled bars from pan and place on a cutting board. Cut into approximately 1¾- by 2¼-inch (4.5 by 5.5 cm) bars.

Cranberry Coconut Squares

● ● ●

A tender shortbread cookie with a hint of orange is topped with a layer of fruit and nut filling.

Tips

These squares are also good made using walnuts, almonds or macadamia nuts in place of the pecans.

Store squares between layers of wax paper in a tightly sealed container. Squares can be stored in the refrigerator for up to 3 days.

● **Preheat oven to 350°F (180°C)**
● **9-inch (2.5 L) square baking pan, lined with foil, greased**

Crust

1½ cups	all-purpose flour	375 mL
½ cup	granulated sugar	125 mL
¼ tsp	salt	1 mL
1 tsp	grated orange zest	5 mL
⅔ cup	unsalted butter, cut into pieces	150 mL

Filling

¾ cup	chopped dried cranberries	175 mL
½ cup	sweetened flaked coconut, coarsely chopped	125 mL
¼ cup	chopped pecans	50 mL
2	eggs	2
¾ cup	granulated sugar	175 mL
2 tbsp	half-and-half (10%) cream	25 mL
1 tsp	grated orange zest	5 mL
½ tsp	vanilla extract	2 mL

1. **Crust:** In a bowl, whisk together flour, granulated sugar and salt until well combined. Stir in orange zest. Using a pastry blender, a fork or your fingers, cut in butter until evenly combined. Mixture will resemble coarse crumbs and start to come together. Using the back of a spoon or your fingers, press crust evenly into bottom of prepared pan. Bake in preheated oven for 12 minutes or until lightly golden. Place pan on a wire cooling rack.

2. **Filling:** In a small bowl, combine cranberries, coconut and pecans until well blended. Set aside.

3. In a large bowl, using a wire whisk, lightly beat eggs. Add granulated sugar and beat until well combined. Beat in cream, orange zest and vanilla. Fold in cranberry mixture. Spread filling evenly over warm crust.

4. Bake for 18 to 22 minutes, or just until filling is set. Let cool completely in baking pan on a wire rack.

5. Using foil, lift cooled squares from pan and place on a cutting board. Cut into 1½-inch (4 cm) squares.

Maple Walnut Squares

● ● ●

The blending of maple and walnuts gives these squares an exquisite flavor.

Tips

Butter is considered to be softened when it is at a temperature of 65°F (18°C).

Store squares between layers of wax paper in a tightly sealed container. Squares can be stored at room temperature for up to 3 days.

● **Preheat oven to 350°F (180°C)**
● **9-inch (2.5 L) square baking pan, lined with foil, greased**

1¾ cups	all-purpose flour	425 mL
1 tsp	baking powder	5 mL
¼ tsp	baking soda	1 mL
¼ tsp	salt	1 mL
½ cup	unsalted butter, softened	125 mL
½ cup	granulated sugar	125 mL
½ cup	packed dark brown sugar	125 mL
2	eggs	2
1½ tsp	maple flavoring	7 mL
½ tsp	vanilla extract	2 mL
1⅓ cups	chopped walnuts	325 mL
	Confectioner's (powdered/icing) sugar	

1. In a bowl, whisk together flour, baking powder, baking soda and salt until well combined. Set aside.

2. In a large bowl, using an electric mixer on medium speed, cream butter, granulated sugar and brown sugar until light and fluffy, about 3 minutes. Add eggs one at a time, beating well after each addition. Beat in maple flavoring and vanilla. Scrape down sides of bowl. On low speed or using a wooden spoon, gradually add flour mixture, stirring just until blended. By hand, fold in walnuts. Spread batter evenly into prepared pan.

3. Bake in preheated oven for 22 to 28 minutes or until a wooden pick inserted into the center comes out with a few moist crumbs. Let cool completely in baking pan on a wire rack.

4. Using foil, lift cooled squares from pan and place on a cutting board. Lightly dust cooled squares with confectioner's sugar. Cut into 2¼-inch (5.5 cm) squares.

Apricot Pineapple Crumb Bars

These thick bars are layered with flavor and have a tangy fruit filling.

Tips

The syrup-packed pineapple adds sweetness to the filling and blends nicely with the apricots and orange juice. If you use juice-packed pineapple, increase the sugar in the filling to ³⁄₄ cup (175 mL).

Let icing set completely before storing bars between layers of wax paper in a tightly sealed container. Bars can be stored at room temperature for up to 3 days.

- Preheat oven to 350°F (180°C)
- 13- by 9-inch (3 L) baking pan, lined with foil, greased

Filling

2¹⁄₂ cups	chopped dried apricots	625 mL
1 cup	freshly squeezed orange juice	250 mL
¹⁄₂ cup	granulated sugar	125 mL
1 tsp	cornstarch	5 mL
1	can (20 oz or 540 mL) crushed pineapple packed in heavy syrup, drained	1

Crust

1²⁄₃ cups	all-purpose flour	400 mL
³⁄₄ cup	granulated sugar	175 mL
¹⁄₂ tsp	baking powder	2 mL
3 cups	quick-cooking rolled oats	750 mL
1 cup	sweetened flaked coconut, coarsely chopped	250 mL
²⁄₃ cup	finely chopped roasted unsalted macadamia nuts	150 mL
1¹⁄₄ cups	unsalted butter, cut into pieces	300 mL

Icing

1¹⁄₄ cups	confectioner's (powdered/icing) sugar	300 mL
1 tsp	grated orange zest	5 mL
2 tbsp	freshly squeezed orange juice	25 mL

1. **Filling:** In a large bowl, combine apricots and orange juice and stir until well combined. Let stand for 30 minutes, stirring occasionally. Set aside.

2. In a small bowl, whisk together granulated sugar and cornstarch until well blended. Set aside.

3. **Crust:** In a bowl, whisk together flour, granulated sugar and baking powder until well combined. Stir in oats, coconut and macadamia nuts until well blended. Using a fork or your fingers, cut in butter until evenly combined. Mixture will resemble coarse crumbs and start to come together. Using the back of a spoon or your fingers, press half of crust mixture evenly into bottom of prepared pan. Reserve remaining crust mixture for topping. Set aside.

Tip

Buy and use roasted
unsalted macadamia
nuts for the best flavor.
Roasting brings out
the nutty flavor of the
macadamias.

4. Add pineapple to apricot mixture and stir until well combined. Stir in sugar mixture until well blended. Spread filling evenly over bottom crust. Crumble reserved crust mixture evenly over filling.

5. Bake in preheated oven for 35 to 40 minutes or until lightly golden. Let cool completely in baking pan on a wire rack.

6. *Icing:* In a small bowl, combine confectioner's sugar, orange zest and orange juice. Using a small whisk or a fork, blend until icing is smooth and thin enough to drizzle from a fork. Drizzle icing over cooled bars. Let stand 20 minutes or until icing is set.

7. Using foil, lift bars from pan and place on a cutting board. Cut into 1- by $2\frac{1}{4}$-inch (2.5 by 5.5 cm) bars.

Raspberry Oat Squares

Oats give squares and bars a crust with lots of texture and a crunchy topping.

Tips

Lining the pan with foil makes it easy to remove squares from the pan after cooling and makes cleanup a breeze.

Store squares between layers of wax paper in a tightly sealed container. Squares can be stored at room temperature for up to 3 days.

- Preheat oven to 350°F (180°C)
- 9-inch (2.5 L) square baking pan, lined with foil, greased

Crust

1½ cups	all-purpose flour	375 mL
⅔ cup	granulated sugar	150 mL
1 tsp	baking powder	5 mL
¼ tsp	baking soda	1 mL
¼ tsp	salt	1 mL
1 cup	quick-cooking rolled oats	250 mL
½ cup	sweetened flaked coconut, coarsely chopped	125 mL
¾ cup	unsalted butter, melted	175 mL
1 tsp	vanilla extract	5 mL
¼ tsp	almond extract	1 mL

Filling

1 cup	seedless raspberry jam	250 mL

Topping

¼ cup	sweetened flaked coconut, coarsely chopped	50 mL

1. **Crust:** In a bowl, whisk together flour, granulated sugar, baking powder, baking soda and salt until well combined. Stir in oats and coconut.

2. In a small bowl, combine melted butter, vanilla and almond extract. Add butter mixture to flour mixture and stir until evenly combined. Mixture will resemble coarse crumbs and start to come together. Reserve ¾ cup (175 mL) of crust mixture for topping. Using the back of a spoon or your fingers, press remaining crust mixture evenly into bottom of prepared pan.

3. **Filling:** Stir raspberry jam to loosen it. Spread jam evenly over crust.

4. **Topping:** Add chopped coconut to reserved crust mixture and stir until well combined. Crumble topping mixture over jam.

5. Bake in preheated oven for 22 to 26 minutes or until lightly golden. Let cool completely in baking pan on a wire rack.

6. Using foil, lift cooled squares from pan and place on a cutting board. Cut into 1½-inch (4 cm) squares.

Creamy Lemon Oat Squares

●●●

These creamy squares have a lovely lemon flavor and are quick and easy to make.

Tips

Combining the filling ingredients before preparing the crust gives the filling time to thicken before baking and gives these squares a creamy texture.

Sweetened condensed milk is sold by weight in the U.S. and by volume in Canada. A U.S. 14-oz can contains $1\frac{1}{3}$ cups (325 mL).

Store squares between layers of wax paper in a tightly sealed container. Squares can be stored in the refrigerator for up to 3 days.

- Preheat oven to 350°F (180°C)
- 9-inch (2.5 L) square baking pan, lined with foil, greased

Filling

$1\frac{1}{3}$ cups	sweetened condensed milk	325 mL
1 tbsp	grated lemon zest	15 mL
6 tbsp	freshly squeezed lemon juice	90 mL

Crust

$1\frac{1}{2}$ cups	all-purpose flour	375 mL
$\frac{2}{3}$ cup	granulated sugar	150 mL
1 tsp	baking powder	5 mL
$\frac{1}{4}$ tsp	salt	1 mL
2 tsp	grated lemon zest	10 mL
1 cup	quick-cooking rolled oats	250 mL
$\frac{3}{4}$ cup	unsalted butter, melted	175 mL

1. *Filling:* Pour sweetened condensed milk into a bowl. Stir in lemon zest. Gradually whisk in lemon juice until well blended. Set aside.

2. *Crust:* In a bowl, whisk together flour, granulated sugar, baking powder and salt until well combined. Stir in lemon zest. Stir in oats. Add melted butter and stir until evenly combined. Mixture will resemble coarse crumbs and start to come together. Using the back of a spoon or your fingers, press half of crust mixture evenly into bottom of prepared pan. Reserve remaining crust mixture for topping. Bake in preheated oven for 10 minutes. Place pan on a wire cooling rack.

3. Stir filling mixture just until smooth. Pour filling over hot crust and spread evenly. Crumble reserved crust mixture over filling.

4. Bake for 18 to 20 minutes or until lightly golden. Let cool completely in baking pan on a wire rack.

5. Using foil, lift cooled squares from pan and place on a cutting board. Cut into $1\frac{1}{2}$-inch (4 cm) squares.

Applesauce Walnut Bars

Makes about 28 bars

With a hint of cinnamon, these applesauce bars are a great treat any time of year.

Tips

Lining the pan with foil makes it easy to remove bars from the pan after cooling and makes cleanup a breeze.

Store bars between layers of wax paper in a tightly sealed container. Bars can be stored at room temperature for up to 3 days.

- Preheat oven to 350°F (180°C)
- 13- by 9-inch (3 L) baking pan, lined with foil, greased

1½ cups	all-purpose flour	375 mL
1½ tsp	baking powder	7 mL
½ tsp	ground cinnamon	2 mL
¼ tsp	salt	1 mL
⅔ cup	unsalted butter, softened	150 mL
¾ cup	granulated sugar	175 mL
¾ cup	packed light brown sugar	175 mL
2	eggs	2
1 cup	unsweetened applesauce	250 mL
2 tsp	vanilla extract	10 mL
¾ cup	chopped walnuts	175 mL
	Confectioner's (powdered/icing) sugar	

1. In a bowl, whisk together flour, baking powder, cinnamon and salt until well combined. Set aside.
2. In a large bowl, using an electric mixer on medium speed, cream butter, granulated sugar and brown sugar until light and fluffy, about 3 minutes. Add eggs one at a time, beating well after each addition. Beat in applesauce and vanilla. Scrape down sides of bowl. On low speed or using a wooden spoon, gradually add flour mixture, beating just until blended. By hand, fold in walnuts. Spread batter evenly into prepared pan.
3. Bake in preheated oven for 22 to 28 minutes or until a wooden pick inserted into the center comes out with a few moist crumbs. Let cool completely in baking pan on a wire rack.
4. Using foil, lift cooled bars from pan and place on a cutting board. Lightly dust cooled bars with confectioner's sugar. Cut into approximately 1¾- by 2¼-inch (4.5 by 5.5 cm) bars.

White Chocolate Raspberry Crumb Squares

There is something quite elegant and luxurious about the combination of white chocolate and raspberries.

Tips

Be sure to use a quality white chocolate containing lots of cocoa butter to make these squares. For best flavor and texture, do not use a vanilla-flavored baking chip or plain white chip that does not contain cocoa butter.

Store squares between layers of wax paper in a tightly sealed container. Squares can be stored at room temperature for up to 3 days.

- Preheat oven to 350°F (180°C)
- 9-inch (2.5 L) square baking pan, lined with foil, greased

Crust

2½ cups	all-purpose flour	625 mL
½ cup	granulated sugar	125 mL
¼ tsp	salt	1 mL
1 cup	unsalted butter, cut into pieces	250 mL

Filling

1 cup	seedless raspberry jam	250 mL
⅔ cup	chopped white chocolate or white chocolate chips	150 mL

1. **Crust:** In a bowl, whisk together flour, granulated sugar and salt until well combined. Using a pastry blender, a fork or your fingers, cut in butter until evenly combined. Mixture will resemble coarse crumbs and start to come together. Using the back of a spoon or your fingers, press two-thirds of crust mixture evenly into bottom of prepared pan. Reserve remaining crust mixture for topping. Bake in preheated oven for 12 minutes or until lightly golden. Place pan on a wire cooling rack.

2. **Filling:** Stir raspberry jam to loosen it. Spread jam evenly over crust. Sprinkle white chocolate over jam. Crumble reserved crust mixture over filling.

3. Bake for 22 to 24 minutes or until lightly golden. Let cool completely in baking pan on a wire rack.

4. Using foil, lift cooled squares from pan and place on a cutting board. Cut into 1½-inch (4 cm) squares.

Blueberry Pie Bars

The touch of cinnamon in the crust and topping is a nice complement to the flavor of the blueberry filling.

Tip

Let icing set completely before storing bars between layers of wax paper in a tightly sealed container. Bars can be stored in the refrigerator for up to 3 days.

Variations

Cherry Pie Bars: Substitute cherry pie filling for blueberry pie filling. Omit cinnamon and substitute ¼ teaspoon (2 mL) almond extract for vanilla extract.

Peach Pie Bars: Substitute peach pie filling for blueberry pie filling. Substitute ¼ teaspoon (1 mL) nutmeg for cinnamon.

- ● Preheat oven to 350°F (180°C)
- ● 13- by 9-inch (3 L) baking pan, lined with foil, greased

Crust

2 cups	all-purpose flour	500 mL
¾ cup	granulated sugar	175 mL
¼ tsp	ground cinnamon	1 mL
¼ tsp	salt	1 mL
½ tsp	vanilla extract	2 mL
1 cup	unsalted butter, cut into pieces	250 mL

Filling

1	can (20 oz or 540 mL) blueberry pie filling	1

Icing

1 cup	confectioner's (powdered/icing) sugar	250 mL
2 tbsp	half-and-half (10%) cream or milk	25 mL
½ tsp	vanilla extract	2 mL

1. **Crust:** In a bowl, whisk together flour, granulated sugar, cinnamon and salt until well combined. Stir in vanilla. Using a pastry blender, a fork or your fingers, cut in butter until evenly combined. Mixture will resemble coarse crumbs and start to come together. Using back of a spoon or your fingers, press two-thirds of crust mixture evenly into bottom of prepared pan. Reserve remaining crust mixture for topping.

2. **Filling:** Spread blueberry pie filling evenly over bottom crust. Crumble reserved crust mixture evenly over filling.

3. Bake in preheated oven for 25 to 30 minutes or until lightly golden brown around edges. Let cool completely in baking pan on a wire rack.

4. **Icing:** In a small bowl, combine confectioner's sugar, cream and vanilla. Using a small whisk or a fork, blend until icing is smooth and thin enough to drizzle from a fork. Drizzle icing over cooled bars. Let stand 20 minutes or until icing is set.

5. Using foil, lift bars from pan and place on a cutting board. Cut into 1- by 2¼-inch (2.5 by 5.5 cm) bars.

Lime Coconut Squares

Lime and coconut make a remarkable flavor combination.

Tips

When zesting limes, remove only the outer colored part of the peel. The white part underneath, called the pith, is very bitter and will give squares an unpleasant flavor.

Store squares between layers of wax paper in a tightly sealed container. Squares can be stored in the refrigerator for up to 3 days.

- Preheat oven to 350°F (180°C)
- 9-inch (2.5 L) square baking pan, lined with foil, greased

Crust

1⅓ cups	all-purpose flour	325 mL
⅓ cup	granulated sugar	75 mL
¼ tsp	salt	1 mL
¼ cup	sweetened flaked coconut, finely chopped	50 mL
1 tsp	grated lime zest	5 mL
⅔ cup	unsalted butter, cut into pieces	150 mL

Filling

¾ cup	granulated sugar	175 mL
1 tbsp	cornstarch	15 mL
4	eggs	4
1 tsp	grated lime zest	5 mL
½ cup	freshly squeezed lime juice	125 mL
1 cup	sweetened flaked coconut, chopped	250 mL

Confectioner's (powdered/icing) sugar

1. **Crust:** In a bowl, whisk together flour, granulated sugar and salt until well combined. Stir in coconut and lime zest. Using a pastry blender, a fork or your fingers, cut in butter until evenly combined. Mixture will resemble coarse crumbs and start to come together. Using the back of a spoon or your fingers, press crust evenly into bottom of prepared pan. Bake in preheated oven for 12 minutes or until lightly golden. Place pan on a wire cooling rack.

2. **Filling:** In a small bowl, whisk together granulated sugar and cornstarch. Set aside.

3. In a bowl, lightly beat eggs. Add sugar mixture and beat until well blended. Stir in lime zest. Gradually whisk in lime juice until well combined. Fold in coconut. Spread filling evenly over warm crust.

4. Bake for 15 to 18 minutes or until lightly golden brown around edges. Let cool completely in baking pan on a wire rack.

5. Using foil, lift cooled squares from pan and place on a cutting board. Lightly dust squares with confectioner's sugar. Cut into 1½-inch (4 cm) squares.

Pineapple Squares

Pineapple is one of my favorite flavors to bake with, and these are a great dessert for a summer evening or a tropical-themed party.

Tips

Save the juice drained from the canned pineapple in filling to use when making the icing.

Let icing set completely before storing squares between layers of wax paper in a tightly sealed container. Squares can be stored in the refrigerator for up to 3 days.

- Preheat oven to 350°F (180°C)
- 9-inch (2.5 L) square baking pan, lined with foil, greased

Crust

1½ cups	all-purpose flour	375 mL
¼ cup	granulated sugar	50 mL
¼ tsp	salt	1 mL
½ cup	unsalted butter, cut into pieces	125 mL

Filling

2	eggs	2
⅓ cup	granulated sugar	75 mL
⅓ cup	packed light brown sugar	75 mL
2 tbsp	all-purpose flour	25 mL
¼ tsp	vanilla extract	1 mL
¼ tsp	almond extract	1 mL
1	can (20 oz or 540 mL) juice-packed crushed pineapple, drained, juice reserved	1

Icing

¾ cup	confectioner's (powdered/icing) sugar	175 mL
1½ tbsp	reserved pineapple juice	22 mL
1½ tsp	unsalted butter, melted	7 mL

1. **Crust:** In a bowl, whisk together flour, granulated sugar and salt until well combined. Using a pastry blender, a fork or your fingers, cut in butter until evenly combined. Mixture will resemble coarse crumbs and start to come together. Using the back of a spoon or your fingers, press crust evenly into bottom of prepared pan. Bake in preheated oven for 12 minutes or until lightly golden. Place pan on a wire cooling rack.

2. **Filling:** In a large bowl, using a wire whisk, lightly beat eggs. Add granulated sugar and brown sugar and stir until well combined. Gradually whisk in flour. Stir in vanilla and almond extract. Scrape down sides of bowl. Fold in pineapple. Spread filling evenly over warm crust.

3. Bake for 20 to 22 minutes, or just until filling is set. Let cool completely in baking pan on a wire rack.

4. **Icing:** In a small bowl, combine confectioner's sugar, pineapple juice and melted butter. Using a small whisk or a fork, blend until icing is smooth and thin enough to drizzle from a fork. Drizzle icing over cooled squares. Let stand 20 minutes or until the icing is set.

5. Using foil, lift squares from pan and place on a cutting board. Cut into 1½-inch (4 cm) squares.

Caramel Pecan Squares

These gooey, nutty treats will satisfy any sweet tooth.

Tips

For the best flavor, use high-quality caramels in this recipe.

For best results, use the pan size and shape called for in the recipe. If you use a different pan, you will need to adjust the baking time to reduce the chance of burning or undercooking.

Store squares between layers of wax paper in a tightly sealed container. Squares can be stored at room temperature for up to 3 days.

- Preheat oven to 350°F (180°C)
- 9-inch (2.5 L) square baking pan, lined with foil, greased

Crust

2¾ cups	all-purpose flour	675 mL
⅔ cup	granulated sugar	150 mL
¼ tsp	salt	1 mL
½ tsp	vanilla extract	2 mL
1 cup	unsalted butter, cut into pieces	250 mL

Filling

30	individually wrapped caramels, unwrapped	30
¼ cup	heavy whipping (36% to 49%) cream	50 mL
½ tsp	vanilla extract	2 mL
1 cup	chopped pecans	250 mL

1. **Crust:** In a bowl, whisk together flour, granulated sugar and salt until well combined. Stir in vanilla. Using a pastry blender, a fork or your fingers, cut in butter until evenly combined. Mixture will resemble coarse crumbs and start to come together. Using the back of a spoon or your fingers, press two-thirds of crust mixture evenly into bottom of prepared pan. Reserve remaining crust mixture for topping. Bake in preheated oven for 12 minutes or until lightly golden. Place pan on a wire cooling rack.

2. **Filling:** In a microwave-safe bowl, heat unwrapped caramels and cream in a microwave at Medium-High (75%) power for 2 minutes. Stir caramels until smooth. If necessary, heat at Medium (50%) power for 20 seconds at a time, stirring between each heating, just until caramels are melted. Do not overheat. Stir in vanilla.

3. Sprinkle pecans over warm crust. Pour caramel filling over pecans and spread evenly. Crumble reserved crust mixture over caramel filling.

4. Bake for 15 to 18 minutes or until lightly golden. Let cool completely in baking pan on a wire rack.

5. Using foil, lift cooled squares from pan and place on a cutting board. Cut into 1½-inch (4 cm) squares.

Mincemeat Bars

● ● ●

With jars of mincemeat pie filling available on grocery store shelves year-round, there's no need to wait for the holidays to enjoy these bars.

Tips

The orange juice and orange zest add a nice touch of citrus to the filling but may be omitted if you prefer.

Store bars between layers of wax paper in a tightly sealed container. Bars can be stored in the refrigerator for up to 3 days.

- Preheat oven to 350°F (180°C)
- 13- by 9-inch (3 L) baking pan, lined with foil, greased

Crust

3⅓ cups	all-purpose flour	825 mL
1¼ cups	granulated sugar	300 mL
¼ tsp	salt	1 mL
1 tsp	vanilla extract	5 mL
1¼ cups	unsalted butter, cut into pieces	300 mL

Filling

1	jar (27 oz or 796 mL) prepared mincemeat pie filling	1
1 tsp	grated orange zest	5 mL
1 tbsp	freshly squeezed orange juice	15 mL

1. **Crust:** In a bowl, whisk together flour, granulated sugar and salt until well combined. Stir in vanilla. Using a pastry blender, fork or your fingers, cut in butter until evenly combined. Mixture will resemble coarse crumbs and start to come together. Using the back of a spoon or your fingers, press two-thirds of crust evenly into bottom of prepared pan. Reserve remaining crust mixture for topping. Bake in preheated oven for 15 minutes or until lightly golden. Place pan on a wire cooling rack.

2. **Filling:** In a bowl, combine mincemeat pie filling, orange zest and orange juice until well blended. Drop spoonfuls of filling on top of hot crust and carefully spread evenly over crust. Crumble reserved crust mixture over filling.

3. Bake for 25 to 27 minutes or until lightly golden. Let cool completely in baking pan on a wire rack.

4. Using foil, lift cooled bars from pan and place on a cutting board. Cut into 1- by 2¼-inch (2.5 by 5.5 cm) bars.

Brownies, Brownies and More Brownies

● ● ●

Chocolate Fudge Brownies. 337

Moist and Chewy Chocolate Syrup
  Brownies. 338

Raspberry Swirl Brownies. 340

Cheesecake Brownies 342

Fudge Nut Brownies. 344

German Chocolate Brownies 346

Layered Cream Cheese Brownies. . . 348

Blue Ribbon Fudge Brownies 349

Espresso Brownies. 350

Classic Brownies 352

Marbled White Chocolate
  Cream Cheese Brownies. 353

Chocolate-Lover's Brownies. 354

Amaretto Brownies. 356

Sour Cream Brownies. 357

Peanut Butter Swirl Brownies 358

Fudgy Brownies 360

Cream Cheese Brownies 361

Mint Brownies. 362

Walnut Brownies. 364

Double Chocolate Brownies 365

Rocky Road Brownies 366

Coconut Macaroon Brownies 368

Raspberry Brownies 369

Chocolate Malt Brownies 370

Buttermilk Brownies 372

Cocoa Brownies. 373

White Chocolate Macadamia
  Brownies. 374

Deluxe Brownies. 375

Peanut Butter Brownies 376

Marbled Cream Cheese Brownies . . 378

Coconut Brownies 380

Eggnog Brownies. 381

Moist, Fudgy Brownies 382

Fudge and Fudge Brownies 383

Espresso Cream Brownies 384

Milk Chocolate Brownies 386

Cocoa Coconut Brownies. 387

Double Chocolate Cream
  Brownies. 388

Toffee Mocha Brownies 389

Chocolate Cream Cheese
  Brownies. 390

Brownies Supreme. 392

About Brownies

Brownies are very versatile treats. More dense and moist than most cakes, brownies contain lots of luscious chocolate. They can be light and cake-like, soft and chewy or dense and fudgy. Brownies are quick and easy to make, using ingredients that are already on hand in most kitchens. Whether intensely flavored with chocolate alone or chocolate combined with added flavors, like nuts, fruit, cream cheese or peanut butter, brownies have legions of devoted fans.

Rich and chocolaty is an absolute must for great brownies. The flavor of good brownies is dependent on the quality of the chocolate in the batter. When making brownies, be sure to use the very best quality of chocolate and cocoa powder that you can afford. Flavor counts. Brownies are all about the chocolate. Why even bother making brownies if you're going to use a chocolate with poor flavor? Heaven forbid that chocolate-*flavored* chips should ever be used in making brownies, or any other cookie for that matter!

The recipes in this chapter are loaded with a variety of different chocolates and other exciting ingredients to enhance the chocolate experience. Whether your preferences lean to dense and fudgy, soft and chewy or cake-like topped with frosting, brownie aficionados will discover several new favorites in this special collection.

Baking Brownies

For very moist, fudgy brownies, start checking the brownies a couple of minutes before the end of the earliest cooking time. A wooden pick inserted near the center should come out with moist, fudgy crumbs clinging to it, and the surface of the brownies should be just set in the center. The middle of the brownies may appear slightly underdone, but the brownies will continue to bake after the pan is removed from the oven. Brownies firm up in the center as they cool.

For cake-like brownies, cook the brownies just until a wooden pick inserted near the center comes out clean and the surface of the brownies springs back when gently pressed. The brownies should not have started to pull away from the edges of the pan.

Cutting Brownies

The aroma of rich, gooey brownies, still warm from the oven, is hard to resist. If you manage to overcome the temptation, cooling the brownies completely before cutting will make it a lot easier to cut them cleanly into bars or squares. A serrated knife is the preferred choice for cutting brownies. The serrated blade will make it easier to cut through the top crust and help prevent the jagged cuts that can be made by a straight-bladed knife.

Chocolate Fudge Brownies

Makes 36 brownies

These quick and easy brownies have an intense chocolate flavor and are one of my favorite brownie recipes.

Tips

All of the recipes in this book use large eggs, the standard size used for baking. If you do not have large eggs, then lightly beat your eggs and substitute ¼ cup (50 mL) beaten egg for each large egg called for in the recipe.

Lining the pan with foil makes it easy to remove brownies from the pan after cooling and makes cleanup a breeze.

Variation

Fold ½ cup (125 mL) chopped walnuts into brownie batter before spreading into pan.

- Preheat oven to 350°F (180°C)
- 9-inch (2.5 L) square baking pan, lined with foil, greased

4 oz	bittersweet chocolate, chopped	125 g
½ cup	unsalted butter, cut into pieces	125 mL
¾ cup	all-purpose flour	175 mL
2 tbsp	unsweetened Dutch-process cocoa powder, sifted	25 mL
¼ tsp	salt	1 mL
1 cup	packed dark brown sugar	250 mL
¾ cup	granulated sugar	175 mL
3	eggs	3
2 tsp	vanilla extract	10 mL

1. In a large microwave-safe bowl, heat chocolate and butter in a microwave at Medium-High (75%) power for 1 minute. Stir chocolate until smooth. If necessary, heat at Medium (50%) power for 10 seconds at a time, stirring between each heating, just until chocolate is melted. Do not overheat. Cool for 5 minutes.

2. In a bowl, whisk together flour, cocoa powder and salt until well combined. Set aside.

3. Using a wire whisk or large spoon, stir brown sugar and granulated sugar into warm chocolate mixture. Add eggs one at a time, beating well after each addition. Beat in vanilla. Scrape down sides of bowl. Gradually add flour mixture, stirring just until blended. Spread batter evenly into prepared pan.

4. Bake in preheated oven for 28 to 32 minutes or until a wooden pick inserted near the center comes out with a few moist crumbs. Let cool completely in baking pan on a wire rack.

5. Use the foil to lift cooled brownies from pan and place on a cutting board. Cut into 1½-inch (4 cm) squares.

Moist and Chewy Chocolate Syrup Brownies

A wonderful brownie from childhood, the fudgy icing makes these a great treat to make with kids.

Tips

Icing will thicken rapidly as it cools, so spread warm icing over cooled brownies immediately.

Store brownies between layers of wax paper in a tightly sealed container. Baked goods such as cookies and brownies can be stored in a tightly sealed container at room temperature for up to 3 days.

● **Preheat oven to 350°F (180°C)**
● **13- by 9-inch (3 L) baking pan, lined with foil, greased**

Brownies

1 cup	all-purpose flour	250 mL
¼ cup	unsweetened Dutch-process cocoa powder, sifted	50 mL
½ tsp	baking powder	2 mL
¼ tsp	instant espresso powder	1 mL
¼ tsp	baking soda	1 mL
¼ tsp	salt	1 mL
½ cup	unsalted butter, softened	125 mL
¾ cup	granulated sugar	175 mL
¼ cup	packed dark brown sugar	50 mL
3	eggs	3
1½ tsp	vanilla extract	7 mL
1 cup	chocolate syrup	250 mL
¾ cup	chopped walnuts	175 mL

Icing

¼ cup	unsalted butter	50 mL
¼ cup	half-and-half (10%) cream	50 mL
¾ cup	superfine sugar	175 mL
½ cup	chopped semisweet chocolate or semisweet chocolate chips	125 mL
1 tsp	vanilla extract	5 mL

1. **Brownies:** In a bowl, whisk together flour, cocoa powder, baking powder, espresso powder, baking soda and salt until well combined. Set aside.

2. In a large bowl, using an electric mixer on medium speed, cream butter, granulated sugar and brown sugar and beat until light and fluffy, about 2 minutes. Add eggs one at a time, beating well after each addition. Beat in vanilla. With mixer running on low, gradually beat in chocolate syrup. Scrape down sides of bowl. On low speed or using a wooden spoon, gradually add flour mixture, beating just until blended. By hand, fold in walnuts. Spread batter evenly into prepared pan.

Tip

These brownies are particularly good made with dark chocolate syrup, which can be found in most grocery stores.

3. Bake in preheated oven for 25 to 30 minutes or until a wooden pick inserted near the center comes out with a few moist crumbs. Let cool completely in baking pan on a wire rack.

4. Use the foil to lift cooled brownies from pan and place on a cutting board.

5. *Icing:* In a small saucepan, over medium-low heat, heat butter and cream until butter melts. Add superfine sugar and stir until completely dissolved. Bring mixture to a boil and boil for 30 seconds, stirring constantly. Remove pan from heat. Add the semisweet chocolate and vanilla. Stir until chocolate is completely melted and mixture becomes smooth and glossy. Immediately pour icing over cooled brownies and spread evenly. Let stand 20 minutes or until frosting is set. Cut into approximately $1\frac{3}{4}$- by $1\frac{1}{2}$-inch (4.5 by 4 cm) bars.

Raspberry Swirl Brownies

These delightful brownies are as pretty as they are tasty.

Tips

Bittersweet chocolate contains a minimum of 35% chocolate liquor, with many brands around 50% and some even higher. The more chocolate liquor, the more intense the flavor. Bittersweet chocolate also differs from unsweetened chocolate in that it contains some sugar and additional cocoa butter to make it richer and smoother.

Store brownies between layers of wax paper in a tightly sealed container. Brownies can be stored in the refrigerator for up to 3 days.

Variation

Substitute apricot jam or seedless blackberry jam for seedless raspberry jam.

- Preheat oven to 350°F (180°C)
- 13- by 9-inch (3 L) baking pan, lined with foil, greased

Cream Cheese Filling

1 lb	cream cheese, softened	500 g
1 cup	granulated sugar	250 mL
2	eggs	2
1 tsp	vanilla extract	5 mL
1 cup	seedless raspberry jam	250 mL

Brownie Batter

6 oz	bittersweet chocolate, chopped	175 g
⅔ cup	unsalted butter, cut into pieces	150 mL
1 cup	all-purpose flour	250 mL
¼ tsp	baking powder	1 mL
¼ tsp	salt	1 mL
4	eggs	4
1½ cups	granulated sugar	375 mL
2 tsp	vanilla extract	10 mL

1. *Filling:* In a large bowl, using an electric mixer on medium speed, beat cream cheese and granulated sugar until smooth and creamy, about 2 minutes. Add eggs one at a time, beating well after each addition. Beat in vanilla. Cover and set aside.

2. *Brownies:* In a large microwave-safe bowl, heat chocolate and butter in a microwave at Medium-High (75%) power for 1 minute. Stir chocolate until smooth. If necessary, heat at Medium (50%) power for 10 seconds at a time, stirring between each heating, just until chocolate is melted. Do not overheat. Cool for 5 minutes.

3. In a bowl, whisk together flour, baking powder and salt until well combined. Set aside.

4. Using a wire whisk or large spoon, add eggs to warm chocolate mixture one at a time, beating well after each addition. Add granulated sugar and stir until well combined. Beat in vanilla. Scrape down sides of bowl. Gradually add flour mixture, stirring just until blended.

Tip

Use shiny or light-colored metal baking pans for making brownies. Dark pans absorb more heat and can cause brownies to overbake and dry out.

5. Spread brownie batter evenly into prepared pan. Carefully spread cream cheese filling evenly over brownie batter. Stir raspberry jam until smooth. Drop small teaspoonfuls (5 mL) of raspberry jam over cream cheese filling. Insert a knife halfway down through fillings. Draw the knife in a swirl pattern through jam and cream cheese to create a marbled effect.

6. Bake in preheated oven for 25 to 30 minutes or until filling is set and a wooden pick inserted near the center comes out with a few moist crumbs. Let cool completely in baking pan on a wire rack.

7. Use the foil to lift cooled brownies from pan and place on a cutting board. Cut into approximately $1\frac{3}{4}$- by $1\frac{1}{2}$-inch (4.5 by 4 cm) bars.

Creative Brownie Shapes

When cutting brownies into serving pieces, think outside the classic square or rectangle shape.

Triangles

Cut brownies into squares, and then cut each square in half to form two triangles.

Diamonds

Diamonds are a great shape for brownies that are baked in a rectangular pan. Make a diagonal cut from one corner of the brownies to the opposite corner, slicing all the way through the brownies. Make a second diagonal cut connecting the two remaining corners, creating an X pattern. Then make a series of parallel cuts, spaced 1 or $1\frac{1}{2}$ inches (2.5 or 4 cm) apart, on either side of the first cuts to create a diamond pattern. If you have trouble making straight cuts, you can use a ruler to keep the lines straight and even.

Cheesecake Brownies

A chocolaty brownie is the base for a creamy cheesecake layer with a sour cream topping.

Tips

Whenever available, use only pure extracts. These are made from the essence of the fruit, herb or other ingredient and have the best, cleanest, purest flavor and will taste wonderful in your cookies and other baked goods. Imitation flavorings can't compare to an extract.

Store brownies between layers of wax paper in a tightly sealed container. Brownies can be stored in the refrigerator for up to 3 days.

- Preheat oven to 350°F (180°C)
- 9-inch (2.5 L) square baking pan, lined with foil, greased

Cream Cheese Filling

10 oz	cream cheese, softened	300 g
⅔ cup	granulated sugar	150 mL
2	eggs	2
½ tsp	vanilla extract	2 mL
¼ tsp	almond extract	1 mL

Brownie Batter

4 oz	bittersweet chocolate, chopped	125 g
½ cup	unsalted butter, cut into pieces	125 mL
¾ cup	all-purpose flour	175 mL
¼ tsp	baking powder	1 mL
¼ tsp	salt	1 mL
2	eggs	2
1 cup	granulated sugar	250 mL
1 tsp	vanilla extract	5 mL

Topping

1¾ cups	sour cream	425 mL
⅔ cup	confectioner's (powdered/icing) sugar	150 mL
½ tsp	vanilla extract	2 mL

1. *Filling:* In a large bowl, using an electric mixer on medium speed, beat cream cheese and granulated sugar until smooth and creamy, about 2 minutes. Add eggs one at a time, beating well after each addition. Beat in vanilla and almond extract. Cover and set aside.

2. *Brownies:* In a large microwave-safe bowl, heat chocolate and butter in a microwave at Medium-High (75%) power for 1 minute. Stir chocolate until smooth. If necessary, heat at Medium (50%) power for 10 seconds at a time, stirring between each heating, just until chocolate is melted. Do not overheat. Cool for 5 minutes.

3. In a bowl, whisk together flour, baking powder and salt until well combined. Set aside.

Tip

Store eggs in their original carton on a shelf in the refrigerator. Do not store eggs in the door, where the temperature fluctuates every time the door is opened.

4. Using a wire whisk or large spoon, add eggs to warm chocolate mixture one at a time, beating well after each addition. Add granulated sugar and stir until well combined. Beat in vanilla. Scrape down sides of bowl. Gradually add flour mixture, stirring just until blended.

5. Spread brownie batter evenly into prepared pan. Carefully spread cream cheese filling evenly over brownie batter.

6. Bake in preheated oven for 25 to 30 minutes or just until cheese filling is set.

7. *Topping:* In a small bowl, whisk together sour cream, confectioner's sugar and vanilla until well blended. Spread topping over hot brownies. Return pan to the oven and bake for 5 minutes or just until topping is set. Let cool completely in baking pan on a wire rack.

8. Use the foil to lift cooled brownies from pan and place on a cutting board. Cut into $1\frac{1}{2}$-inch (4 cm) squares.

Fudge Nut Brownies

This is a great choice for people who like moist brownies with nuts.

Tips

Gently fold in the nuts by hand to keep from overworking the batter after the flour is mixed in. Overworking the batter will make the brownies tough.

Store brownies between layers of wax paper in a tightly sealed container. Brownies can be stored at room temperature for up to 3 days.

- Preheat oven to 350°F (180°C)
- 9-inch (2.5 L) square baking pan, lined with foil, greased

Brownies

6 oz	bittersweet chocolate, chopped	175 g
5 oz	semisweet chocolate, chopped	150 g
½ cup	unsalted butter, softened	125 mL
½ cup	all-purpose flour	125 mL
¼ tsp	baking powder	1 mL
¼ tsp	salt	1 mL
⅔ cup	packed light brown sugar	150 mL
½ cup	granulated sugar	125 mL
2	eggs	2
1 tbsp	vanilla extract	15 mL
1 cup	chopped pecans	250 mL

Frosting

6 oz	bittersweet chocolate, chopped	175 g
¼ cup	unsalted butter, cut into pieces	50 mL
1 tbsp	light (golden) corn syrup	15 mL
1 tbsp	vanilla extract	15 mL
¾ cup	confectioner's (powdered/icing) sugar	175 mL
1 to 2 tbsp	half-and-half (10%) cream or milk	15 to 25 mL

1. **Brownies:** In a large microwave-safe bowl, heat bittersweet chocolate, semisweet chocolate and butter in a microwave at Medium-High (75%) power for 1 minute. Stir chocolate until smooth. If necessary, heat chocolate at Medium (50%) power for 10 seconds at a time, stirring between each heating, just until chocolate is melted. Do not overheat. Cool for 5 minutes.

2. In a bowl, whisk together flour, baking powder and salt until well combined. Set aside.

3. Using a wire whisk or large spoon, stir brown sugar and granulated sugar into warm chocolate mixture. Add eggs one at a time, beating well after each addition. Beat in vanilla. Scrape down sides of bowl. Gradually add flour mixture, stirring just until blended. Fold in chopped pecans. Spread batter evenly into prepared pan.

Tip

Chocolate can be melted in the top of a double boiler placed over simmering water. Stir frequently, until chocolate is completely melted and mixture is smooth. Set aside to cool.

4. Bake in preheated oven for 20 to 24 minutes or until a wooden pick inserted near the center comes out with a few moist crumbs. Let cool completely in baking pan on a wire rack.

5. Use the foil to lift cooled brownies from pan and place on a cutting board.

6. *Frosting:* In a large microwave-safe bowl, heat chocolate and butter in a microwave at Medium-High (75%) power for 1 minute. Stir until smooth. Stir in corn syrup and vanilla. Using an electric mixer on medium speed, gradually beat in confectioner's sugar. Add 1 tablespoon (15 mL) of the cream and beat until smooth and fluffy. Add more cream as needed to achieve the desired consistency. Spread frosting over brownies. Let stand 20 minutes or until frosting is set. Cut into $1\frac{1}{2}$-inch (4 cm) squares.

"With or Without?" That is the Question

Some people love their brownies loaded with nuts or chocolate chips or covered with a thick layer of frosting. Others are purists who love their brownies without any of these adornments. The great thing about brownies is that you can dress them up or down and have them any way you want. Have fun and customize your brownies to match your heart's chocolate desire!

German Chocolate Brownies

Makes about 42 brownies ● ● ●

Adapted from a favorite classic recipe for German Chocolate Cake, these luscious brownies are a big hit at family gatherings and potluck events. The frosting requires careful attention during cooking, but the delicious results more than make up for the extra time and effort.

Tips

Sweet dark chocolate contains as much as 70% chocolate liquor and added cocoa butter. It has more sugar than bittersweet chocolate but less sugar than semisweet chocolate.

Store brownies between layers of wax paper in a tightly sealed container. Brownies can be stored in the refrigerator for up to 3 days. Bring to room temperature before serving.

- **Preheat oven to 350°F (180°C)**
- **13- by 9-inch (3 L) baking pan, lined with foil, greased**

Brownies

9 oz	sweet dark chocolate, chopped	275 g
2/3 cup	unsalted butter, cut into pieces	150 mL
1 1/4 cups	all-purpose flour	300 mL
1/4 tsp	baking powder	1 mL
1/4 tsp	salt	1 mL
3/4 cup	granulated sugar	175 mL
1/2 cup	packed dark brown sugar	125 mL
3	eggs	3
1 tsp	vanilla extract	5 mL
1/2 cup	sweetened flaked coconut	125 mL

Coconut Pecan Frosting

3	egg yolks	3
1/2 cup	granulated sugar	125 mL
2/3 cup	evaporated milk	150 mL
2 tbsp	unsalted butter, cut into pieces	25 mL
1/2 tsp	vanilla extract	2 mL
1 1/2 cups	sweetened flaked coconut	375 mL
1 cup	chopped pecans	250 mL

1. **Brownies:** In a large microwave-safe bowl, heat chocolate and butter in a microwave at Medium-High (75%) power for 1 minute. Stir chocolate until smooth. If necessary, heat at Medium (50%) power for 10 seconds at a time, stirring between each heating, just until chocolate is melted. Do not overheat. Cool for 5 minutes.

2. In a bowl, whisk together flour, baking powder and salt until well combined. Set aside.

3. Using a wire whisk or large spoon, stir granulated sugar and brown sugar into warm chocolate mixture. Add eggs one at a time, beating well after each addition. Beat in vanilla. Scrape down sides of bowl. Gradually add flour mixture, stirring just until blended. Fold in coconut. Spread batter evenly into prepared pan.

Tip

Chilling the brownies before cutting makes it easier to cut them into uniformly shaped bars.

4. Bake in preheated oven for 18 to 22 minutes or until a wooden pick inserted near the center comes out with a few moist crumbs. Let cool completely in baking pan on a wire rack.

5. *Frosting:* In a medium saucepan, whisk together egg yolks and granulated sugar. Gradually whisk in evaporated milk until smooth. Add butter. Over medium-low heat, stirring constantly, cook until mixture thickens, about 10 minutes. Do not allow mixture to boil or eggs may curdle. Remove pan from heat and stir in vanilla. Fold in coconut and pecans. Cover loosely with plastic wrap and chill for 10 minutes.

6. Spoon chilled frosting onto cooled brownies and spread evenly. Cover brownies loosely with plastic wrap and chill for 1 hour.

7. Use the foil to lift cooled brownies from pan and place on a cutting board. Cut into approximately $1\frac{3}{4}$- by $1\frac{1}{2}$-inch (4.5 by 4 cm) bars.

Layered Cream Cheese Brownies

Makes 36 brownies ● ● ●

A smooth cream cheese filling is layered between a brownie base and top for an elegant presentation.

Tips

Overheating chocolate can cause it to seize up and turn lumpy or develop a scorched taste. If chocolate overheats, it should not be used — it will give the cookies an unpleasant flavor.

Always use pure vanilla extract in brownies. Imitation vanilla is made from synthetic flavors and colors, and the taste cannot compare to pure vanilla extract.

Store brownies between layers of wax paper in a tightly sealed container. Baked goods such as cookies and brownies can be stored in a tightly sealed container at room temperature for up to 3 days. Baked goods containing cream cheese should be stored in the refrigerator.

- Preheat oven to 350°F (180°C)
- 9-inch (2.5 L) square baking pan, lined with foil, greased

Cream Cheese Filling

11 oz	cream cheese, softened	330 g
½ cup	granulated sugar	125 mL
1	egg	1
1½ tsp	vanilla extract	7 mL

Brownie Batter

3 oz	bittersweet chocolate, chopped	90 g
⅔ cup	unsalted butter, cut into pieces	150 mL
1⅓ cups	all-purpose flour	325 mL
¼ tsp	salt	1 mL
3	eggs	3
1⅓ cups	granulated sugar	325 mL
1 tsp	vanilla extract	5 mL

1. **Filling:** In a large bowl, using an electric mixer on medium speed, beat cream cheese and granulated sugar until smooth and creamy, about 2 minutes. Add egg and beat well. Beat in vanilla. Cover and set aside.

2. **Brownies:** In a large microwave-safe bowl, heat chocolate and butter in a microwave at Medium-High (75%) power for 1 minute. Stir chocolate until smooth. If necessary, heat at Medium (50%) power for 10 seconds at a time, stirring between each heating, just until chocolate is melted. Do not overheat. Cool for 5 minutes.

3. In a bowl, whisk together flour and salt until well combined. Set aside.

4. Using a wire whisk or large spoon, add eggs to warm chocolate mixture one at a time, beating well after each addition. Add granulated sugar and stir until well combined. Stir in vanilla. Scrape down sides of bowl. Gradually add flour mixture, stirring just until blended.

5. Spread half of brownie batter evenly into prepared pan. Carefully spread cream cheese filling evenly over brownie batter. Spoon remaining brownie batter over filling and spread batter evenly, completely covering filling.

6. Bake in preheated oven for 30 to 35 minutes or until a wooden pick inserted near the center comes out with a few moist crumbs. Let cool completely in baking pan on a wire rack.

7. Use the foil to lift cooled brownies from pan and place on a cutting board. Cut into 1½-inch (4 cm) squares.

Blue Ribbon Fudge Brownies

Makes 36 brownies ● ● ●

These prize-winning brownies are the perfect accompaniment to a cold glass of milk.

Tips

Always use unsweetened cocoa powder for baking. Don't use a cocoa drink mix or powdered ground chocolate. Both of these contain high amounts of sugar, and some contain powdered milk as well.

Baking powder and baking soda are not interchangeable. Always use the specific type and amount of leavener called for in the recipe.

Toasting nuts (see page 32) brings out their flavor and makes them crunchy.

Store brownies between layers of wax paper in a tightly sealed container. Brownies can be stored at room temperature for up to 3 days.

● **Preheat oven to 350°F (180°C)**
● **9-inch (2.5 L) square baking pan, lined with foil, greased**

2 oz	bittersweet chocolate, chopped	60 g
2 oz	sweet dark chocolate, chopped	60 g
½ cup	unsalted butter, softened	125 mL
¾ cup	all-purpose flour	175 mL
½ cup	unsweetened Dutch-process cocoa powder, sifted	125 mL
½ tsp	baking powder	2 mL
¼ tsp	salt	1 mL
1 cup	packed dark brown sugar	250 mL
½ cup	granulated sugar	125 mL
1	egg	1
¼ cup	vegetable oil	50 mL
¼ cup	water	50 mL
1 tbsp	vanilla extract	15 mL
¾ cup	chopped walnuts	175 mL

1. In a large microwave-safe bowl, heat bittersweet chocolate, sweet dark chocolate and butter in a microwave at Medium-High (75%) power for 1 minute. Stir chocolate until smooth. If necessary, heat at Medium (50%) power for 10 seconds at a time, stirring between each heating, just until chocolate is melted. Do not overheat. Cool for 5 minutes.

2. In a bowl, whisk together flour, cocoa powder, baking powder and salt until well combined. Set aside.

3. Using a wire whisk or large spoon, stir brown sugar and granulated sugar into warm chocolate mixture. Add egg and beat well. Gradually whisk in vegetable oil. Stir in water and vanilla. Scrape down sides of bowl. Gradually add flour mixture, stirring just until blended. Fold in walnuts. Spread batter evenly into prepared pan.

4. Bake in preheated oven for 28 to 32 minutes or until a wooden pick inserted near the center comes out with a few moist crumbs. Let cool completely in baking pan on a wire rack.

5. Use the foil to lift cooled brownies from pan and place on a cutting board. Cut into 1½-inch (4 cm) squares.

Espresso Brownies

Intense and fudgy, these decadent brownies are a coffee-lover's dream. They make the perfect treat with a hot cup of coffee for a morning or afternoon snack or even a late-night dessert.

Tips

Instant espresso powder can be found in the coffee aisle of most grocery stores.

Store brownies between layers of wax paper in a tightly sealed container. Brownies can be stored at room temperature for up to 3 days.

- Preheat oven to 350°F (180°C)
- 9-inch (2.5 L) square baking pan, lined with foil, greased

Brownies

4 oz	bittersweet chocolate, chopped	125 g
1/2 cup	unsalted butter, cut into pieces	125 mL
1/2 cup	all-purpose flour	125 mL
2/3 cup	unsweetened Dutch-process cocoa powder, sifted	150 mL
2 tsp	instant espresso powder	10 mL
1/2 tsp	baking powder	2 mL
1/4 tsp	salt	1 mL
1 1/3 cups	granulated sugar	325 mL
3	eggs	3
2 tsp	vanilla extract	10 mL

Frosting

1 tbsp	hot water	15 mL
3/4 tsp	instant espresso powder	3 mL
1 1/2 cups	confectioner's (powdered/icing) sugar	375 mL
2 tsp	half-and-half (10%) cream or milk	10 mL
1 1/2 tsp	unsalted butter, softened	7 mL

1. *Brownies:* In a large microwave-safe bowl, heat chocolate and butter in a microwave at Medium-High (75%) power for 1 minute. Stir chocolate until smooth. If necessary, heat at Medium (50%) power for 10 seconds at a time, stirring between each heating, just until chocolate is melted. Do not overheat. Cool for 5 minutes.

2. In a bowl, whisk together flour, cocoa powder, espresso powder, baking powder and salt until well combined. Set aside.

3. Using a wire whisk or large spoon, stir granulated sugar into warm chocolate mixture. Add eggs one at a time, beating well after each addition. Beat in vanilla. Scrape down sides of bowl. Gradually add flour mixture, stirring just until blended. Spread batter evenly into prepared pan.

4. Bake in preheated oven for 22 to 25 minutes or until a wooden pick inserted near the center comes out with a few moist crumbs. Let cool completely in baking pan on a wire rack.

5. Use the foil to lift cooled brownies from pan and place on a cutting board.

6. *Frosting:* In a small bowl, combine hot water and espresso powder. Stir until completely dissolved. Add confectioner's sugar, cream and butter and beat until smooth and fluffy. Spread frosting over cooled brownies. Let stand 20 minutes or until frosting is set. Cut into $1\frac{1}{2}$-inch (4 cm) squares.

Brownie Add-ins

You can vary the flavor and texture of brownies by adding a creative touch. Try adding one of these ingredients to your favorite brownie recipe.

- A variety of chopped nuts
- Chopped chocolate or chocolate chips
- Mint chips
- Peanut butter chips
- Butterscotch chips
- Toffee bits
- Caramel bits
- Chocolate candies
- Crushed peppermint candies
- Chopped chocolate mint candies
- Chopped dried fruits, such as apricots, cherries or dates

Classic Brownies

Makes about 42 brownies ● ● ●

This is one of my favorite recipes for a traditional brownie — rich, moist, chewy and chocolaty. The walnuts add a nice crunch but may be omitted if you prefer your brownies without nuts.

Tips

For fudgy brownies, bake for the lesser amount of time. For cake-like brownies, bake for the longer amount of time and until the brownies spring back when lightly pressed in the center.

Store brownies between layers of wax paper in a tightly sealed container. Brownies can be stored at room temperature for up to 3 days.

- Preheat oven to 350°F (180°C)
- 13- by 9-inch (3 L) baking pan, lined with foil, greased

1¾ cups	all-purpose flour	425 mL
¼ cup	unsweetened Dutch-process cocoa powder, sifted	50 mL
7 oz	bittersweet chocolate, chopped	210 g
¾ cup	unsalted butter, softened	175 mL
5	eggs	5
⅓ cup	vegetable oil	75 mL
1⅓ cups	granulated sugar	325 mL
1 cup	packed light brown sugar	250 mL
2 tsp	vanilla extract	10 mL
⅔ cup	chopped walnuts	150 mL

1. In a bowl, whisk together flour and cocoa powder until well combined. Set aside.

2. In a microwave-safe bowl, heat chocolate and butter in a microwave at Medium-High (75%) power for 1 minute. Stir chocolate until smooth. If necessary, heat chocolate at Medium (50%) power for 10 seconds at a time, stirring between each heating, just until chocolate is melted. Do not overheat. Set aside.

3. In a large bowl, using an electric mixer on medium speed, lightly beat eggs. Gradually beat in vegetable oil. Add granulated sugar and brown sugar and beat until light and fluffy, about 2 minutes. Beat in vanilla. With mixer running on low, gradually beat in melted chocolate. Scrape down sides of bowl. On low speed or using a wooden spoon, gradually add flour mixture, beating just until blended. By hand, fold in walnuts. Spread batter evenly into prepared pan.

4. Bake in preheated oven for 30 to 35 minutes or until a wooden pick inserted near the center comes out clean. Let cool completely in baking pan on a wire rack.

5. Use the foil to lift cooled brownies from pan and place on a cutting board. Cut into approximately 1¾- by 1½-inch (4.5 by 4 cm) bars.

Marbled White Chocolate Cream Cheese Brownies

Makes 36 brownies

These heavenly cream cheese brownies, with swirls of raspberry jam, are sure to satisfy white chocolate fans.

Tips

White chocolate should not be melted in the microwave as it can easily burn and turn lumpy if overheated.

Don't be concerned if the butter separates from the white chocolate. Simply stir the butter back into the white chocolate before adding it to the egg mixture.

Store brownies between layers of wax paper in a tightly sealed container. Brownies can be stored in the refrigerator for up to 3 days.

- Preheat oven to 350°F (180°C)
- 9-inch (2.5 L) square baking pan, lined with foil, greased

1¼ cups	all-purpose flour	300 mL
¼ tsp	baking powder	1 mL
¼ tsp	salt	1 mL
⅓ cup	unsalted butter, softened	75 mL
6 oz	white chocolate, finely chopped	175 g
4 oz	cream cheese, softened	125 g
½ cup	granulated sugar	125 mL
3	eggs	3
1 tsp	vanilla extract	5 mL
⅓ cup	seedless raspberry jam	75 mL

1. In a bowl, whisk together flour, baking powder and salt until well combined. Set aside.

2. In a microwave-safe bowl, heat butter in a microwave at Medium-High (75%) power just until melted and hot. Add white chocolate and stir until chocolate is completely melted and mixture is smooth. Set aside.

3. In a large bowl, using an electric mixer on medium speed, beat cream cheese and granulated sugar until smooth and creamy, about 2 minutes. Add eggs one at a time, beating well after each addition. Beat in vanilla. With mixer running on low, gradually beat in melted white chocolate mixture until well combined. Scrape down sides of bowl. On low speed or using a wooden spoon, gradually add flour mixture, beating just until blended. Spread batter evenly into prepared pan.

4. Stir raspberry jam until loosened and spreadable. Drop small spoonfuls of jam over brownie layer. Using a knife, gently swirl the jam into the batter, drawing the knife from one side of the pan to the other to create a marbled effect.

5. Bake in preheated oven for 25 to 30 minutes or until a wooden pick inserted near the center comes out clean. Let cool completely in baking pan on a wire rack.

6. Use the foil to lift cooled brownies from pan and place on a cutting board. Cut into 1½-inch (4 cm) squares.

Chocolate-Lover's Brownies

Makes 36 brownies ● ● ●

Sweet dark chocolate adds a special richness to these decadent, fudgy brownies.

Tips

If you don't have sweet dark chocolate, bittersweet chocolate may be used instead. If using bittersweet chocolate, increase brown sugar to 1⅓ cups (325 mL).

Store brownies between layers of wax paper in a tightly sealed container. Brownies can be stored at room temperature for up to 3 days.

- Preheat oven to 350°F (180°C)
- 9-inch (2.5 L) square baking pan, lined with foil, greased

Brownies

1 cup	all-purpose flour	250 mL
¼ cup	unsweetened Dutch-process cocoa powder, sifted	50 mL
¼ tsp	salt	1 mL
10 oz	sweet dark chocolate, chopped	300 g
¼ cup	unsalted butter, softened	50 mL
3	eggs	3
1 cup	packed light brown sugar	250 mL
2 tsp	vanilla extract	10 mL
1 cup	chopped semisweet chocolate or semisweet chocolate chips	250 mL

Icing

2 oz	sweet dark chocolate, chopped	60 g
1 tsp	vegetable shortening	5 mL

1. ***Brownies:*** In a bowl, whisk together flour, cocoa powder and salt until well combined. Set aside.

2. In a microwave-safe bowl, heat sweet dark chocolate and butter in a microwave at Medium-High (75%) power for 1 minute. Stir chocolate until smooth. If necessary, heat chocolate at Medium (50%) power for 10 seconds at a time, stirring between each heating, just until chocolate is melted. Do not overheat. Set aside.

3. In a large bowl, using an electric mixer on medium speed, lightly beat eggs. Add brown sugar and beat until light and fluffy, about 2 minutes. Beat in vanilla. With mixer running on low, gradually beat in melted chocolate. Scrape down sides of bowl. On low speed or using a wooden spoon, gradually add flour mixture, beating just until blended. By hand, fold in chopped semisweet chocolate. Spread batter evenly into prepared pan.

4. Bake in preheated oven for 30 to 35 minutes or until a wooden pick inserted near the center comes out with a few moist crumbs. Let cool completely in baking pan on a wire rack.

5. Use the foil to lift cooled brownies from pan and place on a cutting board.

Tip

Chocolate can be melted in the top of a double boiler placed over simmering water. Stir frequently, until chocolate is completely melted and mixture is smooth. Cool to desired consistency.

6. *Icing:* In a microwave-safe zippered storage bag, combine sweet dark chocolate and vegetable shortening. Microwave on Medium-High (75%) power for 30 seconds. Knead bag until completely combined and smooth, microwaving an additional 5 seconds at a time as needed to fully melt chocolate. Cut off a small corner of bag and drizzle chocolate over brownies. Let stand 20 minutes or until icing is set. Cut into $1\frac{1}{2}$-inch (4 cm) squares.

Amaretto Brownies

● ● ●

Flavored with amaretto and filled with chopped almonds, these lovely brownies have a delightful almond aroma.

Tips

Amaretto is an Italian liqueur with a pleasant almond flavor.

Dutch-process cocoa powder is a refined cocoa treated with a small amount of an alkali solution to neutralize the natural acids. This process improves the flavor and color of the cocoa.

Store brownies in a single layer in a tightly sealed container. Brownies can be stored at room temperature for up to 3 days.

- Preheat oven to 350°F (180°C)
- 9-inch (2.5 L) square baking pan, lined with foil, greased

Brownies

¾ cup	all-purpose flour	175 mL
⅓ cup	unsweetened Dutch-process cocoa powder	75 mL
¼ tsp	baking soda	1 mL
¼ tsp	salt	1 mL
1 cup	unsalted butter, softened	250 mL
¾ cup	granulated sugar	175 mL
½ cup	packed light brown sugar	125 mL
3	eggs	3
3 tbsp	amaretto liqueur	45 mL
¾ cup	chopped unsalted almonds	175 mL

Frosting

2 cups	confectioner's (powdered/icing) sugar	500 mL
2 tbsp	unsweetened Dutch-process cocoa powder	25 mL
⅓ cup	unsalted butter, softened	75 mL
1½ tbsp	half-and-half (10%) cream or milk	22 mL
1 tbsp	amaretto liqueur	15 mL

1. **Brownies:** In a bowl, whisk together flour, cocoa powder, baking soda and salt until well combined. Set aside.
2. In a large bowl, using an electric mixer on medium speed, cream butter, granulated sugar and brown sugar until light and fluffy, about 2 minutes. Add eggs one at a time, beating well after each addition. Scrape down sides of bowl. On low speed or using a wooden spoon, gradually add flour mixture, alternating with amaretto, stirring after each addition just until blended. By hand, fold in almonds. Spread batter evenly into prepared pan.
3. Bake in preheated oven for 22 to 26 minutes or until a wooden pick inserted near the center comes out with a few moist crumbs. Let cool completely in baking pan on a wire rack.
4. Use the foil to lift cooled brownies from pan and place on a cutting board.
5. **Frosting:** In a bowl, whisk together confectioner's sugar and cocoa powder. Set aside. In a large bowl, using an electric mixer on medium speed, beat butter until smooth. Gradually beat in confectioner's sugar mixture, alternating with cream and amaretto. Beat until light and fluffy, about 3 minutes. Spread frosting over cooled brownies. Let stand 20 minutes or until frosting is set. Cut into 1½-inch (4 cm) squares.

Sour Cream Brownies

These brownies are thick, chewy and chocolaty.

Tips

Unsalted butter is the best choice for baked goods. It has a fresh, sweet cream flavor that adds immeasurably to the overall taste of the brownies. Because butter adds so much flavor, always choose a high-quality unsalted butter for baking.

For thin brownies, bake in a 13- by 9-inch (3 L) metal baking pan for 18 to 22 minutes or until a wooden pick inserted near the center comes out with a few moist crumbs.

Store brownies between layers of wax paper in a tightly sealed container. Brownies can be stored at room temperature for up to 3 days.

- Preheat oven to 350°F (180°C)
- 9-inch (2.5 L) square baking pan, lined with foil, greased

1 cup	all-purpose flour	250 mL
1/2 cup	unsweetened Dutch-process cocoa powder, sifted	125 mL
1/4 tsp	baking powder	1 mL
1/4 tsp	salt	1 mL
3 oz	bittersweet chocolate, chopped	90 g
1/3 cup	unsalted butter, cut into pieces	75 mL
2	eggs	2
1 1/4 cups	granulated sugar	300 mL
2/3 cup	sour cream	150 mL
1 tsp	vanilla extract	5 mL
1/2 cup	chopped pecans	125 mL

1. In a bowl, whisk together flour, cocoa powder, baking powder and salt until well combined. Set aside.

2. In a microwave-safe bowl, heat chocolate and butter in a microwave at Medium-High (75%) power for 1 minute. Stir chocolate until smooth. If necessary, heat chocolate at Medium (50%) power for 10 seconds at a time, stirring between each heating, just until chocolate is melted. Do not overheat. Set aside.

3. In a large bowl, using an electric mixer on medium speed, lightly beat eggs. Add granulated sugar and beat until light and fluffy, about 2 minutes. Beat in sour cream and vanilla. With mixer running on low, gradually beat in melted chocolate. Scrape down sides of bowl. On low speed or using a wooden spoon, gradually add flour mixture, beating just until blended. By hand, fold in pecans. Spread batter evenly into prepared pan.

4. Bake in preheated oven for 25 to 30 minutes or until a wooden pick inserted near the center comes out with a few moist crumbs. Let cool completely in baking pan on a wire rack.

5. Use the foil to lift cooled brownies from pan and place on a cutting board. Cut into 1 1/2-inch (4 cm) squares.

Peanut Butter Swirl Brownies

Combining chocolate and peanut butter makes for a winning brownie. These have a pretty appearance and a great blend of flavors.

Tips

Lightly coat the measuring cup with nonstick cooking spray to make it easier to remove the peanut butter after measuring.

Store brownies between layers of wax paper in a tightly sealed container. Brownies can be stored in the refrigerator for up to 3 days.

- Preheat oven to 350°F (180°C)
- 13- by 9-inch (3 L) baking pan, lined with foil, greased

Peanut Butter Filling

6 oz	cream cheese, softened	175 g
2/3 cup	creamy peanut butter	150 mL
1/3 cup	granulated sugar	75 mL
2	eggs	2
1/2 tsp	vanilla extract	2 mL

Brownie Batter

5 oz	bittersweet chocolate, chopped	150 g
3/4 cup	unsalted butter, cut into pieces	175 mL
1 1/3 cups	all-purpose flour	325 mL
1/2 tsp	baking powder	2 mL
1/4 tsp	salt	1 mL
3	eggs	3
1 1/3 cups	granulated sugar	325 mL
2 tsp	vanilla extract	10 mL

1. *Filling:* In a large bowl, using an electric mixer on medium speed, beat cream cheese, peanut butter and granulated sugar until smooth and creamy, about 2 minutes. Add eggs one at a time, beating well after each addition. Beat in vanilla. Cover and set aside.

2. *Brownies:* In a large microwave-safe bowl, heat chocolate and butter in a microwave at Medium-High (75%) power for 1 minute. Stir chocolate until smooth. If necessary, heat at Medium (50%) power for 10 seconds at a time, stirring between each heating, just until chocolate is melted. Do not overheat. Cool for 5 minutes.

3. In a bowl, whisk together flour, baking powder and salt until well combined. Set aside.

4. Using a wire whisk or large spoon, add eggs to warm chocolate mixture one at a time, beating well after each addition. Add granulated sugar and stir until well combined. Stir in vanilla. Scrape down sides of bowl. Gradually add flour mixture, beating just until blended.

Tip

Never store chocolate in the refrigerator or freezer. When melted, moisture on the chocolate will cause it to harden into lumps. It will not melt smoothly and will be unusable for baking.

5. Spread two-thirds of brownie batter evenly into prepared pan. Carefully spread peanut butter filling evenly over brownie batter. Place small spoonfuls of remaining brownie batter over filling. Insert a knife halfway down through filling. Draw the knife in a swirl pattern to create a marbled effect.

6. Bake in preheated oven for 30 to 35 minutes or until a wooden pick inserted near the center comes out with a few moist crumbs. Let cool completely in baking pan on a wire rack.

7. Use the foil to lift cooled brownies from pan and place on a cutting board. Cut into approximately $1\frac{3}{4}$- by $1\frac{1}{2}$-inch (4.5 by 4 cm) bars.

Creative Gift Idea

Do you have a handyman around the house who deserves special recognition for all the wonderful things he does to make your house a home? Or, perhaps, a neighbor or friend who is always willing to lend a hand to fix a leaky pipe or solve a problem?

Reward your special hero with a toolbox full of fresh-baked brownies! Line a small toolbox with colorful napkins, either cloth or paper, and fill it with individually wrapped brownies or packages of a few brownies wrapped together. You can wrap up a variety of different brownies or fill the box with one kind of brownie.

Fudgy Brownies

Makes about 42 brownies ●●●

Loaded with lots of bittersweet chocolate, these brownies are very rich.

Tips

Chocolate can develop a harmless, powdery coating called bloom. When stored in a warm or humid location, a small amount of cocoa butter can separate from the chocolate. This cocoa butter bloom is harmless and will reincorporate back into the chocolate when it is melted. To prevent bloom, store chocolate in a cool, dry place.

Store brownies between layers of wax paper in a tightly sealed container. Brownies can be stored at room temperature for up to 3 days. These moist brownies freeze very well.

Variation

For a less intense brownie, substitute semisweet chocolate for both the melted bittersweet chocolate in the batter and the bittersweet chocolate pieces folded into the batter along with the walnuts.

● Preheat oven to 375°F (190°C)
● 13- by 9-inch (3 L) baking pan, lined with foil, greased

8 oz	bittersweet chocolate, chopped	250 g
1 cup	unsalted butter, cut into pieces	250 mL
2 cups	all-purpose flour	500 mL
¼ tsp	salt	1 mL
1½ cups	granulated sugar	375 mL
¾ cup	packed dark brown sugar	175 mL
4	eggs	4
1½ tsp	vanilla extract	7 mL
1 cup	chopped bittersweet chocolate or bittersweet chocolate chips	250 mL
1 cup	chopped walnuts	250 mL

1. In a large microwave-safe bowl, heat chocolate and butter in a microwave at Medium-High (75%) power for 1 minute. Stir chocolate until smooth. If necessary, heat at Medium (50%) power for 10 seconds at a time, stirring between each heating, just until chocolate is melted. Do not overheat. Cool for 5 minutes.

2. In a bowl, whisk together flour and salt until well combined. Set aside.

3. Using a wire whisk or large spoon, stir granulated sugar and brown sugar into warm chocolate mixture. Add eggs one at a time, beating well after each addition. Beat in vanilla. Scrape down sides of bowl. Gradually add flour mixture, stirring just until blended. Fold in chopped chocolate and walnuts. Spread batter evenly into prepared pan.

4. Bake in preheated oven for 35 to 40 minutes or until a wooden pick inserted near the center comes out with a few moist crumbs. Let cool completely in baking pan on a wire rack.

5. Use the foil to lift cooled brownies from pan and place on a cutting board. Cut into approximately 1¾- by 1½-inch (4.5 by 4 cm) bars.

Cream Cheese Brownies

Cream cheese gives these brownies a luxurious flavor and texture.

Tips

For an extra-special touch, cover the cooled brownies with a cream cheese frosting (see page 211). Store frosted brownies in the refrigerator.

Store brownies between layers of wax paper in a tightly sealed container. Unfrosted brownies can be stored at room temperature for up to 3 days.

- **Preheat oven to 350°F (180°C)**
- **9-inch (2.5 L) square baking pan, lined with foil, greased**

1 cup	all-purpose flour	250 mL
1/4 tsp	baking powder	1 mL
1/4 tsp	salt	1 mL
4 oz	bittersweet chocolate, chopped	125 g
6 tbsp	unsalted butter, softened	90 mL
4 oz	cream cheese	125 g
1 cup	granulated sugar	250 mL
3	eggs	3
2 tsp	vanilla extract	10 mL
1/2 tsp	almond extract	2 mL
1/2 cup	chopped unsalted almonds	125 mL

1. In a bowl, whisk together flour, baking powder and salt until well combined. Set aside.

2. In a microwave-safe bowl, heat chocolate in a microwave at Medium-High (75%) power for 1 minute. Stir chocolate until smooth. If necessary, heat chocolate at Medium (50%) power for 10 seconds at a time, stirring between each heating, just until chocolate is melted. Do not overheat. Set aside.

3. In a large bowl, using an electric mixer on medium speed, cream butter, cream cheese and granulated sugar until light and fluffy, about 3 minutes. Add eggs one at a time, beating well after each addition. Beat in vanilla and almond extract. With mixer running on low, gradually beat in melted chocolate. Scrape down sides of bowl. On low speed or using a wooden spoon, gradually add flour mixture, beating just until blended. By hand, fold in almonds. Spread batter evenly into prepared pan.

4. Bake in preheated oven for 25 to 30 minutes or until a wooden pick inserted near the center comes out with a few moist crumbs. Let cool completely in baking pan on a wire rack.

5. Use the foil to lift cooled brownies from pan and place on a cutting board. Cut into 1 1/2-inch (4 cm) squares.

Mint Brownies

● ● ●

These cool, creamy, minty brownies are great by themselves or with a hot cup of coffee or glass of cold milk.

Tips

A few drops of green food coloring added to the mint filling lends a festive touch during the holidays or for a special treat on St. Patrick's Day.

Only use butter in stick or brick form for baking. Not only is it easy to measure, but stick butter contains a higher fat content that allows the butter to hold its shape. Butter sold in tubs has a higher ratio of water or air than stick butter and will significantly alter the texture of baked goods.

Store brownies between layers of wax paper in a tightly sealed container. Brownies can be stored in the refrigerator for up to 3 days.

● **Preheat oven to 350°F (180°C)**
● **9-inch (2.5 L) square baking pan, lined with foil, greased**

Brownie Batter

3 oz	bittersweet chocolate, chopped	90 g
1/2 cup	unsalted butter, cut into pieces	125 mL
1 cup	all-purpose flour	250 mL
1/4 tsp	baking powder	1 mL
1/4 tsp	salt	1 mL
2	eggs	2
1 cup	granulated sugar	250 mL
1/2 tsp	vanilla extract	2 mL

Mint Filling

3 oz	cream cheese, softened	90 g
3 tbsp	unsalted butter, softened	45 mL
1/4 tsp	mint extract	1 mL
2 cups	confectioner's (powdered/icing) sugar	500 mL

Chocolate Glaze

2 oz	bittersweet chocolate, coarsely chopped	60 mL
1 tbsp	unsalted butter	15 mL
2 tbsp	confectioner's (powdered/icing) sugar	25 mL

1. ***Brownies:*** In a large microwave-safe bowl, heat chocolate and butter in a microwave at Medium-High (75%) power for 1 minute. Stir chocolate until smooth. If necessary, heat at Medium (50%) power for 10 seconds at a time, stirring between each heating, just until chocolate is melted. Do not overheat. Cool for 5 minutes.

2. In a bowl, whisk together flour, baking powder and salt until well combined. Set aside.

3. Using a wire whisk or large spoon, add eggs to warm chocolate mixture one at a time, beating well after each addition. Add granulated sugar and stir until well combined. Stir in vanilla. Scrape down sides of bowl. Gradually add flour mixture, stirring just until blended.

4. Spread brownie batter evenly into prepared pan.

5. Bake in preheated oven for 20 to 25 minutes or until a wooden pick inserted near the center comes out with a few moist crumbs. Let cool completely in baking pan on a wire rack.

Tip

Chilling the brownies first makes them easier to cut and hold their shape.

6. *Filling:* In a large bowl, using an electric mixer on medium speed, beat cream cheese and butter until well blended. Beat in mint extract. Gradually beat in confectioner's sugar until smooth and creamy, about 2 minutes. Spread mint filling evenly over cooled brownies.

7. *Glaze:* In a small microwave-safe bowl, heat chocolate and butter in a microwave at Medium-High (75%) power for 30 seconds. Stir chocolate until smooth. If necessary, heat at Medium (50%) power for 10 seconds at a time, stirring between each heating, just until chocolate is melted. Do not overheat. Whisk in confectioner's sugar until smooth. Drizzle over mint filling. Chill brownies for 1 hour before cutting.

8. Use the foil to lift cooled brownies from pan and place on a cutting board. Cut into 1½-inch (4 cm) squares.

Walnut Brownies

● ● ●

These yummy brownies are loaded with lots of crunchy walnuts.

Tips

Nuts can turn rancid quickly. If you're not going to use them within a couple of weeks of purchase, tightly wrap the nuts and store them in the freezer to preserve their flavor.

Store brownies between layers of wax paper in a tightly sealed container.

● **Preheat oven to 350°F (180°C)**
● **13- by 9-inch (3 L) baking pan, lined with foil, greased**

¾ cup	all-purpose flour	175 mL
¾ cup	unsweetened Dutch-process cocoa powder, sifted	175 mL
½ tsp	baking powder	2 mL
¼ tsp	salt	1 mL
1 cup	unsalted butter, softened	250 mL
1 cup	granulated sugar	250 mL
1 cup	packed light brown sugar	250 mL
4	eggs	4
1 tsp	vanilla extract	5 mL
1½ cups	chopped walnuts	375 mL

1. In a bowl, whisk together flour, cocoa powder, baking powder and salt until well combined. Set aside.

2. In a large bowl, using an electric mixer on medium speed, cream butter, granulated sugar and brown sugar until light and fluffy, about 2 minutes. Add eggs one at a time, beating well after each addition. Beat in vanilla. Scrape down sides of bowl. On low speed or using a wooden spoon, gradually add flour mixture, beating just until blended. By hand, fold in walnuts. Spread batter evenly into prepared pan.

3. Bake in preheated oven for 25 to 30 minutes or until a wooden pick inserted near the center comes out with a few moist crumbs. Let cool completely in baking pan on a wire rack.

4. Use the foil to lift cooled brownies from pan and place on a cutting board. Cut into approximately 1¾- by 1½-inch (4.5 by 4 cm) bars.

Double Chocolate Brownies

Two types of chocolate — sweet dark chocolate and cocoa powder — give these brownies a double punch of flavor.

Tips

Always use pure vanilla extract in cookies. Imitation vanilla is made from synthetic flavors and colors, and the taste cannot compare to pure vanilla extract.

Store brownies between layers of wax paper in a tightly sealed container.

- **Preheat oven to 350°F (180°C)**
- **13- by 9-inch (3 L) baking pan, lined with foil, greased**

5 oz	sweet dark chocolate, chopped	150 g
2/3 cup	unsalted butter, cut into pieces	150 mL
2/3 cup	unsweetened Dutch-process cocoa powder, sifted	150 mL
1/2 cup	all-purpose flour	125 mL
2 cups	granulated sugar	500 mL
4	eggs	4
1 tbsp	vanilla extract	15 mL
1/2 cup	chopped sweet dark chocolate or sweet dark chocolate chips	125 mL
1/2 cup	chopped walnuts	125 mL
	Confectioner's (powdered/icing) sugar	

1. In a large microwave-safe bowl, heat chocolate and butter in a microwave at Medium-High (75%) power for 1 minute. Stir chocolate until smooth. If necessary, heat at Medium (50%) power for 10 seconds at a time, stirring between each heating, just until chocolate is melted. Do not overheat. Cool for 5 minutes.

2. In a bowl, whisk together cocoa powder and flour until well combined. Set aside.

3. Using a wire whisk or large spoon, stir granulated sugar into warm chocolate mixture. Add eggs one at a time, beating well after each addition. Beat in vanilla. Scrape down sides of bowl. Gradually add flour mixture, stirring just until blended. Fold in chopped chocolate and walnuts. Spread batter evenly into prepared pan.

4. Bake in preheated oven for 25 to 30 minutes or until a wooden pick inserted near the center comes out with a few moist crumbs. Let cool completely in baking pan on a wire rack.

5. Use the foil to lift cooled brownies from pan and place on a cutting board. Dust with confectioner's sugar. Cut into approximately 1 3/4- by 1 1/2-inch (4.5 by 4 cm) bars.

Rocky Road Brownies

Makes about 42 brownies

The classic combination of flavors in these wonderful brownies is a variation of the popular ice cream flavor.

Tips

Marshmallows melt quickly in the oven, so watch the baking time carefully after adding the topping.

Fold in the chocolate and nuts by hand to keep from overworking the dough after the flour is mixed in. Overworking the dough will make the cookies tough.

Store brownies between layers of wax paper in a tightly sealed container.

- Preheat oven to 350°F (180°C)
- 13- by 9-inch (3 L) baking pan, lined with foil, greased

Brownies

¾ cup	all-purpose flour	175 mL
1 tbsp	unsweetened Dutch-process cocoa powder, sifted	15 mL
¼ tsp	baking powder	1 mL
¼ tsp	salt	1 mL
3 oz	bittersweet chocolate, chopped	90 g
½ cup	unsalted butter, softened	125 mL
3	eggs	3
¾ cup	granulated sugar	175 mL
1 tsp	vanilla extract	5 mL
½ cup	semisweet chocolate chips	125 mL
½ cup	chopped walnuts	125 mL

Topping

1 cup	miniature marshmallows	250 mL
¾ cup	semisweet chocolate chips	175 mL
¾ cup	chopped walnuts	175 mL

1. **Brownies:** In a bowl, whisk together flour, cocoa powder, baking powder and salt until well combined. Set aside.

2. In a microwave-safe bowl, heat chocolate and butter in a microwave at Medium-High (75%) power for 1 minute. Stir chocolate until smooth. If necessary, heat chocolate at Medium (50%) power for 10 seconds at a time, stirring between each heating, just until chocolate is melted. Do not overheat. Set aside.

3. In a large bowl, using an electric mixer on medium speed, lightly beat eggs. Add granulated sugar and beat until light and fluffy, about 2 minutes. Beat in vanilla. With mixer running on low, gradually beat in melted chocolate. Scrape down sides of bowl. On low speed or using a wooden spoon, gradually add flour mixture, beating just until blended. By hand, fold in chocolate chips and walnuts. Spread batter evenly into prepared pan.

4. Bake in preheated oven for 15 to 18 minutes or until a wooden pick inserted near the center comes out with a few moist crumbs.

Brownies, Brownies and More Brownies

Tip

Peanuts or pecans are also good in this brownie in place of the walnuts.

5. *Topping:* Sprinkle marshmallows, chocolate chips and walnuts over hot brownies. Return pan to oven and bake for 2 minutes. Let cool completely in baking pan on a wire rack.

6. Use the foil to lift cooled brownies from pan and place on a cutting board. Cut into approximately $1\frac{3}{4}$- by $1\frac{1}{2}$-inch (4.5 by 4 cm) bars.

Brownie Sundaes

For a really great dessert, serve brownie sundaes! They are a perfect ending to a warm summer day.

Cut your favorite brownies into large squares and place each on a dessert plate or in a bowl. Top with a generous scoop of vanilla ice cream. (You can also use chocolate, strawberry, chocolate chip or butter pecan ice cream.) Drizzle with warm fudge sauce and adorn with chopped nuts, mini chocolate chips or candy sprinkles, if you desire. Finish it off with a dollop of whipped cream for a grand presentation. Serve immediately and enjoy!

Coconut Macaroon Brownies

Makes about 42 brownies ● ● ●

A chewy coconut layer nestled between the chocolate brownie layers make this treat a big hit with coconut fans.

Tips

Sweetened condensed milk is sold by weight in the U.S. and by volume in Canada. A U.S. 14-oz can contains 1⅓ cups (325 mL).

For best results, use the pan size and shape called for in the recipe. If you use a different pan, you will need to adjust the baking time to reduce the chance of burning or undercooking.

Store brownies between layers of wax paper in a tightly sealed container. Brownies can be stored in the refrigerator for up to 3 days.

- Preheat oven to 350°F (180°C)
- 13- by 9-inch (3 L) baking pan, lined with foil, greased

Coconut Filling

3	egg yolks	3
1⅓ cups	sweetened condensed milk	325 mL
½ tsp	vanilla extract	2 mL
2½ cups	sweetened flaked coconut, coarsely chopped	625 mL

Brownie Batter

6 oz	bittersweet chocolate, chopped	175 g
1 cup	unsalted butter, cut into pieces	250 mL
1½ cups	all-purpose flour	375 mL
¼ tsp	baking powder	1 mL
¼ tsp	salt	1 mL
5	eggs	5
1¾ cups	granulated sugar	425 mL
1½ tsp	vanilla extract	7 mL

1. **Filling:** In a bowl, using a wire whisk, lightly beat egg yolks. Gradually whisk in sweetened condensed milk until well blended. Stir in vanilla. Fold in coconut. Cover and set aside.

2. **Brownies:** In a large microwave-safe bowl, heat chocolate and butter in a microwave at Medium-High (75%) power for 1 minute. Stir chocolate until smooth. If necessary, heat at Medium (50%) power for 10 seconds at a time, stirring between each heating, just until chocolate is melted. Do not overheat. Cool for 5 minutes.

3. In a bowl, whisk together flour, baking powder and salt until well combined. Set aside.

4. Using a wire whisk or large spoon, add eggs to warm chocolate mixture one at a time, beating well after each addition. Add granulated sugar and stir until well combined. Beat in vanilla. Scrape down sides of bowl. Gradually add flour mixture, stirring just until blended.

5. Spread two-thirds of brownie batter evenly into prepared pan. Spoon coconut filling over brownie batter and carefully spread evenly. Spoon remaining brownie batter over filling and carefully spread batter evenly, completely covering filling.

6. Bake in preheated oven for 28 to 34 minutes or until a wooden pick inserted near the center comes out with a few moist crumbs. Let cool completely in baking pan on a wire rack.

7. Use the foil to lift cooled brownies from pan. Cut into approximately 1¾- by 1½-inch (4.5 by 4 cm) bars.

Raspberry Brownies

● ● ●

You can't go wrong with the pairing of raspberries and chocolate.

Tips

It's okay if small spots of jam show through the top layer of brownie batter.

Avoid overmixing brownie batter. Overmixing will develop the gluten in the flour and make the brownies tough and hard.

Store brownies between layers of wax paper in a tightly sealed container.

● **Preheat oven to 350°F (180°C)**
● **9-inch (2.5 L) square baking pan, lined with foil, greased**

Brownie Batter

4 oz	bittersweet chocolate, chopped	125 g
2/3 cup	unsalted butter, cut into pieces	150 mL
1 cup	all-purpose flour	250 mL
1/4 tsp	baking powder	1 mL
1/4 tsp	salt	1 mL
1 1/4 cups	granulated sugar	300 mL
3	eggs	3
1/2 cup	seedless raspberry jam	125 mL
1/2 tsp	vanilla extract	2 mL

Filling

2/3 cup	seedless raspberry jam	150 mL

1. *Brownies:* In a large microwave-safe bowl, heat chocolate and butter in a microwave at Medium-High (75%) power for 1 minute. Stir chocolate until smooth. If necessary, heat at Medium (50%) power for 10 seconds at a time, stirring between each heating, just until chocolate is melted. Do not overheat. Cool for 5 minutes.

2. In a bowl, whisk together flour, baking powder and salt until well combined. Set aside.

3. Using a wire whisk or large spoon, stir granulated sugar into warm chocolate mixture. Add eggs one at a time, beating well after each addition. Beat in raspberry jam and vanilla. Scrape down sides of bowl. Gradually add flour mixture, stirring just until blended. Spread two-thirds of batter evenly into prepared pan.

4. *Filling:* Stir raspberry jam until loosened and spreadable. Spoon jam over brownie layer and spread smooth. Spoon remaining brownie batter over jam and spread evenly.

5. Bake in preheated oven for 25 to 30 minutes or until a wooden pick inserted near the center comes out with a few moist crumbs. Let cool completely in baking pan on a wire rack.

6. Use the foil to lift cooled brownies from pan and place on a cutting board. Cut into 1 1/2-inch (4 cm) squares.

Chocolate Malt Brownies

This brownie is a big hit with people who love the flavor of malted milk.

Tips

Malted milk powder is available at most major supermarkets. Look for it alongside the powdered chocolate drink mixes and packaged hot cocoa mixes.

Store brownies between layers of wax paper in a tightly sealed container. Brownies can be stored at room temperature for up to 3 days.

● **Preheat oven to 350°F (180°C)**
● **9-inch (2.5 L) square baking pan, lined with foil, greased**

Brownies

1 cup	all-purpose flour	250 mL
2/3 cup	malted milk powder	150 mL
1/4 tsp	baking powder	1 mL
1/4 tsp	salt	1 mL
4 oz	bittersweet chocolate, chopped	125 g
1/2 cup	unsalted butter, softened	125 mL
1 cup	granulated sugar	250 mL
2	eggs	2
1 tsp	vanilla extract	5 mL
1/2 cup	chopped pecans	125 mL

Frosting

1 1/4 cups	confectioner's (powdered/icing) sugar	300 mL
1/4 cup	malted milk powder	50 mL
2 tbsp	unsalted butter, softened	25 mL
2 tbsp	half-and-half (10%) cream or milk	25 mL
1/4 tsp	vanilla extract	1 mL

1. **Brownies:** In a bowl, whisk together flour, malted milk powder, baking powder and salt until well combined. Set aside.

2. In a microwave-safe bowl, heat chocolate in a microwave at Medium-High (75%) power for 1 minute. Stir chocolate until smooth. If necessary, heat chocolate at Medium (50%) power for 10 seconds at a time, stirring between each heating, just until chocolate is melted. Do not overheat. Set aside.

3. In a large bowl, using an electric mixer on medium speed, cream butter and granulated sugar until light and fluffy, about 2 minutes. Add eggs one at a time, beating well after each addition. Beat in vanilla. With mixer running on low, gradually beat in melted chocolate. Scrape down sides of bowl. On low speed or using a wooden spoon, gradually add flour mixture, beating just until blended. By hand, fold in pecans. Spread batter evenly into prepared pan.

4. Bake in preheated oven for 24 to 28 minutes or until a wooden pick inserted near the center comes out with a few moist crumbs. Let cool completely in baking pan on a wire rack.

Tip

Lining the baking pan with foil makes it much easier to remove the brownies from the pan after baking and protects the pan from damage from knife cuts. It also makes cleanup a breeze.

5. Use the foil to lift cooled brownies from pan and place on a cutting board.

6. *Frosting:* In a bowl, combine confectioner's sugar and malted milk powder until well blended. Add butter, cream and vanilla. Using an electric mixer on medium speed, beat until frosting is smooth and spreadable. Spread frosting over cooled brownies. Let stand 20 minutes or until frosting is set. Cut into $1\frac{1}{2}$-inch (4 cm) squares.

Giving It All Away

If you're planning to give away a whole pan of uncut brownies to neighbors or to sell them at the community bake sale, try this trick: bake the brownies in a disposable foil pan. This works really well with brownies designed to be baked in a square pan.

Purchase a package of square foil baking pans that will fit into your regular square baking pan. Grease the foil pan with nonstick cooking spray, slip the foil pan into your own baking pan and fill it with the brownie batter. Bake the brownies according to the recipe directions, adding a few extra minutes to the baking time, if necessary. Let cool completely and wrap the foil pan for your event.

If the foil pan does not fit into your regular square pan, you can double-stack the foil pans to make a sturdier pan and help keep the bottom of the brownies from overbaking.

Buttermilk Brownies

Makes 36 brownies ● ● ●

The tangy flavor of buttermilk gives added depth to the dense, fudgy, not-too-sweet brownies and the creamy chocolate frosting.

Tips

Eggs should be at room temperature when added to the creamed butter and sugar mixture. Cold eggs can cause the mixture to break and appear curdled.

Store brownies in a single layer in a tightly sealed container at room temperature.

- Preheat oven to 350°F (180°C)
- 9-inch (2.5 L) square baking pan, lined with foil, greased

Brownies

¾ cup	all-purpose flour	175 mL
½ cup	unsweetened Dutch-process cocoa powder, sifted	125 mL
¼ tsp	baking soda	1 mL
¾ cup	unsalted butter, softened	175 mL
1 cup	granulated sugar	250 mL
½ cup	packed light brown sugar	125 mL
2	eggs	2
1 tsp	vanilla extract	5 mL
½ cup	buttermilk	125 mL

Frosting

1¾ cups	confectioner's (powdered/icing) sugar	425 mL
3 tbsp	unsweetened Dutch-process cocoa powder, sifted	45 mL
⅓ cup	unsalted butter, softened	75 mL
2 tbsp	buttermilk	25 mL
1 tsp	vanilla extract	5 mL

1. **Brownies:** In a bowl, whisk together flour, cocoa powder and baking soda until well combined. Set aside.

2. In a large bowl, using an electric mixer on medium speed, cream butter, granulated sugar and brown sugar until light and fluffy, about 2 minutes. Add eggs one at a time, beating well after each addition. Beat in vanilla. Scrape down sides of bowl. On low speed or using a wooden spoon, gradually add flour mixture, alternating with buttermilk, beating after each addition just until blended. Spread batter evenly into prepared pan.

3. Bake in preheated oven for 24 to 28 minutes or until a wooden pick inserted near the center comes out with a few moist crumbs. Let cool completely in baking pan on a wire rack.

4. Use the foil to lift cooled brownies from pan and place on a cutting board.

5. **Frosting:** In a bowl, whisk together confectioner's sugar and cocoa powder. Set aside. In a large bowl, using an electric mixer on medium speed, beat butter until smooth. Gradually beat in confectioner's sugar mixture, alternating with buttermilk. Add vanilla and beat until light and fluffy, about 3 minutes. Spread frosting over cooled brownies. Let stand 20 minutes or until frosting is set. Cut into 1½-inch (4 cm) squares.

Cocoa Brownies

● ● ●

Brownies made with cocoa powder have many fans, and this recipe is particularly good.

Tips

For fudgy brownies, reduce baking time by a few minutes.

Store brownies between layers of wax paper in a tightly sealed container.

Variation

Fold 1 cup (250 mL) chopped nuts into brownie batter before spreading into prepared pan.

● **Preheat oven to 350°F (180°C)**
● **13- by 9-inch (3 L) baking pan, lined with foil, greased**

1½ cups	all-purpose flour	375 mL
¾ cup	unsweetened Dutch-process cocoa powder, sifted	175 mL
½ tsp	baking powder	2 mL
¼ tsp	salt	1 mL
¾ cup	unsalted butter, softened	175 mL
2 cups	granulated sugar	500 mL
3	eggs	3
1½ tsp	vanilla extract	7 mL

1. In a bowl, whisk together flour, cocoa powder, baking powder and salt until well combined. Set aside.

2. In a large bowl, using an electric mixer on medium speed, cream butter and granulated sugar until light and fluffy, about 2 minutes. Add eggs one at a time, beating well after each addition. Beat in vanilla. Scrape down sides of bowl. On low speed or using a wooden spoon, gradually add flour mixture, beating just until blended. Spread batter evenly into prepared pan.

3. Bake in preheated oven for 25 to 30 minutes or until a wooden pick inserted near the center comes out clean. Let cool completely in baking pan on a wire rack.

4. Use the foil to lift cooled brownies from pan and place on a cutting board. Cut into approximately 1¾- by 1½-inch (4.5 by 4 cm) bars.

White Chocolate Macadamia Brownies

These delightful brownies have lots of white chocolate flavor with chocolate both melted in the batter and chopped pieces added along with the macadamia nuts.

Tips

White chocolate should not be melted in the microwave as it can easily burn and turn lumpy if overheated.

If buying chocolate in blocks or squares, 6 ounces (175 g) of chocolate will yield about 1 cup (250 mL) chopped chocolate.

Store brownies between layers of wax paper in a tightly sealed container at room temperature for up to 3 days.

Variation

White Chocolate Coconut Brownies: Fold ½ cup (125 mL) sweetened flaked coconut into brownie batter along with macadamia nuts.

● Preheat oven to 350°F (180°C)
● 9-inch (2.5 L) square baking pan, lined with foil, greased

1 cup	all-purpose flour	250 mL
¼ tsp	salt	1 mL
½ cup	unsalted butter, softened	125 mL
6 oz	white chocolate, finely chopped	175 g
3	eggs	3
½ cup	granulated sugar	125 mL
2 tsp	vanilla extract	10 mL
¾ cup	chopped white chocolate or white chocolate chips	175 mL
¾ cup	chopped roasted unsalted macadamia nuts	175 mL

1. In a bowl, whisk together flour and salt until well combined. Set aside.
2. In a microwave-safe bowl, heat butter in a microwave at Medium-High (75%) power just until melted and hot. Add white chocolate and stir until chocolate is completely melted and mixture is smooth. Set aside.
3. In a large bowl, using an electric mixer on medium speed, lightly beat eggs. Add granulated sugar and beat until light and fluffy, about 2 minutes. Beat in vanilla. With mixer running on low, gradually beat in melted white chocolate. Scrape down sides of bowl. On low speed or using a wooden spoon, gradually add flour mixture, beating just until blended. By hand, fold in chopped white chocolate and macadamia nuts. Spread batter evenly into prepared pan.
4. Bake in preheated oven for 25 to 30 minutes or until a wooden pick inserted near the center comes out clean. Let cool completely in baking pan on a wire rack.
5. Use the foil to lift cooled brownies from pan and place on a cutting board. Cut into 1½-inch (4 cm) squares.

Deluxe Brownies

Two flavors of chocolate and cocoa powder make these brownies very chocolaty!

Tips

The addition of vegetable oil makes these brownies very moist and good keepers — not that they last long!

Always use an oil with a neutral flavor, such as canola, corn or safflower oil. Oils labeled simply as vegetable oil are usually a blend of neutral-flavored oils and are a good choice for cookie baking. Do not use oils with a strong or distinct flavor, such as olive oil or peanut oil, for baking. These oils will significantly alter the flavor of your brownies in an unpleasant way.

Store brownies between layers of wax paper in a tightly sealed container at room temperature.

- **Preheat oven to 350°F (180°C)**
- **13- by 9-inch (3 L) baking pan, lined with foil, greased**

4 oz	bittersweet chocolate, chopped	125 g
3 oz	semisweet chocolate, chopped	90 g
¾ cup	unsalted butter, cut into pieces	175 mL
1¾ cups	all-purpose flour	425 mL
¼ cup	unsweetened Dutch-process cocoa powder, sifted	50 mL
¼ tsp	salt	1 mL
1⅓ cups	packed dark brown sugar	325 mL
1 cup	granulated sugar	250 mL
5	eggs	5
⅓ cup	vegetable oil	75 mL
2 tsp	vanilla extract	10 mL
⅔ cup	mini semisweet chocolate chips	150 mL
⅔ cup	chopped walnuts	150 mL

I. In a large microwave-safe bowl, heat bittersweet chocolate, semisweet chocolate and butter in a microwave at Medium-High (75%) power for 1 minute. Stir chocolate until smooth. If necessary, heat at Medium (50%) power for 10 seconds at a time, stirring between each heating, just until chocolate is melted. Do not overheat. Cool for 5 minutes.

2. In a bowl, whisk together flour, cocoa powder and salt until well combined. Set aside.

3. Using a wire whisk or large spoon, stir brown sugar and granulated sugar into warm chocolate mixture. Add eggs one at a time, beating well after each addition. Gradually whisk in vegetable oil. Stir in vanilla. Scrape down sides of bowl. Gradually add flour mixture, stirring just until blended. Fold in mini chocolate chips and walnuts. Spread batter evenly into prepared pan.

4. Bake in preheated oven for 30 to 35 minutes or until a wooden pick inserted near the center comes out with a few moist crumbs. Let cool completely in baking pan on a wire rack.

5. Use the foil to lift cooled brownies from pan and place on a cutting board. Cut into approximately 1¾- by 1½-inch (4.5 by 4 cm) bars.

Peanut Butter Brownies

Here's a frosted brownie for people who love chocolate and peanut butter.

Tips

Peanut butter can turn stale after the jar has been open for awhile. Always taste peanut butter to make sure it is fresh before using it in baking.

Store brownies between layers of wax paper in a tightly sealed container. Brownies can be stored at room temperature for up to 3 days.

- **Preheat oven to 350°F (180°C)**
- **9-inch (2.5 L) square baking pan, lined with foil, greased**

Brownies

5 oz	semisweet chocolate, chopped	150 g
1/3 cup	unsalted butter, cut into pieces	75 mL
1 cup	all-purpose flour	250 mL
1/4 tsp	baking powder	1 mL
1/2 cup	creamy peanut butter	125 mL
1/3 cup	granulated sugar	75 mL
1/4 cup	packed light brown sugar	50 mL
3	eggs	3
1 tsp	vanilla extract	5 mL
1/2 cup	mini semisweet chocolate chips	125 mL
1/2 cup	chopped unsalted peanuts	125 mL

Frosting

2 oz	semisweet chocolate, chopped	60 g
1/4 cup	creamy peanut butter	50 mL
2 tbsp	unsalted butter, softened	25 mL
1/2 tsp	vanilla extract	2 mL
1 1/2 cups	confectioner's (powdered/icing) sugar	375 mL

1. **Brownies:** In a large microwave-safe bowl, heat chocolate and butter in a microwave at Medium-High (75%) power for 1 minute. Stir chocolate until smooth. If necessary, heat at Medium (50%) power for 10 seconds at a time, stirring between each heating, just until chocolate is melted. Do not overheat. Cool for 5 minutes.

2. In a bowl, whisk together flour and baking powder until well combined. Set aside.

3. Using a wire whisk or large spoon, stir peanut butter into warm chocolate mixture until smooth. Stir in granulated sugar and brown sugar. Add eggs one at a time, beating well after each addition. Stir in vanilla. Scrape down sides of bowl. Gradually add flour mixture, stirring just until blended. Fold in mini chocolate chips and chopped peanuts. Spread batter evenly into prepared pan.

Tip

Creamy peanut butter gives the brownies and frosting an excellent texture, but, if you prefer it, chunky peanut butter may be used instead.

4. Bake in preheated oven for 25 to 30 minutes or until a wooden pick inserted near the center comes out with a few moist crumbs. Let cool completely in baking pan on a wire rack.

5. Use the foil to lift cooled brownies from pan and place on a cutting board.

6. *Frosting:* In a small microwave-safe bowl, heat chocolate in a microwave at Medium-High (75%) power for 30 seconds. Stir until smooth. Do not overheat. In a large bowl, using an electric mixer on medium speed, cream peanut butter and butter until smooth. Add melted chocolate and beat until well combined. Beat in vanilla. Gradually add confectioner's sugar and beat until smooth and creamy. Spread frosting over cooled brownies. Let stand 20 minutes or until frosting is set. Cut into $1\frac{1}{2}$-inch (4 cm) squares.

Chocolate-Topped Brownies

After removing a pan of brownies from the oven, sprinkle chocolate chips over top of the hot brownies. Let stand until the chocolate is melted, about 5 minutes. Using an offset spatula or the back of a metal spoon, spread the melted chocolate evenly over the brownies. Let cool completely before cutting.

You can use your choice of chocolate — bittersweet, sweet dark, semisweet, milk or white!

Marbled Cream Cheese Brownies

These brownies are a family favorite and also disappear quickly from dessert trays at parties.

Tips

Use shiny or light-colored metal baking pans for making brownies. Dark pans absorb more heat and can cause brownies to overbake and dry out.

Store brownies between layers of wax paper in a tightly sealed container. Brownies can be stored in the refrigerator for up to 3 days.

- **Preheat oven to 350°F (180°C)**
- **9-inch (2.5 L) square baking pan, lined with foil, greased**

Cream Cheese Filling

8 oz	cream cheese, softened	250 g
1/4 cup	granulated sugar	50 mL
1	egg	1
1 tsp	vanilla extract	5 mL

Brownie Batter

5 oz	bittersweet chocolate, chopped	150 g
2/3 cup	unsalted butter, cut into pieces	150 mL
1 cup	all-purpose flour	250 mL
1/2 tsp	baking powder	2 mL
1/4 tsp	salt	1 mL
3	eggs	3
1 cup	granulated sugar	250 mL
2 tsp	vanilla extract	10 mL

1. **Filling:** In a large bowl, using an electric mixer on medium speed, beat cream cheese and granulated sugar until smooth and creamy, about 2 minutes. Add egg and beat well. Beat in vanilla. Cover and set aside.

2. **Brownies:** In a large microwave-safe bowl, heat chocolate and butter in a microwave at Medium-High (75%) power for 1 minute. Stir chocolate until smooth. If necessary, heat at Medium (50%) power for 10 seconds at a time, stirring between each heating, just until chocolate is melted. Do not overheat. Cool for 5 minutes.

3. In a bowl, whisk together flour, baking powder and salt until well combined. Set aside.

4. Using a wire whisk or large spoon, add eggs to warm chocolate mixture one at a time, beating well after each addition. Add granulated sugar and stir until well combined. Stir in vanilla. Scrape down sides of bowl. Gradually add flour mixture, stirring just until blended.

Tip

Brownies containing cream cheese should be stored in the refrigerator.

5. Spread two-thirds of brownie batter evenly into prepared pan. Carefully spread cream cheese filling evenly over brownie batter. Spoon tablespoonfuls of remaining brownie batter over filling. Insert a knife halfway down through filling. Draw the knife through the filling in a swirl pattern to create a marbled effect.

6. Bake in preheated oven for 22 to 25 minutes or until a wooden pick inserted near the center comes out with a few moist crumbs. Let cool completely in baking pan on a wire rack.

7. Use the foil to lift cooled brownies from pan and place on a cutting board. Cut into $1\frac{1}{2}$-inch (4 cm) squares.

Coconut Brownies

Coconut adds a sweet, chewy texture to brownies.

Tips

Coarsely chopping the coconut before adding it to the batter eliminates long pieces and gives the brownies a better texture.

Store brownies between layers of wax paper in a tightly sealed container. Brownies can be stored at room temperature for up to 3 days.

● **Preheat oven to 350°F (180°C)**
● **13- by 9-inch (3 L) baking pan, lined with foil, greased**

1¼ cups	all-purpose flour	300 mL
¼ tsp	baking powder	1 mL
¼ tsp	salt	1 mL
5 oz	bittersweet chocolate, chopped	150 g
1 cup	unsalted butter, softened	250 mL
4	eggs	4
1½ cups	granulated sugar	375 mL
2 tsp	vanilla extract	10 mL
1 cup	sweetened flaked coconut, coarsely chopped	250 mL
½ cup	chopped pecans	125 mL

1. In a bowl, whisk together flour, baking powder and salt until well combined. Set aside.

2. In a microwave-safe bowl, heat chocolate and butter in a microwave at Medium-High (75%) power for 1 minute. Stir chocolate until smooth. If necessary, heat chocolate at Medium (50%) power for 10 seconds at a time, stirring between each heating, just until chocolate is melted. Do not overheat. Set aside.

3. In a large bowl, using an electric mixer on medium speed, lightly beat eggs. Add granulated sugar and beat until light and fluffy, about 2 minutes. Beat in vanilla. With mixer running on low, gradually beat in melted chocolate. Scrape down sides of bowl. On low speed or using a wooden spoon, gradually add flour mixture, beating just until blended. By hand, fold in coconut and pecans. Spread batter evenly into prepared pan.

4. Bake in preheated oven for 22 to 28 minutes or until a wooden pick inserted near the center comes out with a few moist crumbs. Let cool completely in baking pan on a wire rack.

5. Use the foil to lift cooled brownies from pan and place on a cutting board. Cut into approximately 1¾- by 1½-inch (4.5 by 4 cm) bars.

Eggnog Brownies

These brownies are great to make around the holidays when eggnog is available in the grocery store dairy case.

Tips

Butter is considered to be softened when it is at a temperature of 65°F (18°C).

Store brownies between layers of wax paper in a tightly sealed container.

- Preheat oven to 350°F (180°C)
- 13-by 9-inch (3L) baking pan, lined with foil, greased

Brownies

1⅓ cups	all-purpose flour	325 mL
⅓ cup	unsweetened Dutch-process cocoa powder, sifted	75 mL
¼ tsp	baking powder	1 mL
¼ tsp	salt	1 mL
⅔ cup	unsalted butter, softened	150 mL
1½ cups	granulated sugar	375 mL
2	eggs	2
2 tbsp	brandy	25 mL
⅔ cup	dairy eggnog	150 mL

Frosting

⅓ cup	unsalted butter, softened	75 mL
2 tbsp	dairy eggnog	25 mL
2 cups	confectioner's (powdered/icing) sugar	500 mL
1 tsp	brandy	5 mL

1. **Brownies:** In a bowl, whisk together flour, cocoa powder, baking powder and salt until well combined. Set aside.

2. In a large bowl, using an electric mixer on medium speed, cream butter and granulated sugar until light and fluffy, about 2 minutes. Add eggs one at a time, beating well after each addition. Beat in brandy. Scrape down sides of bowl. On low speed or using a wooden spoon, gradually add flour mixture, alternating with eggnog, beating after each addition just until blended. Spread batter evenly into prepared pan.

3. Bake in preheated oven for 20 to 24 minutes or until a wooden pick inserted near the center comes out with a few moist crumbs. Let cool completely in baking pan on a wire rack.

4. Use the foil to lift cooled brownies from pan and place on a cutting board.

5. **Frosting:** In a large bowl, using an electric mixer on medium speed, beat butter until smooth. Beat in eggnog. Gradually beat in confectioner's sugar. Add brandy and beat until smooth and fluffy. Spread frosting over brownies. Let stand 20 minutes or until frosting is set. Cut into approximately 1¾- by 1½-inch (4.5 by 4 cm) bars.

Moist, Fudgy Brownies

These are very fudgy brownies.

Tips

These brownies are also very good made without the nuts or with a combination of nuts.

Store brownies between layers of wax paper in a tightly sealed container.

Variation

Substitute chopped pecans for chopped walnuts.

- Preheat oven to 350°F (180°C)
- 9-inch (2.5 L) square baking pan, lined with foil, greased

4 oz	bittersweet chocolate, chopped	125 g
2/3 cup	unsalted butter, cut into pieces	150 mL
3/4 cup	all-purpose flour	175 mL
1/2 cup	unsweetened Dutch-process cocoa powder, sifted	125 mL
1/2 tsp	baking powder	2 mL
1/4 tsp	salt	1 mL
1 1/2 cups	packed light brown sugar	375 mL
2	eggs	2
1/3 cup	vegetable oil	75 mL
1 tbsp	vanilla extract	15 mL
1 cup	chopped walnuts	250 mL

1. In a large microwave-safe bowl, heat chocolate and butter in a microwave at Medium-High (75%) power for 1 minute. Stir chocolate until smooth. If necessary, heat at Medium (50%) power for 10 seconds at a time, stirring between each heating, just until chocolate is melted. Do not overheat. Cool for 5 minutes.

2. In a bowl, whisk together flour, cocoa powder, baking powder and salt until well combined. Set aside.

3. Using a wire whisk or large spoon, stir brown sugar into warm chocolate mixture. Add eggs one at a time, beating well after each addition. Gradually whisk in vegetable oil. Stir in vanilla. Scrape down sides of bowl. Gradually add flour mixture, stirring just until blended. Fold in walnuts. Spread batter evenly into prepared pan.

4. Bake in preheated oven for 20 to 22 minutes or until a wooden pick inserted near the center comes out with a few moist crumbs. Let cool completely in baking pan on a wire rack.

5. Use the foil to lift cooled brownies from pan and place on a cutting board. Cut into 1 1/2-inch (4 cm) squares.

Fudge and Fudge Brownies

● ● ●

Very fudgy and delicious!

Tips

Lining the pan with foil makes it easy to remove brownies from the pan after cooling and makes cleanup a breeze.

Store brownies between layers of wax paper in a tightly sealed container. Brownies can be stored at room temperature for up to 3 days.

- Preheat oven to 350°F (180°C)
- 9-inch (2.5 L) square baking pan, lined with foil, greased

2 oz	semisweet chocolate, chopped	60 g
2 oz	bittersweet chocolate, chopped	60 g
½ cup	unsalted butter, cut into pieces	125 mL
½ cup	all-purpose flour	125 mL
¼ tsp	salt	1 mL
¾ cup	granulated sugar	175 mL
⅓ cup	packed light brown sugar	75 mL
3	eggs	3
1 tsp	vanilla extract	5 mL
½ cup	chopped walnuts	125 mL

1. In a large microwave-safe bowl, heat semisweet chocolate, bittersweet chocolate and butter in a microwave at Medium-High (75%) power for 1 minute. Stir chocolate until smooth. If necessary, heat at Medium (50%) power for 10 seconds at a time, stirring between each heating, just until chocolate is melted. Do not overheat. Cool for 5 minutes.

2. In a bowl, whisk together flour and salt until well combined. Set aside.

3. Using a wire whisk or large spoon, stir granulated sugar and brown sugar into warm chocolate mixture. Add eggs one at a time, beating well after each addition. Stir in vanilla. Scrape down sides of bowl. Gradually add flour mixture, stirring just until blended. Fold in walnuts. Spread batter evenly into prepared pan.

4. Bake in preheated oven for 20 to 22 minutes or until a wooden pick inserted near the center comes out with a few moist crumbs. Let cool completely in baking pan on a wire rack.

5. Use the foil to lift cooled brownies from pan and place on a cutting board. Cut into 1½-inch (4 cm) squares.

Espresso Cream Brownies

I wanted to create a special coffee-flavored brownie, and this recipe is the result.

Tips

To measure flour properly, stir the flour in the package or container to loosen it and add air, then gently spoon the flour into a dry measuring cup. Use a knife or spatula to level off the flour even with the rim of the cup.

Store brownies between layers of wax paper in a tightly sealed container. Brownies can be stored in the refrigerator for up to 3 days.

- Preheat oven to 350°F (180°C)
- 9-inch (2.5 L) square baking pan, lined with foil, greased

Espresso Cream Cheese Filling

8 oz	cream cheese, softened	250 g
1/3 cup	granulated sugar	75 mL
1 tbsp	instant espresso powder	15 mL
1	egg	1
1 tsp	vanilla extract	5 mL

Brownie Batter

5 oz	bittersweet chocolate, chopped	150 g
2/3 cup	unsalted butter, cut into pieces	150 mL
1 cup	all-purpose flour	250 mL
1 tsp	instant espresso powder	5 mL
1/2 tsp	baking powder	2 mL
1/4 tsp	salt	1 mL
3	eggs	3
1 cup	granulated sugar	250 mL
2 tsp	vanilla extract	10 mL

1. *Filling:* In a large bowl, using an electric mixer on medium speed, beat cream cheese, granulated sugar and espresso powder until smooth and creamy, about 2 minutes. Add egg and beat well. Beat in vanilla. Cover and set aside.

2. *Brownies:* In a large microwave-safe bowl, heat chocolate and butter in a microwave at Medium-High (75%) power for 1 minute. Stir chocolate until smooth. If necessary, heat at Medium (50%) power for 10 seconds at a time, stirring between each heating, just until chocolate is melted. Do not overheat. Cool for 5 minutes.

3. In a bowl, whisk together flour, espresso powder, baking powder and salt until well combined. Set aside.

4. Using a wire whisk or large spoon, add eggs to warm chocolate mixture one at a time, beating well after each addition. Add granulated sugar and stir until well combined. Stir in vanilla. Scrape down sides of bowl. Gradually add flour mixture, beating just until blended.

Tip

Instant espresso powder can be found in the coffee aisle of most grocery stores.

5. Spread two-thirds of brownie batter evenly into prepared pan. Carefully spread filling evenly over brownie batter. Spoon tablespoonfuls of remaining brownie batter over filling. Insert a knife halfway down through filling. Draw the knife through the filling in a swirl pattern to create a marbled effect.

6. Bake in preheated oven for 22 to 25 minutes or until a wooden pick inserted near the center comes out with a few moist crumbs. Let cool completely in baking pan on a wire rack.

7. Use the foil to lift cooled brownies from pan and place on a cutting board. Cut into $1\frac{1}{2}$-inch (4 cm) squares.

Brownie Shapes

For a fun appearance and presentation, cut brownies into creative shapes using cookie cutters. To make clean cuts and brownie portions that hold their shape, choose brownies that do not contain nuts, chocolate chips, or other add-ins and use cookie cutters that do not have small or intricate details.

Milk Chocolate Brownies

Milk chocolate produces brownies with a mellow chocolate flavor.

Tips

To measure flour properly, stir the flour in the package or container to add air to it, then gently spoon the flour into a dry measuring cup. Use a knife or spatula to level off the flour even with the rim of the cup.

Store brownies between layers of wax paper in a tightly sealed container at room temperature for up to 3 days.

- Preheat oven to 350°F (180°C)
- 9-inch (2.5 L) square baking pan, lined with foil, greased

3 oz	milk chocolate, chopped	90 g
1/2 cup	unsalted butter, cut into pieces	125 mL
3/4 cup	all-purpose flour	175 mL
1/2 tsp	baking powder	2 mL
1/4 tsp	salt	1 mL
1 cup	granulated sugar	250 mL
2	eggs	2
1 tsp	vanilla extract	5 mL

1. In a large microwave-safe bowl, heat chocolate and butter in a microwave at Medium-High (75%) power for 30 seconds. Stir chocolate until smooth. If necessary, heat at Medium (50%) power for 10 seconds at a time, stirring between each heating, just until chocolate is melted. Do not overheat. Cool for 5 minutes.

2. In a bowl, whisk together flour, baking powder and salt until well combined. Set aside.

3. Using a wire whisk or large spoon, stir granulated sugar into warm chocolate mixture. Add eggs one at a time, stirring well after each addition. Stir in vanilla. Scrape down sides of bowl. Gradually add flour mixture, stirring just until blended. Spread batter evenly into prepared pan.

4. Bake in preheated oven for 18 to 22 minutes or until a wooden pick inserted near the center comes out with a few moist crumbs. Let cool completely in baking pan on a wire rack.

5. Use the foil to lift cooled brownies from pan and place on a cutting board. Cut into 1 1/2-inch (4 cm) squares.

Cocoa Coconut Brownies

● ● ●

Lots of coconut and lots of flavorful cocoa make for a great brownie combination.

Tips

Use table salt for baking. It has a balanced flavor and very fine grains that blend well into the other ingredients.

Store brownies between layers of wax paper in a tightly sealed container at room temperature for up to 3 days.

- Preheat oven to 350°F (180°C)
- 9-inch (2.5 L) square baking pan, lined with foil, greased

½ cup	all-purpose flour	125 mL
½ cup	unsweetened Dutch-process cocoa powder, sifted	125 mL
½ tsp	baking powder	2 mL
¼ tsp	salt	1 mL
1 cup	sweetened flaked coconut, coarsely chopped	250 mL
½ cup	unsalted butter, softened	125 mL
1 cup	granulated sugar	250 mL
2	eggs	2
1 tsp	vanilla extract	5 mL

1. In a bowl, whisk together flour, cocoa powder, baking powder and salt until well combined. Stir in coconut. Set aside.

2. In a large bowl, using an electric mixer on medium speed, cream butter and granulated sugar until light and fluffy, about 2 minutes. Add eggs one at a time, beating well after each addition. Beat in vanilla. Scrape down sides of bowl. On low speed or using a wooden spoon, gradually add flour mixture, beating just until blended. Spread batter evenly into prepared pan.

3. Bake in preheated oven for 20 to 25 minutes or until a wooden pick inserted near the center comes out with a few moist crumbs. Let cool completely in baking pan on a wire rack.

4. Use the foil to lift cooled brownies from pan and place on a cutting board. Cut into 1½-inch (4 cm) squares.

Double Chocolate Cream Brownies

● ● ●

These luxuriant brownies are definitely worth the indulgence.

Tips

These brownies are also great made with almonds, hazelnuts or walnuts.

Always use pure vanilla extract in brownies. Imitation vanilla is made from synthetic flavors and colors, and the taste cannot compare to pure vanilla extract.

Store brownies between layers of wax paper in a tightly sealed container at room temperature for up to 3 days.

- Preheat oven to 350°F (180°C)
- 9-inch (2.5 L) square baking pan, lined with foil, greased

3 oz	bittersweet chocolate, chopped	90 g
2/3 cup	unsalted butter, cut into pieces	150 mL
1 1/4 cups	all-purpose flour	300 mL
1/4 cup	unsweetened Dutch-process cocoa powder, sifted	50 mL
1/4 tsp	baking powder	1 mL
1/4 tsp	salt	1 mL
1 1/3 cups	granulated sugar	325 mL
2	egg yolks	2
1/3 cup	whipping (35%) cream	75 mL
2 tsp	vanilla extract	10 mL
2/3 cup	chopped pecans	150 mL

1. In a large microwave-safe bowl, heat chocolate and butter in a microwave at Medium-High (75%) power for 1 minute. Stir chocolate until smooth. If necessary, heat at Medium (50%) power for 10 seconds at a time, stirring between each heating, just until chocolate is melted. Do not overheat. Cool for 5 minutes.

2. In a bowl, whisk together flour, cocoa powder, baking powder and salt until well combined. Set aside.

3. Using a wire whisk or large spoon, stir granulated sugar into warm chocolate mixture. Add egg yolks one at a time, beating well after each addition. Stir in cream and vanilla. Scrape down sides of bowl. Gradually add flour mixture, stirring just until blended. Fold in pecans. Spread batter evenly into prepared pan.

4. Bake in preheated oven for 22 to 27 minutes or until a wooden pick inserted near the center comes out with a few moist crumbs. Let cool completely in baking pan on a wire rack.

5. Use the foil to lift cooled brownies from pan and place on a cutting board. Cut into 1 1/2-inch (4 cm) squares.

Toffee Mocha Brownies

● ● ●

Crunchy bits of toffee and pecans enhance the coffee and chocolate flavors in these distinctive treats.

Tips

Avoid overmixing brownie batter. Overmixing will develop the gluten in the flour and make the brownies tough and hard.

Look for bags of toffee bits in the grocery store near the chocolate chips.

Store brownies between layers of wax paper in a tightly sealed container. Brownies can be stored at room temperature for up to 3 days.

● Preheat oven to 350°F (180°C)
● 9-inch (2.5 L) square baking pan, lined with foil, greased

⅓ cup	chopped semisweet chocolate	75 mL
½ cup	unsalted butter, cut into pieces	125 mL
1⅓ cups	all-purpose flour	325 mL
⅓ cup	unsweetened Dutch-process cocoa powder, sifted	75 mL
1 tsp	baking powder	5 mL
¼ tsp	salt	1 mL
¾ cup	granulated sugar	175 mL
¾ cup	packed light brown sugar	175 mL
2	eggs	2
¼ cup	strong brewed coffee	50 mL
1½ tsp	vanilla extract	7 mL
½ cup	toffee bits	125 mL
⅓ cup	chopped pecans	75 mL

1. In a large microwave-safe bowl, heat chocolate and butter in a microwave at Medium-High (75%) power for 1 minute. Stir chocolate until smooth. If necessary, heat at Medium (50%) power for 10 seconds at a time, stirring between each heating, just until chocolate is melted. Do not overheat. Cool for 5 minutes.

2. In a bowl, whisk together flour, coca powder, baking powder and salt until well combined. Set aside.

3. Using a wire whisk or large spoon, stir granulated sugar and brown sugar into warm chocolate mixture. Add eggs one at a time, beating well after each addition. Stir in coffee and vanilla. Scrape down sides of bowl. Gradually add flour mixture, stirring just until blended. Fold in toffee bits and pecans. Spread batter evenly into prepared pan.

4. Bake in preheated oven for 22 to 25 minutes or until a wooden pick inserted near the center comes out with a few moist crumbs. Let cool completely in baking pan on a wire rack.

5. Use the foil to lift cooled brownies from pan and place on a cutting board. Cut into 1½-inch (4 cm) squares.

Chocolate Cream Cheese Brownies

●●●

A chocolate cream cheese layer is nestled between two luscious brownie layers in these elegant squares.

Tips

For best results, use the pan size and shape called for in the recipe. If you use a different pan, you will need to adjust the baking time to reduce the chance of burning or undercooking.

Store brownies between layers of wax paper in a tightly sealed container in the refrigerator for up to 3 days.

- Preheat oven to 350°F (180°C)
- 9-inch (2.5 L) square baking pan, lined with foil, greased

Cream Cheese Filling

3 oz	bittersweet chocolate, chopped	90 g
12 oz	cream cheese, softened	375 g
¾ cup	granulated sugar	175 mL
1	egg	1
1½ tsp	vanilla extract	7 mL

Brownie Batter

3 oz	bittersweet chocolate, chopped	90 g
⅔ cup	unsalted butter, cut into pieces	150 mL
1⅓ cups	all-purpose flour	325 mL
¼ tsp	salt	1 mL
3	eggs	3
1⅓ cups	granulated sugar	325 mL
1 tsp	vanilla extract	5 mL
½ cup	mini semisweet chocolate chips	125 mL
½ cup	finely chopped walnuts	125 mL

1. **Filling:** In a microwave-safe bowl, heat chocolate in a microwave at Medium-High (75%) power for 30 seconds. Stir chocolate until smooth. If necessary, heat at Medium (50%) power for 10 seconds at a time, stirring between each heating, just until chocolate is melted. Do not overheat. Set aside.

2. In a large bowl, using an electric mixer on medium speed, beat cream cheese and granulated sugar until smooth and creamy, about 2 minutes. Add egg and beat well. Beat in melted chocolate and vanilla. Cover and set aside.

3. **Brownies:** In a large microwave-safe bowl, heat chocolate and butter in a microwave at Medium-High (75%) power for 1 minute. Stir chocolate until smooth. If necessary, heat at Medium (50%) power for 10 seconds at a time, stirring between each heating, just until chocolate is melted. Do not overheat. Cool for 5 minutes.

Tip

Bittersweet chocolate
is an excellent choice
for use in brownies.
It contains some
sugar and additional
cocoa butter, making
bittersweet chocolate
richer and smoother than
unsweetened chocolate.

4. In a bowl, whisk together flour and salt until well combined.
Set aside.

5. Using a wire whisk or large spoon, add eggs to warm chocolate
mixture one at a time, beating well after each addition. Add
granulated sugar and stir until well combined. Stir in vanilla.
Scrape down sides of bowl. Gradually add flour mixture,
stirring just until blended. By hand, fold in chocolate chips and
walnuts.

6. Spread half of brownie batter evenly into prepared pan.
Carefully spread cream cheese filling evenly over brownie
batter. Spoon remaining brownie batter over filling and carefully
spread batter evenly, completely covering filling.

7. Bake in preheated oven for 30 to 35 minutes or until a wooden
pick inserted near the center comes out with a few moist
crumbs. Let cool completely in baking pan on a wire rack.

8. Use the foil to lift cooled brownies from pan and place on a
cutting board. Cut into $1\frac{1}{2}$-inch (4 cm) squares.

Brownies Supreme

You can't eat just one of these incredible chocolaty treasures. Packed with cocoa, these moist brownies are outstanding.

Tips

These brownies are particularly good made with the special dark cocoa, a blend of regular and Dutch-process cocoa powder, that is now available in many major supermarkets.

Use a mild-flavored vegetable oil, such as canola oil, that will not alter the taste of the brownies.

Store brownies between layers of wax paper in a tightly sealed container. Brownies can be stored at room temperature for up to 3 days.

Variation

Fold 1 cup (250 mL) chopped walnuts or pecans into brownie batter before spreading into prepared pan.

● **Preheat oven to 350°F (180°C)**
● **13- by 9-inch (3 L) baking pan, lined with foil, greased with nonstick cooking spray**

1¼ cups	all-purpose flour	300 mL
¾ cup	unsweetened Dutch-process cocoa powder, sifted	175 mL
¼ tsp	baking powder	1 mL
¼ tsp	salt	1 mL
4	eggs	4
1 cup	granulated sugar	250 mL
1 cup	packed dark brown sugar	250 mL
¾ cup	vegetable oil	175 mL
2 tsp	vanilla extract	10 mL

1. In a bowl, whisk together flour, cocoa powder, baking powder and salt until well combined. Set aside.

2. In a large bowl, using an electric mixer on medium speed, lightly beat eggs. Add granulated sugar and brown sugar and beat until light and fluffy, about 2 minutes. Gradually beat in vegetable oil. Beat in vanilla. Scrape down sides of bowl. On low speed or using a wooden spoon, gradually add flour mixture, beating just until blended. Spread batter evenly into prepared pan.

3. Bake in preheated oven for 20 to 25 minutes or until a wooden pick inserted near the center comes out with a few moist crumbs. Let cool completely in baking pan on a wire rack.

4. Use the foil to lift cooled brownies from pan and place on a cutting board. Cut into approximately 1¾- by 1½-inch (4.5 by 4 cm) bars.

Biscotti

●●●

Almond Biscotti 396

Apricot Biscotti. 397

Chocolate Walnut Biscotti. 398

Cranberry White Chocolate
   Biscotti 399

Blueberry Lemon Biscotti 400

Spumoni Biscotti 401

Chocolate Chip Biscotti 402

Orange Biscotti. 403

Cinnamon Sugar Biscotti 404

Mocha Biscotti 405

Cherry Almond Biscotti. 406

Brownie Biscotti 407

Pistachio Biscotti 408

Lemon Biscotti 409

Cappuccino Biscotti 410

Hazelnut Chocolate Biscotti 411

White Chocolate Macadamia
   Biscotti 412

Chocolate Cherry Biscotti. 413

Nut Biscotti. 414

Espresso Biscotti 415

Lemon Almond Biscotti 416

Maple Pecan Biscotti 417

Chocolate Chip Orange Biscotti 418

Coconut Biscotti. 419

White Chocolate Lemon
   Biscotti 420

Macadamia Nut Biscotti 421

Currant Almond Biscotti 422

Pumpkin Walnut Biscotti. 423

Triple Chocolate Biscotti 424

Cinnamon Walnut Biscotti. 425

Gingerbread Biscotti. 426

About Biscotti

Biscotti are originally from the Tuscany region of Italy, and the word "biscotti" literally translates as "twice baked." To achieve their crispy texture, these crunchy cookies are baked first as a large log, then cut into slices and baked again.

Biscotti have earned legions of enthusiastic fans. Studded with nuts and dried fruits, these delightful cookies have earned recognition as a unique category all their own. While many people think of biscotti as the perfect treat for dunking in espresso, hot coffee, tea or even a glass of cold milk, Italians traditionally enjoy their biscotti with a sweet dessert wine.

The classic Italian flavor of biscotti is almond, designed to be a complement to the wine. However, biscotti have multiplied in recent years and now include different nuts, dried fruits and even chocolate. I love these cookies and had a lot of fun creating different-flavored biscotti in my kitchen. Some of my favorite flavors are Spumoni Biscotti, Apricot Biscotti, Blueberry Lemon Biscotti, Cranberry White Chocolate Biscotti and Macadamia Nut Biscotti. Mmmm!

While these cookies may look complicated, they are actually quite easy to bake. Get out your mixer and cookie sheets and have some fun. Your family and friends will be impressed with your homemade biscotti.

First Baking

Recipes in some cookbooks call for kneading the biscotti dough before shaping it into logs. I find that kneading develops the gluten in the flour and produces tough biscotti. For the biscotti recipes in this book, I instruct you to spoon the soft dough onto the cookie sheet in a log shape. This will give you tender cookies with a lovely texture that crisp up beautifully during the second baking.

The biscotti logs will nearly double in width as they bake, so be sure to leave 4 inches (10 cm) of space between the logs on the cookie sheet. If your cookie sheet is small, use a sheet for each log. To prevent the logs from burning on the bottom, bake only one cookie sheet at a time. The dough for the second biscotti log can be stored in the refrigerator until you're ready to spoon it onto a cool sheet.

Be sure to line the cookie sheets with parchment paper to prevent the logs from sticking to the sheet and keep the biscotti from burning on the bottom. Insulated cookie sheets are a good choice for baking biscotti. They keep the bottom of the biscotti from overbrowning during the first baking and keep the slices from burning during the second baking to crisp the cookies.

Second Baking

After the first baking, the cookie logs should be cooled for a few minutes to let them set a bit and make them easier to handle. But don't wait too long to slice them. Slicing the logs while they're still warm is a lot easier than waiting until they're cool and hard. If the logs cool too much, they will tend to break or crumble when sliced. If you are baking the logs in two shifts, slice the first log while the second one is in the oven and place the slices on a cooling rack until the oven is available.

Transfer the warm logs from the cooling rack to a sturdy cutting board. To make pretty slices, cut the logs on a diagonal with a serrated knife. A serrated knife will cut through nuts and dried fruits more cleanly than a straight-bladed knife can; a straight blade will tend to tear the cookies. Cut the biscotti into slices that are $\frac{1}{2}$- to $\frac{3}{4}$-inch (1 to 2 cm) thick. Any thicker and the cookies will not dry out properly during the second baking.

Lay the cookie slices flat on a cookie sheet. For a full recipe of biscotti, you will need two large cookie sheets to hold all of the slices. The sheets of sliced biscotti should be baked one at a time. This will provide good air circulation, allowing the biscotti to dry evenly, and keep the slices from burning on the top or bottom. Bake the slices as indicated in the recipe, then turn over and bake again on the second side. The biscotti will crisp as they cool. Be sure the biscotti are completely cool before storing or they can soften.

Finishing Touches

Many flavors of biscotti take on an added flavor dimension when dipped in melted chocolate or drizzled with a pretty chocolate glaze. You can use either chopped chocolate or chocolate chips for melting to create the finishing touch on your biscotti. Choose the same flavor of chocolate, or a complementary chocolate, as the one used in the biscotti recipe. Allow the chocolate to set completely before serving or storing.

Melting Chocolate

Follow these instructions for melting any flavor of chocolate, except white chocolate, for dipping or glazing biscotti. Because white chocolate can easily burn and turn lumpy if overheated, it should be melted in a double boiler on top of the stove rather than in the microwave.

Chocolate-Dipped Biscotti

In a small microwave-proof bowl, combine 2 cups (500 mL) chopped chocolate or chocolate chips and 2 tsp (10 mL) vegetable shortening. Microwave at Medium-High (75%) power for 1 minute. Stir the mixture until it is completely combined and smooth, microwaving an additional 10 seconds at a time as needed to fully melt the chocolate. Dip one end of each cooled cookie in the chocolate. Place biscotti on a piece of parchment paper or wax paper.

Chocolate-Glazed Biscotti

In a 1-quart (1 L) microwave-safe zippered storage bag, combine 1 cup (250 mL) chopped chocolate or chocolate chips and 1 tsp (5 mL) vegetable shortening. Microwave at Medium-High (75%) power for 1 minute. Knead the bag until the mixture is completely combined and smooth, microwaving an additional 10 seconds at a time as needed to fully melt the chocolate. Cut off a small corner of the bag and drizzle the chocolate over the tops and sides of cooled biscotti. Place biscotti on a piece of parchment paper or wax paper.

Melting White Chocolate

For the best flavor, use white chocolate chips rather than vanilla or white chips. White chocolate chips contain cocoa butter, the essential ingredient in white chocolate. Vanilla baking chips or plain white chips do not contain cocoa butter and have little flavor.

White Chocolate-Dipped Biscotti

In the top of a double boiler, combine 2 cups (500 mL) chopped white chocolate or white chocolate chips and 2 tsp (10 mL) vegetable shortening. Place pan over simmering water and heat, stirring frequently, until chocolate softens and begins to melt. Remove pan from heat and stir until completely combined and smooth. Dip one end of each cooled cookie in the chocolate. Place biscotti on a piece of parchment paper or wax paper to set.

White Chocolate-Glazed Biscotti

Melt the white chocolate as described above. Let the chocolate mixture cool in the pan for a minute or two and then spoon it into a zippered storage bag. Cut off a small corner of the bag and drizzle the chocolate over the tops and sides of cooled biscotti. Place biscotti on a piece of parchment paper or wax paper to set.

Storing Biscotti

Biscotti can be stored in a tightly sealed container at room temperature for up to 3 weeks. It may also be wrapped well and frozen for up to 2 months. Do not freeze chocolate-glazed biscotti. Instead, thaw frozen biscotti and allow it to come to room temperature; then dip one end of each cookie in melted chocolate or drizzle the chocolate overtop.

Almond Biscotti

Almond is the classic flavor of biscotti and is one of my absolute favorite varieties of this crunchy, twice-baked cookie. The heavenly scent of almond fills the kitchen as these delightful cookies bake in the oven.

Tip

Biscotti can be stored in a tightly sealed container at room temperature for up to 3 weeks. Biscotti may be wrapped well in foil and frozen for up to 2 months.

- Preheat oven to 350°F (180°C)
- Cookie sheets, lined with parchment paper

3 cups	all-purpose flour	750 mL
2 tsp	baking powder	10 mL
1/4 tsp	salt	1 mL
4	eggs	4
1 1/4 cups	granulated sugar	300 mL
1/3 cup	unsalted butter, melted	75 mL
1 1/2 tsp	vanilla extract	7 mL
1 1/2 tsp	almond extract	7 mL
1 cup	whole unsalted almonds	250 mL

1. In a bowl, whisk together flour, baking powder and salt until well combined. Set aside.

2. In a large bowl, using an electric mixer on medium speed, lightly beat eggs. Add granulated sugar and beat until well combined, about 2 minutes. Gradually beat in melted butter until thoroughly blended. Beat in vanilla and almond extract. Scrape down sides of bowl. On low speed or using a wooden spoon, add flour mixture, one-third at a time, beating well after each addition. By hand, fold in almonds.

3. Spoon dough onto prepared cookie sheet, forming 2 long, flat logs each measuring 12 inches (30 cm) long by 2 to 3 inches (5 to 7.5 cm) wide and spaced 4 inches (10 cm) apart. Biscotti will spread during baking, nearly doubling in width.

4. Bake in preheated oven for 25 to 30 minutes or until firm to the touch and lightly golden brown.

5. Slide parchment paper onto a wire cooling rack. Cool for 10 minutes, then transfer warm loaves to a cutting board. With a sharp serrated knife, cut each loaf on a 45 degree angle into 1/2-inch (1 cm) slices. Place, cut side down, about 1/2 inch (1 cm) apart on prepared cookie sheets.

6. Bake for 7 minutes. Turn slices over and bake an additional 5 to 7 minutes or just until dry. Do not allow biscotti to darken too much in color. Immediately transfer biscotti to cooling rack and cool completely. Biscotti will crisp as they cool.

Apricot Biscotti

This fruity twist on a classic biscotti recipe makes a great cookie to munch with coffee or tea. The orange and almond flavors delicately enhance the apricots in these tender biscotti.

Tips

To keep dried apricots from sticking to your knife when you chop them, give the knife blade a light coat of nonstick cooking spray.

All of the recipes in this book use large eggs, the standard size used for baking. If you do not have large eggs, then lightly beat your eggs and substitute ¼ cup (50 mL) beaten egg for each large egg called for in the recipe.

- Preheat oven to 350°F (180°C)
- Cookie sheets, lined with parchment paper

3 cups	all-purpose flour	750 mL
2 tsp	baking powder	10 mL
¼ tsp	salt	1 mL
4	eggs	4
1¼ cups	granulated sugar	300 mL
¼ cup	unsalted butter, melted	50 mL
2 tsp	grated orange zest	10 mL
1 tsp	vanilla extract	5 mL
½ tsp	almond extract	2 mL
1¼ cups	chopped dried apricots	300 mL
⅔ cup	chopped unsalted almonds	150 mL

1. In a bowl, whisk together flour, baking powder and salt until well combined. Set aside.

2. In a large bowl, using an electric mixer on medium speed, lightly beat eggs. Add granulated sugar and beat until well combined, about 2 minutes. Gradually beat in melted butter until thoroughly blended. Beat in orange zest, vanilla and almond extract. Scrape down sides of bowl. On low speed or using a wooden spoon, add flour mixture, one-third at a time, beating well after each addition. By hand, fold in apricots and almonds.

3. Spoon dough onto prepared cookie sheet, forming 2 long, flat logs each measuring 12 inches (30 cm) long by 2 to 3 inches (5 to 7.5 cm) wide and spaced 4 inches (10 cm) apart. Biscotti will spread during baking, nearly doubling in width.

4. Bake in preheated oven for 25 to 30 minutes or until firm to the touch and lightly golden brown.

5. Slide parchment paper onto a wire cooling rack. Cool for 10 minutes, then transfer warm loaves to a cutting board. With a sharp serrated knife, cut each loaf on a 45-degree angle into ½-inch (1 cm) slices. Place, cut side down, about ½ inch (1 cm) apart on prepared cookie sheets.

6. Bake for 7 minutes. Turn slices over and bake an additional 5 to 7 minutes or just until dry. Do not allow biscotti to darken too much in color. Immediately transfer biscotti to cooling rack and cool completely. Biscotti will crisp as they cool.

Chocolate Walnut Biscotti

Makes about 4 dozen biscotti   ● ● ●

This crispy chocolate cookie is particularly good dunked in hot coffee.

Tip

English walnuts, the kind typically found in grocery stores, have a mild flavor and are the best ones to use in cookies. The intense and slightly bitter taste of black walnuts can overpower the other ingredients.

Variation

Chocolate Almond Biscotti: Substitute 1 tsp (5 mL) almond extract for 1 tsp (5 mL) of the vanilla extract. Substitute chopped unsalted almonds for chopped walnuts.

- Preheat oven to 350°F (180°C)
- Cookie sheets, lined with parchment paper

2¾ cups	all-purpose flour	675 mL
½ cup	unsweetened Dutch-process cocoa powder	125 mL
2 tsp	baking powder	10 mL
¼ tsp	salt	1 mL
4	eggs	4
1¼ cups	granulated sugar	300 mL
⅓ cup	unsalted butter, melted	75 mL
2 tsp	vanilla extract	10 mL
1 cup	chopped walnuts	250 mL

1. In a bowl, whisk together flour, cocoa powder, baking powder and salt until well combined. Set aside.

2. In a large bowl, using an electric mixer on medium speed, lightly beat eggs. Add granulated sugar and beat until well combined, about 2 minutes. Gradually beat in melted butter until thoroughly blended. Beat in vanilla. Scrape down sides of bowl. On low speed or using a wooden spoon, add flour mixture, one-third at a time, beating well after each addition. By hand, fold in walnuts.

3. Spoon dough onto prepared cookie sheet, forming 2 long, flat logs each measuring 12 inches (30 cm) long by 2 to 3 inches (5 to 7.5 cm) wide and spaced 4 inches (10 cm) apart. Biscotti will spread during baking, nearly doubling in width.

4. Bake in preheated oven for 25 to 30 minutes or until firm to the touch.

5. Slide parchment paper onto a wire cooling rack. Cool for 10 minutes, then transfer warm loaves to a cutting board. With a sharp serrated knife, cut each loaf on a 45-degree angle into ½-inch (1 cm) slices. Place, cut side down, about ½ inch (1 cm) apart on prepared cookie sheets.

6. Bake for 7 minutes. Turn slices over and bake an additional 5 to 7 minutes or just until dry. Do not allow biscotti to overbake. Immediately transfer biscotti to cooling rack and cool completely. Biscotti will crisp as they cool.

Cranberry White Chocolate Biscotti

Cranberries and white chocolate pair together beautifully in these wonderful biscotti. The almond extract adds another level to the depth of flavor in these tasty cookies.

Tips

For the best flavor, use white chocolate chips rather than vanilla or white chips. White chocolate chips contain cocoa butter, the essential ingredient in white chocolate. Vanilla baking chips or plain white chips do not contain cocoa butter.

For a pretty appearance, dip cooled biscotti in melted white chocolate (see page 395).

Biscotti may be wrapped well in foil and frozen for up to 2 months. Do not freeze chocolate-dipped biscotti. Thaw frozen biscotti, then dip in melted chocolate.

- Preheat oven to 350°F (180°C)
- Cookie sheets, lined with parchment paper

3 cups	all-purpose flour	750 mL
2 tsp	baking powder	10 mL
1/4 tsp	salt	1 mL
4	eggs	4
1 1/4 cups	granulated sugar	300 mL
1/3 cup	unsalted butter, melted	75 mL
1 tsp	vanilla extract	5 mL
1/2 tsp	almond extract	2 mL
1 cup	dried cranberries	250 mL
3/4 cup	chopped white chocolate or white chocolate chips	175 mL

1. In a bowl, whisk together flour, baking powder and salt until well combined. Set aside.

2. In a large bowl, using an electric mixer on medium speed, lightly beat eggs. Add granulated sugar and beat until well combined, about 2 minutes. Gradually beat in melted butter until thoroughly blended. Beat in vanilla and almond extract. Scrape down sides of bowl. On low speed or using a wooden spoon, add flour mixture, one-third at a time, beating well after each addition. By hand, fold in cranberries and white chocolate.

3. Spoon dough onto prepared cookie sheet, forming 2 long, flat logs each measuring 12 inches (30 cm) long by 2 to 3 inches (5 to 7.5 cm) wide and spaced 4 inches (10 cm) apart. Biscotti will spread during baking, nearly doubling in width.

4. Bake in preheated oven for 25 to 30 minutes or until firm to the touch and lightly golden brown.

5. Slide parchment paper onto a wire cooling rack. Cool for 10 minutes, then transfer warm loaves to a cutting board. With a sharp serrated knife, cut each loaf on a 45-degree angle into 1/2-inch (1 cm) slices. Place, cut side down, about 1/2 inch (1 cm) apart on prepared cookie sheets.

6. Bake for 7 minutes. Turn slices over and bake an additional 5 to 7 minutes or just until dry. Do not allow biscotti to darken too much in color. Immediately transfer biscotti to cooling rack and cool completely. Biscotti will crisp as they cool.

Blueberry Lemon Biscotti

● ● ●

Adding lemon to these cookies really enhances the flavor of the blueberries.

Tip

When zesting lemons, remove only the outer, colored part of the peel. The white part underneath, called the pith, is very bitter and will give cookies an unpleasant flavor. A Microplane grater will finely zest the lemon peel for a wonderful texture in the biscotti.

- Preheat oven to 350°F (180°C)
- Cookie sheets, lined with parchment paper

3 cups	all-purpose flour	750 mL
2 tsp	baking powder	10 mL
¼ tsp	salt	1 mL
4	eggs	4
1¼ cups	granulated sugar	300 mL
¼ cup	unsalted butter, melted	50 mL
3 tbsp	grated lemon zest	45 mL
½ tsp	vanilla extract	2 mL
1 cup	dried blueberries	250 mL

1. In a bowl, whisk together flour, baking powder and salt until well combined. Set aside.

2. In a large bowl, using an electric mixer on medium speed, lightly beat eggs. Add granulated sugar and beat until well combined, about 2 minutes. Gradually beat in melted butter until thoroughly blended. Beat in lemon zest and vanilla. Scrape down sides of bowl. On low speed or using a wooden spoon, add flour mixture, one-third at a time, beating well after each addition. By hand, fold in blueberries.

3. Spoon dough onto prepared cookie sheet, forming 2 long, flat logs each measuring 12 inches (30 cm) long by 2 to 3 inches (5 to 7.5 cm) wide and spaced 4 inches (10 cm) apart. Biscotti will spread during baking, nearly doubling in width.

4. Bake in preheated oven for 25 to 30 minutes or until firm to the touch and lightly golden brown.

5. Slide parchment paper onto a wire cooling rack. Cool for 10 minutes, then transfer warm loaves to a cutting board. With a sharp serrated knife, cut each loaf on a 45-degree angle into ½-inch (1 cm) slices. Place, cut side down, about ½ inch (1 cm) apart on prepared cookie sheets.

6. Bake for 7 minutes. Turn slices over and bake an additional 5 to 7 minutes or just until dry. Do not allow biscotti to darken too much in color. Immediately transfer biscotti to cooling rack and cool completely. Biscotti will crisp as they cool.

Spumoni Biscotti

● ● ●

I really enjoy a good spumoni ice cream made with quality ingredients and thought those same flavors would make a great biscotti. These cookies are very festive and are delightful during the holidays or for other special occasions.

Tips

Dried Bing cherries are wonderful in this recipe. However, other types of dried cherries may be substituted if you cannot find dried Bing cherries.

Store biscotti in a tightly sealed container at room temperature for up to 3 weeks. Biscotti may be wrapped well in foil and frozen for up to 2 months.

- ● Preheat oven to 350°F (180°C)
- ● Cookie sheets, lined with parchment paper

3¼ cups	all-purpose flour	800 mL
2 tsp	baking powder	10 mL
¼ tsp	salt	1 mL
4	eggs	4
1¼ cups	granulated sugar	300 mL
½ cup	unsalted butter, melted	125 mL
2 tsp	almond extract	10 mL
1 cup	dried sweet cherries	250 mL
¾ cup	roasted unsalted pistachio nuts	175 mL
⅔ cup	chopped sweet dark chocolate or sweet dark chocolate chips	150 mL

1. In a bowl, whisk together flour, baking powder and salt until well combined. Set aside.

2. In a large bowl, using an electric mixer on medium speed, lightly beat eggs. Add granulated sugar and beat until well combined, about 2 minutes. Gradually beat in melted butter until thoroughly blended. Beat in almond extract. Scrape down sides of bowl. On low speed or using a wooden spoon, add flour mixture, one-third at a time, beating well after each addition. By hand, fold in cherries, pistachio nuts and sweet dark chocolate.

3. Spoon dough onto prepared cookie sheet, forming 2 long, flat logs each measuring 12 inches (30 cm) long by 2 to 3 inches (5 to 7.5 cm) wide and spaced 4 inches (10 cm) apart. Biscotti will spread during baking, nearly doubling in width.

4. Bake in preheated oven for 28 to 32 minutes or until firm to the touch and lightly golden brown.

5. Slide parchment paper onto a wire cooling rack. Cool for 10 minutes, then transfer warm loaves to a cutting board. With a sharp serrated knife, cut each loaf on a 45-degree angle into ½-inch (1 cm) slices. Place, cut side down, about ½ inch (1 cm) apart on prepared cookie sheets.

6. Bake for 7 minutes. Turn slices over and bake an additional 5 to 7 minutes or just until dry. Do not allow biscotti to darken too much in color. Immediately transfer biscotti to cooling rack and cool completely. Biscotti will crisp as they cool.

Chocolate Chip Biscotti

● ● ●

The crunchy slices are dappled with little bits of yummy chocolate.

Tips

Mini semisweet chocolate chips are available in most grocery stores. If you cannot find mini chocolate chips, chopped semisweet chocolate or regular semisweet chocolate chips may be substituted.

Never store chocolate in the refrigerator or freezer. When melted, moisture on the chocolate will cause it to harden into lumps. It will not melt smoothly and will be unusable for baking.

● **Preheat oven to 350°F (180°C)**
● **Cookie sheets, lined with parchment paper**

3¼ cups	all-purpose flour	800 mL
2 tsp	baking powder	10 mL
¼ tsp	salt	1 mL
4	eggs	4
⅔ cup	granulated sugar	150 mL
⅔ cup	packed light brown sugar	150 mL
⅓ cup	unsalted butter, melted	75 mL
2 tsp	vanilla extract	10 mL
1½ cups	mini semisweet chocolate chips	375 mL
¾ cup	chopped walnuts	175 mL

1. In a bowl, whisk together flour, baking powder and salt until well combined. Set aside.

2. In a large bowl, using an electric mixer on medium speed, lightly beat eggs. Add granulated sugar and brown sugar and beat until well combined, about 2 minutes. Gradually beat in melted butter until thoroughly blended. Beat in vanilla. Scrape down sides of bowl. On low speed or using a wooden spoon, add flour mixture, one-third at a time, beating well after each addition. By hand, fold in chocolate chips and walnuts.

3. Spoon dough onto prepared cookie sheet, forming 2 long, flat logs each measuring 12 inches (30 cm) long by 2 to 3 inches (5 to 7.5 cm) wide and spaced 4 inches (10 cm) apart. Biscotti will spread during baking, nearly doubling in width.

4. Bake in preheated oven for 22 to 27 minutes or until firm to the touch and lightly golden brown.

5. Slide parchment paper onto a wire cooling rack. Cool for 10 minutes, then transfer warm loaves to a cutting board. With a sharp serrated knife, cut each loaf on a 45-degree angle into ½-inch (1 cm) slices. Place, cut side down, about ½ inch (1 cm) apart on prepared cookie sheets.

6. Bake for 7 minutes. Turn slices over and bake an additional 5 to 7 minutes or just until dry. Do not allow biscotti to darken too much in color. Immediately transfer biscotti to cooling rack and cool completely. Biscotti will crisp as they cool.

Orange Biscotti

● ● ●

These are lovely biscotti to enjoy with tea, and the kitchen has a lovely aroma of orange as they bake.

Tips

I strongly advise against substituting margarine in any cookie recipe that calls for butter. In baking, butter adds to the flavor and texture. You just won't get the same results with margarine.

These citrus biscotti are particularly good dipped in melted semisweet chocolate (see page 395).

Variation

Orange Walnut Biscotti: By hand, fold 1 cup (250 mL) chopped walnuts into dough after mixing.

- Preheat oven to 350°F (180°C)
- Cookie sheets, lined with parchment paper

3½ cups	all-purpose flour	875 mL
2 tsp	baking powder	10 mL
¼ tsp	salt	1 mL
4	eggs	4
1¼ cups	granulated sugar	300 mL
¼ cup	unsalted butter, melted	50 mL
3 tbsp	grated orange zest	45 mL
2 tbsp	freshly-squeezed orange juice	25 mL
1 tsp	vanilla extract	5 mL

1. In a bowl, whisk together flour, baking powder and salt until well combined. Set aside.

2. In a large bowl, using an electric mixer on medium speed, lightly beat eggs. Add granulated sugar and beat until well combined, about 2 minutes. Gradually beat in melted butter until thoroughly blended. Beat in orange zest, orange juice and vanilla. Scrape down sides of bowl. On low speed or using a wooden spoon, add flour mixture, one-third at a time, beating well after each addition.

3. Spoon dough onto prepared cookie sheet, forming 2 long, flat logs each measuring 12 inches (30 cm) long by 2 to 3 inches (5 to 7.5 cm) wide and spaced 4 inches (10 cm) apart. Biscotti will spread during baking, nearly doubling in width.

4. Bake in preheated oven for 25 to 30 minutes or until firm to the touch and lightly golden brown.

5. Slide parchment paper onto a wire cooling rack. Cool for 10 minutes, then transfer warm loaves to a cutting board. With a sharp serrated knife, cut each loaf on a 45-degree angle into ½-inch (1 cm) slices. Place, cut side down, about ½ inch (1 cm) apart on prepared cookie sheets.

6. Bake for 7 minutes. Turn slices over and bake an additional 5 to 7 minutes or just until dry. Do not allow biscotti to darken too much in color. Immediately transfer biscotti to cooling rack and cool completely. Biscotti will crisp as they cool.

Cinnamon Sugar Biscotti

Makes about 4 dozen biscotti

● ● ●

The classic pairing of cinnamon and sugar makes for wonderful crisp and sweet biscotti. Reminiscent of the flavor of old-fashioned cinnamon cookies, these biscotti make a tasty and comforting treat for a midmorning coffee break or a late-night snack.

Tips

Bread flour has a high protein content and should not be used for baking biscotti.

Store biscotti in a tightly sealed container at room temperature for up to 3 weeks. Biscotti may be wrapped well in foil and frozen for up to 2 months.

- Preheat oven to 350°F (180°C)
- Cookie sheets, lined with parchment paper

3 cups	all-purpose flour	750 mL
2 tsp	baking powder	10 mL
1½ tsp	ground cinnamon	7 mL
¼ tsp	salt	1 mL
4	eggs	4
1¼ cups	granulated sugar	300 mL
¼ cup	unsalted butter, melted	50 mL
2 tsp	vanilla extract	10 mL

Topping

2 tbsp	granulated sugar	25 mL
1½ tsp	ground cinnamon	7 mL

1. In a bowl, whisk together flour, baking powder, cinnamon and salt until well combined. Set aside.

2. In a large bowl, using an electric mixer on medium speed, lightly beat eggs. Add granulated sugar and beat until well combined, about 2 minutes. Gradually beat in melted butter until thoroughly blended. Beat in vanilla. Scrape down sides of bowl. On low speed or using a wooden spoon, add flour mixture, one-third at a time, beating well after each addition.

3. Spoon dough onto prepared cookie sheet, forming 2 long, flat logs each measuring 12 inches (30 cm) long by 2 to 3 inches (5 to 7.5 cm) wide and spaced 4 inches (10 cm) apart. Biscotti will spread during baking, nearly doubling in width.

4. *Topping:* In a small bowl, whisk together granulated sugar and cinnamon until well blended. Sprinkle 1 tablespoon (15 mL) evenly over top of each loaf. Reserve remaining sugar mixture.

5. Bake in preheated oven for 25 to 30 minutes or until firm to the touch and lightly golden brown.

6. Slide parchment paper onto a wire cooling rack. Cool for 10 minutes, then transfer warm loaves to a cutting board. With a sharp serrated knife, cut each loaf on a 45-degree angle into ½-inch (1 cm) slices. Place, cut side down, about ½ inch (1 cm) apart on prepared cookie sheets. Sprinkle half of the reserved sugar mixture over biscotti slices.

7. Bake for 7 minutes. Turn slices over and sprinkle with the remaining sugar mixture. Bake an additional 5 to 7 minutes or just until dry. Do not allow biscotti to darken too much in color. Immediately transfer biscotti to cooling rack and cool completely. Biscotti will crisp as they cool.

Mocha Biscotti

● ● ●

Espresso powder adds a depth of flavor to the cocoa powder.

Tip

Use regular unsalted butter in stick or brick form for making biscotti. Whipped butters contain air, while "light" butters contain a lot of water, both of which will produce flat, tough biscotti.

Variation

Mocha Almond Biscotti: By hand, fold 1 cup (250 mL) chopped unsalted almonds into dough after mixing.

- Preheat oven to 350°F (180°C)
- Cookie sheets, lined with parchment paper

2¾ cups	all-purpose flour	675 mL
⅓ cup	unsweetened Dutch-process cocoa powder	75 mL
1 tbsp	instant espresso powder	15 mL
2 tsp	baking powder	10 mL
¼ tsp	salt	1 mL
4	eggs	4
⅔ cup	granulated sugar	150 mL
⅔ cup	packed light brown sugar	150 mL
⅓ cup	unsalted butter, melted	75 mL
1½ tsp	vanilla extract	7 mL

1. In a bowl, whisk together flour, cocoa powder, espresso powder, baking powder and salt until well combined. Set aside.

2. In a large bowl, using an electric mixer on medium speed, lightly beat eggs. Add granulated sugar and brown sugar and beat until well combined, about 2 minutes. Gradually beat in melted butter until thoroughly blended. Beat in vanilla. Scrape down sides of bowl. On low speed or using a wooden spoon, add flour mixture, one-third at a time, beating well after each addition.

3. Spoon dough onto prepared cookie sheet, forming 2 long, flat logs each measuring 12 inches (30 cm) long by 2 to 3 inches (5 to 7.5 cm) wide and spaced 4 inches (10 cm) apart. Biscotti will spread during baking, nearly doubling in width.

4. Bake in preheated oven for 25 to 30 minutes or until firm to the touch.

5. Slide parchment paper onto a wire cooling rack. Cool for 10 minutes, then transfer warm loaves to a cutting board. With a sharp serrated knife, cut each loaf on a 45-degree angle into ½-inch (1 cm) slices. Place, cut side down, about ½ inch (1 cm) apart on prepared cookie sheets.

6. Bake for 7 minutes. Turn slices over and bake an additional 5 to 7 minutes or just until dry. Do not allow biscotti to darken too much in color. Immediately transfer biscotti to cooling rack and cool completely. Biscotti will crisp as they cool.

Cherry Almond Biscotti

Makes about 4 dozen biscotti ● ● ●

I like to use dried Bing cherries in this recipe, but dried sour cherries also work well.

Tip

Dried cherries can be found in the grocery aisle with raisins and other dried fruits. Choose dried fruit that is plump, tender and soft. Fruit that is dried out will be tough and draw moisture from the cookies, making them dry.

Variation

Cherry Pecan Biscotti: Substitute chopped pecans for chopped almonds.

- Preheat oven to 350°F (180°C)
- Cookie sheets, lined with parchment paper

3 cups	all-purpose flour	750 mL
2 tsp	baking powder	10 mL
¼ tsp	salt	1 mL
4	eggs	4
1¼ cups	granulated sugar	300 mL
¼ cup	unsalted butter, melted	50 mL
1 tsp	vanilla extract	5 mL
1 tsp	almond extract	5 mL
1 cup	dried cherries	250 mL
¾ cup	chopped unsalted almonds	175 mL

1. In a bowl, whisk together flour, baking powder and salt until well combined. Set aside.

2. In a large bowl, using an electric mixer on medium speed, lightly beat eggs. Add granulated sugar and beat until well combined, about 2 minutes. Gradually beat in melted butter until thoroughly blended. Beat in vanilla and almond extract. Scrape down sides of bowl. On low speed or using a wooden spoon, add flour mixture, one-third at a time, beating well after each addition. By hand, fold in cherries and almonds.

3. Spoon dough onto prepared cookie sheet, forming 2 long, flat logs each measuring 12 inches (30 cm) long by 2 to 3 inches (5 to 7.5 cm) wide and spaced 4 inches (10 cm) apart. Biscotti will spread during baking, nearly doubling in width.

4. Bake in preheated oven for 25 to 30 minutes or until firm to the touch and lightly golden brown.

5. Slide parchment paper onto a wire cooling rack. Cool for 10 minutes, then transfer warm loaves to a cutting board. With a sharp serrated knife, cut each loaf on a 45-degree angle into ½-inch (1 cm) slices. Place, cut side down, about ½ inch (1 cm) apart on prepared cookie sheets.

6. Bake for 7 minutes. Turn slices over and bake an additional 5 to 7 minutes or just until dry. Do not allow biscotti to darken too much in color. Immediately transfer biscotti to cooling rack and cool completely. Biscotti will crisp as they cool.

Brownie Biscotti

Makes about 4 dozen biscotti

With lots of cocoa powder and chopped chocolate, these biscotti are very satisfying.

Tips

Store eggs in their original carton on a shelf in the refrigerator. Do not store eggs in the door, where the temperature fluctuates every time the door is opened.

Store biscotti in a tightly sealed container at room temperature for up to 3 weeks. Biscotti may be wrapped well in foil and frozen for up to 2 months.

- Preheat oven to 350°F (180°C)
- Cookie sheets, lined with parchment paper

2¾ cups	all-purpose flour	675 mL
⅔ cup	unsweetened Dutch-process cocoa powder	150 mL
2 tsp	baking powder	10 mL
1 tsp	instant espresso powder	5 mL
¼ tsp	salt	1 mL
4	eggs	4
¾ cup	granulated sugar	175 mL
¾ cup	packed dark brown sugar	175 mL
½ cup	unsalted butter, melted	125 mL
2 tsp	vanilla extract	10 mL
¾ cup	chopped semisweet chocolate or semisweet chocolate chips	175 mL
¾ cup	chopped walnuts	175 mL

1. In a bowl, whisk together flour, cocoa powder, baking powder, espresso powder and salt until well combined. Set aside.

2. In a large bowl, using an electric mixer on medium speed, lightly beat eggs. Add granulated sugar and brown sugar and beat until well combined, about 2 minutes. Gradually beat in melted butter until thoroughly blended. Beat in vanilla. Scrape down sides of bowl. On low speed or using a wooden spoon, add flour mixture, one-third at a time, beating well after each addition. By hand, fold in chocolate and walnuts.

3. Spoon dough onto prepared cookie sheet, forming 2 long, flat logs each measuring 12 inches (30 cm) long by 2 to 3 inches (5 to 7.5 cm) wide and spaced 4 inches (10 cm) apart. Biscotti will spread during baking, nearly doubling in width.

4. Bake in preheated oven for 30 to 35 minutes or until firm to the touch.

5. Slide parchment paper onto a wire cooling rack. Cool for 10 minutes, then transfer warm loaves to a cutting board. With a sharp serrated knife, cut each loaf on a 45-degree angle into ½-inch (1 cm) slices. Place, cut side down, about ½ inch (1 cm) apart on prepared cookie sheets.

6. Bake for 7 minutes. Turn slices over and bake an additional 5 to 7 minutes or just until dry. Do not allow biscotti to darken too much in color. Immediately transfer biscotti to cooling rack and cool completely. Biscotti will crisp as they cool.

Pistachio Biscotti

Makes about 4 dozen biscotti ● ● ●

Pistachio nuts have a light green color and a mild, sweet flavor.

Tips

If you do not have pistachio flavoring, almond extract may substituted.

Always use pure vanilla extract in baking. Imitation vanilla is made from synthetic flavors and colors, and the taste cannot compare to pure vanilla extract.

Drizzle cooled biscotti with melted sweet dark chocolate for an added dimension of flavor.

● **Preheat oven to 350°F (180°C)**
● **Cookie sheets, lined with parchment paper**

3 cups	all-purpose flour	750 mL
2 tsp	baking powder	10 mL
¼ tsp	salt	1 mL
4	eggs	4
1¼ cups	granulated sugar	300 mL
¼ cup	unsalted butter, melted	50 mL
1 tsp	vanilla extract	5 mL
½ tsp	pistachio flavoring	2 mL
1⅓ cups	chopped unsalted pistachio nuts	325 mL

1. In a bowl, whisk together flour, baking powder and salt until well combined. Set aside.

2. In a large bowl, using an electric mixer on medium speed, lightly beat eggs. Add granulated sugar and beat until well combined, about 2 minutes. Gradually beat in melted butter until thoroughly blended. Beat in vanilla extract and pistachio flavoring. Scrape down sides of bowl. On low speed or using a wooden spoon, add flour mixture, one-third at a time, beating well after each addition. By hand, fold in pistachio nuts.

3. Spoon dough onto prepared cookie sheet, forming 2 long, flat logs each measuring 12 inches (30 cm) long by 2 to 3 inches (5 to 7.5 cm) wide and spaced 4 inches (10 cm) apart. Biscotti will spread during baking, nearly doubling in width.

4. Bake in preheated oven for 25 to 30 minutes or until firm to the touch and lightly golden brown.

5. Slide parchment paper onto a wire cooling rack. Cool for 10 minutes, then transfer warm loaves to a cutting board. With a sharp serrated knife, cut each loaf on a 45-degree angle into ½-inch (1 cm) slices. Place, cut side down, about ½ inch (1 cm) apart on prepared cookie sheets.

6. Bake for 7 minutes. Turn slices over and bake an additional 5 to 7 minutes or just until dry. Do not allow biscotti to darken too much in color. Immediately transfer biscotti to cooling rack and cool completely. Biscotti will crisp as they cool.

Lemon Biscotti

● ● ●

Infused with a delicate citrus scent, these biscotti have a lovely lemon flavor.

Tips

Ripe lemons with a deep yellow color will yield the best flavor.

Store biscotti in a tightly sealed container at room temperature for up to 3 weeks. Biscotti may be wrapped well in foil and frozen for up to 2 months.

Variation

Lemon Poppy Seed Biscotti: Whisk 2 tbsp (25 mL) poppy seeds into flour mixture.

- Preheat oven to 350°F (180°C)
- Cookie sheets, lined with parchment paper

3¼ cups	all-purpose flour	800 mL
2 tsp	baking powder	10 mL
¼ tsp	salt	1 mL
4	eggs	4
1⅓ cups	granulated sugar	325 mL
¼ cup	unsalted butter, melted	50 mL
3 tbsp	grated lemon zest	45 mL
1½ tbsp	freshly squeezed lemon juice	22 mL
1 tsp	vanilla extract	5 mL

1. In a bowl, whisk together flour, baking powder and salt until well combined. Set aside.

2. In a large bowl, using an electric mixer on medium speed, lightly beat eggs. Add granulated sugar and beat until well combined, about 2 minutes. Gradually beat in melted butter until thoroughly blended. Beat in lemon zest, lemon juice and vanilla. Scrape down sides of bowl. On low speed or using a wooden spoon, add flour mixture, one-third at a time, beating well after each addition.

3. Spoon dough onto prepared cookie sheet, forming 2 long, flat logs each measuring 12 inches (30 cm) long by 2 to 3 inches (5 to 7.5 cm) wide and spaced 4 inches (10 cm) apart. Biscotti will spread during baking, nearly doubling in width.

4. Bake in preheated oven for 25 to 30 minutes or until firm to the touch and lightly golden brown.

5. Slide parchment paper onto a wire cooling rack. Cool for 10 minutes, then transfer warm loaves to a cutting board. With a sharp serrated knife, cut each loaf on a 45-degree angle into ½-inch (1 cm) slices. Place, cut side down, about ½ inch (1 cm) apart on prepared cookie sheets.

6. Bake for 7 minutes. Turn slices over and bake an additional 5 to 7 minutes or just until dry. Do not allow biscotti to darken too much in color. Immediately transfer biscotti to cooling rack and cool completely. Biscotti will crisp as they cool.

Cappuccino Biscotti

These crispy slices have a smooth coffee flavor enhanced by chocolate and cream.

Tip

To measure flour properly, stir the flour in the package or container to lighten it up, then gently spoon the flour into a dry measuring cup. Use a knife or spatula to level off the flour even with the rim of the cup.

- Preheat oven to 350°F (180°C)
- Cookie sheets, lined with parchment paper

3½ cups	all-purpose flour	875 mL
2½ tbsp	unsweetened Dutch-process cocoa powder	37 mL
5 tsp	instant espresso powder	25 mL
2¼ tsp	baking powder	11 mL
¼ tsp	salt	1 mL
4	eggs	4
1⅓ cups	granulated sugar	325 mL
⅓ cup	unsalted butter, melted	75 mL
3 tbsp	half-and-half (10%) cream	45 mL
1½ tsp	vanilla extract	7 mL

1. In a bowl, whisk together flour, cocoa powder, espresso powder, baking powder and salt until well combined. Set aside.
2. In a large bowl, using an electric mixer on medium speed, lightly beat eggs. Add granulated sugar and beat until well combined, about 2 minutes. Gradually beat in melted butter until thoroughly blended. Beat in cream and vanilla. Scrape down sides of bowl. On low speed or using a wooden spoon, add flour mixture, one-third at a time, beating well after each addition.
3. Spoon dough onto prepared cookie sheet, forming 2 long, flat logs each measuring 12 inches (30 cm) long by 2 to 3 inches (5 to 7.5 cm) wide and spaced 4 inches (10 cm) apart. Biscotti will spread during baking, nearly doubling in width.
4. Bake in preheated oven for 25 to 30 minutes or until firm to the touch and lightly golden brown.
5. Slide parchment paper onto a wire cooling rack. Cool for 10 minutes, then transfer warm loaves to a cutting board. With a sharp serrated knife, cut each loaf on a 45-degree angle into ½-inch (1 cm) slices. Place, cut side down, about ½ inch (1 cm) apart on prepared cookie sheets.
6. Bake for 7 minutes. Turn slices over and bake an additional 5 to 7 minutes or just until dry. Do not allow biscotti to darken too much in color. Immediately transfer biscotti to cooling rack and cool completely. Biscotti will crisp as they cool.

Hazelnut Chocolate Biscotti

Hazelnuts are very popular for baking, and they make excellent biscotti. These treats are particularly good when glazed with melted chocolate.

Tips

If you don't have hazelnut flavoring, almond extract may be substituted.

Baking powder is a compound leavener. The primary ingredient is baking soda, but baking powder also contains cornstarch and an acid, usually cream of tartar, to activate the baking soda. The cornstarch acts as a buffer to delay the reaction of the baking soda and acid after combination with the liquid.

For extra chocolate flavor, drizzle cooled biscotti with melted semisweet chocolate (see page 395).

- Preheat oven to 350°F (180°C)
- Cookie sheets, lined with parchment paper

3 cups	all-purpose flour	750 mL
2 tsp	baking powder	10 mL
¼ tsp	salt	1 mL
4	eggs	4
1¼ cups	granulated sugar	300 mL
¼ cup	unsalted butter, melted	50 mL
1 tsp	vanilla extract	5 mL
½ tsp	hazelnut flavoring	2 mL
1⅓ cups	chopped unsalted hazelnuts	325 mL
¾ cup	chopped semisweet chocolate or semisweet chocolate chips	175 mL

1. In a bowl, whisk together flour, baking powder and salt until well combined. Set aside.

2. In a large bowl, using an electric mixer on medium speed, lightly beat eggs. Add granulated sugar and beat until well combined, about 2 minutes. Gradually beat in melted butter until thoroughly blended. Beat in vanilla and hazelnut flavoring. Scrape down sides of bowl. On low speed or using a wooden spoon, add flour mixture, one-third at a time, beating well after each addition. By hand, fold in hazelnuts and chocolate.

3. Spoon dough onto prepared cookie sheet, forming 2 long, flat logs each measuring 12 inches (30 cm) long by 2 to 3 inches (5 to 7.5 cm) wide and spaced 4 inches (10 cm) apart. Biscotti will spread during baking, nearly doubling in width.

4. Bake in preheated oven for 25 to 30 minutes or until firm to the touch and lightly golden brown.

5. Slide parchment paper onto a wire cooling rack. Cool for 10 minutes, then transfer warm loaves to a cutting board. With a sharp serrated knife, cut each loaf on a 45-degree angle into ½-inch (1 cm) slices. Place, cut side down, about ½ inch (1 cm) apart on prepared cookie sheets.

6. Bake for 7 minutes. Turn slices over and bake an additional 5 to 7 minutes or just until dry. Do not allow biscotti to darken too much in color. Immediately transfer biscotti to cooling rack and cool completely. Biscotti will crisp as they cool.

White Chocolate Macadamia Biscotti

For complete white chocolate decadence, drizzle cooled biscotti with melted white chocolate.

Tips

White chocolate should not be melted in the microwave as it can easily burn and turn lumpy if overheated.

Store biscotti in a tightly sealed container at room temperature for up to 3 weeks. Biscotti may be wrapped well in foil and frozen for up to 2 months. Do not freeze chocolate-glazed biscotti. Thaw frozen biscotti, then drizzle with melted chocolate.

These biscotti are really good when drizzled with melted white chocolate (see page 395).

Variation

White Chocolate Almond Biscotti: Substitute chopped unsalted almonds for chopped macadamia nuts.

- Preheat oven to 350°F (180°C)
- Cookie sheets, lined with parchment paper

1 cup	chopped white chocolate	250 mL
3⅔ cups	all-purpose flour	900 mL
2½ tsp	baking powder	12 mL
¼ tsp	salt	1 mL
4	eggs	4
1 cup	granulated sugar	250 mL
¼ cup	unsalted butter, melted	50 mL
1½ tsp	vanilla extract	7 mL
1⅓ cups	chopped roasted unsalted macadamia nuts	325 mL
¾ cup	chopped white chocolate or white chocolate chips	175 mL

1. In the top of a double boiler over simmering water, heat the 1 cup (250 mL) white chocolate, stirring frequently, until chocolate softens and melts. Remove pan from heat and stir until chocolate is completely melted and smooth. Set aside.

2. In a bowl, whisk together flour, baking powder and salt until well combined. Set aside.

3. In a large bowl, using an electric mixer on medium speed, lightly beat eggs. Add granulated sugar and beat until well combined, about 2 minutes. Gradually beat in melted butter until thoroughly blended. Beat in melted white chocolate and vanilla. Scrape down sides of bowl. On low speed or using a wooden spoon, add flour mixture, one-third at a time, beating well after each addition. By hand, fold in macadamia nuts and ¾ cup (175 mL) chopped white chocolate.

4. Spoon dough onto prepared cookie sheet, forming 2 long, flat logs each measuring 12 inches (30 cm) long by 2 to 3 inches (5 to 7.5 cm) wide and spaced 4 inches (10 cm) apart. Biscotti will spread during baking, nearly doubling in width.

5. Bake in preheated oven for 25 to 30 minutes or until firm to the touch and lightly golden brown.

6. Slide parchment paper onto a wire cooling rack. Cool for 10 minutes, then transfer warm loaves to a cutting board. With a sharp serrated knife, cut each loaf on a 45-degree angle into ½-inch (1 cm) slices. Place, cut side down, about ½ inch (1 cm) apart on prepared cookie sheets.

7. Bake for 6 minutes. Turn slices over and bake an additional 5 to 6 minutes or just until dry. Do not allow biscotti to darken too much. Transfer biscotti to cooling rack and cool completely.

Chocolate Cherry Biscotti

Makes about 4 dozen biscotti

● ● ●

There is a wonderful synergy between the flavors of chocolate and cherries.

Tip

Parchment paper is a heat- and grease-resistant baking paper used to line cookie sheets to prevent cookies from sticking to the sheet and keep cookies from burning on the bottom. It can be found in most grocery stores.

Variation

Chocolate Cherry Almond Biscotti: By hand, fold 1 cup (250 mL) chopped unsalted almonds into dough along with the cherries.

- ● **Preheat oven to 350°F (180°C)**
- ● **Cookie sheets, lined with parchment paper**

2³⁄₄ cups	all-purpose flour	675 mL
¹⁄₂ cup	unsweetened Dutch-process cocoa powder	125 mL
2 tsp	baking powder	10 mL
¹⁄₄ tsp	salt	1 mL
4	eggs	4
1¹⁄₄ cups	granulated sugar	300 mL
¹⁄₃ cup	unsalted butter, melted	75 mL
1 tsp	vanilla extract	5 mL
1 tsp	almond extract	5 mL
1 cup	dried cherries	250 mL

1. In a bowl, whisk together flour, cocoa powder, baking powder and salt until well combined. Set aside.

2. In a large bowl, using an electric mixer on medium speed, lightly beat eggs. Add granulated sugar and beat until well combined, about 2 minutes. Gradually beat in melted butter until thoroughly blended. Beat in vanilla and almond extract. Scrape down sides of bowl. On low speed or using a wooden spoon, add flour mixture, one-third at a time, beating well after each addition. By hand, fold in cherries.

3. Spoon dough onto prepared cookie sheet, forming 2 long, flat logs each measuring 12 inches (30 cm) long by 2 to 3 inches (5 to 7.5 cm) wide and spaced 4 inches (10 cm) apart. Biscotti will spread during baking, nearly doubling in width.

4. Bake in preheated oven for 25 to 30 minutes or until firm to the touch.

5. Slide parchment paper onto a wire cooling rack. Cool for 10 minutes, then transfer warm loaves to a cutting board. With a sharp serrated knife, cut each loaf on a 45-degree angle into ¹⁄₂-inch (1 cm) slices. Place, cut side down, about ¹⁄₂ inch (1 cm) apart on prepared cookie sheets.

6. Bake for 7 minutes. Turn slices over and bake an additional 5 to 7 minutes or just until dry. Do not allow biscotti to darken too much in color. Immediately transfer biscotti to cooling rack and cool completely. Biscotti will crisp as they cool.

Nut Biscotti

If you love nuts, this is the recipe for you. These biscotti are great plain or drizzle them with chocolate for a special treat.

Tips

This is a very versatile recipe. You can use any combination of nuts you like.

Nuts can turn rancid quickly. If you're not going to use nuts you have on hand within a few weeks of purchase, wrap them tightly and store them in the freezer to preserve their flavor.

Melted semisweet chocolate is an excellent choice for drizzling over these nutty biscotti (see page 395).

- Preheat oven to 350°F (180°C)
- Cookie sheets, lined with parchment paper

3 cups	all-purpose flour	750 mL
2 tsp	baking powder	10 mL
¼ tsp	salt	1 mL
4	eggs	4
⅔ cup	granulated sugar	150 mL
⅔ cup	packed light brown sugar	150 mL
⅓ cup	unsalted butter, melted	75 mL
2 tsp	vanilla extract	10 mL
1 tsp	almond extract	5 mL
1 cup	chopped unsalted almonds	250 mL
1 cup	chopped walnuts	250 mL
1 cup	chopped pecans	250 mL

1. In a bowl, whisk together flour, baking powder and salt until well combined. Set aside.

2. In a large bowl, using an electric mixer on medium speed, lightly beat eggs. Add granulated sugar and brown sugar and beat until well combined, about 2 minutes. Gradually beat in melted butter until thoroughly blended. Beat in vanilla and almond extract. Scrape down sides of bowl. On low speed or using a wooden spoon, add flour mixture, one-third at a time, beating well after each addition. By hand, fold in almonds, walnuts and pecans.

3. Spoon dough onto prepared cookie sheet, forming 2 long, flat logs each measuring 12 inches (30 cm) long by 2 to 3 inches (5 to 7.5 cm) wide and spaced 4 inches (10 cm) apart. Biscotti will spread during baking, nearly doubling in width.

4. Bake in preheated oven for 25 to 30 minutes or until firm to the touch and lightly golden brown.

5. Slide parchment paper onto a wire cooling rack. Cool for 10 minutes, then transfer warm loaves to a cutting board. With a sharp serrated knife, cut each loaf on a 45-degree angle into ½-inch (1 cm) slices. Place, cut side down, about ½ inch (1 cm) apart on prepared cookie sheets.

6. Bake for 7 minutes. Turn slices over and bake an additional 5 to 7 minutes or just until dry. Do not allow biscotti to darken too much in color. Immediately transfer biscotti to cooling rack and cool completely. Biscotti will crisp as they cool.

Espresso Biscotti

● ● ●

I like to dip these intensely coffee-flavored biscotti in sweet dark chocolate. Semisweet chocolate and bittersweet chocolate are also good choices.

Tips

Instant espresso powder can be found in the coffee aisle of most grocery stores.

Store biscotti in a tightly sealed container at room temperature for up to 3 weeks. Biscotti may be wrapped well in foil and frozen for up to 2 months. Do not freeze chocolate-dipped biscotti. Thaw frozen biscotti, then dip in melted chocolate.

- ● **Preheat oven to 350°F (180°C)**
- ● **Cookie sheets, lined with parchment paper**

3 cups	all-purpose flour	750 mL
3 tbsp	instant espresso powder	45 mL
2 tsp	baking powder	10 mL
¼ tsp	salt	1 mL
4	eggs	4
¾ cup	granulated sugar	175 mL
½ cup	packed dark brown sugar	125 mL
¼ cup	unsalted butter, melted	50 mL
1 tsp	vanilla extract	5 mL

1. In a bowl, whisk together flour, espresso powder, baking powder and salt until well combined. Set aside.

2. In a large bowl, using an electric mixer on medium speed, lightly beat eggs. Add granulated sugar and brown sugar and beat until well combined, about 2 minutes. Gradually beat in melted butter until thoroughly blended. Beat in vanilla. Scrape down sides of bowl. On low speed or using a wooden spoon, add flour mixture, one-third at a time, beating well after each addition.

3. Spoon dough onto prepared cookie sheet, forming 2 long, flat logs each measuring 12 inches (30 cm) long by 2 to 3 inches (5 to 7.5 cm) wide and spaced 4 inches (10 cm) apart. Biscotti will spread during baking, nearly doubling in width.

4. Bake in preheated oven for 25 to 30 minutes or until firm to the touch and lightly golden brown.

5. Slide parchment paper onto a wire cooling rack. Cool for 10 minutes, then transfer warm loaves to a cutting board. With a sharp serrated knife, cut each loaf on a 45-degree angle into ½-inch (1 cm) slices. Place, cut side down, about ½ inch (1 cm) apart on prepared cookie sheets.

6. Bake for 7 minutes. Turn slices over and bake an additional 5 to 7 minutes or just until dry. Do not allow biscotti to darken too much in color. Immediately transfer biscotti to cooling rack and cool completely. Biscotti will crisp as they cool.

Lemon Almond Biscotti

Crunchy almonds and a hint of almond extract add a nutty touch that nicely complements the lemon.

Tip

If you have trouble with the bottom of your biscotti browning too much or burning, try using insulated cookie sheets. Insulated sheets are actually two thin sheets with a pocket of air in between that keeps the top sheet from getting too hot.

- Preheat oven to 350°F (180°C)
- Cookie sheets, lined with parchment paper

3 1/4 cups	all-purpose flour	800 mL
2 tsp	baking powder	10 mL
1/4 tsp	salt	1 mL
4	eggs	4
1 1/4 cups	granulated sugar	300 mL
1/4 cup	unsalted butter, melted	50 mL
3 tbsp	grated lemon zest	45 mL
1 1/2 tbsp	freshly squeezed lemon juice	22 mL
1 tsp	vanilla extract	5 mL
1/4 tsp	almond extract	1 mL
1 cup	chopped unsalted almonds	250 mL

1. In a bowl, whisk together flour, baking powder and salt until well combined. Set aside.

2. In a large bowl, using an electric mixer on medium speed, lightly beat eggs. Add granulated sugar and beat until well combined, about 2 minutes. Gradually beat in melted butter until thoroughly blended. Beat in lemon zest, lemon juice, vanilla and almond extract. Scrape down sides of bowl. On low speed or using a wooden spoon, add flour mixture, one-third at a time, beating well after each addition. By hand, fold in almonds.

3. Spoon dough onto prepared cookie sheet, forming 2 long, flat logs each measuring 12 inches (30 cm) long by 2 to 3 inches (5 to 7.5 cm) wide and spaced 4 inches (10 cm) apart. Biscotti will spread during baking, nearly doubling in width.

4. Bake in preheated oven for 25 to 30 minutes or until firm to the touch and lightly golden brown.

5. Slide parchment paper onto a wire cooling rack. Cool for 10 minutes, then transfer warm loaves to a cutting board. With a sharp serrated knife, cut each loaf on a 45-degree angle into 1/2-inch (1 cm) slices. Place, cut side down, about 1/2 inch (1 cm) apart on prepared cookie sheets.

6. Bake for 7 minutes. Turn slices over and bake an additional 5 to 7 minutes or just until dry. Do not allow biscotti to darken too much in color. Immediately transfer biscotti to cooling rack and cool completely. Biscotti will crisp as they cool.

Maple Pecan Biscotti

Makes about 4 dozen biscotti

Maple and pecans are one of those classic flavor combinations that I love, and I couldn't resist using them in this delicious biscotti.

Tip

If you have problems with your biscotti overbaking or underbaking, use an oven thermometer to check the accuracy of your oven's temperature control.

Variation

Maple Walnut Biscotti: Substitute chopped walnuts for chopped pecans.

- ● **Preheat oven to 350°F (180°C)**
- ● **Cookie sheets, lined with parchment paper**

3¼ cups	all-purpose flour	800 mL
2 tsp	baking powder	10 mL
¼ tsp	salt	1 mL
4	eggs	4
1¼ cups	packed light brown sugar	300 mL
⅓ cup	unsalted butter, melted	75 mL
2 tsp	maple flavoring	10 mL
½ tsp	vanilla extract	2 mL
1½ cups	chopped pecans	375 mL

1. In a bowl, whisk together flour, baking powder and salt until well combined. Set aside.

2. In a large bowl, using an electric mixer on medium speed, lightly beat eggs. Add brown sugar and beat until well combined, about 2 minutes. Gradually beat in melted butter until thoroughly blended. Beat in maple flavoring and vanilla. Scrape down sides of bowl. On low speed or using a wooden spoon, add flour mixture, one-third at a time, beating well after each addition. By hand, fold in pecans.

3. Spoon dough onto prepared cookie sheet, forming 2 long, flat logs each measuring 12 inches (30 cm) long by 2 to 3 inches (5 to 7.5 cm) wide and spaced 4 inches (10 cm) apart. Biscotti will spread during baking, nearly doubling in width.

4. Bake in preheated oven for 25 to 30 minutes or until firm to the touch and lightly golden brown.

5. Slide parchment paper onto a wire cooling rack. Cool for 10 minutes, then transfer warm loaves to a cutting board. With a sharp serrated knife, cut each loaf on a 45-degree angle into ½-inch (1 cm) slices. Place, cut side down, about ½ inch (1 cm) apart on prepared cookie sheets.

6. Bake for 7 minutes. Turn slices over and bake an additional 5 to 7 minutes or just until dry. Do not allow biscotti to darken too much in color. Immediately transfer biscotti to cooling rack and cool completely. Biscotti will crisp as they cool.

Chocolate Chip Orange Biscotti

Makes about 4 dozen biscotti

The addition of orange zest has a magical effect on the flavor of chocolate.

Tips

Oranges with a deep orange–colored peel will yield zest with the most intense citrus flavor and aroma.

Store biscotti in a tightly sealed container at room temperature for up to 3 weeks. Biscotti may be wrapped well in foil and frozen for up to 2 months.

- Preheat oven to 350°F (180°C)
- Cookie sheets, lined with parchment paper

3 cups	all-purpose flour	750 mL
2 tsp	baking powder	10 mL
1/4 tsp	salt	1 mL
4	eggs	4
2/3 cup	granulated sugar	150 mL
2/3 cup	packed light brown sugar	150 mL
1/4 cup	unsalted butter, melted	50 mL
2 tbsp	grated orange zest	25 mL
1 tsp	vanilla extract	5 mL
1 1/2 cups	chopped semisweet chocolate or semisweet chocolate chips	375 mL

1. In a bowl, whisk together flour, baking powder and salt until well combined. Set aside.

2. In a large bowl, using an electric mixer on medium speed, lightly beat eggs. Add granulated sugar and brown sugar and beat until well combined, about 2 minutes. Gradually beat in melted butter until thoroughly blended. Beat in orange zest and vanilla. Scrape down sides of bowl. On low speed or using a wooden spoon, add flour mixture, one-third at a time, beating well after each addition. By hand, fold in chocolate chips.

3. Spoon dough onto prepared cookie sheet, forming 2 long, flat logs each measuring 12 inches (30 cm) long by 2 to 3 inches (5 to 7.5 cm) wide and spaced 4 inches (10 cm) apart. Biscotti will spread during baking, nearly doubling in width.

4. Bake in preheated oven for 22 to 27 minutes or until firm to the touch and lightly golden brown.

5. Slide parchment paper onto a wire cooling rack. Cool for 10 minutes, then transfer warm loaves to a cutting board. With a sharp serrated knife, cut each loaf on a 45-degree angle into 1/2-inch (1 cm) slices. Place, cut side down, about 1/2 inch (1 cm) apart on prepared cookie sheets.

6. Bake for 7 minutes. Turn slices over and bake an additional 5 to 7 minutes or just until dry. Do not allow biscotti to darken too much in color. Immediately transfer biscotti to cooling rack and cool completely. Biscotti will crisp as they cool.

Coconut Biscotti

During the second baking, the coconut lightly toasts and takes on a more complex flavor.

Tip

Chopping the coconut will give the biscotti a more uniform texture and make the logs easier to slice.

Variation

Coconut Macadamia Biscotti: By hand, fold 1 cup (250 mL) coarsely chopped unsalted macadamia nuts into dough after mixing.

- ● **Preheat oven to 350°F (180°C)**
- ● **Cookie sheets, lined with parchment paper**

3 cups	all-purpose flour	750 mL
2 tsp	baking powder	10 mL
¼ tsp	salt	1 mL
1⅓ cups	sweetened flaked coconut, chopped	325 mL
4	eggs	4
1 cup	granulated sugar	250 mL
⅓ cup	unsalted butter, melted	75 mL
1 tsp	vanilla extract	5 mL
½ tsp	almond extract	2 mL

1. In a bowl, whisk together flour, baking powder and salt until well combined. Stir in coconut. Set aside.

2. In a large bowl, using an electric mixer on medium speed, lightly beat eggs. Add granulated sugar and beat until well combined, about 2 minutes. Gradually beat in melted butter until thoroughly blended. Beat in vanilla and almond extract. Scrape down sides of bowl. On low speed or using a wooden spoon, add flour mixture, one-third at a time, beating well after each addition.

3. Spoon dough onto prepared cookie sheet, forming 2 long, flat logs each measuring 12 inches (30 cm) long by 2 to 3 inches (5 to 7.5 cm) wide and spaced 4 inches (10 cm) apart. Biscotti will spread during baking, nearly doubling in width.

4. Bake in preheated oven for 25 to 30 minutes or until firm to the touch and lightly golden brown.

5. Slide parchment paper onto a wire cooling rack. Cool for 10 minutes, then transfer warm loaves to a cutting board. With a sharp serrated knife, cut each loaf on a 45-degree angle into ½-inch (1 cm) slices. Place, cut side down, about ½ inch (1 cm) apart on prepared cookie sheets.

6. Bake for 7 minutes. Turn slices over and bake an additional 5 to 7 minutes or just until dry. Do not allow biscotti to darken too much in color. Immediately transfer biscotti to cooling rack and cool completely. Biscotti will crisp as they cool.

White Chocolate Lemon Biscotti

Makes about 4 dozen biscotti

The flavors of white chocolate and lemon blend together nicely. I like to drizzle these yummy biscotti with even more white chocolate.

Tip

Store biscotti in a tightly sealed container at room temperature for up to 3 weeks. Biscotti may be wrapped well in foil and frozen for up to 2 months. Do not freeze chocolate-glazed biscotti. Thaw frozen biscotti, then drizzle with melted chocolate.

- Preheat oven to 350°F (180°C)
- Cookie sheets, lined with parchment paper

3¼ cups	all-purpose flour	800 mL
2 tsp	baking powder	10 mL
¼ tsp	salt	1 mL
4	eggs	4
1¼ cups	granulated sugar	300 mL
¼ cup	unsalted butter, melted	50 mL
3 tbsp	grated lemon zest	45 mL
1½ tbsp	freshly squeezed lemon juice	22 mL
1 tsp	vanilla extract	5 mL
1 cup	chopped white chocolate or white chocolate chips	250 mL

1. In a bowl, whisk together flour, baking powder and salt until well combined. Set aside.

2. In a large bowl, using an electric mixer on medium speed, lightly beat eggs. Add granulated sugar and beat until well combined, about 2 minutes. Gradually beat in melted butter until thoroughly blended. Beat in lemon zest, lemon juice and vanilla. Scrape down sides of bowl. On low speed or using a wooden spoon, add flour mixture, one-third at a time, beating well after each addition. By hand, fold in white chocolate.

3. Spoon dough onto prepared cookie sheet, forming 2 long, flat logs each measuring 12 inches (30 cm) long by 2 to 3 inches (5 to 7.5 cm) wide and spaced 4 inches (10 cm) apart. Biscotti will spread during baking, nearly doubling in width.

4. Bake in preheated oven for 25 to 30 minutes or until firm to the touch and lightly golden brown.

5. Slide parchment paper onto a wire cooling rack. Cool for 10 minutes, then transfer warm loaves to a cutting board. With a sharp serrated knife, cut each loaf on a 45-degree angle into ½-inch (1 cm) slices. Place, cut side down, about ½ inch (1 cm) apart on prepared cookie sheets.

6. Bake for 7 minutes. Turn slices over and bake an additional 5 to 7 minutes or just until dry. Do not allow biscotti to darken too much in color. Immediately transfer biscotti to cooling rack and cool completely. Biscotti will crisp as they cool.

Macadamia Nut Biscotti

● ● ●

Enjoy these nutty biscotti with a cup of Kona coffee for a dreamy island getaway treat.

Tip

Fold in the nuts by hand to keep from overworking the dough after the flour is mixed in. Overworking the dough will make the biscotti tough.

- Preheat oven to 350°F (180°C)
- Cookie sheets, lined with parchment paper

3 cups	all-purpose flour	750 mL
2 tsp	baking powder	10 mL
1/4 tsp	salt	1 mL
4	eggs	4
3/4 cup	granulated sugar	175 mL
1/2 cup	packed light brown sugar	125 mL
1/3 cup	unsalted butter, melted	75 mL
2 tsp	vanilla extract	10 mL
1 1/2 cups	chopped roasted unsalted macadamia nuts	375 mL

1. In a bowl, whisk together flour, baking powder and salt until well combined. Set aside.

2. In a large bowl, using an electric mixer on medium speed, lightly beat eggs. Add granulated sugar and brown sugar and beat until well combined, about 2 minutes. Gradually beat in melted butter until thoroughly blended. Beat in vanilla. Scrape down sides of bowl. On low speed or using a wooden spoon, add flour mixture, one-third at a time, beating well after each addition. By hand, fold in macadamia nuts.

3. Spoon dough onto prepared cookie sheet, forming 2 long, flat logs each measuring 12 inches (30 cm) long by 2 to 3 inches (5 to 7.5 cm) wide and spaced 4 inches (10 cm) apart. Biscotti will spread during baking, nearly doubling in width.

4. Bake in preheated oven for 25 to 30 minutes or until firm to the touch and lightly golden brown.

5. Slide parchment paper onto a wire cooling rack. Cool for 10 minutes, then transfer warm loaves to a cutting board. With a sharp serrated knife, cut each loaf on a 45-degree angle into 1/2-inch (1 cm) slices. Place, cut side down, about 1/2 inch (1 cm) apart on prepared cookie sheets.

6. Bake for 7 minutes. Turn slices over and bake an additional 5 to 7 minutes or just until dry. Do not allow biscotti to darken too much in color. Immediately transfer biscotti to cooling rack and cool completely. Biscotti will crisp as they cool.

Currant Almond Biscotti

Makes about 4 dozen biscotti ● ● ●

Currants are a classic ingredient for scones, and they're also terrific in biscotti.

Tip

Baking powder and baking soda are not interchangeable. Always use the specific type and amount of leavener called for in the recipe.

Variation

Raisin Walnut Biscotti: Omit almond extract. Substitute raisins for currants and chopped walnuts for chopped almonds.

- Preheat oven to 350°F (180°C)
- Cookie sheets, lined with parchment paper

3 cups	all-purpose flour	750 mL
2 tsp	baking powder	10 mL
1/4 tsp	salt	1 mL
4	eggs	4
1 1/4 cups	granulated sugar	300 mL
1/4 cup	unsalted butter, melted	50 mL
1 tsp	vanilla extract	5 mL
1/2 tsp	almond extract	2 mL
1 1/2 cups	dried currants	375 mL
3/4 cup	chopped unsalted almonds	175 mL

1. In a bowl, whisk together flour, baking powder and salt until well combined. Set aside.

2. In a large bowl, using an electric mixer on medium speed, lightly beat eggs. Add granulated sugar and beat until well combined, about 2 minutes. Gradually beat in melted butter until thoroughly blended. Beat in vanilla and almond extract. Scrape down sides of bowl. On low speed or using a wooden spoon, add flour mixture, one-third at a time, beating well after each addition. By hand, fold in currants and almonds.

3. Spoon dough onto prepared cookie sheet, forming 2 long, flat logs each measuring 12 inches (30 cm) long by 2 to 3 inches (5 to 7.5 cm) wide and spaced 4 inches (10 cm) apart. Biscotti will spread during baking, nearly doubling in width.

4. Bake in preheated oven for 25 to 30 minutes or until firm to the touch and lightly golden brown.

5. Slide parchment paper onto a wire cooling rack. Cool for 10 minutes, then transfer warm loaves to a cutting board. With a sharp serrated knife, cut each loaf on a 45-degree angle into 1/2-inch (1 cm) slices. Place, cut side down, about 1/2 inch (1 cm) apart on prepared cookie sheets.

6. Bake for 7 minutes. Turn slices over and bake an additional 5 to 7 minutes or just until dry. Do not allow biscotti to darken too much in color. Immediately transfer biscotti to cooling rack and cool completely. Biscotti will crisp as they cool.

Pumpkin Walnut Biscotti

Makes about 4½ dozen biscotti ● ● ●

Because of the pumpkin, the texture of these flavorful slices is a little bit softer than traditional crunchy biscotti

Tips

To prevent tops or bottoms of cookies from becoming too brown, bake one cookie sheet at a time with the oven rack positioned in the center of the oven.

Store biscotti in a tightly sealed container at room temperature for up to 3 weeks. Biscotti may be wrapped well in foil and frozen for up to 2 months.

Variation

Pumpkin Pecan Biscotti: Substitute chopped pecans for chopped walnuts.

- Preheat oven to 350°F (180°C)
- Cookie sheets, lined with parchment paper

4 cups	all-purpose flour	1 L
2 tsp	baking powder	10 mL
2 tsp	ground cinnamon	10 mL
½ tsp	ground ginger	2 mL
½ tsp	ground nutmeg	2 mL
¼ tsp	salt	1 mL
4	eggs	4
1¼ cups	canned solid pack (purée) pumpkin	300 mL
¾ cup	granulated sugar	175 mL
⅔ cup	packed light brown sugar	150 mL
¼ cup	unsalted butter, melted	50 mL
1 tsp	vanilla extract	5 mL
¾ cup	chopped walnuts	175 mL

1. In a bowl, whisk together flour, baking powder, cinnamon, ginger, nutmeg and salt until well combined. Set aside.

2. In a large bowl, using an electric mixer on medium speed, lightly beat eggs. Beat in pumpkin. Add granulated sugar and brown sugar and beat until well combined, about 2 minutes. Gradually beat in melted butter until thoroughly blended. Beat in vanilla. Scrape down sides of bowl. On low speed or using a wooden spoon, add flour mixture, one-third at a time, beating well after each addition. By hand, fold in walnuts.

3. Spoon dough onto prepared cookie sheet, forming 2 long, flat logs each measuring 12 inches (30 cm) long by 2 to 3 inches (5 to 7.5 cm) wide and spaced 4 inches (10 cm) apart. Biscotti will spread during baking, nearly doubling in width.

4. Bake in preheated oven for 30 minutes or until firm to the touch and lightly golden brown.

5. Slide parchment paper onto a wire cooling rack. Cool for 10 minutes, then transfer warm loaves to a cutting board. With a sharp serrated knife, cut each loaf on a 45-degree angle into ½-inch (1 cm) slices. Place, cut side down, about ½ inch (1 cm) apart on prepared cookie sheets.

6. Bake for 7 minutes. Turn slices over and bake an additional 5 to 7 minutes or just until dry. Do not allow biscotti to darken too much in color. Immediately transfer biscotti to cooling rack and cool completely. Biscotti will crisp as they cool.

Triple Chocolate Biscotti

Makes about 4 dozen biscotti ● ● ●

A chocolate-lover's delight. Drizzle biscotti with sweet dark chocolate to make Quadruple Chocolate Biscotti!

Tips

Dutch-process cocoa powder is a refined cocoa treated with a small amount of an alkali solution to neutralize the natural acids. This process improves the flavor and color of the cocoa.

Homemade cookies make a great gift for family and friends and are perfect for every occasion.

- Preheat oven to 350°F (180°C)
- Cookie sheets, lined with parchment paper

2¾ cups	all-purpose flour	675 mL
½ cup	unsweetened Dutch-process cocoa powder	125 mL
2 tsp	baking powder	10 mL
¼ tsp	salt	1 mL
4	eggs	4
1¼ cups	packed light brown sugar	300 mL
⅓ cup	unsalted butter, melted	75 mL
2 tsp	vanilla extract	10 mL
1 cup	chopped semisweet chocolate or semisweet chocolate chips	250 mL
1 cup	chopped white chocolate or white chocolate chips	250 mL

1. In a bowl, whisk together flour, cocoa powder, baking powder and salt until well combined. Set aside.
2. In a large bowl, using an electric mixer on medium speed, lightly beat eggs. Add brown sugar and beat until well combined, about 2 minutes. Gradually beat in melted butter until thoroughly blended. Beat in vanilla. Scrape down sides of bowl. On low speed or using a wooden spoon, add flour mixture, one-third at a time, beating well after each addition. By hand, fold in semisweet and white chocolate.
3. Spoon dough onto prepared cookie sheet, forming 2 long, flat logs each measuring 12 inches (30 cm) long by 2 to 3 inches (5 to 7.5 cm) wide and spaced 4 inches (10 cm) apart. Biscotti will spread during baking, nearly doubling in width.
4. Bake in preheated oven for 25 to 30 minutes or until firm to the touch.
5. Slide parchment paper onto a wire cooling rack. Cool for 10 minutes, then transfer warm loaves to a cutting board. With a sharp serrated knife, cut each loaf on a 45-degree angle into ½-inch (1 cm) slices. Place, cut side down, about ½ inch (1 cm) apart on prepared cookie sheets.
6. Bake for 7 minutes. Turn slices over and bake an additional 5 to 7 minutes or just until dry. Do not allow biscotti to darken too much in color. Immediately transfer biscotti to cooling rack and cool completely. Biscotti will crisp as they cool.

Cinnamon Walnut Biscotti

Makes about 4 dozen biscotti

● ● ●

Cinnamon- and nut-lovers will enjoy this inviting blend of flavors.

Tips

If you prefer a milder cinnamon flavor, reduce cinnamon to 2 tsp (10 mL).

Store biscotti in a tightly sealed container at room temperature for up to 3 weeks. Biscotti may be wrapped well in foil and frozen for up to 2 months.

Variations

Cinnamon Almond Biscotti: Substitute chopped unsalted almonds for chopped walnuts

Cinnamon Pecan Biscotti: Substitute chopped pecans for chopped walnuts

- ● **Preheat oven to 350°F (180°C)**
- ● **Cookie sheets, lined with parchment paper**

3 cups	all-purpose flour	750 mL
1 tbsp	ground cinnamon	15 mL
2 tsp	baking powder	10 mL
¼ tsp	salt	1 mL
4	eggs	4
1¼ cups	granulated sugar	300 mL
¼ cup	unsalted butter, melted	50 mL
1 tsp	vanilla extract	5 mL
1½ cups	chopped walnuts	375 mL

1. In a bowl, whisk together flour, cinnamon, baking powder and salt until well combined. Set aside.

2. In a large bowl, using an electric mixer on medium speed, lightly beat eggs. Add granulated sugar and beat until well combined, about 2 minutes. Gradually beat in melted butter until thoroughly blended. Beat in vanilla. Scrape down sides of bowl. On low speed or using a wooden spoon, add flour mixture, one-third at a time, beating well after each addition. By hand, fold in walnuts.

3. Spoon dough onto prepared cookie sheet, forming 2 long, flat logs each measuring 12 inches (30 cm) long by 2 to 3 inches (5 to 7.5 cm) wide and spaced 4 inches (10 cm) apart. Biscotti will spread during baking, nearly doubling in width.

4. Bake in preheated oven for 25 to 30 minutes or until firm to the touch and lightly golden brown.

5. Slide parchment paper onto a wire cooling rack. Cool for 10 minutes, then transfer warm loaves to a cutting board. With a sharp serrated knife, cut each loaf on a 45-degree angle into ½-inch (1 cm) slices. Place, cut side down, about ½ inch (1 cm) apart on prepared cookie sheets.

6. Bake for 7 minutes. Turn slices over and bake an additional 5 to 7 minutes or just until dry. Do not allow biscotti to darken too much in color. Immediately transfer biscotti to cooling rack and cool completely. Biscotti will crisp as they cool.

Gingerbread Biscotti

● ● ●

These cookies have a pleasing sweet and spicy flavor.

Tip

Flavors can blend during storage, so store cookies with strong flavors in separate containers.

Variation

Gingerbread Walnut Biscotti: By hand, fold 1 cup (250 mL) chopped walnuts into dough after mixing.

- Preheat oven to 350°F (180°C)
- Cookie sheets, lined with parchment paper

3½ cups	all-purpose flour	875 mL
2½ tsp	baking powder	12 mL
2 tsp	ground cinnamon	10 mL
1½ tsp	ground ginger	7 mL
1 tsp	ground nutmeg	5 mL
¼ tsp	salt	1 mL
4	eggs	4
1 cup	packed dark brown sugar	250 mL
½ cup	fancy molasses	125 mL
¼ cup	unsalted butter, melted	50 mL
1 tsp	vanilla extract	5 mL

1. In a bowl, whisk together flour, baking powder, cinnamon, ginger, nutmeg and salt until well combined. Set aside.

2. In a large bowl, using an electric mixer on medium speed, lightly beat eggs. Add brown sugar and beat until well combined, about 2 minutes. Gradually beat in molasses and melted butter until thoroughly blended. Beat in vanilla. Scrape down sides of bowl. On low speed or using a wooden spoon, add flour mixture, one-third at a time, beating well after each addition.

3. Spoon dough onto prepared cookie sheet, forming 2 long, flat logs each measuring 12 inches (30 cm) long by 2 to 3 inches (5 to 7.5 cm) wide and spaced 4 inches (10 cm) apart. Biscotti will spread during baking, nearly doubling in width.

4. Bake in preheated oven for 25 to 30 minutes or until firm to the touch.

5. Slide parchment paper onto a wire cooling rack. Cool for 10 minutes, then transfer warm loaves to a cutting board. With a sharp serrated knife, cut each loaf on a 45-degree angle into ½-inch (1 cm) slices. Place, cut side down, about ½ inch (1 cm) apart on prepared cookie sheets.

6. Bake for 7 minutes. Turn slices over and bake an additional 5 to 7 minutes or just until dry. Do not allow biscotti to overbake. Immediately transfer biscotti to cooling rack and cool completely. Biscotti will crisp as they cool.

Shortbreads

●●●

Traditional Shortbread. 429

Chocolate Brownie Shortbread. 430

Glazed Lemon Shortbread 432

Brown Sugar and Spice
 Shortbread 433

Coconut Shortbread. 434

Chocolate Chip Shortbread 435

Mocha Shortbread Bites. 436

Maple Pecan Shortbread 437

Cranberry Shortbread. 438

Almond Shortbread 439

Cinnamon Walnut Shortbread. 440

Butterscotch Shortbread 441

Lime Shortbread. 442

Blueberry Lemon Shortbread 443

Macadamia Nut Shortbread 444

Cherry Shortbread 445

Bittersweet Chocolate Shortbread . . 446

Tropical Shortbread 447

Ginger Shortbread 448

Apricot Shortbread. 449

Orange Shortbread. 450

Toffee Shortbread. 451

Walnut Shortbread 452

Lemon Poppy Seed Shortbread 453

White Chocolate Shortbread. 454

Pecan Shortbread 455

Peanut Butter Shortbread. 456

Espresso Shortbread 457

Citrus Shortbread. 458

Cornmeal Shortbread. 459

Oatmeal Shortbread. 460

About Shortbreads

A traditional cookie of Scottish origin, shortbreads were served at Christmas and New Year's to celebrate the winter solstice. We now enjoy these tender treats any day of the year. The name "shortbread" is derived from the minimal handling of the ingredients during mixing, which shortens the development of proteins in the flour. The result is a cookie with a tender, crumbly texture.

Pure shortbreads are made with only three ingredients — butter, sugar and flour. Building on the basic ingredients, a whole assortment of delicious shortbread flavors can be created. Because shortbreads contain so few ingredients, each ingredient plays an important role in the flavor and texture of the finished cookie. Butter is the primary source of flavor in shortbread. It's essential to use fresh, unsalted butter in these cookies as old or salted butter can significantly alter their flavor.

Coarser flours with a high protein count led to the inclusion of rice flour in old-fashioned shortbread recipes to create a cookie with a tender crumb. The lower protein levels in the rice flour balanced the stronger flour proteins and helped prevent the development of the gluten that toughens cookies. Today's all-purpose flours are ground much more finely, and the texture of shortbread is greatly improved. Cake flour contains less protein than all-purpose flour. Many of the recipes in this chapter use a combination of cake flour and all-purpose flour to reduce the development of gluten and produce shortbreads with a nice crumb and texture.

Cornstarch is often used in combination with all-purpose flour to create a shortbread cookie with a tender crumb. Adding cornstarch is particularly helpful in recipes that contain heavy ingredients that can weigh down the dough and make the shortbread more dense. Confectioner's (powdered/icing) sugar contains cornstarch and is a common ingredient in many shortbreads.

Because shortbreads don't contain eggs, this rich and versatile cookie is quite popular with people who are allergic to eggs.

Shaping Shortbread

Early shortbreads were baked as a large, round flat cookie and scored into wedges that represented the rays of the sun. Shortbread doughs can also be rolled out and cut into shapes, pressed into square or round baking pans, or baked in special shortbread molds.

To make traditional shortbread, shape the dough into a flat round and bake it on a cookie sheet. Scoring or cutting the round into wedges before baking makes it easier to cut the finished cookies apart without them breaking into jagged pieces.

Shortbread dough can be rolled out and cut into shapes in the same manner as rolled cutout cookies (see page 205). Use confectioner's sugar instead of flour to dust the board and rolling pin to keep the shortbread from absorbing too much flour and becoming tough. If shortbread dough is too soft to roll out, cover it with plastic wrap and chill for 30 minutes or more until the dough firms a bit and is easier to handle. Don't add more flour to the dough.

A tart pan with a removable bottom is a perfect mold for baking shortbread. The lift-out bottom makes it really easy to remove the shortbread from the pan, and the fluted edge adds a decorative touch to the cookie wedges. Scoring the shortbread before baking makes it easier to cut after removing it from the pan. Shortbread can also be baked in square pans and cut into squares, bars or diamond shapes. Pricking the surface of shortbreads baked in pans helps the dough rise evenly and creates a decorative pattern on top of the cookies.

Finishing Shortbread

For a decorative touch, dust baked and cooled shortbread with a light coating of confectioner's (powdered/icing) sugar. For a special treat, add a glaze or an icing or drizzle cookies with melted chocolate. Shortbread wedges or bars can also be dipped in melted chocolate.

Traditional Shortbread

● ● ●

This classic shortbread is made with only four simple ingredients. It is the high quality of the ingredients that gives these cookies their fresh flavor.

Tips

Butter should be cold so that it does not melt from the warmth of your hands as you work it into the flour.

If using flour to dust pastry board, be careful not to incorporate too much flour into dough during kneading. Too much flour will make the shortbread tough.

- Preheat oven to 325°F (160°C)
- 9-inch (23 cm) shortbread mold or tart pan with removable bottom, greased with unsalted butter

1 cup	all-purpose flour	250 mL
⅓ cup	granulated sugar	75 mL
¼ cup	cornstarch	50 mL
½ cup	chilled unsalted butter, cut into pieces	125 mL

1. In a bowl, whisk together flour, granulated sugar and cornstarch. Using clean fingers, gently rub butter into flour mixture until very crumbly and the texture resembles coarse meal. Gather dough into a ball. Lightly dust a pastry board, clean countertop or other flat surface with confectioner's sugar or flour. Gently knead dough a few strokes until smooth.

2. Using the back of a spoon or your fingers, press dough evenly into prepared mold or bottom of prepared pan. With tines of a fork, prick surface of dough in several places. For tart pan, using a sharp knife, score top of shortbread into 16 wedges. Bake in preheated oven for 25 to 30 minutes or until lightly golden.

3. Let cool in baking pan on a wire rack for 5 minutes. If necessary, gently run knife blade between shortbread and edge of pan to loosen. Unmold or remove sides of pan and slide shortbread onto a wire cooling rack. Cool for 10 minutes. Transfer shortbread to a cutting board. Using a long serrated knife, cut the shortbread into wedges along the score lines. Cool completely.

Chocolate Brownie Shortbread

These rich cookies have a similar flavor and texture to brownies.

Tips

For a truer shortbread texture, bake the cookies 5 to 10 minutes longer.

Let icing set completely before storing shortbread between layers of wax paper in a tightly sealed container. Store cookies at room temperature for up to 3 days.

- Preheat oven to 325°F (160°C)
- 9-inch (23 cm) square baking pan, lined with foil, greased with unsalted butter

Shortbread

1 cup	all-purpose flour	250 mL
1 cup	cake flour	250 mL
2 tbsp	unsweetened Dutch-process cocoa powder	25 mL
¾ cup	unsalted butter, softened	175 mL
¾ cup	confectioner's (powdered/icing) sugar	175 mL
⅓ cup	packed light brown sugar	75 mL
⅓ cup	chocolate syrup	75 mL
½ tsp	vanilla extract	2 mL

Icing

1¼ cups	confectioner's (powdered/icing) sugar	300 mL
2 tbsp	unsweetened Dutch-process cocoa powder	25 mL
3 tbsp	chocolate syrup	45 mL
1 tbsp	unsalted butter, at room temperature	15 mL
2 to 3 tsp	half-and-half (10%) cream or milk	10 to 15 mL
1 tsp	light (golden) corn syrup	5 mL
½ tsp	vanilla extract	2 mL

1. **Shortbread:** In a bowl, whisk together all-purpose flour, cake flour and cocoa powder until well combined. Set aside.

2. In a large bowl, using an electric mixer on medium speed, cream butter, confectioner's sugar and brown sugar until light and fluffy, about 2 minutes. Beat in chocolate syrup and vanilla. Scrape down sides of bowl. On low speed or using a wooden spoon, gradually add flour mixture, beating just until blended.

3. Using the back of a spoon or clean fingers, press dough evenly into bottom of prepared pan. With tines of a fork, prick surface of dough in several places. Bake in preheated oven for 35 to 40 minutes or until set in center. Let cool completely in baking pan on a wire rack.

4. Using foil, lift cooled shortbread from pan and place on a cutting board. Pull edges of foil away from sides. If foil sticks, gently run knife blade between shortbread and foil to loosen.

Tip

Always use unsweetened cocoa powder for baking. Don't use a cocoa drink mix or powdered ground chocolate. Both of these contain high amounts of sugar and some contain powdered milk as well.

5. *Icing:* In a small bowl, whisk together confectioner's sugar and cocoa powder. Add chocolate syrup, butter, 2 teaspoons (10 mL) of the cream, corn syrup and vanilla. Blend until the icing is smooth and thin enough to spread. Add more cream as needed to achieve the desired consistency. Spread icing over cooled shortbread. Let stand 10 to 15 minutes or until the icing is set. Using a long serrated knife, cut shortbread into $1\frac{1}{2}$- by $2\frac{1}{4}$-inch (4 by 5.5 cm) bars.

Cookie Therapy

When it's cold and stormy outside and your mood is low, it's the perfect time to roll up your sleeves, get into the kitchen and bake a batch of cookies. There's something so satisfying about the cookie-baking process. It is a therapeutic activity, and the wonderful aroma of cookies baking in the oven is sure to cheer up a gloomy day. Share some of those cookies with a friend over a cup of hot coffee or tea, and you will brighten their day as well.

Glazed Lemon Shortbread

A lemon-lover's dream, these shortbread squares are sure to please. Topped with a light glaze, they are packed with fresh lemon flavor.

Tips

A ripe medium lemon will yield about 2 teaspoons (10 mL) finely grated zest and 2 to 3 tablespoons (25 to 45 mL) juice.

Let glaze set completely before storing shortbread between layers of wax paper in a tightly sealed container. Shortbread can be stored at room temperature for up to 3 days. Do not freeze glazed cookies.

- Preheat oven to 325°F (160°C)
- 9-inch (23 cm) square baking pan, lined with foil, greased with unsalted butter

Shortbread

1¼ cups	all-purpose flour	300 mL
¾ cup	cake flour	175 mL
¼ tsp	salt	1 mL
¾ cup	unsalted butter, softened	175 mL
⅔ cup	confectioner's (powdered/icing) sugar	150 mL
⅓ cup	granulated sugar	75 mL
3 tbsp	grated lemon zest	45 mL
1½ tbsp	freshly squeezed lemon juice	22 mL

Glaze

1¼ cups	confectioner's (powdered/icing) sugar	300 mL
1½ tsp	grated lemon zest	7 mL
1½ tbsp	freshly squeezed lemon juice	22 mL
2 tsp	unsalted butter, at room temperature	10 mL
1 tsp	light (golden) corn syrup	5 mL

1. **Shortbread:** In a bowl, whisk together all-purpose flour, cake flour and salt until well combined. Set aside.

2. In a large bowl, using an electric mixer on medium speed, cream butter, confectioner's sugar and granulated sugar until light and fluffy, about 2 minutes. Beat in lemon zest and lemon juice. Scrape down sides of bowl. On low speed or using a wooden spoon, gradually add flour mixture, beating just until blended.

3. Using the back of a spoon or clean fingers, press dough evenly into bottom of prepared pan. With tines of a fork, prick surface of dough in several places. Bake in preheated oven for 35 to 40 minutes or until lightly golden. Let cool completely in baking pan on a wire rack.

4. Using foil, lift cooled shortbread from pan and place on a cutting board. Pull edges of foil away from sides. If foil sticks, gently run knife blade between shortbread and foil to loosen.

5. **Glaze:** In a small bowl, combine the confectioner's sugar, lemon zest, lemon juice, butter and corn syrup. Using a small whisk or a fork, blend until the glaze is smooth and thin enough to spread. Spread glaze over cooled shortbread. Let stand 10 to 15 minutes or until the glaze is set. Using a long serrated knife, cut shortbread into 1½- by 2¼-inch (4 by 5.5 cm) bars.

Brown Sugar and Spice Shortbread

Flavors of butterscotch, cinnamon, ginger and nutmeg make these shortbreads a special morning treat with a cup of coffee.

Tips

Sugar adds flavor and texture to cookies and helps keep them fresh longer.

Store shortbread between layers of wax paper in a tightly sealed container. Cookies can be stored at room temperature for up to 3 days.

- Preheat oven to 325°F (160°C)
- 9-inch (23 cm) tart pan with removable bottom or round cake pan with removable bottom, greased with unsalted butter

1⅔ cups	all-purpose flour	400 mL
¾ tsp	ground cinnamon	3 mL
¼ tsp	ground ginger	1 mL
¼ tsp	ground nutmeg	1 mL
¼ tsp	salt	1 mL
⅔ cup	unsalted butter, softened	150 mL
⅔ cup	packed light brown sugar	150 mL

1. In a bowl, whisk together flour, cinnamon, ginger, nutmeg and salt until well combined. Set aside.
2. In a large bowl, using an electric mixer on medium speed, cream butter and brown sugar until light and fluffy, about 2 minutes. Scrape down sides of bowl. On low speed or using a wooden spoon, gradually add flour mixture, beating just until blended.
3. Using the back of a spoon or your fingers, press dough evenly into bottom of prepared pan. With tines of a fork, prick surface of dough in several places. Using a sharp knife, score top of shortbread into 16 wedges. Bake in preheated oven for 30 to 35 minutes or until lightly golden.
4. Let cool in baking pan on a wire rack for 5 minutes. If necessary, gently run knife blade between shortbread and edge of pan to loosen. Remove sides of pan and slide shortbread off pan bottom and onto a wire cooling rack. Cool for 10 minutes. Transfer shortbread to a cutting board. Using a long serrated knife, cut the shortbread into wedges along the score lines. Cool completely.

Coconut Shortbread

● ● ●

Flaked coconut adds wonderful flavor and a bit of texture to these shortbread squares.

Tips

Unsalted butter is the best choice for baking. It gives cookies a rich, fresh flavor and helps them develop a light golden brown color.

Shortbread may be wrapped well in foil and frozen for up to 2 months.

- **Preheat oven to 300°F (150°C)**
- **9-inch (23 cm) square baking pan, lined with foil, greased with unsalted butter**

1¼ cups	all-purpose flour	300 mL
¾ cup	cake flour	175 mL
¼ tsp	salt	1 mL
¾ cup	sweetened flaked coconut, chopped	175 mL
¾ cup	unsalted butter, softened	175 mL
½ cup	confectioner's (powdered/icing) sugar	125 mL
⅓ cup	granulated sugar	75 mL
¼ tsp	vanilla extract	1 mL
¼ tsp	coconut extract	1 mL

1. In a bowl, whisk together all-purpose flour, cake flour and salt until well combined. Stir in coconut. Set aside.

2. In a large bowl, using an electric mixer on medium speed, cream butter, confectioner's sugar and granulated sugar until light and fluffy, about 2 minutes. Beat in vanilla and coconut extract. Scrape down sides of bowl. On low speed or using a wooden spoon, gradually add flour mixture, beating just until blended.

3. Using the back of a spoon or clean fingers, press dough evenly into bottom of prepared pan. With tines of a fork, prick surface of dough in several places. Bake in preheated oven for 40 to 45 minutes or until lightly golden. Let cool completely in baking pan on a wire rack.

4. Using foil, lift cooled shortbread from pan and place on a cutting board. Pull edges of foil away from sides. If foil sticks, gently run knife blade between shortbread and foil to loosen. Using a long serrated knife, cut shortbread into 1½-inch (4 cm) squares.

Chocolate Chip Shortbread

Makes about 24 bars

● ● ●

The mini chocolate chips add a nice touch of chocolate without overpowering the flavor or significantly altering the texture of these shortbread cookies.

Tip

Mini chocolate chips work best in these cookies. The smaller chips make it easier to slice through the shortbread and cut it into bars.

Variation

By hand, fold $\frac{1}{2}$ cup (125 mL) finely chopped walnuts into dough along with chocolate chips.

- Preheat oven to 325°F (160°C)
- 9-inch (23 cm) square baking pan, lined with foil, greased with unsalted butter

$1\frac{1}{2}$ cups	all-purpose flour	375 mL
$\frac{1}{2}$ cup	cake flour	125 mL
$\frac{1}{4}$ tsp	salt	1 mL
$\frac{3}{4}$ cup	unsalted butter, softened	175 mL
$\frac{3}{4}$ cup	granulated sugar	175 mL
$1\frac{1}{2}$ tsp	vanilla extract	7 mL
$\frac{3}{4}$ cup	mini semisweet chocolate chips	175 mL

1. In a bowl, whisk together all-purpose flour, cake flour and salt until well combined. Set aside.
2. In a large bowl, using an electric mixer on medium speed, cream butter and granulated sugar until light and fluffy, about 2 minutes. Beat in vanilla. Scrape down sides of bowl. On low speed or using a wooden spoon, gradually add flour mixture, beating just until blended. By hand, fold in chocolate chips.
3. Using the back of a spoon or clean fingers, press dough evenly into bottom of prepared pan. With tines of a fork, prick surface of dough in several places. Bake in preheated oven for 30 to 35 minutes or until lightly golden. Let cool completely in baking pan on a wire rack.
4. Using foil, lift cooled shortbread from pan and place on a cutting board. Pull edges of foil away from sides. If foil sticks, gently run knife blade between shortbread and foil to loosen. Using a long serrated knife, cut shortbread into $1\frac{1}{2}$- by $2\frac{1}{4}$-inch (4 by 5.5 cm) bars.

Mocha Shortbread Bites

Makes 36 squares

The chocolate glaze adds a decorative and enticing touch that complements the coffee and chocolate flavors in the shortbread.

Tips

Butter is considered to be softened when it is at a temperature of 65°F (18°C).

Chocolate can be melted in the top of a double boiler placed over simmering water. Stir frequently, until chocolate is completely melted and mixture is smooth. Cool to desired consistency.

Let chocolate set completely before storing shortbread between layers of wax paper in a tightly sealed container. Do not freeze glazed cookies.

- Preheat oven to 325°F (160°C)
- 9-inch (23 cm) square baking pan, lined with foil, greased with unsalted butter

Shortbread

1¼ cups	all-purpose flour	300 mL
¾ cup	cake flour	175 mL
2 tbsp	unsweetened Dutch-process cocoa powder	25 mL
1¼ tsp	instant espresso powder	6 mL
1 cup	unsalted butter, softened	250 mL
1 cup	confectioner's (powdered/icing) sugar	250 mL
¼ cup	packed light brown sugar	50 mL
½ tsp	vanilla extract	2 mL

Glaze

⅔ cup	chopped semisweet chocolate or semisweet chocolate chips	150 mL
¾ tsp	vegetable shortening	3 mL

1. **Shortbread:** In a bowl, whisk together all-purpose flour, cake flour, cocoa powder and espresso powder until well combined. Set aside.

2. In a large bowl, using an electric mixer on medium speed, cream butter, confectioner's sugar and brown sugar until light and fluffy, about 2 minutes. Beat in vanilla. Scrape down sides of bowl. On low speed or using a wooden spoon, gradually add flour mixture, beating just until blended.

3. Using the back of a spoon or clean fingers, press dough evenly into bottom of prepared pan. With tines of a fork, prick surface of dough in several places. Bake in preheated oven for 35 to 40 minutes or until set in center. Let cool completely in baking pan on a wire rack.

4. Using foil, lift cooled shortbread from pan and place on a cutting board. Pull edges of foil away from sides. If foil sticks, gently run knife blade between shortbread and foil to loosen.

5. **Glaze:** In a 1-quart (1 L) microwave-safe zippered storage bag, combine semisweet chocolate and vegetable shortening. Microwave on High power for 1 minute. Knead bag until completely combined and smooth, microwaving an additional 10 seconds at a time as needed to fully melt chocolate. Cut off a small corner of bag and drizzle chocolate over top of cooled shortbread. Let stand 10 minutes or until the chocolate is set. Using a long serrated knife, cut shortbread into 1½-inch (4 cm) squares.

Maple Pecan Shortbread

● ● ●

These shortbread rounds have a nice flavor and texture. Be sure to finely chop the pecans so the cookie cutter will cut through the dough cleanly.

Tip

Cut the cookies as close together as possible in order to get as many cookies as you can out of the first rolling of the dough. Rolling the dough scraps multiple times can toughen the cookies.

- **Preheat oven to 325°F (160°C)**
- **Cookie sheets, lined with parchment paper**
- **Cookie cutters**

2½ cups	all-purpose flour	625 mL
¼ tsp	salt	1 mL
1⅓ cups	finely chopped pecans	325 mL
1 cup	unsalted butter, softened	250 mL
⅔ cup	packed light brown sugar	150 mL
1½ tsp	maple flavoring	7 mL
½ tsp	vanilla extract	2 mL

1. In a bowl, whisk together flour and salt until well combined. Stir in pecans. Set aside.

2. In a large bowl, using an electric mixer on medium speed, cream butter and brown sugar until light and fluffy, about 2 minutes. Beat in maple flavoring and vanilla. Scrape down sides of bowl. On low speed or using a wooden spoon, gradually add flour mixture, beating just until blended.

3. Lightly dust a pastry board, clean countertop or other flat surface with confectioner's (powdered/icing) sugar or flour. Gently knead dough a few strokes to form a smooth ball. Divide dough in half. Working with one portion at a time, pat or roll dough to a uniform thickness of ½ inch (1 cm).

4. Dip a 1½-inch (4 cm) round cookie cutter in confectioner's sugar or flour and cut dough into cookies. Cut out as many cookies as possible. Carefully transfer cutouts to prepared cookie sheets, placing 1 inch (2.5 cm) apart. Gather dough remnants into a ball, reroll, cut out more cookies and transfer to cookie sheets.

5. Bake one sheet at a time in preheated oven for 18 to 22 minutes or until edges turn lightly golden.

6. Immediately slide parchment paper onto a wire cooling rack. Cool cookies for 5 minutes, then transfer from parchment paper to cooling rack and cool completely.

Cranberry Shortbread

● ● ●

Dried cranberries are a fun cookie ingredient that add a tangy, fruity flavor to buttery shortbread.

Tips

Use only the freshest ingredients for making shortbread. Because they use so few ingredients, the flavor of every ingredient is extremely important.

Store shortbread between layers of wax paper in a tightly sealed container. Cookies can be stored at room temperature for up to 3 days.

Variation

By hand, fold ⅓ cup (75 mL) finely chopped pecans into dough along with cranberries.

- Preheat oven to 325°F (160°C)
- Cookie sheets, lined with parchment paper

1¼ cups	all-purpose flour	300 mL
¼ tsp	salt	1 mL
½ cup	unsalted butter, softened	125 mL
½ cup	confectioner's (powdered/icing) sugar	125 mL
½ tsp	vanilla extract	2 mL
½ cup	chopped dried cranberries	125 mL

1. In a bowl, whisk together flour and salt until well combined. Set aside.

2. In a large bowl, using an electric mixer on medium speed, cream butter and confectioner's sugar until light and fluffy, about 2 minutes. Beat in vanilla. Scrape down sides of bowl. On low speed or using a wooden spoon, gradually add flour mixture, beating just until blended. By hand, fold in cranberries.

3. On prepared cookie sheet, pat or roll dough into a ½-inch (1 cm) thick circle, approximately 9 inches (23 cm) in diameter. With tines of a fork, prick surface of dough in several places and gently press tines around edge of circle to create a decorative pattern. Using a sharp knife, cut circle into 16 wedges. Bake in preheated oven for 25 to 30 minutes or until lightly golden.

4. Let cool on cookie sheet on a wire rack for 5 minutes. Slide parchment paper onto a wire cooling rack. Cool completely. Cut or break shortbread into wedges.

Almond Shortbread

● ● ●

With a tender texture and lots of almond flavor, these are a satisfying sweet treat any time of day.

Tips

Finely chopping the almonds gives the shortbread a nice texture with little pieces of nut. Do not use ground almonds. They are too fine and would make the shortbread too dry.

For best results, use the pan size and shape called for in the recipe. If you use a different pan, you will need to adjust the baking time to reduce the chance of burning or undercooking.

- **Preheat oven to 325°F (160°C)**
- **9-inch (23 cm) square baking pan, lined with foil, greased with unsalted butter**

1¼ cups	all-purpose flour	300 mL
1 cup	cake flour	250 mL
¼ tsp	salt	1 mL
¾ cup	finely chopped unsalted almonds	175 mL
1 cup	unsalted butter, softened	250 mL
⅔ cup	granulated sugar	150 mL
1 tsp	almond extract	5 mL

1. In a bowl, whisk together all-purpose flour, cake flour and salt until well combined. Stir in almonds. Set aside.

2. In a large bowl, using an electric mixer on medium speed, cream butter and granulated sugar until light and fluffy, about 2 minutes. Beat in almond extract. Scrape down sides of bowl. On low speed or using a wooden spoon, gradually add flour mixture, beating just until blended.

3. Using the back of a spoon or clean fingers, press dough evenly into bottom of prepared pan. With tines of a fork, prick surface of dough in several places. Bake in preheated oven for 35 to 40 minutes or until lightly golden. Let cool completely in baking pan on a wire rack.

4. Using foil, lift cooled shortbread from pan and place on a cutting board. Pull edges of foil away from sides. If foil sticks, gently run knife blade between shortbread and foil to loosen. Using a long serrated knife, cut shortbread into 1½-inch (4 cm) squares.

Cinnamon Walnut Shortbread

Makes 36 squares

Cinnamon and nutmeg enhance the natural nuttiness of the walnuts.

Tips

Bread flour has a high protein content and should not be used for baking shortbread.

Store shortbread between layers of wax paper in a tightly sealed container. Shortbread can be stored at room temperature for up to 3 days.

- Preheat oven to 325°F (160°C)
- 9-inch (23 cm) square baking pan, lined with foil, greased with unsalted butter

Shortbread

2 cups	all-purpose flour	500 mL
1½ tsp	ground cinnamon	7 mL
¼ tsp	ground nutmeg	1 mL
¼ tsp	salt	1 mL
¾ cup	finely chopped walnuts	175 mL
¾ cup	unsalted butter, softened	175 mL
⅓ cup	granulated sugar	75 mL
⅓ cup	packed light brown sugar	75 mL
½ tsp	vanilla extract	2 mL

Topping

1 tbsp	granulated sugar	15 mL
¼ tsp	ground cinnamon	1 mL

1. **Shortbread:** In a bowl, whisk together flour, cinnamon, nutmeg and salt until well combined. Stir in walnuts. Set aside.

2. In a large bowl, using an electric mixer on medium speed, cream butter, granulated sugar and brown sugar until light and fluffy, about 2 minutes. Beat in vanilla. Scrape down sides of bowl. On low speed or using a wooden spoon, gradually add flour mixture, beating just until blended.

3. Using the back of a spoon or clean fingers, press dough evenly into bottom of prepared pan. With tines of a fork, prick surface of dough in several places.

4. **Topping:** In a small bowl, whisk together granulated sugar and cinnamon until well combined. Sprinkle cinnamon sugar evenly over dough. Bake in preheated oven for 35 to 40 minutes or until lightly golden. Let cool completely in baking pan on a wire rack.

5. Using foil, lift cooled shortbread from pan and place on a cutting board. Pull edges of foil away from sides. If foil sticks, gently run knife blade between shortbread and foil to loosen. Using a long serrated knife, cut shortbread into 1½-inch (4 cm) squares.

Butterscotch Shortbread

Makes about 4 dozen cookies

● ● ●

In a twist on classic shortbread, these cookies get their flavor from dark brown sugar.

Tips

Brown sugar adds moisture and rich flavor to cookies.

Creaming the butter and sugar beats air into the mixture. These air pockets give cookies a tender texture.

- Preheat oven to 325°F (160°C)
- Cookie sheets, lined with parchment paper

2½ cups	all-purpose flour	625 mL
¼ tsp	salt	1 mL
1 cup	unsalted butter, softened	250 mL
¾ cup	packed dark brown sugar	175 mL
1 tsp	vanilla extract	5 mL

1. In a bowl, whisk together flour and salt until well combined. Set aside.

2. In a large bowl, using an electric mixer on medium speed, cream butter and brown sugar until light and fluffy, about 2 minutes. Beat in vanilla. Scrape down sides of bowl. On low speed or using a wooden spoon, gradually add flour mixture, beating just until blended.

3. Lightly grease hands with nonstick cooking spray. Roll pieces of dough into 1-inch (2.5 cm) balls. Place on prepared cookie sheets about 2 inches (5 cm) apart. Using the bottom of a glass dipped in confectioner's sugar, press balls to flatten to ½ inch (1 cm) thick. Bake one sheet at a time in preheated oven for 15 to 18 minutes or until edges turn lightly golden.

4. Immediately slide parchment paper onto a wire cooling rack. Cool cookies for 5 minutes, then transfer from parchment paper to cooling rack and cool completely.

Lime Shortbread

● ● ●

The zesty zing of lime works beautifully in shortbread.

Tip

When zesting limes, remove only the outer colored part of the peel. The white part underneath, called the pith, is very bitter and will give cookies an unpleasant flavor.

- Preheat oven to 300°F (150°C)
- 9-inch (23 cm) square baking pan, lined with foil, greased with unsalted butter

1 cup	all-purpose flour	250 mL
1 cup	cake flour	250 mL
¼ tsp	salt	1 mL
¾ cup	unsalted butter, softened	175 mL
½ cup	granulated sugar	125 mL
½ cup	confectioner's (powdered/icing) sugar	125 mL
2 tbsp	grated lime zest	25 mL
1 tbsp	freshly squeezed lime juice	15 mL

1. In a bowl, whisk together all-purpose flour, cake flour and salt until well combined. Set aside.

2. In a large bowl, using an electric mixer on medium speed, cream butter, granulated sugar and confectioner's sugar until light and fluffy, about 2 minutes. Beat in lime zest and lime juice. Scrape down sides of bowl. On low speed or using a wooden spoon, gradually add flour mixture, beating just until blended.

3. Using the back of a spoon or clean fingers, press dough evenly into bottom of prepared pan. With tines of a fork, prick surface of dough in several places. Bake in preheated oven for 40 to 45 minutes or until lightly golden. Let cool completely in baking pan on a wire rack.

4. Using foil, lift cooled shortbread from pan and place on a cutting board. Pull edges of foil away from sides. If foil sticks, gently run knife blade between shortbread and foil to loosen. Using a long serrated knife, cut shortbread into 1½-inch (4 cm) squares.

Blueberry Lemon Shortbread

Makes about 4 dozen cookies

The little pieces of blueberry and grated lemon zest make the shortbread as pretty as it is tasty.

Tips

A ripe medium lemon will yield about 2 teaspoons (10 mL) finely grated zest and 2 to 3 tablespoons (30 to 45 mL) juice.

Prepare and measure all of the ingredients before you start mixing the cookies.

- **Preheat oven to 325°F (160°C)**
- **Cookie sheets, lined with parchment paper**

2 cups	all-purpose flour	500 mL
¼ tsp	salt	1 mL
⅔ cup	unsalted butter, softened	150 mL
⅔ cup	confectioner's (powdered/icing) sugar	150 mL
2 tbsp	grated lemon zest	25 mL
1 tbsp	freshly squeezed lemon juice	15 mL
½ cup	chopped dried blueberries	125 mL

1. In a bowl, whisk together flour and salt until well combined. Set aside.

2. In a large bowl, using an electric mixer on medium speed, cream butter and confectioner's sugar until light and fluffy, about 2 minutes. Beat in lemon zest and lemon juice. Scrape down sides of bowl. On low speed or using a wooden spoon, gradually add flour mixture, beating just until blended. By hand, fold in blueberries

3. Lightly grease hands with nonstick cooking spray. Roll pieces of dough into 1-inch (2.5 cm) balls. Place on prepared cookie sheets about 2 inches (5 cm) apart. Using the bottom of a glass dipped in confectioner's sugar, press balls to flatten to ½ inch (1 cm) thick. Bake one sheet at a time in preheated oven for 15 to 18 minutes or until edges turn lightly golden.

4. Immediately slide parchment paper onto a wire cooling rack. Cool cookies for 5 minutes, then transfer from parchment paper to cooling rack and cool completely.

Macadamia Nut Shortbread

Makes 16 wedges ● ● ●

Macadamia nuts add a rich nuttiness to these wedges that is enhanced by the light scent of coconut.

Tip

To measure flour properly, stir the flour in the package or container to add air to it, then gently spoon the flour into a dry measuring cup. Use a knife or spatula to level off the flour even with the rim of the cup.

- Preheat oven to 325°F (160°C)
- Cookie sheets, lined with parchment paper

1¼ cups	all-purpose flour	300 mL
¼ tsp	salt	1 mL
½ cup	finely chopped roasted unsalted macadamia nuts	125 mL
½ cup	unsalted butter, softened	125 mL
¼ cup	granulated sugar	50 mL
¼ cup	confectioner's (powdered/icing) sugar	50 mL
1 tsp	vanilla extract	5 mL
½ tsp	coconut extract	2 mL

1. In a bowl, whisk together flour and salt until well combined. Stir in macadamia nuts. Set aside.

2. In a large bowl, using an electric mixer on medium speed, cream butter, granulated sugar and confectioner's sugar until light and fluffy, about 2 minutes. Beat in vanilla and coconut extract. Scrape down sides of bowl. On low speed or using a wooden spoon, gradually add flour mixture, beating just until blended.

3. On prepared cookie sheet, pat or roll dough into a ½-inch (1 cm) thick circle, approximately 9 inches (23 cm) in diameter. With tines of a fork, prick surface of dough in several places and gently press tines around edge of circle to create a decorative pattern. Using a sharp knife, cut circle into 16 wedges. Bake in preheated oven for 25 to 30 minutes or until lightly golden.

4. Let cool on cookie sheet on a wire rack for 5 minutes. Slide parchment paper onto a wire cooling rack. Cool completely. Cut or break shortbread into wedges.

Cherry Shortbread

●●●

Either sweet or tart dried cherries can be used in this recipe, and both are enhanced by the flavor of almond.

Tip

To keep cutout shapes from becoming distorted, use a metal spatula to support cookies as you transfer them to the cookie sheet.

- Preheat oven to 325°F (160°C)
- Cookie sheets, lined with parchment paper
- Cookie cutters

1¾ cups	all-purpose flour	425 mL
¼ tsp	salt	1 mL
⅔ cup	unsalted butter, softened	150 mL
½ cup	granulated sugar	125 mL
½ tsp	almond extract	2 mL
½ cup	chopped dried cherries	125 mL

1. In a bowl, whisk together flour and salt until well combined. Set aside.

2. In a large bowl, using an electric mixer on medium speed, cream butter and granulated sugar until light and fluffy, about 2 minutes. Beat in almond extract. Scrape down sides of bowl. On low speed or using a wooden spoon, gradually add flour mixture, beating just until blended. By hand, fold in cherries.

3. Lightly dust a pastry board, clean countertop or other flat surface with confectioner's (powdered/icing) sugar or flour. Gently knead dough a few strokes to form a smooth ball. Divide dough in half. Working with one portion at a time, pat or roll dough to a uniform thickness of ½ inch (1 cm).

4. Dip a 1½-inch (4 cm) round cookie cutter in confectioner's sugar or flour and cut dough into cookies. Cut out as many cookies as possible. Carefully transfer cutouts to prepared cookie sheets, placing 1 inch (2.5 cm) apart. Gather dough remnants into a ball, reroll, cut out more cookies and transfer to cookie sheets.

5. Bake one sheet at a time in preheated oven for 18 to 22 minutes or until edges turn lightly golden.

6. Immediately slide parchment paper onto a wire cooling rack. Cool cookies for 5 minutes, then transfer from parchment paper to cooling rack and cool completely.

Bittersweet Chocolate Shortbread

Makes 52 bars

Bittersweet chocolate gives these bars a full chocolate flavor. For a mellower flavor, use semisweet chocolate.

Tips

Use unsalted butter for cookies. Salted butter can give cookies an "off" flavor or make them too salty.

Shortbread may be wrapped well in foil and frozen for up to 2 months.

- Preheat oven to 325°F (160°C)
- 13- by 9-inch (3 L) baking pan, lined with foil, greased with unsalted butter

5 oz	chopped bittersweet chocolate	150 g
3 cups	all-purpose flour	750 mL
1/4 tsp	salt	1 mL
1 1/4 cups	unsalted butter, softened	300 mL
2/3 cup	packed dark brown sugar	150 mL
1/3 cup	confectioner's (powdered/icing) sugar	75 mL
1 tsp	vanilla extract	5 mL

1. In a microwave-safe bowl, heat chopped chocolate in microwave at Medium-High (75%) power for 30 seconds. Stir until smooth, microwaving an additional 5 seconds at a time as needed to fully melt chocolate. Set aside to cool.

2. In a bowl, whisk together flour and salt until well combined. Set aside.

3. In a large bowl, using an electric mixer on medium speed, cream butter, brown sugar and confectioner's sugar until light and fluffy, about 2 minutes. Beat in melted chocolate and vanilla. Scrape down sides of bowl. On low speed or using a wooden spoon, gradually add flour mixture, beating just until blended.

4. Using the back of a spoon or your fingers, press dough evenly into bottom of prepared pan. With tines of a fork, prick surface of dough in several places. Bake in preheated oven for 40 to 45 minutes or until set in center. Let cool completely in baking pan on a wire rack.

5. Using foil, lift cooled shortbread from pan and place on a cutting board. Pull edges of foil away from sides. If foil sticks, gently run knife blade between shortbread and foil to loosen. Using a long serrated knife, cut shortbread into 1- by 2 1/4-inch (2.5 by 5.5 cm) bars.

Tropical Shortbread

Coconut, pineapple and macadamia nuts make a delicious and unusual shortbread.

Tips

Be sure to use dried pineapple for this shortbread rather than the candied pineapple used in fruitcakes, which will be too sweet and sticky.

A tart pan with a fluted edge makes a pretty mold for shortbread.

● ● ●

- Preheat oven to 325°F (160°C)
- 9-inch (23 cm) tart pan with removable bottom or round cake pan with removable bottom, greased with unsalted butter

1¼ cups	all-purpose flour	300 mL
¾ cup	cake flour	175 mL
¼ tsp	salt	1 mL
¾ cup	unsalted butter, softened	175 mL
⅔ cup	confectioner's (powdered/icing) sugar	150 mL
¼ tsp	almond extract	1 mL
⅓ cup	sweetened flaked coconut, chopped	75 mL
⅓ cup	chopped dried pineapple	75 mL
¼ cup	finely chopped roasted unsalted macadamia nuts	50 mL

1. In a bowl, whisk together all-purpose flour, cake flour and salt until well combined. Set aside.

2. In a large bowl, using an electric mixer on medium speed, cream butter and confectioner's sugar until light and fluffy, about 2 minutes. Beat in almond extract. Scrape down sides of bowl. On low speed or using a wooden spoon, gradually add flour mixture, beating just until blended. By hand, fold in coconut, pineapple and macadamia nuts.

3. Using the back of a spoon or your fingers, press dough evenly into bottom of prepared pan. With tines of a fork, prick surface of dough in several places. Using a sharp knife, score top of shortbread into 16 wedges. Bake in preheated oven for 30 to 35 minutes or until lightly golden.

4. Let cool in baking pan on a wire rack for 5 minutes. If necessary, gently run knife blade between shortbread and edge of pan to loosen. Remove sides of pan and slide shortbread off pan bottom and onto a wire cooling rack. Cool for 10 minutes. Transfer shortbread to a cutting board. Using a long serrated knife, cut the shortbread into wedges along the score lines. Cool completely.

Ginger Shortbread

● ● ●

Candied ginger has an intense flavor, so cut the pieces very small.

Tips

Combining the candied ginger with the flour helps separate the pieces, ensuring they are evenly distributed in the dough.

Flavors can blend during storage, so store cookies with strong flavors in separate containers.

- Preheat oven to 325°F (160°C)
- Cookie sheets, lined with parchment paper

1¼ cups	all-purpose flour	300 mL
½ tsp	ground ginger	2 mL
¼ tsp	salt	1 mL
1 tbsp	minced candied ginger	15 mL
½ cup	unsalted butter, softened	125 mL
½ cup	granulated sugar	125 mL
½ tsp	vanilla extract	2 mL

1. In a bowl, whisk together flour, ginger and salt until well combined. Stir in candied ginger. Set aside.

2. In a large bowl, using an electric mixer on medium speed, cream butter and granulated sugar until light and fluffy, about 2 minutes. Beat in vanilla. Scrape down sides of bowl. On low speed or using a wooden spoon, gradually add flour mixture, beating just until blended.

3. On prepared cookie sheet, pat or roll dough into a ½-inch (1 cm) thick circle, approximately 9 inches (23 cm) in diameter. With tines of a fork, prick surface of dough in several places and gently press tines around edge of circle to create a decorative pattern. Using a sharp knife, cut circle into 16 wedges. Bake in preheated oven for 25 to 30 minutes or until lightly golden.

4. Let cool on cookie sheet on a wire rack for 5 minutes. Slide parchment paper onto a wire cooling rack. Cool completely. Cut or break shortbread into wedges.

Marbled White Chocolate Cream Cheese Brownies (page 353)

Fudge and Fudge Brownies (page 383)

Apricot Biscotti (page 397)

Maple Pecan Biscotti (page 417) and Pumpkin Walnut Biscotti (page 423)

Traditional Shortbread (page 429),
Bittersweet Chocolate Shortbread (page 446)
and Lemon Poppy Seed Shortbread (page 453)

Apricot Pineapple Tassies (page 466)

Almond Pockets (page 478)

Walnut Horns (page 486)
and Strawberry Cream Horns (page 512)

Apricot Shortbread

I like to add a little orange zest to my apricot shortbread because the flavors complement each other so well.

Tips

To keep dried apricots from sticking to your knife when you chop them, give the knife blade a light coat of nonstick cooking spray.

Store shortbread between layers of wax paper in a tightly sealed container. Cookies can be stored at room temperature for up to 3 days.

- Preheat oven to 325°F (160°C)
- Cookie sheets, lined with parchment paper

1 1/4 cups	all-purpose flour	300 mL
1/4 tsp	salt	1 mL
1/2 cup	unsalted butter, softened	125 mL
1/4 cup	granulated sugar	50 mL
1/4 cup	confectioner's (powdered/icing) sugar	50 mL
1 tsp	grated orange zest	5 mL
1/2 tsp	vanilla extract	2 mL
1/2 tsp	almond extract	2 mL
2/3 cup	chopped dried apricots	150 mL

1. In a bowl, whisk together flour and salt until well combined. Set aside.

2. In a large bowl, using an electric mixer on medium speed, cream butter, granulated sugar and confectioner's sugar until light and fluffy, about 2 minutes. Beat in orange zest, vanilla and almond extract. Scrape down sides of bowl. On low speed or using a wooden spoon, gradually add flour mixture, stirring just until blended. By hand, fold in apricots.

3. On prepared cookie sheet, pat or roll dough into a 1/2-inch (1 cm) thick circle, approximately 8 inches (20 cm) in diameter. With tines of a fork, prick surface of dough in several places and gently press tines around edge of circle to create a decorative pattern. Using a sharp knife, cut circle into 16 wedges. Bake in preheated oven for 25 to 30 minutes or until lightly golden.

4. Let cool on cookie sheet on a wire rack for 5 minutes. Slide parchment paper onto a wire cooling rack. Cool completely. Cut or break shortbread into wedges.

Orange Shortbread

● ● ●

Frozen orange juice concentrate in the cookies and a drizzle of orange icing on top gives these delicate bars an intense orange flavor.

Tips

A Microplane grater will finely zest the orange peel for a wonderful texture in cookies.

These citrus-flavored shortbread make a wonderful gift!

Let icing set completely before storing shortbread between layers of wax paper in a tightly sealed container. Do not freeze iced or glazed cookies; store them at room temperature for up to 3 days.

- ● Preheat oven to 325°F (160°C)
- ● 13- by 9-inch (3 L) baking pan, lined with foil, greased with unsalted butter

Shortbread

1½ cups	all-purpose flour	375 mL
1½ cups	cake flour	375 mL
½ tsp	salt	2 mL
1⅓ cups	unsalted butter, softened	325 mL
½ cup	granulated sugar	125 mL
½ cup	confectioner's (powdered/icing) sugar	125 mL
3 tbsp	grated orange zest	45 mL
3 tbsp	frozen orange juice concentrate, thawed	45 mL
½ tsp	vanilla extract	2 mL

Icing

¾ cup	confectioner's (powdered/icing) sugar	175 mL
3 tbsp	freshly squeezed orange juice	45 mL

1. ***Shortbread:*** In a bowl, whisk together all-purpose flour, cake flour and salt until well combined. Set aside.
2. In a large bowl, using an electric mixer on medium speed, cream butter, granulated sugar and confectioner's sugar until light and fluffy, about 2 minutes. Beat in orange zest, orange juice concentrate and vanilla. Scrape down sides of bowl. On low speed or using a wooden spoon, gradually add flour mixture, beating just until blended.
3. Using the back of a spoon or your fingers, press dough evenly into bottom of prepared pan. With tines of a fork, prick surface of dough in several places. Bake in preheated oven for 40 to 45 minutes or until lightly golden. Let cool completely in baking pan on a wire rack.
4. Using foil, lift cooled shortbread from pan and place on a cutting board. Pull edges of foil away from sides. If foil sticks, gently run knife blade between shortbread and foil to loosen.
5. ***Icing:*** In a small bowl, combine the confectioner's sugar and orange juice. Using a small whisk or a fork, blend until the icing is smooth and thin enough to drizzle. Drizzle icing over cooled shortbread. Let stand 10 to 15 minutes or until icing is set. Using a long serrated knife, cut shortbread into 1- by 2¼-inch (2.5 by 5.5 cm) bars.

Toffee Shortbread

● ● ●

Toffee bits and pecans nicely enrich this iced, brown sugar shortbread.

Tip

Use only the freshest ingredients for making shortbread. Because these cookies use so few ingredients, the flavor of every ingredient is extremely important.

- Preheat oven to 325°F (160°C)
- 13- by 9-inch (3 L) baking pan, lined with foil, then with unsalted butter

Shortbread

2 cups	all-purpose flour	500 mL
1/4 tsp	salt	1 mL
3/4 cup	unsalted butter, softened	175 mL
3/4 cup	packed dark brown sugar	175 mL
1 1/2 tsp	vanilla extract	7 mL
1/2 cup	toffee bits	125 mL
1/2 cup	finely chopped pecans	125 mL

Icing

1 cup	confectioner's (powdered/icing) sugar	250 mL
2 to 3 tbsp	half-and-half (10%) cream or milk	25 to 45 mL
1 1/2 tsp	vanilla extract	7 mL

1. **Shortbread:** In a bowl, whisk together flour and salt until well combined. Set aside.

2. In a large bowl, using an electric mixer on medium speed, cream butter and brown sugar until light and fluffy, about 2 minutes. Beat in vanilla. Scrape down sides of bowl. On low speed or using a wooden spoon, gradually add flour mixture, beating just until blended. By hand, fold in toffee bits and pecans.

3. Using the back of a spoon or your fingers, press dough evenly into bottom of prepared pan. With tines of a fork, prick surface of dough in several places. Bake in preheated oven for 35 to 40 minutes or until lightly golden. Let cool completely in baking pan on a wire rack.

4. Using foil, lift cooled shortbread from pan and place on a cutting board. Pull edges of foil away from sides. If foil sticks, gently run knife blade between shortbread and foil to loosen.

5. **Icing:** In a small bowl, combine the confectioner's sugar, 1 tablespoon (15 mL) of the cream and vanilla. Using a small whisk or a fork, blend until the icing is smooth and thin enough to spread. Add more cream as needed to achieve the desired consistency. Spread icing over cooled shortbread. Let stand 10 to 15 minutes or until the icing is set. Using a long serrated knife, cut shortbread into 1- by 2 1/4-inch (2.5 by 5.5 cm) bars.

Walnut Shortbread

Lots of chopped walnuts fill this shortbread with plenty of pleasing flavor and texture.

Tip

Always taste nuts before adding them to cookies to make sure they are fresh.

- Preheat oven to 325°F (160°C)
- 13- by 9-inch (3 L) baking pan, lined with foil, greased with unsalted butter

3 cups	all-purpose flour	750 mL
1/4 tsp	salt	1 mL
1 1/4 cups	unsalted butter, softened	300 mL
1/2 cup	granulated sugar	125 mL
1/2 cup	packed light brown sugar	125 mL
2 tsp	vanilla extract	10 mL
1 1/3 cups	finely chopped walnuts	325 mL

1. In a bowl, whisk together flour and salt until well combined. Set aside.

2. In a large bowl, using an electric mixer on medium speed, cream butter, granulated sugar and brown sugar until light and fluffy, about 2 minutes. Beat in vanilla. Scrape down sides of bowl. On low speed or using a wooden spoon, gradually add flour mixture, beating just until blended. By hand, fold in walnuts.

3. Using the back of a spoon or your fingers, press dough evenly into bottom of prepared pan. With tines of a fork, prick surface of dough in several places. Bake in preheated oven for 35 to 40 minutes or until lightly golden. Let cool completely in baking pan on a wire rack.

4. Using foil, lift cooled shortbread from pan and place on a cutting board. Pull edges of foil away from sides. If foil sticks, gently run knife blade between shortbread and foil to loosen. Using a long serrated knife, cut shortbread into 1- by 2 1/4-inch (2.5 by 5.5 cm) bars.

Lemon Poppy Seed Shortbread

● ● ●

This is an old-fashioned recipe that is great served with afternoon tea.

Tip

To ensure clean cuts, dip cookie cutters in flour or confectioner's (powdered/icing) sugar and shake off the excess before cutting out cookies.

- **Preheat oven to 325°F (160°C)**
- **Cookie sheets, lined with parchment paper**
- **Cookie cutters**

1 cup	all-purpose flour	250 mL
¾ cup	cake flour	175 mL
1 tbsp	poppy seeds	15 mL
¼ tsp	salt	1 mL
⅔ cup	unsalted butter, softened	150 mL
⅔ cup	confectioner's (powdered/icing) sugar	150 mL
2 tbsp	grated lemon zest	25 mL
½ tsp	vanilla extract	2 mL

1. In a bowl, whisk together all-purpose flour, cake flour, poppy seeds and salt until well combined. Set aside.

2. In a large bowl, using an electric mixer on medium speed, cream butter and confectioner's sugar until light and fluffy, about 2 minutes. Beat in lemon zest and vanilla. Scrape down sides of bowl. On low speed or using a wooden spoon, gradually add flour mixture, beating just until blended.

3. Lightly dust a pastry board, clean countertop or other flat surface with confectioner's (powdered/icing) sugar or flour. Gently knead dough a few strokes to form a smooth ball. Divide dough in half. Working with one portion at a time, pat or roll dough to a uniform thickness of ½ inch (1 cm).

4. Dip a 1½-inch (4 cm) round cookie cutter in confectioner's sugar or flour and cut dough into cookies. Cut out as many cookies as possible. Carefully transfer cutouts to prepared cookie sheets, placing 1 inch (2.5 cm) apart. Gather dough remnants into a ball, reroll, cut out more cookies and transfer to cookie sheets.

5. Bake one sheet at a time in preheated oven for 18 to 22 minutes or until edges turn lightly golden.

6. Immediately slide parchment paper onto a wire cooling rack. Cool cookies for 5 minutes, then transfer from parchment paper to cooling rack and cool completely.

White Chocolate Shortbread

Makes 36 squares

A tender shortbread cookie flavored with white chocolate.

Tips

Real white chocolate contains cocoa butter. Always check the ingredients for cocoa butter to be sure you are using white chocolate. Avoid any product labeled as "white" or "vanilla" baking chips.

Store shortbread between layers of wax paper in a tightly sealed container. Shortbread can be stored at room temperature for up to 3 days.

Variations

White Chocolate Macadamia Nut Shortbread: Stir ¼ cup (50 mL) finely chopped roasted unsalted macadamia nuts into flour mixture.

White Chocolate Coconut Shortbread: Stir ⅓ cup (75 mL) sweetened flaked coconut into flour mixture.

- Preheat oven to 325°F (160°C)
- 9-inch (23 cm) square baking pan, lined with foil, greased with unsalted butter

3 oz	chopped white chocolate	90 g
1 cup	all-purpose flour	250 mL
1 cup	cake flour	250 mL
¼ tsp	salt	1 mL
⅔ cup	unsalted butter, softened	150 mL
⅔ cup	granulated sugar	150 mL
½ cup	confectioner's (powdered/icing) sugar	125 mL
1 tsp	vanilla extract	5 mL

1. In the top of a double boiler over simmering water, heat white chocolate, stirring frequently, until chocolate softens and melts. Remove pan from heat and stir until chocolate is completely melted and smooth. Set aside to cool.

2. In a bowl, whisk together all-purpose flour, cake flour and salt until well combined. Set aside.

3. In a large bowl, using an electric mixer on medium speed, cream butter, granulated sugar and confectioner's sugar until light and fluffy, about 2 minutes. Beat in vanilla and melted white chocolate. Scrape down sides of bowl. On low speed or using a wooden spoon, gradually add flour mixture, stirring just until blended.

4. Using the back of a spoon or clean fingers, press dough evenly into bottom of prepared pan. With tines of a fork, prick surface of dough in several places. Bake in preheated oven for 35 to 40 minutes or until lightly golden. Let cool completely in baking pan on a wire rack.

5. Using foil, lift cooled shortbread from pan and place on a cutting board. Pull edges of foil away from sides. If foil sticks, gently run knife blade between shortbread and foil to loosen. Using a long serrated knife, cut shortbread into 1½-inch (4 cm) squares.

Pecan Shortbread

● ● ●

The welcoming nutty aroma as these bake is sure to please.

Tip

Nuts can turn rancid quickly. If you're not going to use them within a few weeks of purchase, tightly wrap the nuts and store them in the freezer to preserve their flavor.

- Preheat oven to 325°F (160°C)
- 9-inch (23 cm) square baking pan, lined with foil, greased with unsalted butter

2 cups	all-purpose flour	500 mL
¼ tsp	salt	1 mL
¾ cup	unsalted butter, softened	175 mL
⅓ cup	granulated sugar	75 mL
⅓ cup	confectioner's (powdered/icing) sugar	75 mL
1 tsp	vanilla extract	5 mL
¾ cup	finely chopped pecans	175 mL

1. In a bowl, whisk together flour and salt until well combined. Set aside.

2. In a large bowl, using an electric mixer on medium speed, cream butter, granulated sugar and confectioner's sugar until light and fluffy, about 2 minutes. Beat in vanilla. Scrape down sides of bowl. On low speed or using a wooden spoon, gradually add flour mixture, stirring just until blended. By hand, fold in pecans.

3. Using the back of a spoon or clean fingers, press dough evenly into bottom of prepared pan. With tines of a fork, prick surface of dough in several places. Bake in preheated oven for 35 to 40 minutes or until lightly golden. Let cool completely in baking pan on a wire rack.

4. Using foil, lift cooled shortbread from pan and place on a cutting board. Pull edges of foil away from sides. If foil sticks, gently run knife blade between shortbread and foil to loosen. Using a long serrated knife, cut shortbread into 1½-inch (4 cm) squares.

Peanut Butter Shortbread

●●●

These have a lovely peanut butter flavor in a tender cookie square.

Tip

Always taste peanut butter to be sure it's fresh before using it for baking. The nut oil in peanut butter can turn stale or rancid after the jar has been open for awhile.

● **Preheat oven to 325°F (160°C)**
● **9-inch (23 cm) square baking pan, lined with foil, greased with unsalted butter**

1½ cups	all-purpose flour	375 mL
¾ cup	cornstarch	175 mL
½ cup	unsalted butter, softened	125 mL
½ cup	creamy peanut butter	125 mL
½ cup	granulated sugar	125 mL
⅓ cup	confectioner's (powdered/icing) sugar	75 mL
1 tsp	vanilla extract	5 mL

I. In a bowl, whisk together flour and cornstarch until well combined. Set aside.

2. In a large bowl, using an electric mixer on medium speed, cream butter, peanut butter, granulated sugar and confectioner's sugar until light and fluffy, about 2 minutes. Beat in vanilla. Scrape down sides of bowl. On low speed or using a wooden spoon, gradually add flour mixture, beating just until blended.

3. Using the back of a spoon or clean fingers, press dough evenly into bottom of prepared pan. With tines of a fork, prick surface of dough in several places. Bake in preheated oven for 35 to 40 minutes or until lightly golden. Let cool completely in baking pan on a wire rack.

4. Using foil, lift cooled shortbread from pan and place on a cutting board. Pull edges of foil away from sides. If foil sticks, gently run knife blade between shortbread and foil to loosen. Using a long serrated knife, cut shortbread into 1½-inch (4 cm) squares.

Espresso Shortbread

● ● ●

Tastes of brown sugar, almond and chocolate are nice additions to these coffee-flavored cookies.

Tips

Lightly spray hands with nonstick cooking spray to prevent dough from sticking while shaping cookies.

Store unopened packages of flour in a cool, dry place for up to 2 years. Always use flour before the date stamped on the package.

Shortbread may be wrapped well in foil and frozen for up to 2 months.

- Preheat oven to 325°F (160°C)
- Cookie sheets, lined with parchment paper

1½ cups	all-purpose flour	375 mL
1 cup	cake flour	250 mL
2 tbsp	instant espresso powder	25 mL
¼ tsp	salt	1 mL
1 cup	unsalted butter, softened	250 mL
¾ cup	packed light brown sugar	175 mL
1 tsp	vanilla extract	5 mL
¼ tsp	almond extract	1 mL
¾ cup	mini semisweet chocolate chips	175 mL

1. In a bowl, whisk together all-purpose flour, cake flour, espresso powder and salt until well combined. Set aside.

2. In a large bowl, using an electric mixer on medium speed, cream butter and brown sugar until light and fluffy, about 2 minutes. Beat in vanilla and almond extract. Scrape down sides of bowl. On low speed or using a wooden spoon, gradually add flour mixture, beating just until blended. By hand, fold in chocolate chips.

3. Lightly grease hands with nonstick cooking spray. Roll pieces of dough into 1-inch (2.5 cm) balls. Place on prepared cookie sheets about 2 inches (5 cm) apart. Using the bottom of a glass dipped in confectioner's sugar, press balls to flatten to ½ inch (1 cm) thick. Bake one sheet at a time in preheated oven for 15 to 18 minutes or until edges turn lightly golden.

4. Immediately slide parchment paper onto a wire cooling rack. Cool cookies for 5 minutes, then transfer from parchment paper to cooling rack and cool completely.

Citus Shortbread

A pleasing blend of orange and lemon flavors gives these shortbread cookies a lovely citrus scent.

Tips

Use any combination of citrus flavors you like in these shortbreads, such as tangerine, tangelo, blood orange, grapefruit or lime.

Store shortbread between layers of wax paper in a tightly sealed container. Cookies can be stored at room temperature for up to 3 days.

- Preheat oven to 325°F (160°C)
- 9-inch (23 cm) tart pan with removable bottom or round cake pan with removable bottom, greased with unsalted butter

⅔ cup	all-purpose flour	150 mL
⅔ cup	cake flour	150 mL
¼ tsp	salt	1 mL
½ cup	unsalted butter, softened	125 mL
¼ cup	granulated sugar	50 mL
¼ cup	confectioner's (powdered/icing) sugar	50 mL
1 tbsp	grated orange zest	15 mL
1 tbsp	grated lemon zest	15 mL
1 tbsp	freshly squeezed orange juice	15 mL

1. In a bowl, whisk together all-purpose flour, cake flour and salt until well combined. Set aside.

2. In a large bowl, using an electric mixer on medium speed, cream butter, granulated sugar and confectioner's sugar until light and fluffy, about 2 minutes. Beat in orange and lemon zests and orange juice. Scrape down sides of bowl. On low speed or using a wooden spoon, gradually add flour mixture, stirring just until blended.

3. Using the back of a spoon or your fingers, press dough evenly into bottom of prepared pan. With tines of a fork, prick surface of dough in several places. Using a sharp knife, score top of shortbread into 16 wedges. Bake in preheated oven for 25 to 30 minutes or until lightly golden.

4. Let cool in baking pan on a wire rack for 5 minutes. If necessary, gently run knife blade between shortbread and edge of pan to loosen. Remove sides of pan and slide shortbread off pan bottom and onto a wire cooling rack. Cool for 10 minutes. Transfer shortbread to a cutting board. Using a long serrated knife, cut the shortbread into wedges along the score lines. Cool completely.

Cornmeal Shortbread

Makes 16 wedges

● ● ●

Cornmeal is a traditional ingredient used to make many European shortbreads.

Tip

Yellow cornmeal gives these shortbread cookies a pleasant corn flavor. White cornmeal, which has a mild flavor, may be substituted if you do not have yellow cornmeal.

● **Preheat oven to 325°F (160°C)**
● **Cookie sheets, lined with parchment paper**

1 cup	all-purpose flour	250 mL
2/3 cup	yellow cornmeal	150 mL
1/4 tsp	salt	1 mL
3/4 cup	unsalted butter, softened	175 mL
3/4 cup	confectioner's (powdered/icing) sugar	175 mL
1 tsp	vanilla extract	5 mL

1. In a bowl, whisk together flour, cornmeal and salt until well combined. Set aside.

2. In a large bowl, using an electric mixer on medium speed, cream butter and confectioner's sugar until light and fluffy, about 2 minutes. Beat in vanilla. Scrape down sides of bowl. On low speed or using a wooden spoon, gradually add flour mixture, beating just until blended.

3. On prepared cookie sheet, pat or roll dough into a 1/2-inch (1 cm) thick circle, approximately 8 inches (20 cm) in diameter. With tines of a fork, prick surface of dough in several places and gently press tines around edge of circle to create a decorative pattern. Using a sharp knife, cut circle into 16 wedges. Bake in preheated oven for 25 to 30 minutes or until lightly golden.

4. Let cool on cookie sheet on a wire rack for 5 minutes. Slide parchment paper onto a wire cooling rack. Cool completely. Cut or break shortbread into wedges.

Oatmeal Shortbread

Oats are a common ingredient in Irish shortbreads.

Tips

For a finer texture, lightly crush oats with a rolling pin before adding to flour mixture.

Store shortbread between layers of wax paper in a tightly sealed container at room temperature for up to 3 days.

Variation

Oatmeal Walnut Shortbread: Stir 3 tbsp (45 mL) finely chopped walnuts into flour mixture along with oats.

- Preheat oven to 325°F (160°C)
- Cookie sheets, lined with parchment paper

1 cup	all-purpose flour	250 mL
1/4 tsp	ground cinnamon	1 mL
1/4 tsp	salt	1 mL
1/3 cup	quick-cooking rolled oats	75 mL
1/2 cup	unsalted butter, softened	125 mL
1/3 cup	granulated sugar	75 mL

1. In a bowl, whisk together flour, cinnamon and salt until well combined. Stir in oats. Set aside.

2. In a large bowl, using an electric mixer on medium speed, cream butter and granulated sugar until light and fluffy, about 2 minutes. Scrape down sides of bowl. On low speed or using a wooden spoon, gradually add flour mixture, beating just until blended.

3. On prepared cookie sheet, pat or roll dough into a 1/2-inch (1 cm) thick circle, approximately 8 inches (20 cm) in diameter. With tines of a fork, prick surface of dough in several places and gently press tines around edge of circle to create a decorative pattern. Using a sharp knife, cut circle into 16 wedges. Bake in preheated oven for 25 to 30 minutes or until lightly golden.

4. Let cool on cookie sheet on a wire rack for 5 minutes. Slide parchment paper onto a wire cooling rack. Cool completely. Cut or break shortbread into wedges.

Extra-Special Cookies

• • •

Raspberry Heart Cookies 464
Apricot Pineapple Tassies 466
Chocolate Cheesecake Bites 468
Cherry Pie Turnovers 470
Blackberry Triangles 472
Hawaiian Pinwheels 474
Blueberry Cheesecake Bites 476
Orange Walnut Spirals 477
Almond Pockets 478
Rugelach 480
Boysenberry Blossoms 482
Pecan Tassies 484
Raspberry Coconut Spirals 485
Walnut Horns 486
Cranberry Orange Walnut Tassies . . . 488
Coconut Pineapple Cups 490
Lemon Cheesecake Bites 492
Strawberry Spirals 493
Orange Curd Cups 494
Sour Cream Fudge Pouches 496
Coconut Macadamia Rugelach 498
Apricot Orange Cups 500
Peach Pie Cookies 501
Pumpkin Walnut Tassies 502
Pineapple Horns 504
Maple Walnut Tartlets 506
Almond Bites 507

Cranberry Pinwheels 508
Luscious Lemon Tartlets 510
Strawberry Cream Horns 512
Raspberry Almond Cream Cheese
   Pockets 514
Apple Butter Turnovers 516
Chocolate Nut Rugelach 518
Cashew Caramel Cups 519
Apricot Horns 520
Blueberry Pillows 522
Maple Pecan Spirals 524
Lemon Cheese Pinwheels 526
Orange Almond Cups 528
Pineapple Tartlets 529
Coconut Lemon Specials 530
Cranberry Orange Spirals 532
Bachelor Buttons 534
Apricot Rugelach 536
Orange Cream Horns 538
Chocolate Mint Pillows 540
Pinwheel Jam Cookies 542
Strawberry Delights 544
Butterhorns 546
Lemon Almond Sticks 548
Apricot Pecan Cups 550
Raspberry Ribbons 552
Cinnamon Spirals 554

About Extra-Special Cookies

When you want to serve something extra-special, the delightful creations in this collection are sure to meet your needs. Each cookie is pretty and delicious, and these flavorful gems will be the highlight of any dessert tray. While they may look complicated and take a little extra time to prepare, none of these treasures are difficult to make, and the superb results are well worth the effort. I'm sure you'll find several new and exciting recipes to fit any occasion or event and impress your family and friends. They're also perfect when you want to treat yourself to something special.

These cookies use the basic cookie-baking techniques we've discussed in other chapters, such as rolling, shaping and slicing the cookie dough. There are a few pieces of baking equipment that haven't been used in other chapters, such as a mini-muffin pan, a dough tamper and a pinwheel cookie cutter.

The majority of these special cookies fall into a few specific cookie categories, each with its own unique characteristics.

Tassies

Tassies, also called cups and bites, are intriguing cookies that resemble tiny tarts. They have a pastry cookie crust that is evenly pressed into the cups of a miniature muffin pan to create the tassie shape. The crust dough can be rolled out thin, cut out with a cookie cutter and fitted into the cups. Or it can be rolled into balls and pressed into the bottom of the cups and evenly up the sides. This can be done with your fingers or a dough tamper, a wooden baking tool shaped like a pestle that is designed specifically for this purpose. The shaped pastry cups are then filled with tantalizing fruit, nut and cream cheese fillings. Sometimes the pastry cups are baked before being filled, while other times the pastry and filling are baked together.

Pinwheels

Fanciful pinwheel cookies use a special square cookie cutter that cuts rolled dough so it can be shaped around a filling. The cutter cuts the dough into a square and also makes cuts from the corners toward the center of the dough. After a spoonful of filling is placed in the center, alternating tips of the dough are brought to the center and sealed. This creates the unique pinwheel shape that these cookies are known for. The finished cookies are eye-catching and make a great gift. Don't worry if you don't have a pinwheel cookie cutter. The same cuts in the dough can be made with a small, sharp knife. A pinwheel cookie cutter just makes the job go a lot faster.

Spirals

Pretty spiral cookies are made using a combination of rolled cutout cookie and refrigerator slice-and-bake cookie techniques. The dough is rolled out into a rectangle and spread with a filling. The rectangle is then rolled up into a log, wrapped and chilled until firm. When set, the dough log is sliced and baked. The finished cookies reveal the decorative spiral pattern of cookie dough and tempting filling.

To make it easier to roll up the dough log, roll the dough out on a piece of floured parchment paper. Rotate the dough during rolling and dust the parchment paper with additional flour to keep it from sticking. After adding the filling, start along the long edge and lift the parchment paper off the rolling surface and use it to help fold the edge of the dough over on itself and roll it into a log. Peel the parchment paper back from the dough as the log starts to form. Continue using the parchment paper to lift and roll the dough until the log is formed. Pinch the edge of the dough to the log and wrap it tightly in parchment paper or in plastic wrap for chilling.

Filled Cookies

Pouches, pockets and turnovers are neat little cookie packages that hide a tasty filling inside. They are made by rolling out and cutting the dough and adding a spoonful of filling to the center. Then either the piece of dough is folded over to make a turnover or it is topped with another piece of dough, and the edges are sealed to make a pouch or pocket. These little packages are frequently topped with a sprinkling of sugar or drizzled with icing to complete the presentation.

Other Creative Cookies

This chapter also contains some distinctive rolled cookies that are cut out or filled and shaped after rolling. These flavorful treats include a variety of horns, rugelach and special cookies. Each recipe gives specific directions for rolling, filling and shaping, and they all have a beautiful finished appearance.

Sharing the Love of Cookies

There are many special ways to share your love of cookies and wonderful cookie creations with family, friends and members of the community. In this chapter, I've included some fun ideas for entertaining with cookie parties and also holding a group fundraiser. Check out these suggestions:

- Cookie Baking Party (page 473)

- Cookie Dessert Buffet (page 521)
- Hosting a Cookie Dessert Buffet (page 523)

- Bake Sales (page 531)
- Planning a Bake Sale Fundraiser (page 533)
- Packaging Cookies for a Bake Sale (page 535)
- Setting Up a Bake Sale Table (page 537)

- Cookie Exchange Party (page 541)
- Planning a Cookie Exchange Party – Part 1 (page 543)
- Planning a Cookie Exchange Party – Part 2 (page 545)
- Hosting a Cookie Exchange Party – Part 1 (page 547)
- Hosting a Cookie Exchange Party – Part 2 (page 549)

Raspberry Heart Cookies

Beautiful heart-shaped cookies with a sweet raspberry filling and glaze make a nice treat throughout the year and are especially pretty when served on Valentine's Day. Bake up a batch of these gems for your sweetheart.

Tips

If you can't find raspberry jelly in your local store, seedless raspberry jam may be substituted for the raspberry jelly. With raspberry jam, the texture of the glaze will be thicker and little more cream may be needed to thin it enough for spreading on top of the cookies.

A small offset spatula is the perfect tool to quickly and easily spread the glaze on these pretty cookies.

- Cookie sheets, lined with parchment paper
- 2-inch (5 cm) heart-shaped cookie cutter

Cookies

2 cups	all-purpose flour	500 mL
2 tsp	baking powder	10 mL
½ tsp	salt	2 mL
½ cup	unsalted butter, softened	125 mL
1 cup	granulated sugar	250 mL
1	egg	1
1 tsp	vanilla extract	5 mL
¼ tsp	almond extract	1 mL

Filling

½ cup	raspberry jelly	125 mL

Glaze

1½ cups	confectioner's (powdered/icing) sugar	375 mL
¼ cup	raspberry jelly	50 mL
1 tbsp	half-and-half (10%) cream or milk	15 mL
¼ tsp	almond extract	1 mL

1. **Cookies:** In a bowl, whisk together flour, baking powder and salt until well combined. Set aside.
2. In a large bowl, using an electric mixer on medium speed, cream butter and granulated sugar until light and fluffy, about 3 minutes. Add egg and beat well. Beat in vanilla and almond extract. Scrape down sides of bowl. On low speed or using a wooden spoon, gradually add flour mixture, beating just until blended.
3. Divide dough in half. Shape each portion into a flat disk. Tightly wrap each dough disk in plastic wrap and chill for at least 1 hour.
4. Preheat oven to 375°F (190°C). Using confectioner's sugar or flour, lightly dust a pastry board, clean countertop or other flat surface and a rolling pin. Working with one dough disk at a time, unwrap dough and roll out to uniform thickness of ⅛ inch (3 mm). Halfway through rolling, rotate the dough a quarter turn and dust the board again to prevent dough from sticking.

Tip

Let glaze set before
storing the cookies
between layers of wax
paper. Cookies can
be stored in a tightly
sealed container at room
temperature for up to
3 days.

5. Dip cookie cutter in confectioner's sugar or flour and cut dough
into desired shapes. Cut out as many cookies as possible from
first rolling. Carefully transfer cutouts to prepared cookie
sheets, placing 1 inch (2.5 cm) apart. Gather dough remnants
into a ball, reroll, cut out more cookies and transfer to cookie
sheets.

6. Bake one sheet at a time in preheated oven for 7 to 9 minutes
or until edges start to turn lightly golden. Immediately slide
parchment paper onto a wire cooling rack. Cool cookies for
5 minutes, then transfer from parchment paper to cooling rack
and cool completely.

7. *Filling:* Gently stir the raspberry jelly to make it spreadable.
Spread a thin layer of jelly on the bottoms of half of the cooled
cookies. Top with remaining cookies.

8. *Glaze:* In a bowl, combine confectioner's sugar, raspberry
jelly, cream and almond extract. Using an electric mixer on
medium speed, beat until glaze is smooth and spreadable. Using
the back of a spoon, spread glaze over tops of filled cookies
following the heart shape and leaving the outside $\frac{1}{4}$ inch
(0.5 cm) of cookie unglazed.

Apricot Pineapple Tassies

Tender pastry cups brimming with a tantalizing tropical filling, these special cookies are hard to resist and disappear fast.

Tips

Use table salt for baking. It has a balanced flavor and very fine grains that blend well into the other ingredients.

Chilling the formed pastry cups before baking will help them bake evenly and give the crusts a tender texture.

- One 24-cup or two 12-cup 1¾-inch (4.5 cm) mini-muffin pans, greased with unsalted butter
- 2½-inch (6 cm) scalloped or round cookie cutter

Crust

1½ cups	all-purpose flour	375 mL
2 tbsp	granulated sugar	25 mL
¼ tsp	salt	1 mL
1 tsp	grated orange zest	5 mL
¼ cup	chilled unsalted butter, cut into pieces	50 mL
2 tbsp	vegetable shortening	25 mL
2 to 3 tbsp	freshly squeezed orange juice	25 to 45 mL

Filling

1 tbsp	all-purpose flour	15 mL
¼ tsp	baking powder	1 mL
1	egg	1
⅓ cup	granulated sugar	75 mL
⅔ cup	apricot pineapple jam or preserves	150 mL
¼ cup	sweetened flaked coconut, coarsely chopped	50 mL
1 tsp	grated orange zest	5 mL

Icing

½ cup	confectioner's (powdered/icing) sugar	125 mL
2 tsp	freshly squeezed orange juice	10 mL
1½ tsp	unsalted butter, melted	7 mL

1. **Crust:** In a large bowl, whisk together flour, granulated sugar, salt and orange zest until well combined. Using a pastry blender or a fork, cut in butter and shortening until mixture resembles coarse crumbs. Add orange juice, 1 tablespoon (15 mL) at a time, stirring with a fork until mixture starts to pull away from sides of the bowl and holds together when formed into a ball. Shape dough into a flat disk. Tightly wrap in plastic wrap and chill for at least 30 minutes.

2. Using confectioner's sugar or flour, lightly dust a pastry board, clean countertop or other flat surface and a rolling pin. Unwrap dough and roll out to uniform thickness of ⅛ inch (3 mm). Halfway through rolling, rotate the dough a quarter turn and dust the board again to prevent dough from sticking.

Tip

Let icing set before storing cookies between layers of wax paper in a tightly sealed container. Cookies can be stored at room temperature for up to 3 days.

3. Dip cookie cutter in confectioner's sugar or flour and cut out 24 circles. Gently fit a cutout into each cup of prepared mini-muffin pan, being careful not to tear or stretch dough. Cover pan loosely with plastic wrap and chill for 15 minutes.

4. Preheat oven to 375°F (190°C).

5. *Filling:* In a small bowl, whisk together flour and baking powder until well combined. Set aside.

6. In a medium bowl, using a wire whisk, lightly beat egg. Add granulated sugar and stir until well combined. Add flour mixture and stir until well blended and smooth. Stir in apricot pineapple jam, coconut and orange zest. Spoon about 1 tablespoon (15 mL) of filling into chilled pastry cups, filling nearly to the top.

7. Bake in preheated oven for 14 to 16 minutes or until top of the crust is golden brown and the filling is set. Remove from oven and cool cookies in pan on a wire cooling rack for 10 minutes. If necessary, use a sharp thin-bladed knife to carefully loosen top edges of cookies from pan. Carefully remove cookies from pan, transfer to cooling rack and cool completely.

8. *Icing:* In a small bowl, combine confectioner's sugar, orange juice and butter. Using a small whisk or a fork, blend until icing is smooth and thin enough to drizzle from a fork. Drizzle icing over cooled cookies.

Chocolate Cheesecake Bites

● ● ●

A creamy chocolate cheesecake filling nestled inside cocoa pastry cups. Try topping these with a tiny dollop of whipped cream and a bit of shaved chocolate. Top the heavenly white chocolate version with a perfect fresh raspberry.

Tips

Use the appropriate measuring tools and techniques to accurately measure ingredients.

Store cookies between layers of wax paper in a tightly sealed container in the refrigerator. Cookies can be stored for up to 3 days.

● **One 24-cup or two 12-cup 1¾-inch (4.5 cm) mini-muffin pans, greased with unsalted butter**

Crust

1¼ cups	all-purpose flour	300 mL
¼ cup	unsweetened Dutch-process cocoa powder, sifted	50 mL
¼ cup	granulated sugar	50 mL
¼ tsp	salt	1 mL
½ cup	chilled unsalted butter, cut into pieces	125 mL
2 to 3 tbsp	cold water	25 to 45 mL

Filling

¾ cup	chopped semisweet chocolate	175 mL
6 oz	cream cheese, softened	175 g
¼ cup	granulated sugar	50 mL
1	egg	1
1 tbsp	half-and-half (10%) cream	15 mL
1 tsp	vanilla extract	5 mL

1. **Crust:** In a large bowl, whisk together flour, cocoa powder, granulated sugar and salt until well combined. Using a pastry blender or a fork, cut in butter until mixture resembles coarse crumbs. Add water, 1 tablespoon (15 mL) at a time, stirring with a fork until mixture starts to pull away from sides of the bowl and holds together when formed into a ball. Add more water as needed. Cover dough with plastic wrap and chill for 15 minutes.

2. Lightly grease hands with nonstick cooking spray. Divide dough into 24 portions and shape each portion into a ball. Using fingers or a dough tamper, press a dough ball evenly against bottom and sides of each prepared muffin cup. Cover pan loosely with plastic wrap and chill for 15 minutes.

3. Preheat oven to 350°F (180°C).

4. **Filling:** In a microwave-safe bowl, heat chopped chocolate in microwave at Medium-High (75%) power for 1 minute. Stir chocolate until smooth. If necessary, heat at Medium (50%) power for 10 seconds at a time, stirring between each heating, just until chocolate is melted. Set aside.

Tip

Chocolate chips contain less cocoa butter than chocolate shaped in bar form, which helps them retain their chip shape when heated during baking. This makes chocolate chips great for making chocolate chip cookies but not a good choice for melting. Bar chocolate melts more uniformly with a smoother texture and combines better with the other ingredients in the filling.

5. In a large bowl, using an electric mixer on medium speed, beat cream cheese and granulated sugar until smooth and creamy, about 2 minutes. Add egg and beat just until blended. Beat in cream and vanilla. Add melted chocolate and stir just until blended. Spoon about 1 tablespoon (15 mL) of cream cheese filling into chilled pastry-lined muffin cups, filling nearly to the top.

6. Bake in preheated oven for 15 to 18 minutes or until the filling is set. Remove from oven and cool cookies in pan on a wire cooling rack for 10 minutes. If necessary, use a sharp thin-bladed knife to carefully loosen top edges of cookies from pan. Carefully remove cookies from pan, transfer to cooling rack and cool completely.

Variation

White Chocolate Cheesecake Bites: Omit cocoa powder from crust and use $1\frac{1}{2}$ cups (375 mL) all-purpose flour. Substitute white chocolate for semisweet chocolate in filling. Do not melt the white chocolate in a microwave; the white chocolate may become lumpy. Melt the white chocolate in the top of a double boiler.

Cherry Pie Turnovers

These pretty cookies look like little turnovers and are packed with cherry and almond flavors.

Tips

Sugar adds flavor and texture to cookies and helps keep them fresh longer.

Let icing set before storing cookies in a tightly sealed container. Cookies can be stored at room temperature for up to 3 days.

Variation

Blueberry, apricot, peach and apple pie fillings are all good choices for this recipe. If using a pie filling other than cherry or apricot, substitute vanilla extract for the almond extract in both the filling and icing.

- Cookie sheets, lined with parchment paper
- 3-inch (7.5 cm) round or scalloped cookie cutter

Cookies

2¾ cups	all-purpose flour	675 mL
½ tsp	baking powder	2 mL
¼ tsp	baking soda	1 mL
½ cup	unsalted butter, softened	125 mL
1 cup	granulated sugar	250 mL
1	egg	1
½ cup	sour cream	125 mL
1 tsp	vanilla extract	5 mL

Filling

1	can (21 oz or 540 mL) cherry pie filling	1
½ tsp	almond extract	2 mL

Icing

1 cup	confectioner's (powdered/icing) sugar	250 mL
4 to 5 tsp	half-and-half (10%) cream	20 to 25 mL
¼ tsp	almond extract	1 mL

1. *Cookies:* In a bowl, whisk together flour, baking powder and baking soda until well combined. Set aside.
2. In a large bowl, using an electric mixer on medium speed, cream butter and granulated sugar until light and fluffy, about 3 minutes. Add egg and beat well. Beat in sour cream and vanilla. Scrape down sides of bowl. On low speed or using a wooden spoon, gradually add flour mixture, beating just until blended.
3. Divide dough in half. Shape each portion into a flat disk. Tightly wrap each dough disk in plastic wrap and chill for 2 to 3 hours.
4. Preheat oven to 375°F (190°C). Using confectioner's sugar or flour, lightly dust a pastry board, clean countertop or other flat surface and a rolling pin. Working with one dough disk at a time, unwrap dough and roll out to uniform thickness of ⅛ inch (3 mm). Halfway through rolling, rotate the dough a quarter turn and dust the board again to prevent dough from sticking.
5. Dip cookie cutter in confectioner's sugar or flour and cut out as many cookies as possible from first rolling.

Tip

On your rolling surface and rolling pin, use only just as much flour as you need to keep the cookies from sticking. If the dough absorbs too much extra flour, the cookies will be tough.

6. **Filling:** In a bowl, combine cherry pie filling and almond extract until well blended. Place a teaspoonful (5 mL) of filling in center of each circle. Fold circles in half and press edges together with tines of a fork to seal. Carefully transfer turnovers to prepared cookie sheets, placing 2 inches (5 cm) apart. Gather dough remnants into a ball, reroll, cut out and fill more cookies; seal and transfer to cookie sheets.

7. Bake one sheet at a time in preheated oven for 8 to 10 minutes or until edges turn lightly golden. Immediately slide parchment paper onto a wire cooling rack. Cool cookies for 5 minutes, then transfer from parchment paper to cooling rack and cool completely.

8. **Icing:** In a small bowl, combine confectioner's sugar, 4 teaspoons (20 mL) of the cream and almond extract. Using a small whisk or a fork, blend until icing is smooth and thin enough to drizzle from a fork. Add more cream as needed to achieve the desired consistency. Drizzle icing over cooled cookies.

Blackberry Triangles

The blackberry jam peeks out from the inside of pretty little triangles.

Tips

Use your favorite flavor of jam or preserves to make these yummy cookies.

Store cookies in a tightly sealed container. Cookies can be stored at room temperature for up to 3 days.

- Cookie sheets, lined with parchment paper
- 3-inch (7.5 cm) round cookie cutter

Cookies

2 cups	all-purpose flour	500 mL
1/4 tsp	salt	1 mL
1/2 cup	unsalted butter, softened	125 mL
3 oz	cream cheese, softened	90 g
1/3 cup	granulated sugar	75 mL
1 tsp	vanilla extract	5 mL

Filling

1 cup	seedless blackberry jam	250 mL

Topping

1	egg yolk	1
1 tsp	water	5 mL
	Coarse sugar or granulated sugar	

1. **Cookies:** In a bowl, whisk together flour and salt until well combined. Set aside.

2. In a large bowl, using an electric mixer on medium speed, cream butter, cream cheese and granulated sugar until light and fluffy, about 3 minutes. Beat in vanilla. Scrape down sides of bowl. On low speed or using a wooden spoon, gradually add flour mixture, beating just until blended.

3. Divide dough in half. Shape each portion into a flat disk. Tightly wrap each dough disk in plastic wrap and chill for at least 2 to 3 hours.

4. Preheat oven to 375°F (190°C). Using confectioner's (powdered/icing) sugar or flour, lightly dust a pastry board, clean countertop or other flat surface and a rolling pin. Working with one dough disk at a time, unwrap dough and roll out to uniform thickness of 1/8 inch (3 mm). Halfway through rolling, rotate the dough a quarter turn and dust the board again to prevent dough from sticking. Using a round cookie cutter, cut dough into circles.

5. Place a teaspoonful (5 mL) of blackberry jam in center of each circle. Fold edges of circle into center to form a triangle, overlapping dough edges, and pinch together to seal. Carefully transfer cookies to prepared cookie sheets, placing 2 inches (5 cm) apart. Gather dough remnants into a ball, reroll, cut out and fill more cookies; seal and transfer to cookie sheets.

Tip

Sugar caramelizes as it bakes and helps give cookies their lovely golden color.

6. *Topping:* In a small bowl, whisk together egg yolk and water until well combined. Lightly brush egg mixture over tops of cookies. Sprinkle with coarse sugar.

7. Bake one sheet at a time in preheated oven for 10 to 12 minutes or until edges start to turn lightly golden. Immediately slide parchment paper onto a wire cooling rack. Cool cookies for 5 minutes, then transfer from parchment paper to cooling rack and cool completely.

Cookie Baking Party

A great way to spend time with family and friends is to host a cookie baking party. You can do this at any time of the year and for any occasion. Cookie baking parties are a lot of fun around the holidays and are also a great way to get together and socialize throughout the year. If your group or organization will be involved in a bake sale fundraiser, consider hosting a cookie baking party to get a lot of the work done in an entertaining setting.

Here's how to make your party go smoothly:

- Poll your guests in advance to decide what kinds of cookies should be baked, to plan what you will need and have copies of the recipes ready for baking.
- Ask each guest to bring specific items, such as flour, oats, butter, peanut butter, granulated sugar, brown sugar, eggs, chocolate chips, nuts, vanilla extract, cookie sheets, baking pans, cooling racks, cookie scoops, parchment paper and other cookie baking essentials.
- Have everyone gather and start baking early in the day so you have plenty of time to finish the cookies before people need to head for home.
- This is an all-day event so plan to have food, other than cookies, available for your guests. A no-fuss way to feed your hungry bakers is to ask one of your guests to prepare a batch of soup or chili in the crock pot and bring it along as their contribution to the party. Add some crusty bread and a salad, and you're all set.

Hawaiian Pinwheels

Not only are these gems pretty, they are bursting with tropical flavors.

Tips

Reserve some of the juice drained from the crushed pineapple to use in the cookie dough and icing.

Tightly wrapped in plastic wrap, this pinwheel cookie dough can be stored in the refrigerator for up to 1 week.

A pinwheel cookie cutter is a nifty tool that not only cuts the dough into squares but also makes the diagonal cuts from the corners toward the center. Pinwheel cutters can often be found where cookie cutters are sold, in many kitchen supply stores and from mail-order suppliers.

- Cookie sheets, lined with parchment paper
- 3-inch (7.5 cm) pinwheel cookie cutter (optional)

Cookies

2 cups	all-purpose flour	500 mL
1½ tsp	baking powder	7 mL
⅛ tsp	salt	0.5 mL
⅓ cup	unsalted butter, softened	75 mL
⅓ cup	vegetable shortening	75 mL
⅔ cup	granulated sugar	150 mL
1	egg	1
2 tsp	reserved pineapple juice	10 mL
¼ tsp	vanilla extract	1 mL
⅛ tsp	almond extract	0.5 mL

Filling

3 oz	cream cheese, softened	90 g
3 tbsp	granulated sugar	45 mL
⅓ cup	drained canned juice-packed crushed pineapple, juice reserved	75 mL
⅓ cup	sweetened flaked coconut, coarsely chopped	75 mL

Icing

¾ cup	confectioner's (powdered/icing) sugar	175 mL
1 tbsp	reserved pineapple juice	15 mL
3 tbsp	finely chopped roasted unsalted macadamia nuts	45 mL

1. **Cookies:** In a bowl, whisk together flour, baking powder and salt until well combined. Set aside.

2. In a large bowl, using an electric mixer on medium speed, cream butter, shortening and granulated sugar until light and fluffy, about 2 minutes. Add egg and beat well. Beat in pineapple juice, vanilla and almond extract. Scrape down sides of bowl. On low speed or using a wooden spoon, gradually add flour mixture, beating just until blended.

3. Divide dough in half. Shape each portion into a flat square. Tightly wrap each dough square in plastic wrap and chill for at least 3 hours.

Tip

Cookies can be stored in a tightly sealed container at room temperature for up to 3 days.

4. Preheat oven to 350°F (180°C). Using confectioner's sugar or flour, lightly dust a pastry board, clean countertop or other flat surface and a rolling pin. Working with one dough square at a time, unwrap dough and roll out to uniform thickness of $\frac{1}{8}$ inch (3 mm). Halfway through rolling, rotate the dough a quarter turn and dust the board again to prevent dough from sticking.

5. Dip pinwheel cookie cutter in confectioner's sugar or flour and cut dough into squares. Or, using a sharp knife, pastry cutter or pizza cutter, cut dough into 3-inch (7.5 cm) squares and make a 1-inch (2.5 cm) diagonal cut from the tip of each corner toward center of each square. Carefully transfer cutouts to prepared cookie sheets, placing 2 inches (5 cm) apart.

6. *Filling:* In a bowl, using an electric mixer on medium speed, beat cream cheese and granulated sugar until well combined and smooth, about 2 minutes. Stir in pineapple and coconut. Place a teaspoon (5 mL) of cream cheese mixture in center of each square. Fold alternating tips to center to form a pinwheel and press lightly to seal. Gather dough remnants into a ball, reroll, cut out more cookies, transfer to cookie sheets, fill and seal.

7. Bake one sheet at a time in preheated oven for 8 to 10 minutes or until edges start to turn lightly golden. Immediately slide parchment paper onto a wire cooling rack. Cool cookies for 5 minutes, then transfer from parchment paper to cooling rack and cool completely.

8. *Icing:* In a small bowl, combine confectioner's sugar and pineapple juice. Using a small whisk or a fork, blend until icing is smooth and thin enough to drizzle from a fork. Drizzle icing over cooled cookies.

9. Sprinkle macadamia nuts over top of iced cookies.

Blueberry Cheesecake Bites

These bite-size treats have all the flavor of a creamy cheesecake filling and a fruity blueberry topping.

Tips

Use a scant tablespoonful (15 mL) of the cream cheese filling. Do not fill the pastry cups all the way to the top because you want to leave a little room to add the pie filling after baking.

Store cookies between layers of wax paper in a tightly sealed container in the refrigerator. Cookies can be stored for up to 3 days.

Variation

Cherry Cheesecake Bites: Add ¼ tsp almond extract to cream cheese filling. Substitute cherry pie filling for blueberry pie filling.

● **One 24-cup or two 12-cup 1¾-inch (4.5 cm) mini-muffin pans, greased with unsalted butter**

Crust

1½ cups	all-purpose flour	375 mL
2 tbsp	granulated sugar	25 mL
¼ tsp	salt	1 mL
½ cup	chilled unsalted butter, cut into pieces	125 mL
2 to 3 tbsp	cold water	25 to 45 mL

Filling

6 oz	cream cheese, softened	175 g
¼ cup	granulated sugar	50 mL
1	egg	1
2 tbsp	half-and-half (10%) cream	25 mL
1 tsp	vanilla extract	5 mL

Topping

1	can (21 oz or 540 mL) blueberry pie filling	1

1. *Crust:* In a large bowl, whisk together flour, granulated sugar and salt until well combined. Using a pastry blender or a fork, cut in butter until mixture resembles coarse crumbs. Add water, 1 tablespoon (15 mL) at a time, stirring with a fork until mixture starts to pull away from sides of the bowl and holds together when formed into a ball. Add more water as needed. Cover dough with plastic wrap and chill for 15 minutes.

2. Lightly grease hands with nonstick cooking spray. Divide dough into 24 portions and shape each portion into a ball. Using fingers or a dough tamper, press a dough ball evenly against bottom and sides of each prepared muffin cup. Cover pan loosely with plastic wrap and chill for 15 minutes.

3. Preheat oven to 350°F (180°C).

4. *Filling:* In a large bowl, using an electric mixer on medium speed, beat cream cheese and granulated sugar until smooth and creamy, about 2 minutes. Add egg and beat just until blended. Beat in cream and vanilla. Spoon a scant tablespoonful (15 mL) of cream cheese filling into chilled pastry-lined muffin cups.

5. Bake in preheated oven for 15 to 18 minutes or until top of the crust is golden brown and the filling is set. Remove from oven and cool cookies in pan on a wire cooling rack for 10 minutes. If necessary, use a sharp thin-bladed knife to carefully loosen top edges of cookies from pan. Carefully remove cookies from pan, transfer to cooling rack and cool completely. Top each cooled cookie with a small spoonful of blueberry pie filling.

Orange Walnut Spirals

These pretty spirals are full of orange flavor.

Tips

Rolling the dough out on a piece of floured parchment paper can make it easier to roll the dough into a log after filling. Use the parchment paper to fold the edge of the dough over on itself and roll up the dough, shaping it into a log.

Halfway through rolling, rotate the dough a quarter turn and dust the board again to prevent dough from sticking.

Store cookies in a tightly sealed container at room temperature. Cookies can be stored for up to 3 days.

● Cookie sheets, lined with parchment paper

Cookies

2⅓ cups	all-purpose flour	575 mL
½ tsp	baking powder	2 mL
¼ tsp	salt	1 mL
¾ cup	unsalted butter, softened	175 mL
1 cup	granulated sugar	250 mL
1	egg	1
2 tsp	grated orange zest	10 mL
½ tsp	vanilla extract	2 mL
⅛ tsp	almond extract	0.5 mL

Filling

¾ cup	orange marmalade	175 mL
¾ cup	finely chopped walnuts	175 mL

1. **Cookies:** In a bowl, whisk together flour, baking powder and salt until well combined. Set aside.

2. In a large bowl, using an electric mixer on medium speed, cream butter and granulated sugar until light and fluffy, about 3 minutes. Add egg and beat well. Beat in orange zest, vanilla and almond extract. Scrape down sides of bowl. On low speed or using a wooden spoon, gradually add flour mixture, beating just until blended.

3. Shape dough into a flat rectangle. Tightly wrap in plastic wrap and chill for at least 1 hour.

4. Using confectioner's (powdered/icing) sugar or flour, lightly dust a pastry board, clean countertop or other flat surface and a rolling pin. Unwrap dough and roll into a 12- by 9-inch (30 by 23 cm) rectangle of uniform thickness.

5. **Filling:** Spread orange marmalade evenly over dough to within ½ inch (1 cm) of edges. Sprinkle walnuts evenly over marmalade. Starting with long edge, tightly roll up dough jelly-roll style to form a log. Tightly wrap in parchment paper or plastic wrap and chill for at least 3 hours or overnight.

6. Preheat oven to 375°F (190°C). Unwrap chilled dough log. Using a sharp knife, cut log into ¼-inch (0.5 cm) slices. Place on prepared cookie sheets about 2 inches (5 cm) apart. Bake one sheet at a time in preheated oven for 8 to 11 minutes or until edges start to turn lightly golden.

7. Immediately slide parchment paper onto a wire cooling rack. Cool cookies for 5 minutes, then transfer from parchment paper to cooling rack and cool completely.

Almond Pockets

Layer upon layer of almond flavors and textures make these pockets extra-special.

Tips

Use regular unsalted butter in stick or brick form for making cookies. Whipped butters contain air, while "light" butters contain a lot of water; both of these will produce flat, tough cookies.

Let icing set before storing cookies in a tightly sealed container. Cookies can be stored at room temperature for up to 3 days.

● **Cookie sheets, lined with parchment paper**

Cookies

3 cups	all-purpose flour	750 mL
¼ tsp	salt	1 mL
¾ cup	unsalted butter, softened	175 mL
6 oz	cream cheese, softened	175 g
¾ cup	granulated sugar	175 mL
½ tsp	vanilla extract	2 mL
½ tsp	almond extract	2 mL

Filling

6 oz	almond paste	175 g
3 tbsp	half-and-half (10%) cream	45 mL

Icing

¾ cup	confectioner's (powdered/icing) sugar	175 mL
1 tbsp	half-and-half (10%) cream	15 mL
¼ tsp	almond extract	1 mL
⅓ cup	finely chopped unsalted sliced almonds	75 mL

1. **Cookies:** In a bowl, whisk together flour and salt until well combined. Set aside.

2. In a large bowl, using an electric mixer on medium speed, cream butter, cream cheese and granulated sugar until light and fluffy, about 3 minutes. Beat in vanilla and almond extract. Scrape down sides of bowl. On low speed or using a wooden spoon, gradually add flour mixture, beating just until blended.

3. Divide dough in half. Shape each portion into a flat square. Tightly wrap each dough square in plastic wrap and chill for 2 to 3 hours.

4. Preheat oven to 375°F (190°C). Using confectioner's sugar or flour, lightly dust a pastry board, clean countertop or other flat surface and a rolling pin. Working with one dough square at a time, unwrap dough and roll out to uniform thickness of ⅛ inch (3 mm). Halfway through rolling, rotate the dough a quarter turn and dust the board again to prevent dough from sticking.

5. Using a sharp knife, pastry cutter or pizza cutter, cut dough into 2-inch (5 cm) squares. Carefully transfer half of squares to prepared cookie sheets, placing 2 inches (5 cm) apart.

Tip

Only use butter in stick or brick form for baking. Not only is it easy to measure, but stick butter contains a higher fat content that allows the butter to hold its shape. Butter sold in tubs has a higher ratio of water or air than stick butter and will significantly alter the texture of baked goods.

6. **Filling:** Crumble almond paste into a large mixer bowl and sprinkle with cream. Using an electric mixer on medium speed, beat until mixture is smooth, about 2 minutes. Place 1 teaspoon (5 mL) of almond filling in center of each square. Top with remaining squares and press edges together with tines of a fork to seal. Gather dough remnants into a ball, reroll, cut out more squares, transfer to cookie sheets, fill, top with additional squares and seal.

7. Bake one sheet at a time in preheated oven for 10 to 12 minutes or until edges start to turn lightly golden. Immediately slide parchment paper onto a wire cooling rack. Cool cookies for 5 minutes, then transfer from parchment paper to cooling rack and cool completely.

8. **Icing:** In a small bowl, combine confectioner's sugar, cream and almond extract. Using a small whisk or a fork, blend until icing is smooth and thin enough to drizzle from a fork. Drizzle icing over cooled cookies.

9. Sprinkle with chopped almonds.

Rugelach

Shaped into little crescents, these tender, crispy cookies are a special treat and make a wonderful accompaniment for a hot cup of tea or coffee.

Tip

If dough becomes too soft to handle when rolling up the wedges, place it in the refrigerator for 15 to 20 minutes to firm up a bit.

• **Cookie sheets, lined with parchment paper**

Cookies

2½ cups	all-purpose flour	625 mL
¼ tsp	salt	1 mL
1 cup	unsalted butter, softened	250 mL
8 oz	cream cheese, softened	250 g
3 tbsp	granulated sugar	45 mL
1 tsp	vanilla extract	5 mL

Filling

⅔ cup	granulated sugar	150 mL
⅔ cup	packed light brown sugar	150 mL
1 tsp	ground cinnamon	5 mL
⅓ cup	unsalted butter, melted	75 mL
1⅓ cups	finely chopped pecans	325 mL

Topping

¼ cup	granulated sugar	50 mL
1½ tsp	ground cinnamon	7 mL
¼ cup	unsalted butter, melted	50 mL

1. **Cookies:** In a bowl, whisk together flour and salt until well combined. Set aside.
2. In a large bowl, using an electric mixer on medium speed, cream butter, cream cheese and granulated sugar until smooth and creamy, about 2 minutes. Beat in vanilla. Scrape down sides of bowl. On low speed or using a wooden spoon, gradually add flour mixture, beating just until blended.
3. Divide dough into 4 equal portions. Shape each portion into a flat disk. Tightly wrap each dough disk in plastic wrap and chill for at least 2 hours.
4. Preheat oven to 350°F (180°C). Using confectioner's (powdered/icing) sugar or flour, lightly dust a pastry board, clean countertop or other flat surface and a rolling pin. Working with one dough disk at a time, unwrap dough and roll out into a 12-inch (30 cm) circle of uniform thickness. Halfway through rolling, rotate the dough a quarter turn and dust the board again to prevent dough from sticking.

Tip

Flour separates and evenly distributes ingredients throughout the dough or batter, binds all the ingredients and contains starches that absorb liquids and act as a thickener. Natural sugars in flour caramelize during baking and aid in browning.

5. *Filling:* In a small bowl, combine granulated sugar, brown sugar and cinnamon until well blended. Brush 1 tablespoon (15 mL) of melted butter over dough circle. Sprinkle with $\frac{1}{3}$ cup (75 mL) of sugar mixture and $\frac{1}{3}$ cup (75 mL) pecans.

6. Using a sharp knife, pastry cutter or pizza cutter, cut circle into 12 equal wedges. Starting at the wide end, roll up wedges. Carefully transfer cookies to prepared cookie sheets, placing pointed side down, 2 inches (5 cm) apart. Curve ends of cookies to form a crescent shape.

7. *Topping:* In a small bowl, combine granulated sugar and cinnamon until well blended. Lightly brush tops of cookies with melted butter and sprinkle with cinnamon sugar mixture.

8. Bake one sheet at a time in preheated oven for 18 to 20 minutes or until edges turn lightly golden. Immediately slide parchment paper onto a wire cooling rack. Cool cookies for 5 minutes, then transfer from parchment paper to cooling rack and cool completely.

Creative Gift Idea

Fill a clear glass cookie jar with a variety of your favorite cookies and tie a decorative ribbon around the top of the jar.
Choose jars of different sizes and shapes to fit the occasion of the gift.

Boysenberry Blossoms

Charming boysenberry centers make these blossoms a delightful and pretty addition to any cookie plate.

Tips

Chilled cookie dough is easier to roll and handle than dough at room temperature.

Let icing set before storing cookies in a tightly sealed container. Do not freeze iced cookies.

Variation

Blackberry Blossoms: Substitute seedless blackberry jam for seedless boysenberry jam.

- Cookie sheets, lined with parchment paper
- 2-inch (5 cm) and 1-inch (2.5 cm) round cookie cutters

Cookies

3 cups	all-purpose flour	750 mL
1 tsp	baking powder	5 mL
½ tsp	salt	2 mL
1 cup	unsalted butter, softened	250 mL
1½ cups	granulated sugar	375 mL
2	eggs	2
2 tsp	vanilla extract	10 mL

Filling

1 cup	seedless boysenberry jam	250 mL

Icing

¾ cup	confectioner's (powdered/icing) sugar	175 mL
4 to 5 tsp	half-and-half (10%) cream or milk	20 to 25 mL
1 tbsp	unsalted butter, softened	15 mL
½ tsp	vanilla extract	2 mL

1. **Cookies:** In a bowl, whisk together flour, baking powder and salt until well combined. Set aside.

2. In a large bowl, using an electric mixer on medium speed, cream butter and granulated sugar until light and fluffy, about 3 minutes. Add eggs one at a time, beating well after each addition. Beat in vanilla. Scrape down sides of bowl. On low speed or using a wooden spoon, gradually add flour mixture, beating just until blended.

3. Divide dough in half. Shape each portion into a flat disk. Tightly wrap each dough disk in plastic wrap and chill for at least 1 hour.

4. Preheat oven to 350°F (180°C). Using confectioner's sugar or flour, lightly dust a pastry board, clean countertop or other flat surface and a rolling pin. Working with one dough disk at a time, unwrap dough and roll out to uniform thickness of ⅛ inch (3 mm). Halfway through rolling, rotate the dough a quarter turn and dust the board again to prevent dough from sticking.

5. Dip a 2-inch (5 cm) round cookie cutter in confectioner's sugar or flour and cut dough into circles. Cut out as many cookies as possible from first rolling. Using a 1-inch (2.5 cm) round cookie cutter, cut out center of half of circles. Carefully transfer whole circles to prepared cookie sheets, placing 2 inches (5 cm) apart.

6. *Filling:* Place a rounded teaspoonful (5 mL) of boysenberry jam in center of each circle. Top with cutout cookies and press edges together with tines of a fork to seal. Gather dough remnants into a ball, reroll, cut out more circles, transfer to cookie sheets, fill, top with cutout circles and seal.

7. Bake one sheet at a time in preheated oven for 8 to 10 minutes or until edges start to turn lightly golden. Immediately slide parchment paper onto a wire cooling rack. Cool cookies for 5 minutes, then transfer from parchment paper to cooling rack and cool completely.

8. *Icing:* In a small bowl, combine confectioner's sugar, 4 teaspoons (20 mL) of the cream, butter and vanilla. Using a small whisk or a fork, blend until icing is smooth and thin enough to drizzle from a fork. Add more cream as needed to achieve the desired consistency. Drizzle icing over cooled cookies.

Pecan Tassies

These little cups are like mini pecan pies.

Tips

If necessary, use a sharp thin-bladed knife to carefully loosen top edges of cookies from pan.

Be sure to taste nuts before using them in baking. Nothing spoils the taste of a nut cookie faster than stale nuts.

Store cookies between layers of wax paper in a tightly sealed container. Cookies can be stored at room temperature for up to 3 days.

● **One 24-cup or two 12-cup 1¾-inch (4.5 cm) mini-muffin pans, greased with unsalted butter**

Crust

1¼ cups	all-purpose flour	300 mL
¼ tsp	salt	1 mL
½ cup	unsalted butter, softened	125 mL
3 oz	cream cheese, softened	90 g
2 tbsp	granulated sugar	25 mL
¼ tsp	vanilla extract	1 mL

Filling

1	egg	1
½ cup	light (golden) corn syrup	125 mL
½ cup	packed light brown sugar	125 mL
2 tbsp	unsalted butter, melted	25 mL
1 tsp	vanilla extract	5 mL
¾ cup	finely chopped pecans	175 mL

1. **Crust:** In a bowl, whisk together flour and salt until well combined. Set aside.

2. In a large bowl, using an electric mixer on medium speed, cream butter, cream cheese and granulated sugar until light and fluffy, about 2 minutes. Beat in vanilla. Scrape down sides of bowl. On low speed or using a wooden spoon, gradually add flour mixture, beating just until blended. Cover dough with plastic wrap and chill for 15 minutes.

3. Lightly grease hands with nonstick cooking spray. Divide dough into 24 portions and shape each portion into a ball. Using fingers or a dough tamper, press a dough ball evenly against bottom and sides of each prepared muffin cup. Cover pan loosely with plastic wrap and chill for 15 minutes.

4. Preheat oven to 350°F (180°C).

5. **Filling:** In a bowl, whisk egg until lightly beaten. Gradually whisk in corn syrup. Add brown sugar, butter and vanilla and stir until well combined. Spoon a rounded teaspoonful (5 mL) of pecans into the bottom of each chilled pastry-lined muffin cup. Spoon about 2 teaspoonfuls (10 mL) of filling on top of pecans, filling nearly to the top.

6. Bake in preheated oven for 15 to 18 minutes or until top of the crust is golden brown and the filling is set. Remove from oven and cool cookies in pan on a wire cooling rack for 10 minutes. Carefully remove cookies from pan, transfer to cooling rack and cool completely.

Raspberry Coconut Spirals

● ● ●

The blending of raspberries, coconut and macadamia nuts in the filling creates a pleasing flavor and colorful presentation.

Tips

Finely chop the macadamia nuts to make it easier to roll the dough into a log and to cut the chilled log into slices.

Rolling the dough out on a piece of floured parchment paper can make it easier to roll the dough into a log after filling. Use the parchment paper to fold the edge of the dough over on itself and roll up the dough, shaping it into a log.

Halfway through rolling, rotate the dough a quarter turn and dust the board again to prevent dough from sticking.

● Cookie sheets, lined with parchment paper

Cookies

2⅓ cups	all-purpose flour	575 mL
½ tsp	baking powder	2 mL
¼ tsp	salt	1 mL
¾ cup	unsalted butter, softened	175 mL
1 cup	granulated sugar	250 mL
1	egg	1
½ tsp	vanilla extract	2 mL
½ tsp	almond extract	2 mL

Filling

⅔ cup	seedless raspberry jam	150 mL
⅔ cup	sweetened flaked coconut, coarsely chopped	150 mL
⅓ cup	chopped roasted unsalted macadamia nuts	75 mL

1. *Cookies:* In a bowl, whisk together flour, baking powder and salt until well combined. Set aside.

2. In a large bowl, using an electric mixer on medium speed, cream butter and granulated sugar until light and fluffy, about 3 minutes. Add egg and beat well. Beat in vanilla and almond extract. Scrape down sides of bowl. On low speed or using a wooden spoon, gradually add flour mixture, beating just until blended.

3. Shape dough into a flat rectangle. Tightly wrap in plastic wrap and chill for at least 1 hour.

4. Using confectioner's (powdered/icing) sugar or flour, lightly dust a pastry board, clean countertop or other flat surface and a rolling pin. Unwrap dough and roll into a 12- by 9-inch (30 by 23 cm) rectangle of uniform thickness.

5. *Filling:* Spread raspberry jam evenly over dough to within ½ inch (1 cm) of edges. Sprinkle coconut and macadamia nuts evenly over jam. Starting with long edge, tightly roll up dough jelly-roll style to form a log. Tightly wrap in parchment paper or plastic wrap and chill for at least 3 hours or overnight.

6. Preheat oven to 375°F (190°C). Unwrap chilled dough log. Using a sharp knife, cut log into ¼-inch (0.5 cm) slices. Place on prepared cookie sheets about 2 inches (5 cm) apart.

7. Bake one sheet at a time in preheated oven for 8 to 11 minutes or until edges start to turn lightly golden. Immediately slide parchment paper onto a wire cooling rack. Cool cookies for 5 minutes, then transfer them to cooling rack and cool completely.

Walnut Horns

These nutty, mini Danish-like cookies are tender and have a tantalizing filling.

Tips

Use a food processor or blender to quickly grind walnuts. You can also use a knife to chop the nuts very finely.

Let icing set before storing cookies in a tightly sealed container. Cookies can be stored at room temperature for up to 3 days.

- Cookie sheets, lined with parchment paper

Cookies

2⅔ cups	all-purpose flour	650 mL
¼ tsp	salt	1 mL
⅔ cup	unsalted butter, softened	150 mL
4 oz	cream cheese, softened	125 g
¾ cup	granulated sugar	175 mL
¼ tsp	vanilla extract	1 mL

Filling

¾ cup	ground walnuts	175 mL
3 tbsp	granulated sugar	45 mL
3 tbsp	packed light brown sugar	45 mL
¼ tsp	ground cinnamon	1 mL
2 tbsp	unsalted butter, melted	25 mL

Confectioner's (powdered/icing) sugar

1. **Cookies:** In a bowl, whisk together flour and salt until well combined. Set aside.

2. In a large bowl, using an electric mixer on medium speed, cream butter, cream cheese and granulated sugar until light and fluffy, about 3 minutes. Beat in vanilla. Scrape down sides of bowl. On low speed or using a wooden spoon, gradually add flour mixture, beating just until blended.

3. Divide dough in half. Shape each portion into a flat square. Tightly wrap each dough square in plastic wrap and chill for at least 2 to 3 hours.

4. Preheat oven to 375°F (190°C). Using confectioner's sugar or flour, lightly dust a pastry board, clean countertop or other flat surface and a rolling pin. Working with one dough square at a time, unwrap dough and roll out to uniform thickness of ⅛ inch (3 mm). Halfway through rolling, rotate the dough a quarter turn and dust the board again to prevent dough from sticking. Using a sharp knife, pastry cutter or pizza cutter, cut dough into 2-inch (5 cm) squares.

Tip

Parchment paper is a heat- and grease-resistant baking paper used to line cookie sheets to prevent cookies from sticking to the sheet and keep cookies from burning on the bottom. It can be found in most grocery stores.

5. *Filling:* In a small bowl, combine walnuts, granulated sugar, brown sugar and cinnamon and stir until well blended. Drizzle melted butter over mixture and stir until well combined. Spoon a teaspoonful (5 mL) of filling diagonally along center of each square. Fold 2 opposite corners of square into center, overlapping dough, and pinch together to seal. Carefully transfer cookies to prepared cookie sheets, placing 2 inches (5 cm) apart. Gather dough remnants into a ball, reroll, cut out and fill more cookies; seal and transfer to cookie sheets.

6. Bake one sheet at a time in preheated oven for 8 to 10 minutes or until edges start to turn lightly golden. Immediately slide parchment paper onto a wire cooling rack. Cool cookies for 5 minutes, then transfer from parchment paper to cooling rack and cool completely. Dust cooled cookies with confectioner's sugar.

Cookie Baking Kit Gift

This makes a wonderful gift for a house warming or wedding shower. Be sure to include your favorite cookie recipe or a copy of this book!

- Two cookie sheets
- Large wire cooling rack
- Rolling pin
- Cookie cutters
- Cookie scoop
- Parchment paper

Cranberry Orange Walnut Tassies

Makes 24 cookies

● ● ●

Perfect for serving at Thanksgiving, these little cups are filled with fall flavor.

Tips

Prepare and measure all of the ingredients before you start mixing the cookies.

English walnuts, the kind typically found in grocery stores, have a mild flavor and are the best ones to use in cookies. The intense and slightly bitter taste of black walnuts can overpower the other ingredients.

Store cookies between layers of wax paper in a tightly sealed container. Cookies can be stored at room temperature for up to 3 days.

- One 24-cup or two 12-cup 1¾-inch (4.5 cm) mini-muffin pans, greased with unsalted butter
- 2½-inch (6 cm) scalloped or round cookie cutter

Crust

1½ cups	all-purpose flour	375 mL
¼ tsp	salt	1 mL
½ cup	unsalted butter, softened	125 mL
3 oz	cream cheese, softened	90 g
2 tbsp	granulated sugar	25 mL
1 tsp	grated orange zest	5 mL

Filling

⅓ cup	finely chopped dried cranberries	75 mL
⅓ cup	finely chopped walnuts	75 mL
2	eggs	2
⅓ cup	light (golden) corn syrup	75 mL
⅔ cup	packed light brown sugar	150 mL
2 tsp	grated orange zest	10 mL
2 tbsp	freshly squeezed orange juice	25 mL

1. **Crust:** In a bowl, whisk together flour and salt until well combined. Set aside.

2. In a large bowl, using an electric mixer on medium speed, cream butter, cream cheese and granulated sugar until light and fluffy, about 2 minutes. Beat in orange zest. Scrape down sides of bowl. On low speed or using a wooden spoon, gradually add flour mixture, beating just until blended. Shape dough into a flat disk. Tightly wrap in plastic wrap and chill for at least 30 minutes.

3. Using confectioner's (powdered/icing) sugar or flour, lightly dust a pastry board, clean countertop or other flat surface and a rolling pin. Unwrap dough and roll out to uniform thickness of ⅛ inch (3 mm). Halfway through rolling, rotate the dough a quarter turn and dust the board again to prevent dough from sticking.

4. Dip cookie cutter in confectioner's sugar or flour and cut out 24 circles. Gently fit a cutout into each cup of prepared mini-muffin pan, being careful not to tear or stretch dough. Cover pan loosely with plastic wrap and chill for 15 minutes.

Tip

When zesting oranges, remove only the outer, colored part of the peel. The white part underneath, called the pith, is very bitter and will give cookies an unpleasant flavor.

5. Preheat oven to 350°F (180°C).

6. *Filling:* In a small bowl, combine cranberries and walnuts. Spoon a rounded teaspoonful of mixture into the bottom of each chilled pastry-lined muffin cup.

7. In a medium bowl, with a wire whisk, lightly beat eggs. Gradually whisk in corn syrup until well blended. Add brown sugar and stir until well combined. Stir in orange zest and orange juice. Spoon 2 teaspoonfuls (10 mL) of filling mixture on top of cranberry-walnut mixture, filling nearly to the top.

8. Bake in preheated oven for 15 to 18 minutes or until top of the crust is golden brown and the filling is set. Remove from oven and cool cookies in pan on a wire cooling rack for 10 minutes. If necessary, use a sharp thin-bladed knife to carefully loosen top edges of cookies from pan. Carefully remove cookies from pan, transfer to cooling rack and cool completely.

Coconut Pineapple Cups

● ● ●

Coconut in the tender pastry cups adds another dimension of texture and taste.

Tips

If you don't have any pineapple juice on hand for the icing, half-and-half (10%) cream or milk may be substituted.

Store cookies between layers of wax paper in a tightly sealed container. Cookies can be stored at room temperature for up to 3 days.

● **One 24-cup or two 12-cup 1¾-inch (4.5 cm) mini-muffin pans, greased with unsalted butter**

Crust

1 cup	all-purpose flour	250 mL
⅓ cup	sweetened flaked coconut, finely chopped	75 mL
¼ tsp	salt	1 mL
½ cup	unsalted butter, softened	125 mL
3 oz	cream cheese, softened	90 g
1 tbsp	granulated sugar	15 mL
⅛ tsp	vanilla extract	0.5 mL
⅛ tsp	almond extract	0.5 mL

Filling

1 cup	pineapple jam or preserves	250 mL
⅔ cup	sweetened flaked coconut, finely chopped	150 mL

Icing

½ cup	confectioner's (powdered/icing) sugar	125 mL
2 tsp	unsweetened pineapple juice	10 mL
1½ tsp	unsalted butter, melted	7 mL

1. **Crust:** In a bowl, whisk together flour, coconut and salt until well combined. Set aside.

2. In a large bowl, using an electric mixer on medium speed, cream butter, cream cheese and granulated sugar until light and fluffy, about 2 minutes. Beat in vanilla and almond extract. Scrape down sides of bowl. On low speed or using a wooden spoon, gradually add flour mixture, beating just until blended. Cover dough with plastic wrap and chill for 15 minutes.

3. Lightly grease hands with nonstick cooking spray. Divide dough into 24 portions and shape each portion into a ball. Using fingers or a dough tamper, press a dough ball evenly against bottom and sides of each prepared muffin cup. Cover pan loosely with plastic wrap and chill for 15 minutes.

4. Preheat oven to 350°F (180°C).

5. **Filling:** In a small bowl, combine pineapple jam and coconut until well blended. Spoon about 1 tablespoon (15 mL) of filling into chilled pastry-lined muffin cups, filling nearly to the top.

Tip

Homemade cookies make a great gift for family and friends and are perfect for every occasion.

6. Bake in preheated oven for 15 to 18 minutes or until top of the crust is golden brown and the filling is set. Remove from oven and cool cookies in pan on a wire cooling rack for 10 minutes. If necessary, use a sharp thin-bladed knife to carefully loosen top edges of cookies from pan. Carefully remove cookies from pan, transfer to cooling rack and cool completely.

7. *Icing:* In a small bowl, combine confectioner's sugar, pineapple juice and butter. Using a small whisk or a fork, blend until icing is smooth and thin enough to drizzle from a fork. Drizzle icing over cooled cookies.

Gift Wrapping on a Budget

You don't have to spend a lot of money on elaborate containers or baskets to hold your cookies. You can package your cookie gifts attractively without breaking the budget.

Arrange cookies on a sturdy, colorful paper plate suitable for the holiday or event. Place the plate inside a clear plastic food storage bag and gather the bag above the cookies or to the side. Secure the bag with a twist tie and cover the tie with a pretty ribbon.

Colored paper sacks (available at party supply and craft stores) are a great way to wrap up cookies for gift-giving. Package the cookies in a clear plastic food storage bag, secure the top with a twist tie and add a ribbon. Use separate bags for different types of cookies. Place the bag or bags of cookies in the sack, padding with tissue paper as needed.

Here's a fun project for kids and adults. Draw designs on the outside of brown paper lunch sacks, decorate them with colorful stickers or leave the bags plain. Package the cookies in a clear plastic food storage bag, secure the top with a twist tie and place in the paper sack. Fold down the top of the sack, punch holes through the top and thread ribbons through the holes and tie into a bow.

Lemon Cheesecake Bites

● ● ●

I've always loved lemon cheesecake, so I just had to create these little gems to share with family and friends.

Tip

Store cookies between layers of wax paper in a tightly sealed container in the refrigerator. Cookies can be stored for up to 3 days.

Variations

Lime Cheesecake Bites: Substitute lime zest for lemon zest in crust. Substitute lime zest and lime juice for lemon zest and lemon juice in cream cheese filling.

Orange Cheesecake Bites: Substitute orange zest for lemon zest in crust. Substitute orange zest and orange juice for lemon zest and lemon juice in cream cheese filling.

● One 24-cup or two 12-cup 1¾-inch (4.5 cm) mini-muffin pans, greased with unsalted butter

Crust

1½ cups	all-purpose flour	375 mL
2 tbsp	granulated sugar	25 mL
¼ tsp	salt	1 mL
1 tsp	grated lemon zest	5 mL
½ cup	chilled unsalted butter, cut into pieces	125 mL
2 to 3 tbsp	cold water	25 to 45 mL

Filling

6 oz	cream cheese, softened	175 g
⅓ cup	granulated sugar	75 mL
1	egg	1
2 tsp	grated lemon zest	10 mL
1 tbsp	freshly squeezed lemon juice	15 mL

1. **Crust:** In a large bowl, whisk together flour, granulated sugar and salt until well combined. Stir in lemon zest. Using a pastry blender or a fork, cut in butter until mixture resembles coarse crumbs. Add water, 1 tablespoon (15 mL) at a time, stirring with a fork until mixture starts to pull away from sides of the bowl and holds together when formed into a ball. Add more water as needed. Cover dough with plastic wrap and chill for 15 minutes.

2. Lightly grease hands with nonstick cooking spray. Divide dough into 24 portions and shape each portion into a ball. Using fingers or a dough tamper, press a dough ball evenly against bottom and sides of each prepared muffin cup. Cover pan loosely with plastic wrap and chill for 15 minutes.

3. Preheat oven to 350°F (180°C).

4. **Filling:** In a large bowl, using an electric mixer on medium speed, beat cream cheese and granulated sugar until smooth and creamy, about 2 minutes. Add egg and beat well. Beat in lemon zest and lemon juice. Spoon about 1 tablespoon (15 mL) of cream cheese filling into chilled pastry-lined muffin cups, filling nearly to the top.

5. Bake in preheated oven for 15 to 18 minutes or until top of the crust is golden brown and the filling is set. Remove from oven and cool cookies in pan on a wire cooling rack for 10 minutes. If necessary, use a sharp thin-bladed knife to carefully loosen top edges of cookies from pan. Carefully remove cookies from pan, transfer to cooling rack and cool completely.

Strawberry Spirals

● ● ●

Strawberry jam is a wonderful filling for buttery spirals.

Tips

Rolling the dough out on a piece of floured parchment paper can make it easier to roll the dough into a log after filling. Use the parchment paper to fold the edge of the dough over on itself and roll up the dough, shaping it into a log.

Butter is considered to be softened when it is at a temperature of 65°F (18°C).

Store cookies in a tightly sealed container. Cookies can be stored at room temperature for up to 3 days.

- Cookie sheets, lined with parchment paper

Cookies

2⅓ cups	all-purpose flour	575 mL
½ tsp	baking powder	2 mL
¼ tsp	salt	1 mL
¾ cup	unsalted butter, softened	175 mL
1 cup	granulated sugar	250 mL
1	egg	1
1½ tsp	vanilla extract	7 mL

Filling

¾ cup	strawberry jam	175 mL
½ cup	finely chopped unsalted almonds	125 mL

1. **Cookies:** In a bowl, whisk together flour, baking powder and salt until well combined. Set aside.

2. In a large bowl, using an electric mixer on medium speed, cream butter and granulated sugar until light and fluffy, about 3 minutes. Add egg and beat well. Beat in vanilla. Scrape down sides of bowl. On low speed or using a wooden spoon, gradually add flour mixture, beating just until blended.

3. Shape dough into a flat rectangle. Tightly wrap in plastic wrap and chill for at least 1 hour.

4. Using confectioner's (powdered/icing) sugar or flour, lightly dust a pastry board, clean countertop or other flat surface and a rolling pin. Unwrap dough and roll into a 12- by 9-inch (30 by 23 cm) rectangle of uniform thickness. Halfway through rolling, rotate the dough a quarter turn and dust the board again to prevent dough from sticking.

5. **Filling:** Spread strawberry jam evenly over dough to within ½ inch (1 cm) of edges. Sprinkle almonds evenly over jam. Starting with long edge, tightly roll up dough jelly-roll style to form a log. Tightly wrap in parchment paper or plastic wrap and chill for at least 3 hours or overnight.

6. Preheat oven to 375°F (190°C). Unwrap chilled dough log. Using a sharp knife, cut log into ¼-inch (0.5 cm) slices. Place on prepared cookie sheets about 2 inches (5 cm) apart.

7. Bake one sheet at a time in preheated oven for 8 to 11 minutes or until edges start to turn lightly golden. Immediately slide parchment paper onto a wire cooling rack. Cool cookies for 5 minutes, then transfer from parchment paper to cooling rack and cool completely.

Orange Curd Cups

● ● ●

The orange juice concentrate in the filling gives these enticing little tarts their citrus zing.

Tips

Do not grate the zest for the curd filling. Slice it thinly so it will be easily caught in the fine sieve when the curd is strained. Be sure to slice only the colored part of the orange; the white pith has a bitter taste.

Store cookies between layers of wax paper in a tightly sealed container in the refrigerator. Cookies can be stored for up to 3 days.

- One 24-cup or two 12-cup 1¾-inch (4.5 cm) mini-muffin pans, greased with unsalted butter
- 2½-inch (6 cm) round or scalloped cookie cutter

Filling

3	eggs	3
3	egg yolks	3
1¾ cups	superfine sugar	425 mL
½ cup	frozen orange juice concentrate, thawed	125 mL
⅓ cup	chilled unsalted butter, cut into pieces	75 mL
2 tbsp	thinly sliced orange zest	25 mL

Crust

1½ cups	all-purpose flour	375 mL
¼ tsp	salt	1 mL
½ cup	unsalted butter, softened	125 mL
2 tbsp	granulated sugar	25 mL
1 tsp	grated orange zest	5 mL
1 tsp	frozen orange juice concentrate, thawed	5 mL

1. ***Filling:*** In top pan of a stainless steel double boiler, using a wire whisk, lightly beat together eggs and egg yolks. Add superfine sugar and beat until well blended. Gradually whisk in orange juice concentrate. Add butter and orange zest.

2. Place pan over boiling water. Stirring constantly, cook until mixture will thickly coat the back of a spoon, about 7 minutes. Do not let mixture boil or it will curdle.

3. Place a fine-meshed sieve over a heatproof bowl or pan and pour curd though sieve to remove the zest and any lumps. Cover curd with plastic wrap and chill until cold and set, about 3 hours.

4. ***Crust:*** In a bowl, whisk together flour and salt until well combined. Set aside.

5. In a large bowl, using an electric mixer on medium speed, cream butter and granulated sugar until light and fluffy, about 2 minutes. Beat in orange zest and orange juice concentrate. Scrape down sides of bowl. On low speed or using a wooden spoon, gradually add flour mixture, beating just until blended. Shape dough into a flat disk. Tightly wrap in plastic wrap and chill for at least 30 minutes.

Tip

Curd can be made a few days in advance and stored in the refrigerator until needed. Press plastic wrap tightly against the surface of curd to prevent a skin from forming on top. Extra curd may be stored in the refrigerator for up to 3 weeks.

6. Preheat oven to 350°F (180°C). Using confectioner's (powdered/icing) sugar or flour, lightly dust a pastry board, clean countertop or other flat surface and a rolling pin. Unwrap dough and roll out to uniform thickness of $\frac{1}{8}$ inch (3 mm). Halfway through rolling, rotate the dough a quarter turn and dust the board again to prevent dough from sticking.

7. Dip a round or scalloped cookie cutter in confectioner's sugar or flour and cut out 24 circles. Gently fit a cutout into each cup of prepared mini-muffin pan, being careful not to tear or stretch dough. Cover pan loosely with plastic wrap and chill for 15 minutes.

8. Bake in preheated oven for 8 to 10 minutes or until top of the crust is lightly golden. Remove from oven and cool crusts in pan on a wire cooling rack for 20 minutes.

9. Carefully remove crusts from pan. Spoon about 1 tablespoon (15 mL) of orange curd into pastry crusts, filling nearly to the top.

Holiday Gift-Giving

Immediately after a holiday (such as Christmas, Thanksgiving, Valentine's Day, Easter, St. Patrick's Day, Independence Day or Halloween), look for sale-priced, decorative holiday-themed plates, bowls and cookie jars in department, discount and closeout stores. You can usually find them at deep discounts of up to seventy-five percent or more off the retail price.

For very little money, you can have a selection of festive dishes to fit any holiday. Store them away until next year, and you are all set for giving away batches of holiday cookie gifts or for setting out plates of cookies when entertaining at home.

Sour Cream Fudge Pouches

The creamy chocolate filling gets a tantalizing tang from sour cream.

Tips

If chocolate is melted in the top of a double boiler, remove the pan from over the hot water and allow the chocolate to cool for 5 minutes before adding the sour cream.

Store cookies in a tightly sealed container. Cookies can be stored at room temperature for up to 3 days.

- Cookie sheets, lined with parchment paper
- 2½-inch (6 cm) round cookie cutter

Cookies

3 cups	all-purpose flour	750 mL
½ tsp	baking powder	2 mL
¼ tsp	salt	1 mL
½ cup	unsalted butter, softened	125 mL
1 cup	granulated sugar	250 mL
1	egg	1
½ cup	sour cream	125 mL
1 tsp	vanilla extract	5 mL

Filling

4 oz	semisweet chocolate, chopped	125 g
½ cup	sour cream	125 mL
½ tsp	vanilla extract	2 mL
3 tbsp	finely chopped walnuts	45 mL

Topping

1	egg	1
1 tbsp	water	15 mL
	Coarse or granulated sugar	

1. **Cookies:** In a bowl, whisk together flour, baking powder and salt until well combined. Set aside.

2. In a large bowl, using an electric mixer on medium speed, cream butter and granulated sugar until light and fluffy, about 2 minutes. Add egg and beat well. Beat in sour cream and vanilla. Scrape down sides of bowl. On low speed or using a wooden spoon, gradually add flour mixture, beating just until blended.

3. Divide dough in half. Shape each portion into a flat disk. Tightly wrap each dough disk in plastic wrap and chill for 2 to 3 hours.

4. **Filling:** In a microwave-safe bowl, heat chopped chocolate in microwave at Medium-High (75%) power for 1 minute. Stir chocolate until smooth. If necessary, heat at Medium (50%) power for 10 seconds at a time, stirring between each heating, just until chocolate is melted. Stir in sour cream and vanilla until mixture is smooth. Fold in walnuts. Set aside to cool.

Tip

To measure flour properly, stir the flour in the package or container to loosen it, then gently spoon the flour into a dry measuring cup. Use a knife or spatula to level off the flour even with the rim of the cup.

5. Preheat oven to 350°F (180°C). Using confectioner's (powdered/icing) sugar or flour, lightly dust a pastry board, clean countertop or other flat surface and a rolling pin. Working with one dough disk at a time, unwrap dough and roll out to uniform thickness of $\frac{1}{8}$ inch (3 mm). Halfway through rolling, rotate the dough a quarter turn and dust the board again to prevent dough from sticking.

6. Dip a round cookie cutter in confectioner's sugar or flour and cut dough into circles. Cut out as many cookies as possible from first rolling. Carefully transfer half of circles to prepared cookie sheets, placing 2 inches (5 cm) apart.

7. Place a rounded teaspoonful (5 mL) of chocolate filling in center of each circle. Top with remaining circles and press edges together with tines of a fork to seal. Gather dough remnants into a ball, reroll, cut out more circles, transfer to cookie sheets, fill, top with additional circles and seal.

8. *Topping:* In a small bowl, whisk together egg and water. Brush over tops of cookies. Sprinkle with coarse sugar.

9. Bake one sheet at a time in preheated oven for 10 to 12 minutes or until edges start to turn lightly golden. Immediately slide parchment paper onto a wire cooling rack. Cool cookies for 5 minutes, then transfer from parchment paper to cooling rack and cool completely.

Coconut Macadamia Rugelach

A tropical take on traditional rugelach, I like to serve these on warm summer evenings after a casual patio dinner with friends.

Tips

If dough becomes too soft to handle when rolling up the wedges, place it in the refrigerator for 15 to 20 minutes to firm up a bit.

Store cookies in a tightly sealed container. Cookies can be stored at room temperature for up to 3 days.

● **Cookie sheets, lined with parchment paper**

Cookies

2½ cups	all-purpose flour	625 mL
¼ tsp	salt	1 mL
1 cup	unsalted butter, softened	250 mL
8 oz	cream cheese, softened	250 g
3 tbsp	granulated sugar	45 mL
1 tsp	vanilla extract	5 mL
½ tsp	almond extract	2 mL

Filling

½ cup	granulated sugar	125 mL
½ cup	packed light brown sugar	125 mL
½ cup	melted unsalted butter	125 mL
1⅓ cups	sweetened flaked coconut, chopped	325 mL
1 cup	finely chopped roasted unsalted macadamia nuts	250 mL

Additional granulated sugar

1. **Cookies:** In a bowl, whisk together flour and salt until well combined. Set aside.

2. In a large bowl, using an electric mixer on medium speed, cream butter, cream cheese and granulated sugar until smooth and creamy, about 2 minutes. Beat in vanilla and almond extract. Scrape down sides of bowl. On low speed or using a wooden spoon, gradually add flour mixture, beating just until blended.

3. Divide dough into four equal portions. Shape each portion into a flat disk. Tightly wrap each dough disk in plastic wrap and chill for at least 2 hours.

4. Preheat oven to 350°F (180°C). Using confectioner's (powdered/icing) sugar or flour, lightly dust a pastry board, clean countertop or other flat surface and a rolling pin. Working with one dough disk at a time, unwrap dough and roll out into a 12-inch (30 cm) circle of uniform thickness. Halfway through rolling, rotate the dough a quarter turn and dust the board again to prevent dough from sticking.

Tip

Buy and use roasted
macadamia nuts
for the best flavor.
Roasting brings out
the nutty flavor of the
macadamias.

5. *Filling:* In a small bowl, combine granulated sugar and brown
sugar. Brush 1 tablespoon (15 mL) of melted butter over dough
circle. Sprinkle with $\frac{1}{4}$ cup (50 mL) of sugar mixture, $\frac{1}{3}$ cup
coconut (75 mL) and $\frac{1}{4}$ cup (50 mL) macadamia nuts.

6. Using a sharp knife, pastry cutter or pizza cutter, cut circle
into 12 equal wedges. Starting at the wide end, roll up wedges.
Carefully transfer cookies to prepared cookie sheets, placing
pointed side down, 2 inches (5 cm) apart. Curve ends of
cookies to form a crescent shape. Lightly brush tops of cookies
with remaining butter and sprinkle with granulated sugar.

7. Bake one sheet at a time in preheated oven for 18 to 20 minutes
or until edges turn lightly golden. Immediately slide parchment
paper onto a wire cooling rack. Cool cookies for 5 minutes,
then transfer from parchment paper to cooling rack and cool
completely.

Tea Party Hostess Gift

A lovely gift to present to the hostess of a tea party is an
assortment of pretty cookies carefully arranged in a tissue-
lined decorated hat box.

Apricot Orange Cups

I love the combination of apricots and oranges so much that I'm always creating new ways to use these flavors.

Tips

To keep dried apricots from sticking to your knife when you chop them, give the knife blade a light coat of nonstick cooking spray.

Store cookies between layers of wax paper in a tightly sealed container.

● **One 24-cup or two 12-cup 1¾-inch (4.5 cm) mini-muffin pans, greased with unsalted butter**

Crust

1¼ cups	all-purpose flour	300 mL
¼ tsp	salt	1 mL
½ cup	unsalted butter, softened	125 mL
3 oz	cream cheese, softened	90 g
2 tbsp	granulated sugar	25 mL
¼ tsp	almond extract	1 mL

Filling

1½ cups	chopped dried apricots	375 mL
½ cup	orange marmalade	125 mL
1 tbsp	freshly squeezed orange juice	15 mL

Icing

½ cup	confectioner's (powdered/icing) sugar	125 mL
2 tsp	freshly squeezed orange juice	10 mL
1½ tsp	unsalted butter, melted	7 mL

1. **Crust:** In a bowl, whisk together flour and salt until well combined. Set aside.

2. In a large bowl, using an electric mixer on medium speed, cream butter, cream cheese and granulated sugar until light and fluffy, about 2 minutes. Beat in almond extract. Scrape down sides of bowl. On low speed or using a wooden spoon, gradually add flour mixture, beating just until blended. Cover dough with plastic wrap and chill for 15 minutes.

3. Preheat oven to 350°F (180°C). Lightly grease hands with nonstick cooking spray. Divide dough into 24 portions and shape each portion into a ball. Using fingers or a dough tamper, press a dough ball evenly against bottom and sides of each prepared muffin cup. Cover pan loosely with plastic wrap and chill for 15 minutes.

4. Bake in preheated oven for 10 to 12 minutes or until top of the crust is lightly golden. Remove from oven and cool crusts in pan on a wire cooling rack for 10 minutes. Carefully remove crusts from pan, transfer to cooling rack and cool completely.

5. **Filling:** In a food processor, combine apricots, orange marmalade and orange juice and process until finely chopped. Spoon about 1 tablespoon (15 mL) of filling into cooled crusts.

6. **Icing:** In a small bowl, combine confectioner's sugar, orange juice and butter. Using a small whisk or a fork, blend until icing is smooth. Drizzle icing over cookies.

Peach Pie Cookies

Tasty little fruit cookie pies in a handy and easy-to-make package.

Tips

Halfway through rolling, rotate the dough a quarter turn and dust the board again to prevent dough from sticking.

Cut cookies close together on rolled dough to get as many cookies as possible from the first rolling. Rolling the dough scraps multiple times can toughen the cookies.

Variation

Apricot Pie Cookies: Substitute apricot jam, apricot preserves or apricot pineapple jam for peach jam.

- Cookie sheets, lined with parchment paper
- 2½-inch (6 cm) round cookie cutter

3 cups	all-purpose flour	750 mL
½ tsp	baking powder	2 mL
¼ tsp	salt	1 mL
⅛ tsp	ground nutmeg	0.5 mL
1 cup	unsalted butter, softened	250 mL
1½ cups	granulated sugar	375 mL
1	egg	1
1 tsp	vanilla extract	5 mL
1 cup	peach jam	250 mL
	Additional granulated sugar	

1. In a bowl, whisk together flour, baking powder, salt and nutmeg until well combined. Set aside.

2. In a large bowl, using an electric mixer on medium speed, cream butter and granulated sugar until light and fluffy, about 3 minutes. Add egg and beat well. Beat in vanilla. Scrape down sides of bowl. On low speed or using a wooden spoon, gradually add flour mixture, beating just until blended.

3. Divide dough in half. Shape each portion into a flat disk. Tightly wrap each dough disk in plastic wrap and chill at least 1 hour.

4. Preheat oven to 350°F (180°C). Using confectioner's (powdered/icing) sugar or flour, lightly dust a pastry board, clean countertop or other flat surface and a rolling pin. Working with one dough disk at a time, unwrap dough and roll out to uniform thickness of ⅛ inch (3 mm).

5. Dip a cookie cutter in confectioner's sugar or flour and cut dough into circles. Cut out as many cookies as possible from first rolling. Carefully transfer half of circles to prepared cookie sheets, placing 2 inches (5 cm) apart.

6. Place a rounded teaspoonful (5 mL) of peach jam in center of each circle. Top with remaining circles and press edges together with tines of a fork to seal. Sprinkle granulated sugar over tops of cookies. Gather dough remnants into a ball, reroll, cut out more circles, transfer to cookie sheets, fill, top with more circles and seal.

7. Bake one sheet at a time in preheated oven for 8 to 10 minutes or until edges start to turn lightly golden. Immediately slide parchment paper onto a wire cooling rack. Cool cookies for 5 minutes, then transfer from parchment paper to cooling rack and cool completely.

Pumpkin Walnut Tassies

Makes 24 cookies

A lightly spiced pumpkin filling is crowned with a crunchy walnut topping in these fabulous cookies that make a perfect treat on cool, blustery days.

Tips

Using egg substitute in place of fresh eggs in cookies and baked goods is not advisable. Egg substitutes are made primarily from egg whites and will significantly affect the quality of your cookies.

Store cookies between layers of wax paper in a tightly sealed container in the refrigerator. Cookies can be stored for up to 3 days.

- One 24-cup or two 12-cup 1¾-inch (4.5 cm) mini-muffin pans, greased with unsalted butter

Crust

1¼ cups	all-purpose flour	300 mL
¼ tsp	salt	1 mL
½ cup	unsalted butter, softened	125 mL
3 oz	cream cheese, softened	90 g
2 tbsp	granulated sugar	25 mL
¼ tsp	vanilla extract	1 mL

Filling

¼ cup	granulated sugar	50 mL
¼ cup	packed light brown sugar	50 mL
¼ tsp	ground cinnamon	1 mL
⅛ tsp	ground nutmeg	0.5 mL
½ cup	canned solid pack (purée) pumpkin	125 mL
2	egg yolks	2
1 tbsp	half-and-half (10%) cream or milk	15 mL
1 tsp	vanilla extract	5 mL

Topping

2 tbsp	light (golden) corn syrup	25 mL
2 tbsp	packed light brown sugar	25 mL
3 tbsp	unsalted butter, melted	45 mL
½ cup	finely chopped walnuts	125 mL

1. **Crust:** In a bowl, whisk together flour and salt until well combined. Set aside.

2. In a large bowl, using an electric mixer on medium speed, cream butter, cream cheese and granulated sugar until light and fluffy, about 2 minutes. Beat in vanilla. Scrape down sides of bowl. On low speed or using a wooden spoon, gradually add flour mixture, beating just until blended. Cover dough with plastic wrap and chill for 15 minutes.

3. Lightly grease hands with nonstick cooking spray. Divide dough into 24 portions and shape each portion into a ball. Using fingers or a dough tamper, press a dough ball evenly against bottom and sides of each prepared muffin cup. Cover pan loosely with plastic wrap and chill for 15 minutes.

Tip

If you have problems
with your cookies
overbaking or
underbaking, use an
oven thermometer to
check the accuracy of
your oven's temperature
control.

4. Preheat oven to 350°F (180°C).

5. *Filling:* In a small bowl, combine granulated sugar, brown sugar, cinnamon and nutmeg until well blended. Set aside. In a medium bowl, whisk together pumpkin and egg yolks until well combined. Stir in cream and vanilla. Add sugar mixture and stir until well combined. Spoon 2 teaspoons (10 mL) of pumpkin filling into chilled pastry-lined muffin cups.

6. *Topping:* In a bowl, whisk together corn syrup, brown sugar and melted butter until well combined. Stir in walnuts. Spoon a teaspoonful (5 mL) of walnut topping over pumpkin filling in each cup.

7. Bake in preheated oven for 18 to 20 minutes or until top of the crust is golden brown and the filling is set. Remove from oven and cool cookies in pan on a wire cooling rack for 15 minutes. If necessary, use a sharp thin-bladed knife to carefully loosen top edges of cookies from pan. Carefully remove cookies from pan, transfer to cooling rack and cool completely.

Pineapple Horns

Pineapple jam makes a perfect filling for these decorative Danish-like cookies.

Tips

If you don't have any pineapple juice on hand for the icing, half-and-half (10%) cream or milk may be substituted.

Let icing set before storing cookies between sheets of wax paper. Cookies can be stored in a tightly sealed container at room temperature for up to 3 days.

● **Cookie sheets, lined with parchment paper**

Cookies

2²⁄₃ cups	all-purpose flour	650 mL
¹⁄₈ tsp	salt	0.5 mL
²⁄₃ cup	unsalted butter, softened	150 mL
4 oz	cream cheese, softened	125 g
¾ cup	granulated sugar	175 mL
2 tsp	unsweetened pineapple juice	10 mL
¼ tsp	vanilla extract	1 mL

Filling

1 cup	pineapple jam or preserves	250 mL

Icing

1 cup	confectioner's (powdered/icing) sugar	250 mL
4 to 5 tsp	unsweetened pineapple juice	20 to 25 mL
¹⁄₈ tsp	vanilla extract	0.5 mL

1. *Cookies:* In a bowl, whisk together flour and salt until well combined. Set aside.

2. In a large bowl, using an electric mixer on medium speed, cream butter, cream cheese and granulated sugar until light and fluffy, about 3 minutes. Beat in pineapple juice and vanilla. Scrape down sides of bowl. On low speed or using a wooden spoon, gradually add flour mixture, beating just until blended.

3. Divide dough in half. Shape each portion into a flat square. Tightly wrap each dough square in plastic wrap and chill for at least 2 to 3 hours.

4. Preheat oven to 375°F (190°C). Using confectioner's sugar or flour, lightly dust a pastry board, clean countertop or other flat surface and a rolling pin. Working with one dough square at a time, unwrap dough and roll out to uniform thickness of ¹⁄₈ inch (3 mm). Halfway through rolling, rotate the dough a quarter turn and dust the board again to prevent dough from sticking. Using a sharp knife, pastry cutter or pizza cutter, cut dough into 2-inch (5 cm) squares.

● ● ●

Tip

Chilled cookie dough is easier to roll and handle than dough at room temperature.

5. **Filling:** Place a teaspoonful (5 mL) of pineapple jam in center of each square. Fold 2 opposite corners of square into center, overlapping dough, and pinch together to seal. Carefully transfer cookies to prepared cookie sheets, placing 2 inches (5 cm) apart. Gather dough remnants into a ball, reroll, cut out and fill more cookies; seal and transfer to cookie sheets.

6. Bake one sheet at a time in preheated oven for 8 to 10 minutes or until edges start to turn lightly golden. Immediately slide parchment paper onto a wire cooling rack. Cool cookies for 5 minutes, then transfer from parchment paper to cooling rack and cool completely.

7. **Icing:** In a small bowl, combine confectioner's sugar, 4 teaspoons (20 mL) of the pineapple juice and vanilla. Using a small whisk or a fork, blend until icing is smooth and thin enough to drizzle from a fork. Add more pineapple juice as needed to achieve the desired consistency. Drizzle icing over cooled cookies.

Creative Gift Idea

Select metal or plastic cookie tins with tight-fitting lids that suit the occasion of your gift.

For soft cookies, line the containers with colored plastic wrap. For crisp cookies, use crumpled colored tissue paper. Carefully arrange cookies in containers and cover with a piece of plastic wrap before securely applying the lid.

Package cookies with strong flavors, such as mint or lots of spices, in separate containers to prevent these flavors from being absorbed by the other cookies.

Maple Walnut Tartlets

● ● ●

Give these little gems a try when you want a special treat.

Tips

If necessary, use a sharp thin-bladed knife to carefully loosen top edges of cookies from pan.

Be sure to taste nuts before using them in baking. Nothing spoils the taste of a nut cookie faster than stale nuts.

Store cookies between layers of wax paper in a tightly sealed container. Cookies can be stored at room temperature for up to 3 days.

● **One 24-cup or two 12-cup 1¾-inch (4.5 cm) mini-muffin pans, greased with unsalted butter**

Crust

1¼ cups	all-purpose flour	300 mL
¼ tsp	salt	1 mL
½ cup	unsalted butter, softened	125 mL
3 oz	cream cheese, softened	90 g
2 tbsp	granulated sugar	25 mL
¼ tsp	vanilla extract	1 mL

Filling

1	egg	1
⅓ cup	light (golden) corn syrup	75 mL
⅓ cup	packed light brown sugar	75 mL
2 tbsp	unsalted butter, melted	25 mL
1 tsp	vanilla extract	5 mL
1 tsp	maple flavoring	5 mL
¾ cup	finely chopped walnuts	175 mL

1. **Crust:** In a bowl, whisk together flour and salt until well combined. Set aside.

2. In a large bowl, using an electric mixer on medium speed, cream butter, cream cheese and granulated sugar until light and fluffy, about 2 minutes. Beat in vanilla. Scrape down sides of bowl. On low speed or using a wooden spoon, gradually add flour mixture, beating just until blended. Cover dough with plastic wrap and chill for 15 minutes.

3. Lightly grease hands with nonstick cooking spray. Divide dough into 24 portions and shape each portion into a ball. Using fingers or a dough tamper, press a dough ball evenly against bottom and sides of each prepared muffin cup. Cover pan loosely with plastic wrap and chill for 15 minutes.

4. Preheat oven to 350°F (180°C).

5. **Filling:** In a bowl, whisk egg until lightly beaten. Gradually whisk in corn syrup. Add brown sugar, butter, vanilla and maple flavoring and stir until well combined. Spoon a rounded teaspoonful (5 mL) of walnuts into the bottom of each chilled pastry-lined muffin cup. Spoon about 2 teaspoonfuls (10 mL) of filling on top of walnuts, filling nearly to the top.

6. Bake in preheated oven for 15 to 18 minutes or until top of the crust is golden brown and filling is set. Remove from oven and cool cookies in pan on a wire rack for 10 minutes. Carefully transfer cookies to rack and cool completely.

Almond Bites

● ● ●

A rich almond filling gives these little bites their nutty flavor.

Tips

Packages of almond paste can be found in the baking aisle of most grocery stores.

Store cookies between layers of wax paper in a tightly sealed container. Cookies can be stored at room temperature for up to 3 days.

● **One 24-cup or two 12-cup 1¾-inch (4.5 cm) mini-muffin pans, greased with unsalted butter**

Crust

1¼ cups	all-purpose flour	300 mL
¼ tsp	salt	1 mL
½ cup	unsalted butter, softened	125 mL
3 oz	cream cheese, softened	90 g
2 tbsp	granulated sugar	25 mL
⅛ tsp	vanilla extract	0.5 mL
⅛ tsp	almond extract	0.5 mL

Filling

6 oz	almond paste	175 g
½ cup	granulated sugar	125 mL
2	eggs	2
	Sliced almonds	

1. **Crust:** In a bowl, whisk together flour and salt until well combined. Set aside.

2. In a large bowl, using an electric mixer on medium speed, cream butter, cream cheese and granulated sugar until light and fluffy, about 2 minutes. Beat in vanilla and almond extract. Scrape down sides of bowl. On low speed or using a wooden spoon, gradually add flour mixture, beating just until blended. Cover dough with plastic wrap and chill for 15 minutes.

3. Lightly grease hands with nonstick cooking spray. Divide dough into 24 portions and shape each portion into a ball. Using fingers or a dough tamper, press a dough ball evenly against bottom and sides of each prepared muffin cup. Cover pan loosely with plastic wrap and chill for 15 minutes.

4. Preheat oven to 350°F (180°C).

5. **Filling:** Crumble almond paste into a mixer bowl. Add granulated sugar and eggs. Using an electric mixer on low speed, beat until well combined and smooth, about 3 minutes. Spoon 2 rounded teaspoonfuls (10 mL) of almond filling into chilled pastry-lined muffin cups. Decorate tops with sliced almonds.

6. Bake in preheated oven for 18 to 20 minutes or until top of the crust is golden brown and the filling is set. Remove from oven and cool cookies in pan on a wire cooling rack for 10 minutes. If necessary, use a sharp thin-bladed knife to carefully loosen top edges of cookies from pan. Carefully remove cookies from pan, transfer to cooling rack and cool completely.

Cranberry Pinwheels

These delicious tangy-sweet cookies have a pretty shape.

Tip

A pinwheel cookie cutter is a nifty tool that not only cuts the dough into squares but also makes the diagonal cuts from the corners toward the center. Pinwheel cutters can often be found where cookie cutters are sold in kitchen supply stores or obtained from mail-order suppliers.

- Cookie sheets, lined with parchment paper
- 3-inch (7.5 cm) pinwheel cookie cutter (optional)

Cookies

2¾ cups	all-purpose flour	675 mL
1 tsp	baking powder	5 mL
⅛ tsp	salt	0.5 mL
⅔ cup	unsalted butter, softened	150 mL
⅔ cup	granulated sugar	150 mL
1	egg	1
½ cup	sour cream	125 mL
1 tsp	grated orange zest	5 mL
½ tsp	vanilla extract	2 mL

Filling

½ cup	cranberry sauce (see Tip, at right)	125 mL
⅓ cup	orange marmalade	75 mL
	Confectioner's (powdered/icing) sugar	

1. **Cookies:** In a bowl, whisk together flour, baking powder and salt until well combined. Set aside.
2. In a large bowl, using an electric mixer on medium speed, cream butter and granulated sugar until light and fluffy, about 2 minutes. Add egg and beat well. Beat in sour cream, orange zest and vanilla. Scrape down sides of bowl. On low speed or using a wooden spoon, gradually add flour mixture, beating just until blended.
3. Divide dough in half. Shape each portion into a flat square. Tightly wrap each dough square in plastic wrap and chill for at least 3 hours.
4. Preheat oven to 350°F (180°C). Using confectioner's sugar or flour, lightly dust a pastry board, clean countertop or other flat surface and a rolling pin. Working with one dough square at a time, unwrap dough and roll out to uniform thickness of ⅛ inch (3 mm). Halfway through rolling, rotate the dough a quarter turn and dust the board again to prevent dough from sticking.

Tip

You can use either whole berry or jellied cranberry sauce in this recipe. For a pretty appearance and stronger cranberry flavor, use the whole berry sauce. If you prefer a milder cranberry flavor and smoother filling, use the jellied sauce.

5. Dip pinwheel cookie cutter in confectioner's sugar or flour and cut dough into squares. Or, using a sharp knife, pastry cutter or pizza cutter, cut dough into 3-inch (7.5 cm) squares and make a 1-inch (2.5 cm) diagonal cut from the tip of each corner toward center of each square. Carefully transfer cutouts to prepared cookie sheets, placing 2 inches (5 cm) apart.

6. *Filling:* In a small bowl, combine cranberry sauce and orange marmalade until well blended. Place a teaspoon (5 mL) of cranberry mixture in center of each square. Fold alternating tips to center to form a pinwheel and press lightly to seal. Gather dough remnants into a ball, reroll, cut out more cookies, transfer to cookie sheets, fill and seal.

7. Bake one sheet at a time in preheated oven for 8 to 10 minutes or until edges start to turn lightly golden. Immediately slide parchment paper onto a wire cooling rack. Cool cookies for 5 minutes, then transfer from parchment paper to cooling rack and cool completely. Dust cooled cookies with confectioner's sugar.

Creative Gift Idea

A colorful glass or ceramic mixing bowl is the perfect container for a batch of homemade cookies. The bowls come in graduated sizes, so you can choose both the size and color that is perfect for presenting your special gift. They're also wonderful because they're inexpensive. You can often find them in discount, overstock and closeout stores for a nominal price.

Luscious Lemon Tartlets

Tartlets filled with lemon curd are a traditional English cookie served with a pot of piping hot, fragrant tea.

Tips

Do not grate the zest for the curd filling. Slice it thinly so it will be easily caught in the fine sieve when the curd is strained.

Store cookies between layers of wax paper in a tightly sealed container in the refrigerator. Cookies can be stored for up to 3 days.

- One 24-cup or two 12-cup 1¾-inch (4.5 cm) mini-muffin pans, greased with unsalted butter
- 2½-inch (6 cm) round or scalloped cookie cutter

Filling

3	eggs	3
3	egg yolks	3
1¾ cups	superfine sugar	425 mL
2 tbsp	thinly sliced lemon zest	25 mL
½ cup	freshly squeezed lemon juice	125 mL
⅓ cup	chilled unsalted butter, cut into pieces	75 mL

Crust

1½ cups	all-purpose flour	375 mL
¼ tsp	salt	1 mL
½ cup	unsalted butter, softened	125 mL
2 tbsp	granulated sugar	25 mL
1 tsp	grated lemon zest	5 mL
½ tsp	vanilla extract	2 mL

1. *Filling:* In top pan of a stainless steel double boiler, using a wire whisk, lightly beat together eggs and egg yolks. Add superfine sugar and beat until well blended. Gradually whisk in lemon zest and lemon juice. Add butter.

2. Place pan over boiling water. Stirring constantly, cook until mixture will thickly coat the back of a spoon, about 7 minutes. Do not let mixture boil or it will curdle.

3. Place a fine-meshed sieve over a heatproof bowl or pan and pour curd though sieve to remove the zest and any lumps. Cover curd with plastic wrap and chill until cold and set, about 3 hours.

4. *Crust:* In a bowl, whisk together flour and salt until well combined. Set aside.

5. In a large bowl, using an electric mixer on medium speed, cream butter and granulated sugar until light and fluffy, about 2 minutes. Beat in lemon zest and vanilla. Scrape down sides of bowl. On low speed or using a wooden spoon, gradually add flour mixture, beating just until blended. Shape dough into a flat disk. Tightly wrap in plastic wrap and chill for at least 30 minutes.

Tip

Curd can be made a few days in advance and stored in the refrigerator until needed. Press plastic wrap tightly against the surface of curd to prevent a skin from forming on top. Extra curd may be stored in the refrigerator for up to 3 weeks. You can substitute store-bought lemon curd for the homemade curd, if you prefer.

6. Preheat oven to 350°F (180°C). Using confectioner's (powdered/icing) sugar or flour, lightly dust a pastry board, clean countertop or other flat surface and a rolling pin. Unwrap dough and roll out to uniform thickness of $1/8$ inch (3 mm). Halfway through rolling, rotate the dough a quarter turn and dust the board again to prevent dough from sticking.

7. Dip a round or scalloped cookie cutter in confectioner's sugar or flour and cut out 24 circles. Gently fit a cutout into each cup of prepared mini-muffin pan, being careful not to tear or stretch dough. Cover pan loosely with plastic wrap and chill for 15 minutes.

8. Bake in preheated oven for 8 to 10 minutes or until top of the crust is lightly golden. Remove from oven and cool crusts in pan on a wire cooling rack for 20 minutes.

9. Carefully remove crusts from pan. Spoon about 1 tablespoon (15 mL) of lemon curd into pastry crusts, filling nearly to the top.

Strawberry Cream Horns

Makes about 4 dozen cookies ● ● ●

These tender cookies are sure to impress your family.

Tips

The combination of butter and cream cheese in the dough creates a flavorful and tender cookie.

Store cookies between layers of wax paper in a tightly sealed container in the refrigerator. Cookies can be stored for up to 3 days.

● **Cookie sheets, lined with parchment paper**

Cookies

2⅔ cups	all-purpose flour	650 mL
¼ tsp	salt	1 mL
⅔ cup	unsalted butter, softened	150 mL
4 oz	cream cheese, softened	125 g
¾ cup	granulated sugar	175 mL
½ tsp	vanilla extract	2 mL

Filling

4 oz	cream cheese, softened	125 g
2 tbsp	granulated sugar	25 mL
1	egg yolk	1
¼ tsp	vanilla extract	1 mL
¼ cup	strawberry jam	50 mL

Confectioner's (powdered/icing) sugar

1. **Cookies:** In a bowl, whisk together flour and salt until well combined. Set aside.
2. In a large bowl, using an electric mixer on medium speed, cream butter, cream cheese and granulated sugar until light and fluffy, about 3 minutes. Beat in vanilla. Scrape down sides of bowl. On low speed or using a wooden spoon, gradually add flour mixture, beating just until blended.
3. Divide dough in half. Shape each portion into a flat square. Tightly wrap each dough square in plastic wrap and chill for at least 2 to 3 hours.
4. Preheat oven to 375°F (190°C). Using confectioner's sugar or flour, lightly dust a pastry board, clean countertop or other flat surface and a rolling pin. Working with one dough square at a time, unwrap dough and roll out to uniform thickness of ⅛ inch (3 mm). Halfway through rolling, rotate the dough a quarter turn and dust the board again to prevent dough from sticking. Using a sharp knife, pastry cutter or pizza cutter, cut dough into 2-inch (5 cm) squares.

Tip

Line cookie sheets with
parchment paper to keep
cookies from sticking to
the sheet.

5. *Filling:* In a bowl, using an electric mixer on medium speed,
   beat cream cheese and granulated sugar until well combined
   and smooth, about 2 minutes. Add egg yolk and beat well. Beat
   in vanilla. Place $1/2$ teaspoon (2 mL) of cream cheese mixture
   in center of each square. Top with $1/4$ teaspoon (1 mL) of
   strawberry jam. Fold 2 opposite corners of square into center,
   overlapping dough, and pinch together to seal. Carefully
   transfer cookies to prepared cookie sheets, placing 2 inches
   (5 cm) apart. Gather dough remnants into a ball, reroll, cut out
   and fill more cookies; seal and transfer to cookie sheets.

6. Bake one sheet at a time in preheated oven for 8 to 10 minutes
   or until edges start to turn lightly golden. Immediately slide
   parchment paper onto a wire cooling rack. Cool cookies for
   5 minutes, then transfer from parchment paper to cooling rack
   and cool completely. Dust tops of cookies with confectioner's
   sugar.

Raspberry Almond Cream Cheese Pockets

An award-winner, this is the recipe to make when you want an elegant cookie for dessert.

Tips

For even baking, cookie sheets should fit inside your oven with at least 2 inches (5 cm) of space between the sheet and the sides of the oven.

Let icing set before storing cookies in a tightly sealed container. Cookies can be stored at room temperature for up to 3 days.

● **Cookie sheets, lined with parchment paper**

Cookies

2 cups	all-purpose flour	500 mL
1/4 tsp	salt	1 mL
3/4 cup	unsalted butter, softened	175 mL
6 oz	cream cheese, softened	175 g
1/2 cup	granulated sugar	125 mL
1/2 tsp	vanilla extract	2 mL

Filling

2 oz	almond paste	60 g
1 tbsp	half-and-half (10%) cream	15 mL
1/2 cup	seedless raspberry jam	125 mL

Topping

1	egg	1
1 tbsp	water	15 mL
	Additional granulated sugar	
1/4 cup	sliced unsalted almonds, coarsely chopped	50 mL

1. *Cookies:* In a bowl, whisk together flour and salt until well combined. Set aside.

2. In a large bowl, using an electric mixer on medium speed, cream butter, cream cheese and granulated sugar until light and fluffy, about 3 minutes. Beat in vanilla. Scrape down sides of bowl. On low speed or using a wooden spoon, gradually add flour mixture, beating just until blended.

3. Divide dough in half. Shape each portion into a flat square. Tightly wrap each dough square in plastic wrap and chill for 2 to 3 hours.

4. Preheat oven to 375°F (190°C). Using confectioner's (powdered/icing) sugar or flour, lightly dust a pastry board, clean countertop or other flat surface and a rolling pin. Working with one dough square at a time, unwrap dough and roll out to uniform thickness of 1/8 inch (3 mm). Halfway through rolling, rotate the dough a quarter turn and dust the board again to prevent dough from sticking.

Tip

Salt should not be eliminated from cookie recipes. Without salt, some cookies will taste bland and unexciting.

5. Using a sharp knife, pastry cutter or pizza cutter, cut dough into 2-inch (5 cm) squares. Carefully transfer half of squares to prepared cookie sheets, placing 2 inches (5 cm) apart.

6. *Filling:* Crumble almond paste into a small bowl and sprinkle with cream. With a fork, work cream into almond paste until mixture is smooth. Spread $\frac{1}{4}$ teaspoon (1 mL) of almond filling in center of each square. Place $\frac{1}{2}$ teaspoon (2 mL) raspberry jam on top of almond filling. Top with remaining squares and press edges together with tines of a fork to seal. Gather dough remnants into a ball, reroll, cut out more squares, transfer to cookie sheets, fill, top with additional squares and seal.

7. *Topping:* In a small bowl, whisk together egg and water. Brush over tops of cookies. Sprinkle with granulated sugar and chopped almonds.

8. Bake one sheet at a time in preheated oven for 10 to 12 minutes or until edges start to turn lightly golden. Immediately slide parchment paper onto a wire cooling rack. Cool cookies for 5 minutes, then transfer from parchment paper to cooling rack and cool completely.

Apple Butter Turnovers

Whether homemade or store-bought, smooth apple butter makes a very flavorful filling for cookies.

Tips

Apple butter can be found alongside jams and jellies in many grocery stores and specialty food stores.

To prevent tops or bottoms of cookies from becoming too brown, bake one cookie sheet at a time with the oven rack positioned in the center of the oven.

● **Cookie sheets, lined with parchment paper**

Cookies

2 cups	all-purpose flour	500 mL
1 tsp	baking powder	5 mL
1/4 tsp	salt	1 mL
1/2 cup	unsalted butter, softened	125 mL
2/3 cup	granulated sugar	150 mL
1	egg	1
1	egg yolk	1
1/4 tsp	vanilla extract	1 mL
2/3 cup	apple butter	150 mL

Topping

2 tbsp	granulated sugar	25 mL
1/2 tsp	ground cinnamon	2 mL
1	egg white	1
1 tsp	water	5 mL

1. *Cookies:* In a bowl, whisk together flour, baking powder and salt until well combined. Set aside.

2. In a large bowl, using an electric mixer on medium speed, cream butter and granulated sugar until light and fluffy, about 3 minutes. Add egg and egg yolk and beat well. Beat in vanilla. Scrape down sides of bowl. On low speed or using a wooden spoon, gradually add flour mixture, beating just until blended.

3. Divide dough in half. Shape each portion into a flat rectangle. Tightly wrap each dough rectangle in plastic wrap and chill for 2 to 3 hours.

4. Preheat oven to 375°F (190°C). Using confectioner's (powdered/icing) sugar or flour, lightly dust a pastry board, clean countertop or other flat surface and a rolling pin. Working with one dough rectangle at a time, unwrap dough and roll into a 12- by 9-inch (30 by 23 cm) rectangle of uniform thickness. Halfway through rolling, rotate the dough a quarter turn and dust the board again to prevent dough from sticking. Using a sharp knife, pastry cutter or pizza cutter, cut dough into 3-inch (7.5 cm) squares.

Tip

Store cookies in a tightly sealed container. Cookies can be stored at room temperature for up to 3 days.

5. Place a rounded teaspoonful (5 mL) of apple butter in center of each square. Fold square in half, forming a triangle, and press edges together with tines of a fork to seal. Carefully transfer turnovers to prepared cookie sheets, placing 2 inches (5 cm) apart.

6. *Topping:* In a small bowl, whisk together granulated sugar and cinnamon until well combined. In another small bowl, whisk together egg white and water until smooth. Lightly brush turnovers with egg white mixture. Sprinkle with cinnamon sugar.

7. Bake one sheet at a time in preheated oven for 8 to 10 minutes or until edges turn lightly golden. Immediately slide parchment paper onto a wire cooling rack. Cool cookies for 5 minutes, then transfer from parchment paper to cooling rack and cool completely.

Cookie Favors

Want to stand out from the crowd and give wedding or anniversary guests a special party favor that they will both enjoy and remember? Give them cookies!

Cookies are an excellent option for wedding and anniversary favors. Unlike many traditional wedding and anniversary favors that wind up in the trash as soon as the guests return home or end up tucked away in a drawer and quickly forgotten, cookies are both fun and edible.

Bake a large batch, or a few batches, of each of the bride's and the groom's favorite homemade cookies. Wrap each cookie individually in a small clear cellophane bag or in plastic wrap. Tie the bags closed with pink and blue ribbons, or ribbons in the bride's and groom's favorite colors or colors from the wedding. Add a label to each one with the cookie's name and identify it as the bride's cookie or the groom's cookie.

Package one of the bride's cookies and one of the groom's cookies in a pretty little gift bag or box for each guest.

Chocolate Nut Rugelach

●●●

Finely chop the chocolate and nuts to get an even blending of flavors and make it easier to roll the dough wedges.

Tips

Halfway through rolling, rotate the dough a quarter turn and dust the board again to prevent dough from sticking.

If dough becomes too soft to handle when rolling up the wedges, place it in the refrigerator for 15 to 20 minutes to firm it up a bit.

Store cookies in a tightly sealed container. Cookies can be stored at room temperature for up to 3 days.

● **Cookie sheets, lined with parchment paper**

Cookies

2½ cups	all-purpose flour	625 mL
¼ tsp	salt	1 mL
1 cup	unsalted butter, softened	250 mL
8 oz	cream cheese, softened	250 g
3 tbsp	granulated sugar	45 mL
1½ tsp	vanilla extract	7 mL

Filling

2 cups	finely chopped or grated semisweet chocolate	500 mL
1 cup	finely chopped walnuts	250 mL

Topping

3 tbsp	unsalted butter, melted	45 mL
	Coarse sugar	

1. **Cookies:** In a bowl, whisk together flour and salt until well combined. Set aside.

2. In a large bowl, using an electric mixer on medium speed, cream butter, cream cheese and granulated sugar until smooth and creamy, about 2 minutes. Beat in vanilla. Scrape down sides of bowl. On low speed or using a wooden spoon, gradually add flour mixture, beating just until blended.

3. Divide dough into four equal portions. Shape each portion into a flat disk. Tightly wrap each dough disk in plastic wrap and chill for at least 2 hours.

4. Preheat oven to 350°F (180°C). Using confectioner's (powdered/icing) sugar or flour, lightly dust a pastry board, clean countertop or other flat surface and a rolling pin. Working with one dough disk at a time, unwrap dough and roll out into a 12-inch (30 cm) circle of uniform thickness.

5. **Filling:** Sprinkle ½ cup (125 mL) of chocolate and ¼ cup (50 mL) walnuts over dough circle. Using a sharp knife, pastry cutter or pizza cutter, cut circle into 12 equal wedges. Starting at the wide end, roll up wedges. Carefully transfer cookies to prepared cookie sheets, placing pointed side down, 2 inches (5 cm) apart. Curve ends of cookies to form a crescent shape.

6. **Topping:** Lightly brush tops of cookies with melted butter and sprinkle with coarse sugar.

7. Bake one sheet at a time in preheated oven for 18 to 20 minutes or until edges turn lightly golden. Immediately slide parchment paper onto a wire rack. Cool cookies for 5 minutes, then transfer to rack and cool completely.

Cashew Caramel Cups

● ● ●

These nutty, sweet treats will satisfy your caramel craving.

Tips

Lightly spray hands with nonstick cooking spray to prevent dough from sticking while shaping cookies.

Let icing set before storing cookies between layers of wax paper. Cookies can be stored in a tightly sealed container at room temperature for up to 3 days.

● **One 24-cup or two 12-cup 1¾-inch (4.5 cm) mini-muffin pans, greased with unsalted butter**

Crust

1½ cups	all-purpose flour	375 mL
3 tbsp	granulated sugar	45 mL
¼ tsp	salt	1 mL
½ cup	chilled unsalted butter, cut into pieces	125 mL
2	egg yolks	2
2 tsp	half-and-half (10%) cream	10 mL
¼ tsp	vanilla extract	1 mL

Filling

½ cup	finely chopped unsalted cashews	125 mL
½ cup	caramel ice cream topping	125 mL

1. **Crust:** In a large bowl, whisk together flour, granulated sugar and salt until well combined. Using a pastry blender or a fork, cut in butter until mixture resembles coarse crumbs. In a small bowl, whisk together egg yolks, cream and vanilla. Add egg mixture to flour mixture and stir with a fork until dough starts to pull away from sides of the bowl and holds together when formed into a ball. Cover dough with plastic wrap and chill for 15 minutes.

2. Lightly grease hands with nonstick cooking spray. Divide dough into 24 portions and shape each portion into a ball. Using fingers or a dough tamper, press a dough ball evenly against bottom and sides of each prepared muffin cup. Cover pan loosely with plastic wrap and chill for 15 minutes.

3. Preheat oven to 350°F (180°C).

4. Bake in preheated oven for 10 minutes. Remove pan from oven and place on a wire cooling rack.

5. **Filling:** In a small bowl, combine cashews and caramel topping. Spoon 2 teaspoons (10 mL) of cashew filling into the bottom of each pastry cup, filling nearly to the top.

6. Return cups to oven. Bake for 8 to 10 minutes or until top of the crust is golden brown. Remove from oven and cool cookies in pan on a wire cooling rack for 10 minutes. If necessary, use a sharp thin-bladed knife to carefully loosen top edges of cookies from pan. Carefully remove cookies from pan, transfer to cooling rack and cool completely.

Apricot Horns

An almond-scented cookie crust and drizzled icing surround a sweet apricot filling.

Tip

Use only just as much flour as you need on your rolling surface and rolling pin to keep the cookies from sticking. If the dough absorbs too much extra flour, the cookies will be tough.

Variation

Substitute apricot pineapple jam for apricot preserves.

● **Cookie sheets, lined with parchment paper**

Cookies

2⅔ cups	all-purpose flour	650 mL
⅛ tsp	salt	0.5 mL
⅔ cup	unsalted butter, softened	150 mL
4 oz	cream cheese, softened	125 g
¾ cup	granulated sugar	175 mL
¼ tsp	almond extract	1 mL

Filling

1 cup	apricot preserves or jam	250 mL

Icing

1 cup	confectioner's (powdered/icing) sugar	250 mL
4 to 5 tsp	half-and-half (10%) cream	20 to 25 mL
¼ tsp	almond extract	1 mL

1. ***Cookies:*** In a bowl, whisk together flour and salt until well combined. Set aside.

2. In a large bowl, using an electric mixer on medium speed, cream butter, cream cheese and granulated sugar until light and fluffy, about 3 minutes. Beat in almond extract. Scrape down sides of bowl. On low speed or using a wooden spoon, gradually add flour mixture, beating just until blended.

3. Divide dough in half. Shape each portion into a flat square. Tightly wrap each dough square in plastic wrap and chill for at least 2 to 3 hours.

4. Preheat oven to 375°F (190°C). Using confectioner's sugar or flour, lightly dust a pastry board, clean countertop or other flat surface and a rolling pin. Working with one dough square at a time, unwrap dough and roll out to uniform thickness of ⅛ inch (3 mm). Halfway through rolling, rotate the dough a quarter turn and dust the board again to prevent dough from sticking. Using a sharp knife, pastry cutter or pizza cutter, cut dough into 2-inch (5 cm) squares.

5. ***Filling:*** Place a teaspoonful (5 mL) of apricot preserves in center of each square. Fold 2 opposite corners of square into center, overlapping dough, and pinch together to seal. Carefully transfer cookies to prepared cookie sheets, placing 2 inches (5 cm) apart. Gather dough remnants into a ball, reroll, cut out and fill more cookies; seal and transfer to cookie sheets.

Tip

Let icing set before storing cookies between layers of wax paper. Cookies can be stored in a tightly sealed container at room temperature for up to 3 days.

6. Bake one sheet at a time in preheated oven for 8 to 10 minutes or until edges start to turn lightly golden. Immediately slide parchment paper onto a wire cooling rack. Cool cookies for 5 minutes, then transfer from parchment paper to cooling rack and cool completely.

7. *Icing:* In a small bowl, combine confectioner's sugar, 4 teaspoons (20 mL) of the cream and almond extract. Using a small whisk or a fork, blend until icing is smooth and thin enough to drizzle from a fork. Add more cream as needed to achieve the desired consistency. Drizzle icing over cooled cookies.

Cookie Dessert Buffet

Dessert parties are a great way to entertain at any time of the year. A cookie dessert buffet works well in the late afternoon as a gathering for family and friends, as a fun way to entertain members of a social or service group following an organization event, or as an after-theater party or a lovely ending to an evening out with a group of friends. A cookie dessert buffet can also be an elegant evening affair where you showcase your best and most elaborate cookies to impress your guests.

The advantage of serving all cookies over more elaborate desserts is that cookies are easy to handle as finger food, they do not require utensils to eat them and the variety of cookies you can serve is endless. Many cookies can be made a week or two in advance, frozen and then defrosted the day of the party. Cookies you want to decorate can be defrosted and pretty embellishments added the day before, allowing the decorations plenty of time to dry before serving. This is a time to show off your best cookies and wow your guests with great flavors.

See also:
* Hosting a Cookie Dessert Buffet (page 523)

Blueberry Pillows

Makes about 3 dozen cookies

I really like the textural contrast of the crunchy sugar topping with the tender cookie and fruity filling.

Tip

To ensure clean cuts, dip knife or pastry or pizza cutters in flour or confectioner's (powdered/icing) sugar and shake off the excess before cutting the dough.

- Cookie sheets, lined with parchment paper

Cookies

3 cups	all-purpose flour	750 mL
1/4 tsp	ground cinnamon	1 mL
1/4 tsp	salt	1 mL
3/4 cup	unsalted butter, softened	175 mL
6 oz	cream cheese, softened	175 g
3/4 cup	granulated sugar	175 mL
1/2 tsp	vanilla extract	2 mL

Filling

3/4 cup	blueberry jam or preserves	175 mL

Topping

1	egg	1
1 tbsp	water	15 mL
	Coarse sugar	

1. **Cookies:** In a bowl, whisk together flour, cinnamon and salt until well combined. Set aside.

2. In a large bowl, using an electric mixer on medium speed, cream butter, cream cheese and granulated sugar until light and fluffy, about 3 minutes. Beat in vanilla. Scrape down sides of bowl. On low speed or using a wooden spoon, gradually add flour mixture, beating just until blended.

3. Divide dough in half. Shape each portion into a flat square. Tightly wrap each dough square in plastic wrap and chill for 2 to 3 hours.

4. Preheat oven to 375°F (190°C). Using confectioner's (powdered/icing) sugar or flour, lightly dust a pastry board, clean countertop or other flat surface and a rolling pin. Working with one dough square at a time, unwrap dough and roll out to uniform thickness of 1/8 inch (3 mm). Halfway through rolling, rotate the dough a quarter turn and dust the board again to prevent dough from sticking.

5. Using a sharp knife, pastry cutter or pizza cutter, cut dough into 2-inch (5 cm) squares. Carefully transfer half of squares to prepared cookie sheets, placing 2 inches (5 cm) apart.

6. **Filling:** Place 1 teaspoon (5 mL) blueberry jam in center of each square. Top with remaining squares and press edges together with tines of a fork to seal. Gather dough remnants into a ball, reroll, cut out more squares, transfer to cookie sheets, fill, top with additional squares and seal.

Tip
Creaming the butter,
cream cheese and
sugar beats air into
the mixture. These air
pockets give cookies a
tender texture.

7. *Topping:* In a small bowl, whisk together egg and water. Brush over tops of cookies. Sprinkle with coarse sugar.

8. Bake one sheet at a time in preheated oven for 10 to 12 minutes or until edges start to turn lightly golden. Immediately slide parchment paper onto a wire cooling rack. Cool cookies for 5 minutes, then transfer from parchment paper to cooling rack and cool completely.

Hosting a Cookie Dessert Buffet

Planning to host a cookie dessert buffet? Here are some pointers to help your event go smoothly:

- Serve a variety of cookie types with different textures, flavors, shapes and colors that will impress your guests.
- If possible, set up the buffet table in the middle of the room, so guests can access the cookies from both sides to improve the traffic flow.
- For a casual afternoon gathering, you can provide sturdy colorful paper plates and paper napkins for guests. For an elegant evening event, set out glass or china plates and quality paper or cloth napkins.
- Arrange the cookies on platters and cake stands with different shapes and heights to add visual interest to your table and make the cookies even more enticing.
- Include some cut up fresh fruit as part of the buffet to complement the cookies and provide guests with a refreshing interlude from all the wonderful sweets.
- Set up the beverage station on a different table or at the far end of the table, away from the busy traffic area around the cookies.
- Serve a variety of hot and cold beverages, including both regular and decaffeinated coffee. For an elegant evening affair, consider serving a dry champagne to accompany your excellent cookie creations.

See also:
- Cookie Dessert Buffet (page 521)

Maple Pecan Spirals

This is an excellent nut cookie.

Tips

Rolling the dough out on a piece of floured parchment paper can make it easier to roll the dough into a log after filling. Use the parchment paper to fold the edge of the dough over on itself and roll up the dough, shaping it into a log.

Butter is considered to be softened when it is at a temperature of 65°F (18°C).

Store cookies in a tightly sealed container. Cookies can be stored at room temperature for up to 3 days.

● Cookie sheets, lined with parchment paper

Cookies

2⅓ cups	all-purpose flour	575 mL
½ tsp	baking powder	2 mL
¼ tsp	salt	1 mL
¾ cup	unsalted butter, softened	175 mL
1 cup	granulated sugar	250 mL
1	egg	1
1½ tsp	maple flavoring	7 mL
½ tsp	vanilla extract	2 mL

Filling

⅔ cup	finely chopped pecans	150 mL
3 tbsp	granulated sugar	45 mL
3 tbsp	packed light brown sugar	45 mL
3 tbsp	unsalted butter, melted	45 mL

1. **Cookies:** In a bowl, whisk together flour, baking powder and salt until well combined. Set aside.
2. In a large bowl, using an electric mixer on medium speed, cream butter and granulated sugar until light and fluffy, about 3 minutes. Add egg and beat well. Beat in maple flavoring and vanilla. Scrape down sides of bowl. On low speed or using a wooden spoon, gradually add flour mixture, beating just until blended.
3. Shape dough into a flat rectangle. Tightly wrap in plastic wrap and chill for at least 1 hour.
4. Using confectioner's (powdered/icing) sugar or flour, lightly dust a pastry board, clean countertop or other flat surface and a rolling pin. Unwrap dough and roll into a 12- by 9-inch (30 by 23 cm) rectangle of uniform thickness. Halfway through rolling, rotate the dough a quarter turn and dust the board again to prevent dough from sticking.
5. **Filling:** In a bowl, combine pecans, granulated sugar and brown sugar until well blended. Brush melted butter evenly over dough. Spread pecan mixture evenly over butter to within ½ inch (1 cm) of edges. Starting with long edge, tightly roll up dough jelly-roll style to form a log. Tightly wrap in parchment paper or plastic wrap and chill for at least 3 hours or overnight.

Tip

Butter is considered to be softened when it is at a temperature of 65°F (18°C).

6. Preheat oven to 375°F (190°C). Unwrap chilled dough log. Using a sharp knife, cut log into $\frac{1}{4}$-inch (0.5 cm) slices. Place on prepared cookie sheets about 2 inches (5 cm) apart.

7. Bake one sheet at a time in preheated oven for 8 to 11 minutes or until edges start to turn lightly golden. Immediately slide parchment paper onto a wire cooling rack. Cool cookies for 5 minutes, then transfer from parchment paper to cooling rack and cool completely.

Creative Gift Idea

Line a decorative basket or other attractive container with a festive napkin and add bundles of cookies wrapped in clear cellophane or plastic wrap, tied with a pretty ribbon.

Lemon Cheese Pinwheels

Makes about 2½ dozen cookies

● ● ●

These citrus gems take a little extra time and patience to prepare but are well worth the effort.

Tips

This recipe requires a total of 2 teaspoons (10 mL) of lemon zest and 3 teaspoons (15 mL) of freshly squeezed lemon juice. Prepare enough of both ingredients when making the dough and store the remaining zest and juice, covered, in the refrigerator for use in the remainder of the recipe.

Store cookies between layers of wax paper in a tightly sealed container in the refrigerator. Cookies can be stored for up to 3 days.

- Cookie sheets, lined with parchment paper
- 3-inch (7.5 cm) pinwheel cookie cutter

Cookies

2 cups	all-purpose flour	500 mL
1½ tsp	baking powder	7 mL
⅛ tsp	salt	0.5 mL
⅓ cup	unsalted butter, softened	75 mL
⅓ cup	vegetable shortening	75 mL
¾ cup	granulated sugar	175 mL
1	egg	1
1 tsp	grated lemon zest	5 mL
1 tsp	freshly squeezed lemon juice	5 mL

Filling

3 oz	cream cheese, softened	90 g
¼ cup	granulated sugar	50 mL
1 tsp	grated lemon zest	5 mL
1 tsp	freshly squeezed lemon juice	5 mL

Icing

¾ cup	confectioner's (powdered/icing) sugar	175 mL
2 tsp	half-and-half (10%) cream	10 mL
1 tsp	freshly squeezed lemon juice	5 mL

1. **Cookies:** In a bowl, whisk together flour, baking powder and salt until well combined. Set aside.

2. In a large bowl, using an electric mixer on medium speed, cream butter, shortening and granulated sugar until light and fluffy, about 2 minutes. Add egg and beat well. Beat in lemon zest and lemon juice. Scrape down sides of bowl. On low speed or using a wooden spoon, gradually add flour mixture, beating just until blended.

3. Divide dough in half. Shape each portion into a flat square. Tightly wrap each dough square in plastic wrap and chill for at least 3 hours.

4. Preheat oven to 350°F (180°C). Using confectioner's sugar or flour, lightly dust a pastry board, clean countertop or other flat surface and a rolling pin. Working with one dough square at a time, unwrap dough and roll out to uniform thickness of ⅛ inch (3 mm). Halfway through rolling, rotate the dough a quarter turn and dust the board again to prevent dough from sticking.

Tip

Cookies made with butter will tend to spread more than cookies made with shortening because shortening melts at a higher temperature. Cookies with only shortening will hold their shape better. Recipes calling for a combination of butter and shortening take advantage of the best qualities of both types of fat.

5. Dip pinwheel cookie cutter in confectioner's sugar or flour and cut dough into squares. Or, using a sharp knife, pastry cutter or pizza cutter, cut dough into 3-inch (7.5 cm) squares and make a 1-inch (2.5 cm) diagonal cut from the tip of each corner toward center of each square. Carefully transfer cutouts to prepared cookie sheets, placing 2 inches (5 cm) apart.

6. *Filling:* In a bowl, using an electric mixer on medium speed, beat cream cheese and granulated sugar until well combined and smooth, about 2 minutes. Beat in lemon zest and lemon juice. Place a teaspoon (5 mL) of cream cheese mixture in center of each square. Fold alternating tips to center to form a pinwheel and press lightly to seal. Gather dough remnants into a ball, reroll, cut out more cookies, transfer to cookie sheets, fill and seal.

7. Bake one sheet at a time in preheated oven for 8 to 10 minutes or until edges start to turn lightly golden. Immediately slide parchment paper onto a wire cooling rack. Cool cookies for 5 minutes, then transfer from parchment paper to cooling rack and cool completely.

8. *Icing:* In a small bowl, combine confectioner's sugar, cream and lemon juice. Using a small whisk or a fork, blend until icing is smooth and thin enough to drizzle from a fork. Drizzle icing over cooled cookies.

Orange Almond Cups

Makes 24 cookies

Combining the wonderful flavors of cream cheese, orange and almond, these cups are really good.

Tips

If necessary, use a sharp thin-bladed knife to carefully loosen top edges of cookies from pan.

Bread flour has a high protein content and should not be used for baking cookies.

Store cookies between layers of wax paper in a tightly sealed container in the refrigerator. Cookies can be stored for up to 3 days.

● **One 24-cup or two 12-cup 1¾-inch (4.5 cm) mini-muffin pans, greased with unsalted butter**

Crust

1½ cups	all-purpose flour	375 mL
3 tbsp	granulated sugar	45 mL
¼ tsp	salt	1 mL
½ cup	chilled unsalted butter, cut into pieces	125 mL
2	egg yolks	2
2 tsp	freshly squeezed orange juice	10 mL

Filling

¼ cup	unsalted butter, softened	50 mL
3 oz	cream cheese, softened	90 g
2 tbsp	granulated sugar	25 mL
1	egg	1
1 tbsp	half-and-half (10%) cream	15 mL
½ tsp	almond extract	2 mL
⅔ cup	orange marmalade	150 mL

1. **Crust:** In a large bowl, whisk together flour, granulated sugar and salt until well combined. Using a pastry blender or a fork, cut in butter until mixture resembles coarse crumbs. In a small bowl, whisk together egg yolks and orange juice. Add egg mixture to flour mixture and stir with a fork until dough starts to pull away from sides of the bowl and holds together when formed into a ball. Cover dough with plastic wrap and chill for 15 minutes.

2. Lightly grease hands with nonstick cooking spray. Divide dough into 24 portions and shape each portion into a ball. Using fingers or a dough tamper, press a dough ball evenly against bottom and sides of each prepared muffin cup. Cover pan loosely with plastic wrap and chill for 15 minutes.

3. Preheat oven to 350°F (180°C).

4. **Filling:** In a bowl, using an electric mixer on medium speed, beat butter, cream cheese and granulated sugar until smooth and creamy, about 2 minutes. Add egg and beat just until blended. Beat in cream and almond extract. Spoon a rounded teaspoonful (5 mL) of orange marmalade into chilled pastry cups. Top with 2 scant teaspoonfuls (10 mL) of cream cheese filling.

5. Bake in preheated oven for 15 to 18 minutes or until top of the crust is golden brown and the filling is set. Remove from oven and cool cookies in pan on a wire rack for 10 minutes. Carefully transfer cookies to rack and cool completely.

Pineapple Tartlets

This cookie is very popular around my house.

Tips

If necessary, use a sharp thin-bladed knife to carefully loosen top edges of cookies from pan.

If you don't have any pineapple juice on hand for the icing, half-and-half (10%) cream or milk may be substituted.

Store cookies between layers of wax paper. Cookies can be stored in a tightly sealed container at room temperature for up to 3 days.

- One 24-cup or two 12-cup 1¾-inch (4.5 cm) mini-muffin pans, greased with unsalted butter

Crust

1¼ cups	all-purpose flour	300 mL
¼ tsp	salt	1 mL
½ cup	unsalted butter, softened	125 mL
3 oz	cream cheese, softened	90 g
2 tbsp	granulated sugar	25 mL
⅛ tsp	vanilla extract	0.5 mL
⅛ tsp	almond extract	0.5 mL

Filling

1½ cups	pineapple jam or preserves	375 mL

Icing

½ cup	confectioner's (powdered/icing) sugar	125 mL
2 tsp	unsweetened pineapple juice	10 mL
1½ tsp	unsalted butter, melted	7 mL

1. *Crust:* In a bowl, whisk together flour and salt until well combined. Set aside.

2. In a large bowl, using an electric mixer on medium speed, cream butter, cream cheese and granulated sugar until light and fluffy, about 2 minutes. Beat in vanilla and almond extract. Scrape down sides of bowl. On low speed or using a wooden spoon, gradually add flour mixture, beating just until blended. Cover dough with plastic wrap and chill for 15 minutes.

3. Lightly grease hands with nonstick cooking spray. Divide dough into 24 portions and shape each portion into a ball. Using fingers or a dough tamper, press a dough ball evenly against bottom and sides of each prepared muffin cup. Cover pan loosely with plastic wrap and chill for 15 minutes.

4. Preheat oven to 350°F (180°C).

5. *Filling:* Spoon about 1 tablespoonful (15 mL) pineapple jam into chilled pastry-lined muffin cups, filling nearly to the top.

6. Bake in preheated oven for 15 to 18 minutes or until top of the crust is golden brown and the filling is set. Remove from oven and cool cookies in pan on a wire cooling rack for 10 minutes. Carefully transfer cookies to rack and cool completely.

7. *Icing:* In a small bowl, combine confectioner's sugar, pineapple juice and butter. Using a small whisk or a fork, blend until icing is smooth and thin enough to drizzle from a fork. Drizzle icing over cooled cookies.

Coconut Lemon Specials

●●●

A creamy lemon filling and a toasted coconut topping make these layered cookies a special treat.

Tips

This recipe requires the juice of 2 lemons (approximately 6½ tablespoons/ 97 mL). Lemons at room temperature yield more juice than lemons just out of the refrigerator.

Finely chopping the coconut for the cookie dough makes it easier to cut out the cookies.

Store eggs in their original carton on a shelf in the refrigerator. Do not store eggs in the door because the temperature fluctuates every time the door is opened.

- Cookie sheets, lined with parchment paper
- 2½-inch (6 cm) scalloped or round cookie cutter

Cookies

2¼ cups	all-purpose flour	550 mL
1 tsp	baking powder	5 mL
¼ tsp	salt	1 mL
1 cup	unsalted butter, softened	250 mL
⅔ cup	granulated sugar	150 mL
1	egg	1
½ tsp	vanilla extract	2 mL
⅔ cup	sweetened flaked coconut, finely chopped	150 mL

Filling

⅔ cup	granulated sugar	150 mL
3 tbsp	cornstarch	45 mL
1⅓ cups	water	325 mL
⅓ cup	freshly squeezed lemon juice	75 mL
3	egg yolks, lightly beaten	3
⅓ cup	unsalted butter, cut into 6 pieces	75 mL

Topping

2	egg whites	2
1 tbsp	freshly squeezed lemon juice	15 mL
1 cup	sweetened flaked coconut	250 mL

1. **Cookies:** In a bowl, whisk together flour, baking powder and salt until well combined. Set aside.

2. In a large bowl, using an electric mixer on medium speed, cream butter and granulated sugar until light and fluffy, about 3 minutes. Add egg and beat well. Beat in vanilla. Scrape down sides of bowl. On low speed or using a wooden spoon, gradually add flour mixture, beating just until blended. By hand, fold in coconut.

3. Divide dough in half. Shape each portion into a flat disk. Tightly wrap each dough disk in plastic wrap and chill for at least 1 hour.

4. **Filling:** In top of a double boiler, whisk together granulated sugar and cornstarch. Gradually whisk in water and lemon juice until smooth. Add egg yolks and whisk until well combined. Add butter. Cook over boiling water, stirring constantly, until mixture starts to thicken and will lightly coat the back of a spoon. Cover with plastic wrap and cool completely.

Tip
Store cookies between layers of wax paper in a tightly sealed container in the refrigerator. Cookies can be stored for up to 3 days.

5. Preheat oven to 350°F (180°C). Using confectioner's (powdered/icing) sugar or flour, lightly dust a pastry board, clean countertop or other flat surface and a rolling pin. Working with one dough disk at a time, unwrap dough and roll out to uniform thickness of $\frac{1}{8}$ inch (3 mm). Halfway through rolling, rotate the dough a quarter turn and dust the board again to prevent dough from sticking.

6. Dip a scalloped or round cookie cutter in confectioner's sugar or flour and cut dough into desired shapes. Cut out as many cookies as possible from first rolling. Carefully transfer cutouts to prepared cookie sheets, placing 1 inch (2.5 cm) apart. Gather dough remnants into a ball, reroll, cut out more cookies and transfer to cookie sheets.

7. *Topping:* In a small bowl, whisk together egg whites and lemon juice. Brush tops of only half of the cookies with egg mixture and sprinkle with coconut.

8. Bake one sheet at a time in preheated oven for 8 to 10 minutes or until edges start to turn lightly golden and coconut is lightly toasted. Immediately slide parchment paper onto a wire cooling rack. Cool cookies for 5 minutes, then transfer from parchment paper to cooling rack and cool completely.

9. Spread a layer of filling over bottom of plain cooled cookies. Top with coconut-topped cookies. Let filling set before storing.

Bake Sales

Bake sales are a fun and popular way to raise money for many organizations including youth sports, school bands and music programs, nonprofit organizations, service groups, churches and charities.

There are a couple of important things to keep in mind when planning a bake sale. Plan to sell some items that will appeal to kids and others that will attract adults, along with a selection that will be enjoyed by people of all ages. Also, choose baked goods that do not require refrigeration. Exposure to heat during transit and while on display during the sale may make treats with perishable ingredients unsafe to eat.

See also:
- Planning a Bake Sale Fundraiser (page 533)
- Packaging Cookies for a Bake Sale (page 535)
- Setting Up a Bake Sale Table (page 537)

Cranberry Orange Spirals

Try these when you are looking for a pretty and delicious special cookie.

Tip

Rolling the dough out on a piece of floured parchment paper can make it easier to roll the dough into a log after filling. Use the parchment paper to fold the edge of the dough over on itself and roll up the dough, shaping it into a log.

● **Cookie sheets, lined with parchment paper**

Cookies

2⅓ cups	all-purpose flour	575 mL
½ tsp	baking powder	2 mL
¼ tsp	salt	1 mL
¾ cup	unsalted butter, softened	175 mL
1 cup	granulated sugar	250 mL
1	egg	1
2 tsp	grated orange zest	10 mL
1 tsp	vanilla extract	5 mL

Filling

⅔ cup	finely chopped dried cranberries	150 mL
½ cup	finely chopped pecans	125 mL
½ cup	orange marmalade	125 mL

1. **Cookies:** In a bowl, whisk together flour, baking powder and salt until well combined. Set aside.

2. In a large bowl, using an electric mixer on medium speed, cream butter and granulated sugar until light and fluffy, about 3 minutes. Add egg and beat well. Beat in orange zest and vanilla. Scrape down sides of bowl. On low speed or using a wooden spoon, gradually add flour mixture, beating just until blended.

3. Shape dough into a flat rectangle. Tightly wrap in plastic wrap and chill for at least 1 hour.

4. Using confectioner's (powdered/icing) sugar or flour, lightly dust a pastry board, clean countertop or other flat surface and a rolling pin. Unwrap dough and roll into a 12- by 9-inch (30 by 23 cm) rectangle of uniform thickness. Halfway through rolling, rotate the dough a quarter turn and dust the board again to prevent dough from sticking.

5. **Filling:** In a bowl, combine cranberries, pecans and orange marmalade until well blended. Spread cranberry mixture evenly over dough to within ½ inch (1 cm) of edges. Starting with long edge, tightly roll up dough jelly-roll style to form a log. Tightly wrap in parchment paper or plastic wrap and chill for at least 3 hours or overnight.

Tip

Eggs should be at room temperature when added to the creamed butter and sugar mixture. Cold eggs can cause the mixture to break and appear curdled.

6. Preheat oven to 375°F (190°C). Unwrap chilled dough log. Using a sharp knife, cut log into ¼-inch (0.5 cm) slices. Place on prepared cookie sheets about 2 inches (5 cm) apart.

7. Bake one sheet at a time in preheated oven for 8 to 11 minutes or until edges start to turn lightly golden. Immediately slide parchment paper onto a wire cooling rack. Cool cookies for 5 minutes, then transfer to cooling rack.

Planning a Bake Sale Fundraiser

If you're in charge of managing a bake sale fundraiser for your group, planning and organizing volunteers are the keys to a successful sale.

- Have volunteer bakers sign up and indicate what they will be making.
- Sign up a few more people than you think you will need to be sure you're covered for any last-minute cancellations.
- Be sure all participants understand that items for the sale are to be homemade, not store-bought.
- Limit the number of batches of chocolate chip cookies and brownies so you will have a wider variety of homemade goodies for the sale.
- Provide bakers with instructions on how they should package and label their items for sale.
- If people want to help but don't want to bake, put them to work as sellers, as helpers to set up for the sale or clean up afterward, or assign them to bring paper plates and cups or beverages.

See also:
- Bake Sales (page 531)
- Packaging Cookies for a Bake Sale (page 535)
- Setting Up a Bake Sale Table (page 537)

Bachelor Buttons

These little bites with their "blue" jam-filled centers are reminiscent of blue bachelor button flowers.

Tip

These cookies are particularly pretty made with round cookie cutters that have a scalloped edge. When folded slightly inward, the scalloped edge adds to the beauty of the flower center.

Variation

Seedless blackberry jam or seedless boysenberry jam can be substituted for blueberry jam.

- One 24-cup or two 12-cup 1¾-inch (4.5 cm) mini-muffin pans, greased with unsalted butter
- 2½-inch (6 cm) scalloped or round cookie cutter

Cookies

1½ cups	all-purpose flour	375 mL
½ tsp	baking powder	2 mL
¼ tsp	salt	1 mL
½ cup	unsalted butter, softened	125 mL
⅓ cup	granulated sugar	75 mL
1	egg	1
1 tsp	vanilla extract	5 mL
1 cup	blueberry jam or preserves	250 mL

Icing

½ cup	confectioner's (powdered/icing) sugar	125 mL
2 tsp	half-and-half (10%) cream or milk	10 mL
1½ tsp	unsalted butter, softened	7 mL
½ tsp	vanilla extract	2 mL

1. **Cookies:** In a bowl, whisk together flour, baking powder and salt until well combined. Set aside.

2. In a large bowl, using an electric mixer on medium speed, cream butter and granulated sugar until light and fluffy, about 2 minutes. Add egg and beat well. Beat in vanilla. Scrape down sides of bowl. On low speed or using a wooden spoon, gradually add flour mixture, beating just until blended. Shape dough into a flat disk. Tightly wrap in plastic wrap and chill for at least 30 minutes.

3. Using confectioner's sugar or flour, lightly dust a pastry board, clean countertop or other flat surface and a rolling pin. Unwrap dough and roll out to uniform thickness of ⅛ inch (3 mm). Halfway through rolling, rotate the dough a quarter turn and dust the board again to prevent dough from sticking.

4. Dip a scalloped or round cookie cutter in confectioner's sugar or flour and cut out 24 circles. Gently fit a cutout into each cup of prepared mini-muffin pan, being careful not to tear or stretch dough. Cover pan loosely with plastic wrap and chill for 15 minutes.

5. Preheat oven to 350°F (180°C).

6. Spoon 2 teaspoonfuls (10 mL) of blueberry jam into chilled pastry cups. Fold sides of pastry slightly toward the center.

Tip

Let icing set before storing cookies between layers of wax paper. Cookies can be stored in a tightly sealed container at room temperature for up to 3 days.

7. Bake in preheated oven for 15 to 18 minutes or until top of the crust is golden brown and the filling is set. Remove from oven and cool cookies in pan on a wire cooling rack for 10 minutes. If necessary, use a sharp thin-bladed knife to carefully loosen top edges of cookies from pan. Carefully remove cookies from pan, transfer to cooling rack and cool completely.

8. *Icing:* In a small bowl, combine confectioner's sugar, cream, butter and vanilla. Using a small whisk or a fork, blend until icing is smooth and thin enough to drizzle from a fork. Drizzle icing around top edge of crust of cooled cookie and let drip down sides.

Packaging Cookies for a Bake Sale

Here are some simple ideas to package up cookies so they will be protected and easy to handle at a bake sale.

- Stack up six cookies and wrap them in clear cellophane to create a cylinder shape. Twist the ends of the cellophane and tie each with a colorful ribbon.
- Carefully pack cookies, bars or brownies in small cellophane bags. Tie the bags closed with pretty ribbons or seal them with a decorative sticker.
- Place individual tartlets, bites or cups in mini-muffin paper liners and pack in a small box, round cookie tin or on top of a cardboard tray that will slide into a plastic bag.
- Stack cookies in a wide-mouth pint-size canning jar. Cover the lid with a round piece of decorative fabric held in place with a small rubber band or tied with a thin ribbon or piece of raffia.
- For larger quantities, fill a quart-size canning jar with one kind of cookie or a variety of cookies to create a "cookie jar."
- Add a tag or label with the cookie name to each package.

See also:
- Bake Sales (page 531)
- Planning a Bake Sale Fundraiser (page 533)
- Setting Up a Bake Sale Table (page 537)

Apricot Rugelach

These pretty little rolled crescents pack a lot of sweet fruit and nut flavor.

Tip

If dough becomes too soft to handle when rolling up the wedges, place it in the refrigerator for 15 to 20 minutes to firm up a bit.

Variation

Raspberry Rugelach: Substitute seedless raspberry jam for apricot jam.

● **Cookie sheets, lined with parchment paper**

Cookies

2½ cups	all-purpose flour	625 mL
¼ tsp	salt	1 mL
1 cup	unsalted butter, softened	250 mL
8 oz	cream cheese, softened	250 g
3 tbsp	granulated sugar	45 mL
1 tsp	vanilla extract	5 mL
½ tsp	almond extract	2 mL

Filling

1⅓ cups	apricot jam or preserves	325 mL
¾ cup	finely chopped unsalted almonds	175 mL
3 tbsp	unsalted butter, melted	45 mL
	Coarse sugar	

1. **Cookies:** In a bowl, whisk together flour and salt until well combined. Set aside.

2. In a large bowl, using an electric mixer on medium speed, cream butter, cream cheese and granulated sugar until smooth and creamy, about 2 minutes. Beat in vanilla and almond extract. Scrape down sides of bowl. On low speed or using a wooden spoon, gradually add flour mixture, beating just until blended.

3. Divide dough into four equal portions. Shape each portion into a flat disk. Tightly wrap each dough disk in plastic wrap and chill for at least 2 hours.

4. Preheat oven to 350°F (180°C). Using confectioner's (powdered/icing) sugar or flour, lightly dust a pastry board, clean countertop or other flat surface and a rolling pin. Working with one dough disk at a time, unwrap dough and roll out into a 12-inch (30 cm) circle of uniform thickness. Halfway through rolling, rotate the dough a quarter turn and dust the board again to prevent dough from sticking.

5. **Filling:** Spread ⅓ cup (75 mL) of apricot jam over dough circle. Sprinkle with 3 tablespoons (45 mL) of almonds. Using a sharp knife, pastry cutter or pizza cutter, cut circle into 12 equal wedges. Starting at the wide end, roll up wedges. Carefully transfer cookies to prepared cookie sheets, placing pointed side down, 2 inches (5 cm) apart. Curve ends of cookies to form a crescent shape.

Tip

Store cookies in a tightly sealed container at room temperature for up to 3 days.

6. Lightly brush tops of cookies with melted butter and sprinkle with coarse sugar.

7. Bake one sheet at a time in preheated oven for 20 to 22 minutes or until edges turn lightly golden. Immediately slide parchment paper onto a wire cooling rack. Cool cookies for 5 minutes, then transfer from parchment paper to cooling rack and cool completely.

Setting Up a Bake Sale Table

Here are some ways to attract customers to your bake sale table and make your sale a success.

- Select a location for your display that allows people to easily see all the goodies you are offering for sale and easy access to the items and cashier.
- If your location is outside, be sure that you have shade cover to keep the baked goods, and your workers and buyers, from getting too warm.
- Cover the display table with an inexpensive tablecloth or piece of fabric to make your table more appealing and showcase the items for sale.
- Arrange packages of cookies and other baked goods in attractive displays in decorative baskets and festive boxes or on pretty trays.
- Clearly post your prices so there is no confusion for buyers and your workers.
- Keep some napkins handy in case buyers want to enjoy their purchases right away rather than take them home.
- Consider selling some simple beverages or bottled drinks to serve with those wonderful baked goods.

See also:
- Bake Sales (page 531)
- Planning a Bake Sale Fundraiser (page 533)
- Packaging Cookies for a Bake Sale (page 535)

Orange Cream Horns

Makes about 4 dozen cookies

● ● ●

This recipe evolved from my love of cream cheese and orange marmalade.

Tips

Unopened packages of flour can be stored in a cool, dry place for up to 2 years. Always use flour before the date stamped on the package.

Let icing set before storing cookies between layers of wax paper in a tightly sealed container in the refrigerator. Cookies can be stored for up to 3 days.

● **Cookie sheets, lined with parchment paper**

Cookies

2⅔ cups	all-purpose flour	650 mL
¼ tsp	salt	1 mL
⅔ cup	unsalted butter, softened	150 mL
4 oz	cream cheese, softened	125 g
¾ cup	granulated sugar	175 mL
1 tsp	grated orange zest	5 mL
¼ tsp	vanilla extract	1 mL

Filling

4 oz	cream cheese, softened	125 g
2 tbsp	granulated sugar	25 mL
1	egg yolk	1
¼ tsp	vanilla extract	1 mL
¼ cup	orange marmalade	50 mL

Icing

1 cup	confectioner's (powdered/icing) sugar	250 mL
4 tsp	freshly squeezed orange juice	20 mL

1. **Cookies:** In a bowl, whisk together flour and salt until well combined. Set aside.

2. In a large bowl, using an electric mixer on medium speed, cream butter, cream cheese and granulated sugar until light and fluffy, about 3 minutes. Beat in orange zest and vanilla. Scrape down sides of bowl. On low speed or using a wooden spoon, gradually add flour mixture, beating just until blended.

3. Divide dough in half. Shape each portion into a flat square. Tightly wrap each dough square in plastic wrap and chill for at least 2 to 3 hours.

4. Preheat oven to 375°F (190°C). Using confectioner's sugar or flour, lightly dust a pastry board, clean countertop or other flat surface and a rolling pin. Working with one dough square at a time, unwrap dough and roll out to uniform thickness of ⅛ inch (3 mm). Halfway through rolling, rotate the dough a quarter turn and dust the board again to prevent dough from sticking. Using a sharp knife, pastry cutter or pizza cutter, cut dough into 2-inch (5 cm) squares.

Tip

For the best texture and flavor in the filling, use a quality orange marmalade with thin pieces of orange peel.

5. *Filling:* In a bowl, using an electric mixer on medium speed, beat cream cheese and granulated sugar until well combined and smooth, about 2 minutes. Add egg yolk and beat well. Beat in vanilla. Place $\frac{1}{2}$ teaspoon (2 mL) of cream cheese filling in center of each square. Top with $\frac{1}{4}$ teaspoon (1 mL) orange marmalade. Fold 2 opposite corners of square into center, overlapping dough, and pinch together to seal. Carefully transfer cookies to prepared cookie sheets, placing 2 inches (5 cm) apart. Gather dough remnants into a ball, reroll, cut out and fill more cookies; seal and transfer to cookie sheets.

6. Bake one sheet at a time in preheated oven for 8 to 10 minutes or until edges start to turn lightly golden. Immediately slide parchment paper onto a wire cooling rack. Cool cookies for 5 minutes, then transfer from parchment paper to cooling rack and cool completely.

7. *Icing:* In a small bowl, combine confectioner's sugar and orange juice. Using a small whisk or a fork, blend until icing is smooth and thin enough to drizzle from a fork. Drizzle icing over cooled cookies.

Chocolate Mint Pillows

Makes 32 cookies ● ● ●

A special surprise is hidden inside each of these delicious cookies.

Tips

Use a high-quality chocolate mint, such as Andes, to make these tantalizing cookies.

Brown sugar adds moisture and rich flavor to cookies.

Store cookies between layers of wax paper in a tightly sealed container. Cookies can be stored at room temperature for up to 3 days.

● **Cookie sheets, lined with parchment paper**

2³⁄₄ cups	all-purpose flour	675 mL
1⁄2 tsp	baking powder	2 mL
1⁄4 tsp	baking soda	1 mL
1⁄4 tsp	salt	1 mL
1⁄2 cup	unsalted butter, softened	125 mL
3⁄4 cup	granulated sugar	175 mL
1⁄2 cup	packed light brown sugar	125 mL
1	egg	1
1⁄2 cup	sour cream	125 mL
1 tsp	vanilla extract	5 mL
55	individually wrapped rectangular layered chocolate mints, unwrapped	55

1. In a bowl, whisk together flour, baking powder, baking soda and salt until well combined. Set aside.

2. In a large bowl, using an electric mixer on medium speed, cream butter, granulated sugar and brown sugar until light and fluffy, about 3 minutes. Add egg and beat well. Beat in sour cream and vanilla. Scrape down sides of bowl. On low speed or using a wooden spoon, gradually add flour mixture, beating just until blended.

3. Divide dough in half. Shape each portion into a flat rectangle. Tightly wrap each dough rectangle in plastic wrap and chill for 2 to 3 hours.

4. Preheat oven to 375°F (190°C). Using confectioner's (powdered/icing) sugar or flour, lightly dust a pastry board, clean countertop or other flat surface and a rolling pin. Working with one dough portion at a time, unwrap dough and roll into a 12- by 8-inch (30 by 20 cm) rectangle of uniform thickness of 1⁄8 inch (3 mm). Halfway through rolling, rotate the dough a quarter turn and dust the board again to prevent dough from sticking.

5. Using a sharp knife, pastry cutter or pizza cutter, cut into 32 rectangles, each 1¹⁄2 by 2 inches (4 by 5 cm). Carefully transfer half of rectangles to prepared cookie sheets, placing 2 inches (5 cm) apart.

6. Place an unwrapped chocolate mint in the center of each rectangle. Top with remaining rectangles and press edges together with tines of a fork to seal.

Tip

Baking powder is a compound leavener. The primary ingredient is baking soda, but baking powder also contains cornstarch and an acid, usually cream of tartar, to activate the baking soda. The cornstarch acts as a buffer to delay the reaction of the baking soda and acid after combination with the liquid.

7. Bake one sheet at a time in preheated oven for 10 to 12 minutes or until edges start to turn lightly golden. Immediately slide parchment paper onto a wire cooling rack. Cool cookies for 5 minutes, then transfer from parchment paper to cooling rack and cool completely.

8. In a microwave-safe bowl, melt remaining chocolate mints in microwave on High power for 30 seconds. Stir until chocolate is completely melted, microwaving an additional 10 seconds at a time as needed to fully melt chocolate. Drizzle chocolate over cooled cookies. Place on parchment or wax paper to set. Allow chocolate to set completely before serving or storing.

Cookie Exchange Party

At the holidays, life can get very hectic. If you like the idea of having lots of different cookies to enjoy, serve and share with family but don't have the time to make all these cookies yourself, then a cookie exchange party, also called a cookie swap, is the perfect way to obtain all those yummy cookies without all the work.

The idea is to host a party and invite a number of guests to bring their favorite cookies to exchange. Each guest bakes enough of their choice of cookie to share with each person who attends. Guests exchange cookies, and each gets to go home with a selection of yummy treats.

A cookie exchange is a great event to host for family, friends or neighbors. You not only get to share cookies, but also get to visit and spend time together during the busy holiday season. You can also host a cookie exchange for members of an organization, service group, social club, or even co-workers.

While traditionally held around the holidays, you can host a cookie exchange at any time of the year and adapt the theme to the occasion.

See also:
- Planning a Cookie Exchange Party (pages 543 and 545)
- Hosting a Cookie Exchange Party (pages 547 and 549)

Pinwheel Jam Cookies

These elegant cookies have a delicate flavor, and their beautiful looks make them a standout on any cookie platter. I like to make them with different-colored jams.

Tip

A pinwheel cookie cutter is a nifty tool that not only cuts the dough into squares but also makes the diagonal cuts from the corners toward the center. Pinwheel cutters can often be found where cookie cutters are sold, in many kitchen supply stores and from mail-order suppliers.

- Cookie sheets, lined with parchment paper
- 3-inch (7.5 cm) pinwheel cookie cutter

Cookies

2¾ cups	all-purpose flour	675 mL
1 tsp	baking powder	5 mL
¼ tsp	salt	1 mL
⅔ cup	unsalted butter, softened	150 mL
⅓ cup	granulated sugar	75 mL
⅓ cup	packed light brown sugar	75 mL
1	egg	1
½ cup	sour cream	125 mL
1½ tsp	vanilla extract	7 mL

Filling

¾ cup	apricot jam	175 mL

Egg Wash

1	egg	1
1 tsp	half-and-half (10%) cream	5 mL

1. **Cookies:** In a bowl, whisk together flour, baking powder and salt until well combined. Set aside.

2. In a large bowl, using an electric mixer on medium speed, cream butter, granulated sugar and brown sugar until light and fluffy, about 2 minutes. Add egg and beat well. Beat in sour cream and vanilla. Scrape down sides of bowl. On low speed or using a wooden spoon, gradually add flour mixture, beating just until blended.

3. Divide dough in half. Shape each portion into a flat square. Tightly wrap each dough square in plastic wrap and chill for at least 3 hours.

4. Preheat oven to 350°F (180°C). Using confectioner's (powdered/icing) sugar or flour, lightly dust a pastry board, clean countertop or other flat surface and a rolling pin. Working with one dough square at a time, unwrap dough and roll out to uniform thickness of ⅛ inch (3 mm). Halfway through rolling, rotate the dough a quarter turn and dust the board again to prevent dough from sticking.

5. Dip pinwheel cookie cutter in confectioner's sugar or flour and cut dough into squares. Or, using a sharp knife, pastry cutter or pizza cutter, cut dough into 3-inch (7.5 cm) squares and make a 1-inch (2.5 cm) diagonal cut from the tip of each corner toward center of each square. Carefully transfer cutouts to prepared cookie sheets, placing 2 inches (5 cm) apart.

Tip

Use a variety of jam flavors to create pinwheel cookies with different colors. Seedless raspberry jam and seedless blackberry jam are excellent choices for these cookies and pair well with the apricot jam. Try all three!

6. *Filling:* Place a teaspoon (5 mL) of jam in center of each square. Fold alternating tips to center to form a pinwheel and press lightly to seal. Gather dough remnants into a ball, reroll, cut out more cookies, transfer to cookie sheets, fill and seal.

7. *Egg Wash:* In a small bowl, whisk together egg and cream until well combined. Lightly brush egg mixture over top of cookies.

8. Bake one sheet at a time in preheated oven for 8 to 10 minutes or until edges start to turn lightly golden. Immediately slide parchment paper onto a wire cooling rack. Cool cookies for 5 minutes, then transfer from parchment paper to cooling rack and cool completely.

Planning a Cookie Exchange Party – Part 1

Careful planning will ensure that your cookie exchange party is a success.

- Well in advance of the party, set a date for the cookie exchange and decide how many people you want to invite. Depending on how many different cookies you want, you can invite anywhere from a few people to a bunch of people. If you want lots of cookie varieties, then 10 to 14 guests is a good number. Each guest will bring lots of cookies made from one recipe, so you could end up with a dozen or so different types of cookies exchanged.
- Send out the invitations early, at least a month in advance, and include a specific date for RSVPs. Follow up with any invitees who don't respond so there won't be any unexpected guests and not enough cookies to go around.
- If you want to stick to a particular theme, such as decorated cookies, international cookies, or something like bars and squares, be sure to indicate this on the invitation. To ensure that the cookies exchanged are special rather than basic cookies, you can also ask guests to bring something other than chocolate chip cookies or brownies.

See also:
- Cookie Exchange Party (page 541)
- Planning a Cookie Exchange Party – Part 2 (page 545)
- Hosting a Cookie Exchange Party (pages 547 and 549)

Strawberry Delights

The center cutout in the top cookie creates a window for the colorful jam to show through. The white chocolate glaze is the perfect finishing touch.

Tip

To keep cutout shapes from becoming distorted, use a metal spatula to support cookies as you transfer them to the cookie sheet.

Variation

Substitute chopped semisweet chocolate for chopped white chocolate.

- Cookie sheets, lined with parchment paper
- 2½-inch (6 cm) and 1-inch (2.5 cm) scalloped or round cookie cutters

Cookies

2¾ cups	all-purpose flour	675 mL
¼ tsp	salt	1 mL
1 cup	unsalted butter, softened	250 mL
⅓ cup	granulated sugar	75 mL
1 tsp	vanilla extract	5 mL
¼ tsp	almond extract	1 mL

Filling

⅔ cup	strawberry jam	150 mL

Glaze

1 cup	white chocolate, chopped	250 mL
1 tsp	vegetable shortening	5 mL

1. **Cookies:** In a bowl, whisk together flour and salt until well combined. Set aside.

2. In a large bowl, using an electric mixer on medium speed, cream butter and granulated sugar until light and fluffy, about 3 minutes. Beat in vanilla and almond extract. Scrape down sides of bowl. On low speed or using a wooden spoon, gradually add flour mixture, beating just until blended.

3. Divide dough in half. Shape each portion into a flat disk. Tightly wrap each dough disk in plastic wrap and chill for 2 to 3 hours.

4. Preheat oven to 375°F (190°C). Using confectioner's (powdered/icing) sugar or flour, lightly dust a pastry board, clean countertop or other flat surface and a rolling pin. Working with one dough disk at a time, unwrap dough and roll out to uniform thickness of ⅛ inch (3 mm). Halfway through rolling, rotate the dough a quarter turn and dust the board again to prevent dough from sticking.

5. Dip a 2½-inch (6 cm) scalloped or round cookie cutter in confectioner's sugar or flour and cut dough into circles. Cut out as many cookies as possible from first rolling. Using a 1-inch (2.5 cm) scalloped or round cookie cutter, cut out center of half of cookies. Carefully transfer cutouts to prepared cookie sheets, placing 1 inch (2.5 cm) apart. Gather dough remnants into a ball, reroll, cut out more cookies and transfer to cookie sheets.

6. Bake one sheet at a time in preheated oven for 7 to 9 minutes or until edges start to turn lightly golden. Immediately slide parchment paper onto a wire cooling rack. Cool cookies for 5 minutes, then transfer from parchment paper to cooling rack and cool completely.

7. *Filling:* Spread a thin layer of strawberry jam on bottoms of whole cookies. Top with cutout cookies.

8. *Glaze:* In the top of a double boiler, combine chopped white chocolate and vegetable shortening. Place pan over simmering water and heat, stirring frequently, until chocolate softens and begins to melt. Remove pan from heat and stir until completely combined and smooth. Spoon melted chocolate into a zippered storage bag. Cut off a small corner of bag and drizzle chocolate over tops of filled cookies. Place on parchment or wax paper to set. Allow chocolate to set completely before serving or storing.

Planning a Cookie Exchange Party – Part 2

- Ask each guest to bring a half-dozen cookies for each guest who will be attending, plus an extra dozen cookies on a plate to share and sample during the party. (If you're only inviting a few people, ask guests to bring a dozen cookies for each attendee.) The cookies to be exchanged should be wrapped in cellophane or packaged in plastic bags for easy handling and to protect them from damage and mingling of the flavors. Guests can transport and display them at the party in baskets, decorative boxes, cookie tins, or on a pretty platter.
- Indicate that all cookies are to be homemade, not store-bought. It really isn't fair to guests who take the time to bake their cookies and make them special to expect them to exchange their homemade goodies for generic store-bought cookies.
- When guests RSVP, ask them which cookie they will be bringing and keep a list to ensure there is no duplication. You want a variety of special cookies, not different versions of just a few. When all the responses are in, let those attending know how many guests will be attending and how many cookies they will need to bring. For example, if there will be 10 guests, ask each guest to bring 6 dozen cookies (5 dozen packaged for the cookie exchange and 1 dozen to share during the party).

Butterhorns

These tasty cookies, similar to rugelach, are made with sour cream in the cookie dough.

Tips

When creamed with sugar, butter traps air that lightens the cookies, adds structure and gives them their tender crumb. During baking, the butter releases moisture in the form of steam that helps cookies cook, set and crisp.

Store cookies in a tightly sealed container at room temperature for up to 3 days.

• **Cookie sheets, lined with parchment paper**

Cookies

2½ cups	all-purpose flour	625 mL
¼ tsp	salt	1 mL
¾ cup	unsalted butter, softened	175 mL
¼ cup	granulated sugar	50 mL
1	egg yolk	1
⅔ cup	sour cream	150 mL
1 tsp	vanilla extract	5 mL

Filling

¾ cup	granulated sugar	175 mL
½ tsp	ground cinnamon	2 mL
⅓ cup	unsalted butter, melted	75 mL
¾ cup	finely chopped walnuts	175 mL

1. **Cookies:** In a bowl, whisk together flour and salt until well combined. Set aside.

2. In a large bowl, using an electric mixer on medium speed, cream butter and granulated sugar until light and fluffy, about 2 minutes. Add egg yolk and beat well. Beat in sour cream and vanilla. Scrape down sides of bowl. On low speed or using a wooden spoon, gradually add flour mixture, beating just until blended.

3. Divide dough into three equal portions. Shape each portion into a flat disk. Tightly wrap each dough disk in plastic wrap and chill for at least 2 hours.

4. Preheat oven to 350°F (180°C). Using confectioner's (powdered/icing) sugar or flour, lightly dust a pastry board, clean countertop or other flat surface and a rolling pin. Working with one dough disk at a time, unwrap dough and roll out into a 12-inch (30 cm) circle of uniform thickness. Halfway through rolling, rotate the dough a quarter turn and dust the board again to prevent dough from sticking.

5. **Filling:** In a small bowl, combine granulated sugar and cinnamon until well blended. Brush 1 tablespoon (15 mL) of melted butter over dough circle. Sprinkle with ¼ cup (50 mL) of sugar mixture and ¼ cup (50 mL) walnuts.

Tip

If dough becomes too soft to handle when rolling up the wedges, place it in the refrigerator for 15 to 20 minutes to firm up a bit.

6. Using a sharp knife, pastry cutter or pizza cutter, cut circle into 12 equal wedges. Starting at the wide end, roll up wedges. Carefully transfer cookies to prepared cookie sheets, placing pointed side down, 2 inches (5 cm) apart. Curve ends of cookies to form a crescent shape.

7. Lightly brush tops of cookies with 2 teaspoons (10 mL) of remaining melted butter.

8. Bake one sheet at a time in preheated oven for 18 to 20 minutes or until edges turn lightly golden. Immediately slide parchment paper onto a wire cooling rack. Cool cookies for 5 minutes, then transfer from parchment paper to cooling rack and cool completely.

Hosting a Cookie Exchange Party – Part 1

Here are a few ideas to help make your Cookie Exchange Party go smoothly and keep your guests entertained.

- Before your guests arrive, arrange a table or two to display the cookies to be exchanged. Decorate the table with a pretty tablecloth and add an attractive centerpiece. Set up separate tables or locations for serving snacks and for the plates of sample cookies.
- If guests will not be bringing their own containers to transport their cookie collection home, provide festive containers, boxes or cookie tins and stage these within easy reach of the cookie exchange table. You can even add nametags to the containers to keep them from getting mixed up before the end of the party.
- As each guest arrives, arrange their basket, platter or container of pre-packaged cookies for the exchange on the table so that it will be easy for guests to walk around the table and collect the packages of each cookie. Place their plate of sample cookies on another table to be enjoyed after everyone has arrived.

See also:
- Cookie Exchange Party (page 541)
- Planning a Cookie Exchange Party (pages 543 and 545)
- Hosting a Cookie Exchange Party – Part 2 (page 549)

Lemon Almond Sticks

Makes about 2½ dozen cookies

● ● ●

Rolling the dough creates intriguing sticks with layers of cookie and filling.

Tips

Always use pure vanilla extract in cookies. Imitation vanilla is made from synthetic flavors and colors, and the taste cannot compare to pure vanilla extract.

Store cookies between layers of wax paper in a tightly sealed container. Cookies can be stored at room temperature for up to 3 days.

● **Cookie sheets, lined with parchment paper**

Cookies

2 cups	all-purpose flour	500 mL
¼ tsp	salt	1 mL
½ cup	unsalted butter, softened	125 mL
⅓ cup	granulated sugar	75 mL
2	egg yolks	2
1 tsp	grated lemon zest	5 mL
½ tsp	vanilla extract	2 mL

Filling

1 cup	ground unsalted almonds	250 mL
½ cup	granulated sugar	125 mL
1 tbsp	grated lemon zest	15 mL
1 tbsp	freshly squeezed lemon juice	15 mL

Confectioner's (powdered/icing) sugar

1. *Cookies:* In a bowl, whisk together flour and salt until well combined. Set aside.

2. In a large bowl, using an electric mixer on medium speed, cream butter and granulated sugar until light and fluffy, about 3 minutes. Add egg yolks one at a time, beating well after each addition. Beat in lemon zest and vanilla. Scrape down sides of bowl. On low speed or using a wooden spoon, gradually add flour mixture, beating just until blended.

3. Divide dough in half. Shape each portion into a flat square. Tightly wrap each dough square in plastic wrap and chill for at least 1 hour.

4. Preheat oven to 375°F (190°C). Using confectioner's sugar or flour, lightly dust a pastry board, clean countertop or other flat surface and a rolling pin. Working with one dough square at a time, unwrap dough and roll out to uniform thickness of ⅛ inch (3 mm). Halfway through rolling, rotate the dough a quarter turn and dust the board again to prevent dough from sticking. Using a sharp knife, pastry cutter or pizza cutter, cut dough into 3-inch (5 cm) squares.

5. *Filling:* In a bowl, combine ground almonds, granulated sugar, lemon zest and lemon juice until well blended. Spread a rounded teaspoonful (5 mL) of filling over each square to within ¼ inch (0.5 cm) of edges. Roll up squares jelly-roll style. Press ends with tines of fork to seal. Place seam side down on prepared cookie sheets, spacing 2 inches (5 cm) apart.

Tip

For zest and juice with the best flavor, use lemons that have a deep yellow color.

6. Bake one sheet at a time in preheated oven for 10 to 12 minutes or until edges start to turn lightly golden. Immediately slide parchment paper onto a wire cooling rack. Cool cookies for 5 minutes, then transfer from parchment paper to cooling rack and cool completely. Sprinkle cooled cookies with confectioner's sugar.

Hosting a Cookie Exchange Party – Part 2

- Depending on the time of day and the season of your party, you can serve finger sandwiches, light appetizers, cheese and crackers, fresh fruit or salty snacks to help counter the sugar rush, or you can focus exclusively on the cookies. You will also want to have some beverages, such as coffee, hot or iced tea, hot cider or cocoa – and don't forget the cold milk – to go with those cookies.
- As guests enjoy the cookie samples, be sure to ask each person to describe their cookies and share any special stories they may have about the recipe.
- After everyone has had a chance to enjoy a bite to eat and sample the cookies, let the exchange begin. Ask guests to walk around the table and fill their take-home container with a package of cookies from each display.
- Depending on the group you are hosting and the length of your party, you can organize some holiday-themed party games for entertainment or simply encourage guests to mingle and visit.

See also:
- Cookie Exchange Party (page 541)
- Planning a Cookie Exchange Party (pages 543 and 545)
- Hosting a Cookie Exchange Party – Part 1 (page 547)

Apricot Pecan Cups

● ● ●

Tender pastry cups hold a delightful fruit and nut filling.

Tips

Always taste nuts before adding them to cookies to make sure they are fresh.

Store cookies between layers of wax paper in a tightly sealed container. Cookies can be stored at room temperature for up to 3 days.

● One 24-cup or two 12-cup 1¾-inch (4.5 cm) mini-muffin pans, greased with unsalted butter

Crust

1¼ cups	all-purpose flour	300 mL
¼ tsp	salt	1 mL
½ cup	unsalted butter, softened	125 mL
3 oz	cream cheese, softened	90 g
2 tbsp	granulated sugar	25 mL
¼ tsp	vanilla extract	1 mL
⅛ tsp	almond extract	0.5 mL

Filling

1	egg	1
¼ cup	light (golden) corn syrup	50 mL
⅓ cup	packed light brown sugar	75 mL
1 tbsp	unsalted butter, melted	15 mL
½ tsp	vanilla extract	2 mL
⅛ tsp	almond extract	0.5 mL
½ cup	finely chopped dried apricots	125 mL
¼ cup	finely chopped pecans	50 mL

1. **Crust:** In a bowl, whisk together flour and salt until well combined. Set aside.
2. In a large bowl, using an electric mixer on medium speed, cream butter, cream cheese and granulated sugar until light and fluffy, about 2 minutes. Beat in vanilla and almond extract. Scrape down sides of bowl. On low speed or using a wooden spoon, gradually add flour mixture, beating just until blended. Cover dough with plastic wrap and chill for 15 minutes.
3. Lightly grease hands with nonstick cooking spray. Divide dough into 24 portions and shape each portion into a ball. Using fingers or a dough tamper, press a dough ball evenly against bottom and sides of each prepared muffin cup. Cover pan loosely with plastic wrap and chill for 15 minutes.
4. Preheat oven to 350°F (180°C).
5. **Filling:** In a bowl, whisk egg until lightly beaten. Gradually whisk in corn syrup. Add brown sugar, butter, vanilla and almond extract and stir until well combined. Stir in apricots and pecans. Spoon about 1 tablespoon (15 mL) of filling into chilled pastry-lined muffin cups, filling nearly to the top.

Tip

Always use pure vanilla and almond extracts in cookies. Imitation vanilla and almond flavorings are made from synthetic flavors and colors, and the taste cannot compare to the pure extracts.

6. Bake in preheated oven for 15 to 18 minutes or until top of the crust is golden brown and the filling is set. Remove from oven and cool cookies in pan on a wire cooling rack for 10 minutes. If necessary, use a sharp thin-bladed knife to carefully loosen top edges of cookies from pan. Carefully remove cookies from pan, transfer to cooling rack and cool completely.

Cookie-of-the-Month

Looking for a unique gift that will be enjoyed throughout the year? Here's a great idea – give the gift of a year of cookies!

We've all heard of the fruit-of-the-month club. Think of this as a cookie-of-the-month club. It makes a wonderful gift for a neighbor or family member, or a friend who has moved across the country or a student away at school. Imagine their joy of looking forward to and opening a monthly or bimonthly gift of delicious homemade cookies.

Pick a theme for your gift and give the recipient a list of the cookies they will receive and what month to expect each gift. You can choose cookie recipes based on seasons of the year, holidays, special events throughout the year, or even the recipient's favorite type or flavor of cookie.

Raspberry Ribbons

Makes about 4 dozen cookies

These pretty sliced cookies are a Scandinavian specialty and very popular at holiday times.

Tips

Slicing the cookies while they are still warm makes it easier to get cleaner cuts, fewer crumbs and a prettier appearance.

Let icing set before storing cookies between layers of wax paper in a tightly sealed container. Cookies can be stored at room temperature for up to 3 days.

- Preheat oven to 350°F (180°C)
- Cookie sheets, lined with parchment paper

Cookies

2¼ cups	all-purpose flour	550 mL
1 tsp	baking powder	5 mL
¼ tsp	salt	1 mL
1 cup	unsalted butter, softened	250 mL
¾ cup	granulated sugar	175 mL
2	egg yolks	2
1 tsp	vanilla extract	5 mL
½ tsp	almond extract	2 mL
½ cup	finely chopped unsalted almonds	125 mL
1 cup	seedless raspberry jam	250 mL

Icing

1 cup	confectioner's (powdered/icing) sugar	250 mL
2 tbsp	half-and-half (10%) cream or milk	25 mL
½ tsp	vanilla extract	2 mL
¼ tsp	almond extract	1 mL

1. **Cookies:** In a bowl, whisk together flour, baking powder and salt until well combined. Set aside.

2. In a large bowl, using an electric mixer on medium speed, cream butter and granulated sugar until light and fluffy, about 2 minutes. Add egg yolks one at a time, beating well after each addition. Beat in vanilla and almond extract. Scrape down sides of bowl. On low speed or using a wooden spoon, gradually add flour mixture, beating just until blended.

3. Divide dough into four equal portions. Lightly grease hands with nonstick cooking spray. Shape each portion into a 12- by 2-inch (30 by 5 cm) log and place 4 inches (10 cm) apart on prepared cookie sheets. Using the back of a spoon, make a 1-inch (2.5 cm) wide by ½-inch (1 cm) deep depression down the center of each log. Sprinkle logs with almonds.

4. Bake one sheet at a time in preheated oven for 10 minutes. Remove pan from oven and fill the depressions with raspberry jam. Bake an additional 10 to 12 minutes or until edges start to turn lightly golden.

Tip

Seedless raspberry jam
gives these cookies a
lovely texture. However,
if you prefer, use a
seeded jam.

5. Immediately slide parchment paper onto a wire cooling
   rack. Cool cookies for 5 minutes then carefully transfer from
   parchment paper to a cutting board. Using a sharp knife, cut
   cookies into 1-inch (2.5 cm) slices. Transfer to a cooling rack
   and cool completely.

6. *Icing:* In a small bowl, combine confectioner's sugar, cream,
   vanilla and almond extract. Using a small whisk or a fork, blend
   until icing is smooth and thin enough to drizzle from a fork.
   Drizzle icing over cooled cookies.

Variations

Blackberry Ribbons: Substitute seedless blackberry jam for
seedless raspberry jam. Substitute vanilla extract for almond
extract in both cookies and icing.

Apricot Ribbons: Substitute apricot jam or preserves for
seedless raspberry jam.

Strawberry Ribbons: Substitute strawberry jam or preserves for
seedless raspberry jam. Substitute vanilla extract for almond
extract in both cookies and icing.

Cinnamon Spirals

A cinnamon sugar filling gives lots of flavor and a fanciful spiral pattern to the sliced cookies.

Tips

Halfway through rolling, rotate the dough a quarter turn and dust the board again to prevent dough from sticking.

Rolling the dough out on a piece of floured parchment paper can make it easier to roll the dough into a log after filling. Use the parchment paper to fold the edge of the dough over on itself and roll up the dough, shaping it into a log.

Use unsalted butter for cookies. Salted butter can give cookies an "off" flavor or make them too salty.

● **Cookie sheets, lined with parchment paper**

Cookies

2⅓ cups	all-purpose flour	575 mL
½ tsp	baking powder	2 mL
¼ tsp	salt	1 mL
¾ cup	unsalted butter, softened	175 mL
1 cup	granulated sugar	250 mL
1	egg	1
1½ tsp	vanilla extract	7 mL

Filling

½ cup	granulated sugar	125 mL
2 tbsp	ground cinnamon	25 mL
2 tbsp	unsalted butter, melted	25 mL

1. **Cookies:** In a bowl, whisk together flour, baking powder and salt until well combined. Set aside.

2. In a large bowl, using an electric mixer on medium speed, cream butter and granulated sugar until light and fluffy, about 3 minutes. Add egg and beat well. Beat in vanilla. Scrape down sides of bowl. On low speed or using a wooden spoon, gradually add flour mixture, beating just until blended.

3. Shape dough into a flat rectangle. Tightly wrap in plastic wrap and chill for at least 1 hour.

4. Using confectioner's (icing) sugar or flour, lightly dust a pastry board, clean countertop or other flat surface and a rolling pin. Unwrap dough and roll into a 12- by 9-inch (30 by 23 cm) rectangle of uniform thickness.

5. **Filling:** In a small bowl, combine granulated sugar and cinnamon until well blended. Spread melted butter evenly over dough to within ½ inch (1 cm) of edges. Sprinkle cinnamon sugar evenly over butter. Starting with long edge, tightly roll up dough jelly-roll style to form a log. Tightly wrap in parchment paper or plastic wrap and chill for at least 3 hours or overnight.

6. Preheat oven to 375°F (190°C). Unwrap chilled dough log. Using a sharp knife, cut log into ¼-inch (0.5 cm) slices. Place on prepared cookie sheets about 2 inches (5 cm) apart. Bake one sheet at a time in preheated oven for 8 to 11 minutes or until edges start to turn lightly golden.

7. Immediately slide parchment paper onto a wire cooling rack. Cool cookies for 5 minutes, then transfer from parchment paper to rack and cool completely.

Blue Ribbon Cookies

● ● ●

Entering cookie competitions at fairs can be very rewarding and a lot of fun. Nothing beats the joy and excitement of winning your first ribbon, and if that ribbon is blue, you'll be walking on air. I competed in quite a few baked foods and preserved foods fair competitions in the United States and earned over 900 awards, including over 600 blue ribbons and special awards for excellence, for my entries. Now classified as a food "professional" and no longer eligible to compete in amateur fair competitions, I enjoy serving as a state and county fair judge and sharing my expertise with exhibitors. I love fairs and fair competitions and am thrilled to give back to events that have brought me so much fun and joy.

For those of you who would like to enter your cookies into a fair competition for the first time, and for those who already enter but would like to improve your entries and increase your win ratio, I'm happy to share with you my expert cookie competition advice, garnered from years as a successful exhibitor and experienced judge.

Fair Entry Requirements

The first step toward success at a fair competition is to familiarize yourself with the individual fair's rules and entry requirements. Following these rules and requirements means your entry won't be disqualified on a technicality before it's even tasted by the judge. Here are some important items to pay careful attention to:

- Be sure to submit your entry form before the entry deadline.
- Include all information needed on the form.
- Make note of entry delivery dates and times.
- If you can't deliver on that date, ask the fair if someone else can deliver your entries for you (some fairs allow this, some do not).
- Allow plenty of time to deliver your entries on delivery day (allow extra time for traffic on the way to the fair and at the fairgrounds).
- Deliver your entries on time (many fairs are very strict about delivery times and won't accept entries even a few minutes late).
- Submit the exact number of items required for each entry (usually 6 to 8 of each type of cookie).
- Submit entries on appropriate plates or in containers as specified in the fair rules (delivery requirements vary by fair).
- Bring a few extras for each entry so you can replace any cookies damaged during transport.
- Submit any additional information, such as recipes, when required.

Some fairs require that recipes be submitted for all food entries, while others only require recipes for special contests. Cookie recipes for regular competitions don't need to be original, and you can use recipes from any source. However, most specialty contests, especially sponsored contests, require original recipes that have not been submitted into any other contest and have never been published. If you are required to submit the recipe, be sure it is complete. Include all ingredients, directions, baking pans, oven temperature, baking times and finishing instructions needed to complete the recipe. Some bakers don't like to reveal the "secret" ingredients that make their cookies special and conveniently leave out those little details. But, trust me, judges can taste those unlisted ingredients, and many an outstanding entry has been given "no award" because ingredients tasted in the cookie were missing from the required written recipe.

What Judges Look For in Cookie Entries

Understanding the judging process and how and why judges pick one entry out of dozens to receive first place can sometimes be a bit mystifying. So let me take away some of that mystery and explain what judges look for in an entry.

There are three basic criteria that judges use to evaluate a cookie entry: appearance, texture and flavor. The best entries score high in all of these areas.

Appearance

First impressions are important. When an entry comes before a judge, the first thing he or she notices is how the cookie looks. Is it attractive and appealing? Does it look like it would taste good? The judge also looks at the size and shape of the cookies. Are they all about the same size? Do they look like they came from the same batch? The color of the cookies is also important. Are the cookies evenly browned? Are they too pale or too dark? Are they burned on the bottom? All of these elements determine the appearance of the cookies.

Texture

Each type of cookie has its own texture. Some are supposed to be soft and chewy, while others should be crisp and tender. Judges look for these specific characteristics when they judge a particular type of cookie. If cookies are underdone and doughy or overbaked and hard, they will not score well on texture. There is also an element of texture called mouth feel. If a cookie has a grainy texture in the mouth, such as from undissolved sugar, the cookie will lose texture points.

Flavor

Flavor is the most important element in judging cookies and other baked foods. If the entry doesn't taste good, it doesn't matter if it's attractive or has a great texture. A cookie with bad flavor won't win awards. Judges look for cookies that have a great, balanced flavor. It may be complex, bold, refined or delicate. If the ingredients don't taste fresh or the flavor of one ingredient overpowers the others, the cookie won't score well. Stale butter, rancid nuts, too much spice or salt or bland chocolate are just some of the negative flavors that keep cookies from winning awards. When it comes to flavor, wow the judges with a great-tasting cookie to win those blue ribbons.

Judging Standards for Cookies

Use this quick guide to make sure your cookies are award-worthy.

Flavor
- Overall good, balanced flavor
- One ingredient does not overpower another
- No "off" or unpleasant taste

Texture
- Appropriate texture for the type of baked goods
- Uniform crumb structure — no air pockets or open texture
- A tender texture, not tough, dry, crumbly or gummy
- Item is not overbaked or underbaked

Appearance
- Entry has a pleasing and attractive appearance
- Uniform shape and color
- Cookies have appropriate thickness for type — not too thick or too thin
- Not overly browned or pale in color
- All items in entry are of similar shape, size and color

Judging Systems

There are two systems of judging that are used to determine the placings and awards for fair entries. These are the American System of Judging and the Danish System of Judging.

American System of Judging

In the American System of Judging, the system used by most fairs, all entries within a class are judged against each other. The judges award only one first place, one second place and one third place within the class. Some fairs give awards down through fifth place and/or encourage judges to choose entries to receive honorable mention awards. While there may be several entries in a class that are worthy of winning first place, only one entry can be chosen for the top award.

Danish System of Judging

In the Danish System of Judging, each entry in a class is judged against a standard for that

Expert Tips for Baking Success

This baker's dozen of expert tips will help make your cookie baking go more smoothly and improve your results.

- Use a tested recipe. Baking for a fair competition is not the time to try a recipe for the first time.
- Make sure you have all ingredients on hand before starting to bake
- Organize your recipes, ingredients and baking equipment so everything is ready when you need it.
- Use fresh, quality ingredients with good flavor.
- Check nuts for freshness before baking. Nothing ruins the flavor of a cookie faster than stale or rancid nuts.
- Use fresh baking powder and baking soda for best results.
- If you're baking several entries, measure and combine dry ingredients and chop chocolate, nuts and dried fruit the day before. Cover tightly with plastic wrap or seal in zippered plastic bags to preserve freshness.
- Test your oven temperature to be sure it is accurate. Make note of any temperature adjustments needed for each recipe.
- Never clean your oven just before baking for a competition. Ash residue and cleaning fluids can impart an unpleasant flavor to your baked goods.
- Make sure your oven is fully preheated before baking and that the rack is in the center position.
- Bake only one sheet of cookies or one pan of bars in the oven at a time to ensure uniform baking and browning.
- Bake more cookies than needed and select the best-looking, most uniform cookies to enter.
- Don't waste your money on fancy plates to impress the judges. Unless you're entering a specialty contest where presentation is part of the score, the judge won't give you any extra points for pretty plates.

---

particular type of cookie and awards are given based on individual merit. Judges can award as many first place awards as the quality of the entries warrants. Any entry earning 90 to 100 points wins first place. Between 80 and 89 points, the entry is awarded second place. For scores from 70 to 79 points, the entry earns third place. If an entry is scored lower than 70 points, then no award is given. The American System of Judging is used to determine special awards for Best of Class, Best of Division and Best of Show, where only one entry can win the top prize.

Closed and Open Judgings

Most fairs conduct a closed judging, meaning the judging is done in private and is not open to the public. Baked foods entries are delivered to the fair, often a day or two before the fair opens, and the judging takes place the same day or the next morning. The entries and awards are then arranged in the display cases before the fair opens. Competitors usually have to visit the fair to learn what awards they may have won. Some fairs will provide entrants with a judge's scorecard that may provide some insight on what the judge liked or did not like about the entry. Most fairs, however, do not provide scorecards and competitors are left to wonder why their entry didn't win an award.

If you're lucky, your fair will conduct an open judging where the entries are judged in front of an audience and the judges will explain why an entry did or didn't win a ribbon. Open judgings are usually held during the fair, with entries delivered the morning of the judging. They are very educational, and competitors can really learn a lot about how to improve their entries. Some judges are uncomfortable working in front of an audience, but I have found that competitors are very appreciative of the opportunity to learn from the judges. The highlight of my judging year is the California State Fair held in Sacramento each August. All of the food competitions are conducted with open judgings. We discuss each entry and offer advice for improvement. The audience has the opportunity to ask questions about baking or home canning, depending on the entries being judged, and receive answers from the judges. It is a great experience for all. If your fair conducts open judgings, I strongly encourage you to attend.

Most specialty food contests held at fairs are open judging events. The competitors deliver their entries about an hour before judging and can then sit and watch the judging. If they're lucky, the judges will share information about the winning entries and why they earned awards.

15 Biggest Cookie Mistakes

These are the most common mistakes that competitors make that reduce their entry's score and take their cookies out of competition for the awards. To give yourself the best chance of winning a ribbon, make sure your cookies don't have any of these problems.

- Cookies are too brown on top or around the edges
- Cookies are dark brown or burnt on the bottom
- Cookies spread too much during baking and are too flat for the type of cookie
- Cookies are dry, hard and crumbly
- Using low-quality ingredients that lack flavor
- Using stale nuts in cookies
- Adding too much spice, particularly cloves, and overpowering the flavor of other cookie ingredients
- Using too much salt in cookies
- Using too much leavener, giving cookies a soapy or metallic aftertaste
- Cookies are significantly mismatched in size and shape
- Bars and brownies are underdone in the center
- Bars and squares have soggy bottom crusts
- Bars have a bottom crust that is too thick or too thin
- Overbaked and dry brownies
- Bars or squares are cut into pieces considered too large for a cookie portion

Packaging Cookies for Mailing

The arrival in the mail of a thoughtful gift of homemade cookies is always appreciated. It's even better if those cookies are intact and taste fresh. There are a few things you can do to help your cookies arrive safe and sound in one piece, rather than in lots of little pieces. You'll want to choose cookies that will travel well and arrive in good condition, and the cookies need to be packaged carefully to preserve their freshness and to survive shipping.

Selecting Cookies for Mailing

Some cookies are better choices for shipping than others. I don't recommend mailing any cookies or bars that require refrigeration, including those with cream cheese, custard or curd fillings, as they will likely spoil before reaching their destination. Be sure to select cookies that are sturdy and will travel well; otherwise, your wonderful gift of beautiful cookies may turn into a box of crumbs. Here are some pointers to help you select the best cookies for shipping:

- Crispy cookies can crumble, while delicate cookies like pinwheels don't travel well because their points tend to break off during shipping. Bars and cookies with a cake-like texture may crush easily under the weight of other cookies and lose their shape.
- Cookies with a firm texture, like biscotti, shortbread and slice-and-bake cookies, are excellent choices for shipping. You don't have to worry about them drying out, and their sturdy texture keeps breakage to a minimum.
- Drop and hand-shaped cookies with a moist, chewy texture survive mailing quite well. Chocolate chip, oatmeal, peanut butter, coconut and sugar cookies, snickerdoodles and cookies containing dried fruit, such as apricots and cranberries, are all good choices.

- Frostings, icings and glazes can soften during shipping, so it's best to send unfrosted cookies.
- Bars and brownies are another great choice for mailing. They can either be cut and wrapped individually or left uncut and wrapped whole.

Choose cookies of similar type to pack and ship together. Just like the guidelines for storing cookies, you don't want to pack crispy cookies and soft cookies together in the same container. The crisp cookies will absorb moisture from the soft cookies and lose their crunch, while the soft cookies will turn dry and lose their chewy texture.

Planning Ahead

Have all of your shipping materials ready and organized so you don't have to run to the store for a missing item when you're ready to pack your cookies. Planning ahead and having everything organized will make the packing and shipping process go much more smoothly.

It is important to pack cookies in an airtight container to preserve their moisture and freshness during shipping. Choose a decorative cookie tin with a tight-fitting lid or a sturdy plastic storage container with a resealable lid for shipping cookies. You will also need a sturdy cardboard shipping box that's large enough to allow 2 to 3 inches (5 to 7.5 cm) of cushioning packing material between the container and the walls of the outside box.

Ship your cookies as quickly as you can after baking so they arrive as fresh as possible. Plan to bake and ship your cookies early in the week so they won't be delayed over the weekend. Choose a fast shipping method so your cookies will arrive at their freshest.

Packing Your Cookies

Use care to pack your cookies to ensure they arrive as pretty and as tasty as when you baked them. You want to wrap the cookies tightly to preserve their freshness and use lots of padding to prevent them from breaking. Start by lining the cookie container with two layers of plastic wrap, leaving the ends of the wrap long enough to overlap on top of the packed cookies. Place a piece of bubble wrap in the bottom of the container and add a layer of crumpled wax paper, parchment paper or tissue paper to cushion and protect the cookies.

Wrap cookies individually or place two cookies back-to-back, with their bottoms together, and wrap tightly in plastic wrap. Wrap cut bars and brownies individually or wrap bars in uncut blocks.

Pack wrapped cookies snugly into the container, placing the heaviest cookies on the bottom so they won't crush more delicate cookies. Fill any gaps between the cookies and the side of the container with crumpled paper. Separate the layers of cookies with crumpled paper. When you've packed the cookies, wrap the ends of plastic wrap over top. Add a layer of crumpled paper and a piece of bubble wrap on top of cookies to completely fill the container so the cookies won't have room to shift during shipping.

Be sure to pack cookies with strong flavors such as cinnamon, ginger or peppermint in a separate container to prevent their flavor from transferring to other cookies. Pack just one mint-flavored cookie in a container with other cookies, and all of the cookies in the tin will take on the mint flavor by the time the package reaches its destination.

Packing the Shipping Box

Place a layer of shipping peanuts or crumpled paper in the bottom of the shipping box. Set your cookie container on top of this bottom layer. Fill in the space along the sides and top of the cookie container with more shipping peanuts or crumpled paper. Make sure the cookie container is snuggly packed in the shipping box so that it won't shift around during shipping. Insert a card with the recipient's name and address on it inside the box just in case the outside label gets damaged.

Securely seal the shipping box with reinforced shipping tape. Securely place a mailing label on top and mark the box as perishable and fragile. Now you're ready to send your package of homemade cookies off to the lucky recipient.

Cookie Problem Solver

Sometimes cookies don't turn out the way they're supposed to and an adjustment in technique or measuring needs to be made to get the right results. If you're having trouble with your cookies, one or more of these reasons may be the cause of the problem.

Cookies have crumbly texture
- Not enough fat
- Not enough liquid
- Too much flour
- Flour not evenly distributed through dough
- Dough was overmixed
- Baking time too long

Cookies are dry or hard
- Not enough fat
- Not enough liquid
- Brown sugar replaced with granulated sugar
- Too much salt
- Too much flour
- Egg substitute used in place of eggs
- Oven temperature too high
- Baking time too long

Cookies are tough
- Dough was overmixed
- Rolled cutout cookies absorbed too much flour
- Dough scraps rerolled too many times.
- Baking time too long

Cookies are dense or heavy
- Butter too warm during creaming
- Butter and sugar not creamed long enough
- Protein content too high in flour
- Not enough leavener
- Not enough liquid
- Oven temperature too low

Cookies spread too much
- Too much fat
- Too much liquid
- Too much sugar
- "Light" butter or margarine substituted for butter
- Butter substituted for shortening
- Butter too warm during creaming
- Dough not chilled to firm fat before baking
- Dough placed on warm cookie sheets
- Cookie sheets greased instead of lined with parchment paper
- Oven temperature too low

Cookies don't spread enough
- Not enough fat
- Not enough liquid
- Not enough sugar
- Shortening or margarine substituted for butter
- Dough too cold or frozen
- Oven temperature too high

Cookies bake unevenly

- Dough not portioned evenly
- Dough rolled or sliced unevenly
- Different-sized cutouts baked on same cookie sheet
- Cookies placed too close to each other on cookie sheet
- Cookie sheet too large for oven to allow air circulation around pan
- Oven has hot spots

Cookies are too dark

- Too much sugar
- Dark or nonstick cookie sheet used instead of light-colored sheets
- Oven rack position too high
- Oven temperature too high
- Baking time too long

Cookies are too pale

- Not enough sugar
- Shortening or margarine substituted for butter
- "Light" butter or margarine substituted for butter
- Oven temperature too low
- Baking time too short

Cookies are too brown on bottom

- Dark or nonstick cookie sheet used instead of light-colored sheets
- Thin or lightweight cookie sheet used instead of heavy-gauge metal or insulated sheet
- Cookie sheets greased instead of lined with parchment paper
- Cookie sheet too large for oven to allow air circulation around pan
- Oven rack position too low, too close to heating element
- Oven temperature too high
- Baking time too long

Cookies stick to pan

- Too much sugar
- Oven temperature too high
- Cookies overbaked
- Cookies left on cookie sheet too long
- Cookie sheets greased instead of lined with parchment paper

Cookies are underbaked

- Oven temperature too low
- Baking time too short

Cookies are overbaked

- Oven temperature too high
- Baking time too long

Cookies have white streaks

- Flour not evenly distributed through dough
- Leavener not evenly distributed through dough

Cookies have large holes, tunnels or open crumb texture

- Too much leavener
- Leavener not evenly combined into flour mixture
- Leavener not evenly distributed through dough
- Oven temperature too high

Cookies have soapy taste

- Too much baking soda

Cookies have metallic taste

- Too much baking powder

Cookies taste salty

- Too much salt
- Too much baking soda

Cookie Supply Sources

● ● ● ●

Department stores, kitchen supply stores, craft stores and some discount stores are good places to find quality baking equipment and supplies. Many large shopping malls have a kitchen gadgets store where you can find all kinds of specialty baking tools. Most supermarkets carry a wide selection of baking ingredients; however, some items, such as instant espresso powder or coarse decorating sugar, may not be available in all areas. If you have trouble finding baking pans, tools and utensils, or quality ingredients, try these sources to help fill your needs.

Equipment

KitchenAid®
800-541-6390
www.shopkitchenaid.com
Electric mixers and attachments, kitchen appliances, silicone spatulas
Ships to U.S. only

A Cook's Wares
211 37th Street
Beaver Falls, PA 15010
800-915-9788
724-846-9490
www.cookswares.com
Cookie sheets, baking pans, utensils and specialty tools, scales, thermometers
Ships to U.S. only

Amazon.com
www.amazon.com (USA)
www.amazon.ca (Canada)
Baking pans, cookie sheets, silicone baking mats, miniature muffin pans, wire cooling racks, mixing bowls, rolling pins, cookie cutters, cookie scoops, cookie presses, baking utensils

The Baker's Catalogue
(King Arthur Flour)
P.O. Box 876
Norwich, VT 05055-0876
800-827-6836
www.kingarthurflour.com
www.bakerscatalogue.com
Cookie sheets, baking utensils and tools, cooling racks, cookie cutters, scales, measuring tools, thermometers

Chef's Catalog
5070 Centennial Boulevard
Colorado Springs, CO 80919
800-338-3232
www.chefscatalog.com
Baking equipment, mini-muffin pans, measuring tools, scales, thermometers
Ships to U.S. only

Country Kitchen
(SweetArt, Inc.)
4261 Speedway Drive
Fort Wayne, IN 46825
260-482-4835
800-497-3927 (orders only)
www.countrykitchensa.com
Baking pans, cooling racks, decorating supplies

Kitchen Krafts, Inc.
P.O. Box 442
Waukon, IA 52172-0442
800-776-0575
www.kitchenkrafts.com
Baking supplies, utensils and tools, cooling racks, cookie cutters, decorating supplies

The Kitchen Shoppe Inc.
101 Shady Lane
Carlisle, PA 17013
800-391-2665
www.kitchenshoppe.com
Cookie sheets, baking pans, cooling racks, specialty tools
Ships to U.S. only

Shop Taste of Home
Suite 1046T, P.O. Box 26820
Lehigh Valley, PA 18002 USA
800-880-3012
Fax: 610-997-8057
www.shoptasteofhome.com
Pinwheel cookie cutters, other cookie cutters

Sur La Table
Catalogue Division
1765 Sixth Avenue S.
Seattle, WA 98134
800-243-0852 (U.S. only)
866-328-5412 (Canada only)
www.surlatable.com
Baking pans, mini-muffin pans, baking equipment, cookie cutters

Sweet Celebrations Inc.
P.O. Box 39426
Edina, MN 55439-0426
800-328-6722
www.sweetc.com
Baking pans, baking equipment, huge selection of cookie cutters, shortbread molds, decorating supplies

Williams-Sonoma
Mail Order Department
P.O. Box 7456
San Francisco, CA 94120-7456
877-812-6235
www.williams-sonoma.com
Cookie sheets, baking pans, baking equipment and utensils
Ships to U.S. only

Wilton Industries
2240 W. 75th Street
Woodbridge, IL 60517-0750
800-794-5866
www.wilton.com
Cookie sheets, baking pans, baking equipment and utensils, cookie cutters, decorating supplies
Ships to U.S. only (see Golda's Kitchen for Canadian orders)

Canada

Golda's Kitchen
700 Matheson Boulevard W.
Mississauga, Ontario, Canada L5R 3T2
866-465-3299
905-712-1475
www.goldaskitchen.com
Cookie sheets, baking pans, mini-muffin pans, cooling racks, utensils, cookie cutters, decorating supplies

McCall's Bakers Warehouse
1290 Fewster Drive
Mississauga, Ontario, Canada L4W 1B6
905-602-9622
www.mccalls.ca
Cookie sheets, baking pans, mini-muffin pans, baking utensils and tools, cookie cutters, decorating supplies

Ingredients

The Baker's Catalogue
(King Arthur Flour)
P.O. Box 876
Norwich, VT 05055-0876
800-827-6836
www.kingarthurflour.com
www.bakerscatalogue.com
Instant espresso powder, chocolate powder, cocoa powder, black cocoa powder, vanilla and other extracts, colored sugars and decorating supplies

Penzeys Spices
800-741-7787
www.penzeys.com
Premium spices and extracts

The Spice House
847-328-3711
www.thespicehouse.com
Premium spices

Trader Joe's
www.traderjoes.com
Over 300 stores in 26 states across the United States
Nuts, chocolate, dried fruit, dairy products and other ingredients

The Vanilla.COMpany
www.vanilla.com
Premium vanilla extracts

High–Altitude Baking Information

Colorado State University
Food Science Extension Office
Fort Collins, CO 80523-1571
Answers to questions regarding high–altitude baking

Library and Archives Canada Cataloguing in Publication

Amendt, Linda J.
       400 sensational cookies / Linda J. Amendt.

Includes index.
ISBN 978-0-7788-0229-7

1. Cookies. I. Title. II. Title: Four hundred sensational cookies.

TX772.A44 2009   641.8'654   C2009-902262-1

Index

(v) = variation

A

almond paste, 24
 Almond Pockets, 478–79
 Almond Squares, 313
 Amaretti, 60
almonds, 24
 Almond Biscotti, 396
 Almond Bites, 507
 Almond Cutouts, 222–23
 Almond Logs, 114
 Almond Pockets, 478–79
 Almond Shortbread, 439
 Amaretto Brownies, 356
 Apricot Biscotti, 397
 Apricot Coconut Dreams, 187
 Apricot Coconut Oatmeal Drops,
  166
 Apricot Ribbons (v), 552–53
 Apricot Rugelach, 536–37
 Cherry Almond Biscotti, 406
 Chinese Almond Cookies, 111
 Chocolate Almond Biscotti (v),
  398
 Chocolate Almond Dreams, 181
 Chocolate Almond Toffee Bars,
  295
 Chocolate Cherry Almond
  Biscotti (v), 413
 Chocolate Chip Almond Cookies,
  133
 Cinnamon Almond Biscotti (v),
  425
 Coconut Almond Cookies (v), 100
 Coconut Cookies (v), 50
 Coffee Almond Rounds, 105
 Cranberry Almond Slices, 268,
  287
 Cream Cheese Brownies, 361
 Currant Almond Biscotti, 422
 Deluxe Nut Bars, 304
 Double Almond Cookies, 98
 English Toffee Cookies, 106–07
 Glazed Almond Slices, 261
 Lemon Almond Biscotti, 416
 Lemon Almond Sticks, 548–49
 Lemon Wedding Cake Cookies
  (v), 95
 Mocha Almond Biscotti (v), 405
 Nut Biscotti, 414
 Oatmeal Almond Cookies, 164

 Orange Almond Cups, 528
 Orange Wedding Cake Cookies,
  95
 Raspberry Almond Cream Cheese
  Pockets, 514–15
 Raspberry Ribbons, 552–53
 Raspberry Rugelach (v), 536–37
 Raspberry Rugelach (v), 536–37
 Strawberry Ribbons (v), 552–53
 Strawberry Spirals, 493
 Swedish Tea Cookies, 108
 Triple Chocolate Chip Nut
  Cookies (v), 129
 Viennese Vanilla Crescents, 84
 White Chocolate Almond Biscotti
  (v), 412
altitude adjustments, 40, 563
Amaretto Brownies, 356
Apple Butter Turnovers, 516–17
Apple Pie Crumb Squares, 277
Apple Walnut Cookies, 68–69
Applesauce Oatmeal Cookies, 167
Applesauce Walnut Bars, 328
apricots, 24
 Apricot Biscotti, 397
 Apricot Coconut Dreams, 187
 Apricot Coconut Oatmeal Drops,
  166
 Apricot Cranberry Oat Dreams,
  201
 Apricot Cream Sandwich Cookies
  (v), 236–37
 Apricot Crunch Squares, 289
 Apricot Dreams, 175
 Apricot Horns, 520–21
 Apricot Orange Cups, 500
 Apricot Pecan Cups, 550–51
 Apricot Pie Cookies (v), 501
 Apricot Pineapple Bars, 278–79
 Apricot Pineapple Crumb Bars,
  324–25
 Apricot Pineapple Tassies,
  466–67
 Apricot Ribbons (v), 552–53
 Apricot Rugelach, 536–37
 Apricot Shortbread, 449
 Apricot Slices, 273
 Cranberry Apricot Coconut
  Cookies (v), 80
 Cranberry Apricot Dreams, 191
 Nutty Fruit Bars, 299
 Pineapple Apricot Oatmeal
  Drops, 152

 Pinwheel Jam Cookies, 542–43
 Tropical Oat Squares, 285
artificial sweeteners, 16–17

B

Bachelor Buttons, 534–35
bake sales, 463, 531
 cookie packaging, 535
 planning, 533
 setting up, 537
baker's sugar, 14
baking equipment, 6–11
 cookie cutters, 10–11
 cookie presses, 11
 cookie scoops, 10
 cookie sheets, 6–7, 28–29
 cutting boards, 8
 decorating bag, to improvise, 205
 dough tampers, 11, 462
 electric mixers, 6
 foil, 10
 foil pans, 371
 food processors, 6
 ingredient bowls, 8
 kitchen timers, 9
 measuring equipment, 9
 microplane graters, 11
 mini-muffin pans, 7, 462
 mixing bowls, 6, 7–8
 parchment paper, 10
 pastry bags, 241
 pastry blenders, 9–10
 pastry boards, 8–9
 pastry cloths, 8
 pinwheel cookie cutters, 462
 rolling pins, 8
 silicone baking mats, 11
 spatulas, 10, 11
 supply sources, 562–63
 tart pans, 7
 utensils, 9–11
 wire cooling racks, 9
 wire whisks, 9
baking fundamentals, 27–40
 baking process, 37–38
 baking terms, 27–28
 cookie storage, 38–40
 cookie texture, 13–17, 20–21,
  38, 556
 cooling process, 38
 finishing touches, 38
 high altitude adjustments, 40, 563

mixing methods, 34–37
oven temperature, checking, 29–30
problem solver, 560–61
successful baking, tips for, 557
baking pans
choosing, 6–7
preparing, 28–29
baking powder, 19–20
baking soda, 19
baking terms, 27–28
Banana Rum Oatmeal Cookies, 160
Banana Walnut Oatmeal Cookies, 165
bars and squares
about, 276
Almond Squares, 313
Apple Pie Crumb Squares, 277
Applesauce Walnut Bars, 328
Apricot Crunch Squares, 289
Apricot Pineapple Bars, 278–79
Apricot Pineapple Crumb Bars, 324–25
baking pans, 7, 28–29, 371
bar shapes, to cut, 281, 309
Blackberry Cream Squares (v), 310
Blackberry Squares (v), 296
Blueberry Pie Bars, 330
Boysenberry Squares, 296
Buttermilk Spice Bars, 306
Cappuccino Cheesecake Bars, 320
Caramel Pecan Squares, 333
Cashew Caramel Blondies, 305
Cherry Cheesecake Squares, 283
Cherry Crumb Squares, 301
Cherry Pie Bars (v), 330
Chocolate Almond Toffee Bars, 295
Chocolate Chip Coffee Bars, 308–09
Chocolate Mint Bars, 291
Chocolate Walnut Bars, 298
Coconut Pecan Bars, 282
Coconut Pineapple Bars, 292
cooling process, 38
Cranberry Almond Bars, 287
Cranberry Coconut Squares, 322
Cream Cheese Blondies, 290
Creamy Lemon Oat Squares, 327
Deluxe Nut Bars, 304
Golden Coconut Cashew Squares, 316–17
Golden Coconut Macadamia Nut Squares (v), 316–17
Lime Coconut Squares, 331
Lime Squares, 293

Maple Date Pecan Squares, 307
Maple Walnut Squares, 323
Marmalade Crumb Bars, 321
Mincemeat Bars, 334
Nutty Chocolate Squares, 288
Nutty Fruit Bars, 299
Oatmeal Coconut Bars, 311
Orange Cream Squares (v), 310
Peach Pie Bars (v), 330
Peach Squares (v), 312
Peaches and Cream Squares, 310
Peanut Butter Oat Bars, 297
Pecan Pie Bars, 294
Pineapple Nut Cheese Squares, 314–15
Pineapple Squares, 332
Pumpkin Crunch Bars, 302–03
Raspberry Cream Squares (v), 310
Raspberry Oat Squares, 326
Raspberry Streusel Squares, 280–81
Sour Cream Blueberry Squares, 286
Sour Cream Lemon Squares, 300
storing, 38–39
Strawberry Squares, 312
Sunshine Lemon Squares, 284
Tropical Oat Squares, 285
White Chocolate Pumpkin Blondies, 318–19
White Chocolate Raspberry Crumb Squares, 329
biscotti
about, 394–95
Almond Biscotti, 396
Apricot Biscotti, 397
Blueberry Lemon Biscotti, 400
Brownie Biscotti, 407
Cappuccino Biscotti, 410
Cherry Almond Biscotti, 406
Cherry Pecan Biscotti (v), 406
Chocolate Almond Biscotti (v), 398
Chocolate Cherry Almond Biscotti (v), 413
Chocolate Cherry Biscotti, 413
Chocolate Chip Biscotti, 402
Chocolate Chip Orange Biscotti, 418
Chocolate Walnut Biscotti, 398
chocolate-dipped biscotti, 395
chocolate-glazed biscotti, 395
Cinnamon Almond Biscotti (v), 425
Cinnamon Pecan Biscotti (v), 425
Cinnamon Sugar Biscotti, 404
Cinnamon Walnut Biscotti, 425

Coconut Biscotti, 419
Coconut Macadamia Biscotti (v), 419
Cranberry White Chocolate Biscotti, 399
Currant Almond Biscotti, 422
Espresso Biscotti, 415
Gingerbread Biscotti, 426
Gingerbread Walnut Biscotti (v), 426
Hazelnut Chocolate Biscotti, 411
Lemon Almond Biscotti, 416
Lemon Biscotti, 409
Lemon Poppy Seed Biscotti (v), 409
Macadamia Nut Biscotti, 421
Maple Pecan Biscotti, 417
Maple Walnut Biscotti (v), 417
Mocha Almond Biscotti (v), 405
Mocha Biscotti, 405
Nut Biscotti, 414
Orange Biscotti, 403
Pistachio Biscotti, 408
Pumpkin Pecan Biscotti (v), 423
Pumpkin Walnut Biscotti, 423
Raisin Walnut Biscotti (v), 422
Spumoni Biscotti, 401
Triple Chocolate Biscotti, 424
White Chocolate Almond Biscotti (v), 412
White Chocolate Lemon Biscotti, 420
White Chocolate Macadamia Biscotti, 412
white chocolate-dipped biscotti, 395
white chocolate-glazed biscotti, 395
bites. See tassies
Bittersweet Chocolate Chunk Cookies, 132
Bittersweet Chocolate Shortbread, 446
Black and White Chocolate Dreams, 185
blackberries
Blackberry Blossoms (v), 482–83
Blackberry Cream Squares (v), 310
Blackberry Ribbons (v), 552–53
Blackberry Squares (v), 296
Blackberry Triangles, 472–73
blondies. See bars and squares
Blue Ribbon Chocolate Chip Cookies, 120
Blue Ribbon Fudge Brownies, 349
Blue Ribbon Sugar Cookies, 206

blueberries, dried, 24
  Blueberry Lemon Biscotti, 400
  Blueberry Lemon Cookies, 66
  Blueberry Lemon Shortbread, 443
blueberry pie filling
  Blueberry Cheesecake Bites, 476
  Blueberry Pie Bars, 330
  Sour Cream Blueberry Squares, 286
blueberry preserves
  Bachelor Buttons, 534–35
  Blueberry Pillows, 522–23
Boysenberry Blossoms, 482–83
Boysenberry Squares, 296
brown sugar, 14–15, 33
Brown Sugar and Spice Shortbread, 433
Brown Sugar Cookies, 82
Brown Sugar Cutouts, 216–17
Browned Butter Frosting, 64
Brownie Biscotti, 407
brownies
  about, 336
  add-ins, 351
  Amaretto Brownies, 356
  baking pans, 7, 371
  Blue Ribbon Fudge Brownies, 349
  brownie shapes, 341, 385
  Brownie Sundaes, 367
  Brownies Supreme, 392
  Buttermilk Brownies, 372
  Cheesecake Brownies, 342–43
  Chocolate Cream Cheese Brownies, 390–91
  Chocolate Fudge Brownies, 337
  Chocolate Malt Brownies, 370–71
  Chocolate-Lover's Brownies, 354–55
  Chocolate-Topped Brownies, 377
  Classic Brownies, 352
  Cocoa Brownies, 373
  Cocoa Coconut Brownies, 387
  Coconut Brownies, 380
  Coconut Macaroon Brownies, 368
  cooling process, 38
  Cream Cheese Brownies, 361
  Deluxe Brownies, 375
  Double Chocolate Brownies, 365
  Double Chocolate Cream Brownies, 388
  Eggnog Brownies, 381
  Espresso Brownies, 350–51
  Espresso Cream Brownies, 384–85
  Fudge and Fudge Brownies, 383

Fudge Nut Brownies, 344–45
Fudgy Brownies, 360
German Chocolate Brownies, 346–47
Layered Cream Cheese Brownies, 348
Marbled Cream Cheese Brownies, 378–79
Marbled White Chocolate Cream Cheese Brownies, 353
Milk Chocolate Brownies, 386
Mint Brownies, 362–63
Moist, Fudgy Brownies, 382
Moist and Chewy Chocolate Syrup Brownies, 338–39
Peanut Butter Brownies, 376–77
Peanut Butter Swirl Brownies, 358–59
Raspberry Brownies, 369
Raspberry Swirl Brownies, 340–41
Rocky Road Brownies, 366–67
Sour Cream Brownies, 357
storing, 38–39
Toffee Mocha Brownies, 389
Walnut Brownies, 364
White Chocolate Coconut Brownies (v), 374
White Chocolate Macadamia Brownies, 374
butter, about, 17–18, 30–31
Butter Pecan Cookies, 110
Butterhorns, 546–47
buttermilk, about, 21
Buttermilk Brownies, 372
Buttermilk Chocolate Chip Cookies, 122
Buttermilk Spice Bars, 306
Butterscotch Dreams, 186
Butterscotch Pecan Cookies, 63
Butterscotch Shortbread, 441
Butterscotch Slices, 252

C

candied ginger
  Ginger Shortbread, 448
Cappuccino Biscotti, 410
Cappuccino Cheesecake Bars, 320
caramel
  Caramel Pecan Squares, 333
  Cashew Caramel Blondies, 305
  Cashew Caramel Cups, 519
cashews, 24
  Butterscotch Dreams, 186
  Cashew Caramel Blondies, 305
  Cashew Caramel Cups, 519
  Cashew Cookies, 64
  Deluxe Nut Bars, 304

Golden Coconut Cashew Squares, 316–17
Cheesecake Brownies, 342–43
cherries, dried, 24
  Cherry Almond Biscotti, 406
  Cherry Oatmeal Dreams, 198
  Cherry Shortbread, 445
  Chocolate Cherry Biscotti, 413
  Spumoni Biscotti, 401
cherry pie filling
  Cherry Cheesecake Bites (v), 476
  Cherry Pie Bars (v), 330
  Cherry Pie Turnovers, 470–71
cherry preserves
  Cherry Cheesecake Squares, 283
  Cherry Crumb Squares, 301
Chewy Chocolate Chip Cookies, 123
Chewy Oatmeal Cookies, 148
Chewy Peanut Butter Cookies, 74
Chinese Almond Cookies, 111
chocolate. See also white chocolate
  about, 21–23
  Bittersweet Chocolate Shortbread, 446
  Black and White Chocolate Dreams, 185
  Chocolate Almond Dreams, 181
  Chocolate Almond Toffee Bars, 295
  Chocolate Brownie Shortbread, 430–31
  Chocolate Cheesecake Bites, 468–69
  Chocolate Cherry Biscotti, 413
  Chocolate Chocolate Chip Cookies, 138
  Chocolate Coffee Cream Cookies (v), 232–33
  Chocolate Cookies, 78
  Chocolate Cutouts, 244–45
  Chocolate Decadence Dreams, 177
  Chocolate Dreams, 172
  Chocolate Glaze, 55
  Chocolate Mint Bars, 291
  Chocolate Mint Pillows, 540–41
  Chocolate Mint Thins, 256
  Chocolate Nut Rugelach, 518
  Chocolate Sandwich Cookies, 232–33
  Chocolate Spritz Cookies, 116
  Chocolate Thumbprint Cookies, 90
  Chocolate Walnut Bars, 298
  Chocolate Walnut Biscotti, 398
  to chop, 31
  Double Chocolate Dreams, 173

Fudgy Brownie Cookies, 53
Gary's Chocolate Cookies, 87
to melt, 31, 395
Mocha Chip Thins, 266
Mocha Fudge Dreams, 193
Mocha Fudge Truffle Cookies, 46
Mocha Shortbread Bites, 436
Nutty Chocolate Squares, 288
Peanut Butter Oat Bars, 297
Sour Cream Fudge Pouches, 496–97
Triple Chocolate Biscotti, 424
Ultimate Dark Chocolate Espresso Cookies, 73
chocolate chip cookies
about, 22–23, 118
Bittersweet Chocolate Chunk Cookies, 132
Blue Ribbon Chocolate Chip Cookies, 120
Buttermilk Chocolate Chip Cookies, 122
Chewy Chocolate Chip Cookies, 123
Chocolate Chip Almond Cookies, 133
Chocolate Chip Biscotti, 402
Chocolate Chip Coffee Bars, 308–09
Chocolate Chip Dreams, 171
Chocolate Chip Espresso Cookies, 143
Chocolate Chip Heaven Cookies, 119
Chocolate Chip Oatmeal Dreams, 182
Chocolate Chip Orange Biscotti, 418
Chocolate Chip Orange Cookies, 128
Chocolate Chip Shortbread, 435
Chocolate Chip Slices, 260
Chocolate Chip Walnut Cookies, 124
Chocolate Chip Wedding Cookies (v), 94
Chocolate Chocolate Chip Cookies, 138
Chocolate Chunk Cookies, 126
Chocolate Decadence Dreams, 177
Classic Chocolate Chip Cookies, 131
Cream Cheese Chocolate Chip Cookies, 139
Crispy Chocolate Chip Cookies, 141

Deluxe Chocolate Chip Cookies, 137
Double Chocolate Chip Cookies, 121
Double Chocolate Dreams, 173
Glazed Chocolate Chip Cookies, 130
Hazelnut Chocolate Biscotti, 411
Jumbo Chocolate Chip Cookies, 135
Milk Chocolate Chip Cookies, 134
Mini M&M Candy Cookies, 65
Oatmeal Chippers, 150
Orange Chocolate Oat Drops (v), 163
Peanut Butter Chocolate Chippers, 140
Peanut Butter Oat Chippers, 156
Pistachio Chip Dreams (v), 199
Sour Cream Chocolate Chip Cookies, 142
Special Chocolate Chip Cookies, 144
Spumoni Biscotti, 401
Sweet Dark Chocolate Chip Cookies, 127
Tender Chocolate Chip Cookies, 136
Triple Chocolate Chip Cookies, 129
Ultimate Chocolate Chip Heaven Cookies (v), 119
White Chocolate Chip Cookies, 125
Chocolate Cream Cheese Brownies, 390–91
Chocolate Fudge Brownies, 337
Chocolate Malt Brownies, 370–71
Chocolate Syrup Brownies, Moist and Chewy, 338–39
Chocolate-Dipped Cappuccino Sticks, 83
Chocolate-Glazed Coffee Cookies, 269
Chocolate-Glazed Oatmeal Cookies, 159
Chocolate-Lover's Brownies, 354–55
Cinnamon Almond Biscotti (v), 425
Cinnamon Crisps, 253
Cinnamon Pecan Biscotti (v), 425
Cinnamon Spirals, 554
cinnamon sugar, 77
Cinnamon Sugar Biscotti, 404
Cinnamon Sugar Cookies, 240–41
Cinnamon Walnut Biscotti, 425
Cinnamon Walnut Shortbread, 440

citrus fruit, *see also* specific kinds
about, 24–25
lemon yields, 48
lime yields, 99
Meyer lemons, 195
orange yields, 259
Citrus Shortbread, 458
Classic Brownies, 352
Classic Chocolate Chip Cookies, 131
Cocoa Brownies, 373
Cocoa Coconut Brownies, 387
cocoa powders, about, 23, 33
stencil designs, 227
coconut
about, 24
Apricot Coconut Dreams, 187
Apricot Coconut Oatmeal Drops, 166
Apricot Crunch Squares, 289
Apricot Pineapple Crumb Bars, 324–25
Apricot Pineapple Tassies, 466–67
Banana Rum Oatmeal Cookies, 160
Chocolate-Glazed Oatmeal Cookies, 159
Cocoa Coconut Brownies, 387
CocoMac Dreams, 189
Coconut Almond Cookies (v), 100
Coconut Biscotti, 419
Coconut Brownies, 380
Coconut Cookies, 50
Coconut Crisps, 263
Coconut Dreams, 183
Coconut Lemon Cookies (v), 86
Coconut Lemon Specials, 530–31
Coconut Lime Cookies, 86
Coconut Macadamia Rugelach, 498–99
Coconut Macaroon Brownies, 368
Coconut Macaroons, 55
Coconut Oat Chews, 155
Coconut Oat Dreams, 194
Coconut Pecan Bars, 282
Coconut Pecan Cookies, 100
Coconut Pecan Frosting, 346–47
Coconut Pineapple Bars, 292
Coconut Pineapple Cups, 490–91
Coconut Shortbread, 434
Coconut Walnut Cookies (v), 100
Cranberry Coconut Cookies, 80
Cranberry Coconut Squares, 322
German Chocolate Brownies, 346–47

coconut (*continued*)
  Golden Coconut Cashew Squares, 316–17
  Hawaiian Cookies, 62
  Hawaiian Pinwheels, 474–75
  Lime Coconut Squares, 331
  Nutty Chocolate Squares, 288
  Nutty Fruit Bars, 299
  Oatmeal Ambrosia Dreams, 192
  Oatmeal Coconut Bars, 311
  Piña Colada Cookies (v), 62
  Pineapple Apricot Oatmeal Drops, 152
  Raspberry Coconut Spirals, 485
  Raspberry Oat Squares, 326
  Tropical Dreams, 196
  Tropical Oat Cookies, 158
  Tropical Oat Squares, 285
  Tropical Shortbread, 447
  White Chocolate Chip Coconut Cookies (v), 125
  White Chocolate Coconut Brownies (v), 374
  White Chocolate Coconut Cookies, 43
  White Chocolate Coconut Shortbread (v), 454
coffee, 26
  Cappuccino Biscotti, 410
  Cappuccino Cheesecake Bars, 320
  Chocolate Chip Coffee Bars, 308–09
  Chocolate Chip Espresso Cookies, 143
  Chocolate Coffee Cream Cookies (v), 232–33
  Chocolate-Dipped Cappuccino Sticks, 83
  Chocolate-Glazed Coffee Cookies, 269
  Coffee Almond Rounds, 105
  Espresso Biscotti, 415
  Espresso Brownies, 350–51
  Espresso Cream Brownies, 384–85
  Espresso Dreams, 184
  Espresso Sandwich Cookies, 242–43
  Espresso Shortbread, 457
  Mocha Biscotti, 405
  Mocha Chip Thins, 266
  Mocha Fudge Dreams, 193
  Mocha Fudge Truffle Cookies, 46
  Mocha Shortbread Bites, 436
  Toffee Mocha Brownies, 389
  Ultimate Dark Chocolate Espresso Cookies, 73

confectioner's sugar, 15, 33
Cookie Baking 101, 27
cookie baking parties, 473
cookie competitions, 555–58
  cookie mistakes, 558
  fair entry requirements, 555
  judges evaluation criteria, 556
  judging standards, 556
  judging systems, 556–57
cookie crusts, method for, 276
cookie cutter ornaments, 225
cookie cutters, 10–11, 233
cookie decorating
  cocoa powder stencil designs, 227
  cookie doughs, tinting, 209
  cookie ornaments, 235
  egg paint, 211
  finishing touches, 38
  iced cookies, painting, 219
  lollipop cookies, 231
  milk paint, 223
  pastry bags, 241
  sugar sparkles, 221
  sugar stencil designs, 245
cookie decorating parties, 215
cookie dessert buffets, 521, 523
cookie doughs
  chilling, 37
  freezing, 39–40
  mixing methods, 34–37
  to roll out, 204–05
  to shape for slice-and-bake cookies, 250, 255, 265
  to tint, 209
cookie exchange parties, 463, 541
  hosting, 547, 549
  planning, 543, 545
cookie place cards, 217
cookie presses, 11
cookie scoops, 10
cookie sheets
  choosing, 6–7
  preparing, 28–29
cookie texture, 556
  and baking time, 38
  and dairy products, 20–21
  effect of sugar on, 13–17
  problem solver, 560–61
cookie therapy, 431
corn syrup, 13, 16, 33
Cornmeal Shortbread, 459
cornstarch, 13
cranberries, dried, 24
  Applesauce Cranberry Oatmeal Cookies (v), 167
  Apricot Cranberry Oat Dreams, 201
  Cranberry Almond Slices, 268

  Cranberry Apricot Dreams, 191
  Cranberry Coconut Cookies, 80
  Cranberry Coconut Squares, 322
  Cranberry Nut Cookies, 47
  Cranberry Oat Cookies, 151
  Cranberry Orange Cookies, 56
  Cranberry Orange Spirals, 532–33
  Cranberry Orange Walnut Tassies, 488–89
  Cranberry Shortbread, 438
  Cranberry White Chocolate Biscotti, 399
  Nutty Fruit Bars, 299
  Oatmeal Cranberry Pecan Dreams, 180
cranberries, fresh
  Cranberry Almond Bars, 287
cranberry sauce
  Cranberry Pinwheels, 508–09
cream, types of, 21
cream cheese
  about, 21
  Almond Bites, 506
  Almond Pockets, 478–79
  Apricot Horns, 520–21
  Apricot Pecan Cups, 550–51
  Apricot Rugelach, 536–37
  Blackberry Triangles, 472–73
  Blueberry Cheesecake Bites, 476
  Blueberry Pillows, 522–23
  Cappuccino Cheesecake Bars, 320
  Cheesecake Brownies, 342–43
  Cherry Cheesecake Bites (v), 476
  Cherry Cheesecake Squares, 283
  Chocolate Cheesecake Bites, 468–69
  Chocolate Cream Cheese Brownies, 390–91
  Chocolate Nut Rugelach, 518
  Coconut Macadamia Rugelach, 498–99
  Coconut Pineapple Cups, 490–91
  Cranberry Orange Walnut Tassies, 488–89
  Cream Cheese Blondies, 290
  Cream Cheese Brownies, 361
  Cream Cheese Chocolate Chip Cookies, 139
  Cream Cheese Citrus Rounds, 267
  Cream Cheese Sugar Cookies, 210–11
  Cream Cheese Walnut Cookies, 102
  Espresso Cream Brownies, 384–85

Hawaiian Pinwheels, 474–75
Layered Cream Cheese Brownies, 348
Lemon Cheese Pinwheels, 526–27
Lemon Cheesecake Bites, 492
Lime Cheesecake Bites (v), 492
Maple Walnut Tartlets, 506
Marbled Cream Cheese Brownies, 378–79
Marbled White Chocolate Cream Cheese Brownies, 353
Mint Brownies, 362–63
Orange Almond Cups, 528
Orange Cheesecake Bites (v), 492
Orange Cream Horns, 538–39
Peaches and Cream Squares, 310
Peanut Butter Swirl Brownies, 358–59
Pecan Tassies, 484
Pineapple Horns, 504–05
Pineapple Nut Cheese Squares, 314–15
Pineapple Tartlets, 529
Pumpkin Walnut Tassies, 502–03
Raspberry Almond Cream Cheese Pockets, 514–15
Raspberry Rugelach (v), 536–37
Raspberry Swirl Brownies, 340–41
Rugelach, 480–81
Strawberry Cream Horns, 512–13
Walnut Horns, 486–87
White Chocolate Cheesecake Bites (v), 468–69
cream of tartar, 20
Crispy Chocolate Chip Cookies, 141
crumb toppings, 276
Currant Almond Biscotti, 422
cutout cookies. See rolled cutout cookies
cutting boards, 8

D

dairy products, about, 20–21, 31
dates, 24
    Date Walnut Slices, 264
    Maple Date Pecan Squares, 307
decorating bag, to improvise, 205
decoration of cookies
    cocoa powder stencil designs, 227
    cookie doughs, tinting, 209
    cookie ornaments, 235
    egg paint, 211
    finishing touches, 38
    iced cookies, painting, 219
    lollipop cookies, 231

milk paint, 223
pastry bags, 241
sugar sparkles, 221
sugar stencil designs, 245
Deluxe Brownies, 375
Deluxe Chocolate Chip Cookies, 137
Deluxe Nut Bars, 304
dessert parties, 521, 523
Doodle Dreams, 197
Double Almond Cookies, 98
Double Butterscotch Dreams (v), 186
Double Chocolate Brownies, 365
Double Chocolate Chip Cookies, 121
Double Chocolate Cream Brownies, 388
Double Chocolate Dreams, 173
dough tampers, 11, 462
dream cookies
    about, 170
    Apricot Coconut Dreams, 187
    Apricot Cranberry Oat Dreams, 201
    Apricot Dreams, 175
    Black and White Chocolate Dreams, 185
    Butterscotch Dreams, 186
    Cherry Oatmeal Dreams, 198
    Chocolate Almond Dreams, 181
    Chocolate Chip Dreams, 171
    Chocolate Chip Oatmeal Dreams, 182
    Chocolate Decadence Dreams, 177
    Chocolate Dreams, 172
    Chocolate Hazelnut Dreams (v), 181
    Chocolate Pecan Dreams (v), 181
    Chocolate Walnut Dreams (v), 181
    CocoMac Dreams, 189
    Coconut Dreams, 183
    Coconut Oat Dreams, 194
    Cranberry Apricot Dreams, 191
    Doodle Dreams, 197
    Double Butterscotch Dreams (v), 186
    Double Chocolate Dreams, 173
    Double White Chocolate Dreams, 179
    Espresso Dreams, 184
    Golden Oatmeal Dreams, 188
    Lemon Dreams, 195
    Maple Pecan Dreams, 176
    Mocha Fudge Dreams, 193
    Oatmeal Ambrosia Dreams, 192

Oatmeal Cranberry Pecan Dreams, 180
Oatmeal Dreams, 174
Orange Dreams, 190
Pineapple Dreams, 200
Pistachio Dreams, 199
Toffee Dreams, 202
Tropical Dreams, 196
White Chocolate Chip Dreams, 178
dried fruit, about, 24–25, 31–32
drop cookies
    about, 42
    Amaretti, 60
    Apple Walnut Cookies, 68–69
    Blueberry Lemon Cookies, 66
    Butterscotch Pecan Cookies, 63
    Cashew Cookies, 64
    chilling, 37
    Coconut Cookies, 50
    Coconut Macaroons, 55
    cookie sheets, 6–7, 28–29
    Cranberry Nut Cookies, 47
    Cranberry Orange Cookies, 56
    to freeze dough, 40
    Fudgy Brownie Cookies, 53
    giant cookies, to bake, 42
    Hawaiian Cookies, 62
    Lemon Drops, 48
    Malted Milk Cookies, 70
    Maple Walnut Cookies, 51
    Michael's Mom's Persimmon Cookies, 58
    Mincemeat Cookies, 67
    Mini M&M Candy Cookies, 65
    Mocha Fudge Truffle Cookies, 46
    Orange Cookies, 61
    Orange Marmalade Cookies, 52
    Peanut Butter Cookies, 49
    Piña Colada Cookies (v), 62
    Pineapple Cookies, 54
    Pumpkin Spice Cookies, 44–45
    Tangy Lime Cookies, 57
    Toffee Cookies, 59
    White Chocolate Coconut Cookies, 43

E

egg paint, 211
egg substitutes, about, 174
Eggnog Brownies, 381
Eggnog Cookies, 254–55
Eggnog Sugar Cookies, 113
eggs, about, 20, 31
Eier Kringle, 218–19
English Toffee Cookies, 106–07
Espresso Biscotti, 415
Espresso Brownies, 350–51

Espresso Cream Brownies, 384–85
Espresso Dreams, 184
Espresso Sandwich Cookies, 242–43
Espresso Shortbread, 457
evaporated milk, 21
extracts and flavorings, about, 25–26
extra-special cookies
  about, 462–63
  Almond Bites, 507
  Almond Pockets, 478–79
  Apple Butter Turnovers, 516–17
  Apricot Horns, 520–21
  Apricot Orange Cups, 500
  Apricot Pecan Cups, 550–51
  Apricot Pie Cookies (v), 501
  Apricot Pineapple Tassies, 466–67
  Apricot Ribbons (v), 552–53
  Apricot Rugelach, 536–37
  Bachelor Buttons, 534–35
  Blackberry Blossoms (v), 482–83
  Blackberry Ribbons (v), 552–53
  Blackberry Triangles, 472–73
  Blueberry Cheesecake Bites, 476
  Blueberry Pillows, 522–23
  Boysenberry Blossoms, 482–83
  Butterhorns, 546–47
  Cashew Caramel Cups, 519
  Cherry Cheesecake Bites (v), 476
  Cherry Pie Turnovers, 470–71
  Chocolate Cheesecake Bites, 468–69
  Chocolate Mint Pillows, 540–41
  Chocolate Nut Rugelach, 518
  Cinnamon Spirals, 554
  Coconut Lemon Specials, 530–31
  Coconut Macadamia Rugelach, 498–99
  Coconut Pineapple Cups, 490–91
  Cranberry Orange Spirals, 532–33
  Cranberry Orange Walnut Tassies, 488–89
  Cranberry Pinwheels, 508–09
  Hawaiian Pinwheels, 474–75
  Lemon Almond Sticks, 548–49
  Lemon Cheese Pinwheels, 526–27
  Lemon Cheesecake Bites, 492
  Lime Cheesecake Bites (v), 492
  Luscious Lemon Tartlets, 510–11
  Maple Pecan Spirals, 524–25
  Maple Walnut Tartlets, 506
  Orange Almond Cups, 528
  Orange Cheesecake Bites (v), 492
  Orange Cream Horns, 538–39
  Orange Curd Cups, 494–95
  Orange Walnut Spirals, 477
  Peach Pie Cookies, 501
  Pecan Tassies, 484
  Pineapple Horns, 504–05
  Pineapple Tartlets, 529
  Pinwheel Jam Cookies, 542–43
  Pumpkin Walnut Tassies, 502–03
  Raspberry Almond Cream Cheese Pockets, 514–15
  Raspberry Coconut Spirals, 485
  Raspberry Heart Cookies, 464–65
  Raspberry Ribbons, 552–53
  Raspberry Rugelach (v), 536–37
  Rugelach, 480–81
  Sour Cream Fudge Pouches, 496–97
  Strawberry Cream Horns, 512–13
  Strawberry Delights, 544–45
  Strawberry Ribbons (v), 552–53
  Strawberry Spirals, 493
  Walnut Horns, 486–87
  White Chocolate Cheesecake Bites (v), 468–69

F

fats, about, 17–19
Favorite Sugar Cookies, 81
Festive Sugar Cookies, 112
filled cookies
  about, 463
  Almond Pockets, 478–79
  Apricot Horns, 520–21
  Apricot Pie Cookies (v), 501
  Apricot Ribbons (v), 552–53
  Blackberry Blossoms (v), 482–83
  Blackberry Triangles, 472–73
  Blueberry Pillows, 522–23
  Boysenberry Blossoms, 482–83
  Cherry Pie Turnovers, 470–71
  Chocolate Mint Pillows, 540–41
  Coconut Lemon Specials, 530–31
  Lemon Almond Sticks, 548–49
  Orange Cream Horns, 538–39
  Peach Pie Cookies, 501
  Pineapple Horns, 504–05
  Raspberry Almond Cream Cheese Pockets, 514–15
  Raspberry Heart Cookies, 464–65
  Raspberry Ribbons, 552–53
  Sour Cream Fudge Pouches, 496–97
  Strawberry Cream Horns, 512–13
  Strawberry Delights, 544–45
  Strawberry Ribbons (v), 552–53
  Walnut Horns, 486–87
flours, about, 12–13, 32
foil, 10
foil pans, 371
food processors, 6, 35
Frosted Marmalade Oat Cookies, 168
frostings, glazes and icings
  about, 38
  Browned Butter Frosting, 64
  Chocolate Glaze, 55, 362
  Chocolate-Topped Brownies, 377
  Coconut Pecan Frosting, 346–47
  decorating bag, to improvise, 205
  to keep soft, 237
  pastry bags, 241
  Royal Icing, 212–13
fruit ingredients
  about, 24–25, 31–32
Fudge and Fudge Brownies, 383
Fudge Nut Brownies, 344–45
Fudgy Brownie Cookies, 53
Fudgy Brownies, 360
fundraisers, 463, 531
  cookie packaging, 535
  planning, 533
  setting up, 537

G

Gary's Chocolate Cookies, 87
German Chocolate Brownies, 346–47
giant cookies, to bake, 42
gift ideas
  basket containers, 525
  beach pail packaging, 247
  cookie baking kits, 487
  cookie favors, 517
  cookie jars, 107, 481
  cookie place cards, 217
  cookie shapes, 243
  cookie tins, 505
  cookie-of-the-month, 551
  gift wrapping ideas, 491
  holiday gift giving, 495
  host or hostess gifts, 303, 499
  lollipop cookies, 231
  mailing packages, 558–59
  mixing bowl containers, 509
  plant pot cookie container, 317
  toolbox cookie container, 359
  "Welcome to the Neighborhood", 69
Ginger Cookies, 103
Ginger Shortbread, 448
Gingerbread Biscotti, 426
Gingerbread Cookies, Old-time, 212–13
Gingerbread Walnut Biscotti (v), 426
Glazed Almond Slices, 261

Glazed Chocolate Chip Cookies, 130
Glazed Lemon Shortbread, 432
Glazed Lime Cookies, 99
Glazed Orange Cutouts, 228–29
glazes. *See* frostings, glazes and icings
Golden Coconut Cashew Squares, 316–17
Golden Coconut Macadamia Nut Squares (v), 316–17
Golden Oatmeal Dreams, 188
grains, about, 13

H

hand-shaped cookies
    about, 72
    Almond Logs, 114
    Brown Sugar Cookies, 82
    Butter Pecan Cookies, 110
    Chewy Peanut Butter Cookies, 74
    chilling, 37
    Chinese Almond Cookies, 111
    Chocolate Chip Wedding Cookies (v), 94
    Chocolate Cookies, 78
    Chocolate Spritz Cookies, 116
    Chocolate Thumbprint Cookies, 90
    Chocolate-Dipped Cappuccino Sticks, 83
    Chocolate-Glazed Oatmeal Cookies, 159
    Classic Peanut Butter Cookies, 96
    Coconut Almond Cookies (v), 100
    Coconut Lemon Cookies (v), 86
    Coconut Lime Cookies, 86
    Coconut Pecan Cookies, 100
    Coconut Walnut Cookies (v), 100
    Coffee Almond Rounds, 105
    cookie sheets, 6–7, 28–29
    Cranberry Apricot Coconut Cookies (v), 80
    Cranberry Coconut Cookies, 80
    Cream Cheese Walnut Cookies, 102
    Double Almond Cookies, 98
    Eggnog Sugar Cookies, 113
    English Toffee Cookies, 106–07
    Favorite Sugar Cookies, 81
    Festive Sugar Cookies, 112
    to freeze dough, 40
    Gary's Chocolate Cookies, 87
    Ginger Cookies, 103
    Glazed Lime Cookies, 99
    Lemon Balls, 101
    Lemon Crinkles, 76
    Lemon Spritz Cookies (v), 115

Lemon Sugar Cookies, 88
Lemon Wedding Cake Cookies (v), 95
Mexican Wedding Cake Cookies, 94
Molasses Cookies, 79
Oatmeal Almond Cookies, 164
Orange Balls (v), 101
Orange Spritz Cookies (v), 115
Orange Sugar Cookies (v), 88
Orange Wedding Cake Cookies, 95
Peanut Butter Chews, 104
Peanut Butter Jam Thumbprints, 91
Pecan Sandies, 75
Rum Cookies, 97
Snickerdoodles, 77
Spice Cookies, 85
Spritz Cookies, 115
Swedish Tea Cookies, 108
Thumbprint Cookies, 89
Tropical Oat Cookies, 158
Ultimate Dark Chocolate Espresso Cookies, 73
Viennese Vanilla Crescents, 84
White Chocolate Cookies, 109
White Chocolate Raspberry Thumbprints, 92–93
Hawaiian Cookies, 62
Hawaiian Pinwheels, 474–75
hazelnuts
    about, 24
    Chocolate Hazelnut Dreams (v), 181
    Hazelnut Chocolate Biscotti, 411
holiday cookies
    Almond Logs, 114
    Apricot Ribbons (v), 552–53
    calendar suggestions, 239
    cookie exchange parties, 541
    Eggnog Brownies, 381
    Eggnog Cookies, 254–55
    Eggnog Sugar Cookies, 113
    Eier Kringle, 218–19
    Festive Sugar Cookies, 112
    Holiday Sugar Cookies, 214–15
    Mincemeat Cookies, 67
    Raspberry Ribbons, 552–53
    Snowflake Cookies, 224–25
    Strawberry Ribbons (v), 552–53
    Sugar Cookie Slices, 272
    Swedish Tea Cookies, 108
    Vanilla Cookie Cutter Cookies, 208–09
honey, 13, 16, 33
horn cookies
    about, 463

Apricot Horns, 520–21
Orange Cream Horns, 538–39
Pineapple Horns, 504–05
Strawberry Cream Horns, 512–13
Walnut Horns, 486–87

I

icebox cookies. *See* refrigerator slice-and-bake cookies
icings. *See* frostings, glazes and icings
ingredients, about, 12–26
    chocolate, 21–23, 31
    cocoa powders, 23
    cornstarch, 13
    cream of tartar, 20
    dairy products, 20–21, 31
    eggs, 20, 31
    extracts and flavorings, 25–26
    fats, 17–19, 30–32
    flours, 12–13
    fruit ingredients, 24–25, 31–32
    grains, 13
    leaveners, 19–20
    measurement equivalents, 34
    measuring, 9, 32–33
    mixing methods, 34–37
    nuts, 23–24, 31–32
    oats, 13
    preparation of, 30–32
    salt, 26
    spices, 26
    sugars and sweeteners, 13–17, 32–33
instant pudding mixes. *See* dream cookies

J

jams, as fillings, 25
Jumbo Chocolate Chip Cookies, 135

K

kitchen equipment. *See* baking equipment

L

Layered Cream Cheese Brownies, 348
leaveners, about, 19–20
lemon
    Blueberry Lemon Biscotti, 400
    Blueberry Lemon Cookies, 66
    Blueberry Lemon Shortbread, 443
    Citrus Shortbread, 458
    Coconut Lemon Cookies (v), 86
    Coconut Lemon Specials, 530–31

lemon (*continued*)
Cream Cheese Citrus Rounds, 267
Creamy Lemon Oat Squares, 327
fresh fruit yields, 48
Glazed Lemon Shortbread, 432
Lemon Almond Biscotti, 416
Lemon Almond Sticks, 548–49
Lemon Balls, 101
Lemon Biscotti, 409
Lemon Cheese Pinwheels, 526–27
Lemon Cheesecake Bites, 492
Lemon Crinkles, 76
lemon curd, 510
Lemon Dreams, 195
Lemon Drops, 48
Lemon Poppy Seed Biscotti (v), 409
Lemon Poppy Seed Shortbread, 453
Lemon Sandwich Cookies, 262
Lemon Slices, 251
Lemon Spritz Cookies (v), 115
Lemon Sugar Cookies, 88, 220–21
Lemon Wedding Cake Cookies (v), 95
Luscious Lemon Tartlets, 510–11
Meyer lemons, 195
Sour Cream Lemon Squares, 300
Sunshine Lemon Squares, 284
White Chocolate Lemon Biscotti, 420
lime
Coconut Lime Cookies, 86
fresh fruit yields, 99, 238
Glazed Lime Cookies, 99
Lime Cheesecake Bites (v), 492
Lime Coconut Squares, 331
Lime Cutouts, 238–39
Lime Shortbread, 442
Lime Squares, 293
Margarita Cookies, 274
Tangy Lime Cookies, 57
liquid sweeteners, 13, 16, 33
lollipop cookies, 231
Lots of Oats Cookies, 161

M
macadamia nuts
about, 24
Apricot Dreams, 175
Apricot Pineapple Crumb Bars, 324–25
Black and White Chocolate Dreams, 185
CocoMac Dreams, 189

Coconut Macadamia Biscotti (v), 419
Coconut Macadamia Rugelach, 498–99
Cranberry Apricot Dreams, 191
Double White Chocolate Dreams, 179
Golden Coconut Macadamia Nut Squares (v), 316–17
Hawaiian Cookies, 62
Hawaiian Pinwheels, 474–75
Macadamia Nut Biscotti, 421
Macadamia Nut Shortbread, 444
Oatmeal Ambrosia Dreams, 192
Pineapple Apricot Oatmeal Drops, 152
Pineapple Nut Cheese Squares, 314–15
Raspberry Coconut Spirals, 485
Tropical Dreams, 196
Tropical Oat Cookies, 158
Tropical Shortbread, 447
White Chocolate Chip Cookies, 125
White Chocolate Cookies, 109
White Chocolate Macadamia Biscotti, 412
White Chocolate Macadamia Brownies, 374
White Chocolate Macadamia Shortbread (v), 454
mailing, packaging for, 558–59
Malted Milk Cookies, 70
maple
Maple Date Pecan Squares, 307
Maple Leaf Cookies, 230–31
Maple Nut Wafers, 257
Maple Pecan Biscotti, 417
Maple Pecan Dreams, 176
Maple Pecan Shortbread, 437
Maple Pecan Spirals, 524–25
Maple Walnut Cookies, 51
Maple Walnut Squares, 323
Maple Walnut Tartlets, 506
Oatmeal Walnut Cookies, 149
maple syrup, 13
Marbled Cream Cheese Brownies, 378–79
margarine, about, 18
Margarita Cookies, 274
Marmalade Crumb Bars, 321
marshmallows, 366
measurement equivalents, 34
measuring equipment, 9, 32–33
Mexican Wedding Cake Cookies, 94
Microplane graters, 11
Milk Chocolate Brownies, 386

Milk Chocolate Chip Cookies, 134
milk paint, 223
Mincemeat Bars, 334
Mincemeat Cookies, 67
Mini M&M Candy Cookies, 65
mint
Chocolate Mint Bars, 291
Chocolate Mint Pillows, 540–41
Chocolate Mint Thins, 256
Mint Brownies, 362–63
Mocha Almond Biscotti (v), 405
Mocha Biscotti, 405
Mocha Chip Thins, 266
Mocha Fudge Dreams, 193
Mocha Shortbread Bites, 436
Moist, Fudgy Brownies, 382
molasses, 13, 16, 33
Molasses Cookies, 79
Molasses Oat Cookies, 162
Molasses Slices, 270

N
Nut Biscotti, 414
Nutmeg Cookies, 246–47
nutmeg sugar, 113
nuts, *see also* specific kinds (almonds, pecans, etc.)
about, 23–24, 31–32
to toast, 32
Nutty Chocolate Squares, 288
Nutty Fruit Bars, 299

O
oatmeal cookies
about, 146
Applesauce Oatmeal Cookies, 167
Apricot Coconut Oatmeal Drops, 166
Apricot Cranberry Oat Dreams, 201
Banana Rum Oatmeal Cookies, 160
Banana Walnut Oatmeal Cookies, 165
Cherry Oatmeal Dreams, 198
Chewy Oatmeal Cookies, 148
Chocolate Chip Oatmeal Dreams, 182
Chocolate-Glazed Oatmeal Cookies, 159
Coconut Oat Chews, 155
Coconut Oat Dreams, 194
Cranberry Oat Cookies, 151
Frosted Marmalade Oat Cookies, 168
Golden Oatmeal Dreams, 188
Lots of Oats Cookies, 161

Molasses Oat Cookies, 162
Oatmeal Almond Cookies, 164
Oatmeal Ambrosia Dreams, 192
Oatmeal Chippers, 150
Oatmeal Cranberry Pecan
   Dreams, 180
Oatmeal Dreams, 174
Oatmeal Nut Chippers (v), 150
Oatmeal Pumpkin Cookies, 157
Oatmeal Raisin Cookies, 147
Oatmeal Shortbread, 460
Oatmeal Walnut Cookies, 149
Old-Fashioned Oatmeal Cookies,
   153
Orange Oat Drops, 163
Peanut Butter Oat Chippers, 156
Pineapple Apricot Oatmeal
   Drops, 152
Tropical Oat Cookies, 158
White Chocolate Oatmeal
   Cookies, 154
oats
   about, 13
   Apricot Pineapple Crumb Bars,
      324–25
   Creamy Lemon Oat Squares, 327
   measuring, 32
   Oatmeal Coconut Bars, 311
   Peanut Butter Oat Bars, 297
   Raspberry Oat Squares, 326
   Tropical Oat Squares, 285
oil, about, 17, 19
orange
   Apricot Biscotti, 397
   Apricot Coconut Dreams, 187
   Apricot Orange Cups, 500
   Apricot Pineapple Crumb Bars,
      324–25
   Chocolate Chip Orange Biscotti,
      418
   Chocolate Chip Orange Cookies,
      128
   Citrus Shortbread, 458
   Cranberry Orange Cookies, 56
   Cranberry Orange Spirals,
      532–33
   Cranberry Orange Walnut
      Tassies, 488–89
   Cream Cheese Citrus Rounds,
      267
   fresh fruit yields, 259
   Frosted Marmalade Oat Cookies,
      168
   Glazed Orange Cutouts, 228–29
   Marmalade Crumb Bars, 321
   Nutty Fruit Bars, 299
   Orange Almond Cups, 528
   Orange Balls (v), 101

Orange Biscotti, 403
Orange Cheesecake Bites (v), 492
Orange Chocolate Oat Drops (v),
   163
Orange Clouds, 259
Orange Cookies, 61
Orange Cream Horns, 538–39
Orange Cream Squares (v), 310
Orange Curd Cups, 494–95
Orange Dreams, 190
Orange Marmalade Cookies, 52
Orange Oat Drops, 163
Orange Shortbread, 450
Orange Spritz Cookies (v), 115
Orange Sugar Cookies (v), 88
Orange Walnut Spirals, 477
Orange Wedding Cake Cookies,
   95
ornaments, cookies as, 235
oven temperature, checking, 9,
   29–30

P

pastry bags, 241
pastry boards, 8–9
Peach Pie Bars (v), 330
Peach Pie Cookies, 501
Peach Squares (v), 312
Peaches and Cream Squares, 310
peanut butter
   Chewy Peanut Butter Cookies, 74
   Classic Peanut Butter Cookies, 96
   measuring, 33
   Peanut Butter Brownies, 376–77
   Peanut Butter Chews, 104
   Peanut Butter Chocolate
      Chippers, 140
   Peanut Butter Cookies, 49
   Peanut Butter Cutouts, 248
   Peanut Butter Jam Thumbprints,
      91
   Peanut Butter Oat Bars, 297
   Peanut Butter Oat Chippers, 156
   Peanut Butter Shortbread, 456
   Peanut Butter Swirl Brownies,
      358–59
peanuts, 24
pecans, 24
   Apricot Pecan Cups, 550–51
   Butter Pecan Cookies, 110
   Buttermilk Chocolate Chip
      Cookies, 122
   Butterscotch Pecan Cookies, 63
   Caramel Pecan Squares, 333
   Cherry Pecan Biscotti (v), 406
   Chewy Oatmeal Cookies, 148
   Chocolate Chip Espresso Cookies
      (v), 143

Chocolate Pecan Dreams (v), 181
Chocolate Thumbprint Cookies,
   90
Cinnamon Pecan Biscotti (v), 425
Classic Chocolate Chip Nut
   Cookies (v), 131
Coconut Brownies, 380
Coconut Pecan Bars, 282
Coconut Pecan Cookies, 100
Coconut Pecan Frosting, 346–47
Cranberry Nut Cookies, 47
Cranberry Oat Cookies, 151
Cranberry Orange Spirals,
   532–33
Crispy Chocolate Chip Nut
   Cookies (v), 141
Deluxe Chocolate Chip Cookies,
   137
Deluxe Nut Bars, 304
Double Chocolate Cream
   Brownies, 388
Fudge Nut Brownies, 344–45
Glazed Chocolate Chip Cookies
   (v), 130
Maple Date Pecan Squares, 307
Maple Pecan Biscotti, 417
Maple Pecan Dreams, 176
Maple Pecan Shortbread, 437
Maple Pecan Spirals, 524–25
Mexican Wedding Cake Cookies,
   94
Mocha Fudge Truffle Cookies, 46
Nut Biscotti, 414
Nutty Chocolate Squares, 288
Nutty Fruit Bars, 299
Oatmeal Cranberry Pecan
   Dreams, 180
Oatmeal Nut Chippers (v), 150
Oatmeal Pumpkin Cookies, 157
Oatmeal Raisin Cookies, 147
Orange Pecan dreams (v), 190
Pecan Pie Bars, 294
Pecan Rounds, 265
Pecan Sandies, 75
Pecan Shortbread, 455
Pecan Tassies, 484
Pumpkin Crunch Bars, 302–03
Pumpkin Pecan Biscotti (v), 423
Pumpkin Spice Cookies, 44–45
Rugelach, 480–81
Sour Cream Brownies, 357
Toffee Dreams, 202
Toffee Mocha Brownies, 389
Toffee Shortbread, 451
Triple Chocolate Chip Nut
   Cookies (v), 129
White Chocolate Pumpkin
   Blondies, 318–19

Persimmon Cookies, Michael's
Mom's, 58
Piña Colada Cookies (v), 62
pineapple
Apricot Pineapple Bars, 278–79
Apricot Pineapple Crumb Bars,
324–25
Apricot Pineapple Tassies,
466–67
Coconut Pineapple Bars, 292
Coconut Pineapple Cups, 490–91
Hawaiian Cookies, 62
Hawaiian Pinwheels, 474–75
Nutty Fruit Bars, 299
Oatmeal Ambrosia Dreams, 192
Piña Colada Cookies (v), 62
Pineapple Apricot Oatmeal
Drops, 152
Pineapple Cookies, 54
Pineapple Dreams, 200
Pineapple Horns, 504–05
Pineapple Nut Cheese Squares,
314–15
Pineapple Squares, 332
Pineapple Tartlets, 529
Tropical Dreams, 196
Tropical Oat Cookies, 158
Tropical Shortbread, 447
pinwheel cookies
about, 462
Cranberry Pinwheels, 508–09
Hawaiian Pinwheels, 474–75
Lemon Cheese Pinwheels,
526–27
Pinwheel Jam Cookies, 542–43
pistachio nuts, 24
Pistachio Biscotti, 408
Pistachio Dreams, 199
Spumoni Biscotti, 401
problem solver, 560–61
pumpkin
Oatmeal Pumpkin Cookies, 157
Pumpkin Crunch Bars, 302–03
Pumpkin Spice Cookies, 44–45
Pumpkin Walnut Biscotti, 423
Pumpkin Walnut Tassies,
502–03
White Chocolate Pumpkin
Blondies, 318–19

R

raisins, 24
Applesauce Raisin Oatmeal
Cookies (v), 167
Chewy Oatmeal Cookies, 148
Golden Oatmeal Dreams, 188
Lots of Oats Cookies, 161
Oatmeal Raisin Cookies, 147

Oatmeal Raisin Dreams (v), 174
Raisin Walnut Biscotti (v), 422
raspberries
Marbled White Chocolate Cream
Cheese Brownies, 353
Raspberry Almond Cream Cheese
Pockets, 514–15
Raspberry Brownies, 369
Raspberry Coconut Spirals, 485
Raspberry Cream Sandwich
Cookies, 236–37
Raspberry Cream Squares (v),
310
Raspberry Heart Cookies, 464–65
Raspberry Oat Squares, 326
Raspberry Ribbons, 552–53
Raspberry Rugelach (v), 536–37
Raspberry Streusel Squares,
280–81
Raspberry Swirl Brownies,
340–41
White Chocolate Raspberry
Crumb Squares, 329
White Chocolate Raspberry
Thumbprints, 92–93
raw sugar, 15–16
refined sugar, 13–14
refrigerator slice-and-bake cookies
about, 250
Apricot Slices, 273
Butterscotch Slices, 252
chilling dough, 37
Chocolate Chip Slices, 260
Chocolate Mint Thins, 256
Chocolate-Glazed Coffee
Cookies, 269
Cinnamon Crisps, 253
Coconut Crisps, 263
cookie shapes, 255, 265
Cranberry Almond Slices, 268
Cream Cheese Citrus Rounds,
267
Date Walnut Slices, 264
Eggnog Cookies, 254–55
to freeze dough, 40
Glazed Almond Slices, 261
Lemon Sandwich Cookies, 262
Lemon Slices, 251
Maple Nut Wafers, 257
Margarita Cookies, 274
Mocha Chip Thins, 266
Molasses Slices, 270
Orange Clouds, 259
Pecan Rounds, 265
Sugar Cookie Slices, 272
Vanilla Slices, 258
White Chocolate Rounds, 271
Rocky Road Brownies, 366–67

rolled cutout cookies
about, 204–05
Almond Cutouts, 222–23
Apricot Cream Sandwich Cookies
(v), 236–37
Blue Ribbon Sugar Cookies, 206
Brown Sugar Cutouts, 216–17
chilling, 37
Chocolate Coffee Cream Cookies
(v), 232–33
Chocolate Cutouts, 244–45
Chocolate Sandwich Cookies,
232–33
Cinnamon Sugar Cookies,
240–41
cookie shapes, 233
cookie sheets, 6–7, 28–29
Cream Cheese Sugar Cookies,
210–11
Eier Kringle, 218–19
Espresso Sandwich Cookies,
242–43
to freeze dough, 40
Glazed Orange Cutouts, 228–29
Holiday Sugar Cookies, 214–15
Lemon Sugar Cookies, 220–21
Lime Cutouts, 238–39
Maple Leaf Cookies, 230–31
Nutmeg Cookies, 246–47
Old-time Gingerbread Cookies,
212–13
Peanut Butter Cutouts, 248
Raspberry Cream Sandwich
Cookies, 236–37
Snowflake Cookies, 224–25
Sour Cream Cookies, 226–27
Spice Cookies, 234–35
Tender Cutouts, 207
Vanilla Cookie Cutter Cookies,
208–09
rolling pins, 8
Royal Icing, 212–13
rugelach
about, 463
Apricot Rugelach, 536–37
Butterhorns, 546–47
Chocolate Nut Rugelach, 518
Coconut Macadamia Rugelach,
498–99
Rugelach, 480–81
Rum Cookies, 97

S

salt, 26
shortbreads
about, 7, 15, 428
Almond Shortbread, 439
Apricot Shortbread, 449

Bittersweet Chocolate Shortbread, 446
Blueberry Lemon Shortbread, 443
Brown Sugar and Spice Shortbread, 433
Butterscotch Shortbread, 441
Cherry Shortbread, 445
Chocolate Brownie Shortbread, 430–31
Chocolate Chip Shortbread, 435
Cinnamon Walnut Shortbread, 440
Citrus Shortbread, 458
Coconut Shortbread, 434
Cornmeal Shortbread, 459
Cranberry Shortbread, 438
Espresso Shortbread, 457
Ginger Shortbread, 448
Glazed Lemon Shortbread, 432
Lemon Poppy Seed Shortbread, 453
Lime Shortbread, 442
Macadamia Nut Shortbread, 444
Maple Pecan Shortbread, 437
Mocha Shortbread Bites, 436
Oatmeal Shortbread, 460
Oatmeal Walnut Shortbread (v), 460
Orange Shortbread, 450
Peanut Butter Shortbread, 456
Pecan Shortbread, 455
Toffee Shortbread, 451
Traditional Shortbread, 429
Tropical Shortbread, 447
Walnut Shortbread, 452
White Chocolate Coconut Shortbread (v), 454
White Chocolate Macadamia Shortbread (v), 454
White Chocolate Shortbread, 454
shortening, about, 17, 18–19, 31, 33
slice-and-bake cookies. See refrigerator slice-and-bake cookies
Snickerdoodles, 77
snowballs, 94
Snowflake Cookies, 224–25
sour cream, 21, 33
Sour Cream Blueberry Squares, 286
Sour Cream Brownies, 357
Sour Cream Chocolate Chip Cookies, 142
Sour Cream Cookies, 226–27
Sour Cream Fudge Pouches, 496–97
Sour Cream Lemon Squares, 300

Special Chocolate Chip Cookies, 144
Spice Cookies, 85, 234–35
spices, 26
spiral cookies
  about, 462
  Cinnamon Spirals, 554
  Cranberry Orange Spirals, 532–33
  Maple Pecan Spirals, 524–25
  Orange Walnut Spirals, 477
  Raspberry Coconut Spirals, 485
  Strawberry Spirals, 493
Spritz Cookies, 115, 116
Spumoni Biscotti, 401
squares. See bars and squares
stencil designs, 227
strawberries
  Strawberry Cream Horns, 512–13
  Strawberry Delights, 544–45
  Strawberry Ribbons (v), 552–53
  Strawberry Spirals, 493
  Strawberry Squares, 312
sugar cookies
  Blue Ribbon Sugar Cookies, 206
  Brown Sugar Cookies, 82
  Brown Sugar Cutouts, 216–17
  Cinnamon Sugar Cookies, 240–41
  Cream Cheese Sugar Cookies, 210–11
  Favorite Sugar Cookies, 81
  Festive Sugar Cookies, 112
  Holiday Sugar Cookies, 214–15
  Lemon Sugar Cookies, 88, 220–21
  Orange Sugar Cookies (v), 88
  Snickerdoodles, 77
  Sour Cream Cookies, 226–27
  Sugar Cookie Slices, 272
sugar sparkles, 221
sugar stencil designs, 245
sugars and sweeteners
  about, 13–17
  measuring, 32–33
Sunshine Lemon Squares, 284
supply sources, 562–63
Swedish Tea Cookies, 108
Sweet Dark Chocolate Chip Cookies, 127
sweetened condensed milk
  about, 21
  Chocolate Walnut Bars, 298
  Coconut Macaroon Brownies, 368
  Creamy Lemon Oat Squares, 327
  Nutty Chocolate Squares, 288
  Nutty Fruit Bars, 299

T
Tangy Lime Cookies, 57
tart pans, 7
tassies
  about, 7, 462
  Almond Bites, 507
  Apricot Orange Cups, 500
  Apricot Pecan Cups, 550–51
  Apricot Pineapple Tassies, 466–67
  Bachelor Buttons, 534–35
  Blueberry Cheesecake Bites, 476
  Cashew Caramel Cups, 519
  Cherry Cheesecake Bites (v), 476
  Chocolate Cheesecake Bites, 468–69
  Coconut Pineapple Cups, 490–91
  Cranberry Orange Walnut Tassies, 488–89
  Lemon Cheesecake Bites, 492
  Lime Cheesecake Bites (v), 492
  Luscious Lemon Tartlets, 510–11
  Maple Walnut Tartlets, 506
  Orange Almond Cups, 528
  Orange Cheesecake Bites (v), 492
  Orange Curd Cups, 494–95
  Pecan Tassies, 484
  Pineapple Tartlets, 529
  Pumpkin Walnut Tassies, 502–03
  White Chocolate Cheesecake Bites (v), 468–69
Tender Chocolate Chip Cookies, 136
Tender Cutouts, 207
thimble cookies, 89
Thumbprint Cookies, 89
toffee
  Chocolate Almond Toffee Bars, 295
  Toffee Cookies, 59
  Toffee Dreams, 202
  Toffee Mocha Brownies, 389
  Toffee Shortbread, 451
Traditional Shortbread, 429
Triple Chocolate Biscotti, 424
Tropical Dreams, 196
Tropical Oat Cookies, 158
Tropical Oat Squares, 285
Tropical Shortbread, 447
turbinado sugar (raw sugar), 15–16
turnovers
  Apple Butter Turnovers, 516–17
  Raspberry Almond Cream Cheese Pockets, 514–15

U
Ultimate Chocolate Chip Heaven Cookies (v), 119

Ultimate Dark Chocolate Espresso
Cookies, 73

V

Vanilla Cookie Cutter Cookies,
208–09
Vanilla Slices, 258
vanilla sugar, 84
Viennese Vanilla Crescents, 84

W

walnuts, 24
Apple Walnut Cookies, 68–69
Applesauce Oatmeal Cookies,
167
Applesauce Walnut Bars, 328
Banana Walnut Oatmeal Cookies,
165
Blue Ribbon Fudge Brownies,
349
Brownie Biscotti, 407
Butterhorns, 546–47
Chocolate Chip Biscotti, 402
Chocolate Chip Dreams, 171
Chocolate Chip Espresso Cookies
(v), 143
Chocolate Chip Heaven Cookies,
119
Chocolate Chip Oatmeal Dreams,
182
Chocolate Chip Shortbread (v),
435
Chocolate Chip Walnut Cookies,
124
Chocolate Nut Rugelach, 518
Chocolate Walnut Bars, 298
Chocolate Walnut Biscotti, 398
Chocolate Walnut Decadence
Dreams (v), 177
Chocolate Walnut Dreams (v),
181
Cinnamon Walnut Biscotti, 425
Cinnamon Walnut Shortbread,
440
Classic Chocolate Chip Nut
Cookies (v), 131
Coconut Walnut Cookies (v), 100
Cranberry Orange Cookies, 56
Cranberry Orange Walnut
Tassies, 488–89
Cream Cheese Walnut Cookies,
102

Crispy Chocolate Chip Nut
Cookies (v), 141
Date Walnut Slices, 264
Deluxe Brownies, 375
Deluxe Chocolate Chip Cookies,
137
Deluxe Nut Bars, 304
Double Chocolate Brownies, 365
Double Chocolate Dreams, 173
Fudge and Fudge Brownies, 383
Fudgy Brownie Cookies, 53
Fudgy Brownies, 360
Gingerbread Walnut Biscotti (v),
426
Glazed Chocolate Chip Cookies,
130
Golden Oatmeal Dreams, 188
Jumbo Chocolate Chip Cookies,
135
Maple Nut Wafers, 257
Maple Walnut Biscotti (v), 417
Maple Walnut Cookies, 51
Maple Walnut Dreams (v), 176
Maple Walnut Squares, 323
Maple Walnut Tartlets, 506
Mincemeat Cookies, 67
Mocha Fudge Truffle Cookies
(v), 46
Moist, Fudgy Brownies, 382
Nut Biscotti, 414
Nutty Fruit Bars, 299
Oatmeal Nut Chippers (v), 150
Oatmeal Pumpkin Cookies, 157
Oatmeal Walnut Cookies, 149
Oatmeal Walnut Shortbread (v),
460
Orange Walnut Biscotti (v), 403
Orange Walnut Dreams (v), 190
Orange Walnut Spirals, 477
Persimmon Cookies, Michael's
Mom's, 58
Pumpkin Walnut Biscotti, 423
Pumpkin Walnut Tassies,
502–03
Raisin Walnut Biscotti (v), 422
Rocky Road Brownies, 366–67
Special Chocolate Chip Cookies,
144
Tender Chocolate Chip Cookies,
136
Triple Chocolate Chip Nut
Cookies (v), 129

Walnut Brownies, 364
Walnut Horns, 486–87
Walnut Shortbread, 452
weight equivalents, 34
white chocolate
about, 23
Black and White Chocolate
Dreams, 185
Butterscotch Dreams, 186
CocoMac Dreams, 189
Cranberry Nut Cookies, 47
Cranberry White Chocolate
Biscotti, 399
Double White Chocolate Dreams,
179
Marbled White Chocolate Cream
Cheese Brownies, 353
to melt, 395
Strawberry Delights, 544–45
White Chocolate Cheesecake
Bites (v), 468–69
White Chocolate Chip Coconut
Cookies (v), 125
White Chocolate Chip Cookies,
125
White Chocolate Chip Dreams,
178
White Chocolate Coconut
Brownies (v), 374
White Chocolate Coconut
Cookies, 43
White Chocolate Coconut
Shortbread (v), 454
White Chocolate Cookies, 109
White Chocolate Lemon Biscotti,
420
White Chocolate Macadamia
Biscotti, 412
White Chocolate Macadamia
Brownies, 374
White Chocolate Oatmeal
Cookies, 154
White Chocolate Pumpkin
Blondies, 318–19
White Chocolate Raspberry
Crumb Squares, 329
White Chocolate Raspberry
Thumbprints, 92–93
White Chocolate Rounds,
271
White Chocolate Shortbread,
454